- Cover just the modules for a very technical perspective

- Omit any chapter you don't want – you can still cover the corresponding module

- Omit any module you don't want – it will not affect your ability to cover the chapters

XLM/A	Computer Hardware and Software
XLM/B	The World Wide Web and the Internet
XLM/C	Designing Databases and Entity-Relationship Diagramming
XLM/D	Decision Analysis with Spreadsheet Software
XLM/E	Network Basics
XLM/F	Building a Web Page with HTML
XLM/G	Object-Oriented Technologies
XLM/H	Computer Crime and Forensics
XLM/I	Building an E-Portfolio
XLM/J	Implementing a Database with Microsoft Access
XLM/K	Careers in Business

Management Information Systems

FOR THE INFORMATION AGE

Management Information Systems

FOR THE INFORMATION AGE

FIFTH EDITION

Stephen Haag

DANIELS COLLEGE OF BUSINESS

UNIVERSITY OF DENVER

Maeve Cummings

KELCE COLLEGE OF BUSINESS

PITTSBURG STATE UNIVERSITY

Donald J. McCubbrey

DANIELS COLLEGE OF BUSINESS

UNIVERSITY OF DENVER

**McGraw-Hill
Irwin**

Boston   Burr Ridge, IL   Dubuque, IA   Madison, WI   New York   San Francisco   St. Louis
Bangkok   Bogotá   Caracas   Kuala Lumpur   Lisbon   London   Madrid   Mexico City
Milan   Montreal   New Delhi   Santiago   Seoul   Singapore   Sydney   Taipei   Toronto

Irwin

MANAGEMENT INFORMATION SYSTEMS FOR THE INFORMATION AGE

Published by McGraw-Hill/Irwin, a business unit of The McGraw-Hill Companies, Inc., 1221 Avenue of the Americas, New York, NY, 10020. Copyright © 2005, 2004, 2002, 2000, 1998 by The McGraw-Hill Companies, Inc. All rights reserved. No part of this publication may be reproduced or distributed in any form or by any means, or stored in a database or retrieval system, without the prior written consent of The McGraw-Hill Companies, Inc., including, but not limited to, in any network or other electronic storage or transmission, or broadcast for distance learning.

Some ancillaries, including electronic and print components, may not be available to customers outside the United States.

This book is printed on acid-free paper.

2 3 4 5 6 7 8 9 0 VNH/VNH 0 9 8 7 6 5

ISBN 0-07-293586-3

Editorial director: *Brent Gordon*
Publisher: *Stewart Mattson*
Senior sponsoring editor: *Paul Ducham*
Developmental editor: *Jennifer Wisnowski*
Senior marketing manager: *Douglas Reiner*
Media producer: *Greg Bates*
Lead project manager: *Mary Conzachi*
Senior production supervisor: *Sesha Bolisetty*
Senior designer: *Mary E. Kazak*
Photo research coordinator: *Jeremy Cheshareck*
Photo researcher: *Jennifer Blankenship*
Senior supplement producer: *Carol Loreth*
Senior digital content specialist: *Brian Nacik*
Cover and interior design: *Amanda Kavanaugh/Ark Design Studio*
Cover image: © *Corbis*
Typeface: *11/13 Bulmer MT*
Compositor: *ElectraGraphics, Inc.*
Printer: *Von Hoffmann Corporation*

Library of Congress Cataloging-in-Publication Data

Haag, Stephen.
    Management information systems for the information age / Stephen Haag, Maeve
Cummings, Donald J. McCubbrey.—5th ed.
        p. cm.
    Includes bibliographical references and index.
    ISBN 0-07-293586-3 (alk. paper)
    1. Management information systems. 2. Information technology. I. Cummings, Maeve.
II. McCubbrey, Donald J. III. Title.
T58.6.H18 2005
658.4'038'011—dc22

                                        2004053851

www.mhhe.com

Homer and Marilyn. They have devoted their lives to helping children and in that devotion they have found happiness and joy. We can only hope to be so lucky.

Stephen Haag

To David:
You have brains in your head
You're as strong as a tree
Oh, the places you'll go
Oh, the things you will see
(Adapted from Dr. Seuss)

Maeve Cummings

To Jani: My wife and best friend. Your warmth and acceptance lights up my life. You're more fun to be with than anyone I've ever known. I am blessed, truly blessed.

Donald J. McCubbrey

BRIEF CONTENTS

CONTENTS

GROUP PROJECTS

PREFACE

The fifth edition of *Management Information Systems for the Information Age* provides you the ultimate in flexibility to tailor content to the exact needs of your MIS or IT course. The nine chapters and eleven Extended Learning Modules may be presented in logical sequence, or you may choose your own mix of technical topics and business/managerial topics.

The nine chapters form the core of material covering business and managerial topics, from strategic and competitive technology opportunities to the organization and management of information using databases and data warehouses. If you covered only the chapters and none of the modules, the focus of your course would be MIS from a business and managerial point of view.

The eleven Extended Learning Modules provide a technical glimpse into the world of IT, covering topics ranging from building a Web site, to computer crimes and forensics, to how to use Microsoft Access. If you chose only the modules and none of the chapters, the focus of your course would be on the technical and hands-on aspects of IT.

Each module follows its corresponding chapter, but chapters and modules may usefully be presented independently. For example, Module H on computer crime and forensics follows logically after Chapter 8 on protecting people and information. But you can cover Chapter 8 and omit Module H—that's completely up to you. On the other hand, you can omit Chapter 8 and cover Module H—you have flexibility to do what suits your needs.

You can easily select a course format that represents your own desired blend of topics. While you might not choose to cover the technologies of networks, for example, you might require your students to build a small database application. In that case, you would omit Module E (Network Basics) and spend more time on Module C (Designing Databases and Entity-Relationship Diagramming) and Module J (Implementing a Database with Microsoft Access).

On the facing page, we've provided a table of the chapters and the modules. As you put your course together and choose the chapters and/or modules you want to cover, we would offer the following:

- Cover any or all of the chapters as suits your purposes.
- Cover any or all of the modules as suits your purposes.
- If you choose a chapter, you do not have to cover its corresponding module.
- If you choose a module, you do not have to cover its corresponding chapter.
- You may cover the modules in any order you wish.

Please note that your students will find Modules E, F, G, J, and K on the CD that accompanies the textbook. In the book, we provide a two-page introduction to the modules. All your students have to do is go to the CD to read the full modules.

The unique organization of this text is aimed at giving you **complete flexibility** to design your course as you see fit.

THE CHAPTERS	THE EXTENDED LEARNING MODULES
CHAPTER 1 The Information Age in Which You Live	**Extended Learning Module A** Computer Hardware and Software
CHAPTER 2 Major Business Initiatives	**Extended Learning Module B** The World Wide Web and the Internet
CHAPTER 3 Databases and Data Warehouses	**Extended Learning Module C** Designing Databases and Entity-Relationship Diagramming
CHAPTER 4 Decision Support and Artificial Intelligence	**Extended Learning Module D** Decision Analysis with Spreadsheet Software
CHAPTER 5 Electronic Commerce	**Extended Learning Module E*** Network Basics
CHAPTER 6 Systems Development	**Extended Learning Module F*** Building a Web Page with HTML
CHAPTER 7 IT Infrastructures	**Extended Learning Module G*** Object-Oriented Technologies
CHAPTER 8 Protecting People and Information	**Extended Learning Module H** Computer Crime and Forensics
CHAPTER 9 Emerging Trends and Technologies	**Extended Learning Module I** Building an e-Portfolio
	Extended Learning Module J** Implementing a Database with Microsoft Access
	Extended Learning Module K* Careers in Business

*The complete text for modules E, F, G, J, and K are on the CD that accompanies this text.
**Extended Learning Module J is a bonus module that you would typically cover in conjunction with Chapter 3 (Databases and Data Warehouses) and/or Extended Learning Module C (Designing Databases and Entity-Relationship Diagramming).

- Management Focus—By focusing on the chapters, your class will take on a managerial approach to MIS.
- Technical Focus—If hands-on, technical skills are more important, focus your MIS course on the modules.

Organization—The Haag Advantage

The separation of content between the chapters and the Extended Learning Modules is very simple. We can sum it up by saying:

- The **chapters** address what you want your students **to know.**
- The **modules** address what you want your students **to be able to do.**

Together, both combine to provide a well-balanced repository of important information aimed at developing a prospective business professional equipped with both foundational knowledge and application experience, ready to take on today's highly competitive job market.

Each chapter and module contains full pedagogical support:

- Student Learning Outcomes
- On Your Own Projects
- Team Work Projects
- Summary
- Key Terms and Concepts
- Short-Answer Questions
- Assignments and Exercises

The **chapters** focus on the *business and managerial* applications of MIS and information technology.

The **modules** focus on giving your students real *hands-on-knowledge* they can apply in both their personal and professional experiences.

Figure 3.8

A Multidimensional Data Warehouse with Information from Multiple Operational Databases

ligence, many organizations are building data warehouses and providing data-mining tools. A data warehouse is simply the next step (beyond databases) in the progression of building business intelligence. And data-mining tools are the tools you use to mine a data warehouse and extrapolate the business intelligence you need to make a decision, solve a problem, or capitalize on an opportunity to create a competitive advantage.

WHAT IS A DATA WAREHOUSE?

A *data warehouse* is a logical collection of information—gathered from many different operational databases—used to create business intelligence that supports business analysis activities and decision-making tasks (see Figure 3.8). Sounds simple enough on the surface, but data warehouses represent a fundamentally different way of thinking about organizing and managing information in an organization. Consider these key features of a data warehouse, detailed in the sections that follow.

DATA WAREHOUSES ARE MULTIDIMENSIONAL In the relational database model, information is represented in a series of two-dimensional files or tables. Not so in a data warehouse—most data warehouses are multidimensional, meaning that they contain layers of columns and rows. For this reason, most data warehouses are really *multidimensional databases.* The layers in a data warehouse represent information according to different dimensions. This multidimensional representation of information is referred to as a *hypercube.*

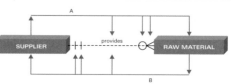

Figure C.3

Reading an Entity-Relationship (E-R) Diagram

Once you determine that a relationship does exist, you must then determine the numerical nature of the relationship, what we refer to as "minimum and maximum cardinality." To describe this, you use a | to denote a single relationship, a 0 to denote a zero or optional relationship, and/or a crow's foot (<) to denote a multiple relationship. By way of illustration, let's consider the portion of your E-R diagram in Figure C.3. To help you read the symbols and diagram, we've added blue lines and arrows. Following the line marked A, you would read the E-R diagram as:

"A *Supplier* may not provide any *Raw Material* (denoted with the 0) but may provide more than one *Raw Material* (denoted with the crow's foot)."

So, that part of the E-R diagram states that the logical relationship between *Supplier* and *Raw Material* is that a *Supplier* may provide no *Raw Material* currently in inventory but may provide more than one *Raw Material* currently in inventory. This is exactly what business rule 4 (on page 163) states.

Following the blue line marked B, you would read the E-R diagram as:

Student Learning Outcomes and Summary

Student learning outcomes drive each chapter and module. We then summarize each chapter and module by revisiting the student learning outcomes. It's the old adage . . .

1. Tell them what you're going to tell them.
2. Tell them.
3. Tell them what you told them.

At the beginning of each chapter and module, you'll find a list of **Student Learning Outcomes,** providing your students with a road map of what they should learn and accomplish while reading a chapter or module.

Summary: Student Learning Outcomes Revisited

1. **Describe supply chain management (SCM) systems, their strategic and competitive opportunities, the challenges businesses face in employing them successfully, and available IT support.** A *supply chain management (SCM) system* is an IT system that supports supply chain management activities by automating the tracking of inventory and information among business processes and across companies. Supply chain management systems can increase revenues, reduce costs, and increase customer satisfaction. The biggest challenge to their successful implementation is the lack of effective communication between individual areas within a company. Two well-known providers of SCM software are i2 and Manugistics. Dell Computer gets well-deserved recognition as well as competitive advantage from its IT-enabled SCM system.

2. **Describe customer relationship management (CRM) systems, their strategic and competitive opportunities, the challenges businesses face in employing them successfully, and available IT support.** *Customer relationship management (CRM) systems* use information about customers to gain insights into their needs, wants, and behaviors in order to serve them better. CRM is not just software but also a business objective which encompasses many different aspects of a business including software, hardware, services, support, and strategic business goals. CRM systems provide competitive advantage by increasing revenues, by cutting costs, and by treating your customers in ways that encourage them to choose your company over the competition. CRM system installations fail for many reasons, but chief among them is that companies focus on the software and fail to pay enough attention to business processes and acceptance by people within the organization. There are many CRM applications available. The two most prominent ones are Siebel Systems and Salesforce.com.

3. **Describe business intelligence (BI) systems, their strategic and competitive opportunities, the challenges businesses face in employing** them successfully, and available IT support. *Business intelligence (BI) systems* are the IT applications and tools that support the business intelligence function within an organization. Their objective is to improve the timeliness and quality of the input for decision making. Higher quality managerial decision making is an important way companies gain an advantage over their competitors. The biggest challenge to the effective use of BI systems is that, in too many cases, knowledge workers do not know how to use them effectively. While the Web is used to support BI applications in some firms, specialized software is at the heart of BI, and there are many packages available. Brio Software Systems and Cognos are but two examples.

4. **Describe integrated collaboration environments (ICE), their strategic and competitive opportunities, the challenges businesses face in employing them successfully, and available IT support.** An *integrated collaboration environment (ICE)* is the environment in which virtual teams do their work. Virtual teams are teams whose members are located in varied geographic locations and whose work in ICEs is supported by specialized ICE software or by more basic collaboration systems. A *collaboration system* is software that is designed specifically to improve the performance of teams by supporting the sharing and flow of information. There are many varieties of collaboration systems including basic e-mail systems as well as *workflow systems, document management systems, knowledge management systems,* and *social network systems.* Companies can gain huge competitive advantages from collaboration systems through more effective coordination of the work of virtual teams and by fully utilizing available knowledge within their organizations. Knowledge management systems have been less successful than other forms of collaboration systems primarily because knowledge workers do not believe they add value to their work. ICE software combines

A **Summary** of these outcomes appears with the EOC elements per chapter/module, providing an invaluable tool for your students as they prepare to take an exam.

xix

Case Studies

CLOSING CASE STUDY TWO

USING NEURAL NETWORKS TO CATEGORIZE PEOPLE

Would your banker give you an A, B, or C? What about your supermarket? You know you're being graded in your classes, but did you know that you're also being graded by businesses?

Special treatment for certain customers is not new. Airline customers who fly first class have always received preferential treatment, even when flights were cancelled or delayed. You won't find them napping on a stone floor with their backpacks as pillows. This makes business sense to the airlines, since these are the customers who are most profitable.

Although companies have always offered preferential treatment to their more profitable customers, the speed and capacity of computers today are making the

BANKS

The First Union Bank uses software that categorizes people into red, green, and yellow classes depending on the customer's history and value to the bank. Customers who are green might get better credit card rates than customers who are red and are judged to add less to the bank's bottom line.

Say you called the bank that issued you your credit card and said that you didn't want to pay the annual fee anymore. The bank could look at your credit card activity and decide whether it's more profitable to the bank to waive your fee rather than risk your not using the credit card anymore.

...IES

...ars using neural network
...determine which of their
...o bankrupt. Neural net-
...tterns, and if your profile
...have defaulted, you'll be

Opening Case

Each chapter begins with a one-page opening case study, highlighting how an organization has successfully implemented many of that chapter's concepts.

CHAPTER ONE

The Information Age in Which You Live
Changing the Face of Business

OPENING CASE STUDY
PAY-PER-TUNE GENERATION AND DISRUPTIVE TECHNOLOGIES ROCK THE RECORD INDUSTRY

In 1999, the record industry raked in $14.6 billion in revenue and was growing 6 percent annually. Then, Napster appeared on the scene and forever changed the record industry. Napster's innovative disruptive technology—file sharing via peer-to-peer technology—appealed to the growing "pay-per-tune" generation, seeking only a particular song instead of the entire album.

Of course, you probably know that the federal government eventually deemed Napster's activities illegal and put it out of business. But the pay-per-tune notion of purchasing music never went away. Apple's iTunes provides a catalog of over 400,000 songs, each of which can be purchased without buying the whole album. Paid down-...d to reach

tion? We believe not, along with many other people. As Dave Allison, owner of Times Beach Records, explains, "The entire industry has to redefine itself and change . . . We're all in this together, and we have to move forward together . . ." Indeed, the record industry must undergo dramatic transformation if it is to survive and thrive.

This story of the record industry isn't really about the disruptive technologies of the Internet, file-sharing peer-to-peer systems, and MP3 players. It is about the challenge of those technologies and the willingness of organizations—or, in this case, an industry—to embrace those disruptive technologies and determine how to use them instead to create a competitive advantage.

And that's the focus of our text. Although it will introduce you to a wide array of technology terms and concepts and teach you the technology, we want you to always keep in mind the challenge of how to apply technology to create a competitive advantage. In this first chapter, we

CLOSING CASE STUDY TWO

TOTING THE E-COMMERCE LINE WITH EBAGS

For a true e-commerce success story you don't have to look any further than eBags (www.ebags.com). While many pure-play e-commerce Web sites have fallen by the wayside, eBags is not only surviving, it is thriving. It is the world's leading online provider of bags and accessories for all lifestyles. With 180 brands and over 8,000 products, eBags has sold more than 2.5 million bags since its launch in March 1999. It carries a complete line of premium and popular brands, including Samsonite, JanSport, The North Face, Liz Claiborne, and Adidas. You can buy anything from backpacks and carry-ons to computer cases and handbags at extremely competitive prices from its Web site.

eBags has received several awards for excellence in online retailing, among them:

- Circle of Excellence Platinum Award, Bizrate.com
- Web Site of the Year, *Catalog Age Magazine* (for the second year in a row)
- Email Marketer of the Year, ClickZ.MessageMedia
- Marketer of the Year, Colorado AMA
- Rocky Mountain Portal Award
- Gold Peak Catalog, Colorado AMA
- Entrepreneur of the Year—Rocky Mountain Region, Ernst and Young
- E-Commerce Initiative Award of Merit, Colorado

A good part of the reason for eBags's success is its commitment to providing each customer with superior service, 24 hours a day, 365 days a year. eBags provides customers with the ability to contact customer service representatives for personal assistance by telephone or e-mail and also provides convenient, real-time UPS order tracking. According to Jon Nordmark, CEO of eBags.com, "From a customer perspective, we've spent a great deal of time developing pioneering ways to guide our shoppers to the bags and accessories that enhance their lifestyles through function and fashion."

Although you would never know it, this superior customer service is not provided by eBags employees. For the past several years, eBags has outsourced both the handling of phone orders and customer service calls to Finali Corporation (www.finali.com). "The call center is often the only human contact customers have with our brand," says eBags CEO Jon Nordmark. "By maintaining a call center staff that can think on its feet, Finali delivers real value to our customers and a measurable return on our call center investment."

Typically, the conversion rate of inbound customer calls to sales at the call center has been about 25 percent. But during the 2001 holiday season, special training and incentives for Finali call center reps servicing the eBags Web site helped raise that number to 44 percent. In addition, the average size of orders placed

Closing Cases

To help your students apply what they have just learned, you'll find two closing case studies at the end of each chapter. Each case has a set of questions that are great for class discussion.

Team Work and On Your Own Projects

There are now 72 Team Work and On Your Own projects spread throughout the text, in both the chapters and modules. Many of these can be used as break-out exercises, and just as many can be assigned as homework. In the Instructor's Manual, you'll find our discussions of and solutions to each of these projects.

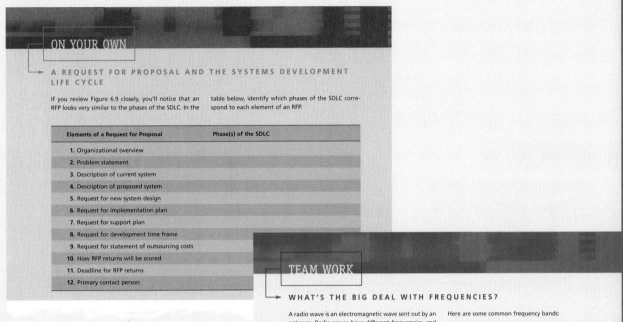

ON YOUR OWN

A REQUEST FOR PROPOSAL AND THE SYSTEMS DEVELOPMENT LIFE CYCLE

If you review Figure 6.9 closely, you'll notice that an RFP looks very similar to the phases of the SDLC. In the table below, identify which phases of the SDLC correspond to each element of an RFP.

Elements of a Request for Proposal	Phase(s) of the SDLC
1. Organizational overview	
2. Problem statement	
3. Description of current system	
4. Description of proposed system	
5. Request for new system design	
6. Request for implementation plan	
7. Request for support plan	
8. Request for development time frame	
9. Request for statement of outsourcing costs	
10. How RFP returns will be scored	
11. Deadline for RFP returns	
12. Primary contact person	

On Your Own

Assign these to students for individual reflection and work.

TEAM WORK

WHAT'S THE BIG DEAL WITH FREQUENCIES?

A radio wave is an electromagnetic wave sent out by an antenna. Radio waves have different frequencies, and by tuning a radio receiver, a cell phone (which has a receiver), or a baby monitor (which also has a receiver) to a certain frequency you can pick up a specific signal. Frequencies are measured in KHz (kilohertz—thousands of cycles per second), MHz (megahertz—millions of cycles per second), and GHz (gigahertz—billions of cycles per second).

You may have heard that there is a fixed number of channels, and competition for control of those available is fierce. All wireless gizmos require a radio frequency to transmit and receive, so communications companies spend billions of dollars for the rights to the part of the spectrum that's for sale. Other parts are free (like the WiFi part) and still others are set aside for government agencies like the Department of Defense.

The figure below shows the part of the spectrum in common use for wireless information delivery all day, every day.

Here are some common frequency bands:

FM radio: 88 megahertz to 108 megahertz

AM radio: 535 kilohertz to 1.7 megahertz

Television stations: 174 to 220 megahertz for channels 7 through 13.

Place on the spectrum the following wireless services:

WiFi

GPS devices

Microwave ovens

Police radar guns

TV channels 2–6

Wildlife tracking collars

CB radio

Aviation navigation

Cordless phones

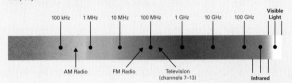

Team Work

These are designed for small groups of two to four. Many are great for in class assignments.

Electronic Commerce and Group Projects

Electronic Commerce

These projects are designed to impart to your students hands-on, technological experiences, many requiring Web exploration. You'll find an Electronic Commerce project at the end of each chapter. To support these projects, we've provided more than 1,000 links on the Web site for this text at www.mhhe.com/haag.

Group Projects

After the last module in the text, you'll find 20 Group Projects. These require your students to use technology to solve a problem or take advantage of an opportunity. A quick warning to instructors: Some of these take an entire weekend to solve. Be careful not to assign too many at one time.

Electronic COMMERCE

Searching Online Databases and Information Repositories

As you find sites on the Internet that provide information, many of them will do so in the form of a database—a searchable grouping of information that allows you to find specific information by entering key words and key phrases. These words and phrases are, in fact, some sort of key (similar to primary and forei that are used as matching criteria in a field of the d

In this section, you'll explore a variety of inforr Internet. To help you, we've included a number of database and information repositories. On the (www.mhhe.com/haag), we've provided direct lir many, many more. These are a great starting point merce section.

FINANCIAL AID RESOURCES

On the Internet, you can find valuable databases tl sources as you attend school. These resources c money you don't have to pay back—and standard of financial aid lenders, ranging from traditional ba ties wanting to give something back to society. Fina a financial aid database and answer the following

A. Do you have to register as a user to access i

B. Do you have to pay a fee to access informat

C. Can you build a profile of yourself and use

D. Can you apply for aid while at the site or m that you need to complete and return?

E. By what sort of categories of aid can you se

CASE 16:
STRATEGIC AND COMPETITIVE ADVANTAGE: ANALYZING OPERATING LEVERAGE

PONY ESPRESSO

Pony Espresso is a small business that sells specialty coffee drinks at office buildings. Each morning and afternoon, trucks arrive at offices' front entrances, and the office employees purchase various beverages with names such as Java du Jour and Café de Colombia. The business is profitable. But Pony Espresso offices are located to the north of town, where lease rates are less expensive, and the principal sales area is south of town. This means that the trucks must drive cross-town four times each day.

The cost of transportation to and from the sales area, plus the power demands of the trucks' coffee brewing equipment, is a significant portion of the variable costs. Pony Espresso could reduce the amount of driving—and, therefore, the variable costs—if it moves the offices much closer to the sales area.

Pony Espresso presently has fixed costs of $10,000 per month. The lease of a new office, closer to the sales area, would cost an additional $2,200 per month. This would increase the fixed costs to $12,200 per month.

Although the lease of new offices would increase the fixed costs, a careful estimate of the potential savings in gasoline and vehicle maintenance indicates that Pony Espresso could reduce the variable costs from $0.60 per unit to $0.35 per unit. Total sales are unlikely to increase as a result of the move, but the savings in variable costs should increase the annual profit.

You have been hired by Pony Espresso to assist in the cost analysis and new lease options to determine a growth in profit margin. You will also need to calculate a degree of operating leverage to better understand the company's profitability. Degree of operating leverage (DOL) will give the CEO of Pony Espresso, Darian Presley, a great deal of information for setting operating targets and planning profitability.

SOME PARTICULARS YOU SHOULD KNOW

1. Consider the information provided—especially look at the change in the variability of the profit from month to month. From November through January, when it is much more difficult to lure office workers out into the cold to purchase coffee, Pony Espresso barely breaks even. In fact, in December of 2003, the business lost money.

2. First, develop the cost analysis on the existing lease information using the monthly sales figures provided to you in the file PONYESPRESSO.xls. Second, develop the cost analysis from the new lease information provided above.

3. You need to calculate the variability that is reflected in the month-to-month standard deviation of earnings for the current cost structure and the projected cost structure.

4. Do not consider any association with downsizing such as overhead; simply focus on the information provided to you.

5. You will need to calculate the EBIT—earnings before interest and taxes.

6. Would the DOL and business risk increase or decrease if Pony Espresso moved its office? *Note:* Variability in profit levels, whether measured as EBIT, operating income, or net income, does not necessarily increase the level of business risk as the DOL increases.

7. File: PONYESPRESSO.xls (Excel file).

End-of-Chapter Elements

Short-Answer Questions

1. How will free Internet phone calls work?
2. What is a push technology environment?
3. How will push technologies support personalization?
4. Why may you someday rent personal productivity software from an ASP?
5. What is the concept of information supplier convergence?
6. What is the role of physiological interfaces?
7. What are the three steps in automatic speech recognition?
8. What is virtual reality?
9. What type of special input and ou[...] does virtual reality make use of?
10. What are CAVEs?
11. What are some examples of biom[...] applications?

12. How will biometrics aid in providing security and identification?
13. What is the function of a biochip?
14. What is the role of an implant chip?
15. How will digital cash someday work on the Internet?
16. What is a wearable computer?
17. How do multi-state CPUs differ from today's standard CPUs?
18. Why will holographic storage devices be able to store more information than today's [...]

Discussion Questions

1. When selling antiques, you can usually obtain a higher price for those that have a provenance, which is information detailing the origin and history of the object. For example, property owned by Jacqueline Kennedy Onassis and Princess Diana sold for much more than face value. What kinds of products have value over and above a comparable product because of such information? What kind of information makes products valuable? Consider both tangible (resale value) and intangible value (sentimental appeal).
2. Personal checks that you use to buy merchandise have a standard format. Checks have very few different sizes, and almost no variation in format. Consider what would happen if everyone could create his or her own size, shape, and layout of personal check. What would the costs and benefits be to business and the consumer in terms of buying checks, exchanging them for merchandise, and bank check processing?
3. Consider society as a business that takes steps to protect itself from the harm of illegal acts. Discuss the mechanisms and costs that are involved. Examine ways in which our society would be different if no one ever broke a law. Are there ever benefits to our society when people break the law, for example, when they claim that the law itself is unethical or unjust?
4. Can you access all the IT systems at your college or university? What about payroll or grade information on yourself or others? What kinds of controls has your college or university implemented to prevent the misuse of information?
5. You know that you generally can't use a PC to

formatted disk. What other instances of the lack of difficulty in accessing information have you experienced personally or heard of? For example, have you used different versions of MS PowerPoint or MS Access that won't work on all the PCs that you have access to?
6. Have you, or someone you know, experienced computer problems caused by a virus? What did the virus do? Where do you think you got it? How did you fix the problem? What was the cost to you in time, trouble, and stress?
7. What laws do you think the United States should pass to protect personal information? None? Laws such as the European Union has? Stricter laws than the EU? Why? Should some personal information be more protected than other information? Why or why not?
8. The issue of pirated software is one that the software industry fights on a daily basis. The major centers of software piracy are in places like Russia and China where salaries and [...]

Assignments and E[...]

1. **SELLING THE IDEA OF IMPLANT CHI[...]** favor of using implant chips that c[...] information. Your task is to put tog[...] students obtain implant chips. With[...]
   A. The school-related information [...]
   B. The nonschool-related informat[...]
   C. The processes within your scho[...]
   D. The benefits your school would [...]
   E. The benefits students would rea[...]
   Your presentation should be no mo[...]
2. **RESEARCHING WEARABLE COMPU[...]** Xybernaut. Connect to its Web site [...]

Assignments and Exercises

1. **AN EIP FOR YOUR COURSE** Enterprise information portals (EIPs) allow knowledge workers to access company information via a Web interface. You have been asked to create an EIP for this course. Answer the following questions in order to determine how the EIP should be developed.
   - What type of information would be contained on the EIP?
   - Who would have access to the EIP?
   - How long would information remain on the EIP?
   - What is the difference between a collaborative processing EIP and a decision processing EIP?
   - Which type of EIP would you implement and why?
2. **SPONSOR OF THE IT INFRASTRUCTURE** To build a solid IT infrastructure you must have executive sponsorship. Your current boss doesn't understand the importance of building a solid IT infrastructure. In fact, your boss doesn't even understand the term IT infrastructure. First, explain to your boss what an IT infrastructure is and why it is critical for any organization. Second, explain three primary components of an IT infrastructure.
3. **IT INFRASTRUCTURE COMPONENTS AND THE REAL WORLD** Throughout this chapter we discussed several IT infrastructure components including client/server, Web services, integrations, among others. Pick two of the components discussed in this chapter and try to find business examples of how companies are using these components in the real world. We also mentioned that there are thousands of additional components you can use to build an IT infrastructure. Research the Internet to see if you can find two additional IT infrastructure components that were not discussed in this chapter along with business examples of how businesses are using the components in the real world.
4. **CREATING THE IDEAL INFRASTRUCTURE** This chapter focused on many different IT infrastructure components. Choose three of the different components discussed in this chapter and explain how you could use them to improve the IT infrastructure at your school. Be sure to think of current requirements as well as future requirements for the IT infrastructure.

Each chapter and module contains complete pedagogical support in the form of:

- **Summary of Student Learning Outcomes** These mirror the chapter's or module's opener.
- **Two Closing Case Studies** Reinforcing important concepts with prominent examples from businesses and organizations (chapters only).
- **Key Terms and Concepts** With page numbers where discussions of them are found.
- **Assignments and Exercises** One full page of problems designed to give your students the chance to apply key concepts of the text.
- **Discussion Questions** Challenging questions aimed at promoting an atmosphere of critical thinking in your classroom (chapters only).

Changes for the Fifth Edition

The content changes for the fifth edition were driven by:

1. Instructor feedback on the fourth edition.
2. Changes that have occurred in the business world.
3. Advances that have occurred in the technology arena.
4. Changes made by our competitors.

As a group of authors and contributors working together, we carefully sifted through all the competitive scanning information we could gather to create a fifth edition that builds on the success of the fourth edition.

Throughout the text, you'll find new or updated opening and closing case studies, Industry Perspectives, Global Perspectives, Group Projects, and Team Work and On Your Own projects, as well as new or expanded coverage of such topics as *business intelligence, customer relationship management, supply chain management, n-tier architectures, application service providers,* and *Web Services.*

We've provided all these content updates and new pedagogical features in a visually appealing, streamlined format.

Most important, we're pleased to have been able to respond to reviewer suggestions and provide the following:

- New *Extended Learning Module K* on careers in business and what IT skills your students need to learn to compete effectively in the job market.
- Updated *Chapter 2* on major business initiatives focusing on the role of IT in support of customer relationship management, supply chain management, business intelligence systems, and integrated collaboration environments.
- Updated *Extended Learning Module D* on decision support with spreadsheet software including 3-D pivot tables.
- Updated *Chapter 5* on electronic commerce focusing on fundamental differences in Business to Business and Business to Consumer electronic commerce.
- Updated *Chapter 7* on IT infrastructures.
- Updated *Chapter 9* on emerging trends and technologies.
- Updated *Extended Learning Module I* on building an e-portfolio.
- Enhanced *Extended Learning Module J* on using Microsoft Access to implement a database including building input forms and making changes to reports.

The Support Package

We realize that no text is complete without a well-rounded and value-added support package. Our support package is designed to ease your teaching burden by providing you with a Web site full of valuable information, a test bank with more than 2,000 questions and easy-to-use test generating software, an Instructor's Manual that walks you through each chapter and module and provides value-added teaching notes and suggestions, and PowerPoint presentations.

ONLINE LEARNING CENTER AT WWW.MHHE.COM/HAAG

As in previous editions, the Web site for the fifth edition contains a wealth of valuable information and supplements for both the instructor and the student.

INSTRUCTOR'S MANUAL

The Instructor's Manual is provided to you in an effort to help you prepare for your class presentations. In its new format, you will find a separate box for each PowerPoint slide. In that box, you will find an overview of the slide and a list of key points to cover. This presentation enables you to prepare your class presentation by working solely with the Instructor's Manual because you also see the PowerPoint slide presentations. We've also provided embedded links within each Instructor's Manual document to the various in-text pedagogical elements including:

- **On Your Own and Team Work projects**—when to use them, how to grade them, how long they should take, etc.
- **The Global and Industry Perspectives boxes**—how to introduce them, key points to address, possible discussion questions to ask, etc.

At the beginning of each Instructor's Manual document you'll find other useful information including the appropriate author to contact if you have questions or comments, a list of the Group Projects that you can cover, and a list of any associated data files.

We've provided the Instructor's Manual files in Word format and placed them on both the Instructor's CD and the text's Web site.

TEST BANK

For each chapter and module, there are approximately 125 multiple-choice, true/false, and fill-in-the-blank questions aimed at challenging the minds of your students.

POWERPOINT PRESENTATIONS

The PowerPoint presentations are ready for you to use in class. In preparing to use these, you simply work through the Instructor's Manual which includes thumbnails of each slide and important points to cover. Of course, we realize that you'll probably want to customize some of the presentations. So, we've made available to you most of the images and photos in the text. You can find these on your Instructor's CD as well as the text's Web site at www.mhhe.com/haag.

Supplements:

- Online Learning Center
- Instructor's Manual
- Test Bank
- PowerPoint Presentations
- Student CD
- MISource CD
- Classroom Performance System
- Problem Solving Video Vignettes
- MBA MIS Cases
- Application Cases for MIS

Empowered Instruction

Classroom Performance System

Engage students and assess real-time lecture retention with this simple yet powerful wireless application. You can even deliver tests that instantly grade themselves.

Instructor Resource CD

Everything you need on one CD: PowerPoint slides, Test Item File (in Word and Diploma format), Solutions to end-of-chapter exercises and real world case questions, and much more.

PowerPoint Presentation

Robust, detailed, and designed to keep students engaged.

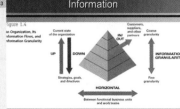

M?SOURCE

Software Skills & Computer Concepts

MISource provides animated tutorials and simulated practice of the core skills in Microsoft Excel, Access, and PowerPoint. MISource also animates 47 important computer concepts.

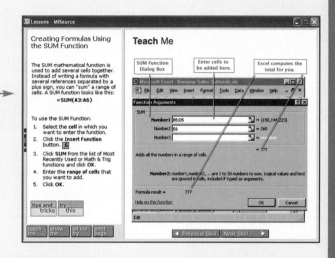

Spend less time reviewing software skills and computer literacy. Each text includes a copy of MISource.

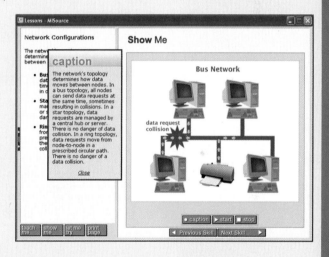

MIS Practice and Principles

MISource includes three video vignettes about the problems and opportunities facing a growing beverage company. Use the questions that follow each vignette as homework assignments or for discussion. Animated presentations of data mining, online transaction processing, and the systems development life cycle give students more perspective.

PROBLEM SOLVING VIDEO VIGNETTES

Three separate segments show how a growing beverage company comes to terms with problems and opportunities that can be addressed with database systems, telecommunications technology, and system development. Use the questions that follow each segment to inspire discussion or test students' critical thinking skills.

POWERWEB

PowerWeb is dynamic and easy to use. It automatically finds and delivers newly published supplemented MIS-specific content. PowerWeb is the first online supplement to offer your students access to

- Course-specific current articles refereed by content experts
- Course-specific real-time news
- Weekly course updates
- Interactive exercises and assessment tools
- Student study tips
- Web research tips and exercises
- Refereed and updated research links
- Daily news
- Access to the Northernlight.com Special Collection™ of journals and articles

MBA MIS CASES

Developed by Richard Perle of Loyola Marymount University, these 14 comprehensive cases allow you to add MBA-level analysis to your course. Visit our Web site to review a sample case.

APPLICATION CASES FOR MIS

Looking for a more substantial hands-on component? The Fifth Edition of Application Cases in MIS (ISBN 0072933631) by James Morgan is the proven answer.

ONLINE LEARNING CENTER

Visit www.mhhe.com/haag for additional instructor and student resources.

ONLINE COURSES

Content for the Fifth Edition is available in WebCT, Blackboard, and PageOut formats to accommodate virtually any online delivery platform.

EXTENDED LEARNING MODULE CD-ROM

This text is packaged with a student CD (0072962593) that contains five Extended Learning Modules (E, F, G, J, and K). There is a two-page introduction to each module in the book itself. All your students have to do is go to the CD to read the full module.

ACKNOWLEDGMENTS

As we now enter our fifth edition of this text, it has become increasingly obvious that the authors are only a small part of the overall equation that makes a good text. At McGraw-Hill/Irwin, there are several groups of people who have made this project successful. They are strategic management, EDP, and editorial.

McGraw-Hill/Irwin's strategic management is simply second to none. We gratefully acknowledge the dedicated work of Ed Stanford, J. P. Lenney, and David Littlehale. Their guidance is invaluable.

EDP includes all those people who take our thoughts on paper and bring them to life in the form of an exciting and dynamic book. Merrily Mazza leads this wonderful group of people, including Mary Conzachi (the book's project manager), Peter de Lissovoy (our manuscript editor), Jeremy Cheshareck (photo research coordinator), and Mary Kazak (cover and interior design specialist).

Editorial comprises those people who determine which projects to publish, and they have guided us every step of the way with a wealth of market intelligence. Stuart Mattson (publisher) leads the editorial group that includes Paul Ducham (our senior sponsoring editor) and Jennifer Wisnowski (the book's developmental editor). We are indebted to them for leading the way.

We would also like to acknowledge the dedicated work of the following people at McGraw-Hill/Irwin: Greg Bates (media producer), Rose Range (supplement producer), and Douglas Reiner (marketing manager). Without Greg and Rose, our text would be just a text, with no supplements or great supporting Web site. Without Douglas, you might never know we created this text.

We wish to acknowledge the wonderful efforts of our contributor team: Paige Baltzan, Amy Phillips, Dan Connolly, David Cox, Kathleen Davisson, Jeff Engelstad, and Syl Houston. Each has brought to the table unique talents and knowledge indispensable to the success of this text. As authors, we have come to realize that it's an impossible task to single-handedly keep up with technology—its advancements and how it's being used in the business world.

Last, but certainly not least, we offer our gratitude to our reviewers, who took on a thankless job that paid only a fraction of its true worth. We had the best. They include

Ajith Abraham
Oklahoma State University, Tulsa

Kamal Agarwal
Howard University

Rodney Alles
Chattahoochee Valley Community College

Beverly Amer
Northern Arizona University

Martin Anderson
Bowling Green State University

John Atkinson
West Kentucky University

David Bahn
Metropolitan State University

James Borden
Villanova University

Ronald Brando
Hudson Valley Community College

Kathryn Brohman
The University of Georgia

Bobby Burby
Webster University, Crystal Lake

Genard Catalano
Columbia College, Marysville

Dave Chatterjee
The University of Georgia

James Cumbo
Emory & Henry College

Andy Curran
The University of Cincinnati, Batavia

Mohammad Dadashzadeh
Wichita State University

Marvin Darter
Rider University

Subhankar Dhar
San Jose State University

Joyce Early
Fashion Institute Technology

Gary Fisher
Angelo State University

Mary Ellen Frank
Duquesne University

James Frost
Idaho State University

Bob Fulkerth
Golden Gate University, San Francisco

Joe Gagne
The University of South Carolina, Sumter

FROM STEPHEN HAAG . . . As I look back on my 20-year book publishing career, it dawns on me that writing a book is simply an extension of teaching. The entire author team—coauthors and contributors—are dedicated to the task of education, and I commend them all for their efforts. I specifically acknowledge the work of Maeve, Don, Paige, and Amy, who make writing a true pleasure.

I am also grateful to the many people who helped me along the career path of writing books. They include Peter Keen, JD Ice, David Brake, Rick Williamson, and a host of people still working at McGraw-Hill.

My colleagues in the Daniels College of Business at the University of Denver also provide support. I wish I could name all of you, but there isn't enough room. To James Griesemer (Dean), Sam Cassidy, the ITEC faculty, and Erin Hirsch, I thank you all.

And my writing efforts would not be successful nor would my life be complete without my family. My mother and father live just a few minutes from me and give me unending love and support. My two sons—Darian and Trevor—make me smile after long nights of working. My two four-legged sons—Indiana and Zippy—don't really even care that I write books; they offer me unconditional love. Finally, my wife, Pam, should be listed as a coauthor on many of my books. Her work is never done, and she loves every minute of it.

FROM MAEVE CUMMINGS . . . My sincere thanks goes to the many people who helped directly and indirectly with this edition and the previous four. Thanks to Steve, who is every bit as good a friend as he is a lead author. Thanks to Don, who is great to work with. Thanks to all the people at McGraw-Hill/Irwin who put in long hours and a lot of work to bring this book to completion.

A special thanks to Keith Neufeld, who is an expert on networks and generous with his knowledge, and to Lanny Morrow, who keeps me in touch with the fascinating world of computer forensics. Felix Dreher and Barbara Clutter were, and always have been, unwaveringly supportive and helpful, and a special thanks to my wonderful graduate assistant Nadir Bilge.

Thanks to the Holy Faith and Loreto nuns who gave me an excellent early education, which served as a solid foundation on which I was able to build. These were exceptionally dedicated teachers and I learned much more from them than the basics of reading, writing, and arithmetic.

As always, I want to thank my great family: my parents (Dolores and Steve), sisters (Grainne, Fiona, and Clodagh), and brother (Colin). And last, but by no means least, thanks to my husband, Slim, for making everything I do possible.

FROM DON McCUBBREY . . . The joy of this profession is working with students. Thanks go to them for keeping me on my toes by getting better every year. Thanks to my colleagues at the Daniels College of Business for surrounding me with an atmosphere of excellence. Thanks to my friends from the business community in Colorado, from IT consultants to EC entrepreneurs, who provide students and faculty with the seamless connectivity to the business world so essential in our field.

Special thanks go to my friends from academe, industry, and government from many countries around the world. Many of us meet each year in Bled, Slovenia, for our annual Electronic Commerce Conference. Thanks to Stephen for his high standards as leader of the band, and to Maeve, who is not only talented, but a true delight to work with. Amy and Paige, our contributors, have much to offer as writers, and we will see great things from them. Thanks to the team from McGraw-Hill: Paul, Jennifer, and all the others behind the scenes. Your counsel and support added much value.

Finally, thanks to my children, Heather, Stuart, and CJ, all of whom found success in the IT field, each with their own special focus. Thanks to my 97-year-old mother, who has read all my books. Most of all, thanks to my wife, Janis, who puts up with me and is truly one in a million.

STEPHEN HAAG is a professor in and Chair of the Department of Information Technology and Electronic Commerce in the Daniels College of Business at the University of Denver. Stephen is also the Director of the Masters of Science in Information Technology program and the Director of the Advanced Technology Center. Stephen holds a B.B.A. and M.B.A. from West Texas State University and a Ph.D. from the University of Texas at Arlington.

Stephen is the coauthor of numerous books including *Interactions: Teaching English as a Second Language* (with his mother and father), *Information Technology: Tomorrow's Advantage Today* (with Peter Keen), *Excelling in Finance,* and more than 40 books within the *I-Series.* He has also written numerous articles appearing in such journals as *Communications of the ACM, Socio-Economic Planning Sciences,* the *International Journal of Systems Science, Managerial and Decision Economics, Applied Economics,* and the *Australian Journal of Management.* Stephen lives with his wife, Pam, and their four sons—Indiana, Darian, Trevor, and Zippy—in Highlands Ranch, Colorado.

MAEVE CUMMINGS is a professor of Information Systems at Pittsburg State University. She holds a B.S. in Mathematics and Computer Science and an M.B.A from Pittsburg State and a Ph.D. in Information Systems from the University of Texas at Arlington. She has published in various journals including the *Journal of Global Information Management* and the *Journal of Computer Information Systems.* She serves on various editorial boards and is a coauthor of *Case Studies in Information Technology* and the concepts books of the *I-Series,* entitled *Computing Concepts.* Maeve has been teaching for 20 years and lives in Pittsburg, Kansas, with her husband, Slim.

DONALD J. MCCUBBREY is a professor in the Department of Information Technology and Electronic Commerce and Director of the Center for the Study of Electronic Commerce in the Daniels College of Business at the University of Denver. He holds a B.S.B.A. in Accounting from Wayne State University, a Master of Business from Swinburne University of Technology in Victoria, Australia, and a Ph.D. in Information Systems from the University of Maribor, Slovenia.

Prior to joining the Daniels College faculty in 1984, he was a partner with a large international accounting and consulting firm. During his career as an IT consultant he participated in client engagements in the United States as well as in several other countries in the Americas and Europe. He has published articles in *Communications of the Association for Information Systems, Information Technology and People* and *MIS Quarterly,* and coauthored the systems analysis and design text entitled *Foundations of Business Systems.* He is an associate editor of the *Communications of the Association for Information Systems.* He is a cofounder and director emeritus of the Colorado Software and Internet Association and lives in the Colorado foothills with his wife, Janis.

ABOUT THE CONTRIBUTORS

PAIGE BALTZAN teaches in the Department of Information Technology and Electronic Commerce in the Daniels College of Business at the University of Denver. Paige holds a B.S.B.A. in MIS and Accounting from Bowling Green State University and an M.B.A. specializing in MIS from the University of Denver. Paige's primary concentration focuses on object-oriented technologies and systems development methodologies. Paige has been teaching at the University of Denver for the past five years. A few of the courses Paige teaches include Systems Analysis and Design, Telecommunications and Networking, Software Engineering, Database Management Systems, and The Global Information Economy. Paige is the coauthor of *Microsoft Word 2003* with Stephen Haag and James Perry. This book is part of the well-received *I-Series* from McGraw-Hill. Paige is also working on a new book with Stephen Haag and Amy Phillips entitled *Business Driven Technology*.

Prior to joining the University of Denver, Paige spent three years working at Level(3) Communications as a technical architect and four years working at Accenture as a technology consultant specializing in the telecommunications industry. Paige lives in Lakewood, Colorado, with her husband, Tony, and daughters, Hannah and Sophie.

AMY PHILLIPS is a professor in the Department of Information Technology and Electronic Commerce in the University of Denver's Daniels College of Business. Amy has been teaching for more than 20 years—five years in public secondary education and 15 years in higher education. Amy has also been an integral part of both the academic and administrative functions within the higher educational system.

Amy's main concentration is database-driven Web sites, focusing on dynamic Web content, specifically ASP, XML, and .NET technologies. Some of the main core course selections that Amy teaches at the University of Denver include Analysis and Design, Elements of .NET, ASP.NET, and C#.NET. Her other publications include *Internet Explorer 6.0, PowerPoint 2003,* and a new book due out in 2005, *Business Driven Technology*.

CAREERS IN BUSINESS CONTRIBUTORS are the people who offered great insight into the new Module K on Careers in Business. No single person could have compiled information on the many business careers that appear in that module. The contributor team includes:

- Dan Connolly (Hospitality and Tourism Management)
- David Cox (Finance)
- Kathleen Davisson (Accounting)
- Jeff Engelstad (Real Estate and Construction Management)
- Syl Houston (Management)

Management Information Systems

FOR THE INFORMATION AGE

CHAPTER ONE OUTLINE

STUDENT LEARNING OUTCOMES

1. Define management information systems (MIS) and information technology (IT) and describe their relationship.

2. Validate information as a key resource and describe both personal and organizational dimensions of information.

3. Explain why people are the most important organizational resource, define their information and technology literacy challenges, and discuss their ethical responsibilities.

4. Describe the important characteristics of information technology (IT) as a key organizational resource.

5. Define competitive advantage and illustrate the role of information technology in supporting operational excellence, major business initiatives, decision making, and organizational transformation.

6. Discuss the impacts information technology can and will have on your life.

CHAPTER ONE

The Information Age in Which You Live
Changing the Face of Business

OPENING CASE STUDY:
PAY-PER-TUNE GENERATION
AND DISRUPTIVE TECHNOLOGIES ROCK
THE RECORD INDUSTRY

In 1999, the record industry raked in $14.6 billion in revenue and was growing 6 percent annually. Then, Napster appeared on the scene and forever changed the record industry. Napster's innovative disruptive technology—file sharing via peer-to-peer technology—appealed to the growing "pay-per-tune" generation, seeking only a particular song instead of the entire album.

Of course, you probably know that the federal government eventually deemed Napster's activities illegal and put it out of business. But the pay-per-tune notion of purchasing music never went away. Apple's iTunes provides a catalog of over 400,000 songs, each of which can be purchased without buying the whole album. Paid downloads of individual songs is expected to reach $3.2 billion in 2008.

Unfortunately, this isn't good for the record industry. Album sales, which account for the majority of revenue, ended at about $600 million in 2003, down from $711 million in 1999. That decrease is greater than the projected increase of pay-per-tune revenue by a wide margin.

But pay-per-tune isn't the only culprit. It's estimated worldwide that the illegal downloading, piracy, and file-sharing of music accounts for 40 percent of the decline in record sales. In these areas without a doubt we confront the illegal and unethical use of technology. The technology involved itself obviously isn't illegal or unethical. The use of the technology is.

So, what is the record industry supposed to do? Accept its fate as a dinosaur doomed to extinction? We believe not, along with many other people. As Dave Allison, owner of Times Beach Records, explains, "The entire industry has to redefine itself and change . . . We're all in this together, and we have to move forward together . . ." Indeed, the record industry must undergo dramatic transformation if it is to survive and thrive.

This story of the record industry isn't really about the disruptive technologies of the Internet, file-sharing peer-to-peer systems, and MP3 players. It is about the challenge of those technologies and the willingness of organizations—or, in this case, an industry—to embrace those disruptive technologies and determine how to use them instead to create a competitive advantage.

And that's the focus of our text. Although it will introduce you to a wide array of technology terms and concepts and teach you the technology, we want you to always keep in mind the challenge of how to apply technology to create a competitive advantage. In this first chapter, we will start by seeing how organizations can use technology to support operational excellence, major business initiatives, decision making, and—yes—organizational transformation.

Technology is a set of tools you use to work with information. The competitive advantage of technology really lies in <u>how</u> you and your organization decide to use it. As in the case of the record industry and moving to a pay-per-tune environment, many times you'll find it necessary to transform what you do to meet the changing needs and desires of your customers. Other times, you may simply find how much more efficient you can be by using technology. In either case, technology can be an enabler of competitive advantage and innovation. It can also spell doom for your organization if you choose to ignore it.[1,2]

Introduction

It is the ***information age***—a time when knowledge is power. Today, more than ever, businesses are using information (and information technology) to gain and sustain a competitive advantage. You'll never find a successful business whose slogan is "What you don't know can't hurt you." Businesses understand that what they don't know can become an Achilles' heel and a source of advantage for the competition.

Whether your major is marketing, finance, accounting, human resource management, or any of the many other specializations in a business program, you're preparing to enter the business world as a *knowledge worker*. Simply put, a ***knowledge worker*** works with and produces information as a product. According to *U.S. News & World Report* in 1994 (10 years ago), knowledge workers in the United States outnumbered all other workers by a four-to-one margin.[3] Today, that margin is even greater, probably five-to-one or six-to-one.

In the information age, *management information systems* and *information technology* are vitally important tools and topics. Why? Because management information systems deals with the coordination and use of three very important organizational resources—information, people, and information technology. Formally, we define management information systems and information technology as follows:

- ***Management information systems (MIS)*** deals with the planning for, development, management, and use of information technology tools to help people perform all tasks related to information processing and management.
- ***Information technology (IT)*** is any computer-based tool that people use to work with information and support the information and information-processing needs of an organization.

From those definitions you can gather that people or knowledge workers use information technology to work with information.

Statistically, there are any number of ways to validate the impact information technology is having on the business world. Consider the graph in Figure 1.1. It shows that 29.6 million households in the United States took advantage of online banking in 2003 with 50 percent of those paying their bills online. It is estimated that 56 million households will use online banking in 2008, with 85 percent paying bills online. Those are startling and insightful statistics for the financial services industry. Most notably—with so many

Figure 1.1

Online Banking and Bill Paying[4]

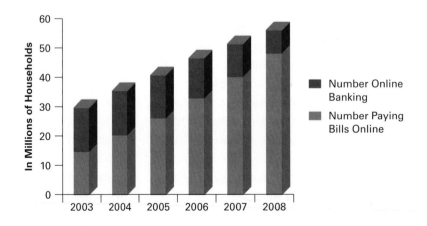

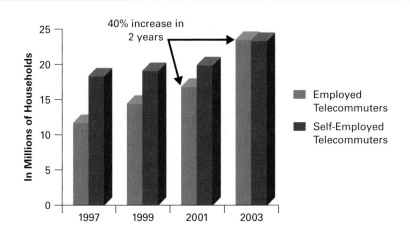

Figure 1.2

Telecommuting on the Rise[5]

people now performing online banking, what will happen to the numerous small bank branches you see in malls and on street corners? And that's just the banking side. Already, more than one-third of all stock transactions take place over the Internet.[6] In the coming years, you can expect to see the financial services industry, as a whole, transform itself around providing customer self-service systems, those systems that customers use to process their own transactions.

Think about your future job. It may include ***telecommuting,*** the use of communications technologies (such as the Internet) to work in a place other than a central location. In Figure 1.2, you can see that telecommuting among employed workers in the United States rose to 23.5 million in 2003, a more than 100 percent increase from 1997 and an almost 40 percent increase from 2001.

From a personal point of view, telecommuting presents wonderful "quality of life" opportunities. From a business point of view, it is also good but presents new challenges. Now more than ever businesses must consider the issue of security. With the advent of the Internet, wireless communications, and telecommuting, the security of information is a top priority. People working from home are more vulnerable to virus attacks than are workers at a central location behind company firewall hardware and software. Communications across the Internet (either wired or wireless) are more susceptible to interception than communications on a secure local area network in an office building. Management information systems (MIS) encompasses all of these issues and many more, as well as the enabling technologies.

This is an MIS book, but what you need to keep in mind is that technology is not the sole focus of MIS. Technology is a set of tools that enables you to work more efficiently and effectively with information. Pragmatically speaking, people and information are the most important resources within MIS, not technology. Of course, every organization today needs all three (and many others such as capital) to compete effectively in the marketplace.

In this first chapter, we will explore with you the three key resources of MIS—information, people, and information technology. We'll do so at a fairly high level in the hope of providing you with a solid understanding of the roles of each and their interrelationships. In subsequent chapters (and modules), we'll focus specifically on the strategic and competitive opportunities of IT (Chapters 2 and 5), provide you technology-centric coverage (the extended learning modules and Chapters 3, 4, 6, and 7), ask why protection is necessary for organizations and you in cyberspace (Chapter 8), and finally look at emerging trends that we see on the horizon (Chapter 9).

Information as a Key Resource

Information is crucially important today. We are in the "information age," a time when knowledge is power. Information is one of the three key components of management information systems (MIS) along with information technology and people. Knowledge comes from having timely access to information and knowing what to do with it, the province of MIS.

DATA, INFORMATION, AND BUSINESS INTELLIGENCE

To understand the nature of information and *business intelligence,* you must first understand another term—*data.* **Data** are raw facts that describe a particular phenomenon. For example, the current temperature, the price of a movie rental, and your age are all data. **Information** then is simply data that have a particular meaning within a specific context. For example, if you're trying to decide what to wear, the current temperature is information because it's pertinent to your decision at hand (what to wear); in this situation the price of a movie rental is not pertinent information.

Information may be data that have been processed in some way or presented in a more meaningful fashion. In business, for instance, the price of a movie rental may be information to a checkout clerk, but it may represent only data to an accountant who is responsible for determining net revenues at the end of the month.

Business intelligence is information "on steroids," so to speak. **Business intelligence (BI)** is knowledge—knowledge about your customers, your competitors, your business partners, your competitive environment, and your own internal operations—that gives you the ability to make effective, important, and often strategic business decisions. It enables your organization to extract the true meaning of information to take creative and powerful steps to ensure a competitive advantage. So, business intelligence is much more than just a list of the products you sell. It could combine your product information with your advertising strategy information and customer demographics information to help you determine the effectiveness of various advertising media on demographic groups segmented by location. You'll learn more about business intelligence, how to gather it, how to use it, and how to use IT to generate it throughout this text, and especially in Chapters 2 and 3.

PERSONAL DIMENSIONS OF INFORMATION

As a knowledge worker, you work with and produce information. As you do, you can consider it from three points of view or dimensions: time, location, and form (see Figure 1.3).

THE TIME DIMENSION   The time dimension of information has two aspects: (1) having access to information when you need it, or *timeliness,* and (2) having information that describes the time period you're considering. Information, like many organizational resources, can become old and obsolete. For example, if you want to make a stock trade today, you need to know the price of the stock right now. If you have to wait a day to view stock prices, you may not survive in the turbulent securities market. It's no wonder that over one-third of all stock transactions today occur over the Internet.

Figure 1.3

Personal Dimensions of Information

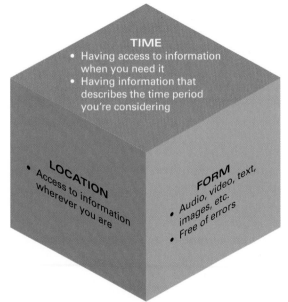

TIME
- Having access to information when you need it
- Having information that describes the time period you're considering

LOCATION
- Access to information wherever you are

FORM
- Audio, video, text, images, etc.
- Free of errors

OVERCOMING LANGUAGE BARRIERS ON THE INTERNET

The Internet is certainly a disruptive technology that has eliminated geographical and location barriers. With almost one-sixth of the world's population having access to the Internet, "location, location, location" in the physical world is becoming less and less and less important.

However, now we have new issues to deal with, notably, a language barrier. What happens if you connect to a site that offers information in a language you don't understand? How can you send an e-mail to someone in Japan who doesn't speak English?

One solution is language translation software, and one company leading the way in the development of language translation software is SYSTRAN. SYSTRAN Enterprise is a suite of software tools that enables you, among other things, to translate about 3,700 words per minute, translate both e-mail and Web page content, and display Asian fonts.

Is it perfect? Not according to SYSTRAN's disclaimer. It states specifics about what its products will do, but does encourage you to carefully review any translation before making it a part of your business communications.

Indeed, when Kentucky Fried Chicken wanted to translate its slogan "finger-lickin' good" into Chinese, it came out as "eat your fingers off." Now, KFC wasn't using SYSTRAN's software, but this example does illustrate the difficulty of translating idiomatic phrases from one language to another. Product names are another example. When General Motors (GM) tried to sell the Chevy Nova in South America, people didn't buy it. As it turns out, *No va* means "it won't go" in Spanish. GM subsequently changed the name to Caribe for its Spanish markets.

By the way, you should connect to SYSTRAN's Web site at www.systransoft.com. There, you can type in a phrase and choose the language into which you would like it translated.

Your information is useful and relevant only if it describes the appropriate time period. For example, most utility companies provide you with a bill that not only tells you of your current usage and the average temperature but also compares that information to the previous month and perhaps the same month last year. This type of information can help you better manage your utilities or simply understand that this month's high utility bill was caused by inclement weather.

THE LOCATION DIMENSION Information is no good to you if you can't access it. The location dimension of information means having access to information no matter where you are. Ideally, in other words, your location or the information's location should not matter. You should be able to access information in a hotel room, at home, in the student center of your campus, at work, on the spur of the moment while walking down the street, or even while traveling on an airplane. This location dimension is closely related to mobile and wireless computing which we'll discuss in an upcoming section.

To keep certain information private and secure while providing remote access for employees, many businesses are creating intranets. An *intranet* is an internal organizational Internet that is guarded against outside access by a special security feature called a *firewall* (which can be software, hardware, or a combination of the two). So, if your organization has an intranet and you want to access information on it while away from the office, all you need is Web access and the password that will allow you through the firewall.

For example, Sutter Health, a nonprofit network of 33 hospitals with 4.5 million patients, uses an intranet to allow doctors, specialists, lab technicians, and patients to communicate via the Internet.[7] Sutter's intranet even supports a virtual emergency room. It allows doctors—from various locations throughout a given hospital—to view and perform a preliminary diagnosis on emergency room patients.

THE FORM DIMENSION The form dimension of information deals with two primary aspects. The first is simply having information in a form that is most usable and understandable by you—audio, text, video, animation, graphical, and others. The second deals with accuracy. That is, you need information that is free of errors. Think of information as you would think of a physical product. If you buy a product and it's defective, you become an unsatisfied customer. Likewise, if you receive information that is incorrect, you're very unhappy as well.

ORGANIZATIONAL DIMENSIONS OF INFORMATION

Even if your choice in life is to be an entrepreneur, you also need to consider various organizational dimensions of information. These include information flows, information granularity, what information describes, and how information is used (whether for transaction processing or analytical processing, which we'll discuss in an upcoming section).

INFORMATION FLOWS Information in an organization flows in four directions: up, down, horizontally, and inward/outward. To consider these flows, let's briefly review the structure of an organization. Most people view a traditional organization as a pyramid with four levels and many sides (see Figure 1.4). From top to bottom, the levels are:

- *Strategic management,* which provides an organization with overall direction and guidance.
- *Tactical management,* which develops the goals and strategies outlined by strategic management.
- *Operational management,* which manages and directs the day-to-day operations and implementations of the goals and strategies.
- Nonmanagement employees, who actually perform daily activities, such as order processing, developing and producing goods and services, and serving customers.

If you consider your school as an example, strategic management might include the chancellor, president, and various vice presidents. Tactical management would include the deans. Operational management would include the department chairs and directors of academic programs. The final level would include instructors who are responsible for teaching your classes.

Figure 1.4

An Organization, Its Information Flows, and Information Granularity

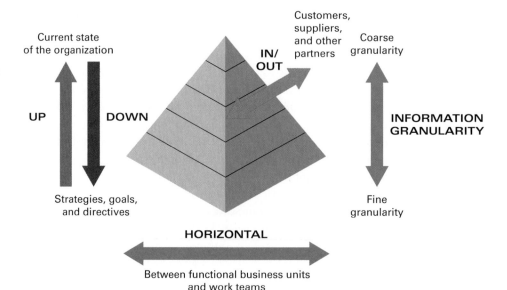

Information that flows upward, or the *upward flow of information,* describes the current state of the organization based on its daily transactions. When a sale occurs, for example, that information originates at the lowest level of the organization that then is passed up through various levels of management. Information that is gathered as a part of everyday operations is consolidated by information technology and passed upward to decision makers who monitor and respond to problems and opportunities.

The *downward flow of information* consists of the strategies, goals, and directives that originate at one level and are passed to lower levels. Many organizations are taking advantage of collaborative technologies and systems to share and move this type of information. You'll learn more about these types of technologies later in this chapter and in Chapter 2.

Information that flows horizontally, or the *horizontal flow of information,* is between functional business units and work teams. For example, at your school various departments are responsible for scheduling courses. That information is passed horizontally to the registrar's office, which creates a course schedule for your entire campus (which may be online—timely and accessible from anywhere by you). Again, collaborative technologies and systems support the horizontal flow of information.

Finally, the *outward and inward flows of information* consist of information that is communicated to customers, suppliers, distributors, and other partners for the purpose of doing business. These flows of information are really what electronic commerce is all about. Today, no organization is an island, and you must ensure that your organization has the right information technology to communicate with all types of business partners. We cover these important topics in Chapter 5 (on e-commerce), *Extended Learning Module E* (network basics), and Chapter 7 (IT infrastructures).

INFORMATION GRANULARITY   Figure 1.4 also illustrates another dimension of information—granularity. ***Information granularity*** refers to the extent of detail within the information. On one end of this spectrum is coarse granularity, or highly summarized information. At the other end is fine granularity, or information that contains a great amount of detail. As you might guess, people in the highest levels of the organization deal mainly with a coarse granularity of information, with sales by year being an example. People in the lowest levels of the organization, on the other hand, need information with fine granularity. If you consider sales again, nonmanagement employees need information in great detail that describes each transaction—when it occurred, whether by credit or cash, who made the sale, to whom that sale was made, and so on.

So, when transaction information originates at the lowest level of an organization (with fine granularity), it is consolidated to a coarser granularity as it moves up through the organization (the upward flow of information).

WHAT INFORMATION DESCRIBES   Another organizational dimension of information is what the information describes. Information can be internal, external, objective, subjective, or some combination of the four.

1. ***Internal information*** describes specific operational aspects of an organization.
2. ***External information*** describes the environment surrounding the organization.
3. ***Objective information*** quantifiably describes something that is known.
4. ***Subjective information*** attempts to describe something that is unknown.

Consider a bank that faces a decision about what interest rate to offer on a CD. That bank will use internal information (how many customers it has who can afford to buy a CD), external information (what rate other banks are offering), objective information (what is today's prime interest rate), and subjective information (what prime interest rate

DIFFERENT SOFT DRINKS AND DIFFERENT TASTES, BUT CONSOLIDATED INFORMATION

"Consolidated sales information is critical to our business. Our field people need combined data on all product lines for sales presentations to distributors. And our managers need information constantly to make key marketing and distribution decisions," offers Harish Ramani, Director of Strategic Systems and Support with Dr Pepper/7 Up, IT department.

Dr Pepper/7 Up is a subsidiary of Cadbury Schweppes, the global beverage giant and owner of highly visible beverage brands such as Dr Pepper, 7 Up, Canada Dry, Schweppes, Sunkist, A&W Root Beer, and many others. The challenges associated with owning and distributing so many different brands are numerous, including:

- Needing to consolidate information on all product brands.
- Providing business intelligence so managers can make strategic decisions.

To support its varied information-processing needs, Cadbury Schweppes turned to technology.

Specifically, Cadbury implemented Cognos Business Intelligence (BI) software. Cognos is the world's leading provider of business intelligence software. Cognos BI is software that, among other things, provides the ability to aggregate information from many different sources. In this case, Cadbury uses Cognos BI to aggregate information from all its beverage lines.

Using the software, Cadbury is able to provide a single user interface to all its field people and management personnel. No matter how many different product lines a person may be looking at, the interface is the same as if that person were viewing only one product line.

Technology tools, such as Cognos BI, that consolidate information from different sources to support the creation and use of business intelligence are vitally important in today's business world. Like Cadbury, most businesses have multiple product lines. Those businesses need to consolidate information, make it available in a usable form to nonmanagement employees, and present it as business intelligence to managers making business decisions.[8]

is expected in the future). Actually, the rate other banks are offering is not only external information (it describes the surrounding environment) but objective information (it is quantifiably known).

As a general rule, people in the lowest level of the organization deal mainly with internal and objective information (the price of a movie rental is an example). People in the highest levels of the organization, on the other hand, deal with all types of information.

People as the Key Resource

The single most important resource in any organization is its people. People set goals, carry out tasks, make decisions, serve customers, and, in the case of IT specialists, provide a stable and reliable technology environment so the organization can run smoothly and gain a competitive advantage in the marketplace. This discussion is all about you. You're preparing to be a knowledge worker.

INFORMATION AND TECHNOLOGY LITERACY

In business, your most valuable asset is <u>not</u> technology but rather your *mind*. IT is simply a set of tools that helps you work with and process information, but it's really just a *mind support* tool set. Technology such as spreadsheet software can help you quickly create a high-quality and revealing graph. But it can't tell you whether you should build a bar or a pie graph, and it can't help you determine whether you should show sales by territory or sales by salesperson. Those are your tasks, and that's why your business curriculum includes classes in human resource management, accounting, finance, marketing, and perhaps production and operations management.

Nonetheless, technology is an important set of tools for you. Technology can help you be more efficient and can help you dissect and better understand problems and opportunities. So, it's important for you to learn how to use your technology tool set. And it's equally important that you understand the information to which you're applying your technology tools.

A *technology-literate knowledge worker* is a person who knows how and when to apply technology. The "how" aspect includes knowing what technology to buy, how to exploit the many benefits of application software, and what technology infrastructure is required to get businesses connected to each other, just to name a few. From your personal perspective, we've provided many extended learning modules in this text to help you become a technology-literate knowledge worker. These include:

- *Extended Learning Module A*—basic computer hardware and software terminology.
- *Extended Learning Module B*—how to search and use the Web.
- *Extended Learning Modules C* and *J*—how to design and implement a database.
- *Extended Learning Module D*—advanced decision support tools in Excel including filtering, conditional formatting, and pivot tables.
- *Extended Learning Module E*—the basics of networks including how to set up a home network.
- *Extended Learning Module F*—how to write HTML to create a Web site.
- *Extended Learning Module I*—how to build an e-portfolio to advertise yourself on the Web.

A technology-literate knowledge worker also knows "when" to apply technology. Unfortunately, in many cases, people and organizations have blindly decided to use technology to help solve some sort of business problem. What you need to understand is that technology is not a panacea. You can't simply apply technology to any given process and expect that process instantly to become more efficient and effective. Look at it this way— if you apply technology to a process that doesn't work correctly, then you'll only be doing things wrong millions of times faster. There are cases when technology is not the solution. Being a technology-literate knowledge worker will help you determine when and when not to apply technology.

Information-literate knowledge workers

- Can define what information they need.
- Know how and where to obtain that information.
- Understand the information once they receive it (i.e., can transform it into business intelligence).
- Can act appropriately based on the information to help the organization achieve the greatest advantage.

Consider a unique, real-life example of an information-literate knowledge worker.

Several years ago, a manager of a retail store on the East Coast received some interesting information: diaper sales on Friday evening accounted for a large percentage of total sales for the week. Most people in this situation would immediately jump to the decision to ensure that diapers are always well stocked on Friday evenings or to run a special on diapers during that time to increase sales further, but not our information-literate

E-LEARNING: NOT JUST FOR SCHOOL

To become effective in your use of information, you can use technology to *learn*—not only about what certain information means—but more basically how to perform your work responsibilities better. Brink's Home Security recently implemented an *e-learning* management system to help (1) train its 2,600 employees, (2) increase customer retention, (3) improve profits, and (4) reduce employee turnover.

Many of Brink's field personnel work nights and weekends installing home security systems. For them, instructor-led training classes in a central location (Brink's has a nationwide field workforce) created problems and simply didn't work.

The new e-learning management system helps managers develop customized online training modules and allows field personnel to access those modules 24 hours per day, seven days per week. The system even provides skills assessment and other forms of evaluation.

The total investment in the system for Brink's was $300,000. It expects to save $500,000 in the first three years as a result of replacing instructor-led classes with the e-learning modules. Brink's has already noticed that its better-trained field personnel have improved profit margins and increased customer retention.[9]

knowledge worker. She first looked at the information and decided it was not complete. That is, she needed more information before she could act.

She decided the information she needed was *why* a rash of diaper sales (pardon the pun) occurred on Friday evenings and *who* was buying the diapers. That information was not stored within the computer system, so she stationed an employee in the diaper aisle on Friday evening to record any information pertinent to the situation (i.e., she knew how and where to obtain information). The store manager learned that young businessmen purchased the most diapers on Friday evenings. Apparently, they had been instructed to buy the weekend supply on their way home from work. The manager's response was to stock premium domestic and imported beer near the diapers. Since then, Friday evening has been not only a big sale time for diapers but also for premium domestic and imported beer.

There are a couple of important lessons you can learn from this story. First, as we've already stated, technology is not a panacea. Although a computer system generated the initial report detailing the sale of diapers on Friday evenings, our retail store manager did not make any further use of technology to design and implement her innovative and highly effective solution. Second, this story can help you distinguish between information and business intelligence. In this case, the information was the sale of diapers on Friday evening. The business intelligence included:

- *Who* was making diaper purchases on Friday evening.
- *Why* those people were purchasing diapers on Friday evening.
- *What* complementary product(s) those people might also want or need.

As a good rule of thumb, when you receive information and need to make a decision based on it, ask yourself questions that start with who, what, when, why, where, and how. Answers to those questions will help you create business intelligence and make better decisions.

YOUR ETHICAL RESPONSIBILITIES

Your roles as a technology-literate and information-literate knowledge worker extend far beyond using technology and information to gain a competitive advantage in the marketplace for your organization. You must also consider your social responsibilities: This is where ethics become important. ***Ethics*** are the principles and standards that guide our behavior toward other people. Your ethics have consequences for you just as laws do. But ethics are different from laws. Laws either clearly require or prohibit an action. Ethics are more subjective, more a matter of personal or cultural interpretation, and thus a decision or an action might have an outcome that is right or wrong according to different people's ethics. Thus, ethical decision making can be complex. Consider the following examples:

1. Copying software you purchase, making copies for your friends, and charging them for the copies.
2. Making an extra backup of your software just in case both the copy you are using and the primary backup fail for some reason.
3. Giving out the phone numbers of your friends and family, without their permission, to a telecom provider of some sort of calling plan so you can receive a discount.

Each of these examples is either ethically (according to you or some people) and/or legally (according to the government) incorrect. In the second example, you might be ethically okay in making an extra backup copy (because you didn't share it with anyone), but according to most software licenses you're prohibited by law from making more than one backup copy. What do you think about the first and third examples? Illegal? Unethical? Both?

To help you better understand the relationship between ethical acts and legal acts, consider Figure 1.5. The graph is composed of four quadrants, and the complexity of ethical decisions about behavior is suggested by quadrant III. Do any of the three examples above fall in quadrant III? Perhaps you can think of some other actions that although legal might still be unethical (how about gossiping?). You always want your actions to remain in quadrant I. If all your actions fall into that quadrant, you'll always be acting legally *and* ethically, and thus in a socially responsible way. Technology has further increased the complexity of ethics in our society because of the speed and casual ease with which people can access, distribute, and use information.

Being socially and ethically responsible in the information age involves not only the actions you initiate yourself but also what you do to protect yourself and your organization against the actions of others—that is, protecting yourself against cyber crimes. There are many types of cyber crimes—such as viruses, worms, identity theft, and Web defacing—performed by a variety of hackers such as black-hat hackers and cyberterrorists, and it is your responsibility to guard against them. It might even be considered an ethical lapse not to do so. We cannot stress enough how important it is for you to protect yourself and your organization's assets in cyberspace. We'll talk more about these issues later in this chapter, and we'll explore them in great detail in *Extended Learning Module H* (Computer Crime and Forensics) and Chapter 8 (Protecting People and Information).

Figure 1.5

Acting Ethically and Legally[10]

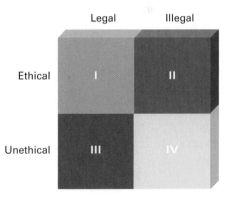

E-MAIL: ELECTRONIC MAIL OR EXPENSIVE MAIL?

In February 1995, an employee at Chevron came across what he thought was an interesting and funny list— "25 Reasons Why Beer Is Better Than Women." He quickly logged into his e-mail and distributed the list to many people. The only problem was that one of the people who received the e-mail was a woman, and she was offended by it. What followed was a lot of legal mumbo jumbo and an eventual out-of-court settlement worth $2 million that Chevron had to pay to the offended employee—definitely an example of when e-mail becomes expensive mail.

Most people agree that the original sender should not have distributed the list. It was mail that was potentially embarrassing and offensive to some people and, therefore, should not have been distributed as a matter of ethics. What people don't agree on, however, is whether or not the company was at fault for not monitoring and stopping the potentially offensive mail. What are your thoughts? Before you decide, follow the accompanying diagram and consider the consequences of your answers.[11]

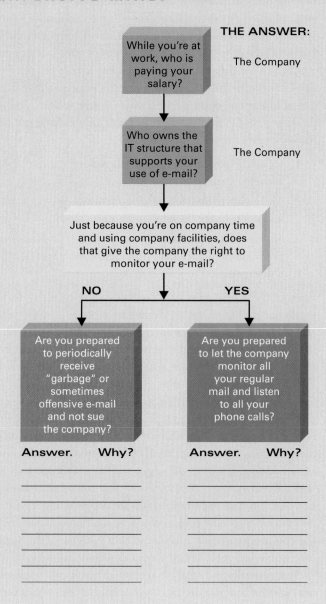

Information Technology as a Key Resource

Within management information systems (MIS), the third key resource is information technology. As we have already defined it, **information technology (IT)** is any computer-based tool that people use to work with information and support the information and information-processing needs of an organization. So, IT includes a cell phone or PDA that you might use to obtain stock quotes, your home computer that you use to write term papers, large networks that businesses use to connect to one another, and the Internet that almost one in every six people in the world currently uses.[12]

KEY TECHNOLOGY CATEGORIES

There are two basic categories of technology: hardware and software (see Figure 1.6). *Hardware* consists of the physical devices that make up a computer (often referred to as a *computer system*). *Software* is the set of instructions that your hardware executes to carry out a specific task for you. So, your PDA is the actual hardware; it contains software that you use to maintain your calendar, update your address book, and so on. Let's briefly look at hardware and software; for a more thorough discussion, read *Extended Learning Module A* (Computer Hardware and Software), which follows this chapter.

TECHNOLOGY HARDWARE   All hardware falls into one of the following six categories:

1. ***Input device***—tool you use to enter information and commands. Input devices include such tools as a keyboard, mouse, touch screen, game controller, and bar code reader.

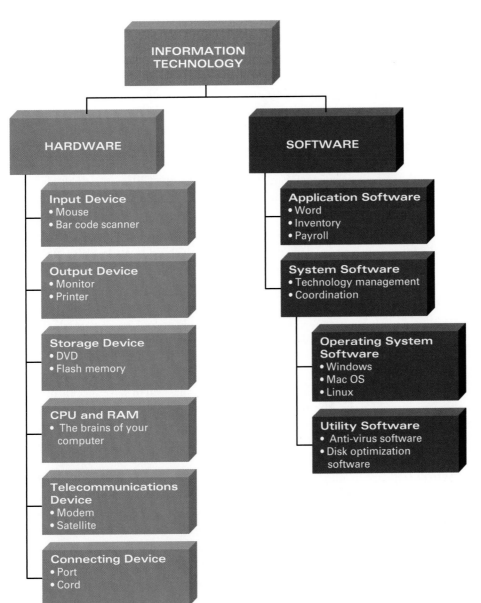

Figure 1.6

Information Technology
Hardware and Software

IDENTIFYING HARDWARE AND SOFTWARE

Pick up a recent copy of your local newspaper or perhaps a computer magazine such as *PC Magazine* or *Wired* and find an ad for a personal computer system. What is the price of the complete system? What hardware devices does it include? What software does it include?

Now, compare that system to a similar one that you can find on the Internet (you might want to start at Dell at www.dell.com). Which is cheaper? Does this surprise you? Why or why not?

Finally, identify all of the various computer components and place them in the graphical depiction of information technology hardware and software in Figure 1.6 on page 15.

2. *Output device*—tool you use to see, hear, or otherwise recognize the results of your information-processing requests. Output devices include such tools as a printer, monitor, and set of speakers.

3. *Storage device*—tool you use to store information for use at a later time. Storage devices include such tools as a hard disk, flash memory card, and DVD.

4. *Central processing unit (CPU)*—the hardware that interprets and executes the system and application software instructions and coordinates the operation of all the hardware. Popular personal CPUs include the Intel Pentium and Xeon product lines and the AMD Athlon series. *RAM*, or *random access memory*, is a temporary holding area for the information you're working with as well as the system and application software instructions that the CPU currently needs. Together, the CPU and RAM make up the brains of your computer.

5. *Telecommunications device*—tool you use to send information to and receive it from another person or computer in a network. For example, if you connect to the Internet using a modem, the modem (which could be a telephone, DSL, cable, wireless, or satellite modem) is a telecommunications device.

6. Connecting hardware—includes such things as parallel ports into which you would connect a printer, connector cables to connect your printer to the parallel port, and internal connecting devices that mainly include buses over which information travels from one piece of hardware to another.

TECHNOLOGY SOFTWARE   There are two main types of software: application and system. *Application software* is the software that enables you to solve specific problems or perform specific tasks. Microsoft Word, for example, can help you write term papers, so it's application software. From an organizational perspective, payroll software, collaborative software such as videoconferencing, and inventory management software are all examples of application software.

System software handles tasks specific to technology management and coordinates the interaction of all technology devices. Within system software, you'll find operating system software and utility software. *Operating system software* is system software that controls your application software and manages how your hardware devices work together. Popular operating systems include Microsoft Windows (and all its variations), Mac OS, Linux (an open-source operating system), and Unix.

Utility software is software that provides additional functionality to your operating system software. Utility software includes anti-virus software, screen savers, disk optimization software, uninstaller software (for properly removing unwanted software), file security software (which usually includes encryption), and a host of others. Again, in the extended learning module that follows this chapter, we discuss both hardware and software in greater detail.

DECENTRALIZED COMPUTING, SHARED INFORMATION, AND MOBILE COMPUTING

All organizations use hardware and software to connect people to each other; to reach out to customers, distributors, suppliers, and business partners; and to provide a reliable and stable computing environment for smooth operations. Because so many people perform so many different tasks in so many different places within a business environment, the concepts of decentralized computing, shared information, and mobile computing are very important (see Figure 1.7).

Decentralized computing is an environment in which an organization distributes computing power and locates it in functional business areas as well as on the desktops of knowledge workers. This is possible because of the proliferation of less expensive, more powerful, and smaller systems including tablet PCs, notebooks, desktop computers, minicomputers, and servers. Equally important are technology infrastructures such as integrations and middleware that enable different computers and networks to communicate with each other and share information. You'll learn more about technology infrastructures in Chapter 7.

Shared information is an environment in which an organization's information is organized in one or more central locations, allowing anyone to access and use it as he or she needs to. Shared information enables people in the sales department, for example, to access work-in-progress manufacturing information to determine which products will be available to ship. At your school, the registrar's office can access the information within the financial aid office to determine how much of your tuition bill is covered by a scholarship or loan. To support shared information, most businesses organize information in the form of a database. In fact, databases have become the standard by which businesses organize their information and provide everyone access to it. We'll talk more

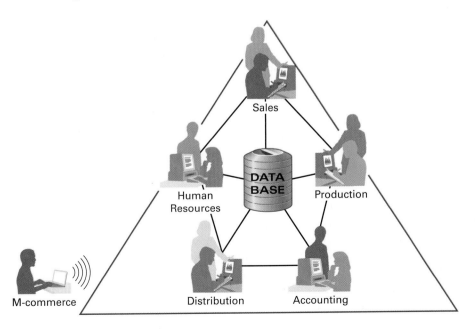

Figure 1.7

Decentralized Computing, Shared Information, and Mobile Computing about databases in a moment within the context of IT support for operational excellence, and we've devoted all of Chapter 3, *Extended Learning Module C* (Designing Databases and E-R Diagramming), and *Extended Learning Module J* (Implementing a Database with Microsoft Access) to the topic of databases.

Finally, ***mobile computing*** is a broad general term describing your ability to use technology to wirelessly connect to and use centrally located information and/or application software. As such, mobile computing is all about wireless connectivity. For example, ***m-commerce,*** the term used to describe electronic commerce conducted over a wireless device such as a cell phone, PDA, or notebook, now gives you the ability to buy and sell stocks, check weather forecasts, download music, and read your e-mail while sitting in an airport waiting to catch a flight. Business is now global and knows no geographical boundaries. You need mobile computing and wireless access to information and software no matter where you are.

Information Technology in Support of Business

Information technology has many uses in business. But if we had to sum up all those in one simple sentence, we would say: Businesses use information technology to give themselves a competitive advantage. A ***competitive advantage*** is providing a product or service in a way that customers value more than what the competition is able to do. Your organization can use technology to achieve a competitive advantage by supporting and enabling operational excellence, major business initiatives, decision making, and organizational transformation.

OPERATIONAL EXCELLENCE

At its most fundamental level, information technology can aid your organization in achieving operational excellence. Here, we look narrowly toward *operational excellence* within the context of efficiency, doing things right—in the least amount of time (this is the commonly accepted meaning of efficiency), at the least expense, with the fewest number of errors, and optimizing the use of resources. In support of operational excellence, almost all businesses use transaction processing systems, customer-self service systems, databases, and database management system software.

A ***transaction processing system (TPS)*** is exactly what its name implies—a system that processes transactions within an organization. TPSs include payroll systems, inventory stocking systems, sales processing systems, and a host of others. It is incumbent on your organization to support these types of functions in the operationally efficient way. This will add to your bottom-line profits by reducing costs.

An extension of a TPS is a customer self-service system. A ***customer self-service system*** is an extension of a TPS that places technology in the hands of an organization's customers and allows them to process their own transactions. Online banking, to which we alluded earlier, is a good example. Online banking provides you with the ability to do your own banking anywhere at anytime (except to withdraw or deposit cash of course). You can check your account balance, move funds from one account to another, pay your bills electronically, and even request that your bank send a physical check to a business or another person. Customer self-service systems further decentralize computing power in an organization by placing that power in the hands of customers.

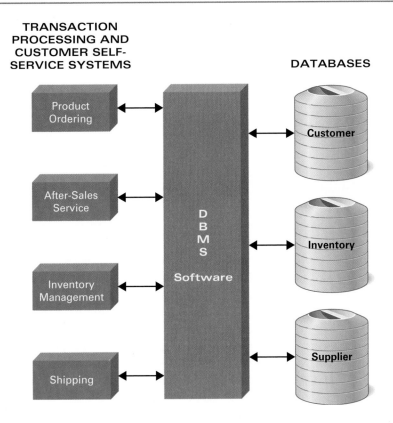

Figure 1.8

Information Technology Support for Operational Excellence

Behind every TPS and customer self-service system are one or more databases and database management system software (see Figure 1.8). Databases (which we focus on in Chapter 3) are large repositories of information that maintain tremendous detail on every transaction. Between a database and a TPS or customer self-service system is database management system (DBMS) software. DBMS software provides a bridge between a database (the information) and a software system (e.g., inventory management). It allows each different TPS and customer self-service system to access, use, and update the database information according to specific business rules.

Consider Amazon.com. Its world-renowned "1-Click ordering" customer self-service system on the Web provides a tremendous competitive advantage because of its ease of ordering, its filtering capabilities that match complementary products to your past purchases and that make recommendations concerning what might interest you, and its ability to maintain your billing and shipping information (so you're not forced to enter that information every time you make a purchase). Behind Amazon's customer self-service system is a large database that stores product information and information about your previous purchases along with DBMS software that gives you the ability to access and use that information.

Amazon has other systems as well—such as order fulfillment, inventory management, and supply chain management—that also use the DBMS software to access product and customer information. Together, all of these systems provide Amazon with a competitive advantage in the fiercely competitive online retail environment.

Operational excellence is key in the business world. Your organization cannot afford to process transactions incorrectly or have customers click through numerous Web pages to finally order a product. Information technology can definitely help your organization achieve operational excellence, which can in turn become a competitive advantage in the marketplace.

"NO-SWIPE" CREDIT CARDS OFFER CUSTOMER CONVENIENCE AND OPERATIONAL EXCELLENCE

The standard for using a credit card at a store has long been based on the swiping process to read the information from it. Wireless technologies—specifically RFID or radio-frequency identification—promise to be the disruptive technologies that set the new standard for no-swipe credit card use.

ExxonMobil, with its Speedpass RFID system embedded in a key chain, was the first to exploit no-swipe credit cards, beginning as early as 1997. Speedpass cards (or key chains), however, are good only at Exxon-Mobil gas stations.

RFID is a seemingly simple technology. An RFID-enabled computer chip is embedded into the credit card. The computer chip contains all the information normally found in the magnetic stripe of today's credit cards. When the card comes within close proximity to a wireless reader (6 to 12 inches), the computer chip is literally jolted to life by the electromagnetic waves the reader emits. So, you don't have to swipe an RFID credit card; instead, you just wave it at the reader.

MasterCard, American Express, and Visa USA have all transformed their own credit cards to make them capable of using RFID technology. Those companies have been testing their new systems for the past couple of years and plan full-scale rollouts in 2004 and 2005. MasterCard has even explored combining its credit card with a Nokia phone. (Most people carry cell phones today.) In this case, your cell phone would contain the RFID computer chip representing your credit card. So, you wouldn't even have to carry your credit card, as long as you had your cell phone in hand.

RFID-based credit cards offer greater customer convenience and should create additional efficiencies as you pay using your credit card. According to Betsy Foran-Owens, a MasterCard vice president, "In some instances it's faster than cash. You're eliminating the fumble factor."[13]

MAJOR BUSINESS INITIATIVES

To apply technology successfully in the business world, you need an integrated plan that encompasses your entire organization. That is, you can't have different departments within your organization with differing goals and strategies. Integrating the use of technology throughout your organization is key, and it must be based on your business strategies and initiatives.

Following this line of thinking, organizations plan their integrated use of technology around such major business initiatives as customer relationship management, enterprise resource planning, sales force automation, and supply chain management. These are all hot topics in the business world right now and will be for many years to come. Just as important, your organization needs to define how it will use technology in support of these initiatives.

Let's consider supply chain management. *Supply chain management (SCM)* tracks inventory and information among business processes and across companies. Therefore, a *supply chain management (SCM) system* is an IT system that supports supply chain management activities by automating the tracking of inventory and information among business processes and across companies. Consider the supply chain in Figure 1.9 and suppose your organization is a wholesaler of office furniture. You have customers—retail outlets such as Office Max and Office Depot. Those organizations have other customers, namely, businesses and individuals who purchase and use the office furniture. So, moving forward, your supply chain includes your customers and your customers' customers. Moving backward, your supply chain is even more extensive. You have distributing lines

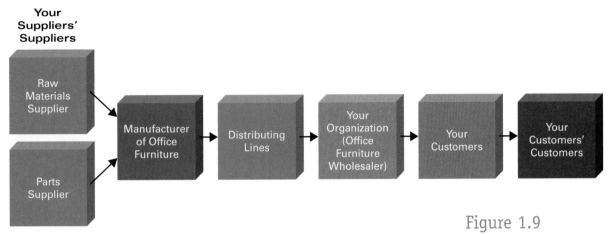

Figure 1.9

Suppliers' Suppliers and Customers' Customers in a Supply Chain

(e.g., truck and rail companies) that move products from manufacturers to you. You have manufacturers, and those manufacturers have suppliers of raw materials and suppliers of parts. So, your supply chain includes your suppliers and your suppliers' suppliers.

The goal of a comprehensive supply chain management system is to automate the flow of inventory and information across the entire supply chain. Ideally, your organization would use *electronic data interchange (EDI)*—the direct computer-to-computer transfer of transaction information contained in standard business documents, such as invoices and purchase orders, in a standard format—to order needed inventory from various manufacturers. Those electronic orders would trigger other systems within the manufacturing companies including the ordering of raw materials and parts from their suppliers and drop shipment schedules sent to the distributing lines.

Likewise, when an end customer ordered furniture from a retail outlet, that retail outlet would communicate its needed inventory in similar fashion to your organization. To be effective and offer the greatest competitive advantage in the marketplace, all processes that move information (including the electronic transfer of funds to reconcile accounts) would be handled in an automated fashion by EDI within an SCM system.

Another important initiative that many businesses are implementing today deals with managing the knowledge within the organization. "Knowledge," in this case, refers to your organization's *know-how*. This is the expertise your organization uses to run itself, make important decisions, and set its strategic direction. Knowledge management deals with almost every type of knowledge in your organization, including how processes work, failed and successful attempts at reengineering, and the strategies your organization uses to target customer segments with various products and services. In the case of the latter, the information that your organization uses to make decisions regarding how to target customer segments is business intelligence. The actual decisions themselves and the strategies are knowledge.

In support of knowledge management, you can create and use a knowledge management system. A *knowledge management (KM) system* is an IT system that supports the capturing, organization, and dissemination of knowledge (i.e., know-how) throughout an organization. The use and application of knowledge management systems are as numerous as there are types of organizations. In the accompanying Global Perspective box, you can learn how Unilever used a knowledge management system to share product branding knowledge among its employees. You will also learn more about knowledge management systems in Chapter 2, including challenges to success and strategic and competitive opportunities.

INTERNAL BRANDING WITH KNOWLEDGE MANAGEMENT

Product and image branding are just as important internally to your employees as externally to your customers. That is, your employees must recognize and embrace your branding strategies just as much as your customers.

Unilever Bestfoods Netherlands (UBF NL)—one of the largest international manufacturers of widely recognized food, home care, and personal care brand products—understood this key element and implemented a document management and knowledge management system (called Livelink Skins) for its employees.

According to Teun Potjewijd, an IT manager for UBF NL, "The Livelink Skins solution has helped Unilever Bestfoods Netherlands develop a unified way of working. It has improved internal communication and has helped create a stronger awareness of our new internal brand identity among our employees."

Livelink is actually a series of Web pages on UBF NL's intranet. Those Web pages present all employees with a standardized interface including document, news items, and discussions that all reflect UBF NL's branding efforts. As employees access the intranet to perform any of their work, they immediately see items related to branding efforts.

When undertaking branding efforts, don't forget that your employees need to be as brand conscious as your customers. Knowledge management systems can help.[14]

DECISION MAKING

When we discussed operational excellence a little earlier, you learned about the role of transaction processing and customer self-service systems, systems that process transactions. These support the concept of *online transaction processing (OLTP),* the gathering of input information, processing that information, and updating existing information to reflect the gathered and processed information. The counterpart to OLTP is *online analytical processing (OLAP),* the manipulation of information to support decision making. Just as with operational excellence, information technology is an important enabler of the decision-making process in business.

Some decisions in business are relatively easy to make while others are not. For example, deciding how many inventory units to reorder may be relatively easy (and structured using a reorder point algorithm), while deciding where to build a new distribution center may not be. In the case of the latter, you need to take into account numerous logistical issues, including proximity to major highways, proximity to a major airport, the workforce in a proposed area, tax incentives, and so on.

Technology to support decision making falls into one of two general categories: (1) systems that help you analyze a situation and then leave the decision entirely up to you and (2) systems that actually make some sort of recommendation concerning what action to take. The first category includes such IT tools as decision support systems and executive information systems. For example, an *executive information system (EIS)* is a highly interactive IT system that allows you to first view highly summarized information and then choose how you would like to see greater detail, which may alert you to potential problems or opportunities. In Figure 1.10, you can see three graphs that might appear in an EIS. The first one at the left shows sales by year. By clicking on a particular year, you can view sales by territory for that year. Then, by clicking on a particular terri-

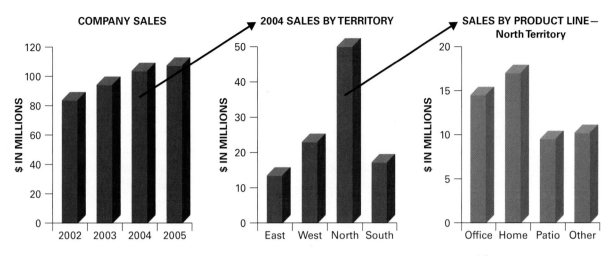

Figure 1.10

Drilling Down with an
Executive Information
System (EIS)

tory, you can view sales by product line for that territory within a given year. These types of IT systems offer you great speed in massaging information, developing alternatives, and viewing information from various perspectives. However, they do not make a recommendation concerning what you should do.

When making important business decisions, the old adage of "two heads are better than one" definitely applies. In the business world, you'll work on a number of teams, performing processes and making decisions. In this instance, technology plays an important role by providing tools that allow teams of people to work together, sharing ideas and addressing problems and opportunities. Most notably, you'll be working with a **collaboration system,** a system that is designed specifically to improve the performance of teams by supporting the sharing and flow of information. Many of these systems support "anonymous voting." That is, you can post a possible alternative to solving a problem and every team member can vote concerning whether they like the idea without specifying who they are. This helps teams develop innovative solutions and avoid such traps as "groupthink" or dominance by a particular team member. We'll talk more about EISs, collaboration systems, and other decision support technologies in Chapters 2 and 4.

The second category includes technologies in the area of artificial intelligence. **Artificial intelligence (AI)** is the science of making machines imitate human thinking and behavior. For example, a neural network is an artificial intelligence system that is capable of finding and differentiating patterns within information. Your credit card company probably uses a neural network to monitor your card use and identify possible fraud in case someone else happened to steal your card and attempted to use it. In this instance, the neural network has been fed every single credit card transaction you've performed, and it has developed a pattern of how, when, and why you use your card. Then, when a transaction occurs that doesn't fit the pattern of your profile, the neural network alerts someone that your credit card may have been stolen. You may have, in fact, received a call from your credit card company to verify a transaction. If so, it was most likely a neural network that "sent up a red flag" concerning the transaction.

Artificial intelligence is growing in use every day in the business world. Although you may not be directly involved in the development of such tools, you will very likely use them sometimes. So, it's important that you understand to which situations you should apply each AI tool. We'll cover those issues and many more in Chapter 4.

USING TECHNOLOGY WHEN MILLIONS OF POSSIBLE SOLUTIONS EXIST

Another important artificial intelligence tool is a genetic algorithm. A *genetic algorithm* is an artificial intelligence system that mimics the evolutionary, survival-of-the-fittest process to generate increasingly better solutions to a problem. Organizations apply genetic algorithms to problems for which (1) there are literally millions of possible solutions and (2) there is no appropriate problem-solving algorithm that will generate the perfect solution.

Consider the development of a new home area. Assume that someone has purchased a large parcel of land and intends to build 5,000 homes for residential sale. The task of laying out the design of the new home area is a daunting one. This is further complicated when having to determine how to optimally lay utility lines (fresh water lines, sewer lines, electrical lines, phone lines, gas lines, and cable TV lines). There are extensive sets of constraints concerning the laying of utility lines, but no simple algorithm that will help you find the right solution.

For example, depending on the grade of the terrain, fresh water and sewer lines must be sized to accommodate the slope of the terrain. And you can't run electrical or gas lines under a bridge. Furthermore, cable TV substations have to be positioned appropriately to ac-commodate the use of high-speed cable TV modems. Those are just a few of the many considerations, never mind the most basic one of optimizing lot tracts to build the most homes while minimizing unused land.

Many residential home developers turn to a genetic algorithm for this problem. Once the genetic algorithm has been fed all the necessary information (maximum and minimum lot tract sizes, topographical information of the terrain, performance criteria for evaluating solutions, and so on), it sets out creating solutions. As it comes across a fairly good solution, it attempts to alter the solution (using evolutionary, survival-of-the-fittest processes such as crossover, selection, and mutation) to create a better one. Eventually, the genetic algorithm exhausts all possible solutions and makes a recommendation concerning the best one, given the constraints and performance criteria that were specified.

Of course, the decision is still yours to make. While a genetic algorithm can determine the best possible solution, you need to carefully analyze the solution and determine if it really is "best." Technology can make recommendations, but the ultimate decision is still yours. In the end, you receive either the credit for making a good decision or the reprimand for making a bad one.

ORGANIZATIONAL TRANSFORMATION

As you read in the opening case, information technology—specifically, disruptive technologies—often forces an entire industry to transform itself and the way it does business. Indeed, it will be interesting to watch as the record industry transforms itself in the coming years from an album-based music provider to a pay-per-tune music provider.

Let's focus right now on just one organization—your organization—instead of an entire industry. In the business world, if you're standing still, you're falling behind. It's a simple fact—your competition is always trying to do better than you. Therefore, your organization must constantly seek to evolve, and, in most cases, transform itself. Quite the opposite of the record industry's initial reactionary approach to using information technology, your organization can take a proactive approach to using technology to transform itself.

eBay is a good example. It was never content with being the world's premier online auction house. A few years ago, it acquired PayPal and began offering payment services to its buyers and sellers. In 2003, it began offering its own credit card, with its "Anything Points" program offering eBay members the ability to buy products and pay for seller services with points accumulated from using the credit card. The integration of PayPal into its auction format and the offering of a credit card are simply not possible without sophisticated IT systems.

General Motors (GM) is another good example. Its financing business segment (GMAC) is now more profitable than manufacturing and selling of automobiles. GM doesn't want you to pay cash for a car—it wants you to finance the purchase or lease the car through GMAC. Many people believe that GM's core competency is its production of automobiles. While that may be true, it makes more money financing automobiles than it does manufacturing them. Again, it requires extensive use of technology to create financing and leasing systems in the automotive industry.

The business world is certainly a global one as well. Your organization will have business partners, competitors, suppliers, and customers worldwide. IT systems can support the movement of information and money in native languages and currencies. IT systems can eliminate geographical and time boundaries, enabling your organization to take advantage of a worldwide market of customers and talent. Going global is one way in which your organization can transform itself, and information technology can help.

In many instances, your business's transformation may be about deciding what information technology facilities and services to keep in house and what facilities and services to outsource. Like many others, your organization may choose to outsource many of its IT operations and focus solely on its core competencies. In this case, you may use an application service provider. An ***application service provider (ASP)*** supplies software applications (and often related services such as maintenance, technical support, and the like) over the Internet that would otherwise reside on its customers' in-house computers.

Your school is probably a good example of an organization that focuses on its core competencies and outsources other functions. Your school's core competency is education, providing you with the necessary knowledge to be successful. In focusing on that core competency, your school may have chosen to outsource other functions such as its bookstore operations, food services, and security. By outsourcing these types of activities, your school can focus on its core competency and spend more time determining how to transform itself by offering new degree programs, offering distance learning formats, and so on.

Whatever the case, your organization must seek to constantly transform itself. The highly competitive business environment necessitates this focus.

Information Technology in Your Life

Information technology plays an important role in every aspect of your life. From a personal point of view, you probably use a home computer to surf the Web, talk through Instant Messaging to your friends all over the world, buy products, and search for information. In the business world, information technology is everywhere and inescapable. This text shows you what you need to know about information technology in the business world to effectively use it and manage it to be more efficient at what you do and to help your organization gain competitive advantage.

YOUR CAREER

No matter what career you choose, information technology will have a great impact. Just as no person or organization is an island, neither is any specific function within an organization ever isolated. All functions in an organization need to work together, sharing information to achieve the greatest possible competitive advantage.

RESEARCHING YOUR CAREER AND INFORMATION TECHNOLOGY

To position yourself in the best possible way to succeed in the business world, you need to start researching your career right now. Here, we would like you to focus on the IT skills your career requires.

First, consider what career you want to have. Record that career in this box. Second, visit Monster.com (www.monster.com) and search for jobs that relate to your career. Read through several of the job postings and determine what IT skills you need to acquire. Write down those skills in this box as well.

Finally, compare your findings to other students in your class interested in a similar career. Together, you should be able to create a comprehensive list of IT skills you need to be successful.

CAREER: _____

IT SKILLS

_____

_____

_____

_____

IT SKILLS

_____

_____

_____

_____

Sharing information occurs through information technology, most notably decentralized computing, which we discussed in a previous section of the chapter. Powerful central information repositories or databases maintain a wealth of organizational information, everything from planned shipments of raw materials from suppliers to detailed information on customer inquiries, and perhaps complaints. If your customers consistently complain about the quality of a product, for instance, you need to be able to determine the cause of the problem, which may include looking at which supplier provided the raw materials that went into the production of the product, the production process itself such as which machines were used to produce the product, the salesperson who sold the product, and perhaps even how long the product sat in inventory before being sold.

So clearly, you need to learn a variety of business information technology tools. Many of these tools (called *vertical market software*) are specific to a given industry, such as the health care industry. Others (called *horizontal market software*) are more general, including accounting software or customer relationship management which can be used in numerous industries.

As you work with organizational information, you'll have the opportunity to download parts of it to your personal technology environment. From there, you can explore problems and opportunities by using personal productivity tools such as spreadsheet and database management system software. Your ability to use these personal productivity tools effectively will, in part, define your career success. We would encourage you to learn as much about these tools as you can. In this text, we've provided several extended learning modules to help you learn about the true productivity power of spreadsheet and database management system software.

In the business world, you'll be working with information technology, managing people, and most probably managing a budget. That doesn't mean you have to major in IT, human resource management, and finance. Information, people, and money pervade every aspect of business. You must learn to use and manage them well.

ETHICS, SECURITY, AND PRIVACY

As we close this first chapter, let's turn our attention back to ethics and a couple of new topics—security and privacy. We cannot stress enough how important it is for you to be ethical in your use of information and information technology. Even if you're not breaking the law, "shady" ethical acts can have a great impact on other people, and serious consequences for you. As a general rule of thumb when developing your ethical position, we encourage you to follow one simple rule—Do unto others as you would have them do unto you.

Unfortunately, you can't expect everyone to follow that rule, so much so that you must be vigilant in protecting yourself, your information, and your technology tools. As we said earlier, the easy power of information tools today increases the odds they will be misused by some people too, and not to guard your organization against bad actors out there is almost unethical in itself. You're probably familiar with viruses and worms, special types of software designed to do damage to your information and technology tools. You may also encounter *spyware* (also called *sneakware* or *stealthware*), software that comes hidden in free downloadable software and tracks your online movements, mines the information stored on your computer, or uses your computer's CPU and storage for some tasks you know nothing about. Spyware can invade your privacy, collect information about you, and send it—via the Internet—to an organization that might later sell that information.

Perhaps the greatest threat today (and on the horizon) to your personal safety in cyberspace is identity theft. *Identity theft* is the forging of someone's identity for the purpose of fraud. If you become a victim of identity theft, the "thief" will steal and use your credit cards, driver's license, and numerous other forms of identification. In today's IT-based and often virtual world, the thief has only to steal the information associated with those forms of identifications, not the actual documents themselves.

In 2003, financial losses from identity theft were estimated to be approximately $100 billion in the United States and $300 billion worldwide. Those are astounding numbers, but pale in comparison to what many experts are predicting for 2005—$1.8 trillion in the United States and almost $5 trillion worldwide.[15]

It is crucially important that you protect yourself, your information, and your technology tools. For starters, below are a few things to keep in mind (there are many more):

- Keep your anti-virus software up to date.
- Use only secure Web sites when submitting personal or financial information.
- Never give out your personal information to enter a contest on the Internet.
- Change your passwords frequently and intersperse capital letters and digits in them.
- Never assume that everyone has the same ethical standards you do.

DEVELOPING STRATEGIES FOR PROTECTING YOURSELF AGAINST IDENTITY THEFT

Identity theft is not something that happens to someone else. Almost 10 million people in the United States reported themselves as victims of identity theft in 2002—that's about one in every 29 people (even less when you take children out of the equation).

We provided a short list on the previous page of things you can do to protect yourself, your information, and your technology tools. As a group, focus on creating a comprehensive list of steps you can take to avoid identity theft. Write down the most important

steps in the table provided below. To help you start, consider visiting these sites:

- Federal Trade Commission—www.ftc.gov
- Identity Theft Prevention and Survival— www.identitytheft.org
- MSN's MoneyCentral—moneycentral.msn.com (search on Financial Privacy)
- Identity Theft Resource Center— www.idtheftcenter.org

1.	6.
2.	7.
3.	8.
4.	9.
5.	10.

Summary: Student Learning Outcomes Revisited

1. **Define management information systems (MIS) and information technology (IT) and describe their relationship.** *Management information systems (MIS)* deals with the planning for, development, management, and use of information technology tools to help people perform all tasks related to information processing and management. *Information technology (IT)* is any computer-based tool that people use to work with information and support the information and information-processing needs of an organization. IT is one of the three key elements, along with people and information, of management information systems.

2. **Validate information as a key resource and describe both personal and organizational**

dimensions of information. Information is one of the three key elements within MIS. We are in the "information age," a time when knowledge is power. Information is the foundation for business intelligence. The personal and organizational dimensions of information include

- Personal
  - Time—Access to information when you need it and information that describes the time period you're considering
  - Location—Access to information no matter where you are
  - Form—Information in a form that is most usable and understandable and information that is free of errors

- Organizational
  - Information flows—Up, down, horizontal, and inward/outward
  - *Granularity*—The extent of detail within information
  - What information describes—*Internal* (specific operational aspects), *external* (the surrounding environment), *objective* (quantifiably known), and *subjective* (something unknown)

3. **Explain why people are the most important organizational resource, define their information and technology literacy challenges, and discuss their ethical responsibilities.** People are the single most important resource in any organization, setting goals, carrying out tasks, and making decisions.

   - *Technology-literate knowledge workers* are people who know how and when to apply technology.

   - *Information-literate knowledge workers* (1) can define what information they need; (2) know how and where to obtain that information; (3) understand the information once they receive it; and (4) can act appropriately based on the information.

   - Most important, knowledge workers must be ethical. *Ethics* are the principals and standards that guide our behavior toward other people.

4. **Describe the important characteristics of information technology (IT) as a key organizational resource.** Information technology is a set of tools you use to work with information. All technology is either *hardware* (the physical devices that make up a computer) or *software* (the set of instructions that your hardware executes).

5. **Define competitive advantage and illustrate the role of information technology in supporting operational excellence, major business initiatives, decision making, and organizational transformation.** A *competitive advantage* is providing a product or service in a way that customers value more than what the competition is able to do.

   - Operational excellence—The use of technology for efficiency (doing things right, in the least amount of time, with the fewest number of errors, and so on)

   - Major business initiatives—The use of technology to support initiatives such as customer relationship management, enterprise resource planning, sales force automation, and supply chain management

   - Decision making—The use of technology tools—such as decision support systems, executive information systems, and artificial intelligence (AI)—to (1) help you analyze a situation and/or (2) make some sort of recommendation concerning what to do

   - Organizational transformation—The use of technology to enable your organization to evolve and transform itself into new modes of operation, market segments, and so on

6. **Discuss the impacts information technology can and will have on your life.** Technology is everywhere in the business world. For your career, you need to learn to use technology tools specific to your job and industry and personal productivity tools. You also need to protect yourself, your technology, and your information in cyberspace. The issues of security and privacy are vitally important.

CLOSING CASE STUDY ONE

YOU AND YOUR INFORMATION

No matter what you do or where you go, your information travels with you and is eventually captured and stored by a number of organizations. In this all-encompassing information and IT environment, let's consider two issues: trust and accuracy. As you'll see, both are related.

First, answer the questions on the next page (with a simple *yes* or *no*), which pertain to your everyday life.

1. Do you keep a paper record of all your long-distance phone calls—when you placed them by date and time, to whom, and the length—and then compare that list to your monthly phone bill?

Yes ☐   No ☐

2. Do you meet with the meter reader to verify the correct reading of your water, gas, or electricity usage?

Yes ☐   No ☐

3. As you shop, do you keep a record of the prices of your groceries and then compare that record to the register receipt?

Yes ☐   No ☐

4. Do you frequently ask to see your doctor's medical record on you to ensure that it's accurate?

Yes ☐   No ☐

5. When you receive a tuition bill, do you pull out your calculator, add up the amounts, and verify that the total is correct?

Yes ☐   No ☐

6. Have you ever purchased a credit report on yourself to make sure your credit information is accurate?

Yes ☐   No ☐

7. Have you ever called the police department to verify that no outstanding traffic violations have been inadvertently assigned to you?

Yes ☐   No ☐

8. Do you count your coin change when you receive it from a store clerk?

Yes ☐   No ☐

9. Do you verify your credit card balance by keeping all your credit card receipts and then matching them to charges on your statement?

Yes ☐   No ☐

10. Do you keep all your paycheck stubs to verify that the amounts on your W-2 form at the end of the year are accurate?

Yes ☐   No ☐

How many of these questions did you answer *yes?* How many did you answer *no?* More than likely, you probably answered *no* to almost all the questions (if not all of them). What does that have to say about your trust that organizations are maintaining accurate information about you? Well, it basically says that you trust organizations to keep accurate information about you. The real question is, Is that necessarily the case?

Now answer the set of questions below, which relate to the level of confidence organizations have in the accuracy of information you give them.

1. When interviewing with potential employers, do they take your word that you have a college degree?

Yes ☐   No ☐

2. If you deposit several checks into your checking account at once, does the bank trust you to correctly add the amounts?

Yes ☐   No ☐

3. When you register for a class that has a prerequisite, does your school assume that you have actually taken the prerequisite class?

Yes ☐   No ☐

4. When you make a deposit at an ATM and enter the amount, does the bank assume that you entered the correct amount?

Yes ☐   No ☐

5. When you're buying a house and negotiating a loan, does the bank assume that the price you're paying for the house is correct and not inflated?

Yes ☐   No ☐

6. When insuring your car, does the insurance company assume that you have a good driving record?

Yes ☐   No ☐

7. When you apply for a parking permit at your school, does it assume that the car belongs to you?

Yes ☐   No ☐

8. When you file your taxes, does the IRS assume that you've correctly reported all your income over the past year?

Yes ☐   No ☐

The answer to each of these questions is probably *no.* And what does that say about the extent to which organizations trust you to provide accurate information? In this instance, it may not be strictly a matter of trust. Organizations today can't afford to have dirty information—information that's not accurate. Because organizations base so many of their decisions on information, inaccurate information creates a real problem that may equate to inefficient processes and lost revenue.

So, on the one side, you're probably very trusting in your assumptions that organizations are maintaining accurate information about you. On the other side, organizations don't really depend on you to provide accurate information.

Questions

1. Should you really trust organizations to maintain accurate information about you? In many instances, is it even worth your time and energy to verify the accuracy of that information?

2. What other examples can you think of in which you simply trust that your information is accurate? What other examples can you think of in which specific organizations don't assume that you're providing accurate information?

3. What sort of impact will cyberspace business have on the issues of trust and accuracy? Will it become easier or more difficult for cyberspace business to assume that you're providing accurate information? Will you trust cyberspace business to maintain your information more accurately than traditional organizations?

4. What are the ethical issues involved in organizations sharing information about you? In some instances it may be okay and in your best interest. But what if the shared information about you is inaccurate? What damage could it cause? What recourse do you have, if any?

5. It's a real dilemma: Most people think that credit card offerers charge extremely high interest rates. But how many people do you know who actually go through the process of calculating their average daily balances, applying the interest rates, and then verifying that the interest charged on their accounts is correct? Why do people complain that they are being charged excessive interest rates and then fail to check the accuracy of the interest calculations?

6. What about the future? As more organizations maintain even more information about you, should you become more concerned about accuracy? Why or why not?

CLOSING CASE STUDY TWO

TECHNOLOGY METRICS—MEASURING EFFICIENCY AND EFFECTIVENESS

If you want to study the single largest organization in the world undergoing transformation because of information technology, you only have to look as far as the United States government. According to the President's Management Agenda (PMA), one of the top five federal government initiatives is expanded electronic government, an initiative that focuses on transforming the government into a click-and-mortar enterprise.

According to comScore Media Metrix in October 2003, the U.S. government ranked sixth among the most popularly visited sites, behind Microsoft, Time Warner (AOL), Yahoo!, Google, and eBay but ahead of the likes of Lycos, Walt Disney, RealNetworks, Amazon, and even Ask Jeeves. With populations now flocking to various government sites, the U.S. government has turned its attention to transformational activities using information technology.

An important question that any organization must ask when undertaking transformation is the extent to which the transformation is successful. To address that, you must be able to measure the success. Here, you can use two different types of metrics—efficiency metrics and effectiveness metrics. Efficiency metrics deal with measuring "doing things right," that is, how efficient you are in using resources, decreasing processing time, decreasing downtimes, decreasing costs, and decreasing errors. Effectiveness metrics deal with measuring "doing the right things," that is, how effective you are at achieving your initiatives, increasing your customer base, expanding your market share, and so on.

Comparing Governments by Efficiency and Effectiveness	
Efficiency Rankings	**Effectiveness Rankings**
1. United States	1. Canada
2. Australia	2. Singapore
3. New Zealand	3. United States
4. Singapore	4. Denmark
5. Norway	5. Australia
6. Canada	6. Finland
7. United Kingdom	7. Hong Kong
8. Netherlands	8. United Kingdom
9. Denmark	9. Germany
10. Germany	10. Ireland

In 2002 and 2003, two interesting reports revealed dramatic differences in the efficiency and effectiveness of the U.S. government as it undertook its click-and-mortar transformation (see the accompanying table). The first report was presented by the United Nations, which ranked the United States first in terms of efficiency. Metrics here included number of computers per 100 citizens, number of Internet hosts per 1,000 citizens, the percentage of population online, the number of telephone lines per 100 citizens, a human development index (technology literacy of citizens), and an information access index (the ease with which government information can be found).

The second report was released by Accenture. Accenture's research focused on citizen satisfaction with the provision of government services via the Internet. Customer satisfaction is an important metric tool for measuring effectiveness. The research concluded that Canada ranked first and the United States third. Metrics here included the extent to which the government was performing customer relationship management, the maturity level of delivering services electronically, the number of multi-channel service delivery options, and the extent to which agencies within the government shared citizen information.[16,17,18]

Questions

1. Consider the relationship between efficiency and effectiveness. In mathematical terms, efficiency is necessary and effectiveness is sufficient. That is, you must be efficient in your transformational activities but that efficiency doesn't necessarily mean that you'll be successful. As well, your transformational activities must be effective and can really only be effective if you're also efficient. Discuss how the United States can be ranked first in terms of efficiency but only third in terms of effectiveness.

2. The portal for the United States government is FirstGov (www.firstgov.gov). Visit that site and review the services provided to citizens. What sort of services is the government providing online to its citizens? Were you aware that all of these services were available on the Internet? Which services are you currently using online? Which services do you see as being beneficial? Will you start to use them? Why or why not?

3. What must the United States government do to become more effective in its electronic delivery of services?

4. Using any of the Industry or Global perspectives in this chapter, develop a set of efficiency and effectiveness metrics for assessing the success of the discussed initiative. How could being efficient not necessarily imply that your chosen organization will be successful?

5. What metrics would you use to measure such concepts as "anywhere" and "anytime"? How could you gather information to use in support of the development of those metrics?

Key Terms and Concepts

Application service provider (ASP), 25
Application software, 16
Artificial intelligence (AI), 23
Business intelligence (BI), 6
Central processing unit (CPU), 16
Collaboration system, 23
Competitive advantage, 18
Customer self-service system, 18
Data, 6
Decentralized computing, 17
Electronic data interchange (EDI), 21
Ethics, 13
Executive information system (EIS), 22
External information, 9
Genetic algorithm, 24
Hardware, 15
Identity theft, 27
Information, 6
Information age, 4
Information granularity, 9
Information-literate knowledge worker, 11
Information technology (IT), 4
Input device, 15
Internal information, 9
Intranet, 7
Knowledge management (KM) system, 21

Knowledge worker, 4
Management information systems (MIS), 4
M-commerce, 18
Mobile computing, 18
Objective information, 9
Online analytical processing, (OLAP), 22
Online transaction processing (OLTP), 22
Operating system software, 16
Operational management, 8
Output device, 16
Random access memory (RAM), 16
Shared information, 17
Software, 15
Spyware (sneakware or stealthware), 27
Storage device, 16
Strategic management, 8
Subjective information, 9
Supply chain management (SCM), 20
Supply chain management (SCM) system, 20
System software, 16
Tactical management, 8
Technology-literate knowledge worker, 11
Telecommunications device, 16
Telecommuting, 5
Transaction processing system (TPS), 18
Utility software, 16

Short-Answer Questions

1. How does a knowledge worker differ from other types of workers?
2. What are the three key resources within management information systems (MIS)?
3. What is telecommuting? What new challenges does telecommuting pose for businesses?
4. What is the relationship among data, information, and business intelligence?
5. What are the personal dimensions of information?
6. What are the four types of information flows in an organization?
7. What is information granularity? How does it relate to the levels of an organization?
8. What are the four types of information according to what information describes?
9. How are information-literate knowledge workers and technology-literate knowledge workers different and how are they similar?

10. What are ethics? Why are ethics so important?
11. What are the key categories of information technology?
12. What is the relationship between decentralized computing and shared information?
13. What is mobile computing and m-commerce?
14. What types of technology support operational excellence?
15. How can businesses use technology to support their major business initiatives?
16. What are the roles of technology in support of decision making?
17. What is spyware and what is identity theft? How can you protect yourself, your technology, and your information in cyberspace?

Assignments and Exercises

1. **INTERNAL, EXTERNAL, OBJECTIVE, AND SUBJECTIVE INFORMATION** Consider a local video rental store. It must make a decision regarding how many copies of a new video rental release to carry in its inventory. In making this decision, the video rental store will use a variety of specific information, all of which will be internal, external, objective, subjective, or some combination of the four. Complete the table below by identifying specific pieces of information that the video rental store would use in making such a decision—list each piece of information in the left column. In the remaining four columns, place appropriate check marks to designate the information as internal, external, objective, subjective, or some combination of the four.

INFORMATION	INTERNAL	EXTERNAL	OBJECTIVE	SUBJECTIVE

2. **SURVEYING GLOBAL INFORMATION TECHNOLOGY** Visit Internet.com (http://cyberatlas.internet.com) to review Internet statistics. Click on **Stats Toolbox** and then **Online Population.** You will find a breakdown of information by country including total population, number of Internet users, number of active Internet users, and number of ISPs. Load that information into spreadsheet software. Now, consider that you want to launch a new ISP (Internet service provider) service in three countries around the world. Using your spreadsheet software, determine which countries you would choose. Which countries did you choose? What was your selection criteria? How did spreadsheet software help you transform information into business intelligence?

3. **FINDING TRUST IN TRUSTe** Truste (www.truste.org) is an organization that has created specific guidelines for the use of your private information by Web sites to whom you offer it. If a Web site adheres to all of TRUSTe's guidelines, that Web site can then display the TRUSTe logo on its site. That way, you know your private information is protected. TRUSTe has four main guidelines or principles that Web sites displaying its logo must follow. Connect to TRUSTe. What are the four guidelines? Are any or all of these guidelines important to you as an individual? If so, which one or ones and why? Should the government require that all Web sites follow these guidelines or a similar set? Why or why not?

4. **REVIEWING THE 100 BEST COMPANIES TO WORK FOR** Each year *Fortune* magazine devotes an issue to the top 100 best companies to work for. Find the most recent issue of *Fortune* that does this (or visit its Web site at www.fortune.com). First, develop a numerical summary that describes the 100 companies in terms of their respective industries. Which industries are the most dominant? Pick one of the more dominant industries (preferably one in which you would like to work) and choose a specific highlighted company. Prepare a short class presentation on why that company is among the 100 best to work for.

Discussion Questions

1. Knowledge workers dominate today's business environment. However, many industries still need workers who do not fall into the category of knowledge workers. What industries still need skilled workers who are not knowledge workers? Can you see a time when these jobs will be replaced by knowledge workers? Can you envision circumstances that would actually cause an economy to do an "about-face" and begin needing more non-knowledge skilled workers than knowledge workers?

2. The three key resources in management information systems (MIS) are information, information technology, and people. Which of these three resources is the most important? Why? The least important? Why?

3. Telecommuting is like everything else: it has a good side and it has a bad side. What are some of the disadvantages or pitfalls of telecommuting? How can these be avoided?

4. As an information-literate knowledge worker for a local distributor of imported foods and spices, you've been asked to prepare a customer mailing list that will be sold to international cuisine restaurants in your area. If you do so, would you be acting ethically? If you don't consider the proposal ethical, what if your boss threatened to fire you if you didn't prepare the list? Do you believe you would have any legal recourse if you didn't prepare the list and were subsequently fired?

5. Consider the ATM system that is now worldwide. How does it address your personal dimensions of time, location, and form? Besides just tracking what transactions you've completed using an ATM, what other information might your bank want to know and use concerning your use of the ATM system?

6. In addition to using neural networks to monitor credit card fraud, the same companies also use neural networks to determine whether or not you are a creditworthy risk. By feeding in thousands of credit card applications, the neural network develops a pattern of who is and isn't a creditworthy risk. Basically, the neural network compares your credit application to those of past ones and recommends an action. What do you think about that? Should you be given or denied a credit card based on what others have done (or failed to do)? Why or why not?

7. Many schools use collaboration systems to offer distance learning classes. Instead of going to class, you communicate with your instructors and classmates via technology. Would you like to take distance learning classes? What are the advantages? Can you learn as much without going to class and personally interacting with your instructor and classmates? What might be some of the disadvantages of distance learning? Is there a happy medium—how about going to school for only one class session per week and then attending the others virtually via technology? Is this a good or bad idea?

8. We often say that hardware is the *physical* interface to a technology system while software is the *intellectual* interface. How is your hardware your physical interface to your computer? How is your software your intellectual interface to your computer? Do you see technology progressing to the point that we may no longer distinguish between hardware and software and thus no longer perceive differing physical and intellectual interfaces?

9. Consider your school within the context of a supply chain. It has suppliers and it has customers. The entire supply chain also exhibits suppliers' suppliers and customers' customers. Draw a supply chain for your school similar to the one in Figure 1.9 on page 21. Be sure to include suppliers' suppliers, suppliers, customers' customers, and customers. It may be helpful to first ask yourself what your school actually provides.

Using the Internet as a Tool to Find a Job

Are you taking advantage of the Internet to find a job? Locate an internship? Learn about interviewing and negotiating skills? We'd like to help you learn how. Complete the project on this page and the next and visit the Web site for this text (www.mhhe.com/ haag, select "Electronic Commerce Projects") to find approximately 100 valuable links for using the Internet as a tool to find a Job.

JOB DATABASES

There are, quite literally, thousands of sites that provide you with databases of job postings. Some are better than others. Some focus on specific industries, others offer postings for only executive managers.

Think for a moment about the job you want. What would be its title? In which industry do you want to work? In what part of the country do you want to work? Connect to a couple of different databases, search for your job, and answer the following questions for each database.

A. What is the date of the last update?

B. Are career opportunities abroad listed as a separate category or are they integrated with domestic jobs?

C. Can you search for a specific organization?

D. Can you search by geographic location? If so, how? By state? By city? By zip code?

E. Can you apply for a position online? If so, how do you submit your résumé?

CREATING AND POSTING AN ELECTRONIC RÉSUMÉ

Most, if not all, job databases focus on two groups: employers and employees. As a potential employee, you search to find jobs that meet your qualifications and desires. Likewise, employers search job databases that contain résumés so they can find people (like you) who meet their qualifications and desires. In this instance, you need to build an electronic résumé (or e-portfolio which we discuss in *Extended Learning Module I*) and leave it at the various job database sites as you perform your searches. That way, organizations performing searches can find you.

Most job database sites give you the ability to create and post an electronic résumé. Visit two job database sites (different from those you visited to find a job). In each, go through the process of creating an e-résumé, posting it, and making some sort of modifications to it. As you do, answer the following questions for each of the sites.

A. Do you have to register as a user to build an e-résumé?

B. Once a potential employer performs a search that matches your e-résumé, how can that employer contact you?

C. What five valuable tips for building a good e-résumé are available?

D. Once you build your e-résumé, can you use it to perform a job search?

E. When you modify your e-résumé, can you update your existing e-résumé or must you delete the old one and create a new one?

F. How many key terms concerning your qualifications can you include in your e-résumé?

G. For what time frame does your e-résumé stay active?

LOCATING THAT "ALL IMPORTANT" INTERNSHIP

Have you ever noticed that a large number of jobs require expertise? That being the case, how does someone gain relevant experience through a job when experience is required to get the job? As it turns out, that has always been a perplexing dilemma for many college students, and one way to solve it is by obtaining an internship. Internships provide you with valuable knowledge about your field, pay you for your work, and offer you that valuable experience you need to move up in your career.

On the Web site for this text (www.mhhe.com/haag, select "Electronic Commerce Projects"), we provided you with a number of Web sites that offer internship possibilities—visit a few of them. Did you find any internships in line with your career? What about pay? Did you find both paying and nonpaying internships? How did these internship sites compare to the more traditional job database sites you looked at earlier? Why do you think this is true?

INTERVIEWING AND NEGOTIATING

The Internet is a vast repository of information—no doubt more information than you'll ever need in your entire life. During the job search process, however, the Internet can offer you very valuable specific information. In the area of interviewing and negotiating, for example, the Internet contains more than 5,000 sites devoted to interviewing skills, negotiating tips, and the like.

Interviewing and negotiating are just as important as searching for a job. Once you line up that first important interview, you can still not land the job if you're not properly prepared. If you do receive a job offer, you may be surprised to know that you can negotiate such things as moving expenses, signing bonuses, and allowances for technology in your home.

We've provided Web sites for you that address the interviewing and negotiating skills you need in today's marketplace. Review some of these sites (and any others that you may find). Then, develop a list of do's and don'ts for the interviewing process. Finally, develop a list of tips that seem helpful to you that will increase your effectiveness during the negotiation process. Once you've developed these two lists, prepare a short class presentation.

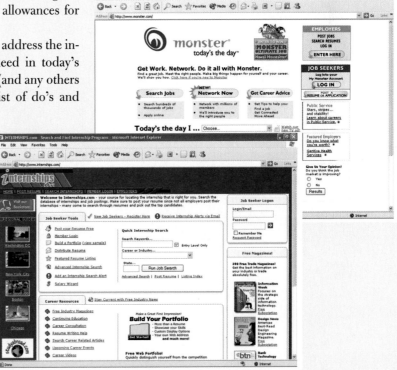

EXTENDED LEARNING MODULE A

COMPUTER HARDWARE AND SOFTWARE

Student Learning Outcomes

1. DEFINE INFORMATION TECHNOLOGY (IT) AND ITS TWO BASIC CATEGORIES: HARDWARE AND SOFTWARE.

2. DESCRIBE THE CATEGORIES OF COMPUTERS BASED ON SIZE.

3. COMPARE THE ROLES OF PERSONAL PRODUCTIVITY, VERTICAL MARKET, AND HORIZONTAL MARKET SOFTWARE.

4. DESCRIBE THE ROLES OF OPERATING SYSTEM AND UTILITY SOFTWARE AS COMPONENTS OF SYSTEM SOFTWARE.

5. DEFINE THE PURPOSE OF EACH OF THE SIX MAJOR CATEGORIES OF HARDWARE.

Introduction

In this extended learning module, we cover the basics of computer hardware and software, including terminology, characteristics of various devices, and how all the parts work together to create a complete and usable computer system. If you've had a previous computing concepts course, this material will be a quick, solid review for you. If this is your first real exposure to hardware and software technologies, you'll definitely learn a great deal from this module.

Information technology (IT) is any computer-based tool that people use to work with information and support the information and information-processing needs of an organization. So information technology (IT) includes the Internet, a personal computer, a cell phone that can access the Web, a personal digital assistant you use for note taking and appointment scheduling, presentation software you use to create a slide show, a printer, a joystick or gamepad for playing video games . . . the list is almost endless (see Figure A.1).

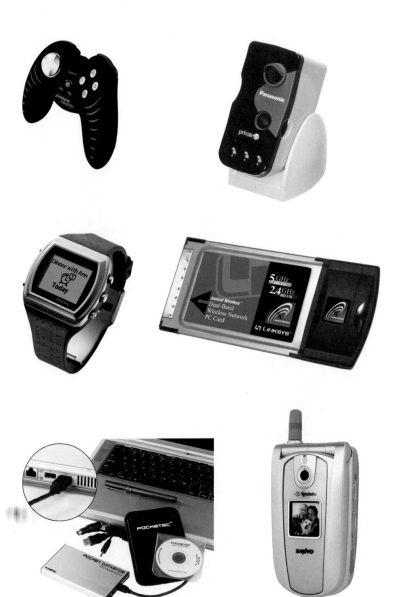

Figure A.1

Information Technology (IT) Includes Many Tools

All of these technologies help you perform specific information-processing tasks. For example, a printer allows you to create a paper version of a document, the Internet connects you to people all over the world, a CD allows you to store information for use at a later time, and word processing software helps you create letters, memos, and term papers.

So, do you need all these various technologies? Yes and no. As you read this module, you'll see categories of both hardware and software. More than likely, you'll need something from each category. But you certainly won't need every one.

A Quick Tour of Technology

There are two basic categories of information technology: hardware and software. *Hardware* consists of the physical devices that make up a computer (often referred to as a *computer system*). *Software* is the set of instructions that your hardware executes to carry out a specific task for you. If you create a graph, you would use various hardware devices such as a keyboard to enter information and a monitor to see the graph, and you would use software such as Microsoft Excel, the most popular spreadsheet software.

All hardware falls into one of six categories. Here's a quick summary (see Figure A.2).

Figure A.2

Six Categories of
Computer Hardware

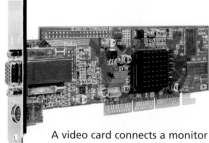

A video card connects a monitor to the motherboard inside the system unit.

Mice and keyboards are the most popular input devices. This keyboard has a fingerprint scanner.

A cable modem allows you to access the Internet.

CDs are common storage media.

The Intel Pentium 4 is a CPU.

A monitor is an output device.

1. Input: **Input devices** are tools you use to enter information and commands.
2. Output: **Output devices** are tools you use to see, hear, or otherwise recognize the results of your information-processing requests.
3. Storage: **Storage devices** are tools you use to store information for use at a later time.
4. Processing: The **central processing unit (CPU)** is the actual hardware that interprets and executes the software instructions and coordinates the operation of all other hardware. **RAM,** or **random access memory,** is a temporary holding area for the information you're working with, as well as the system and application software instructions that the CPU currently needs.
5. Telecommunications: A **telecommunications device** is a tool you use to send information to and receive it from another person or computer in a network. Telecommunications, as a field, and its associated devices is so broad that we've devoted an entire module to the topic. Please read *Extended Learning Module E* to learn about cable and DSL modems, home networks, fiber optics, and much more.
6. Connecting: Connecting hardware include such things as parallel ports into which you would connect a printer and connector cords to connect your printer to the parallel port.

The two main types of software are application and system software. **Application software** is the software that enables you to solve specific problems or perform specific tasks (see Figure A.3). Microsoft PowerPoint, for example, can help you create slides for

Figure A.3

Print Shop and Excel Are Application Software Tools

Pareto chart of the Excel information. A pareto chart graphically summarizes and displays the relative importance of numeric values.

With Excel you can manipulate numeric and label information. You can also create various types of charts and graphs with the numerical values.

a presentation, so it's application software. So is Microsoft FrontPage because it helps you create and publish a Web page or Web site. A business would use payroll software, collaborative software such as videoconferencing and inventory management software.

System software handles tasks specific to technology management and coordinates the interaction of all technology devices. System software includes both operating system software and utility software. *Operating system software* is system software that controls your application software and manages how your hardware devices work together. Popular personal operating system software includes Microsoft Windows XP, Mac OS (for Apple computers), and Linux (an open source operating system). There are also operating systems for networks (Microsoft Windows NT is an example), operating systems for personal digital assistants (Windows CE is an example), and operating systems for just about every other type of technology configuration, even for sewing machines.

Utility software is software that provides additional functionality to your operating system software. Utility software includes anti-virus software, screen savers, disk optimization software, uninstaller software (for properly removing unwanted software), and a host of other types. Some types of utility software are nice to have, like screen savers, while others are essential. For example, anti-virus software protects you from computer viruses that can be deadly for your computer. You definitely need anti-virus software.

So ends our quick tour of technology. In the remainder of this module we'll explore categories of computers by size, software in more detail, and hardware in more detail.

Categories of Computers by Size

Computers come in different shapes, sizes, and colors. Some are small enough that you can carry them around with you, while others are the size of a family refrigerator. Size is usually related to power and speed, and thus price (See Figure A.4).

PERSONAL DIGITAL ASSISTANTS (PDAS)

A *personal digital assistant (PDA)* is a small hand-held computer that helps you surf the Web and perform simple tasks such as note taking, calendaring, appointment scheduling, and maintaining an address book. The PDA screen is touch sensitive, allowing you to write directly on the screen with the screen capturing what you're writing. PDAs today cost between $100 and $500.

TABLET PCS

A *tablet PC* is a pen-based computer that provides the screen capabilities of a PDA with the functional capabilities of a notebook or desktop computer. Similar to PDAs, tablet PCs allow you to use a writing pen or stylus to write notes on the screen and touch the screen to perform functions such as clicking on a link while visiting a Web site. Tablet PCs come in two designs—convertibles and slates. Convertible tablet PCs look like notebook computers, including a screen that you lift up and set in position with a full keyboard and touch pad underneath. Using a convertible PC, you can swivel the screen and lay it flat on the keyboard, converting it into a notebook with no top that closes.

Slate tablet PCs come with no integrated physical keyboard, making the tablet the entire computer. You can buy a docking station for a slate tablet PC, giving you the ability to connect a keyboard and mouse.

Notebooks are fully functional portable personal computers.

Convertible tablet PCs have screens that swivel and lie flat on top of the system unit.

Some desktops are built especially for gaming.

PDAs are small hand-held computers.

Figure A.4

PDAs, Desktops, Tablet PCs, and Notebooks

NOTEBOOK COMPUTERS

A *notebook computer* is a small, portable, fully functional, battery-powered computer. Notebooks come equipped with all the technology you need to meet your personal needs and weigh as little as 4 pounds. If you need a fully functional computer in a variety of places—home, work, school, and/or on the road—then a notebook computer may be just the answer. Notebook computers range in price from about $800 to several thousand dollars.

DESKTOP COMPUTERS

A *desktop computer* is the most popular choice for personal computing needs. You can choose a desktop computer with a horizontal system box (the box is where the CPU, RAM, and storage devices are held) or choose a desktop computer with a vertical system box (called a tower) that you usually place on the floor near your work area. Desktop computers range in price from a little less than $500 to several thousand dollars. Dollar for dollar with comparable characteristics, a desktop computer is faster and more powerful than a notebook computer.

Which one you need—PDA, tablet PC, notebook, or desktop computer—is a function of your unique individual needs. PDAs offer great portability and allow you to keep a calendar, send and receive e-mail, take short notes, and even access the Web. But they're not designed to help you write a term paper, build a Web site, or create a complex graph with statistical software. For these and more complex tasks, you would need a notebook, tablet PC, or a desktop computer.

So, the next question is, should you buy a notebook or a tablet PC? Most likely, you need a computer that supports full word processing, spreadsheet, presentation, Web site development, and some other capabilities. You need to decide where you'll need your computer. If you need to use your computer both at home and at school (or perhaps at work), then you should buy one of these because they are, in fact, portable. So, if you'd like to be able to surf the Web and get e-mail in your hotel room while on a business or vacation trip, a notebook computer or a tablet PC may be what you need.

In the future, we believe the capabilities of PDAs will improve so that you can in fact perform "complex" tasks such as creating an elaborate spreadsheet or graph and even integrating speech recognition. To learn more about some of today's best PDAs, connect to the Web site that supports this text at www.mhhe.com/haag.

MINICOMPUTERS, MAINFRAME COMPUTERS, AND SUPERCOMPUTERS

PDAs, notebooks, and desktop computers are designed to meet your personal information-processing needs. In business, however, many people often need to access and use the same computer simultaneously. In this case, businesses need computing technologies that multiple people can access and use at the same time. Computers of this type include minicomputers, mainframe computers, and supercomputers (see Figure A.5).

Figure A.5

Minicomputers, Mainframes, and Supercomputers

Minicomputers are well suited for small to medium size businesses.

Mainframe computers support the information-processing tasks of large businesses.

Supercomputers are very expensive and fast number-crunching machines. They are usually scalable, meaning that you get as many units as you need and they work together on your processing tasks.

A *minicomputer* (sometimes called a *mid-range computer*) is designed to meet the computing needs of several people simultaneously in a small to medium-size business environment. Minicomputers are more powerful than desktop computers but also cost more, ranging in price from $5,000 to several hundred thousand dollars. Businesses often use minicomputers as servers, either for creating a Web presence or as an internal computer on which shared information and software is placed. For this reason, mini-computers are well suited for business environments in which people need to share common information, processing power, and/or certain peripheral devices such as high-quality, fast laser printers.

A *mainframe computer* (sometimes just called a *mainframe*) is a computer de-signed to meet the computing needs of hundreds of people in a large business environment. So mainframe computers are a step up in size, power, capability, and cost from minicomputers. Mainframes can easily cost in excess of $1 million. With processing speeds greater than 1 trillion instructions per second (compared to a typical desktop that can process more than three billion instructions per second), mainframes can easily handle the processing requests of hundreds of people simultaneously.

A *supercomputer* is the fastest, most powerful, and most expensive type of computer. Organizations such as NASA and the National Weather Service that are heavily involved in research and "number crunching" employ supercomputers because of the speed with which they can process information. Other large, customer-oriented businesses such as General Motors and AT&T employ supercomputers just to handle customer informa-tion and transaction processing.

How much do you really need to know about the technical specifics (CPU speed, storage disk capacity, and so on), prices, and capabilities of minicomputers, mainframe computers, and supercomputers? Probably not much, unless you plan to major in infor-mation technology. What you should definitely concentrate on, though, is the technical specifics, prices, and capabilities of PDAs, tablet PCs, notebooks, and desktop comput-ers. These will be your companions for your entire business career. Learn and know them well.

Software: Your Intellectual Interface

The most important tool in your technology tool set is software. Software contains the instructions that your hardware executes to perform an information-processing task for you. So, software is really your *intellectual interface,* designed to automate processing tasks that you would undertake with your mind. Without software, your computer is lit-tle more than a very expensive doorstop. As we've stated before, there are two categories of software: application and system.

APPLICATION SOFTWARE

Application software is the software you use to meet your specific information-processing needs, including payroll, customer relationship management, project management, training, word processing, and many, many others.

PERSONAL PRODUCTIVITY SOFTWARE

Personal productivity software helps you perform personal tasks—such as writing a memo, creating a graph, and creating a slide presentation—that you can usually do even if you don't own a computer. You're probably already familiar with some personal pro-ductivity software tools including Microsoft Word and Excel, Netscape Communicator or Internet Explorer, and Quicken (personal finance software).

Category	Examples*
Word processing—Helps you create papers, letters, memos, and other basic documents	• Microsoft Word • Corel WordPerfect
Spreadsheet—Helps you work primarily with numbers, including performing calculations and creating graphs	• Microsoft Excel • LotusIBM Lotus 1-2-3
Presentation—Helps you create and edit information that will appear in electronic slides	• Corel Presentations • LotusIBM Freelance Graphics
Desktop publishing—Extends word processing software by including design and formatting techniques to enhance the layout and appearance of a document	• Microsoft Publisher • Quark QuarkXPress
Personal information management (PIM)—Helps you create and maintain (1) to-do lists, (2) appointments and calendars, and (3) points of contact	• Corel Central • LotusIBM Organizer
Personal finance—Helps you maintain your checkbook, prepare a budget, track investments, monitor your credit card balances, and pay bills electronically	• Quicken Quicken • Microsoft Money
Web authoring—Helps you design and develop Web sites and pages that you publish on the Web	• Microsoft FrontPage • LotusIBM FastSite
Graphics—Helps you create and edit photos and art	• Microsoft PhotoDraw • Kodak Imaging for Windows
Communications—Helps you communicate with other people	• Microsoft Outlook • Internet Explorer
Database management system (DBMS)—Helps you specify the logical organization for a database and access and use the information within a database	• Microsoft Access • FileMaker FileMaker Pro

* Publisher name given first.

Figure A.6

Categories of Personal
Productivity Software

In fact, two modules in this text help you learn how to use two of these tools—*Extended Learning Module D* (for Microsoft Excel, spreadsheet software) and *Extended Learning Module J* (for Microsoft Access, database management system software). Figure A.6 lists and describes the 10 major categories of personal productivity software and includes some of the more popular packages within each.

VERTICAL AND HORIZONTAL MARKET SOFTWARE

While performing organizational processes in your career, you'll also frequently use two other categories of application software: vertical market software and horizontal market software.

Vertical market software is application software that is unique to a particular industry. For example, the health care industry has a variety of application software unique to that market segment, including radiology software, patient-scheduling software, nursing allocation software, and pharmaceutical software. This type of software is written specifically for an industry. Health care industry patient-scheduling software wouldn't work well for scheduling hair styling and manicure appointments in a beauty salon.

BUYING PERSONAL PRODUCTIVITY SOFTWARE SUITES

When you buy personal productivity software, we recommend that you do so in the form of a suite. A *software suite (suite)* is bundled software that comes from the same publisher and costs less than buying all the software pieces individually.

In this project, your team has two tasks. First, research the most popular personal productivity software suites. These include Microsoft Office, Corel WordPerfect Office, and LotusIBM SmartSuite. For each, identify which specific software pieces fall into the 10 categories of personal productivity software listed in Figure

A.6. Then, try to find some information that describes the market share of each personal productivity software suite.

Second, choose one specific personal productivity software suite. Determine the individual price for each piece of software included in it. Now, perform a price comparison. How much cheaper is the entire suite? Can you think of a situation in which someone would buy the individual pieces as opposed to the entire suite? If so, please describe it.

Horizontal market software is application software that is general enough to be suitable for use in a variety of industries. Examples of horizontal market software include

- Inventory management
- Payroll
- Accounts receivable
- Billing
- Invoice processing
- Human resource management

The preceding functions (and many others) are very similar, if not identical, across many different industries, enabling software publishers to develop one particular piece of software (e.g., accounts receivable) that can be used by many different industries.

Personal productivity software is actually a type of horizontal market software in that it is general enough to be suitable for use in a variety of industries. No matter what industry you work in, you need basic word processing software for creating memos, business plans, and other basic documents.

There are, however, some key differences between personal productivity software and horizontal and vertical market software. First is the issue of price. You can buy a full suite of personal productivity software for less than $400. In contrast, some individual horizontal and vertical market software packages may cost $500,000 or more. Second is the issue of customizability. When you purchase personal productivity software, you cannot change the way it works. That is, you're buying the right to use it but not to change how it operates. With horizontal and vertical market software you may in fact also be able to purchase the right to change the way the software works. So, if you find a payroll software package that fits most of your organizational needs, you can buy the software and the right to change the operation of the software so that it meets your needs precisely. This is a very common business practice when purchasing and using horizontal and vertical market software.

In Chapter 6 (Systems Development), we discuss how organizations go about the process of developing software for their particular needs, including how organizations can and do purchase vertical and horizontal market software and then customize that software.

SYSTEM SOFTWARE

System software is that category of software that controls how your various technology tools work together as you use your application software to perform specific information-processing tasks. System software includes two basic categories: operating system and utility.

OPERATING SYSTEM SOFTWARE

Operating system software is system software that controls your application software and manages how your hardware devices work together. For example, while using Excel to create a graph, if you choose to print the graph, your operating system software would take over, ensure that you have a printer attached, ensure that the printer has paper (and notify you if it doesn't), and send your graph to the printer along with instructions on how to print it.

Your operating system software also supports a variety of useful features, one of which is multitasking. *Multitasking* allows you to work with more than one piece of software at a time. Suppose you wanted to create a graph in Excel and insert it into a word processing document (see Figure A.7). With multitasking, you can have both pieces of application software open at the same time, and even see both on the screen. So, when you complete the creation of your graph, you can easily copy and paste it into your word processing document without having to exit the spreadsheet software and then start your word processing software.

Figure A.7

Most Modern Operating Systems Support Multitasking

The task bar area tells you what software you're currently working with.

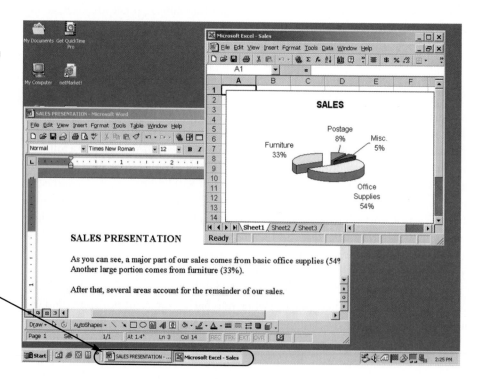

TEAM WORK

EVALUATING UTILITY SOFTWARE SUITES

Just as you can purchase personal productivity software suites that contain many pieces of software, you can also purchase utility software suites. In the table below, we've included the three most popular utility software suites: McAfee Office Pro, Norton SystemWorks, and Ontrack SystemSuite.

As a team, do some research and determine what major pieces of software are included in each. As you do, fill in the table.

Now, pick a particular utility suite and visit its Web site. What is the process for updating your software? Is it free? How often does the site recommend that you update your utility software?

Utility software piece	McAfee Office Pro	Norton SystemWorks	Ontrack SystemSuite

Within operating system software, there are different types for personal environments and for organizational environments that support many users simultaneously (these are called *network operating systems* or *NOSs*, and we explore some of these in greater detail in *Extended Learning Module E: Network Basics*). Popular personal operating systems include

- **Microsoft Windows XP Home**—Microsoft's latest upgrade to Windows 2000, with enhanced features for allowing multiple people to use the same computer.
- **Microsoft Windows XP Professional (Windows XP Pro)**—Microsoft's latest upgrade to Windows 2000 Pro.
- **Mac OS**—The operating system for today's Apple computers.
- **Linux**—An open-source operating system that provides a rich operating environment for high-end workstations and network servers.

If you're considering purchasing a notebook computer that you'll use extensively at school connected to a network there, we recommend that you contact your school's technology support department to determine which operating system is best for you.

UTILITY SOFTWARE

Utility software is software that adds functionality to your operating system software. A simple example is that of screen saver software (which is probably also a part of your operating system). Most important, utility software includes anti-virus software. *Anti-virus software* is utility software that detects and removes or quarantines computer viruses. Viruses are everywhere today, with 200 to 300 new ones surfacing each month. Some viruses are benign: they do something annoying like causing your screen to go blank but do not corrupt your information. Other viruses are deadly, perhaps reformatting your hard disk or altering the contents of your files. You definitely need anti-virus software to protect your computer. We talk much more about this vitally important topic and other possible attacks that can be launched against your computer from cyberspace in Chapter 8.

Other types of utility software include

- **Crash-proof software**—Utility software that helps you save information if your system crashes and you're forced to turn it off and then back on again.
- **Uninstaller software**—Utility software that you can use to remove software from your hard disk that you no longer want.
- **Disk optimization software**—Utility software that organizes your information on your hard disk in the most efficient way.

We would once again state that utility software is not optional software just because it adds *additional* functionality to your computer. You definitely need utility software. The four examples we described above are just a few of the many you'll find in a utility software suite.

Hardware: Your Physical Interface

To properly understand the significant role of your hardware (the physical components of your computer), it helps to know something about how your computer works. You work with information in the form of characters (A–Z, a–z, and special ones such as an asterisk) and numbers (0–9). Computers, on the other hand, work only with 1s and 0s in terms of bits and bytes. Computers use electricity to function, and electrical pulses have two states: on and off, which are assigned the values of 0 and 1, respectively.

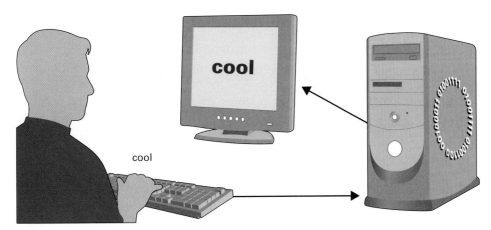

Figure A.8

Representations of Information as It Moves throughout Your Computer

A ***binary digit (bit)*** is the smallest unit of information that your computer can process. A bit can either be a 1 (on) or a 0 (off). The challenge from a technological point of view is to be able to represent all our natural language characters, special symbols, and numbers in binary form. ASCII is one agreed-upon standard to do this. ***ASCII (American Standard Code for Information Interchange)*** is the coding system that most personal computers use to represent, process, and store information. In ASCII, a group of eight bits represents one natural language character and is called a ***byte.***

For example, if you were to type the word *cool* on the keyboard, your keyboard (a hardware device) would change it into four bytes—one for each character—that would look like the following used by other parts of your computer (see Figure A.8):

01100011	01001111	01001111	01001100
c	o	o	l

This grouping of 1s and 0s is used for all information moving around or stored on your computer, as it travels from one device to another, is stored on a storage device, and is processed by your CPU.

There are three important conclusions that you should draw from the previous discussion. First, your hardware works with information in a different form (although with the same meaning) than you do. You work with characters, special symbols, and the numbers 0–9. Your computer, on the other hand, represents all these in a binary form, a collection of unique 1s and 0s. Second, the term *byte* is the bridge between people and a computer. A computer can store one character, special symbol, or number in a byte. One byte is essentially one character. So, a Zip disk with a storage capacity of 100 megabytes can hold approximately 100 million characters of information.

Third, the primary role of your input and output devices is to convert information from one form to another. Input devices convert information from human-readable form into bits and bytes, while output devices convert the 1s and 0s to something a human can recognize. All other hardware internally works with information in the form of bits and bytes.

COMMON INPUT DEVICES

An *input device* is a tool you use to enter information and commands (see Figure A.9). You can use a keyboard to type in information, for example, and use a mouse to point and click on buttons and icons. As you saw in the previous section, input devices are responsible for converting information in human-readable form to the binary code that computers use. For example, a c would be 01100011 as it moves around a computer. Below are the principle types of input devices being used today (see Figure A.10).

- *Keyboards* are the most often used input devices for desktop and notebook computers, while *styluses* are the most frequently used input devices for PDAs and tablet PCs. Both allow you to input both information and commands and are used in business and personal settings.
- *Pointing devices* are devices that are used to input commands.
  - *Mouse*—a pointing device that you use to click on icons or buttons. The three types are mechanical (using a ball), optical (using red light), and wireless (uses waves).
  - *Trackball*—is similar to a mechanical mouse, but it has the ball on the top.
  - *Touchpad*—is the little dark rectangle that you use to move the cursor with your finger, often found on notebook computers.
  - *Pointing stick*—is a little rod (like a pencil-top eraser) used almost exclusively on notebook computers.
- *Game controllers* are used for gaming to better control screen action.
  - *Gaming wheel*—is a steering wheel and foot pedals for virtual driving.
  - *Joystick*—controls action with a vertical handle and programmable buttons.
  - *Gamepad*—is a multifunctional input device with programmable buttons, thumb sticks, and a directional pad.

Figure A.9

Common Input Devices

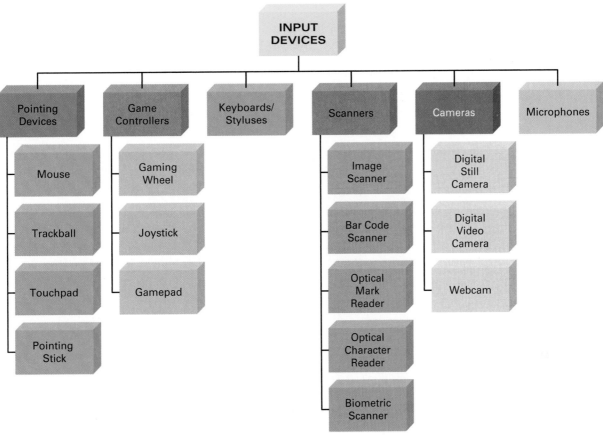

Figure A.10

Categories of Input Devices

- *Scanners* are used to convert information that exists in visible form into electronic form.
  - *Image scanner*—captures images, photos, text, and artwork that already exist on paper.
  - *Bar code scanner*—reads information that is in the form of vertical bars, where their width and spacing represent digits (often used in point-of-sale [POS] systems in retail environments).
  - *Optical mark reader*—detects the presence or absence of a mark in a predetermined spot on the page (often used for true/false and multiple choice exams answers).
  - *Optical character reader*—reads characters that appear on a page or sales tag (often used in point-of-sale [POS] systems in retail environments).
  - *Biometric scanner*—scans some human physical attribute, like your fingerprint or iris for security purposes.
- *Digital cameras* capture still images or video as a series of 1s and 0s. Some will capture only stills, others do both.
  - *Digital still camera*—digitally captures still images in varying resolutions.
  - *Digital video camera*—captures video digitally.
  - *Webcam*—captures digital video to upload to the Web.
- *Microphones* capture audio for conversion into electronic form.

Figure A.11

Categories of Output Devices

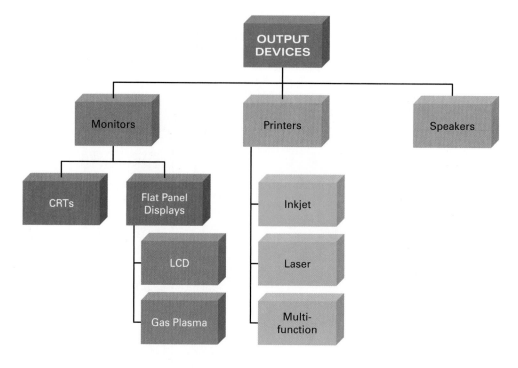

COMMON OUTPUT DEVICES

An **output device** is a tool you use to see, hear, or otherwise recognize the results of your information-processing requests. The most common output devices for both business and personal computing environments are monitors and printers (see Figure A.11), but speakers and plotters (printers that generate drawings) are also output devices. Any device that converts the digital form of information in a computer to something that you can see, read, or hear is an output device.

MONITORS

Monitors come in two varieties: CRT or flat-panel displays (see Figure A.12). **CRTs** are the monitors that look like traditional television sets, while **flat-panel displays** are thin, lightweight monitors that take up much less space than CRTs. Flat-panel displays are either liquid crystal display or gas plasma display. **Liquid crystal display (LCD) monitors** make the image by sending electricity through crystallized liquid trapped between two layers of glass or plastic. **Gas plasma displays** send electricity through gas trapped between two layers of glass or plastic to create an image. A gas plasma display usually provides a better image, but is more expensive than a comparably sized LCD monitor.

Figure A.12

Monitors Are Common Output Devices

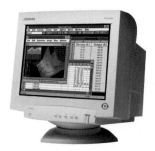

When selecting a monitor, the important features to consider, besides its price and physical size, are the monitor's (1) viewable image size, (2) resolution, and (3) dot pitch.

1. The *viewable image size (VIS)* is the size of the image. The quoted size (17", 19", etc.) is measured diagonally from corner to corner. In a flat-panel display, this size is the same as the distance from corner to opposite corner of the monitor's frame, while in a CRT it's slightly less since the image doesn't completely fill the screen area on a CRT. The physical size of a CRT, for a comparable image size, is usually larger since it's much deeper than the flat-panel displays.

2. The *resolution of a screen* is the number of pixels it has. *Pixels (picture elements)* are the dots that make up the image on your screen. For example, a monitor with a resolution of 1,280 × 1,024 has 1,280 pixels across and 1,024 down the screen. The higher the resolution the better the image.

3. *Dot pitch* is the distance between the centers of a pair of like-colored pixels. So, a monitor with .24 mm dot pitch is better than one with .28 mm dot pitch because the dots are smaller and closer together, giving you a better quality image.

PRINTERS

Printers are another common type of output device (see Figure A.13). The sharpness and clarity of a printer's output depend on the printer's resolution. The *resolution of a printer* is the number of dots per inch (dpi) it produces. This is the same principle as the resolution in monitors. As is the case with monitors, the more dots per inch, the better the image, and consequently, the more costly the printer. High-end personal printers usually have a resolution of 1,200 × 1,200 or better. Multiplying these numbers together gives you 1,440,000 dots per square inch. Some printers, especially those that advertise high-quality photo output, achieve resolutions of 5,760 × 1,440 by making multiple passes across the image.

- *Inkjet printers* make images by forcing ink droplets through nozzles. Standard inkjet printers use four colors: black, cyan (blue), magenta (purplish pink), and yellow. Some inkjet printers produce high-quality images and are often advertised as photo printers. These have two shades each of magenta and cyan for a total of six colors.

Figure A.13

Printers Are Also Common Output Devices

- *Laser printers* form images using the same sort of electrostatic process that photocopiers use. Laser printers are usually more expensive than inkjets, but have become dramatically cheaper lately. They usually provide better quality images than inkjets. They come in black and white and in color versions.
- *Multifunction printers* scan, copy, and fax, as well as print. These devices are very popular in homes and small offices since they offer so many features all in one box. Multifunction printers can be either inkjet or laser.

COMMON STORAGE DEVICES

As opposed to RAM, which is temporary memory, storage media don't lose their contents when you turn off your computer. The main issues to consider when choosing a storage medium are (1) whether you want portability, (2) how much storage space you need, and (3) whether you need to change the information on the medium.

Some storage devices, such as hard disks, offer you easy update capabilities and high storage capacity, but may not be portable. Others, like floppy disks, while they are portable and updateable, don't have much storage space. Still others like DVD-ROMs are portable with high capacity, but the information that comes on them can't be changed (see Figure A.14).

Figure A.14

Categories of Storage Media

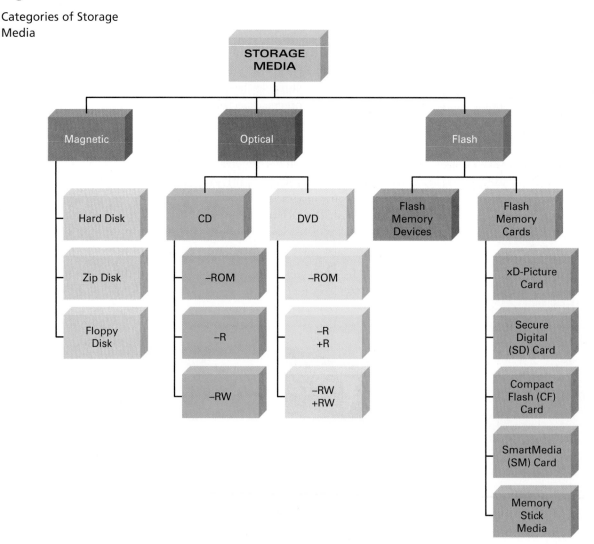

Capacities of storage media are measured in megabytes, gigabytes, and terabytes. A **megabyte (MB or M or Meg)** is roughly 1 million bytes; a **gigabyte (GB or Gig)** is roughly 1 billion bytes; and a **terabyte (TB)** is roughly 1 trillion bytes. A consumer hard disk would have a capacity of between 1 and 250 gigabytes while a hard disk for a large organization (also called a *hard disk pack*) can hold in excess of 100 TB of information. Common storage devices include

- Magnetic storage media (see Figure A.15) include
  - *Hard disk*—magnetic storage device with one or more thin metal platters or disks that store information sealed inside the disk drive. You usually get one installed in your system unit (the computer box) when you buy a computer. If you need more hard disk space or want portability, you can get an external unit that you can plug into the USB ports. (We'll discuss USB ports in a later section.) A hard disk offers ease of updating and large storage capacity.
  - *Zip disk*—a high capacity (100 Meg, 250 Meg, and 750 Meg) removable storage medium. The big advantage of Zip disks is that they're portable and have a large storage capacity, but they are expensive compared to other high capacity removable storage media.
  - *Floppy disk*—a removable magnetic storage medium that holds 1.44 Meg of information.

Figure A.16

Optical Storage Media

- *Optical storage media* are plastic discs on which information is stored, deleted, and/or changed using laser light (see Figure A.16) and include CDs and DVDs, of which there are several types:
  - *CD-ROM (compact disc — read-only memory)*—an optical or laser disc whose information cannot be changed. A CD stores up to 800 Meg of information.
  - *CD-R (compact disc — recordable)*—an optical or laser disc that you can write to one time only.
  - *CD-RW (compact disc — rewritable)*—an optical or laser disc on which you can save, change, and delete files as often as you like.
  - *DVD-ROM*—a high-capacity optical or laser disc whose information cannot be changed. The capacity of a DVD, unlike that of a CD, varies according to type.
  - *DVD-R* or *DVD+R (DVD — recordable)*—a high-capacity optical or laser disc to which you can write one time only.
  - *DVD-RW* or *DVD+RW* (depending on the manufacturer)—a high-capacity optical or laser disc on which you can save, change, and delete files.
- Flash memory comes in two varieties: flash memory device and flash memory cards (see Figure A.17). A *flash memory device* is a flash memory storage device that is small enough to fit on a key ring and plugs directly into the USB port on your computer. A flash memory card, on the other hand, has to be inserted into a reader, which in turn plugs into the USB port. *Flash memory cards* have high-capacity storage laminated inside a small piece of plastic. There are several different types.
  - *xD-Picture (xD) cards*—flash memory card that looks like a rectangular piece of plastic smaller than a penny and about as thick, with one edge slightly curved. xD cards have capacities ranging from 32 to 512 megabytes.
  - *Secure Digital (SD) cards* and *MultiMediaCards (MMC)*—flash memory cards that look identical to each other (but SD cards have copy protection built-in), are a little larger than a quarter, and are slightly thicker than a credit card.
  - *CompactFlash (CF) cards*—flash memory cards slightly larger than a half-dollar, with capacities up to 6 gigabytes.

Figure A.17

Common Types of Flash
Memory

- *SmartMedia (SM) cards*—flash memory cards that are a little longer than a
  CF card and about as thick as a credit card with capacities of up to 512
  megabytes.
- *Memory Stick Media cards*—elongated flash memory cards about the width
  of a penny developed by Sony with capacities up to 512 megabytes.

CPU AND RAM

Together, your CPU and RAM make up the real brains of your computer (see Figure
A.18). Your CPU largely determines the power (and also the price) of your computer.
The *central processing unit (CPU)* is the hardware that interprets and executes the system and application software instructions and coordinates the operation of all other
hardware. *Random access memory (RAM)* is a temporary holding area for the information you're working with as well the system and application software instructions that
the CPU currently needs.

   You'll often hear the CPU referred to as a microprocessor or a CPU chip. The dominant manufacturers of CPUs include Intel (with its Celeron, Pentium, and Xeon series
for personal computers) and AMD (with its Athlon and Opteron series). As a consumer,
you'll probably find the most useful information about CPUs is their relative speeds.

Figure A.18

CPU and RAM

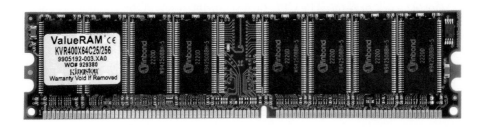

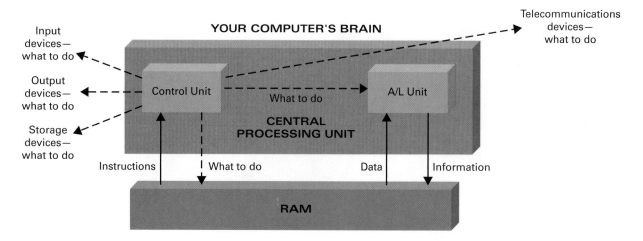

Figure A.19

Your CPU and RAM at Work

Today's CPU speed is usually quoted in gigahertz. **Gigahertz (GHz)** is the number of billions of CPU cycles per second that the CPU can handle. The more cycles per second, the faster the processing and the more powerful the computer. Gigahertz refers to how fast the CPU can carry out the steps it takes to execute software instructions—a process sometimes called the CPU cycle or machine cycle. A **CPU cycle (machine cycle)** consists of retrieving, decoding, and executing the instruction, then returning the result to RAM, if necessary (see Figure A.19). When you load (or open) a program, you're telling your computer to send a copy of the program from the storage device (hard disk or CD) into RAM. In carrying out the software instructions, the CPU repeatedly performs machine cycles as follows:

1. *Retrieve an instruction:* The **control unit,** which is the component of the CPU that directs what happens in your computer, sends to RAM for instructions and the information it needs. If the instruction says to add 4 and 6, the two numbers travel as information with the *add* instruction. The instruction travels from RAM on the system bus. The **system bus** consists of electrical pathways that move information between basic components of the motherboard, including between RAM and the CPU. When the instruction reaches the CPU it waits temporarily in **CPU cache,** which is a type of memory on the CPU where instructions called up by the CPU wait until the CPU is ready to use them. It takes much less time to get the instruction from cache to the control unit than from RAM, so cache speeds up processing.

2. *Decode the instruction:* The CPU gets the instruction out of cache, examines it to see what needs to be done, in this case, add 4 and 6.

3. *Execute the instruction:* The CPU then does what the instruction says to do. In our example, it sends the two numbers to the arithmetic logic unit to be added. The **arithmetic logic unit (ALU)** is a component of the CPU that performs arithmetic, as well as comparison and logic operations.

4. *Store the result in RAM:* The CPU then sends the result of the addition, 10, to RAM. There's not always a result to send back to RAM. Sometimes the CPU does intermediate calculations that don't get saved.

You'll sometimes hear the CPU speed referred to as the "clock speed." This refers to the CPU clock. Every CPU has its own **CPU clock,** which is simply a sliver of quartz that beats at regular intervals in response to an electrical charge. The beat of the CPU clock is like the drummer in a marching band. Just as the drummer keeps everyone marching in time, the CPU clock keeps all your computer's operations synchronized. Each beat or tick of the CPU clock is called a clock cycle and is equivalent to a CPU cycle (machine cycle). The CPU uses the CPU clock to keep instructions and information marching through your CPU at a fixed rate.

RAM is a sort of chalkboard that your CPU uses while it processes information and software instructions. When you turn off your computer, everything in RAM disappears—that's why we call it "temporary." When you first start your computer, system instructions that are necessary to keep your computer running get written into RAM. Then, as you open applications, like Word or Excel, the instructions to make those programs run join the operating system in RAM. As you type in your document or enter information into your workbook, that too is stored in RAM. When you've finished your work and save it, a copy is transferred from RAM to your disk or CD.

The most important thing you need to know about RAM is its capacity for storing instructions and information. RAM capacity is expressed in megabytes or gigabytes. You'll remember that a megabyte is roughly 1 million bytes. A byte is equivalent to a character. So RAM with a capacity of 256 Meg can hold 256 million characters—that includes operating system instructions as well as the applications and information that you're currently using.

NOTEBOOK COMPUTER CPUS AND RAM

A notebook computer is to a desktop computer as a recreational vehicle is to a traditional home—everything is smaller, and power to run devices is limited since you have to carry the power sources with you. A **mobile CPU** is a special type of CPU for a notebook computer that changes speed, and therefore power consumption, in response to fluctuation in use. A desktop CPU, running at 1 GHz, uses between 75 and 1,090 watts of power whereas a mobile CPU might run at a much smaller 34 watts.

RAM modules for notebook computers are smaller than those for desktop computers. To install or swap RAM in a notebook, you probably open up the small bay door on the system unit.

CONNECTING THE HARDWARE OUTSIDE TO THE HARDWARE INSIDE

Since the CPU controls all computer hardware, all hardware devices must be connected to the CPU, just as your limbs are connected to your brain through your spinal cord.

The CPU, along with RAM, is located on the large circuit board (called the *motherboard*) inside your system unit. The connector (or plug) on the end of the cable coming out of your printer connects it to the motherboard which then carries information between the CPU and the printer.

WIRED CONNECTIONS

All devices that are not wireless have connectors on the ends of cables that plug into ports on the system unit. A **port** is the place on your system unit, monitor, or keyboard through which information and instructions flow to and from your computer system. For wired connections it's the opening or socket where you insert the connector, and for wireless devices a port is where the wave information goes in and out.

Figure A.20

Categories of Connectors
and Ports

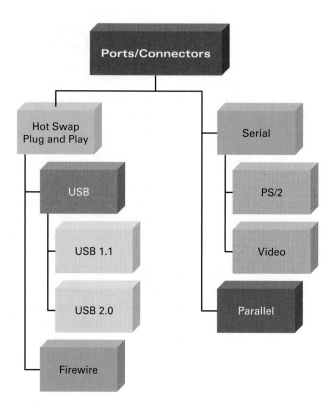

The ports are accessible on the outside of the system unit and that means that you don't have to open up the system unit to plug in your scanner. There are various types of connectors/ports (see Figure A.20) including:

- **USB (universal serial bus) port**—fit small flat plug-and-play, hot-swap USB connectors, and, using USB hubs, you can connect up to 127 devices to a single USB port on your computer. **Hot swap** is an operating system feature that allows you—while your computer is running—to unplug a device and plug in a new one (without first shutting down your computer). **Plug and play** is an operating feature that finds and installs the device driver for a device that you plug into your computer. USB connectors/ports comes in two speeds: USB 1.1 and USB 2.0 (which is faster), and in two physical shapes called Type A and Type B, respectively. Type A USB connectors/ports are all the same size and shape (see Figure A.21), but Type B USB connectors are smaller, squarer, and come in several different sizes. Type B connectors are usually on the end of the cable that plugs into the device (like a digital camera).
- **Firewire ports**—(also called **IEEE 1394** or **I-Link**) fit hot-swap, plug-and-play Firewire connectors, and you can connect up to 63 Firewire devices to a single Firewire port by daisy-chaining the devices together (see Figure A.21).
- **PS/2 ports**—fit PS/2 connectors, which you often find on keyboards and mice (see Figure A.21). PS/2 is a special type of serial connector/port. Serial connectors/ports are gradually being replaced by USB and Firewire.
- **Parallel ports**—fit parallel connectors, which are large flat connectors found almost exclusively on printer cables, but which are losing popularity in favor of USB (see Figure A.21).

Summary:

1. **Define informa** **basic categorie** *Information te* based tool that information and information-pro IT includes cell spreadsheet sof consists of the computer (often system). *Softwa* your hardware task for you.

2. **Describe the c** **size.** Categories personal digital computers, desl mainframe com *personal digita* hand-held com and perform si calendaring, ap maintaining an pen-based com capabilities of a capabilities of a A *notebook com* functional batte for you to carry *computer* is the computing nee designed for us *minicomputer* designed to me people simultar business enviro *(mainframe)* is computing nee business enviro fastest, most po of computer. In smallest, least p supercomputer and most exper

3. **Compare the r** **vertical marke**

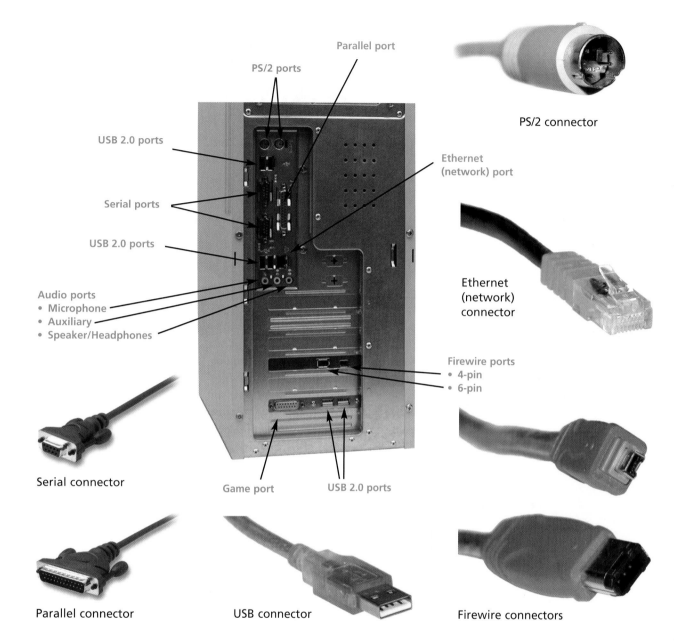

PS/2 ports

Parallel port

USB 2.0 ports

Serial ports

USB 2.0 ports

Audio ports
• Microphone
• Auxiliary
• Speaker/Headphones

PS/2 connector

Ethernet (network) port

Ethernet (network) connector

Firewire ports
• 4-pin
• 6-pin

Serial connector

Game port

USB 2.0 ports

Parallel connector

USB connector

Firewire connectors

Figure A.21

Ports and Connectors to Connect Devices to the CPU on the Motherboard

WIRELESS CONNECTIONS

Wireless devices transfer and receive information in the form of waves, either infrared or radio waves. Different types of waves have different frequencies. The three types most frequently used in personal and business computer environments are infrared, Bluetooth, and WiFi.

- *Infrared*—also called *IR* or *IrDA (infrared data association)* uses red light to send and receive information. Infrared light has a frequency that's below what the eye can see. It's used for TV remotes and other devices that operate over short distances that are free of obstacles.

- *Bluetooth*—is a standard for transmitting information in the form of short range radio waves over distances of up to 30 feet and is used for purposes such as wirelessly connecting a cell phone or a PDA to a computer.

Figure A.22

The Expansion Bus, Expansion Slots, and Expansion Cards

information-processing requests and convert information in a form that your computer understands into a form that you can understand.

- **CPU and RAM**—The real brains of your computer that execute software instructions (CPU) and hold the information, application software, and operating system software you're working with (RAM).

- **Storage devices**—Help you store information for use at a later time.
- **Telecommunications devices**—Help you send information to and receive it from another person or location.
- Connecting devices—Help you connect all your hardware devices to each other.

Key Terms and Concepts

Anti-virus software, 50
Application software, 41
Arithmetic logic unit (ALU), 60
ASCII (American Standard Code for Information Interchange), 51
Bar code scanner, 53
Binary digit (bit), 51
Biometric scanner, 52
Bluetooth, 63
Byte, 51
CD-R (compact disc-recordable), 58
CD-ROM (compact disc read-only memory), 58
CD-RW (compact disc-rewritable), 58
Central processing unit (CPU), 41
Communications software, 46
CompactFlash (CF) card, 58
Control unit, 60
CPU cache, 60
CPU clock, 61
CPU (machine) cycle, 60
Crash-proof software, 50
CRT, 54
Database management system (DBMS), 46
Desktop computer, 43
Desktop publishing software, 46
Digital camera, 53
Digital still camera, 53
Digital video camera, 53
Disk optimization software, 50
Dot pitch, 55
DVD-R or DVD+R (DVD-recordable), 58
DVD-ROM, 58
DVD-RW or DVD+RW, 58
Expansion bus, 64
Expansion card (board), 64
Expansion slot, 64
Firewire (IEEE 1394 or I-Link), 62
Flash memory card, 58
Flash memory device, 58
Flat-panel display, 54
Floppy disk, 57

Game controller, 52
Gamepad, 52
Gaming wheel, 52
Gas plasma display, 54
Gigabyte (GB or Gig), 57
Gigahertz (GHz), 60
Graphics software, 46
Hard disk, 57
Hardware, 40
Horizontal market software, 47
Hot swap, 62
Image scanner, 53
Information technology (IT), 39
Infrared, IR, or IrDA (infrared data association), 63
Inkjet printer, 55
Input device, 41
Joystick, 52
Keyboard, 52
Laser printer, 56
Linux, 60
Liquid crystal display (LCD), 54
Mac OS, 50
Mainframe computer (mainframe), 45
Megabyte (MB or M or Meg), 57
Memory Stick Media card, 59
Microphone, 53
Microsoft Windows XP Home, 50
Microsoft Windows XP Professional (Windows XP Pro), 50
Minicomputer (mid-range computer), 45
Mobile CPU, 61
Mouse, 52
Multifunction printer, 56
MultiMediaCard (MMC), 58
Multitasking, 48
Notebook computer, 43
Operating system software, 42
Optical character reader, 52
Optical mark reader, 52
Optical storage media, 58
Output device, 41

Figure A.23

PC Cards Connect External Devices to Notebook Comput

Short-Answer Questions

1. What are the two categories of information technology (IT)?
2. What are the six categories of hardware?
3. What is the difference between application and system software?
4. Dollar for dollar with comparable characteristics, which is faster and more powerful—a desktop computer or a notebook computer?
5. What are the major categories of personal productivity software?
6. What is the difference between vertical and horizontal market software?
7. Why is anti-virus software so important?
8. What do the terms bit and byte mean?
9. What is the difference between a tablet PC and a PDA?
10. What are two types of pointing devices?
11. What is a gaming wheel and how does it differ from a gamepad?
12. What purpose does a biometric scanner serve?
13. What does a microphone do?
14. What is the difference between a CRT and a flat-panel display?
15. How would you measure the size of a screen?
16. How is the resolution of a printer comparable to the resolution of a screen?
17. What does dot pitch tell you?
18. What are the two main types of printers for personal computers?
19. How does a CD differ from a floppy disk?
20. What are three types of flash memory cards?
21. What is a mobile CPU?
22. What is the expansion bus?
23. Which wireless standard is used by networks?
24. What is an expansion slot?
25. What is a PC Card?

Assignments and Exercises

1. **COMPARING DIFFERENT TYPES OF COMPUTER SYSTEMS** Computers come in varying sizes and levels of power and performance. Use the Web to find out about computer system configurations. Do some comparison shopping for three types of computers: desktops, notebooks, and tablet PCs. Choose three Web sites that sell computer systems. From each of these sites, choose the most expensive and least expensive computer systems you can find for each of the three types of computers. Create a table for each of the three types of computers and compare them based on the following criteria:
   - Type and speed of CPU
   - Type and speed of RAM
   - Amount of CPU cache
   - System bus speed
   - Hard disk capacity and speed (revolutions per minute or rpm)
   - Number and type of ports

2. **CUSTOMIZING A COMPUTER PURCHASE** One of the great things about the Web is the number of e-tailers that are now online offering you a variety of products and services. One such e-tailer is Dell, which allows you to customize and buy a computer. Connect to Dell's site at www.dell.com. Go to the portion of Dell's site that allows you to customize either a notebook or desktop computer. First, choose an already-prepared system and note its price and capability in terms of CPU speed, RAM size, monitor quality, and storage capacity. Now, customize that system to increase CPU speed, add more RAM, increase monitor size and quality, and add more storage capacity. What's the difference in price between the two? Which system is more in your price range? Which system has the speed and capacity you need?

3. **UNDERSTANDING THE COMPLEXITY OF SOFTWARE** Software instructions on how to open Word or send information to a printer must be provided to a computer in great detail and with excruciating accuracy. Writing code to make the computer execute these instructions properly and in the right order is not a simple task. To understand how detailed you must be, pick a partner for this project and envision that you are standing in a kitchen. The task for one of you is to write down all the instructions that are necessary to make a peanut butter and jelly sandwich. When the instructions are complete, have the other person follow those instructions exactly. How successful was the second person in making the sandwich? Did your instructions include every single step? What did you leave out?

4. **WEB-ENABLED CELL PHONES AND WEB COMPUTERS** When categorizing computers by size for personal needs, we focused on PDAs, tablet PCs, notebook computers, and desktop computers. There are several other variations including Web-enabled cell phones that include instant text messaging and Web computers. For this project, you'll need a group of four people, split into two groups of two. Have the first group research Web-enabled cell phones, their capabilities, and their costs. Have that group make a purchase recommendation based on price and capability. Have the second group do the same for Web computers. What's your vision of the future? Will we ever get rid of clunky notebooks and desktops in favor of more portable and cheaper devices such as Web-enabled cell phones and Web computers? Why or why not?

5. **ADDING MEDIA TO A PRESENTATION** We certainly live in a "multimedia" society, in which it's often easy to present and receive information using a variety (multi) of media. Presentation tools such as Microsoft's PowerPoint can help you easily build presentations that include audio, animation, and video. And this may help you get a better grade in school. Using your preferred presentation software, document the steps necessary to add a short audio or video clip to a presentation. How does the representation of the clip appear on a slide? How can you initiate it? Does your presentation software include any clips that you can insert or do you have to record your own? Now, try recording a short audio clip. What steps must you perform?

6. **OPERATING SYSTEM SOFTWARE FOR PDAS** The personal digital assistant (PDA) market is a ferocious, dynamic, and uncertain one. One of the uncertainties is what operating system for PDAs will become the dominant one. For notebooks and desktops right now, you're pretty well limited to the Microsoft family

unless you buy an Apple computer (in which case your operating system is Mac OS) or want to venture into using Linux (which we wouldn't recommend for most people). Do some research on the more popular PDAs available today. What are the different operating systems? What different functionality do they offer? Are they compatible with each other? Take a guess—which one will come out on top?

7. **TYPES OF MONITORS AND THEIR QUALITY** The monitor you buy will greatly affect your productivity. If you get a high-resolution, large screen monitor, you'll see the screen content better than if you get a low-resolution, small screen monitor. One factor in this is the monitor type. The various levels of monitor resolution are called QXGA, SVGA, SXGA, UXGA, VGA, and XGA. Do a little research on these resolution levels. Rank them from best monitor to worst (the higher the resolution, the better the quality and clarity of the picture). Also, determine a price for each.

CHAPTER TWO OUTLINE

STUDENT LEARNING OUTCOMES

1. Describe supply chain management (SCM) systems, their strategic and competitive opportunities, the challenges businesses face in employing them successfully, and available IT support.

2. Describe customer relationship management (CRM) systems, their strategic and competitive opportunities, the challenges businesses face in employing them successfully, and available IT support.

3. Describe business intelligence (BI) systems, their strategic and competitive opportunities, the challenges businesses face in employing them successfully, and available IT support.

4. Describe integrated collaboration environments (ICE), their strategic and competitive opportunities, the challenges businesses face in employing them successfully, and available IT support.

5. Describe how individual systems that work together in an integrated manner can give airline companies a competitive advantage.

WEB SUPPORT

www.mhhe.com/haag

- Books and music
- Clothing and accessories
- Auction houses
- Automobiles

CHAPTER TWO

Major Business Initiatives
Gaining Competitive Advantage with IT

OPENING CASE STUDY:
DIGITAL LOYALTY NETWORK MAKES
GM MORE COMPETITIVE

Under the direction of CEO Rick Wagoner, General Motors (GM) recently launched a coordinated IT initiative to make GM more competitive. Wagoner's goal was to strengthen and integrate GM's customer and supply chain management systems, as well as some of its business intelligence and collaboration systems, into a "digital loyalty network" (DLN). Wagoner viewed the DLN as one of the keys to GM's success (and survival) in an increasingly competitive global automotive market.

GM's supply chain encompasses a large network of suppliers located all over the world. Inaccurate projections of market demand had led to high levels of inventory in the supply chain as well as unsold cars sitting on dealers' lots.

One of the innovations GM came up with is called Order-to-Delivery (OTD), a digitized process designed to migrate from a build-to-stock model to a more balanced build-to-stock and build-to-order model. OTD reduced delivery lead times of ordered vehicles by 50 percent in less than a year after its implementation (from 80 days to just over 40 days).

GM also participates in Covisint, a large B2B (Business to Business) e-marketplace. It expects Covisint processes to reduce its inventory, help the company respond to changes in consumer demand on a more timely basis, and reduce the time to develop new vehicles by fostering closer collaboration between GM and its suppliers.

GM and its dealers have many customer "touch points" at which customer information is collected: dealer contacts, contacts through GM's OnStar interactive vehicle telematics service, GM's consumer Web site (www.BuyPower.com), corporate call centers, trade shows, and response from direct mail campaigns. Customer information, however, was not being consistently fed back to GM to use for product improvements, sales and marketing campaigns, and personalization efforts.

The BuyPower Web site is one exception. BuyPower is accessible to 3.5 billion of the world's 6.4 billion people. By analyzing customer behavior on the Web site using clickstream data and business intelligence analytical tools, GM has a more complete understanding of shifts in global market demand.

One clear outcome of the DLN project was an enhanced understanding of how seemingly separate IT applications that focused on supply chain management, customer relationship management, business intelligence, and collaboration were all interrelated. GM realized that these stand-alone IT systems had to be integrated for the DLN project to yield meaningful business benefits. Accordingly, U.S. call centers were consolidated from 40 to 3, and 19 global customer databases were reduced to 3 data warehouses. Business intelligence is now readily available to GM planners. The data warehouses track customers over time as they move across brands, locations, and other GM businesses (finance, mortgage, etc).

GM hopes that its DLN initiative will pay off in the long run. One sign that the trend is in the right direction is that in 2003 GM won the Polk Automotive Loyalty Award in the Overall Manufacturer category for the fourth consecutive year, beating out such tough competitors as Honda, Toyota, and BMW.[1,2,3]

Introduction

Recent studies have shown that as competition intensifies in almost every industry, companies must develop innovative products and business processes to survive and thrive, and that information technology (IT) is a powerful tool to help them do so.[4] In this chapter, we discuss some of the most important IT applications businesses are using today:

- Supply chain management (SCM)
- Customer relationship management (CRM)
- Business intelligence (BI)
- Integrated collaboration environments (ICE)

We also discuss the competitive advantages that businesses can achieve by integrating their IT applications so that they operate in a holistic manner. We begin with supply chain management, an application many companies consider an absolute necessity for the smooth functioning of their daily operations.

Supply Chain Management

Dell Computer's supply chain management system is the envy of the industry. Its direct sell model gives the company a huge advantage over any competitor still using a traditional model of selling through retailers. Traditional PC manufacturers build PCs and ship them to wholesalers, distributors, or directly to retailers. The PCs sit on the retailers' shelves or in a warehouse until you come in and buy one. If you took a look at a typical distribution chain you will see that there are too many PCs in inventory. A ***distribution chain*** is simply the path followed from the originator of a product or service to the end consumer. Holding on to inventory in a distribution chain costs money, because whoever owns the inventory has to pay for it as well as pay for the operation of the warehouses or stores while waiting for someone to buy it.

Dell's model is different. It sells computers directly from its Web site so there is no inventory in its distribution chain. Dell has enhanced its supply chain as well. It uses i2 supply chain management software to send orders for parts to suppliers every two hours, enabling it to manufacture and deliver exactly what its customers want with little or no inventory in its supply chain.[5]

The differences between Dell's "sell, source, and ship" model and the traditional "buy, hold, and sell" model are illustrated in Figure 2.1.

WHAT ARE SUPPLY CHAIN MANAGEMENT SYSTEMS?

For a company the size of General Motors, with operations all over the world and tens of thousands of suppliers, supply chain management and IT-based supply chain management systems are critical necessities to ensure the smooth flow of parts to GM factories. As we discussed in Chapter 1, ***supply chain management (SCM)*** tracks inventory and information among business processes and across companies. A ***supply chain management (SCM) system*** is an IT system that supports supply chain management activities by automating the tracking of inventory and information among business processes and across companies.

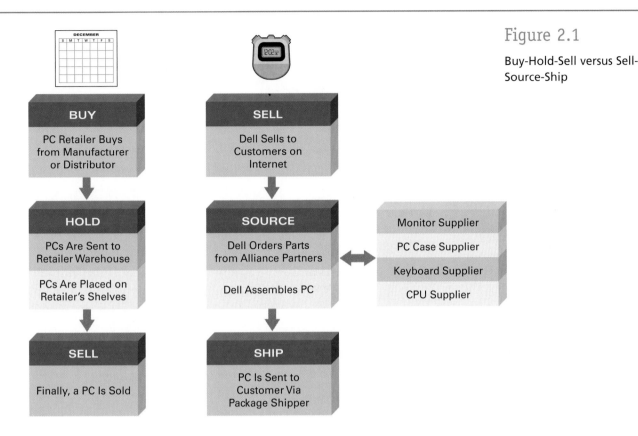

Figure 2.1

Buy-Hold-Sell versus Sell-Source-Ship

Most large manufacturing companies use just-in-time manufacturing processes, which ensure that the right parts are available as products in process move down the assembly line. *Just-in-time (JIT)* is an approach that produces or delivers a product or service just at the time the customer wants it. For retailers, like Target, this means that products customers want to buy are on the shelves when customers walk by. Supply chain management systems also focus on making sure that the *right number* of parts or products are available, not too many and not too few. Too many products on hand means that too much money is tied up in inventory and also increases the risk of obsolescence. Too few products on hand is not a good thing either, because it could force an assembly line to shut down or, in the case of retailers, lose sales because an item is not in stock when a customer is ready to buy.

While modern supply chain management systems focus on assuring that the right amount of inventory is available when needed, they also encompass other essential functions such as selecting suppliers and monitoring their performance. For example, it does GM no good to have the right number of component parts on hand if their quality is so poor that they cause problems on the assembly line. As a consequence, many companies monitor the quality of parts received from their suppliers and, if quality is below expectations, either work with suppliers to improve their quality or put them on notice that they will not get any more of the company's business unless quality improves.

Managing logistics is another important process in modern supply chain management systems. *Logistics* is the set of processes that plans for and controls the efficient and effective transportation and storage of supplies from suppliers to customers. Many companies now have suppliers located in all parts of the globe. Coordinating logistics to

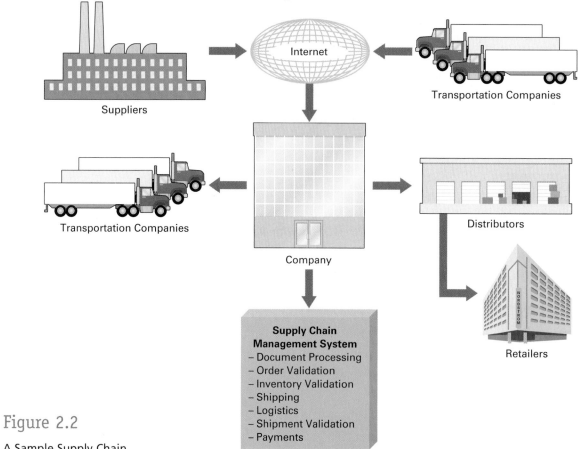

Figure 2.2

A Sample Supply Chain Management (SCM) System Infrastructure

be sure that parts reach their intended destination at the lowest cost is a critical and complicated part of supply chain management systems. A sample supply chain management system is illustrated in Figure 2.2.

STRATEGIC AND COMPETITIVE OPPORTUNITIES WITH SUPPLY CHAIN MANAGEMENT

A well-designed supply chain management system chain helps a business by optimizing the following processes:

- Fulfillment—Ensuring the right quantity of parts for production or products for sale arrive at the right time.
- Logistics—Keeping the cost of transporting materials as low as possible consistent with safe and reliable delivery.
- Production—Ensuring production lines function smoothly because high quality parts are available when needed.
- Revenue and profit—Ensuring no sales are lost because shelves are empty.
- Spend—Keeping the cost of purchased parts and products at acceptable levels.

Cooperation among supply chain partners for mutual success is another hallmark of modern supply chain management systems. For example, many manufacturing companies share product concepts with suppliers early in the product development process.

PERDUE TALKS TURKEY

Most folks have all they can handle on Thanksgiving Day to serve up one turkey for their family feast. The managers and employees of Perdue Farms have to move more than 1 million turkeys across the United States at Thanksgiving-time.

This task is a whole lot more manageable since Perdue invested some $20 million in a Manugistics (www.manugistics.com) supply chain management system. Using the SCM system's forecasting software and supply chain planning applications, Perdue finds it much easier to deliver the right number of turkeys to the right stores at just the right time. According to Don Taylor, Perdue's CIO, "As we get to November, we have live information at our fingertips."

Because getting turkeys from the farm to your local supermarket is a race against time, Perdue uses its SCM logistics module to be sure the turkeys arrive in fresh condition. Each of Perdue's trucks is equipped with a global positioning system that enables Perdue's dispatchers to know each truck's location at all times. If a truck has mechanical trouble en route, another truck is dispatched to rescue the turkeys and speed them on their way. Perdue uses a variety of technologies to keep in touch with customers, including telephone, e-mail, and videoconferencing. Some retailers have computer systems that communicate with Perdue's systems, allowing Perdue to track sales of its turkeys with real-time information obtained from in-store checkout scanners. "We're always looking for new technologies as they come along to see what makes sense for us," says CIO Taylor. When Thanksgiving rolls around, Taylor will give thanks for his SCM system for making his job a bit easier and for getting turkeys fresh to his retail customers' tables.[6]

This lets suppliers contribute their ideas on how to make high quality parts at a lower cost.

In the retail industry, several companies recently completed a successful pilot study to demonstrate the practical feasibility of a process innovation called collaborative planning, forecasting, and replenishment.[7] **Collaborative planning, forecasting, and replenishment (CPFR)** is a concept that encourages and facilitates collaborative processes between supply chain partners. One of the techniques used in CPFR is to have retailers share sales information they obtain from store checkout scanners with manufacturers on a daily basis. This gives manufacturers more current and accurate information with which to schedule production. Excess inventory is eliminated from manufacturers' warehouses, distribution centers, and retail store shelves. Stock-outs are reduced, as are total costs in the supply chain. The winners are the companies in the supply chain who use CPFR (their sales are higher) and the customers who shop at the retail outlets (the prices they pay are lower because of the cost savings produced by CPFR).

CHALLENGES TO SUCCESS WITH SUPPLY CHAIN MANAGEMENT

To be successful with supply chain management, you can learn from the experiences of companies who have achieved business benefits with SCM. A recent survey noted the following four key issues:

1. High level executives must recognize the importance of supply chain management to the company's success.
2. You must work closely with your company's customers and suppliers to build world-class business processes.

EVEN NATIONS CAN GAIN A COMPETITIVE ADVANTAGE WITH IT

Using IT for competitive advantage is not restricted to companies. Singapore is a well-known example that a nation can use IT for competitive advantage as well.

As a small island nation with few natural resources, Singapore concluded some time ago that its most valuable resource was its people. The government decided that the wave of the future was IT, and that it should invest in training a cadre of IT workers and focus on becoming what they called the "Intelligent Island." Singapore subsequently became renowned for the way it used IT to speed up the flow of goods through its port facilities by replacing cumbersome paperwork processes with e-commerce techniques.

On its Web site, the Singapore Economic Development Board (SEDB) invites companies to "Plug into one of the best business environments in the world. Big or small, new or established, this is where you can inno-

vate and create, grow and globalize. Be part of the Singapore success story!"

As evidence of its continuing efforts, the SEDB recently recognized 17 Singapore-based companies for their success in harnessing Internet technologies for their supply chain management systems by presenting them with the eSupply Chain Management (eSCM) Certificate. Each company met the standards set by the eSCM Assessment Program sponsored by the Singapore Manufacturers Federation with the support of several government agencies. The goal of the eSCM program is to improve the SCM capabilities of Singapore companies by benchmarking their performance against world-class practices, and thereby help to ensure that Singapore maintains its position as a leader in the use of information technology for competitive advantage.[8]

---

3. Your supply chain management should be innovative in the way it integrates with internal IT systems as well as with the IT systems of key customers and suppliers.

4. You must continuously adapt your supply chain management strategies and systems as market needs change.[9]

Problems with supply chain management often arise because individual areas *within* a company do not communicate effectively with each other. One well-known example of this is the case of Volvo, which in one year made too many green cars and was not able to sell them. So, when the inventory of green cars started to build up, the sales and marketing staff at headquarters offered incentives to dealers in the form of price reductions. When the supply chain managers saw the resultant rise in the sale of green cars, they doubled their production of green cars. As a result, Volvo dealers again had more green cars on their hands than they knew what to do with until someone figured out that poor communication between sales and production was causing the problem.[10]

IT SUPPORT FOR SUPPLY CHAIN MANAGEMENT

The solution for a successful supply chain management system includes either purchasing sophisticated software with Web interfaces or hiring a third-party Web-based application service provider who promises to provide part or all of the SCM service. An ***application service provider (ASP)*** supplies software applications (and often related services such as maintenance, technical support, and the like) over the Internet that would otherwise reside on its customers' in-house computers (see Figure 2.3). Knowledge workers query the SCM software for information or to order inventory. The SCM software connects to potential suppliers, distributors, and transporting companies to determine where to purchase the inventory and the best way to have the inventory deliv-

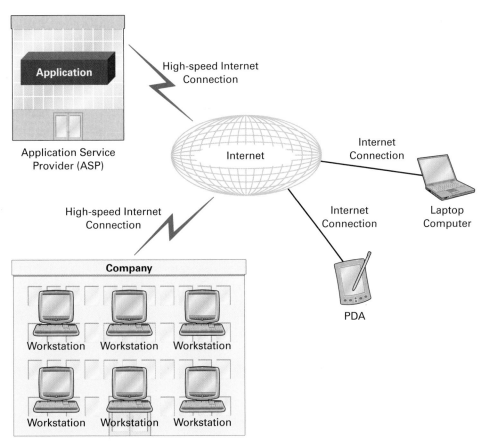

Figure 2.3

A Sample Application
Service Provider (ASP)
Infrastructure

ered. The SCM system also performs such functions as order validation, message validation to potential suppliers and distributors, inventory routing and validation, and electronic payments. While the SCM software market was pioneered by specialist companies such as i2 and Manugistics, it is now dominated by enterprise software providers SAP, Oracle, and PeopleSoft.[11]

Customer Relationship Management

Wells Fargo Bank's customer relationship management system tracks and analyzes every transaction made by its 10 million retail customers at its branches, its ATMs, and through its Web-based online banking systems. It has become so good at predicting customer behavior that it knows what customers need before many of them even realize they need it. Wells Fargo's system collects every customer transaction and combines it with personal information provided by the customer. The system is able to predict tailored offerings that will appeal to individual customers (a money-saving second mortgage, for example), at just the right time. As a result, Wells Fargo sells four additional banking products or services to its customers compared with an industry average of 2.2.[12]

Another example is the American Cancer Society, which depends on donations from the public to carry out its educational and service programs. It recently installed a Siebel eBusiness CRM application (www.siebel.com) to better target members of its donor base to include planned giving. Terry Music, National Vice President for Information Delivery, notes, "Our donor base contains many individuals who, through their wills or other financial instruments, are able to make substantial gifts to our cancer fighting efforts. With our CRM system, we are able to target them as a contained group within our fundraising efforts."[13]

You don't have to be a part of a traditional for-profit organization to get into the habit of looking for ways to improve how customers are treated. Not-for-profits and governmental agencies can serve people better and also gain benefits for themselves from the way they use IT. For example, see if you can come up with ways that one of the local governmental bodies in your region, such as a city, county, or state, could get a competitive advantage from the way it uses IT to serve you as a citizen. Take the customer's perspective (yours). For example, how complicated is it to get your driver's license renewed? How difficult is it to get information on various governmental services? Can you pay a traf-

fic ticket online with your credit card or do you have to mail in a check? If you feel a traffic ticket was issued unfairly, are you able to dispute it online or do you have to go to some office downtown and stand in line?

Once you have evaluated a local Web site, go to unpan1.un.org/intradoc/groups/public/documents/aspa/unpan012904.pdf. This site picked the 100 best city Web sites in the world as of mid-2003. How does your local site compare with some of the sites on the list? What suggestions can you come up with to improve the customer service your local site provides to the citizenry?

WHAT ARE CUSTOMER RELATIONSHIP MANAGEMENT SYSTEMS?

What do you think is the primary driver for your organization? If you said the *customers*—congratulations, you are correct. Without customers, a business couldn't exist; and so, many businesses' primary goal is to increase customer satisfaction.

Acquiring and retaining customers are the basic objectives of any organization and, as a result, customer relationship management systems has become one of the hottest IT systems in business today. A *customer relationship management (CRM) system* uses information about customers to gain insights into their needs, wants, and behaviors in order to serve them better. Customers interact with companies in many ways, and each interaction should be easy, enjoyable, and error free. Have you ever had an experience with a company that made you so angry you changed companies or returned the product? It's not uncommon for a customer to change companies after having a negative experience. The goal of CRM is to limit such negative interactions and provide customers with positive experiences.

CRM systems typically include such functions as:

- Sales force automation
- Customer service and support
- Marketing campaign management and analysis

It's important to note that CRM is not just software. It is a total business objective which encompasses many different aspects of a business including software, hardware, services, support, and strategic business goals. The CRM system you adopt should support all these functions and should also be designed to provide the organization with detailed customer information. In many cases, companies begin with a sales force automation application and then progress to the other two functions. *Sales force automation (SFA)*

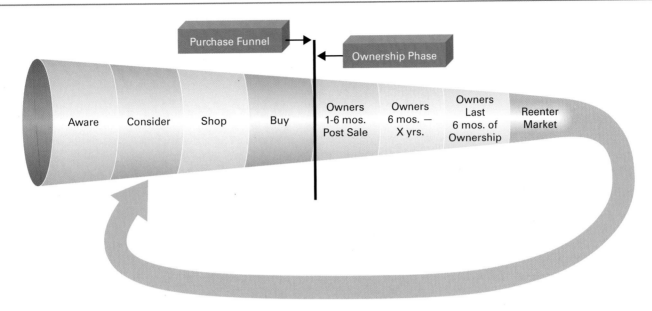

Figure 2.4

General Motors' Purchase Funnel[14]

systems automatically track all the steps in the sales process. The sales process contains many steps including contact management, sales lead tracking, sales forecasting and order management, and product knowledge.

Some basic SFA systems perform sales lead tracking or listing potential customers for the sales team to contact. They also perform contact management, which tracks all the times a salesperson contacts a potential customer, what they discussed, and the next steps. More sophisticated SFA systems perform detailed analysis of the market and customers and can even offer product configuration tools enabling customers to configure their own products (see Figure 2.4).

STRATEGIC AND COMPETITIVE OPPORTUNITIES WITH CUSTOMER RELATIONSHIP MANAGEMENT

One of the results of CRM is competitive advantage through achieving superior performance in CRM functions, in particular:

- Devising more effective marketing campaigns based on more precise knowledge of customer needs and wants.
- Assuring that the sales process is efficiently managed.
- Providing superior after-sale service and support through, for example, well-run call centers.

Successful CRM systems provide a competitive advantage for your organization versus your competitors. All of the classic goals of CRM—treating customers better, understanding their needs and wants, tailoring offerings in response—are likely to result in the buyer choosing your product or service instead of the competition's. However, attempting to predict the amount or degree to which the CRM-enabled organization will gain market share can be a difficult task. Certainly, it is something that can be measured after-the-fact, thus allowing your organization to understand the true results of better CRM on customers' buying decisions. But predicting the degree of gain in market share and then forecasting a net result in terms of incremental revenues is difficult. One way to measure the benefits of CRM systems, according to one expert, is to place the benefits

HOW CONTINENTAL AIRLINES CREATES FANATICALLY LOYAL CUSTOMERS

According to Gordon Bethune, Chairman and CEO of Continental Airlines, the airline industry is getting so impersonal it's becoming like mass transit. Continental's strategy to differentiate itself from other airlines is to reestablish the concept that "if you pay more, you get more." Continental uses technology to identify its best customers, those who generate 10 percent of the company's revenue. Continental's CRM software identifies them as CO, which stands for "costars." The software tracks each touch point with the company and enables employees to recognize the costars by name. Costars receive extra attention even though they may be sitting in the coach section on a particular flight. The software even provides flight attendants with information on which beverage a costar prefers, and all beverages are free. Continental employees put a special tag on costars' bags and their bags are unloaded first.

Even so, Bethune recognizes that Continental's first obligation is to have its planes leave and arrive on time and get all its customers to their destinations safely. CRM can't do this for the company. What CRM does, however, is assure that the company's costars are given the special attention they have earned.[15]

Figure 2.5

Example Revenue Enhancers and Cost Cutters

Revenue Enhancers	Cost Cutters
• Increase sales effectiveness	• Decrease cost of sales
• Add new customers at a higher rate	• More time to sell, less time on administration
• Offer new products/services	• Decrease cost of service
• Provide a better customer experience	• Cost per service interaction
• Increase revenue per customer	• Transition to more self-service
• Sell more of current products/services	
• Improve customer retention	

into two principal categories, revenue enhancers and cost cutters.[16] Examples of revenue enhancers and cost cutters are shown in Figure 2.5.

CHALLENGES TO SUCCESS WITH CUSTOMER RELATIONSHIP MANAGEMENT

While many CRM systems provide substantial business benefits, other CRM projects are considered less than successful. As a matter of fact, a recent Gartner Group study found that 40 percent of companies surveyed hadn't made an investment in CRM—and that more than 50 percent of those that had saw the installations as failures.[17] Despite the fact that so many CRM software installations fail, and that some companies haven't even given them a try, a company that does its homework beforehand can look forward to a successful installation.

One analyst listed some of the most common reasons why CRM installations are less than successful:

- **The company's goals are too broad.** Too often a CRM initiative tries to encompass everything that should be done to attain the vision of a customer-centric company. While there is nothing wrong with having this vision, companies need to realize that the vision is more easily achieved with a series of small, tactical steps rather than with one giant leap forward.

- **Strategies are too generic.** CRM strategies must be business-specific. The CRM industry—analysts and consultants as well as vendors—have been saying that every company can use technology the same way to gain the same results. The truth is that each company needs a solution tailored to its unique requirements.

- **Implementations are often too software-centric.** Technology can and should play a role in enhancing customer relationships—but a supporting role, not a leading one. Software should support the specific CRM processes each company needs to get real business benefits.[18]

One widely held view is that CRM is the most important step your firm will take, because it is all about the most important asset your company has: the customer. True enough. It is important to remember, however, CRM is not only a technology, but also a set of processes and people and skills. There must be a fit. This is true with any IT application, of course.

IT SUPPORT FOR CUSTOMER RELATIONSHIP MANAGEMENT

Figure 2.6 is an example of a sample CRM infrastructure. The *front office systems* are the primary interface to customers and sales channels; they send all the customer information they collect to the database. The *back office systems* are used to fulfill and support customer orders and they also send all their customer information to the database.

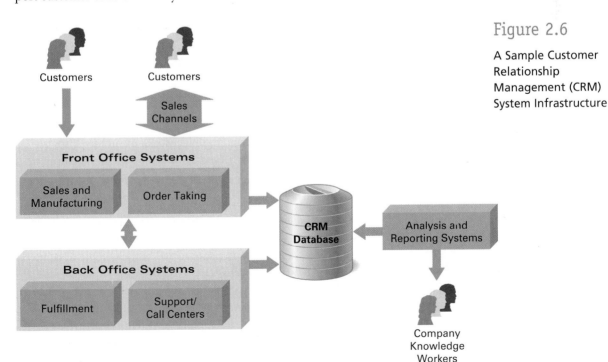

Figure 2.6

A Sample Customer Relationship Management (CRM) System Infrastructure

The CRM system analyzes and distributes the customer information and provides the organization with a complete view of each customer's experience with the business. There are many systems available today a company can purchase that offer CRM functionality. Some of the big providers of these packages are Clarify, Oracle, SAP, and Siebel Systems. Clarify and Siebel are also some of the most prominent SFA software providers; others are Salesforce.com and Vantive. Salesforce.com was the first company to offer CRM using an ASP model and others have since followed suit.

Business Intelligence

FiberMark North America, a manufacturer of specialty packaging and paper, could not easily retrieve business intelligence from its expensive transaction processing systems. "We were desperate to get good information quickly," said Joel Taylor, Director of IS. Taylor spent less than $75,000 on QlikView — BI software from QlikTech (www. qliktech.com), which grabs FiberMark's information from its transaction processing systems and stores it in a readily accessible database.

Now, instead of printing 1,000-page monthly sales reports for each of FiberMark's 29 salespeople, the salespeople can access business intelligence from the corporate intranet. "With a very short training cycle (15 minutes), they're up and flying," says Taylor. "They print four pages, not 1,000." He stated the system paid for itself in nine months in saved paper and related costs alone. More important, though, salespeople and executives can get the specific, up-to-date business intelligence they want anytime they want it.[19]

WHAT ARE BUSINESS INTELLIGENCE SYSTEMS?

Business intelligence sounds like a great term, but what exactly is it? ***Business intelligence (BI)*** is knowledge—knowledge about your customers, your competitors, your business partners, your competitive environment, and your own internal operations—that gives you the ability to make effective, important, and often strategic business decisions. ***Business intelligence (BI) systems*** are the IT applications and tools that support the business intelligence function within an organization. The objective of BI is to improve the timeliness and quality of the input for decision making by helping knowledge workers to understand the

- Capabilities available in the firm.
- State of the art, trends, and future directions in the markets.
- Technological, demographic, economic, political, social, and regulatory environments in which the firm competes.
- Actions of competitors and the implications of these actions.[20]

As illustrated in Figure 2.7, business intelligence encompasses both internal and external information. Some business people treat competitive intelligence as a specialized branch of business intelligence. ***Competitive intelligence (CI)*** is business intelligence focused on the external competitive environment. There is even an organization for people who specialize in competitive intelligence called the Society for Competitive Intelligence Professionals (SCIP). Visit its Web site at www.scip.org to find out more about its activities, programs, and publications.

Figure 2.7

Building Business Intelligence

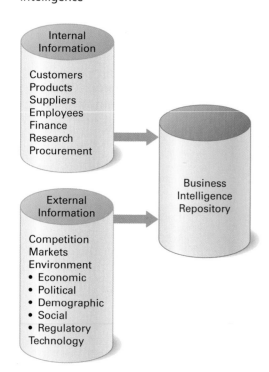

Internal Information

Customers
Products
Suppliers
Employees
Finance
Research
Procurement

Business Intelligence Repository

External Information

Competition
Markets
Environment
• Economic
• Political
• Demographic
• Social
• Regulatory
Technology

IBM AND FACTIVA JOIN FORCES TO TRANSFORM GLOBAL CONTENT BUSINESS

IBM and Factiva, a Dow Jones and Reuters Company, recently agreed to codevelop text analytics solutions built on the IBM WebFountain platform.

IBM's WebFountain is a mining and discovery tool that extracts trends, patterns, and relationships from massive amounts of information stored on proprietary databases, Internet pages, and newsgroups. Factiva's first application on WebFountain will offer an independent, external view of a company's reputation by analyzing information from a comprehensive collection of information sources. The resulting analysis will provide a view on relevant business issues, show new industry trends, and disclose relationships. Using this information, executives can gain new insights into the way that outsiders perceive their company or brand, see how perceptions change over time, and identify emerging issues associated with their company or brand. As Factiva subscribers, they will also be able to access the underlying sources from which the analysis was derived.

"It's the information that organizations don't know—outside their four walls and beyond the typical market research and outdated surveys—that can be the most critical for decision making, but until now, there was no single tool that could derive real intelligence from billions of pages," said Robert Carlson, IBM Web-Fountain Vice President. "With WebFountain, customers can use the Internet's immense amount of data as a business tool, and Factiva's authoritative sources and classification expertise make the results even more powerful."

The IBM-Factiva partnership will allow executives tasked with enhancing a brand's image to gain insight, manage risk, and, perhaps most important, identify new business opportunities more quickly and cost effectively than ever. "This is the next logical step toward giving people intelligence that they can act upon," said Clare Hart, President and CEO of Factiva. "Companies that can assimilate vast amounts of information and quickly determine market opportunities will emerge as leaders in today's extremely competitive environment. We expect this type of service to become a key business asset and a must-have for the most ambitious enterprises."[21]

Business intelligence has information as its foundation. Most often, it is information collected from various sources within an organization and from external sources as well. For example, as described in Chapter 1, information is collected from transaction processing systems and stored in various databases. A company may have databases for different applications, including separate databases for customers, products, suppliers, and employees, among many others. Such databases are necessary to support the processing of day-to-day transactions. On the other hand, they contain more detailed information than is needed to support most decisions that managers need to make.

To deal with this, most organizations summarize information from their various databases into a summarized data repository called a data warehouse. A **data warehouse** is a logical collection of information—gathered from many different operational databases—used to create business intelligence that supports business analysis activities and decision-making tasks. Often, a data warehouse is subdivided into smaller repositories called data marts for use by a single department within an organization. A **data mart** is a subset of a data warehouse in which only a focused portion of the data warehouse information is kept. For example, if an organization has a separate group which focuses on competitive intelligence, it may find it more effective to use its own data mart rather than the organization's data warehouse. Data warehouses and data marts are covered in Chapter 3.

Some of the tools used to derive business intelligence from data warehouses and data marts include the OLAP tools discussed in Chapter 1. They are discussed more thoroughly in Chapters 3 and 4. Other technical components of business intelligence include such tools as

- Data mining (discussed in Chapter 3).
- Automated exception detection with proactive alerting and automatic recipient determination.
- Automatic learning.[22]

A ***data-mining tool*** is a software tool you use to query information in a data warehouse. We discuss data-mining tools in Chapters 3 and 4. Automated anomaly and exception detection is software that detects an unusual or unexpected condition, and proactively alerts the right person(s) that it has occurred. Some BI systems use artificial intelligence techniques to automatically learn and thus anticipate the kinds of business intelligence knowledge workers want and need. Artificial intelligence is discussed in detail in Chapter 4.

STRATEGIC AND COMPETITIVE OPPORTUNITIES WITH BUSINESS INTELLIGENCE

Business managers face many kinds of decisions ranging from routine decisions (such as whether to order additional stock) to decisions with long-range strategic implications (such as whether to expand into international markets). A survey by the Gartner Group of the strategic uses of business intelligence found that such uses were ranked by firms in the following order of importance:

1. Corporate performance management.
2. Optimizing customer relations, monitoring business activity, and traditional decision support.
3. Packaged stand-alone BI applications for specific operations or strategies.
4. Management reporting of business intelligence.[23]

Earlier, we mentioned that one of the primary purposes of BI is to improve the timeliness and quality of input to the decision process. Companies with well-designed BI systems available to their managers will find that their managers make better decisions on a variety of business issues. Higher quality managerial decision making lets companies gain an advantage over their competitors who operate without the benefit of BI systems for their managers to use. BI systems provide managers with actionable information and knowledge

- at the right time,
- in the right location,
- in the right form[24]

Despite the fact that the benefits of BI systems are self-evident, you will find that many companies today do not yet have them. One of the reasons for this is that knowledge of their value as a competitive tool is not widely understood by business managers. Another reason is that, in some cases, they have been installed in companies but not used effectively. Some of the challenges in using BI systems are discussed in the next section. (See Figure 2.8 for an illustration of how GM has integrated its various customer-facing systems with BI applications.)

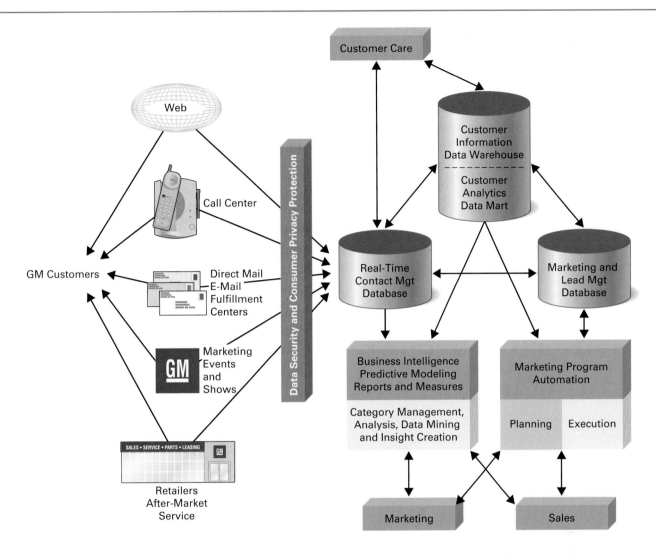

Figure 2.8

Aggregating Customer
Touch Points at General
Motors[25]

CHALLENGES TO SUCCESS WITH BUSINESS INTELLIGENCE

As we discussed in Chapter 1, IT systems are of no value unless knowledge workers know how to use them effectively. BI systems are a great example of this. To ensure that BI systems have a high impact on business decisions, you must

- Focus on using information provided by the BI systems to deal with an important business issue.
- Provide the ability to customize BI information to each knowledge worker involved in the decision-making process.
- Build discipline and precision into decision-making processes.
- Recognize that knowledge workers must understand BI tools and know how to use them effectively.
- Understand that many BI systems are complex systems and continually change as information provided them changes.[26]

IS HUGEHATS A GOOD INVESTMENT?

Assume that one of your teammates has a good friend named Brad, who is a born entrepreneur. Starting with lemonade stands when he was eleven and moving on to used golf balls and CDs, Brad always seemed to have a knack for "buying low and selling high." Brad has approached your teammates with an idea for an Internet business called "HugeHats." Brad has a larger than average–sized head and finds it hard to find hats that fit him. As a result, he thinks there is a large under-served market for people like him. He wants to start a company to sell large-size baseball and other types of hats over the Internet, but needs $20,000 to get started. He wants your team to borrow from your credit cards, if necessary, to invest in his venture. Brad has not done any formal analysis, but "just knows" this business will make all of you rich and that there is little, if any, competition. Your team tells him you will consider it but only after you gather some competitive intelligence to find out if this is a good idea or not.

Normally you would scan all the trade publications, talk to industry analysts, key participants in the indus-

try, and other retailers. For this exercise, however, you are artificially restricted to obtaining information from electronic sources.

Assignment: Use the Internet to scan for similar sites, competitor news, and possible industry trends. Prepare a written summary of your findings followed by a recommendation as to whether or not your team should consider an investment in HugeHats. A good write-up will cover at least the following points:

- An assessment of the competition.
- Evidence of your information search (at least six sources).
- A recommendation on whether or not to invest in HugeHats and, if so, how much.
- Other points you believe to be relevant to the decision.

Please limit your write-up to three pages plus any attachments you wish to add.

IT SUPPORT FOR BUSINESS INTELLIGENCE

While the World Wide Web is used to support BI systems in many firms, specialized software is at the heart of BI. In the past, a large number of companies built their own systems. Now the trend is toward buying packages. Gartner Research found that the number of firms that plan to manage their BI integration internally dropped from 49 percent in 2001 to 37 percent in 2002.[27] The reason for this change is that the traditional custom-design, build, and integrate model for BI systems takes too long (at least six months) and costs too much ($2 to $3 million). Implemented quickly, specialized BI software packages can deliver immediate benefits and a quick return on a company's investment.[28]

A large number of firms are involved in aspects of the BI business. For example, several companies identified as companies to watch in the BI field are Aydatum, Brio Software Decisions, Cognos, Crystal Decisions, E-Intelligence, Hyperion, MicroStrategy, ProClarity, Siebel, and Spotfire.[29] One interesting feature of many BI software packages is a digital dashboard. A *digital dashboard* displays key information gathered from several sources on a computer screen in a format tailored to the needs and wants of an individual knowledge worker (see Figure 2.9).

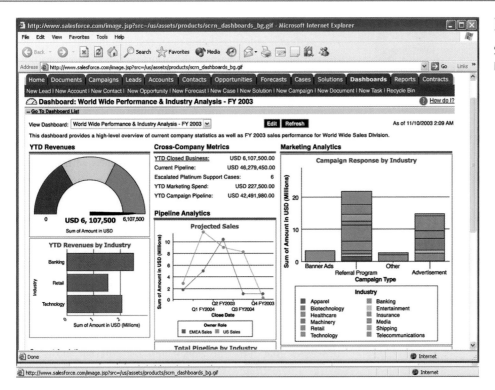

Figure 2.9

Sample Digital
Dashboard

Integrated Collaboration Environments

Siemens AG, based in Munich, Germany, is a 150-year-old electrical engineering and electronics company with 440,000 employees in 190 countries. Much of its work is done in teams, whose members work in integrated collaborative environments supported by a state-of the-art collaborative software suite, SiteScape's Forum (www.sitescape.com). A top Siemens executive describes his experience with the software this way: "A perfect example of the value Forum brings to Siemens is when I had to institute a cross-functional team of 18–20 people spread across the United States and Germany. We needed a communication channel that would be up 24 × 7. Because of the six-hour time difference, we set 9 A.M. and 3 P.M. as the push time. People were able to discuss ideas and share web-enabled documents." He also hopes to use Forum in an extranet capacity, streamlining the supply chain management process and exploring Business to Business functions with the tool.

"I'm really happy with Forum," the executive says. "It helps productivity to have a web-based collaboration solution which allows each team member to contribute freely to discussions and documents from anywhere, at any time."[30]

WHAT ARE INTEGRATED COLLABORATION ENVIRONMENTS?

Almost everything you do in your organization will be performed in a team environment. So, improving team collaboration greatly increases your organization's productivity and competitive advantage. An *integrated collaboration environment (ICE)* is the environment in which virtual teams do their work. *Virtual teams* are teams whose members are located in varied geographic locations and whose work is supported by specialized ICE

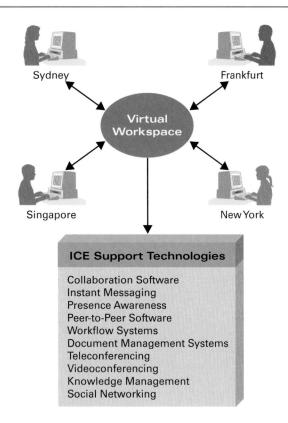

Figure 2.10

An Integrated Collaboration Environment

software or by more basic collaboration systems. A *collaboration system* is software that is designed specifically to improve the performance of teams by supporting the sharing and flow of information. Integrated collaboration environments are supported by combinations of collaboration systems and other technologies as illustrated in Figure 2.10.

More and more, virtual teams are composed of people from your company's alliance partners as well. An *alliance partner* is a company your company does business with on a regular basis in a collaborative fashion, usually facilitated by IT systems.

Many companies first use e-mail and then move on to collaboration systems incorporating more advanced features such as giving employees access to each other's calendars, group scheduling, imaging, workflow systems, and document management systems. *Workflow* defines all of the steps or business rules, from beginning to end, required for a business process. For example, in order for a bank to process a loan application correctly, there are a specified series of business processes that must be performed by different knowledge workers. *Workflow systems* facilitate the automation and management of business processes. For example, all of the steps to process that loan application could be performed by a workflow system with the necessary documents updated and passed from knowledge worker to knowledge worker as electronic documents. Large companies produce millions of documents each month and they need to be organized and managed. A *document management system* manages a document through all the stages of its processing. It is similar to a workflow system except that the focus is more on document storage and retrieval. Banks, for example, retain copies of your checks in electronic form and can produce a copy for you should you ever need one.

Companies will soon migrate to more sophisticated collaboration systems that utilize tele-, video-, and Web-conferencing in real time and that incorporate project management and work flow automation.

KNOWLEDGE MANAGEMENT Knowledge management systems are a variant of ICE. A *knowledge management (KM) system* is an IT system that supports the capturing, organization, and dissemination of knowledge (i.e., know-how) throughout an organization. The objective of knowledge management systems is to be sure that a company's knowledge of facts, sources of information, and solutions are available to all of its employees whenever needed.

SOCIAL NETWORK SYSTEMS Social network systems are another, newer form of ICE. *Social network systems* are IT systems that link you to people you know and, from there, to people your contacts know. For example, if a salesperson at your company wants an introduction to an influential executive at another company, a social network system could find out if someone in your company has good enough connections to arrange an introduction. This is exactly the kind of question that could get a quick reply from the right kind of social network system. Figure 2.11 describes the way social network systems work.

Linkedin is one of the best-known social network sites focused on business professionals. Here is a summary of the way its software works. It's a three-step process:

1. **Build your network.** You start out by asking people you know to sign up. After they do, they are encouraged to invite their friends and colleagues to join as well. That's how your network grows.

2. **Find the people you need.** Once you've built your network, it's easy to search it to find the people you need. It could be someone who could help you get a job, for example.

3. **Make a trusted contact.** Once you've located the person you want to reach, all you have to do is compose a message for her and send it via the network. When she receives it, she knows it came to her through a network of trusted friends and colleagues.

That's the way it works. For more details, check out Linkedin's Web site at www.linkedin.com.

Figure 2.11

The Way Social Network Systems Work[31]

STRATEGIC AND COMPETITIVE OPPORTUNITIES WITH INTEGRATED COLLABORATION ENVIRONMENTS

The payoffs from collaboration can be huge. For example, while oil and gas exploration companies usually form joint ventures on large projects, they often do not collaborate on purchases of high-dollar value commodities for the project. A recent survey estimated that the industry could realize up to $7 billion in annual savings by using collaborative technologies and seeking more collaborative preferred provider relationships.[32]

There are many successful examples of knowledge management systems adding value. For example, in making the case for a knowledge system at Hewlett-Packard (HP), John Doyle, the former head of HP Labs is credited with saying, "If only HP knew what HP knows."[33] What he meant by this was that there was a huge amount of valuable knowledge in the brains and files (both paper and computer) of HP employees. If HP knew what knowledge was there, and it was shared and accessible to others, it could be useful in solving critical problems, or could lead to ideas for new products and services.

CHALLENGES TO SUCCESS WITH INTEGRATED COLLABORATION ENVIRONMENTS

Although gaining acceptance of integrated collaboration environments has not been a problem for most of their variants, it has been a problem for one of them—knowledge management systems.

Two academic researchers found that the reason lies not with knowledge management technologies, but in the lack of commitment and motivation by knowledge workers, professionals, and managers to use them.[34] Another observer sums it up this way:

• People don't realize how important the knowledge they possess actually is and therefore don't submit it to the knowledge repository.

• People believe that "knowledge is power" and are reluctant to share what they know with others.

WALKING THE TALK

The IT industry is developing an international supply chain for software development. Although hardware manufacturing and assembly have been done offshore for years, moving software development to other countries in large amounts is a relatively new phenomenon. Most offshore development is moving to India, but it is also going to countries such as Bulgaria, China, Rumania, Russia, and Vietnam.

The development center of Wipro Technologies, an Indian IT services giant, is located near Bangalore, India. Currently, about 6,500 people work in several new buildings there, and by 2005, the campus is scheduled to have three times as many employees as it does today.

U.S. software firms are setting up captive development shops offshore. Smaller companies have done this for some time: for example, more than half of Agile Software's 200 developers work in India, Hong Kong, and southern China.

Bigger firms have joined the trend. In June 2003, SAP announced that it would double its workforce in India to 2,000 within three years. Oracle plans to double (to about 6,000) the workforce at its two Indian research centers, one of them in Bangalore. Microsoft and IBM both recently announced plans to expand their IT operations in India.

A programmer in Bangalore costs an American firm about one-quarter of what it would pay for comparable skills in the United States. Even when the extra infrastructure and telecommunications costs are added, savings from moving development offshore are still in excess of 30 percent. Technology, of course, makes it all possible. High-speed networks and collaboration software tools have made it cheaper and easier for geographically dispersed teams to function effectively.

Firms that develop software programs to facilitate such collaboration are among the offshore pioneers. Agile is one example; CollabNet is another. CollabNet offers a Web-based service that allows teams of programmers to coordinate their work, and it has recently bought Enlite Networks, another collaboration start-up which develops many of its programs in India.[35]

- People don't have time to submit information. This can be a real problem and one where technology can help. By being closely tied to existing working practices, knowledge management applications transparently capture and store information back in the knowledge repository.[36]

IT SUPPORT FOR INTEGRATED COLLABORATION ENVIRONMENTS

A comparison of ICE software is shown in Figure 2.12. Three ICE vendors dominate the market—IBM/Lotus, Microsoft, and Novell. Each incorporates "presence awareness" in the latest releases of their collaboration products. *Presence awareness* is a software function that determines whether a user is immediately reachable or is in a less-available status. Based on Instant Messaging (IM) technology, presence awareness is built into or will soon be included in all sorts of applications, from e-mail and CRM to knowledge management and social networking.

Groove and NextPage are both examples of a special kind of information-sharing software called peer-to-peer. *Peer-to-peer collaboration software* permits users to communicate in real time and share files without going through a central server. The peer-to-peer file-sharing feature in the collaboration software is combined with the ability to create and edit documents collaboratively and to send and receive text and voice messages.

While there are literally scores of knowledge management software packages available, social network software is relatively new. Still, there are several social network pack-

DO YOU WANT SPOKE POKING AROUND?

Assume that you and your teammates work in the accounting department at a large software company that sells CRM packages. Your company is in a highly competitive business and sometimes people wonder whether or not the company will survive. It has to compete against such big-name players as Seibel Systems and Salesforce.com, as well as scores of other companies.

Your company's management recently purchased a copy of Spoke (www.spoke.com), which we discussed briefly on this page. Management announced to employees in every department of the company, including yours, that it needed help in getting new sales leads and that Spoke would help in the effort. You know that Spoke's application software searches the names and company affiliations stored in your e-mail contact list on your office computer's hard drive. It looks for companies the sales department is trying to reach, and if it finds one, refers the contact to someone in the sales department.

Let's say that Spoke finds a few likely companies in your contact list, or the contact list of one of your teammates, and someone from the sales department gives you a call and asks you to arrange an introduction. Would you be willing to make an introduction or do you feel it would be inappropriate? How do you feel about the Spoke software examining your contact lists whether you like it or not? Do you think a better way for employees to help the company get the additional sales it needs would be for employees to submit names of good prospects to the sales department rather than putting you in a position where you might feel pressure to cooperate?

Prepare a team position statement on this issue for class discussion. You may find that your team cannot agree on a single position. In this case, team members may divide into two or more camps, each with a different opinion. In either event, be prepared to justify your position(s) for the class discussion.

ages currently available, and more are becoming available each month. Some of them, like Friendster.com and Tickle, focus on dating. Others, like Tribe.net and Linkedin, focus on professional contacts. One of the more interesting and controversial social network packages is Spoke, which allows companies to mine their employees' computerized contact databases. Spoke searches employees' computer contact lists for contacts at other companies that can be used (with the employees' permission, of course) to arrange introductions for salespeople and thereby avoid cold calling.[37]

Figure 2.12

A Comparison of ICE Software

Type	Basic Functions	Example	Web site
Collaboration	Real time collaboration and conferencing	LiveMeeting	www.microsoft.com
Workflow	Business process management	Metastorm	www.metastorm.com
Document Management	Enterprise content management	FileNet	www.filenet.com
Peer to Peer	Desktop and mobile collaboration	Groove	www.groove.net
Knowledge Management	Knowledge capture, organization, location, and reuse	IBM Knowledge Discovery	www-306.ibm.com/software/lotus/knowledge/
Social Network	Leveraging your personal and professional network	Linkedin	www.linkedin.com

A View of the Integrated Enterprise

So far in this chapter, we've discussed four major categories of IT applications:

1. Supply chain management
2. Customer relationship management
3. Business intelligence
4. Integrated collaboration environments

When effectively deployed and utilized, applications such as these help businesses meet the challenges of an ever-changing competitive environment. One of the biggest challenges companies face today is to find ways to share information from different systems. When information is shared effectively, companies stand to gain many benefits in efficiency, effectiveness, and innovation. This is the concept of shared information that we discussed in Chapter 1.

To give you an appreciation of how much of what we have been discussing in this chapter can come together in a single industry, it's hard to think of a better example than the airline industry. The large airline companies, in particular, have given ample evidence over a number of years that they know how to integrate supply chain management systems, customer relationship management systems, business intelligence systems, and integrated collaboration environments for competitive advantage, as illustrated in Figure 2.13. The following discussion will show you how they do it.

AIRLINE RESERVATION SYSTEMS

The airlines really got started using IT in a significant way when American Airlines and United Airlines introduced the first airline reservation systems, SABRE and APOLLO. Airline companies that did not have their own reservation system, Frontier Airlines, for example, paid for the privilege of being a "cohost" on SABRE or APOLLO, which permitted its flights to be listed on the systems and available to travel agents. American and United got a tremendous competitive advantage from being the owners of the reservation systems. First, the systems were very profitable. Second, American and United had access to business intelligence on their own flights (for example, which ones were filled to capacity, and which ones were taking off with too many empty seats). In addition, they had immediate access to competitive intelligence on other airlines because it was all available in the reservation systems' databases. If Frontier wanted to have special competitive analyses prepared, it could request special reports, but it had to pay for them and wait for them to be prepared.

Figure 2.13

Integration of SCM, CRM, BI, and ICE in the Airline Industry

SCM	CRM	BI	ICE
• Spare parts	• Reservation systems	• Yield management	• Virtual team projects
• Fuel	• Frequent flyer programs	• Profitability analysis	• Knowledge management
• Food/beverages	• Consumer Web sites	• Competitive analysis	• Social networking
• Other supplies	• Check-in kiosks	• Cost management	• Competitive threat

IT BRIDGES THE LANGUAGE GAP

One of the challenges most companies face when they try to integrate their systems is that the same information within different applications is represented in different ways. For example, a product description in the manufacturing module of a company's ERP system might be ASIC GMAC6 620TBGA. Believe it or not, descriptions like this are not uncommon in the business world. And while manufacturing specialists and the computer applications they use can understand what such cryptic descriptions mean, other people and different computer applications can have problems. The same physical description of a product might be completely different in the company's CRM system, and customers and competitors probably label it as something completely different as well. Obviously, this creates a need for a solution that can standardize information descriptions so that they mean the same thing to different users and different computer applications. Otherwise, effective enterprise application integration will never occur, nor will companies be able to achieve effective application integration with third parties such as customers and suppliers.

Silver Creek Systems (www.silvercreeksystems.com) is a start-up software company located in Colorado. It has a solution to offer to companies who struggle with this problem. Silver Creek developed a software application capable of taking internal information (like product information) and automatically transforming it, in real time, to the format needed by other applications within the company and in the formats needed by customers and suppliers. The software also has the capability to translate information into one of several widely used foreign languages at the same time. The features its software offers should go a long way to easing the technical challenges of application system integration. Perhaps most important, however, is its language translation capability, which should make it easier for companies to customize their sales Web sites for doing business around the world.

FREQUENT FLYER PROGRAMS

When the airlines introduced frequent flyer programs, it was to increase the likelihood that their most valued customers, their frequent business travelers, would fly with them instead of the competition.

After frequent flyer programs came into being, with their mileage and other perks, air travelers saw that it made sense to concentrate their travel with a single airline in order to get free trips and upgrades. Frequent flyer programs are a great example of a successful customer relationship management system because they collect, store, and use information about customers' behavior, enabling airlines to offer more personalized customer service. For example, IBM is working with FinnAir applying complex business intelligence systems to increase frequent flyers' loyalty and reduce marketing costs. Eero Ahol, FinnAir's Senior Vice President for business development and strategy, says that, so far, the technology has reduced marketing costs by 20 percent and improved response rates by 10 percent.[38] Much of the information needed to manage frequent flyer programs is collected from the airlines' reservation systems, which share it with the frequent flyer program's IT systems.

AIRLINE MAINTENANCE SYSTEMS

Have you ever been on an airplane that was getting ready to take off when all of a sudden the pilot announced that the flight would be delayed because of a "mechanical"? As the Chairman of Continental Airlines noted in the Industry Perspective on page 80 of this chapter, the safety of an airline's passengers is its highest concern. If a faulty part is detected prior to take-off, everyone waits until it is replaced. Airlines use up-to-date supply chain management systems to be sure they have the right replacement parts on hand when they are needed. By integrating their supply chain management systems with their business intelligence systems, airlines know how many air miles have been logged by each plane in their fleet. Information of this kind is used to predict how many spare parts should be stocked at each airport location. It is also used to schedule preventative maintenance. For example, certain parts may be replaced after specified time or mileage intervals whether or not an actual failure has occurred.

YIELD MANAGEMENT SYSTEMS

Yield management systems are a great example of a business intelligence system that can increase revenues. *Yield management systems* are a specialized kind of decision support system designed to maximize the amount of revenue an airline generates on each flight. Basically, what they do is alter the price of available seats on a flight minute by minute as the date of the flight approaches, depending on the number of seats that have been sold compared to an estimate of what was expected. So, if fewer seats have been sold, more low-cost seats are made available for sale. If more seats have been sold than what was originally estimated, fewer low-cost seats will be made available for sale. The objective is to have the airplane take off full at the highest possible average cost per seat, as illustrated in Figure 2.14. (Airlines would rather make at least some money on a low cost seat than make nothing on an empty seat.) Yield management systems are the reason that an airfare you're quoted over the phone can be $100 higher when you call back an hour later. They're a good example of how business intelligence gathered from an airline's reservation system can be used to maximize revenues on each individual flight.

INTEGRATED COLLABORATION ENVIRONMENTS

As in all large corporations, employees at airline companies often work in teams. Airline companies, however, are much more likely to have employees based in many different locations. For example, United Airlines has its headquarters in Chicago, but headquarters employees may work with team members located in places like New York, London, Frankfurt, and Sydney. So, United Airlines, like other airline companies, uses some of the integrated collaboration environments we discussed earlier in the chapter, even though for an airline company, there is no airfare to pay to bring team members together. Integrated collaboration environments, however, are an interesting competitive threat for

Figure 2.14

The Payoff from Yield Management

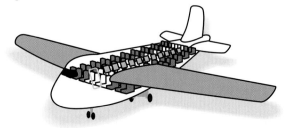

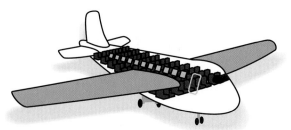

Average seat = $420
Yield = $50,400

120 seats occupied at average price of $420 per seat = $50,400 total yield for the flight.

Average seat = $325
Yield = $65,000

200 seats occupied at average price of $325 per seat = $65,000 total yield for the flight.

PUSHING THE STATE OF THE ART

It's good to get into the habit of noticing the ways that companies are using or not using IT effectively. You can start to build up your own catalog of ideas for your organization. It's always good to use a state-of-the-art application and see if you can build on it to come up with something even better. Pick a company that you think is getting a competitive advantage from IT and try to suggest ways that it could be improved. This is the time to let your imagination run free and to consider using some new and emerging technologies. If you like, you can read Chapter 9 to learn about emerging technologies.

airline companies as more and more companies adopt them. This is because companies will be able to avoid the cost and burdens on their employees (time away from their offices and families, for example) by using integrated collaboration environments to hold team meetings rather than flying employees to a central point for a face-to-face meeting.

Summing It Up

Now that we've talked about some of the ways companies use IT for competitive advantage, we'll summarize four of the most important considerations you should keep in mind as you work to bring an IT-enabled competitive advantage to your organization. These include:

1. Competition is all around you.
2. IT competitive advantages are only temporary.
3. Be efficient *and* effective.
4. Push the state of the art.

First, remember that your organization is in a competitive environment. The reason we emphasize competitive advantage is that you and your competitors are both trying to attract and retain the same customers. Second, using IT for competitive advantage usually provides only a temporary advantage. This is because your competitors are forced to duplicate (or to better) what you have. This also means that your organization must be continually looking for ways to use IT for competitive advantage so you stay ahead of, or don't fall behind, the competition. That may sound like a lot of work, and a never-ending cycle, but the reassuring reality is that there will be continuing opportunities for you to come up with creative IT solutions to business problems.

Third, remember that what you are trying to do is to make your organization both more efficient and more effective. This means that you should be applying IT to solving the most important business problems, as well as being more efficient generally. It's the difference between doing things right and doing the right things. You need to do *both*. Finally, if an IT system is going to give you a competitive advantage, it should push the state of the art. Do some research on what your competition does best and then try to surpass it. Don't let your imagination be limited by just considering technologies that are currently available or reject currently available technologies because they're too expensive. If you place artificial boundaries like these on candidate solutions, you may inhibit creativity unnecessarily. You can always bring an overly ambitious solution back to reality, but if you don't evaluate it, the opportunity will be lost.

Summary: Student Learning Outcomes Revisited

1. **Describe supply chain management (SCM) systems, their strategic and competitive opportunities, the challenges businesses face in employing them successfully, and available IT support.** A *supply chain management (SCM) system* is an IT system that supports supply chain management activities by automating the tracking of inventory and information among business processes and across companies. Supply chain management systems can increase revenues, reduce costs, and increase customer satisfaction. The biggest challenge to their successful implementation is the lack of effective communication between individual areas within a company. Two well-known providers of SCM software are i2 and Manugistics. Dell Computer gets well-deserved recognition as well as competitive advantage from its IT-enabled SCM system.

2. **Describe customer relationship management (CRM) systems, their strategic and competitive opportunities, the challenges businesses face in employing them successfully, and available IT support.** *Customer relationship management (CRM) systems* use information about customers to gain insights into their needs, wants, and behaviors in order to serve them better. CRM is not just software but also a business objective which encompasses many different aspects of a business including software, hardware, services, support, and strategic business goals. CRM systems provide competitive advantage by increasing revenues, by cutting costs, and by treating your customers in ways that encourage them to choose your company over the competition. CRM system installations fail for many reasons, but chief among them is that companies focus on the software and fail to pay enough attention to business processes and acceptance by people within the organization. There are many CRM applications available. The two most prominent ones are Siebel Systems and Salesforce.com.

3. **Describe business intelligence (BI) systems, their strategic and competitive opportunities, the challenges businesses face in employing**
them successfully, and available IT support. *Business intelligence (BI) systems* are the IT applications and tools that support the business intelligence function within an organization. Their objective is to improve the timeliness and quality of the input for decision making. Higher quality managerial decision making is an important way companies gain an advantage over their competitors. The biggest challenge to the effective use of BI systems is that, in too many cases, knowledge workers do not know how to use them effectively. While the Web is used to support BI applications in some firms, specialized software is at the heart of BI, and there are many packages available. Brio Software Systems and Cognos are but two examples.

4. **Describe integrated collaboration environments (ICE), their strategic and competitive opportunities, the challenges businesses face in employing them successfully, and available IT support.** An *integrated collaboration environment (ICE)* is the environment in which virtual teams do their work. Virtual teams are teams whose members are located in varied geographic locations and whose work in ICEs is supported by specialized ICE software or by more basic collaboration systems. A *collaboration system* is software that is designed specifically to improve the performance of teams by supporting the sharing and flow of information. There are many varieties of collaboration systems including basic e-mail systems as well as *workflow systems, document management systems, knowledge management systems,* and *social network systems.* Companies can gain huge competitive advantages from collaboration systems through more effective coordination of the work of virtual teams and by fully utilizing available knowledge within their organizations. Knowledge management systems have been less successful than other forms of collaboration systems primarily because knowledge workers do not believe they add value to their work. ICE software combines collaborative tools focused on such virtual team activities as document management and workflow

systems with network connectivity. Three ICE vendors dominate the market—IBM/Lotus, Microsoft, and Novell. There are scores of KM software packages available. Social network software is still quite new, but more packages are becoming available all the time.

5. **Describe how individual systems that work together in an integrated manner can give airline companies a competitive advantage.** Large airline companies have long used information technology for competitive advantage. Airline reservation systems give the airlines business intelligence information on their flight activities as well as competitive information on other airlines who do not have reservation systems of their own. Their frequent flyer programs are great examples of customer relationship management systems, and now some airlines are using decision support systems to make them more effective. Airlines use supply chain management systems to ensure that spare parts are always there when needed. Finally, while airlines use integrated collaboration environments to support teamwork, at the same time the technology is a potential threat to their business because it has the potential to reduce the need for business travel.

SALESFORCE.COM LEADS THE WAY IN HOSTED CRM SYSTEMS

Salesforce.com is the world leader in providing hosted CRM software and is giving CRM industry leaders like Siebel Systems a run for their money. Salesforce.com customers have access to their CRM applications from any Web browser and from a number of access devices ranging from desktop PCs to laptops, PDAs, and cell phones. The actual application software resides on one of several Salesforce.com servers. In this way, Salesforce.com customers get the best of both worlds. Their employees have access to the software functions they need no matter where they happen to be. And customers do not have to deal with setting up and managing hardware of their own in order to run the software.

The quality of the Salesforce.com application software combined with the convenience of its hosted model offering has been popular with customers. At the beginning of 2004, Salesforce.com had 8,400 customers and its software was offered in 11 languages.

Salesforce.com launched its CRM application suite in 1999 with a sales force automation (SFA) application. Many previous attempts at providing IT support to field sales forces had failed because sales people found the software applications difficult to use and more trouble than they were worth. There are more than 18 modules in the Salesforce.com SFA application including:

- Lead management
- Real-time alerts
- Team selling
- Workflow automation

Sales are the life-blood of most companies. Without cash flow from sales, companies cannot remain in business very long. Yet, you would be surprised at how many companies lose sales because customer inquiries are not managed promptly and effectively. The lead management module in Salesforce.com's SFA application helps companies track inquiries from prospective customers and automatically sends them to the right people within the sales organization. This ensures that sales people get instant access to the new prospective customers and that customer leads are never lost or forgotten. The software also tracks leads to give sales managers assurance that all leads are qualified (i.e. that they come from a customer with the ability to pay) and that sales people follow up on qualified leads in a timely manner.

The real-time alerts module ensures that sales people receive immediate notification of events that may affect a sales lead. Real-time alerts can be sent to the sales person's computer, PDA, or cell phone. For example, a company's BI application connected to its CRM application in an integrated IT corporate environment can be instructed to do a continuous scan of online news sources. It could then alert the SFA application when a news event occurs that would be useful for a sales person to know.

As we discussed in this chapter, much of the work done in companies today is done in teams. The Salesforce.com team-selling module supports team selling by identifying members for team sales efforts and providing a means for them to share information on a customer or prospective customer among all members of the team. This feature of the Salesforce.com SFA application helps individual team members coordinate their efforts and ensures that the customer hears a consistent message from each member of the sales team.

The workflow automation module permits companies to standardize and automate their sales, marketing, and service workflow processes to achieve greater efficiency, consistency, and control. Users can create custom workflow rules tailored to the way they want to operate their sales and marketing processes and even initiate special workflow rules which are triggered when special circumstances arise. For example, if the SFA application detects that there has been no contact with a prospective customer for two weeks, it can send a reminder notice to the sales team that it is time to get back in touch with the customer in some way. Workflow rules can be quickly and easily modified to keep pace with changing business needs.

Going beyond SFA, the Salesforce.com application suite contains application modules for areas such as customer service and support as well as marketing campaign management and analysis. The software also includes the ability to build a digital dashboard to display key performance indicators to sales and marketing managers on a current basis. Time will tell whether or not the ASP model will increase in popularity among customers for application software. In the meantime, CRM software industry leader Siebel Systems has taken notice of Salesforce.com's success. It recently released a hosted version of its software called CRM OnDemand.[39,40]

Questions

1. A Mercedes-Benz dealer might want the lead management module of the SFA application to qualify a lead before having a sales person contact the prospect for follow-up. Why is qualifying a lead important? How could software qualify a prospect?

2. Do you agree that hosted services will enjoy a surge in popularity? Why or why not?

3. Which of the other applications discussed in the chapter do you think would be good candidates for hosted application offerings by software vendors? Which of the applications discussed in the chapter do you think would not be good candidates for hosted offerings? Please state the reasons for your answers.

4. The case suggested some examples of real-time events that sales people would want to know about right away. Please suggest at least five additional examples of real-time events that sales people would want to know about if they had sales leads at companies in each of the following industries:
   - High-fashion retail
   - Health care
   - Higher education

5. What risks does a company take if it does not use collaboration software to support a sales team?

CLOSING CASE STUDY TWO

PARTNERS HEALTH CARE: JUST-IN-TIME KNOWLEDGE MANAGEMENT

The knowledge management system developed at Partners Health Care is a model for the way knowledge management (KM) systems should work. Partners Health Care, located in Boston, Massachusetts, is an umbrella organization which includes Brigham and Women's Hospital, as well as several other hospitals and physicians' groups. Partners has a KM system that not only works, but also saves lives and reduces costs at the same time. The trick that Partners found to make its KM system work is to embed knowledge into the normal work processes of physicians. Partners found this works better than trying to get busy physicians to make contributions and references to a knowledge repository as a separate stand-alone process.

Dr. Bob Goldszer is the associate chief medical officer and head of the Special Services Department at Brigham and Women's Hospital, which was recently ranked as one of the top 15 hospitals in the United States. Dr. Goldszer is also on the faculty of the Harvard Medical School and has both an M.D. and an MBA. Clearly, he is at the top of a profession which puts a premium on the knowledge of practitioners.

And keeping up with advances in medical science and clinical practice is no easy task. For example, Dr. Goldszer needs to know something about almost 10,000 separate diseases and syndromes, 3,000 different medications, and 1,100 lab tests. At the same time, he must try to stay current on many of the 400,000 learned papers that are added to the biomedical literature each year. Not only is the task of keeping up on new knowledge in a field that changes as quickly as medical science a near-impossible one, it is a critically important one as well. Errors in diagnosis and treatment of patients happen all too often, and the results of such errors can be serious, even fatal. In addition, treating complications caused by errors only adds to the already out-of-control national health care costs in the United States and many other countries. For example, studies at Partners showed that more than 5 percent of patients had adverse reactions to drugs while under medical care, and 43 percent of those adverse reactions were life threatening or fatal. Of the adverse reactions that were preventable, more than half were the result of inappropriate drug prescriptions. Another study found that more than half of the prescriptions for a particular medication to treat a heart condition were inappropriate.

The method Partners chose to embed KM into the work processes of its physicians was to focus on the physicians' order entry system. Any time Partners physicians prescribe medications or order tests, they must enter the order into an IT system which not only accepts the order, but runs it against an integrated database of patients' medical records and clinical knowledge. For example, if a physician enters an order for a particular drug, the KM system compares the order against the patient's medical record to determine if there is a potential negative interaction with other medications he is taking or if the patient had an allergic reaction to that medication in the past. Or the system may check the order against the patient's diagnosis and the clinical knowledge base and note that the medication order is an unusual one. If so, the physician is so advised and she can withdraw or change the order. On the other hand, the physician can override the system's advice if her medical judgment tells her there is little risk.

Embedding a knowledge management system into the work process system of high-end professionals like physicians is a relatively new technique, but it could have payoffs for KM in other disciplines as well. In the case of Partners, studies so far show that its KM system reduced serious medication errors by 55 percent. As another example of the system's value, when the clinical knowledge base was changed to include a new drug found to be particularly beneficial for heart patients, the drug was prescribed for 81 percent of patients, an increase from 12 percent. For physicians like Dr. Goldszer and their patients, improvements like these make an important difference.[41,42]

Questions

1. Partners got acceptance of its KM system by embedding knowledge into the normal work processes of physicians, in this case their order entry systems. Give at least three additional examples of instances in which knowledge could be embedded in the work of physicians.

2. Pick at least two other examples of high-level knowledge workers. You might consider attorneys, accountants, financial analysts, or university professors. For each of the two knowledge workers you pick, give at least three specific examples of how knowledge could be embedded in their work.

3. Discuss alternative procedures physicians could follow to continue to enter orders for medication in the event of a system failure such as a hard disk crash that takes up to an hour to restore.

4. What risks are Partners exposed to if incorrect medical procedures are ordered based on information in the KM system that is inaccurate or out of date? How can Partners be sure information in the KM systems is accurate?

5. Should physicians at Partners be *required* to use the KM system? Why or why not?

Key Terms and Concepts

Alliance partner, 88
Application service provider (ASP), 76
Back office system, 81
Business intelligence (BI), 82
Business intelligence (BI) system, 82
Collaboration system, 88
Collaborative planning, forecasting, and
  replenishment (CPFR), 75
Competitive intelligence (CI), 82
Customer relationship management (CRM) system, 78
Data mart, 83
Data-mining tool, 84
Data warehouse, 83
Digital dashboard, 86
Distribution chain, 72
Document management system, 88

Front office system, 81
Integrated collaboration environment (ICE), 87
Just-in-time (JIT), 73
Knowledge management (KM) system, 88
Logistics, 73
Peer-to-peer collaboration software, 90
Presence awareness, 90
Sales force automation (SFA) system, 78
Social network system, 88
Supply chain management (SCM), 72
Supply chain management (SCM) system, 72
Virtual team, 87
Workflow, 88
Workflow system, 88
Yield management system, 94

Short-Answer Questions

1. What is a supply chain management (SCM) system? List three aspects of supply chain management that can give a business a competitive advantage.
2. What are the principal advantages of Dell's "sell, source, and ship" model over a traditional distribution chain?
3. What is a customer relationship management (CRM) system?
4. Why have many CRM and SFA systems been less than successful?
5. What is business intelligence? Why is it more than just information?

6. What is competitive intelligence? What is the relationship between competitive intelligence and business intelligence?
7. What is an integrated collaboration environment (ICE)?
8. Define virtual teams. Why are virtual teams so important in today's business world?
9. What is the purpose of knowledge management (KM) systems?
10. What are social network systems? How are they being used?

Assignments and Exercises

1. **COLLABORATION WORK** In a group of three or more students, collaborate on a project to make a list of 100 music CDs or video DVDs. Classify them into groups. For example, if you choose DVDs, your categories might be adventure, comedy, classic, horror, musicals, among others. All communication about the project must be electronically communicated (but not by phone). You could use e-mail, set up a Web site, use a chat room, use instant messaging, or use a collaboration e-room, if your school has that facility. Print out a copy of all correspondence on the project and put the correspondence together in a folder in chronological order. Was this task very different from collaborating face to face with your partners? In what ways was it better, in what ways worse? What additional problems or advantages would you expect if the people you're working with were in a different hemisphere?

2. **REAL WORLD APPLICATIONS** In the chapter we mentioned that many CRM installations have been less than successful. On the other hand, there are many satisfied users of CRM applications. Log on to the Internet and find at least three examples of companies who are getting real business benefits from their CRM systems. Prepare a report on the results they are getting and the way they achieved them. One place to start your search is at www.searchcrm.com. Another good source is the Web sites of CRM application software vendors Siebel and Salesforce.com (www.siebel.com and www.salesforce.com). At least one of your examples must be from a site other than the three mentioned.

3. **UNUSUAL APPLICATIONS OF GROOVE** Groove is one of the best known peer-to-peer collaboration software companies. It has a Web log (or "blog") on its Web site which is full of current information on the benefits of peer-to-peer collaboration software and the experiences of people who use Groove on team collaboration projects. Log on to the Groove Web site at www.groove.net and navigate your way to its blog. Find two examples of unusual ways that people are using Groove and be prepared to summarize your findings in a class discussion. The more unusual the application the better.

4. **WAL-MART'S SCM SYSTEM** Wal-Mart is famous for its low prices, and you may have experienced its low prices first-hand. At least, you have probably seen its motto, "Always Low Prices—Always." One of the biggest reasons Wal-Mart is able to sell at prices lower than almost everyone else is that it has a super-efficient supply chain. Its IT-enabled supply chain management system is the envy of the industry because it drives excess time and unnecessary costs out of the supply chain. So, because Wal-Mart can buy low, it sells low. As a matter of fact, if your company wants to sell items to Wal-Mart for it to sell in its stores, you will have to do business with it electronically. If your company can't do that, Wal-Mart won't buy anything from you. Log on to Wal-Mart's Web site (www.walmart.com), search for supplier information, and find out what Wal-Mart's requirements are for its suppliers to do business with it electronically. Prepare a brief summary of its requirements for presentation in class.

Discussion Questions

1. Do you think that your school would benefit from installing a customer relationship management (CRM) system? How might it benefit you as a student? How could it benefit your school?

2. Many companies believe the ASP model is the best way to use CRM. What are some of the disadvantages of the ASP model?

3. What advantages can you see for a manager to have a digital dashboard at her disposal? Are there any words of caution regarding the development and use of a digital dashboard she should hear from you before her company spends money on it?

4. If you were a member of a virtual team using collaboration software, would you want the presence awareness feature as part of the software? Why or why not?

5. As discussed in the chapter, Spoke software examines employees' e-mail contact lists searching for people at potential customer sites who may be known to employees. Do you think a company has an ethical obligation to notify employees it is going to use Spoke, or (because it will only search PC files on company-owned PCs) is it none of the employees' business?

6. Assume you are the chief financial officer (CFO) for a large company. Your company has hundreds of IT applications that have been installed over the years. Recently, the chief information officer (CIO) proposed a project to install some new software that would enable the applications to share information easily. Develop a list of at least four questions for the CIO to answer to your satisfaction before you will consider supporting the project.

Ordering Products and Services on the Internet

For most people, electronic commerce is all about business-to-consumer (B2C). On the Internet, you (as an individual consumer) can purchase groceries, clothes, computers, automobiles, music, antiques, books, and much more. If you want to buy it, there's probably an Internet site selling it. Even more, there are probably hundreds of Internet sites selling what it is you want, giving you the opportunity to shop for the best buy.

You can indeed find almost anything you want to buy on the Internet. However, you should carefully consider the person or organization from whom you're making the purchase. You want to be sure you are doing business with someone you can trust. This is especially true if you have to provide a credit card number to make the purchase.

BOOKS AND MUSIC

Books and music make up one category of products you can readily find to purchase on the Internet. One of the most widely known and acclaimed Internet sites performing electronic commerce is Amazon.com at www.amazon.com. Amazon offers several million book and music titles for sale.

Of course, as with all products you buy on the Internet, you need to consider price and the amount you'll save on the Internet compared to purchasing books and music from local stores. Sometimes prices are higher on the Internet, and you can certainly expect to pay some sort of shipping and handling charges. We know that there are several sites that let you buy individual songs and download them to your computer in MP3 format, but for right now let's just focus on buying traditional CDs.

Make a list of books and music CDs that you're interested in purchasing. Find their prices at a local store. Next, visit three Web sites selling books and music and answer the following questions.

A. What are the books, CDs, or cassettes you're interested in?

B. What are their prices at a local store?

C. Can you find them at each Internet site?

D. Are the local prices higher or lower than the Internet prices?

E. How do you order and pay for your products?

F. How long is the shipping delay?

G. What is the shipping charge?

H. Overall, how would you rate your Internet shopping experience compared to your local store shopping experience?

CLOTHING AND ACCESSORIES

It might seem odd, but many people purchase all types of clothing on the Internet from shoes to pants to all kinds of accessories (including perfume). The disadvantage in shopping for clothes on the Internet is that you can't actually try them on and stand in front of the mirror. But if you know exactly what you want (by size and color), you can probably find and buy it on the Internet.

Connect to several clothing and accessory sites and experience cyber–clothes shopping. As you do, consider the following.

A. How do you order and pay for merchandise?

B. What sort of description is provided about the clothing? Text, photos, perhaps 3D views?

C. What is the return policy for merchandise that you don't like or that doesn't fit?

D. Finally, is shopping for clothes on the Internet as much fun as going to the Mall? Why or why not?

AUCTION HOUSES

Auction houses act as clearing stations at which you can sell your products or purchase products from other people in an auction format (essentially, consumer-to-consumer or C2C electronic commerce). EBay, the most popular auction house, boasts millions of items for sale.

It works quite simply. First, you register as a user at a particular auction house. Once you do, you'll have a unique user ID and password that allow you to post products for sale or bid on other products. When the auction is complete for a particular product (auction houses set time limits that last typically from one to 10 days), the auction house will notify the seller and the winning bidder. Then, it's up to you and the other person to exchange money and merchandise.

So, think of a product you'd like to buy or sell—perhaps a rare coin, a computer, a hard-to-find Beanie Baby, or a car. Connect to a couple of different Internet auction houses and answer the following questions for each.

A. What is the registration process to become a user?

B. Do you have to pay a fee to become a user?

C. Is your product of interest listed?

D. How do you bid on a product?

E. What does the auction house charge you to sell a product?

F. What is the duration of a typical auction?

G. Can you set a minimum acceptable bid for a product you want to sell?

H. How does the auction house help you evaluate the credibility of other people buying and selling products?

AUTOMOBILES

Another product category that you may not expect to find on the Internet is automobiles. That's right—on the Internet you can find literally any automobile you'd be interested in purchasing. Muscle cars, Jaguars, Rolls Royces, Hondas, and thousands more are for sale on the Internet.

Try connecting to a few of these sites and browse for an automobile you'd like to own. As you do, think about these issues: What variety can you find (color, engine size, interior, etc.)? Are financing options available? How do you "test drive" a car for sale on the Internet? What happens if you buy a car and then don't like it? What about used cars? Can you trust people selling a used car on the Internet? How do you pay for a car, typically a relatively large purchase?

You can find a variety of sites that provide competitive pricing information concerning cars. Many of these sites are for all cars in general, not just those for sale on the Internet. One of the best sites is AutoSite at www.autosite.com. If you're ever shopping for a new or used car, you should definitely check out that site.

EXTENDED LEARNING MODULE B

THE WORLD WIDE WEB AND THE INTERNET

Student Learning Outcomes

1. DEFINE THE RELATIONSHIPS AMONG WEB SITE, WEB SITE ADDRESS, DOMAIN NAME, WEB PAGE, AND UNIFORM RESOURCE LOCATOR (URL).

2. EXPLAIN HOW TO INTERPRET THE PARTS OF AN ADDRESS ON THE WEB.

3. IDENTIFY THE MAJOR COMPONENTS AND FEATURES OF WEB BROWSER SOFTWARE.

4. DESCRIBE THE DIFFERENCES BETWEEN DIRECTORY AND TRUE SEARCH ENGINES.

5. DESCRIBE THE VARIOUS TECHNOLOGIES THAT MAKE UP THE INTERNET.

6. IDENTIFY KEY CONSIDERATIONS IN CHOOSING AN INTERNET SERVICE PROVIDER (ISP).

7. DESCRIBE THE COMMUNICATIONS SOFTWARE AND TELECOMMUNICATIONS HARDWARE YOU NEED TO CONNECT TO THE INTERNET.

Introduction

Perhaps the most visible and explosive information technology tool is the Internet, and subsequently the World Wide Web (Web). No matter where you look or what you read, someone always seems to be referring to one of the two. On television commercials, you find Web site addresses displayed (such as www.ibm.com for an IBM commercial or www.toyota.com for a Toyota commercial). In almost every magazine these days, you'll find articles about the Internet because of its growing significance in our society. Most major business publications, such as *Fortune, Forbes,* and *Business Week,* devote entire issues each year to the Internet and how to use it for electronic commerce. Of course, many such publications have been carrying articles detailing how and why so many dot-coms failed in recent years (now affectionately referred to as *dot-bombs*).

The Internet really is everywhere—and it's here to stay. What's really great about the Internet is that it takes only a couple of hours to learn. Once you've read the text for this module, you should try your hand at the Internet scavenger hunts on page 122. You'll be surprised to learn how easy it is to find information on the Internet.

World Wide Web

The **World Wide Web,** or **Web** as you probably know it, is a multimedia-based collection of information, services, and Web sites supported by the Internet. The **Internet** is a vast network of computers that connects millions of people all over the world. Schools, businesses, government agencies, and many others have all connected their internal networks to the Internet, making it truly a large network of networked computers. So the Internet and all its technological infrastructure is really what makes the Web possible. Most people consider the Web and the Internet to be the same. Although there are both subtle and distinct differences between the two, we'll not delve into those differences here.

WEB SITES, ADDRESSES, AND PAGES

As you use the Web, you'll most often be accessing Web sites. A **Web site** is a specific location on the Web where you visit, gather information, and perhaps even order products. Each Web site has a specific Web site address. A **Web site address** is a unique name that identifies a specific site on the Web. Technically, this address is called a domain name. A **domain name** identifies a specific computer on the Web and the main page of the entire site. Most people use the term *Web site address* instead of the technical term *domain name.* For example, the Web site address for *USA Today* is www.usatoday.com (see Figure B.1).

Most Web sites include several and perhaps hundreds of Web pages. A **Web page** is a specific portion of a Web site that deals with a certain topic. The address for a specific Web page is called a URL. A **URL (uniform resource locator)** is an address for a specific Web page or document within a Web site. Most people opt for the common term of *Web page address* when referring to a URL. As you can see in Figure B.1, you can click on the link for **Sports** on the main page for the *USA Today.* By clicking on that link, you

Figure B.1

The *USA Today* Web Site and Sports Web Page

will then be taken to a specific Web page within the *USA Today* Web site. The URL or Web page address for that page is www.usatoday.com/sports/sfront.htm. Links are important on the Web. A ***link*** (the technical name is ***hyperlink***) is clickable text or an image that takes you to another site or page on the Web.

UNDERSTANDING ADDRESSES

When you access a certain Web site or page, you do so with its unique address, such as www.usatoday.com (for our *USA Today* example). Addresses, because they are unique, tell you some important information about the site or page. Let's consider two different examples (see Figure B.2): Yahoo! (www.yahoo.com) and the University of Technology in Sydney, Australia (www.uts.edu.au).

Most addresses start with http://www, which stands for *hypertext transfer protocol* (http) and *World Wide Web* (www). The http:// part is so common now that you don't even have to use it in most cases. The remaining portion of the address is unique for each site or page. If you consider www.yahoo.com, you know that it's the address for Yahoo!. You can also tell it's a commercial organization by the last three letters: com. This three-letter extension can take on many forms and is referred to as the ***top-level domain.*** Top-level domains include

- **com**—Commercial or for-profit business
- **coop**—Cooperative
- **edu**—Educational institution
- **gov**—U.S. government agency
- **mil**—U.S. military organization
- **net**—Internet administrative organization
- **org**—Professional or nonprofit organization
- **int**—International treaties organization
- **info**—General information

- **biz**—Business
- **museum**—Accredited museum
- **name**—Personal
- **pro**—Accountant, doctor, lawyer, etc.

The top-level domain ".com" identifies Yahoo! as a commercial or for-profit organization.

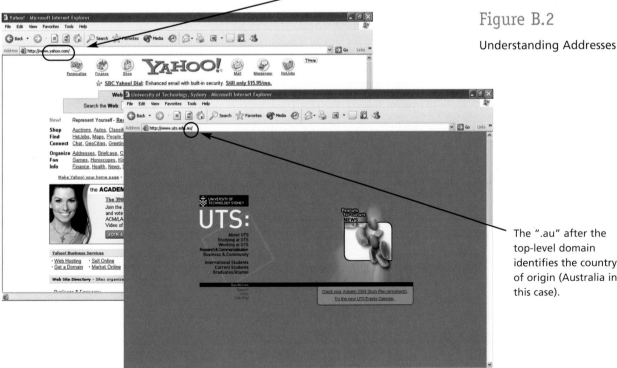

The ".au" after the top-level domain identifies the country of origin (Australia in this case).

Figure B.2

Understanding Addresses

Some addresses have a two-character extension that follows the top-level domain. In this case, it's to identify the country location of the site. For example, the site address for the University of Technology in Sydney, Australia, is www.uts.edu.au. From that address, you can tell it's for an educational institution (edu) located in Australia (au).

USING WEB BROWSER SOFTWARE

Web browser software enables you to surf the Web. It is, in fact, the software we used to view sites for the *USA Today,* Yahoo!, and University of Technology in Sydney, Australia. The most popular Web browsers today are Internet Explorer and Netscape Communicator. They are free for you to use; Internet Explorer is standard on most computers today.

To demonstrate how you use Web browser software, let's take a quick tour of Internet Explorer and Netscape Communicator. In Figures B.3 (on this page) and B.4 (on the opposite page), you can see we are using Internet Explorer and Netscape Communicator, respectively, to view the Web site for eBay (www.ebay.com). In Figure B.3, you can see the menu bar for Internet Explorer that includes the functions for **File, Edit, View, Favorites, Tools,** and **Help.** In Figure B.4, you can see the menu bar for Netscape Communicator that includes the functions of **File, Edit, View, Go, Communicator,** and **Help.** Both menu bars are very similar and support the same basic functions. For example, if you click on **File** in either Internet Explorer or Netscape Communicator, you'll see a pull-down menu that allows you to initiate other actions such as printing the Web site and sending the Web site via e-mail to someone else.

Below the menu bar, you'll find a button bar on both Web browsers that supports more functions. We won't go into any of these in detail here; you can play with them at your leisure. Below the button bar is the **Address** field for Internet Explorer and the **Location** field for Netscape Communicator. Both are the same. If you know the address for where you want to go, click in either of these two fields, type in the address, and then hit **Enter.**

Figure B.3

Internet Explorer

Menu bar

Button bar

Address field

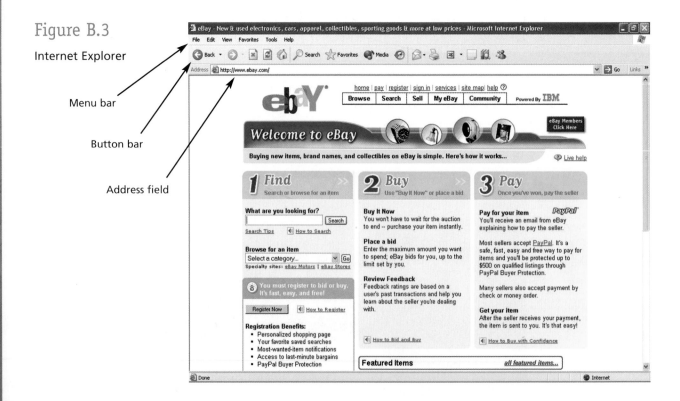

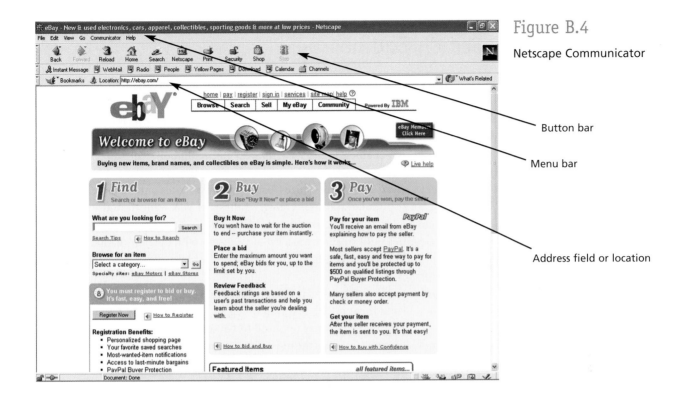

Button bar

Menu bar

Address field or location

One of the most important features of any Web browser is that you can create and edit a list of your most commonly visited places on the Web. In Internet Explorer, it's called a **Favorites list,** and in Netscape Communicator it's called a **Bookmarks list.** So, if you frequently visit eBay, you can save the address in one of these lists while you're viewing it. In Internet Explorer, click on the **Favorites** button and then **Add.** In Netscape Communicator, click on the **Bookmarks** button and then **Add Bookmark.** Later, when you want to visit eBay, click on the appropriate button (**Favorites** for Internet Explorer or **Bookmarks** for Netscape Communicator) and then click on the eBay link. That's all there is to it.

Web browser software is the easiest personal productivity software to learn. Most people find that they need very little instruction and seldom need a book. Just connect to the Web, start the Web browser of your choice, play around for an hour or so, and you'll soon be a Web surfing expert.

It really is quite simple. When you start your Web browser software, you'll first see what is called a *home page*—the Web site that your Web browser automatically connects to and displays when you first start surfing. Once you're there, you can click on any of the links that interest you, or you can type in a new address and go to any other site.

If you're not sure of the exact Web site address, you begin to search for it in one of two ways. The first is to use a search engine, which we'll discuss in the next section. The second is to type in a logical name in the **Address** field (using Internet Explorer) or the **Location** field (using Netscape Communicator). For example, if you want to download tax forms from the IRS Web site but don't know the address of the IRS, you can simply type in "IRS" or "internal revenue service" in the **Address** or **Location** field. Your Web browser will automatically begin a search for Web sites related to those terms and hopefully will find the right site for you. (In the instance of searching for the IRS, both Internet Explorer and Netscape Communicator do take you to the site you need.)

Search Engines

There will be occasions when you want to find information and services on the Web, but you don't know exactly which site to visit. In this case, you can type in a logical name as we just demonstrated, or you can use a search engine. A *search engine* is a facility on the Web that helps you find sites with the information and/or services you want. There are many types of search engines on the Web, the two most common being directory search engines and true search engines.

A *directory search engine* organizes listings of Web sites into hierarchical lists. Yahoo! is the most popular and well known of these. If you want to find information using a directory search engine, start by selecting a specific category and continually choose subcategories until you arrive at a list of Web sites with the information you want. Because you continually narrow down your selection by choosing subcategories, directory search engines are hierarchical.

A *true search engine* uses software agent technologies to search the Internet for key words and then places them into indexes. In doing so, true search engines allow you to ask questions or type in key terms as opposed to continually choosing subcategories to arrive at a list of Web sites. *Google* is the most popular and well-known true search engine.

Let's now consider the task of finding who won the Academy Awards in 2003 to see how directory and true search engines differ.

USING A DIRECTORY SEARCH ENGINE

As we stated, Yahoo! is the most popular and well-known directory search engine. Figure B.5 shows the sequence of pages (categories) through which you would traverse using Yahoo! to determine who won the Academy Awards in 2003. The sequence of categories includes

- **Arts & Humanities**
- **Awards**
- **Movies and Film@**
- **Academy Awards**
- **75th Annual Academy Awards**

In the final screen you can see a list of Web sites from which you can choose.

There are some definite advantages to performing a search in this way. If you look at the next-to-last screen, for example **Academy Awards,** it also includes subcategories for the Academy Awards in each of the last seven years (1996–2002). So, you can easily find related information using a directory search engine.

You can also use directory search engines in a different fashion. For example, in the first screen, we could have entered **academy +awards +2003** in the field immediately to the left of the **Search** button and then clicked on the **Search** button. This particular search would yield a list of Web sites that is very similar to the list we received by choosing subcategories.

You might notice that we included the plus sign ($+$) in a couple of different places in our key terms list. By doing so, we limited the search to finding just sites that included all three words. Likewise, if you want to limit a search so that it won't show Web sites that contain certain key words, you would use a minus sign ($-$). For example, if you wanted to find Web sites that contain information about the Miami Dolphins NFL team, you could enter **Miami +Dolphins.** That would probably yield a list of suitable sites, but it might also include sites that include information about watching dolphins (the

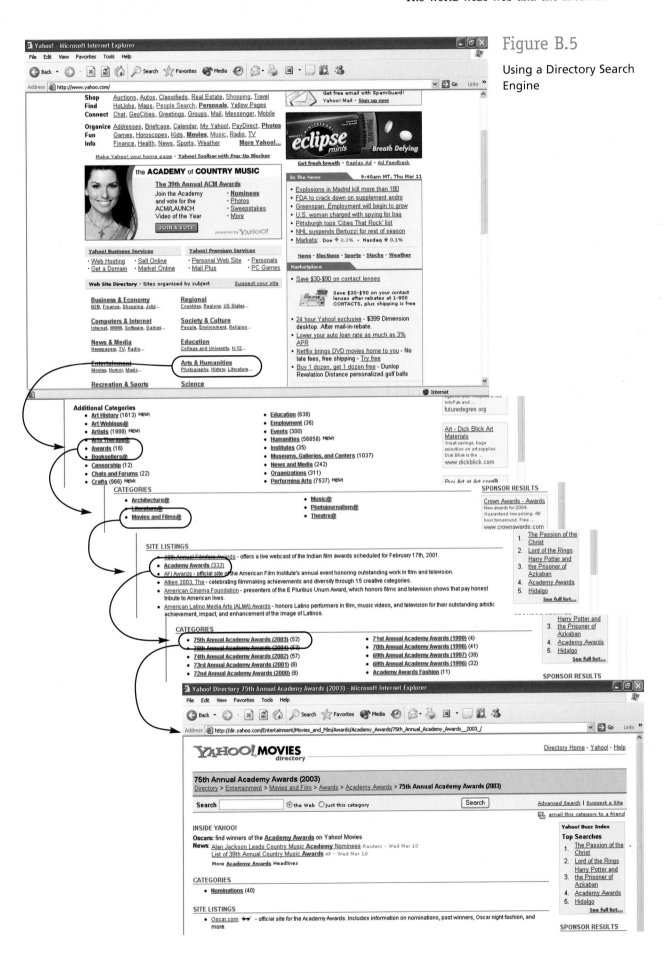

Figure B.5

Using a Directory Search Engine

aquatic version) in Miami. You can further refine your search by entering something like **Miami +Dolphins −aquatic −mammal.** That search will yield a list of Web sites that have the terms *Miami* and *Dolphins* but will eliminate any sites that have the term *aquatic* or *mammal.*

When you use a directory search engine and type in specific terms instead of traversing through subcategories, we definitely recommend that you make use of the plus sign and/or minus sign. For example, if you want to find sites about wind tunnels, using **wind tunnel** will return a list of sites related to wind tunnels but also the wind (weather sites) and tunnels in general. On the other hand, **wind +tunnel** will yield a more refined list of sites. We recommend that you complete the Team Work project (Finding and Using Search Engines) on page 113. As you do, you'll find that some search engines support advanced and unique capabilities that can help you further refine your search criteria.

USING A TRUE SEARCH ENGINE

Google is the most popular and well-known true search engine. Using Google (www.google.com), you simply ask a question or type in some key terms. For finding out who won the Academy Awards in 2003, we would simply enter **Who won the Academy Awards in 2003** and hit the **Google Search** button. As you can see in Figure B.6, Google returned a list of possible Web sites.

Both types of search engines are very easy to use. Which you choose is really a function of how you think. Some people think in terms of hierarchical lists while others think in terms of questions. What you'll undoubtedly find is that directory search engines are better in some cases while true search engines are better in others.

Figure B.6

Using a True Search Engine

Our question

Possible Web sites with answers

FINDING AND USING SEARCH ENGINES

Search engines are easy to find on the Web and even easier to use. In fact, there are about 100 search engines that you can use to find almost any information you need.

Your group's tasks include (1) creating a list of the 10 most popular search engines on the Web and (2) per-

forming a search on each for the same information. As you complete the second task, evaluate how easy or difficult it was to use each search engine. Also, evaluate the quality of the Web site list you received from each search engine.

Internet Technologies

To best take advantage of everything the Web has to offer, it often helps to understand what's going on behind the Web, that is, the Internet. The Internet is really the enabling structure that makes the Web possible. Without the Web, the Internet still exists and you can still use it. But the reverse is not true. The Internet is the set of underlying technologies that makes the Web possible. The Web is somewhat of a graphical user interface (GUI) that sets on top of the Internet. The Web allows you to click on links to go to other sites, and it allows you to view information in multiple forms of media.

THE INTERNET BACKBONE

The **Internet backbone** is the major set of connections for computers on the Internet (see Figure B.7). A **network access point (NAP)** is a point on the Internet where several connections converge. At each NAP is at least one computer that simply routes Internet traffic from one place to another (much like an airport which allows you to switch planes in an attempt to get to your final destination). These NAPs are owned and maintained by network service providers. A **network service provider (NSP),** such as MCI or AT&T, owns and maintains routing computers at NAPs and even the lines that connect the NAPs to each other. In Figure B.7, you can see that Dallas is a NAP, with lines converging from Atlanta, Phoenix, Kansas City, and Austin.

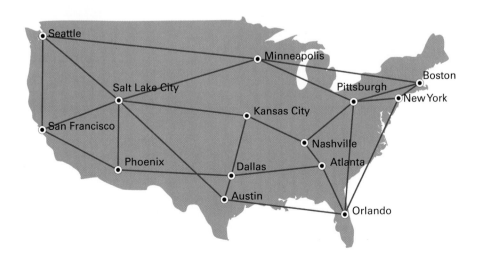

Figure B.7

The Internet Backbone in the United States

At any given NAP, an Internet service provider may connect its computer or computers to the Internet. An ***Internet service provider (ISP)*** is a company that provides individuals, organizations, and businesses access to the Internet. ISPs include AOL, Juno, and perhaps even your school. In turn, you "dial up" or connect your computer to an ISP computer. So, your ISP provides you access to the Internet (and thus the Web) by allowing you to connect your computer to its computer (which is already connected to the Internet).

If you live in the San Francisco area and send an e-mail to someone living near Boston, your e-mail message might travel from San Francisco to Salt Lake City, then to Minneapolis, and finally to Boston. Of course, your e-mail message may very well travel the route of San Francisco, Phoenix, Dallas, Atlanta, Nashville, Pittsburgh, Orlando, New York, and then Boston. But, no matter—your message will get there. Can you imagine the route that your e-mail message would travel if you were in San Francisco sending it to someone in Venice, Italy? One time, it might go west around the world through Australia. The next time, it might go east around the world through New York and then on to London.

INTERNET SERVERS

There are many types of computers on the Internet, namely, router (which we've already discussed), client, and server computers (see Figure B.8). The computer that you use to

Figure B.8

Servers on the Internet

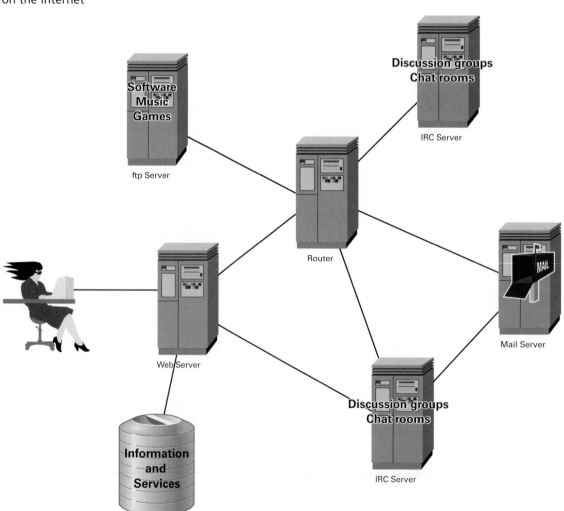

USING A WEB PORTAL

Most Web browser software is already configured to take you to a certain Web site when you start surfing. For example, Internet Explorer usually starts at the Microsoft Network site (MSN at www.msn.com). Sites such as MSN, Yahoo!, and The Go Network (www.go.com) are often referred to as Web portals. A **Web portal** is a site that provides a wide range of services, including search engines, free e-mail, chat rooms, discussion boards, and links to hundreds of different sites.

The nice thing about Web portals is that they often let you customize the first page you see. So, you can request a ticker of your favorite stocks, the weather forecast for your area over the next three days, and a list of sites you commonly visit.

In this project, you are to create a customized and personal Web portal at two different places on the Web. We recommend that you do so at one of these sites (although there are many others):

- www.msn.com
- www.go.com
- www.excite.com
- www.yahoo.com

As you build each personalized Web portal, answer the following questions.

1. What is the registration process required to build a Web portal?
2. Can you receive a free e-mail account? If so, must you establish it?
3. Can you create categories of your most commonly visited sites?
4. Can you request customized local information for your area? If so, what type of information?
5. How do you adjust your Web browser settings so that it automatically takes you to your Web portal page?

---

access the Internet and surf the Web is called a *client computer*. Your client computer can be a traditional desktop or notebook computer, a Web or Internet appliance, a PDA, or perhaps even a cell phone.

Internet server computers are computers that provide information and services on the Internet. There are four main types of server computers on the Internet: Web, mail, ftp, and IRC servers. A *Web server* provides information and services to Web surfers. So, when you access www.ebay.com, you're accessing a Web server (for eBay) with your client computer. Most often, you'll be accessing and using the services of a Web server.

A *mail server* provides e-mail services and accounts. Many times, mail servers are presented to you as a part of a Web server. For example, Hotmail is a free e-mail server and service provided by MSN. An *ftp (file transfer protocol) server* maintains a collection of files that you can download. These files can include software, screen savers, music files (many in MP3 format), and games. An *IRC (Internet Relay Chat) server* supports your use of discussion groups and chat rooms. IRC servers are popular hosting computers for sites such as www.epinions.com. There, you can share your opinions about various products and services, and you can also read the reviews written by other people.

COMMUNICATIONS PROTOCOLS

As information moves around the Internet, bouncing among network access points until it finally reaches you, it does so according to various communications protocols. A *communications protocol (protocol)* is a set of rules that every computer follows to transfer information. The most widely used protocols on the Internet include TCP/IP, http, and ftp (and a few others such as PPP, Point-to-Point Protocol, and POP, Post Office Protocol).

TCP/IP, or *transport control protocol/Internet protocol,* is the primary protocol for transmitting information over the Internet. Whenever any type of information moves over the Internet, it does so according to TCP/IP. *Hypertext transfer protocol (http)* is the communications protocol that supports the movement of information over the Web, essentially from a Web server to you. That's why Web site addresses start with "http://." Most Web browser software today assumes that you want to access a Web site on the Internet. So you don't even have to type in the "http://" if you don't want to.

File transfer protocol (ftp) is the communications protocol that allows you to transfer files of information from one computer to another. When you download a file from an ftp server (using ftp), you're using both TCP/IP (the primary protocol for the Internet) and ftp (the protocol that allows you to download the file). Likewise, when you access a Web site, you're using both TCP/IP and http (because the information you want is Web based).

Connecting to the Internet

To access the Web (via the Internet), you need an Internet service provider (ISP), as we discussed earlier. ISPs can include your school, your place of work, commercial ISPs such as AOL, and free ISPs such as NetZero. Which you choose is a function of many things.

One of the nice benefits of going to school or being employed is that you often get free Web access through school or your work. All you have to do is connect your home computer to your school's or work's computer (we'll talk about this process in a moment) and you're ready to surf. However, some schools and places of business may restrict where you can go on the Web. And they may even monitor your surfing.

Commercial ISPs charge you a monthly fee, just as your telephone company charges you a monthly fee for phone service. This fee usually ranges from a few dollars a month to about $20. Popular worldwide commercial ISPs include Microsoft (MSN), AOL, CompuServe, and AT&T WorldNet, just to name a few.

Free ISPs are absolutely free, as their names suggest—you don't pay a setup fee, you don't pay a monthly fee, and you usually have unlimited access to the Web. But there are some catches. Many free ISPs do not offer you Web space, as opposed to most commercial ISPs which do. *Web space* is a storage area where you keep your Web site. So, if you want to create and maintain a Web site, you may have to choose a commercial ISP over a free ISP (your school probably also offers you Web space). Also when using a free ISP, you will often see banner ads that you can't get rid of. You can move them around and from side to side, but you can't remove them completely from your screen. Technical support is often limited with a free ISP. Some offer only e-mail support, while others do offer phone support but no toll-free number.

In spite of those drawbacks, many people do choose free ISPs over commercial ISPs, mainly because of cost (remember, $20 per month equals $240 per year). Popular free ISPs include Myfreei (www.access-4-free.com), Dotnow (www.dotnow.com), and NetZero (www.netzero.com, see Figure B.9). To decide which type of ISP is best for you, ask these questions:

- *Do you need Web space?* If yes, a free ISP may not be the right choice.
- *Is great technical support important?* If yes, then a commercial ISP may be the right choice.

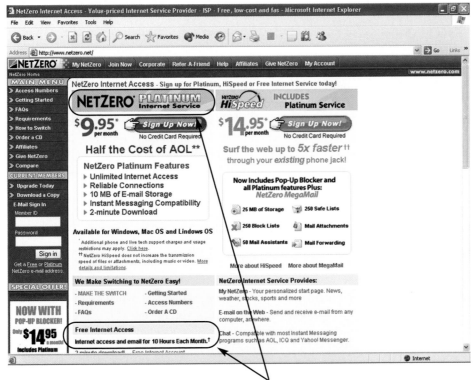

Figure B.9

NetZero Is a Popular Free ISP

NetZero, in addition to offering free Internet access, also offers a subscription service with more features.

- *Is money a serious consideration?* If yes, then a commercial ISP may not be the right choice.
- *Is privacy important to you?* If yes, then your school or work may not be the right choice.

COMMUNICATIONS SOFTWARE

To access and use the Web, you need communications software, namely,

- ***Connectivity software***—Enables you to use your computer to dial up or connect to another computer.
- ***Web browser software***—Enables you to surf the Web.
- ***E-mail software*** (short for ***electronic mail software***)—Enables you to electronically communicate with other people by sending and receiving e-mail.

Connectivity software is the first and most important. With connectivity software, while using a standard telephone modem, you essentially use your computer (and a phone line) to call up and connect to the server computer of your ISP. Connectivity software is standard on most personal computers today. To use connectivity software, you really only need to know the number to call. Then it's a relatively easy process: within Microsoft Windows, click on **Start, Programs, Accessories, Communications, Network and Dial-up Connections,** and then select **Make New Connection** (your exact sequence may vary slightly according to which version of Windows you're using).

Alternatively, if you're using connectivity software in conjunction with a high-speed modem connection such as a cable, DSL, or satellite modem (we'll discuss these further

EVALUATING ISP OPTIONS

Choosing an Internet service provider (ISP) is an important, but not too terribly complicated, task. In this project, your group is to evaluate three different ISPs: a well-recognized commercial ISP such as AOL or AT&T WorldNet, a free ISP such as NetZero (there are many others), and a local or regional ISP in your area (you may need to look in your phone book to find one of these).

As you evaluate these three different ISPs, do so in terms of (1) price per month, (2) amount of Web space provided, (3) monthly limit of hours you can be connected without paying an additional fee, (4) customer support, and (5) the ability to have e-mail.

Of the three, which would you choose and why?

in a moment), you don't really "make a call" to connect to your ISP. Instead, you probably have an "always-on" high-speed Internet connection. So, when you turn on your computer, it goes through the process of connecting you to your ISP.

Web browser software and e-mail software are also standard software today. If your school or work is your ISP, then you'll most often be using commercially available Web browser software such as Internet Explorer or Netscape Communicator, and the e-mail software you use will vary according to your school's or work's preference. If you're using a commercial or free ISP, then your choice of Web browser software and e-mail software will depend on that particular organization.

Regardless of your choice of ISP, the unique Web browser software and e-mail software provided work in similar fashion. So, if you're used to using Internet Explorer and then choose AOL as your ISP, you will see that AOL has its own Web browser software. It will look different on the screen, but it supports the same functionality (favorites list, moving forward and backward through your list of visited Web sites, and so on). All you have to do is get used to a new interface. Different e-mail software will also look different but support the same functionality.

TELECOMMUNICATIONS HARDWARE

In addition to communications software, you also need some telecommunications hardware to access the Web (again, via the Internet). If you're at school or work, you'll probably be able to connect your computer directly to a network that is then connected to the Internet. This often amounts to simply plugging a network line into your computer and starting your preferred Web browser or e-mail software. We discuss this type of connection to the Internet in more detail in *Extended Learning Module E.*

If you're connecting from home, you'll need some sort of modem. There are many types of modems, including

- A *telephone modem (modem)*—A device that connects your computer to your phone line so that you can access another computer or network.
- *Digital Subscriber Line (DSL)*—A high-speed Internet connection using phone lines, which allows you to use your phone line for voice communication at the same time.
- A *cable modem*—A device that uses your TV cable to deliver an Internet connection.

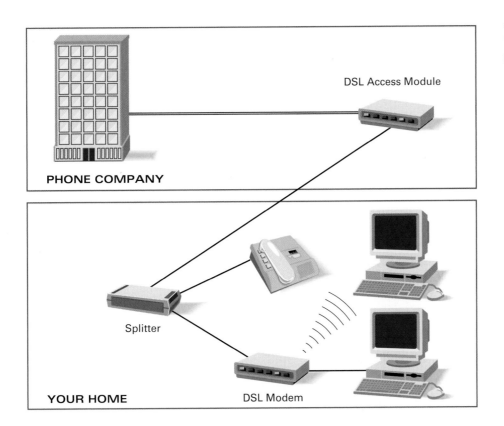

- A **satellite modem**—A modem that allows you to get Internet access from your satellite dish.

DSL, cable, and satellite modems are among the newest, most expensive, and fastest. They also don't tie up your phone line. If, for example, you're using a basic telephone modem, you can't use your telephone line for voice communications at the same time. A DSL modem on the other hand, for example, basically splits your telephone line so that you can use it simultaneously for voice communications and for connecting to the Internet (see Figure B.10). Even more so, DSL, cable, and satellite modems offer you an "always-on" Internet connection.

With these high-speed Internet connection options, you may also have the ability to connect wirelessly to the modem using a router or other piece of equipment. As you can see in Figure B.10, the DSL modem is wired directly to one computer and wirelessly connected to another computer. This gives you the ability to connect multiple computers to the DSL modem. Again, we'll cover both wired and wireless connections to the Internet in *Extended Learning Module E*.

The biggest factor in determining your choice of telecommunications hardware (beyond price) may be that of availability. In many areas of the country, phone companies and cable TV service providers do not yet support the use of DSL, cable, and satellite modems. So, you may be limited to just using a basic telephone modem. If some of the other options are available to you, we definitely recommend that you research them.

Summary: Student Learning Outcomes Revisited

1. **Define the relationships among Web site, Web site address, domain name, Web page, and uniform resource locator (URL).** A ***Web site*** (such as www.usatoday.com for the *USA Today*) is a specific location on the Web where you visit, gather information, and perhaps even order products. A ***Web site address*** (www.usatoday.com) is a unique name that identifies a specific site on the Web. Technically, a Web site address is called a ***domain name.*** A ***Web page*** is a specific portion of a Web site that deals with a certain topic. Technically, the address for a specific Web page is called a ***URL (uniform resource locator).***

2. **Explain how to interpret the parts of an address on the Web.** Most Web site addresses start with http://www. Beyond that, the address is unique. The first part (using www.uts.edu.au as an example) provides the name of the organization or Web site (UTS or University of Technology in Sydney). The next part tells the type of organization and is called the ***top-level domain.*** For UTS, it is "edu," describing it as an educational institution. If something follows after that, it usually provides a country of origin ("au" for UTS which identifies its country of origin as Australia).

3. **Identify the major components and features of Web browser software.** The two most popular Web browsers are Internet Explorer and Netscape Communicator. Each includes a menu bar (with functions such as **File, Edit,** and **View**), a button bar (for commonly performed tasks such as printing), and an address or location field into which you can type a Web site address. Web browsers also include capabilities for maintaining a list of commonly visited sites. In Internet Explorer, these are called a **Favorites list,** while Netscape Communicator refers to them as a **Bookmarks list.**

4. **Describe the differences between directory and true search engines.** *Search engines* are facilities on the Web that help you find sites with the information and/or services you want. A ***directory search engine*** organizes listings of Web sites into hierarchical lists. Using a directory search engine, you start by selecting a specific category and continually refine your search by choosing subsequent subcategories. A ***true search engine*** uses software agent technologies to search the Internet for key words and then places them into indexes. You use a true search engine by asking a question or providing key terms.

5. **Describe the various technologies that make up the Internet.** At the heart of the Internet is the ***Internet backbone,*** the major set of connections for computers on the Internet. A ***network access point (NAP)*** is a point on the Internet where several connections converge. ***Network service providers (NSPs),*** such as MCI or AT&T, own and maintain routing computers at NAPs and even the lines that connect the NAPs to each other. Besides your computer (called a client computer) which you use to access the Internet, there are also four types of ***Internet server computers*** that provide information and services on the Internet. These include ***Web servers*** (providing information and services to Web surfers), ***mail servers*** (providing e-mail services and accounts), ***ftp servers*** (maintaining a collection of files that you can download), and ***IRC servers*** (supporting your use of discussion groups and chat rooms). As information travels from these servers to you, it follows a set of ***communications protocols***—sets of rules that every computer follows to transfer information. The most common protocols include ***TCP/IP*** (the primary protocol for transmitting information), ***http*** (for supporting the movement of information over the Web), and ***ftp*** (for allowing you to transfer files of information from one computer to another).

6. **Identify key considerations in choosing an Internet service provider (ISP).** When choosing an ISP—whether it is a commercial ISP, a free ISP, your school, or your work—you need to consider the following:

- Web space—If you want to publish a Web site, then your ISP must provide you with Web space
- Technical support—Which can be in the form of e-mail, 24-hour toll-free assistance, or perhaps none at all
- Money—Commercial ISPs are the most expensive, while free ISPs, your school, and your work are free
- Privacy—Your school or work may monitor your surfing activities

7. **Describe the communications software and telecommunications hardware you need to connect to the Internet.** Communications software for connecting to the Internet includes *connectivity software* (for dialing up another computer), *Web browser software* (for actually surfing the Web), and *e-mail software* (for electronically communicating with other people). Telecommunications hardware includes the device that you use to physically connect your computer to a network, which may connect through a phone line or cable line. These devices are called modems and include a *telephone modem, DSL modem, cable modem,* and *satellite modem.*

Key Terms and Concepts

Cable modem, 118
Communications protocol (protocol), 115
Connectivity software, 117
Digital Subscriber Line (DSL), 118
Directory search engine, 110
Domain name, 106
E-mail (electronic mail) software, 117
File transfer protocol (ftp), 116
Ftp (file transfer protocol) server, 115
Hypertext transfer protocol (http), 116
Internet, 106
Internet backbone, 113
Internet server computer, 115
Internet service provider (ISP), 114
IRC (Internet Relay Chat) server, 115
Link (hyperlink), 107
Mail server, 115
Network access point (NAP), 113

Network service provider (NSP), 113
Satellite modem, 119
Search engine, 110
TCP/IP (transport control protocol/Internet protocol), 116
Telephone modem (modem), 118
Top-level domain, 107
True search engine, 110
Uniform resource locator (URL), 106
Web browser software, 108
Web page, 106
Web portal, 115
Web server, 115
Web site, 106
Web site address, 106
Web space, 116
World Wide Web (Web), 106

Short-Answer Questions

1. How do the Web and Internet differ?
2. What is the relationship between a Web site and a Web page?
3. What is the difference between a directory search engine and a true search engine?
4. How can you use plus signs (+) and minus signs (−) to refine a search?
5. What is the relationship between the Internet backbone, a network access point, and a network service provider?
6. What is the role of an ISP?
7. What are the four major types of servers on the Internet?
8. What are the advantages and disadvantages of choosing a commercial ISP?
9. What communications software do you need to use the Web?
10. What are the four main types of modems you can use to access the Internet while at home?

Assignments and Exercises

For each of the following Internet scavenger hunts, find the answer on the Web. When you do, write down the answer as well as the address where you found it. One restriction: You are not allowed to use encyclopedia sites such as *Encyclopedia Britannica.*

1. What is the weight of the moon?

Answer: _____

Address: _____

2. Who was the first U.S billionaire?

Answer: _____

Address: _____

3. Who is Olive Oyl's brother?

Answer: _____

Address: _____

4. Who wrote "It was the worst of times . . ."?

Answer: _____

Address: _____

5. What does the Seine River empty into?

Answer: _____

Address: _____

6. What is a lacrosse ball made of?

Answer: _____

Address: _____

7. Who lives at 39 Stone Canyon Drive?

Answer: _____

Address: _____

8. What is the color of Mr. Spock's blood?

Answer: _____

Address: _____

9. At what did the Nasdaq stock market close yesterday?

Answer: _____

Address: _____

10. What is the most frequently broken bone in the human body?

Answer: _____

Address: _____

11. What is a pregnant goldfish called?

Answer: _____

Address: _____

12. Who was the first pope to visit Africa?

Answer: _____

Address: _____

13. How many tusks does an Indian rhinoceros have?

Answer: _____

Address: _____

14. What does a pluviometer measure?

Answer: _____

Address: _____

15. What is the fear of the number 13 called?

Answer: _____

Address: _____

16. Which ear can most people hear best with?

Answer: _____

Address: _____

17. Who is the patron saint of England?

Answer: _____

Address: _____

18. What boxer's life story was titled *Raging Bull*?

Answer: _____

Address: _____

19. What was the first domesticated bird?

Answer: _____

Address: _____

20. What is the population of the United States right now?

Answer: _____

Address: _____

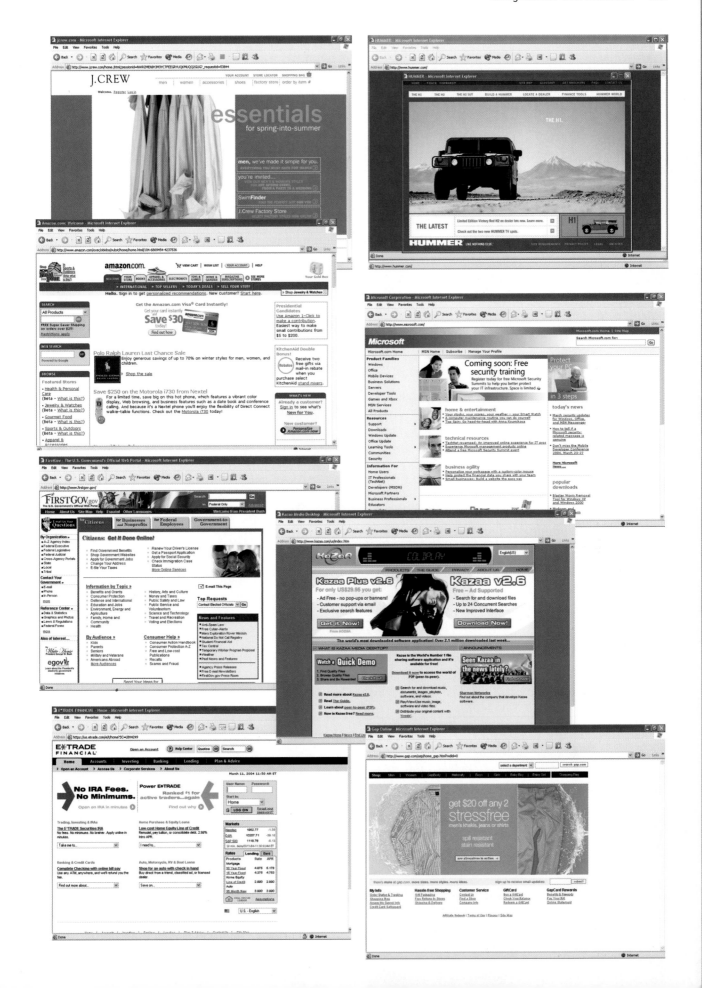

CHAPTER THREE OUTLINE

STUDENT LEARNING OUTCOMES

1. Describe business intelligence and its role in an organization.

2. Differentiate between databases and data warehouses with respect to their focus on online transaction processing and online analytical processing.

3. List and describe the key characteristics of a relational database.

4. Define the five software components of a database management system.

5. List and describe the key characteristics of a data warehouse.

6. Define the four major types of data-mining tools in a data warehouse environment.

7. List key considerations in managing the information resource in an organization.

WEB SUPPORT

www.mhhe.com/haag

- Financial aid resources
- Libraries
- Consumer information
- Demographics
- Real estate
- Data warehouses and data-mining tools

CHAPTER THREE

Databases and Data Warehouses
Building Business Intelligence

OPENING CASE STUDY: CHRYSLER SPINS A COMPETITIVE ADVANTAGE WITH SUPPLY CHAIN MANAGEMENT SOFTWARE

According to John Kay, DaimlerChrysler's manager of electronic commerce, "Being able to get critical product information to our external suppliers as soon as it becomes available is a definite competitive advantage for all concerned." John is talking about Chrysler's Supply Partner Information Network (SPIN), a Web-based supply chain management system that increased productivity by 20 percent and reduced operating costs in the first year of its implementation.

The two technology tools critical to the success of SPIN, which already boasts over 3,500 suppliers accessing and using it, are the Internet and databases. The Internet, of course, allows 24 × 7 access to SPIN by Chrysler's suppliers for providing parts, bidding on contracts, and submitting purchase invoices. The Internet also allows Chrysler to send to its suppliers in real time vitally important information updates on procurement requirements, strategy applications, and the like.

What's internal to SPIN is a powerful set of databases that track, organize, and maintain all of Chrysler's inventory, material requirements planning, work-in-progress, and supplier information. A database is a technology tool that enables you to organize vast amounts of information in the most logical way that suits your business needs. For SPIN to be successful, databases are an absolute necessity. As Jeremy Hamilton-Wright, the team leader in Chrysler's IS department, describes it, "SPIN supports everything from developing products to delivering parts and sending payments. SPIN works for all of Chrysler's different types of suppliers: production suppliers, parts suppliers, and the suppliers that package parts."

All businesses today are using databases to organize and manage their information. Why? Because databases allow you to create logical relationships within your information. At Chrysler, for example, recall notices for a defective part or assembly are logically tracked back through the production process, including human operators and equipment, through database information. If Chrysler determines that the error didn't occur in the production process, it tracks information further back through its databases to its inventory and suppliers.

Many organizations also use databases in support of their customer relationship management (CRM) strategies, another source of competitive advantage. Using CRM-enabled databases, organizations today can track customer purchases, purchases by credit card or cash, purchases by time of the day and day of the week, purchases by store location, and an array of customer demographics. All that information can then be logically organized in such a way that you could easily find the answer to the following question: "Which of our customers who have purchased over $1,500 in the last six months at a store within a five-mile radius of their homes have a household income above $75,000 and no children?"

Answers to those types of questions are what we call *business intelligence.* Business intelligence helps you make sense of your information by allowing you to view it from different perspectives and ask insightful and thought-provoking questions. To support the creation of business intelligence, many organizations are taking information from their databases and creating data warehouses, another technology tool that supports the logical organization of information.[1]

Introduction

As we've discussed in the first two chapters, you and your organization need more than just data and information. You need **business intelligence (BI)**—knowledge about your customers, your competitors, your business partners, your competitive environment, and your own internal operations—that gives you the ability to make effective, important, and often strategic business decisions. It enables your organization to extract the true meaning of information so that you can take creative and powerful steps to ensure a competitive advantage. Many such actions by your organization support some or all the initiatives we discussed in Chapter 2—customer relationship management, supply chain management, and collaboration, to name just a few.

Of course, to create business intelligence you need both data and *information* (we'll commonly refer to both as *information* in this chapter). So, business intelligence doesn't just magically appear. You must first gather and organize all your information. Then, you have to have the right IT tools to define and analyze various relationships within the information. In short, knowledge workers such as you use IT tools to create business intelligence from information. The technology, by itself, simply won't do it for you. However, technology such as databases, database management systems, data warehouses, and data-mining tools can definitely help you build and use business intelligence.

As you begin working with these IT tools (which we'll discuss in great detail throughout this chapter), you'll be performing the two types of information processing we alluded to in Chapter 1: online transaction processing and online analytical processing. **Online transaction processing (OLTP)** is the gathering of input information, processing that information, and updating existing information to reflect the gathered and processed information. Databases and DBMSs are the technology tools that directly support OLTP. Databases that support OLTP are most often referred to as **operational databases.** Inside these operational databases is valuable information that forms the basis for business intelligence.

As you can see in Figure 3.1 (on the facing page), you can also query operational databases to gather basic forms of business intelligence, such as how many products individually sold over $10,000 last month and how much money was spent last month on radio advertising. While the results of these queries may be helpful, you really need to combine product and advertising information (with several other types of information including customer demographics) to perform online analytical processing.

Online analytical processing (OLAP) is the manipulation of information to support decision making. At Australian P&C Direct, OLAP within a data warehouse is a must. P&C has created a data warehouse that supports its customer relationship management activities, cross-selling strategies, and marketing campaigns. By creating a data warehouse with customer information (including census data and lifestyle codes), its wide array of insurance and financial products, and its marketing campaign information, P&C agents can view all the products a given customer has purchased and more accurately determine cross-selling opportunities and what marketing campaigns a given customer is likely to respond to.[2]

A data warehouse is, in fact, a special form of a database that contains information gathered from operational databases for the purpose of supporting decision-making tasks. When you build a data warehouse and use data-mining tools to manipulate the data warehouse's information, your single goal is to create *business intelligence.* So, data warehouses support only OLAP; they do not at all support OLTP. As you can see in Figure 3.1, you can perform more in-depth queries to gather business intelligence from a

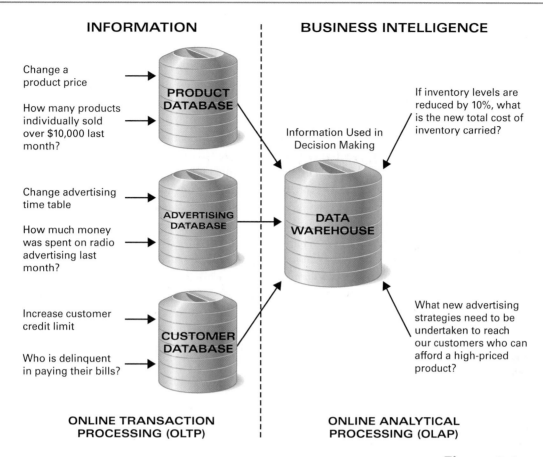

INFORMATION | **BUSINESS INTELLIGENCE**

Change a product price

How many products individually sold over $10,000 last month?

PRODUCT DATABASE

Change advertising time table

How much money was spent on radio advertising last month?

ADVERTISING DATABASE

Increase customer credit limit

Who is delinquent in paying their bills?

CUSTOMER DATABASE

Information Used in Decision Making

DATA WAREHOUSE

If inventory levels are reduced by 10%, what is the new total cost of inventory carried?

What new advertising strategies need to be undertaken to reach our customers who can afford a high-priced product?

ONLINE TRANSACTION PROCESSING (OLTP) | **ONLINE ANALYTICAL PROCESSING (OLAP)**

Figure 3.1

Building Business Intelligence

data warehouse than you can with a single database. For example, "What new advertising strategies need to be undertaken to reach our customers who can afford a high-priced product?" is a query that would require information from multiple databases. Data warehouses better support creating that type of business intelligence than do databases.

As this chapter unfolds, we'll look specifically at (1) databases and database management systems and (2) data warehouses and data-mining tools. Databases today are the foundation for organizing and managing information, and database management systems provide the tools you use to work with a database. Data warehouses are relatively new technologies that help you organize and manage business intelligence, and data-mining tools help you extract that vitally important business intelligence. Data warehouses and data-mining tools are a subset of the business intelligence software that we discussed in Chapter 2.

As we first look at databases and database management systems in this chapter, we'll be exploring their use by Solomon Enterprises in support of customer relationship management and order processing. Solomon Enterprises specializes in providing concrete to commercial builders and individual homeowners in the greater Chicago area. Solomon tracks detailed information on its concrete types, customers, raw materials, raw materials' suppliers, trucks, and employees. It uses a database to organize and manage all this information. As we discuss Solomon Enterprises and its use of a database, we'll focus mostly on CRM and ordering processing. In *Extended Learning Module C,* which follows this chapter, we'll look at how to design the supply chain management side of Solomon's database.

The Relational Database Model

For organizing and storing basic and transaction-oriented information (that is eventually used to create business intelligence), businesses today use databases. There are actually four primary models for creating a database. The object-oriented database model is the newest and holds great promise; we'll talk more about the entire object-oriented genre in Chapter 7 and in *Extended Learning Module G*. Right now, let's focus on the most popular database model: the relational database model.

As a generic definition, we would say that any ***database*** is a collection of information that you organize and access according to the logical structure of that information. In reference to a ***relational database,*** we say that it uses a series of logically related two-dimensional tables or files to store information in the form of a database. The term ***relation*** often describes each two-dimensional table or file in the relational model (hence its name *relational* database model). A relational database is actually composed of two distinct parts: (1) the information itself, stored in a series of two-dimensional tables, files, or relations (people use these three terms interchangeably) and (2) the logical structure of that information. Let's look at a portion of Solomon's database to further explore the characteristics of the relational database model.

COLLECTIONS OF INFORMATION

In Figure 3.2 (on the facing page), we've created a view of a portion of Solomon's database. Notice that it contains five files: *Order, Customer, Concrete Type, Employee,* and *Truck.* (It will contain many more as we develop it completely in *Extended Learning Module C.*) These files are all related for numerous reasons—customers make orders, employees drive trucks, an order has a concrete type, and so on. And you need all these files to manage your customer relationships and process orders.

Within each file, you can see specific pieces of information (or *attributes*). For example, the *Order* file contains *Order Number, Order Date, Customer Number, Delivery Address, Concrete Type, Amount* (this is given in cubic yards), *Truck Number,* and *Driver ID.* In the *Customer* file, you can see specific information including *Customer Number, Customer Name, Customer Phone,* and *Customer Primary Contact.* These are all important pieces of information that Solomon's database should contain. Moreover, Solomon needs all this information (and probably much more) to effectively process orders and manage customer relationships.

CREATED WITH LOGICAL STRUCTURES

Using the relational database model, you organize and access information according to its logical structure, not its physical position. So, you don't really care in which row of the *Employee* file Allison Smithson appears. You really need to know only that Allison's *Employee ID* is 984568756 or, for that matter, that her name is Allison Smithson. In the relational database model, a ***data dictionary*** contains the logical structure for the information in a database. When you create a database, you first create its data dictionary. The data dictionary contains important information (or logical properties) about your information. For example, the data dictionary for *Customer Phone* in the *Customer* file would require 10 digits. The data dictionary for *Date of Hire* in the *Employee* file would require a month, day, and year, as well.

This is quite different from other ways of organizing information. For example, if you want to access information in a certain cell in most spreadsheet applications, you must know its physical location—row number and column character. With a relational

ORDER FILE

Order Number	Order Date	Customer Number	Delivery Address	Concrete Type	Amount	Truck Number	Driver ID
100000	9/1/2004	1234	55 Smith Lane	1	8	111	123456789
100001	9/1/2004	3456	2122 E. Biscayne	1	3	222	785934444
100002	9/2/2004	1234	55 Smith Lane	5	6	222	435296657
100003	9/3/2004	4567	1333 Burr Ridge	2	4	333	435296657
100004	9/4/2004	4567	1333 Burr Ridge	2	8	222	785934444
100005	9/4/2004	5678	1222 Westminster	1	4	222	785934444
100006	9/5/2004	1234	222 East Hampton	1	4	111	123456789
100007	9/6/2004	2345	9 W. Palm Beach	2	5	333	785934444
100008	9/6/2004	6789	4532 Lane Circle	1	8	222	785934444
100009	9/7/2004	1234	987 Furlong	3	8	111	123456789
100010	9/9/2004	6789	4532 Lance Circle	2	7	222	435296657
100011	9/9/2004	4567	3500 Tomahawk	5	6	222	785934444

CUSTOMER FILE

Customer Number	Customer Name	Customer Phone	Customer Primary Contact
1234	Smelding Homes	3333333333	Bill Johnson
2345	Home Builders Superior	3334444444	Marcus Connolly
3456	Mark Akey	3335555555	Mark Akey
4567	Triple A Homes	3336666666	Janielle Smith
5678	Sheryl Williamson	3337777777	Sheryl Williamson
6789	Home Makers	3338888888	John Yu

CONCRETE TYPE FILE

Concrete Type	Type Description
1	Home foundation and walkways
2	Commercial foundation and infrastructure
3	Premier speckled (concrete with pea-size smooth gravel aggregate)
4	Premier marble (concrete with crushed marble aggregate)
5	Premier shell (concrete with shell aggregate)

EMPLOYEE FILE

Employee ID	Employee Last Name	Employee First Name	Date of Hire
123456789	Johnson	Emilio	2/1/1985
435296657	Evaraz	Antonio	3/3/1992
785934444	Robertson	John	6/1/1999
984568756	Smithson	Allison	4/1/1997

TRUCK FILE

Truck Number	Truck Type	Date of Purchase
111	Ford	6/17/1999
222	Ford	12/24/2001
333	Chevy	1/1/2002

Figure 3.2

A Portion of Solomon Enterprises' Database for Customer Relationship Management and Ordering Processing

database, however, you need only know the field name of the column of information (for example, *Amount*) and its logical row, not its physical row. As a result, in Solomon's database example, you could easily change the amount for an order, without having to know where that information is physically stored (by row or column).

And with spreadsheet software, you can immediately begin typing in information, creating column headings, and providing formatting. You can't do that with a database. Using a database, you must clearly define the characteristics of each field by creating a data dictionary. So, you must carefully plan the design of your database before you can start adding information.

WITH LOGICAL TIES WITHIN THE INFORMATION

In a relational database, you must create ties or relationships in the information that show how the files relate to each other. Before you can create these relationships among files, you must first specify the primary key of each file. A ***primary key*** is a field (or group of fields in some cases) that uniquely describes each record. In Solomon's database, *Order Number* is the primary key for the *Order* file and *Customer Number* is the primary key for the *Customer* file. That is to say, every order in the *Order* file must have a unique *Order Number* and every customer in the *Customer* file must have a unique *Customer Number*.

When you define that a specific field in a file is the primary key, you're also stating as well that the field cannot be blank. That is, you cannot enter the information for a new employee in the *Employee* file and leave the *Employee ID* field blank. If that were possible, you could potentially have two employees with identical primary keys (blank), which is not possible in a database environment.

Again, this is quite different from working with spreadsheets. Using a spreadsheet, it would be almost impossible to ensure that each field in a given column is unique. This reinforces the notion that, while spreadsheets work with information according to physical location, databases work with information logically.

If you look back at Figure 3.2, you can see that *Customer Number* appears in both the *Customer* and *Order* files. This creates a logical relationship between the two files and is an example of a foreign key. A ***foreign key*** is a primary key of one file that appears in another file. Now look at Figure 3.3. In it, we've provided the logical relationships among all five files. Notice, for example, that *Truck Number* is the primary key for the *Truck* file. It also appears in the *Order* file. This enables Solomon to track which trucks were used to deliver the various orders. So, *Truck Number* is the primary key in the *Truck* file and is also a foreign key that appears in the *Order* file. There are other examples of foreign keys as well in Figure 3.3.

Figure 3.3

Creating Logical Ties with Primary and Foreign Keys

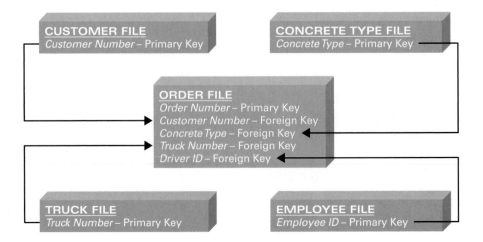

CUSTOMER FILE
Customer Number – Primary Key

CONCRETE TYPE FILE
Concrete Type – Primary Key

ORDER FILE
Order Number – Primary Key
Customer Number – Foreign Key
Concrete Type – Foreign Key
Truck Number – Foreign Key
Driver ID – Foreign Key

TRUCK FILE
Truck Number – Primary Key

EMPLOYEE FILE
Employee ID – Primary Key

PRIMARY KEYS, FOREIGN KEYS, AND INTEGRITY CONSTRAINTS

Let's consider the information that your school tracks for a class. In this instance, a class is a scheduled course. For example, your school may have FINA 2100—Introduction to International Financial Markets as a course. If the school offers it in the fall, then it becomes a class. Below, we've provided many pieces of information that your school probably tracks about the class. First, which is the primary key (place an X in the second column)? Second, for each piece of information, identify if it's a foreign key (a primary key of another file). If it is, write down the filename in the third column. Finally, in the fourth column for each piece of information, write down any integrity constraints you can think of. For example, can it be blank or must it contain something? Can it be duplicated across multiple records (classes)? If it's a number, does it have a specific range in which it must fall? There are many others.

Information	Primary Key?	Foreign Key?	Integrity Constraints
Department designation (e.g., FINA)			
Course number (e.g., 2100)			
Course name			
Course description			
Prerequisite			
Number of credit hours			
Lab fee			
Instructor name			
Room number			
Time of day			
Day of week			

Foreign keys are essential in the relational database model. Without them, you have no way of creating logical ties among the various files. As you might guess, we use these relationships extensively to create business intelligence because they enable us to track the logical relationships within many types of information.

WITH BUILT-IN INTEGRITY CONSTRAINTS

By defining the logical structure of information in a relational database, you're also developing *integrity constraints*—rules that help ensure the quality of the information. For example, by stating that *Customer Number* is the primary key of the *Customer* file and a foreign key in the *Order* file, you're saying (1) that no two customers can have the same *Customer Number* and (2) that a *Customer Number* that is entered into the *Order* file must have a matching *Customer Number* in the *Customer* file. So, as Solomon creates a new order and enters a *Customer Number* in the *Order* file, the database management system must find a corresponding and identical *Customer Number* in the *Customer* file. This makes perfect sense. You cannot create an order for a customer who does not exist.

Consumer Reports magazine has rated the Ritz-Carlton first among luxury hotels.[3] Why? It's simple: Ritz-Carlton has created a powerful guest preference database to provide customized, personal, and high-level service to guests of any of its hotels. For example, if you leave a message at a Ritz-Carlton front desk that you want the bed turned down at 9 P.M., prefer no chocolate mints on your pillow, and want to participate in the 7 A.M. aerobics class, that information is passed along to the floor maid (and others) and is also stored in the guest preference database. By assigning to you a unique customer ID that creates logical ties to your various preferences, the Ritz-Carlton transfers your information to all of its other hotels. The next time you stay in a Ritz-Carlton hotel, in Palm Beach for example, your information is already there, and the hotel staff immediately knows of your preferences.

For the management at Ritz-Carlton, achieving customer loyalty starts first with knowing each customer individually (the concept of customer relationship management). That includes your exercise habits, what you most commonly consume from the snack bar in your room, how many towels you use daily, and whether you like a chocolate on your pillow. To store and organize all this information, Ritz-Carlton uses a relational database, and employees use it to meet your needs (or whims).

Database Management System Tools

When working with word processing software, you create and edit a document. When working with spreadsheet software, you create and edit a workbook. The same is true in a database environment. A database is equivalent to a document or a workbook because they all contain information. And while word processing and spreadsheet are the software tools you use to work with documents and workbooks, you use database management system software to work with databases. A ***database management system (DBMS)*** helps you specify the logical organization for a database and access and use the information within a database. A DBMS contains five important software components (see Figure 3.4):

1. DBMS engine
2. Data definition subsystem
3. Data manipulation subsystem
4. Application generation subsystem
5. Data administration subsystem

The DBMS engine is perhaps the most important, yet seldom recognized, component of a DBMS. The ***DBMS engine*** accepts logical requests from the various other DBMS subsystems, converts them into their physical equivalent, and actually accesses the database and data dictionary as they exist on a storage device. Again, the distinction between logical and physical is important in a database environment. The ***physical view*** of information deals with how information is physically arranged, stored, and accessed on some type of storage device such as a hard disk. The ***logical view*** of information, on the other hand, focuses on how you as a knowledge worker need to arrange and access information to meet your particular business needs.

Databases and DBMSs provide two really great advantages in separating the logical from the physical view of information. First, the DBMS handles the physical tasks. So you, as a database user, can concentrate solely on your logical information needs. Second, although there is only one physical view of information, there may be numerous knowledge workers who have different logical views of the information in a database.

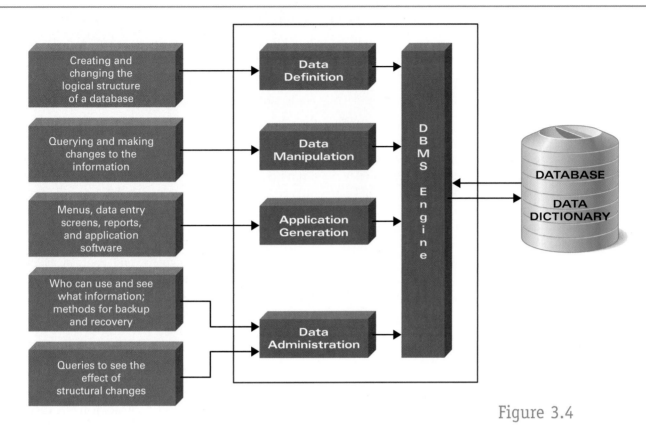

Figure 3.4

Software Subsystems of a
Database Management
System

That is, according to what business tasks they need to perform, different knowledge workers logically view information in different ways. The DBMS engine can process virtually any logical information view or request into its physical equivalent.

DATA DEFINITION SUBSYSTEM

The *data definition subsystem* of a DBMS helps you create and maintain the data dictionary and define the structure of the files in a database.

When you create a database, you must first use the data definition subsystem to create the data dictionary and define the structure of the files. This is very different from using something like spreadsheet software. When you create a workbook, you can immediately begin typing in information and creating formulas and functions. You can't do that with a database. You must define its logical structure before you can begin typing in any information. Typing in the information is the easy part: Defining the logical structure is more difficult. In *Extended Learning Module C* that follows this chapter, we take you through the process of defining the logical structure for the supply chain management (SCM) side of Solomon Enterprises' database. We definitely recommend that you read that module—knowing how to define the correct structure of a database can be a substantial career opportunity for you.

If you ever find that a certain file needs another piece of information, you have to use the data definition subsystem to add a new field in the data dictionary. Likewise, if you want to delete a given field for all the records in a file, you must use the data definition subsystem to do so.

TRACKING SHOE MOVEMENT WITH WIRELESS AND DATABASE TECHNOLOGIES

Managing your inventory is an important task and often a daunting one. Simply knowing where your inventory is scattered across multiple warehouses may often not be easy but it can certainly save you money. Consider Skechers USA, for example, a footwear maker in Ontario, California. It recently implemented a wireless tracking and database-enabled system to improve inventory management, which saves approximately $1 million annually.

When a shipment of shoes arrives from a Far East manufacturer (each box with 12 pairs of shoes), an employee uses a hand-held scanner to verify its receipt.

Next, the employee logs the warehouse destination of each box. That information is all stored in a database. Then, at any time and from any location, an employee can determine the warehouse in which any given box of shoes is stored. This enables Skechers to efficiently schedule shipments out of its four different warehouse locations.

As Paul Galliher, VP of distribution, describes it, "We can now use logical pick paths and improve all the shipping processes with the proper documentation generated that allows us to see at which of our four buildings we can schedule a pickup."[4]

As you create the data dictionary, you're essentially defining the logical properties of the information that the database will contain. Logical structures of information include the following:

Logical Properties	Examples
Field name	*Customer Number, Order Date*
Type	Alphabetic, numeric, date, time, etc.
Form	Is an area code required for a phone number?
Default value	If no *Order Date* is entered, the default is today's date.
Validation rule	Can *Amount* exceed 8?
Is an entry required?	Must you enter *Delivery Address* for an order or can it be blank?
Can there be duplicates?	Primary keys cannot be duplicates; but what about amounts?

These are all important logical properties to a lesser or greater extent depending on the type of information you're describing. For example, a typical concrete delivery truck can hold at most eight cubic yards of concrete. Further, Solomon may not accept orders for less than four cubic yards of concrete. Therefore, an important validation rule for *Amount* in the *Order* file is "must be greater than or equal to 4 and cannot be greater than 8."

DATA MANIPULATION SUBSYSTEM

The ***data manipulation subsystem*** of a DBMS helps you add, change, and delete information in a database and query it for valuable information. Software tools within the data manipulation subsystem are most often the primary interface between you as a user and the information contained in a database. So, while the DBMS engine handles your information requests from a physical point of view, it is the data manipulation tools within a DBMS that allow you to specify your logical information requirements. Those logical information requirements are then used by the DBMS engine to access the information you need from a physical point of view.

In most DBMSs, you'll find a variety of data manipulation tools, including views, report generators, query-by-example tools, and structured query language.

VIEWS   A *view* allows you to see the contents of a database file, make whatever changes you want, perform simple sorting, and query to find the location of specific information. Views essentially provide each file in the form of a spreadsheet workbook. The screen in Figure 3.5 shows a view in Microsoft Access for the *Order* file in Solomon's database. At this point, you can click on any specific field and change its contents. You could also point at an entire record and click on the Cut icon (the scissors) to remove a record. If you want to add a record, simply click in the *Order Number* field of the first blank record and begin typing.

Note: we've sorted the file in ascending order by *Concrete Type*. You can easily achieve this by clicking on the A→Z Sort button in the view window. If you want to sort in descending order by *Concrete Type*, simply point to any *Concrete Type* field and click on the Z→A Sort button. You can also perform searches within views. For example, if you wanted to find all orders for *Customer Number* 3456, simply point anywhere in that column, click on the Find Text button (the binoculars), and enter 3456. Access will respond by highlighting each *Customer Number* field where 3456 appears.

As with most other types of personal productivity software, DBMSs support such functions and tasks as cutting and pasting, formatting (for example, bolding a field), spell checking, hiding columns (just as you would do using spreadsheet software), filtering, and even adding links to Web sites.

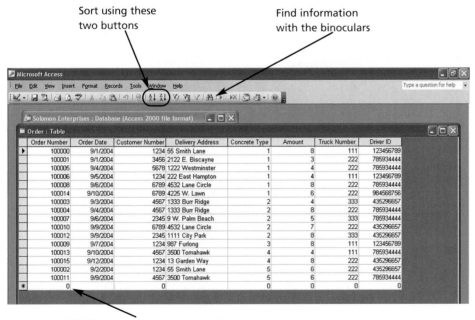

Figure 3.5

A View in Microsoft Access

REPORT GENERATORS   *Report generators* help you quickly define formats of reports and what information you want to see in a report. Once you define a report, you can view it on the screen or print it. Figure 3.6 shows two intermediate screens in Microsoft Access. The first allows you to specify which fields of information are to appear in a report. We have chosen to include *Order Number, Order Date, Customer Number,* and *Amount* from the *Order* file. The second allows you to choose from a set of predefined report formats. Following a simple and easy-to-use set of screens (including the two in Figure 3.6), we went on to specify that sorting should take place by *Customer Number* and that the name of the report should be "Customer and Amount Report." The completed report is also shown in Figure 3.6. Notice that it displays only those fields we requested, that it's sorted by *Customer Number,* and that the title is "Customer and Amount Report."

A nice feature about report generators is that you can save a report format that you use frequently. For example, if you think you'll use the report in Figure 3.6 often, you can save it by giving it a unique name. Later, you can request that report and your DBMS will generate it, using the most up-to-date information in the database. You can also choose from a variety of report formats (we chose a simple one for our illustration). And you can choose report formats that create intermediate subtotals and grand totals, which can include counts, sums, averages, and the like.

Figure 3.6

Using a Report Generator

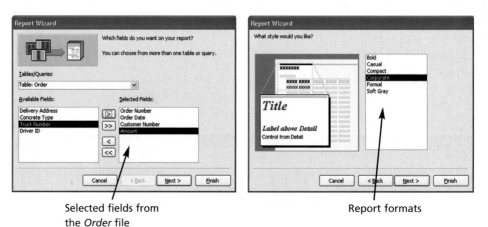

Selected fields from the *Order* file

Report formats

CUSTOMER AND AMOUNT REPORT

Customer Number	Order Number	Order Date	Amount
1234	100000	9/1/2004	8
1234	100002	9/2/2004	6
1234	100006	9/5/2004	4
1234	100009	9/7/2004	8
1234	100015	9/12/2004	8
2345	100007	9/6/2004	5
2345	100012	9/9/2004	8
3456	100001	9/1/2004	3
4567	100003	9/3/2004	4
4567	100004	9/4/2004	8
4567	100011	9/9/2004	6
4567	100013	9/10/2004	4
5678	100005	9/4/2004	4
6789	100008	9/6/2004	8
6789	100010	9/9/2004	7
6789	100014	9/10/2004	6

QUERY-BY-EXAMPLE TOOLS   *Query-by-example (QBE) tools* help you graphically design the answer to a question. Suppose for example that Janelle Smith from Triple A Homes (*Customer Number* 4567) has called and ordered a delivery of concrete. Although she can't remember the name of the driver, she would like to have the driver that comes out the most often to deliver concrete to Triple A Homes. Solomon's task, from a customer relationship management point of view, is to go through all the orders and determine which employee most often delivers concrete to Triple A Homes. The task may seem simple considering that Solomon currently has very few orders in its database. However, can you imagine trying to answer that question if there were thousands of orders in Solomon's database? It would not be fun.

Fortunately, QBE tools can help you answer this question and perform many other queries in a matter of seconds. In Figure 3.7, you can see a QBE screen that formulates the answer to the question. When you perform a QBE, you (1) identify the files in which the needed information is located, (2) drag any necessary fields from the identified files to the QBE grid, and (3) specify selection criteria.

For the names of employees who have delivered concrete to Triple A Homes, we identified the two files of *Order* and *Employee*. Second, we dragged *Customer Number* from the *Order* file to the QBE grid and dragged *Employee Last Name* and *Employee First Name* from the *Employee* file to the QBE grid. Finally, we specified in the Criteria box that we wanted to view only the orders for *Customer Number* 4567 (Triple A Homes). Access did the rest and provided the information in Figure 3.7.

QBEs rely heavily on the logical relationships within a database to find information. For example, *Order Number* 100004 has the *Customer Number* of 4567 (Triple A Homes). So, the QBE tool took the *Driver ID* from the *Order* file for that order and found a match in the *Employee* file. When it found a match, it presented the *Employee Last Name* and *Employee First Name* (John Robertson). Without the logical relationships being correctly defined, this QBE query would not have worked properly.

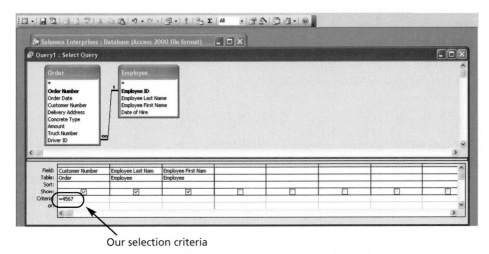

Our selection criteria

Figure 3.7

Using a Query-by-Example to Find Information

Customer Number	Employee Last Name	Employee First Name
4567	Evaraz	Antonio
4567	Robertson	John
4567	Robertson	John
4567	Robertson	John

STRUCTURED QUERY LANGUAGE *Structured query language (SQL)* is a standardized fourth-generation query language found in most DBMSs. SQL performs the same function as QBE, except that you perform the query by creating a statement instead of pointing, clicking, and dragging. The basic form of an SQL statement is

SELECT . . . FROM . . . WHERE . . .

After the SELECT, you list the fields of information you want; after the FROM, you specify what logical relationships to use; and after the WHERE, you specify any selection criteria. If you consider our QBE above of Who most often delivers concrete to *Customer Number* 4567? the SQL statement would look like the following:

SELECT Order.[Customer Number], Employee.[Employee Last
Name], Employee.[Employee First Name]
FROM Employee INNER JOIN [Order] ON Employee.[Employee ID]
= Order.[Driver ID]
WHERE (((Order.[Customer Number])=4567));

Thoroughly introducing you to the syntax of building SQL statements is outside the scope of this text and would easily require almost 100 pages of material. But you should be aware that SQL does exist. If you're majoring in IT or MIS, you'll undoubtedly take a course in SQL.

APPLICATION GENERATION SUBSYSTEM

The *application generation subsystem* of a DBMS contains facilities to help you develop transaction-intensive applications. These types of applications usually require that you perform a detailed series of tasks to process a transaction. Application generation subsystem facilities include tools for creating visually appealing and easy-to-use data entry screens, programming languages specific to a particular DBMS, and interfaces to commonly used programming languages that are independent of any DBMS.

As with SQL, application generation facilities are most often used by IT specialists. As a knowledge worker, we recommend that you leave application generation to IT specialists as much as you can. You need to focus on views, report generators, and QBE tools. These will help you find information in a database and perform queries so you can start to build and use business intelligence.

DATA ADMINISTRATION SUBSYSTEM

The *data administration subsystem* of a DBMS helps you manage the overall database environment by providing facilities for backup and recovery, security management, query optimization, concurrency control, and change management. The data administration subsystem is most often used by a data administrator or database administrator—someone responsible for assuring that the database (and data warehouse) environment meets the entire information needs of an organization.

Backup and recovery facilities provide a way for you to (1) periodically back up information contained in a database and (2) restart or recover a database and its information in case of a failure. These are important functions you cannot ignore in today's information-based environment. Organizations that understand the importance of their information take precautions to preserve it, often by running backup databases, a DBMS, and storage facilities parallel to the primary database environment. In Chapters 7 and 8, we talk specifically about how to develop plans and strategies in the event of some sort of failure. We call this contingency planning or disaster recovery planning.

LUFTHANSA WANTS YOUR COMPLAINTS

In a time when all airlines are seeking ways to gain passengers and their loyalty, Lufthansa is taking an approach like no other. Simply put, if you don't like something about your flight—the late departure/arrival, uncomfortable seats, hot meals that weren't hot, or anything else you care to complain about—Lufthansa wants to know about it.

This approach isn't to let you vent so that you'll feel better. Lufthansa takes every complaint and enters it into a database. The database, Oracle 9i, supports Lufthansa's COSMIC project—Customer Oriented Service Management Improvement in the Cabin. In any given month, Lufthansa employees enter 6,000 to 7,000 complaints about arrival/departure, boarding, meals, and other aspects of in-flight service. The system tracks such a level of detail that a complaint can even be recorded for a portion of food (e.g., your bread or meat) that you didn't feel was sufficient in size.

That many complaints may seem high, but consider that Lufthansa uses 14,000 cabin attendants to fly 45 million passengers each year to 350 different destinations in 94 countries. That means Lufthansa receives and records only one complaint per 650 passengers. That's good, but not good enough for Lufthansa.

Lufthansa uses Oracle's Discoverer data-mining tools to carefully sift through all the complaints. Lufthansa can easily categorize complaints by each outsourcing caterer. It uses that information to impose penalties on caterers who continually provide substandard food and beverages.

The Discoverer tool set has allowed Lufthansa to cut the time spent handling customer complaints by an amazing 70 percent. That not only saves money, but also increases customer loyalty and retention.

Soon, Lufthansa plans to create satellite links between its in-flight planes and the home office, which will allow cabin attendants to enter complaints on board a flight and have the complaints immediately analyzed.

Customer service is about providing exceptional service. But it's also about rectifying customer complaints. Using databases and tool sets that allow you to sift through and organize customer complaints, your organization can gain a competitive advantage, just like Lufthansa.[5]

Security management facilities allow you to control who has access to what information and what type of access those people have. In many database environments, for example, some people may need only view access to database information, but not change privileges. Still others may need the ability to add, change, and/or delete information in a database. Through a system of passwords and access privileges, the data administration subsystem allows you to define which users can perform which tasks and what information they can see. At car dealership JM Family Enterprises (JMFE), security management facilities are an absolute must because its technology is highly decentralized and includes users of mobile technologies.[6] JMFE's system supports encryption and passwords to protect databases, files, and many hardware resources. The system even supports automatic log-offs after a certain amount of time if users accidentally leave their systems running.

Query optimization facilities often take queries from users (in the form of SQL statements or QBEs) and restructure them to minimize response times. In SQL, for example, you can build a query statement that might involve working with as many as 10 different files. As you might well guess, when working with 10 different files, there may be several different solutions for combining them to get the information you need. Fortunately, you don't have to worry about structuring the SQL statement in the most optimized fashion. The query optimization facilities will do that for you and provide you with the information you need in the fastest possible way.

RESEARCHING PERSONAL DBMSs

We believe the ability to use a personal DBMS is becoming more essential every day in finding a good job. All businesses want you to possess expertise in word processing, spreadsheet, and presentation software. Many more are now beginning to place a high priority on your ability to use a personal DBMS. To the left below are seven well-known personal DBMSs. For each, find the information for the topics to the right.

- Alpha Five
- askSam Professional
- FileMaker Pro
- Microsoft Access
- MyDatabase
- Paradox
- QuickBase

1. Latest version number

2. Security features

3. Support for SQL

4. Export information to HTML format

5. Support for mail merge

6. Support for creating relationships among tables

7. Report wizard support

8. Form wizard support

Reorganization facilities continually maintain statistics concerning how the DBMS engine physically accesses information. In maintaining those statistics, reorganization facilities can optimize the physical structure of a database to further increase speed and performance. For example, if you frequently access a certain file by a specific order, the reorganization facilities may maintain the file in that presorted order by creating an index that maintains the sorted order in that file. What's really nice is that you don't have to be aware of the changes to your database with respect to physical locations—the DBMS engine will take care of it for you.

Concurrency control facilities ensure the validity of database updates when multiple users attempt to access and change the same information. This is crucial in today's networked business environment. Consider your school's online registration system. What if you and another student try to register for a class with only one seat remaining at exactly the same time? Who gets enrolled in the class? What happens to the person who does not get his or her desired class schedule? These are important questions that must be answered according to your business rules and, once answered, defined in the database environment using concurrency control facilities.

PROTECTING YOUR MOST SENSITIVE DATABASE INFORMATION

According to a recent study by the Gartner Group, it is estimated that 70 percent of unauthorized access to information occurs by internal employees. Further, the study found that internal employees are responsible for more than 95 percent of the intrusions that result in significant financial loss.

Consider, moreover, that law enforcement experts estimate that more than 50 percent of all identity thefts are committed by employees who have access to large financial databases. These statistics are certainly evidence that your organization needs to take action to protect your most sensitive database information, since over 90 percent of all corporate information is stored in databases.

As you undertake the task of creating a protection plan for your information, here are a few helpful things to keep in mind.

- **Database security does not equal network security**—Network security—firewalls and the like—does not protect your databases from the inside. You need additional security mechanisms for your databases that allow you to specify who can access what information and how (read-only, create, delete, and/or update).

- **Database security should be application transparent**—Your applications should not change as a result of implementing database security. Your employees should notice no difference in how the applications work. Transparent security is the best security.

- **Database security should not prevent the right people from obtaining the right information when they need it**—This is important. In a database environment, you need to carefully determine who *can* access various kinds of information. Even if it means more work for your database administrator and staff, you should never implement global database security measures that prohibit the right people from obtaining the right information.

The significance and proliferation of databases demands that your organization develop security mechanisms that protect your information. If you don't believe it, reread the first paragraph and understand that it's mostly internal employees stealing your information.[7]

Change management facilities allow you to assess the impact of proposed structural changes to a database environment. For example, if you decide to add a character identifier to a numeric truck number, you can use the change management facilities to see how many files will be affected. Recall that *Truck Number* would be the primary key for a *Truck* file and that it would also be a foreign key in many other files. Sometimes, structural changes may not have much effect on the database (adding a four-digit zip code extension), but others can cause widespread changes that you must assess carefully before implementing.

All these—backup and recovery, security management, query optimization, reorganization, concurrency control, and change management—are vitally important facilities in any DBMS and thus any database environment. As a user and knowledge worker, you probably won't deal with these facilities specifically as far as setting them up and maintaining them is concerned. But how they're set up and maintained will affect what you can do. So knowing that they do exist and understanding their purposes are important.

Data Warehouses and Data Mining

Suppose as a manager at Victoria's Secret, you wanted to know the total revenues generated from the sale of shoes last month. That's a simple query, which you could easily implement using either SQL or a QBE tool. But what if you wanted to know, "By actual versus budgeted, how many size 8 shoes in black did we sell last month in the southeast and southwest regions, compared with the same month over the last 5 years?" That task seems almost impossible, even with the aid of technology. If you were actually able to build a QBE query for it, you would probably bring the organization's operational database environment to its knees.

This example illustrates the two primary reasons so many organizations are opting to build data warehouses. First, while operational databases may have the needed information, the information is not organized in a way that lends itself to building business intelligence within the database or using various data manipulation tools. Second, if you could build such a query, your operational databases, which are probably already supporting the processing of hundreds of transactions per second, would seriously suffer in performance when you hit the Start button to perform the query.

To support such intriguing, necessary, and complex queries to create business intelligence, many organizations are building data warehouses and providing data-mining tools. A data warehouse is simply the next step (beyond databases) in the progression of building business intelligence. And data-mining tools are the tools you use to mine a data warehouse and extrapolate the business intelligence you need to make a decision, solve a problem, or capitalize on an opportunity to create a competitive advantage.

Figure 3.8

A Multidimensional Data Warehouse with Information from Multiple Operational Databases

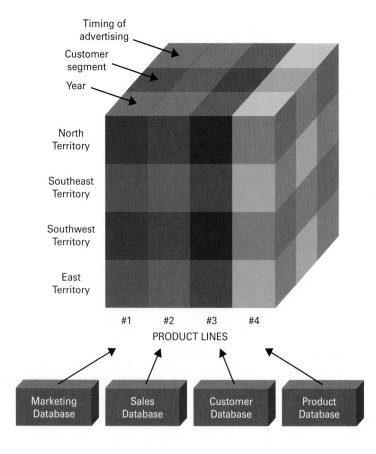

WHAT IS A DATA WAREHOUSE?

A ***data warehouse*** is a logical collection of information—gathered from many different operational databases—used to create business intelligence that supports business analysis activities and decision-making tasks (see Figure 3.8). Sounds simple enough on the surface, but data warehouses represent a fundamentally different way of thinking about organizing and managing information in an organization. Consider these key features of a data warehouse, detailed in the sections that follow.

DATA WAREHOUSES ARE MULTIDIMENSIONAL In the relational database model, information is represented in a series of two-dimensional files or tables. Not so in a data warehouse—most data warehouses are multidimensional, meaning that they contain layers of columns and rows. For this reason, most data warehouses are really *multidimensional databases*. The layers in a data warehouse represent information according to different dimensions. This multidimensional representation of information is referred to as a *hypercube*.

In Figure 3.8, you can see a hypercube that represents product information by product line and region (columns and rows), by year (the first layer), by customer segment (the second layer), and by the timing of advertising media (the third layer). Using this hypercube, you can easily ask, According to customer segment A, what percentage of total sales for product line 1 in the southwest territory occurred immediately after a radio advertising blitz? The information you would receive from that query constitutes business intelligence.

Any specific subcube within the larger hypercube can contain a variety of summarized information gathered from the various operational databases. For example, the forward-most and top-left subcube contains information for the North territory, by year, for product line 1. So, it could contain totals, average, counts, and distributions summarizing in some way that information. Of course, what it contains is really up to you and your needs.

DATA WAREHOUSES SUPPORT DECISION MAKING, NOT TRANSACTION PROCESSING   In an organization, most databases are transaction-oriented. That is, most databases support online transaction processing (OLTP) and, therefore, are operational databases. Data warehouses are not transaction-oriented: They exist to support decision-making tasks in your organization. Therefore, data warehouses support only online analytical processing (OLAP).

As we just stated, the subcubes within a data warehouse contain summarized information. So, while a data warehouse may contain the total sales for a year by product line, it does not contain a list of each individual sale to each individual customer for a given product line. Therefore, you simply cannot process transactions with a data warehouse. Instead, you process transactions with your operational databases and then use the information contained within the operational databases to build the summary information in a data warehouse.

WHAT ARE DATA-MINING TOOLS?

Data-mining tools are the software tools you use to query information in a data warehouse. These data-mining tools support the concept of OLAP—the manipulation of information to support decision-making tasks. Data-mining tools include query-and-reporting tools, intelligent agents, multidimensional analysis tools, and statistical tools (see Figure 3.9). Essentially, data-mining tools are to data warehouse users what data manipulation subsystem tools are to database users.

Figure 3.9

The Data Miner's Tool Set

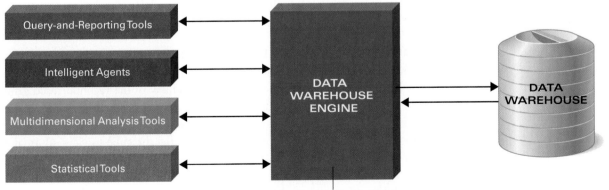

As in a DBMS, a data warehouse system
has an engine responsible for converting your
logical requests into their physical equivalent.

A PERFECT MATCH—DATA WAREHOUSES, BUSINESS INTELLIGENCE, AND CUSTOMER RELATIONSHIP MANAGEMENT

Bank Hapoalim is Israel's largest bank, serving almost 2 million customers with a wide array of financial services and products. Bank Hapoalim's customer relationship management (CRM) focus is to offer superior customer care and unique financial services to maintain and expand its customer base.

As a part of this effort, Bank Hapoalim turned to Cognos, the world leader in business intelligence software and data warehouses. According to Tal Shlasky, data warehouse project manager at Bank Hapoalim, "We continue to devote our resources and energy to the individual customer in our quest to be more efficient and better suited to banking in the 21st century. Using an industry-leading solution like Cognos, we are doing just that. Cognos gives us an integrated view of the enterprise, allowing us to target customers based on their individual needs. Without a doubt, that capability gives us a competitive edge in the market."

To grow a customer base of 2 million, any organization needs data warehouses that support business intelligence.[8]

QUERY-AND-REPORTING TOOLS *Query-and-reporting tools* are similar to QBE tools, SQL, and report generators in the typical database environment. In fact, most data warehousing environments support simple and easy-to-use data manipulation subsystem tools such as QBE, SQL, and report generators. Most often, data warehouse users use these types of tools to generate simple queries and reports.

INTELLIGENT AGENTS Intelligent agents utilize various artificial intelligence tools such as neural networks and fuzzy logic to form the basis of "information discovery" and building business intelligence in OLAP. For example, Wall Street analyst Murray Riggiero uses OLAP software called Data/Logic, which incorporates neural networks to generate rules for his highly successful stock and bond trading system.[9] Other OLAP tools, such as Data Engine, incorporate fuzzy logic to analyze real-time technical processes.

Intelligent agents represent the growing convergence of various IT tools for working with information. Previously, intelligent agents were considered only within the context of artificial intelligence and were seldom thought to be a part of the data organizing and managing functions in an organization. Today, you can find intelligent agents being used not only for OLAP in a data warehouse environment but also for searching for information on the Web. In Chapter 4, we'll explore artificial intelligence techniques such as intelligent agents.

MULTIDIMENSIONAL ANALYSIS TOOLS *Multidimensional analysis (MDA) tools* are slice-and-dice techniques that allow you to view multidimensional information from different perspectives. For example, if you completed any of the recommended group projects for Chapter 1, you were using spreadsheet software to literally slice and dice the provided information. Within the context of a data warehouse, we refer to this process as "turning the cube." That is, you're essentially turning the cube to view information from different perspectives.

This turning of the cube allows you to quickly see information in different subcubes. If you refer back to the data warehouse in Figure 3.8 on page 142, you'll notice that information by customer segment and timing of advertising is actually hidden. Using MDA tools, you can easily bring this to the front of the data warehouse for viewing. What you've essentially done is to slice the cube vertically by layer and bring some of the background layers to the front. As you do this, the values of the information are not affected.

STATISTICAL TOOLS   Statistical tools help you apply various mathematical models to the information stored in a data warehouse to discover new information. For example, you can perform a time-series analysis to project future trends. You can also perform a regression analysis to determine the effect of one variable on another.

Sega of America, one of the largest publishers of video games, uses a data warehouse and statistical tools to effectively distribute its advertising budget of more than $50 million a year.[10,11] With its data warehouse, product line specialists and marketing strategists "drill" into trends of each retail store chain. Their goal is to find buying trends that will help them better determine which advertising strategies are working best (and at what time of the year) and how to reallocate advertising resources by media, territory, and time. Sega definitely benefits from its data warehouse, and so do retailers such as Toys "Я" Us, Wal-Mart, and Sears—all good examples of customer relationship management through technology.

To learn more about today's best data warehousing and data-mining tools, visit the Web site that supports this text at www.mhhe.com/haag.

DATA MARTS: SMALLER DATA WAREHOUSES

Data warehouses are often perceived as organizationwide, containing summaries of all the information that an organization tracks. However, some people need access to only a portion of that data warehouse information as opposed to all of it. In this case, an organization can create one or more data marts. A ***data mart*** is a subset of a data warehouse in which only a focused portion of the data warehouse information is kept (see Figure 3.10).

Lands' End first created an organizationwide data warehouse for everyone to use, but soon found out that there can be "too much of a good thing."[12] In fact, many Lands' End employees wouldn't use the data warehouse because it was simply too big, too complicated, and included information they didn't need access to. So, Lands' End created several smaller data marts. For example, Lands' End created a data mart just for the merchandising department. That data mart contains only merchandising-specific information and not any information, for instance, that would be unique to the finance department.

Figure 3.10

Data Marts Are Subsets of Data Warehouses

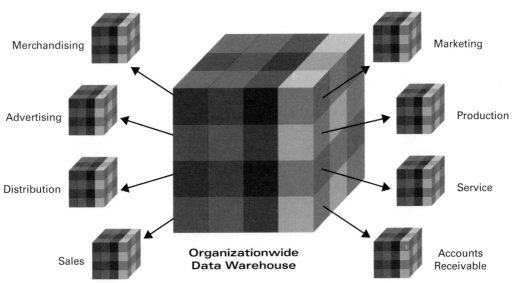

Merchandising

Advertising

Distribution

Sales

Organizationwide Data Warehouse

Marketing

Production

Service

Accounts Receivable

Because of the smaller, more manageable data marts, knowledge workers at Lands' End are making better use of information. If some of your employees don't need access to organizationwide data warehouse information, consider building a smaller data mart for their particular needs.

If you do choose to build smaller data marts for your employees, the data-mining tools are the same. That is, data marts support the use of query-and-reporting tools, intelligent agents, multidimensional analysis tools, and statistical tools. This yields efficiency in an organization with respect to training. Once you've trained your employees to use any or all data-mining tools, they can apply them to an organizationwide data warehouse or smaller data marts.

DATA MINING AS A CAREER OPPORTUNITY

Data mining represents a substantial career opportunity for you, no matter what your career choice. In the business world, you'll face numerous situations in which you need business intelligence to make the right and most effective decisions.

Fortunately, you don't have to be an IT expert to perform data mining. As you'll learn in *Extended Learning Module D* (Decision Analysis with Spreadsheet Software), you can actually use a spreadsheet tool such as Microsoft Excel to build a three-dimensional cube similar to the one in Figure 3.8. You can then use Excel's other decision support features to build a graph, perform a regression analysis, and "turn the cube" by bringing new layers of information forward. You can do the same with Microsoft Access, by building a three-dimensional cube (i.e., data warehouse) of information stored in a database. We definitely recommend that you learn to use these tools and then note your proficiency in your e-portfolio under "Technology Skills."

Beyond personal productivity tools, you should consider learning how to use some data-mining tools specific to the data warehouse environment. Some of the more popular ones include:

HOW UP-TO-DATE SHOULD DATA WAREHOUSE INFORMATION BE?

Information timeliness is a must in a data warehouse—old and obsolete information leads to poor decision making. Below is a list of decision-making processes that people go through for different business environments. For each, specify whether the information in the data warehouse should be updated monthly, weekly, daily, or by the minute. Be prepared to justify your decision.

1. To adjust class sizes in a university registration environment
2. To alert people to changes in weather conditions
3. To predict scores for professional football games
4. To adjust radio advertisements in light of demographic changes
5. To monitor the success of a new product line in the clothing retail industry
6. To adjust production levels of foods in a cafeteria
7. To switch jobs to various printers in a network
8. To adjust CD rates in a bank
9. To adjust forecasted demands of tires in an auto parts store

- Query and Analysis and Enterprise Analytic tools in Business Objects (www.businessobjects.com)
- Business Intelligence and Information Access tools in SAS (www.sas.com)
- ReportNet, PowerPlay, Visualizer, NoticeCast, and DecisionStream tools in Cognos (www.cognos.com)
- PowerAnalyzer tools in Informatica (www.informatica.com)

There are many, many others. You should have a look at your school's catalog of courses in data mining—you may find them offered in the technology department, statistics department, and other departments. We recommend that at the very least you become acquainted with the following: SAS (the leading vendor in statistical software), Cognos (the leading vendor in data warehousing and data-mining tools), and Informatica (the second-leading vendor in data warehousing and data-mining tools).

IMPORTANT CONSIDERATIONS IN USING A DATA WAREHOUSE

As is true with all types of technology, you can't simply implement a data warehouse and use data-mining tools just because they're a "hot" set of technologies and expect automatically to increase your efficiency and effectiveness. Always let your business needs drive your technology decisions. You have to need the technology and the technology has to fit your needs. With respect to data warehouse and data-mining tools, consider your answers to the following questions.

1. **Do you need a data warehouse?** Although great IT tools, they are not necessarily the best technologies for all businesses because (1) they are expensive, (2) they may not be necessary since some businesses can easily extract all the business intelligence they need from databases, and (3) they require extensive and often expensive support.

2. **Do all your employees need an entire data warehouse?** If not, consider building data marts.

3. **How up-to-date must the information be?** To create a data warehouse, you take "snapshots" of database information and load it into a data warehouse. If crucial information changes every second, this may not be possible.

4. **What data-mining tools do you need?** User needs should always drive the answer to this question. Whichever you choose, training will be key. If your users can fully exploit all the features of their chosen data-mining tools, your entire organization will reap the benefits.

Managing the Information Resource

As you prepare to enter today's fast-paced, exciting, and information-based business world, you must be prepared to help your organization manage and organize its information. After all, you will be a knowledge worker—a person who works primarily with information. Your organization will be successful, in part, because of your ability to organize and manage information in a way that best moves the organization toward its goals. We would offer you three important questions to keep in mind. The answers to them are definitely moving targets. As business and technology change, your answers may have to change as well.

WHO SHOULD OVERSEE YOUR ORGANIZATION'S INFORMATION RESOURCE?

Organizations today can have chief executive officers (CEOs), chief operating officers (COOs), and chief financial officers (CFOs), among others. You can also find another title—chief information officer. The *chief information officer (CIO)* is responsible for overseeing an organization's information resource. A CIO's responsibilities may range from approving new development activities for data warehouses and data marts to monitoring the quality and use of information within those data warehouses and data marts.

Two important functions associated with overseeing an organization's information resource are data administration and database administration. *Data administration* is the function in an organization that plans for, oversees the development of, and monitors the information resource. It must be completely in tune with the strategic direction of the organization to assure that all information requirements can and are being met.

Database administration is the function in an organization that is responsible for the more technical and operational aspects of managing the information contained in organizational information repositories (databases, data warehouses, and data marts). Database administration functions include defining and organizing database structures and contents, developing security procedures, developing database and DBMS documentation, approving and monitoring the development of databases and database applications, reporting/rectifying intrusions or operational anomalies, and maintaining overall system integrity.

In large organizations, both administrative functions are usually handled by steering committees rather than by a single individual. These steering committees are responsible for their respective functions and for reporting to the CIO. It's definitely a team effort to manage most organizational resources—information is no different from other assets in that it needs careful oversight and management.

However, in certain ways information is different from many "typical" organizational resources. For example, information is intangible, so it becomes extremely difficult to measure its worth. What dollar value would you attach to a customer record? Realistically, it is impossible to set a precise dollar value on information. So, how can you know how much you should spend on information technology tools? It is a difficult question to answer.

Since information is intangible, it can also be shared by numerous people and not actually be "consumed." Money is different. If you have money in your department budget and spend it on travel, you can't very well use that same money for employee education expenses. In this way, then, the intangibility of information is good because many people can use it without "consuming" it. But as we've alluded to many times, this is also why you have to make special and unique considerations for the security of information that you do not have to make for other organizational resources, such as money. Security is mostly the responsibility of database administration.

IS INFORMATION OWNERSHIP A CONSIDERATION?

Information sharing in your organization means that anyone—regardless of title or department—can access and use whatever information he or she needs. But information sharing brings to light an important question: Does anyone in your organization own any information? In other words, if everyone shares information, who is ultimately responsible for providing that information and assuring the quality of the information? Information ownership is a key consideration in today's information-based business environment. Someone must accept full responsibility for providing specific pieces of information and ensuring the quality of that information. If you find that the wrong information is stored in the organization's data warehouse, you must be able to determine the source of the problem and whose responsibility it is.

This issue of information ownership is similar to other management functions. If you manage a department, you're responsible for the work in that department as well as its expenses and people. The same is true for information. If information originates in your department, you essentially own that information because you're providing it to those who need it and ensuring its quality.

HOW "CLEAN" MUST YOUR INFORMATION BE?

Information "cleanliness" (closely related to information ownership) is an important topic today and will be for many years. Have you ever received the same piece of advertising mail (snail mail, that is) multiple times from the same company on the same day?

CRUD: DEFINING INFORMATION OWNERSHIP

One easy way to determine information ownership is to think in terms of **CRUD**—**c**reate, **r**ead, **u**pdate, and **d**elete. If you can create, update, and/or delete information, then in some way you own that information because you are responsible for its quality.

Here again, let's consider your school as an example and focus on your personal and transcript information. That information includes your student ID, name, address, phone number, GPA, declared major, declared minor (if you have one), and courses completed (this is your transcript).

For each of those pieces, first identify who has create, update, and delete privileges. There may be many individuals or departments that have these sorts of information privileges. If so, who is ultimately responsible for your personal and transcript information? Second, identify all the groups of people at your school who can only view your information.

Many people have, and it's an example of "unclean" information. In this instance, your name may appear twice in a database, once without your middle initial and once with your middle initial. Likewise, your name may appear twice in a database with two different spellings of your last name.

In all popular business-oriented databases and DBMSs, such as Oracle, you can find utilities to help you "clean" your information. In the example above of having your information twice in a database (with different spellings of your last name), the utility would probably determine that the two records actually belong to the same person (you) because of the identical nature of other associated information such as your address and phone number.

In a data warehouse environment, recall that information comes from multiple databases. It becomes even more important then to consolidate and "clean" the information so no duplicate or erroneous information exists in the data warehouse. To accomplish this, you go through *extraction, transformation, and loading (ETL)*. ETL is a process in which you specify what information you want from each database, how that information is to be associated, and what rules to follow in consolidating the information to ensure its cleanliness. You certainly don't want duplicate information weakening the foundation for your business intelligence.

Summary: Student Learning Outcomes Revisited

1. **Describe business intelligence and its role in an organization.** *Business intelligence* is knowledge—knowledge about your customers, your competitors, your partners, your competitive environment, and your own internal operations—that gives you the ability to make effective, important, and often strategic business decisions. Business intelligence is much more than just a list of your products or to whom you've sold them. It would combine your product information perhaps with your advertising strategy information and customer demographics to help you determine the effectiveness of various advertising media on demographic groups segmented by location.

2. **Differentiate between databases and data warehouses with respect to their focus on online transaction processing and online analytical processing.** A *database* is a collection of information that you organize and access according to the logical structure of that information. Databases support both online

transaction processing (OLTP) and online analytical processing (OLAP). Databases that support OLTP are often referred to as *operational databases.* These databases contain detailed information about transactions that have taken place. And using various data manipulation tools, you can query a database to extract meaningful information. A *data warehouse* is a collection of information—gathered from many different operational databases—used to create business intelligence that supports business analysis activities and decision-making tasks. So, data warehouses support only OLAP, not OLTP.

3. **List and describe the key characteristics of a relational database.**   The *relational database model* uses a series of logically related two-dimensional tables or files to store information in the form of a database. Key characteristics include

- A collection of information—Composed of many files or tables of information that are related to each other

- Contain logical structures—You care only about the logical information and not about how it's physically stored or where it's physically located

- Have logical ties among the information—All the files in a database are related in that some primary keys of certain files appear as foreign keys in others

- Possess built-in integrity constraints—When creating the data dictionary for a database, you can specify rules by which the information must be entered (e.g., not blank, etc.)

4. **Define the five software components of a database management system.**   The five software components of a database management system include

- *DBMS engine*—Accepts logical requests from the various other DBMS subsystems, converts them into their physical equivalent, and actually accesses the database and data dictionary as they exist on a storage device

- *Data definition subsystem*—Helps you create and maintain the data dictionary and define the structure of the files in a database

- *Data manipulation subsystem*—Helps you add, change, and delete information in a database and query it for valuable information

- *Application generation subsystem*—Contains facilities to help you develop transaction-intensive applications

- *Data administration subsystem*—Helps you manage the overall database environment by providing facilities for backup and recovery, security management, query optimization, concurrency control, and change management

5. **List and describe the key characteristics of a data warehouse.**   The key characteristics of a data warehouse include

- Multidimensional—While databases store information in two-dimensional tables, data warehouses include layers to represent information according to different dimensions

- Support decision making—Data warehouses, because they contain summarized information, support business activities and decision-making tasks, not transaction processing

6. **Define the four major types of data-mining tools in a data warehouse environment.**   The four major types of data-mining tools in a data warehouse environment include

- *Query-and-reporting tools*—Similar to QBE tools, SQL, and report generators in the typical database environment

- **Intelligent agents**—Utilize various artificial intelligence tools such as neural networks and fuzzy logic to form the basis of "information discovery" and building business intelligence in OLAP

- *Multidimensional analysis (MDA) tools*—Slice-and-dice techniques that allow you to view multidimensional information from different perspectives

- **Statistical tools**—Help you apply various mathematical models to the information stored in a data warehouse to discover new information

7. **List key considerations in managing the information resource in an organization.**   Key considerations in managing the information resource in an organization include these questions:

- Who should oversee the organization's information?

- Is information ownership a consideration?

- How "clean" must your information be?

BEN & JERRY'S, STAPLES, AND BUSINESS INTELLIGENCE

Organizations want information. Organizations need information. However, information must be in an organized format that supports the creation of business intelligence. Otherwise, according to Rebecca Wettemann, Vice President of Research at Nucleus Research, "It's like having a bank account with millions of dollars in it but no ATM card. If you can't get it [business intelligence] and can't make it work for you, then it is not really useful."

In support of creating and using business intelligence, companies have focused much of their spending efforts on business intelligence software and data-mining tools. According to a Merrill Lynch survey in 2003, business intelligence software and data-mining tools were at the top of the technology spending list of CIOs. And according to A. G. Edwards, the market for that type of software is expected to grow from $4.7 billion in 2003 to $7.5 billion in 2006.

Consider two companies—Ben & Jerry's and Staples—and their approach to creating and using business intelligence.

BEN & JERRY'S

Ben & Jerry's, located in Waterbury, Vermont, produces 190,000 pints of ice cream and frozen yogurt daily and ships to over 50,000 grocery stores in the United States and 12 other countries. Every single pint is meticulously tracked, first by being entered into an Oracle database. With that information carefully organized, Ben & Jerry's uses a sophisticated data-mining tool set from a company called Business Objects.

For example, the sales people can easily monitor sales to determine how much ground Cherry Garcia Frozen Yogurt is gaining on Cherry Garcia Ice Cream, its number one selling product. The consumer affairs staff can even correlate each of the several hundred calls and e-mails received each week to the exact pint of ice cream. If complaints are consistent concerning a specific batch, the consumer affairs staff can drill down to the supplier who provided the ingredients such as milk or eggs.

In one particular instance, Ben & Jerry's received a large number of complaints that its Cherry Garcia Ice Cream didn't have enough cherries. The complaints were coming in from all over the country, so it wasn't a regional problem. Employees continued drilling through business intelligence with Business Objects and determined that the manufacturing process (from the supplies of raw materials to the mixing) was satisfactory and had no anomalies. Eventually the problem was determined to be that the ice cream box for Cherry Garcia Ice Cream had on it a photo of frozen yogurt, a product with more cherries than the ice cream. Simply changing the photo on the box solved the problem.

STAPLES

Staples, a $10.7-billion-a-year office-supply chain, extensively uses statistical tools on its data warehouse information to create business intelligence. Alan Gordon, Director of Sales Forecasting, joined the company in 1993 when the company had 150 stores. His charge was to determine where to build new stores. Using a variety of programs from SAS (the leading provider of statistical tools within business intelligence software), Alan created a sophisticated system that evaluates 40 variables, including proximity to competitors and sales tax by zip code. Of the some 4,000 sites that Alan now targets each year, approximately 100 become a new store. That has translated into 950 new stores since his arrival.

Marci Lerner, Staples' Vice President of Finance, also discovered the true value of statistical data-mining tools and business intelligence. Marci decided to use a suite of statistical tools provided by Hyperion Solutions. Using her new business intelligence, Marci gained valuable insights into not only the company's financial situation but also how to display merchandise in the stores.

For example, Marci determined that Staples had been misusing its floor space. Typically, each store devoted a great deal of space to large items such as file cabinets, desks, and other furniture. It made logical sense because bigger items yielded better gross margins than pens and pencils. However, Marci's analysis of Staples' business intelligence pointed out that the costs of storage, distribution, handling, damage, and labor associated with large items made them less profitable than smaller, less space-intensive categories of office supplies. Because of that finding, Staples has decreased its furniture department in most stores, in favor of more room for labels, paper, desk organizers, calendars, and the like. This has helped the company grow its net income to the tune of 12 percent compounded over the last five years.[15,16]

QUESTIONS

1. Ben & Jerry's tracks a wealth of information on each pint of ice cream and frozen yogurt. If you were to design Ben & Jerry's data warehouse, what dimensions of information would you include? As you develop your list of dimensions, consider every facet of Ben & Jerry's business operations, from supply chain management to retail store monitoring.

2. Databases are the underlying technology that allows Ben & Jerry's to track ice cream and frozen yogurt information. Based on your knowledge of databases, what sort of tables or files of information would Ben & Jerry's need in its database? What would be the primary keys for each of those? What would be the foreign keys among those to create the necessary relationships?

3. Marci Lerner, of Staples, used financial business intelligence to determine the best utilization of floor space for product displays and the like. What other business questions and issues can be addressed by looking at financial information within the context of business intelligence? For example, could Marci also use her financial information to determine the optimal distribution lines for moving products to the various stores?

4. Alan Gordon, of Staples, takes into consideration 40 variables to evaluate a potential location for a new store. In this case study, we identified two of those as being proximity to competitors and sales tax by zip code. Make a list of 10 other variables that Alan might also use in his analysis. For each, provide justification.

5. Neil Hastie, CIO at TruServe Corporation, once described most decision making in all types of businesses as "a lot of by-guess and by-golly, a lot of by-gut, and a whole lot of paper reports." That statement is not kind to managers in general or to IT specialists charged with providing the right people with the right technology to make the right decisions. What's the key to turning Neil's statement into a positive one? Is it training? It is providing timely information access? Is it providing everyone with a wide assortment of data-mining tools? Other solutions? Perhaps it's a combination of several answers.

CLOSING CASE STUDY TWO

MINING DINING DATA

Restaurants, fast-food chains, casinos, and others use data warehouses to determine customer purchasing habits and to determine what products and promotions to offer and when to offer them. Some of the leading data warehouse users include AFC Enterprises (operator and franchiser of more than 3,300 Church's Chicken, Popeyes' Chicken and Biscuits, Seattle Coffee Company, Cinnabon, and Torrefazione outlets worldwide); Red Robin International (a 170-unit casual-dining chain); Harrah's Entertainment (owner of 26 U.S. casinos); Pizzeria Uno; and Einstein/Noah Bagel (operator of 428 Einstein's and 111 Noah's New York Bagel stores).

AFC ENTERPRISES

AFC Enterprises cultivates a loyal clientele by slicing and dicing its data warehouse to strategically configure promotions and tailor menus to suit local preferences. AFC's data warehouse helps it better understand its core customers and maximize its overall profitability. AFC tracks customer-specific information from name and address to order history and frequency of visits. This enables AFC to determine exactly which customers are likely to respond to a given promotion on a given day of the week.

AFC also uses its data warehouse to anticipate and manipulate customer behavior. For example, AFC can use its data warehouse to determine that coffee is added to the tab 65 percent of the time when a particular dessert is ordered and 85 percent of the time when that dessert is offered as a promotional item. Knowing that, AFC can run more promotions for certain desserts figuring that customers will respond by ordering more desserts and especially more coffee (coffee is a high-margin item in the restaurant business).

RED ROBIN INTERNATIONAL

Red Robin's terabyte-size data warehouse tracks hundreds of thousands of point-of-sale (POS) transactions, involving millions of menu items and more than 1.5 million invoices. As Howard Jenkins, Red Robin's Vice President of Information Systems, explains it, "With data mining in place, we can ask ourselves, 'If we put the items with high margins in the middle of the menu, do we sell more versus putting it at the top or bottom, [and if so], to whom and where?' We can also tell if something cannibalizes the sale of other items and can give the marketing department an almost instant picture of how promotions are being sold and used."

The placement of items on a menu is strategic business, just as the placement of promotional items in a grocery store can mean increased sales for one item and reduced sales for another. The job of finding the right mix is definitely suited to mining a data warehouse.

Using Cognos Business Intelligence, Red Robin now has measurable results of promotion and menu changes, makes better and more timely decisions, and has realized seven-figure savings in operational costs.

HARRAH'S ENTERTAINMENT

Harrah's Entertainment uses its data warehouse to make decisions for its highly successful Total Gold customer recognition program. Depending on their spending records, Total Gold members can receive free vouchers for dining, entertainment, and sleeping accommodations. Knowing which rewards to give to which customers is key.

John Boushy, Senior Vice President of Entertainment and Technology for Harrah's, says, "We can determine what adds value to each customer and provide that value at the right time." Dining vouchers or free tickets for shows are awarded to day visitors, not sleeping accommodations. Customers who consistently visit a particular restaurant and order higher-end foods receive free dinners and cocktails, not vouchers for free (and cheaper) breakfasts.

PIZZERIA UNO

Pizzeria Uno uses its data warehouse to apply the 80/20 rule. That is, it can determine which 20 percent of its customers contribute to 80 percent of its sales and adjust menus and promotions to suit top patron preferences. These changes can often lead to converting some of the other 80 percent of Pizzeria Uno's customers to the more profitable 20 percent.

EINSTEIN/NOAH BAGEL

Einstein/Noah Bagel uses its data warehouse in real time to maximize cross-selling opportunities. For example, if data warehouse information reveals that a manager in a given store might be missing a cross-selling opportunity on a particular day, an e-mail is automatically sent out to alert managers to the opportunity. Salespeople can then respond by offering the cross-selling opportunity ("How about a cup of hot chocolate with that bagel since it's so cold outside?") to the next customer.[17,18,19]

QUESTIONS

1. Consider the issue of timely information with respect to the businesses discussed in the case. Which of the businesses must have the most up-to-date information in its data warehouse? Which business can have the most out-of-date information in its data warehouse and still be effective? Rank the five businesses discussed with a 1 for the one that needs the most up-to-date information and a 5 for the one that is least sensitive to timeliness of information. Be prepared to justify your rankings.

2. Harrah's Entertainment tracks a wealth of information concerning customer spending habits. If you were to design Harrah's Entertainment's data warehouse, what dimensions of information would you include? As you develop your list of dimensions, consider

every facet of Harrah's business operations, including hotels, restaurants, and gaming casinos.

3. AFC Enterprises includes information in its data warehouse such as customer name and address. Where does it (or could it) gather such information? Think carefully about this, because customers seldom provide their names and addresses when ordering fast food at a Church's or Popeyes. Is AFC gathering information in an ethical fashion? Why or why not?

4. Visit a local grocery store and walk down the breakfast cereal aisle. You should notice something very specific about the positioning of the various breakfast cereals. What is it? On the basis of what information do you think grocery stores determine cereal placement? Could they have determined that information from a data warehouse or from some other source? If another source, what might that source be?

5. Suppose you're opening a pizza parlor in the town where you live. It will be a "take and bake" pizza parlor in which you make pizzas for customers but do not cook them. Customers buy the pizzas uncooked and take them home for baking. You will have no predefined pizza types but will make each pizza to the customer's specifications. What sort of data warehouse would you need to predict the use of toppings by time of day and by day of the week? What would your dimensions of information be? If you wanted to increase the requests for a new topping (such as mandarin oranges), what information would you hope to find in your data warehouse that would enable you to do so?

Key Terms and Concepts

Application generation subsystem, 138
Business intelligence (BI), 126
Chief information officer (CIO), 148
Data administration, 148
Data administration subsystem, 138
Database, 128
Database administration, 148
Database management system (DBMS), 132
Data definition subsystem, 133
Data dictionary, 128
Data manipulation subsystem, 134
Data mart, 145
Data-mining tool, 143
Data warehouse, 142
DBMS engine, 132
Foreign key, 130

Integrity constraint, 131
Logical view, 132
Multidimensional analysis (MDA) tool, 144
Online analytical processing (OLAP), 126
Online transaction processing (OLTP), 126
Operational database, 126
Physical view, 132
Primary key, 130
Query-and-reporting tool, 144
Query-by-example (QBE) tool, 137
Relation, 128
Relational database, 128
Report generator, 136
Structured query language (SQL), 138
View, 135

Short-Answer Questions

1. What is business intelligence? Why is it more than just information?
2. What is online transaction processing (OLTP)?
3. What is online analytical processing (OLAP)?
4. What is the most popular database model?
5. How are primary and foreign keys different?
6. What are the five important software components of a database management system?
7. How are QBE tools and SQL similar? How are they different?

8. What is a data warehouse? How does it differ from a database?
9. What are the four major types of data-mining tools?
10. What is a data mart? How is it similar to a data warehouse?
11. What is the role of a chief information officer (CIO)?

Assignments and Exercises

1. **FINDING "HACKED" DATABASES**   *The Happy Hacker* (www.happyhacker.org/news/newsfeed.shtml) is a Web site devoted to "hacking"—breaking into computer systems. When people hack into a system, they often go after information in databases. There, they can find credit card information and other private and sensitive information. Sometimes, they can even find designs of yet-to-be-released products and other strategic information about a company. Connect to *The Happy Hacker* Web site and find an article that discusses a database that was hacked. Prepare a short report for your class detailing the incident.

2. **DEFINING QUERIES FOR A VIDEO RENTAL STORE**   Consider your local video rental store. It certainly has an operational database to support its online transaction processing (OLTP). The operational database supports such things as adding new customers, renting videos (obviously), ordering videos, and a host of other activities. Now, assume that the video rental store also uses that same database for online analytical processing (OLAP) in the form of creating queries to extract meaningful information. If you were the manager of the video rental store, what kinds of queries would you build? What answers are you hoping to find?

3. **CREATING A QUERY**   On the Web site that supports this text (www.mhhe.com/haag, choose Chapter 3 and then Solomon Enterprises), we've provided the database (in Microsoft Access) we illustrated in this chapter. Connect to the text's Web site and download that database. Now, create three queries using the QBE tool. The first one should extract information from only one file (your choice). The second one should extract information found in at least two files. The third should include some sort of selection criteria. How easy or difficult was it to perform these three queries? Would you say that a DBMS is just as easy to use as something like word processing or spreadsheet software? Why or why not? (By the way, *Extended Learning Module J* takes you through the step-by-step process of creating a query in Access.)

4. **CAREER OPPORTUNITIES IN YOUR MAJOR**   Knowledge workers throughout the business world are building their own desktop databases (often called end-user databases or knowledge worker databases). To do so, they must understand both how to design a database and how to use a desktop DBMS such as Microsoft Access or FileMaker (made by FileMaker). The ability to design a database and use a desktop DBMS offers you a great career advantage. Research your chosen major by looking at job postings (the Web is the best place to start). How many of those jobs want you to have some database knowledge? Do they list a specific DBMS package? What's your take—should you expand your education and learn more about databases and DBMSs? Why or why not?

5. **SALARIES FOR DATABASE ADMINISTRATORS**   Database administrators (DBAs) are among the highest paid professionals in the information technology field. Many people work for 10 to 20 years to get a promotion to DBA. Connect to Monster.com (www.monster.com) or another job database of your choice and search for DBA job openings. As you do, select all locations and job categories and then use "dba" as the keyword search criteria. How many DBA job postings did you find? In what industries were some of the DBA job openings? Read through a couple of the job postings. What was the listed salary range (if any)? What sort of qualifications were listed?

6. Throughout this chapter, we compared the power of databases to spreadsheet software. In many instances, databases provide greater support for enforcing integrity constraints. However, you can achieve some level of enforcing integrity constraints with spreadsheet software. For example, you can specify that entries into a cell or cells must be in a date format. You can also specify a range of values for a numeric field. Start your preferred spreadsheet software and explore some of the features that enable you to enforce integrity constraints. If you're using Excel, click on **Data** and then **Validation**. What integrity constraint features did you find? How would you use them in building a spreadsheet application? What is the role of an **Input Message** and an **Error Alert**?

Discussion Questions

1. Databases and data warehouses clearly make it easier for people to access all kinds of information. This will lead to great debates in the area of privacy. Should organizations be left to police themselves with respect to providing access to information or should the government impose privacy legislation? Answer this question with respect to (1) customer information shared by organizations, (2) employee information shared within a specific organization, and (3) business information available to customers.

2. Business intelligence sounds like a fancy term with a lot of competitive advantage potentially rolled into it. What sort of business intelligence does your school need? Specifically, what business intelligence would it need to predict enrollments in the coming years? What business intelligence would it need to determine what curriculums to offer? Do you think your school gathers and uses this kind of business intelligence? Why or why not?

3. Consider your school's registration database that enforces the following integrity constraint: to enroll in a given class, the student must have completed or currently be enrolled in the listed prerequisite (if any). Your school, in fact, probably does have that integrity constraint in place. How can you get around that integrity constraint and enroll in a class for which you are not taking nor have completed the prerequisite? Is this an instance of when you should be able to override an integrity constraint? What are the downsides to being able to do so?

4. In this chapter, we listed the five important software components of a DBMS: the DBMS engine, the data definition, data manipulation, application generation, and data administration subsystems. Which of those are most and least important to users of a database? Which of those are most and least important to technology specialists who develop data applications? Which of those are most and least important to the chief information officer (CIO)? For each of your responses, provide justification.

5. Some people used to believe that data warehouses would quickly replace databases for both online transaction processing (OLTP) and online analytical processing (OLAP). Of course, they were wrong. Why can data warehouses not replace databases and become "operational data warehouses"? How radically would data warehouses (and their data-mining tools) have to change to become a viable replacement for databases? Would they then essentially become databases that simply supported OLAP? Why or why not?

6. Consider that you work in the human resources management department of a local business and that many of your friends work there. Although you don't personally generate payroll checks, you still have the ability to look up anyone's pay. Would you check on your friends to see if they're earning more money than you? For that matter, would you look up their pay just out of simple curiosity, knowing that you would never do anything with the information or share it with anyone else? Why or why not? People working at the Internal Revenue Service (IRS) were caught just curiously looking up the reported incomes of movie stars and other high-profile public figures. Is this acceptable? Why or why not?

7. As we discussed in the Industry Perspective on page 149, the government is beginning to mandate that organizations turn over sensitive customer information. You've probably also watched a number of movies in which a government made extensive use of personal information. Make a list of movies you've recently seen in which a government uses personal information to monitor the lives of people. What ethical questions do you see? Do you find yourself wanting to protect your personal information from the government after watching any of the movies? Why or why not?

Searching Online Databases and Information Repositories

As you find sites on the Internet that provide information, many of them will do so in the form of a database—a searchable grouping of information that allows you to find specific information by entering key words and key phrases. These words and phrases are, in fact, some sort of key (similar to primary and foreign keys we discussed in this chapter) that are used as matching criteria in a field of the database.

In this section, you'll explore a variety of information topics that you can find on the Internet. To help you, we've included a number of Web sites related to searching online database and information repositories. On the Web site that supports this text (www.mhhe.com/haag), we've provided direct links to all these Web sites as well as many, many more. These are a great starting point for completing this Electronic Commerce section.

FINANCIAL AID RESOURCES

On the Internet, you can find valuable databases that give you access to financial aid resources as you attend school. These resources can be in the form of scholarships—money you don't have to pay back—and standard student loans. And there are a variety of financial aid lenders, ranging from traditional banks, the government, and private parties wanting to give something back to society. Find at least three Web sites that provide a financial aid database and answer the following questions for each.

A. Do you have to register as a user to access information?

B. Do you have to pay a fee to access information?

C. Can you build a profile of yourself and use it as you search?

D. Can you apply for aid while at the site or must you request paper applications that you need to complete and return?

E. By what sort of categories of aid can you search?

LIBRARIES

LEXIS-NEXIS is now completely on the Internet. Many libraries and other such sites even offer full books online for you to read. You may never have to go to a physical library again. Think for a moment about a term paper you're currently writing or may have to write soon. What is the major topic? Now connect to a couple of different library sites and try to find some of the information you'll need. As you do, answer the following questions for each site.

A. What organization supports the site? Is the organization reputable?

B. Do you have to pay a subscription fee to access the information provided?

C. How good are the search capabilities?

D. How can you obtain printed versions of information you find?

E. Is finding information in libraries on the Internet easier or more difficult than finding information in a traditional library?

CONSUMER INFORMATION

Many consumer organizations also provide databases of information on the Internet. At those sites you can read about the latest product reviews, search for new pharmaceuticals that cure diseases (or alleviate symptoms of them), and access safety information for products such as automobiles and children's toys.

Connect to several consumer organization sites and do some digging around. As you do, think about a product you're considering buying or perhaps have just bought. Is the information helpful? Is the information opinion only, completely factual, or a combination of the two? How important will this type of consumer information become as electronic commerce becomes more widespread on the Internet?

DEMOGRAPHICS

For organizations focusing on meeting wants or desires of end consumers, the demographic makeup of the target audience is key. It's simple: The more you know about your target audience, the better equipped you are to develop and market products.

And you can find all sorts of demographic information on the Internet. Connect to a couple of different demographic-related Web sites and see what they have to offer. As you do, answer the following questions for each.

A. Who is the target audience of the site?

B. Who is the provider of the site?

C. Is the provider a private (for-profit) organization or a not-for-profit organization?

D. How often is the demographic information updated?

E. Does the site require that you pay a subscription fee to access its demographic information?

F. How helpful would the information be if you wanted to start a new business or sell various types of products?

REAL ESTATE

You can't actually live on the Internet, although some people may seem as though they want to try. But you can find real estate for sale and rent. You can find sites that take you through a step-by-step process for buying your first home, that provide mortgage and interest rate calculators, that offer financing for your home, and that even offer crime reports by neighborhood. Connect to several real estate–related sites and see what they have to offer. As you do, answer the following questions for each.

A. What is the focus of the site (residential, commercial, rental, and so forth)?

B. Does the site require you to register as a user to access its services?

C. Can you request that e-mail be sent to you when properties in which you are interested become available?

D. How can you search for information (by state, by zip code, by price range, by feature such as swimming pool)?

E. Does the site offer related information such as loans and mortgage calculators?

EXTENDED LEARNING MODULE C

DESIGNING DATABASES AND ENTITY-RELATIONSHIP DIAGRAMMING

Student Learning Outcomes

1. IDENTIFY HOW DATABASES AND SPREADSHEETS ARE BOTH SIMILAR AND DIFFERENT.

2. LIST AND DESCRIBE THE FOUR STEPS IN DESIGNING AND BUILDING A RELATIONAL DATABASE.

3. DEFINE THE CONCEPTS OF ENTITY CLASS, INSTANCE, PRIMARY KEY, AND FOREIGN KEY.

4. GIVEN A SMALL OPERATING ENVIRONMENT, BUILD AN ENTITY-RELATIONSHIP (E-R) DIAGRAM.

5. LIST AND DESCRIBE THE STEPS IN NORMALIZATION.

6. DESCRIBE THE PROCESS OF CREATING AN INTERSECTION RELATION TO REMOVE A MANY-TO-MANY RELATIONSHIP.

Introduction

As you learned in Chapter 3, databases are quite powerful and can aid your organization in both transaction and analytical processing. But you must carefully design and build a database for it to be effective. Relational databases are similar to spreadsheets in that you maintain information in two-dimensional files. In a spreadsheet, you place information in a cell (the intersection of a row and column). To use the information in a cell, you must know its row number and column character. For example, cell C4 is in column C and row 4.

Databases are similar and different. You still create rows and columns of information. However, you don't need to know the physical location of the information you want to see or use. For example, if cell C4 in your spreadsheet contained sales for Able Electronics (one of your customers), to use that information in a formula or function, you would reference its physical location (C4). In a database, you simply need to know you want *sales* for *Able Electronics*. Its physical location is irrelevant. That's why we say that a ***database*** is a collection of information that you organize and access according to the logical structure of that information.

So, you do need to design your databases carefully for effective utilization. In this module, we'll take you through the process of designing and building a relational database, the most popular of all database types. A ***relational database*** uses a series of logically related two-dimensional tables or files to store information in the form of a database. There are well-defined rules to follow, and you need to be aware of them.

As far as implementation is concerned, you then just choose the DBMS package of your choice, define the tables or files, determine the relationships among them, and start entering information. We won't deal with the actual implementation in this module. However, we do show you how to implement a database using Microsoft Access in *Extended Learning Module J*.

Once you've implemented your database, you can then change the information as you wish, add rows of information (and delete others), add new tables, and use simple but powerful reporting and querying tools to extract the exact information you need.

Designing and Building a Relational Database

Using a database amounts to more than just using various DBMS tools. You must also know *how* to actually design and build a database. So, let's take a look at how you would go about designing a database. The four primary steps include

1. Defining entity classes and primary keys.
2. Defining relationships among entity classes.
3. Defining information (fields) for each relation (the term *relation* is often used to refer to a file while designing a database).
4. Using a data definition language to create your database.

Let's continue with the example database we introduced you to in Chapter 3, that of Solomon Enterprises. Solomon Enterprises specializes in providing concrete to commercial builders and individual home owners in the greater Chicago area. On page 130 (Figure 3.3) in Chapter 3, we provided a graphical depiction of some of the tables in

Solomon's database, including *Customer, Concrete Type, Order, Truck,* and *Employee*. As you recall, an order is created when a customer calls in for the delivery of a certain concrete type. Once the concrete is mixed, Solomon has an employee drive the truck to the customer's location. That illustrates how you can use a database in support of your customer relationship management initiative and order-processing function.

In this module, we want to design and model the supply chain management side for Solomon Enterprises. Figure C.1 contains a supply chain management report that Solomon frequently generates. Let's make some observations.

Figure C.1

A Supply Chain Management Report for Solomon Enterprises

SOLOMON ENTERPRISES
Supply Report Ending October 14, 2005

Concrete		Raw Material				Supplier	
Type	Name	ID	Name	Unit	QOH	ID	Nane
1	Home	B	Cement paste	1	400	412	Wesley Enterprises
		C	Sand	2	1200	444	Juniper Sand & Gravel
		A	Water	1.5	9999	999	N/A
			TOTAL:	4.5			
2	Comm	B	Cement paste	1	400	412	Wesley Enterprises
		C	Sand	2	1200	444	Juniper Sand & Gravel
		A	Water	1	9999	999	N/A
			TOTAL:	4			
3	Speckled	B	Cement paste	1	400	412	Wesley Enterprises
		C	Sand	2	1200	444	Juniper Sand & Gravel
		A	Water	1.5	9999	999	N/A
		D	Gravel	3	200	444	Juniper Sand & Gravel
			TOTAL:	7.5			
4	Marble	B	Cement paste	1	400	412	Wesley Enterprises
		C	Sand	2	1200	444	Juniper Sand & Gravel
		A	Water	1.5	9999	999	N/A
		E	Marble	2	100	499	A&J Brothers
			TOTAL:	6.5			
5	Shell	B	Cement paste	1	400	412	Wesley Enterprises
		C	Sand	2	1200	444	Juniper Sand & Gravel
		A	Water	1.5	9999	999	N/A
		F	Shell	2.5	25	499	A&J Brothers
			TOTAL:	7			

- Solomon provides five concrete types: 1—home foundation and walkways; 2—commercial foundation and infrastructure; 3—premier speckled (with gravel); 4—premier marble; 5—premier shell.
- Solomon uses six raw materials: A—water; B—cement paste; C—sand; D—gravel; E—marble; F—shell.
- Mixing instructions are for a cubic yard. For example, one cubic yard of commercial concrete requires 1 part cement paste, 2 parts sand, and 1 part water. The terms "part" and "unit" are synonymous.
- Some raw materials are used in several concrete types. Any given concrete type requires several raw materials.
- QOH (quantity on hand) denotes the amount of inventory for a given raw material.
- Suppliers provide raw materials. For a given raw material, Solomon uses only one supplier. A given supplier can provide many different raw materials.
- QOH and supplier information are not tracked for water (for obvious reasons). However, Solomon places the value 9999 in the QOH for water and uses 999 for the ID of the supplier.

When you begin to think about designing a database application, you first need to capture your business rules. Business rules are statements concerning the information you need to work with and the relationships within the information. These business rules will help you define the correct structure of your database. From the report in Figure C.1 and the observations above, we derived the following business rules.

1. A given concrete type will have many raw materials in it.
2. A given raw material may appear in many types of concrete.
3. Each raw material has one and only one supplier.
4. A supplier may provide many raw materials. Although not displayed in Figure C.1, Solomon may have a supplier in its database that doesn't currently provide any raw materials.

Before you begin the process of designing a database, it's important that you first capture and understand the business rules. These business rules will help you define the correct structure of your database.

STEP 1: DEFINING ENTITY CLASSES AND PRIMARY KEYS

The first step in designing a relational database is to define the various entity classes and the primary keys that uniquely define each record or instance within each entity class. An *entity class* is a concept—typically people, places, or things—about which you wish to store information and that you can identify with a unique key (called a primary key). A *primary key* is a field (or group of fields in some cases) that uniquely describes each record. Within the context of database design, we often refer to a record as an instance. An *instance* is an occurrence of an entity class that can be uniquely described with a primary key.

From the supply chain management report in Figure C.1, you can easily identify the entity classes of *Concrete Type, Raw Material,* and *Supplier.* Now, you have to identify their primary keys. For most entity classes, you cannot use names as primary keys because duplicate names can exist. For example, your school provides you with a unique student ID and uses that ID as your primary key instead of your name (because other students may have the same name as you).

DEFINING ENTITY CLASSES AND PRIMARY KEYS

Learning how to design a relational database really requires that you roll up your sleeves and practice, practice, practice. To help with this, you'll be designing a relational database that might be used at your school while we go carefully through the process of designing the relational database for Solomon Enterprises' supply chain management function. Below is a description of a hypothetical relational database that might be used at your school.

In conjunction with taking an introductory computer concepts course, your school has decided to test the idea of offering weekend seminars to cover the basics of the Internet and the Web. Initially, your school will offer two such seminars: Web101—The Basics of the Web and Internet; and Web205—Building a Web Site. Web101 will have five different sections, and Web205 will have four different sections.

Although they are not required to, students can enroll in one or both seminars. The seminars are held for eight hours on a single day. There is no cost associated with taking the seminars. One teacher, from a pool of qualified teachers, will be assigned to each section of each seminar. Some teachers will obviously not be assigned to teach any sections, and some teachers may be assigned to several different sections.

Finally, the system should track the final grades assigned to each student. One more thing. Your school is simply testing this idea in this particular term. So, don't worry about the term (e.g., Fall, Winter, Spring, or Summer) or the year.

For this particular scenario, you are to create a simple two-column table that lists all the entity classes in the left column and their associated primary keys in the right column. Finally, record as many business rules as you can find provided in the description.

From the report, you can see that the entity class *Concrete Type* includes two pieces of information—*Concrete Type* and a name or *Type Description*. Although *Type Description* is unique, the logical choice for the primary key is *Concrete Type* (e.g., 1 for home, 2 for commercial, and so on). Notice that the primary key name is the same as the entity class name. This is perfectly acceptable; if it is a potential point of confusion for you, change the primary key name to something like *Concrete Type ID* or *Concrete Type Identifier*. For our purposes, we'll use *Concrete Type* as the primary key name.

If you consider *Raw Material* as an entity class, you'll find several pieces of information including *Raw Material ID*, *Raw Material Name*, and *QOH*. The logical choice for a primary key here is *Raw Material ID* (e.g., A for water, B for cement paste, and so on). Although *Raw Material Name* is unique, we still suggest that you not use names.

Likewise, if you consider *Supplier* as an entity class, you'll find two pieces of information: *Supplier ID* and *Supplier Name*. Again, we recommend that you use *Supplier ID* as the primary key.

STEP 2: DEFINING RELATIONSHIPS AMONG THE ENTITY CLASSES

The next step in designing a relational database is to define the relationships among the entity classes. To help you do this, we'll use an entity-relationship diagram. An ***entity-relationship (E-R) diagram*** is a graphic method of representing entity classes and their relationships. An E-R diagram includes five basic symbols:

1. A rectangle to denote an entity class
2. A dotted line connecting entity classes to denote a relationship

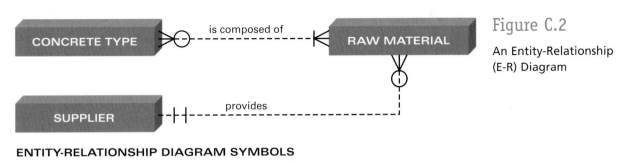

Figure C.2

An Entity-Relationship
(E-R) Diagram

ENTITY-RELATIONSHIP DIAGRAM SYMBOLS

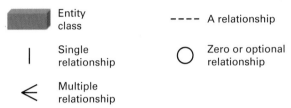

Entity
class

\- - - - A relationship

| Single
relationship

○ Zero or optional
relationship

⟨ Multiple
relationship

3. A | to denote a single relationship

4. A 0 to denote a zero or optional relationship

5. A crow's foot (shown as <) to denote a multiple relationship

To use these symbols, you must first decide among which entity classes relationships exist. If you determine that two particular entity classes have a relationship, you simply draw a dotted line to connect them and then write some sort of verb that describes the relationship.

In Figure C.2, you can see the E-R diagram for the supply chain management side of Solomon's database. To determine where the relationships exist, simply ask some questions and review your business rules. For example, is there a relationship between concrete type and raw material? The answer is yes because raw materials are used in mixing the various concrete types. Likewise, the raw materials are provided by suppliers (another relationship). However, there is no logical relationship between concrete type and supplier. So, we drew dotted lines between *Concrete Type* and *Raw Material* and between *Raw Material* and *Supplier*. We then added some verbs to describe the relationships. For example, a *Concrete Type* is composed of *Raw Material,* and a *Supplier* provides a *Raw Material.*

It should also make sense (both business and logical) when you read the relationships in reverse. To do this, simply flip the location of the nouns in the sentence and change the verb accordingly. For example,

- *Concrete Type–Raw Material:* A *Concrete Type* is composed of *Raw Material.*
- *Raw Material–Concrete Type:* A *Raw Material* is used to create a *Concrete Type.*
- *Supplier–Raw Material:* A *Supplier* provides a *Raw Material.*
- *Raw Material–Supplier:* A *Raw Material* is provided by a *Supplier.*

Each of the preceding statements makes logical sense, follows the relationships we identify in Figure C.2, and reflects the business rules listed on page 163. Again, we stress the importance of using business rules. Technology (databases, in this instance) is a set of tools that you use to process information. So, your implementations of technology should match the way your business works. If you always start by defining business rules and using those rules as guides, your technology implementations will most likely mirror how your business works. And that's the way it should be.

DEFINING RELATIONSHIPS AMONG ENTITY CLASSES

Let's continue exploring how to design a relational database for your school and its offering of weekend seminars. If your group correctly completed the tasks in the Team Work on page 164, you know that there are four entity classes. They include (along with their primary keys):

Entity Class	Primary Key
Seminar	Seminar 3-character identifier and number (e.g., Web101 and Web205)
Seminar Section	Seminar 3-character identifier, number, and section number (e.g., Web101-1 through Web101-5 and Web205-1 through Web205-4)
Student	Student ID (whatever your school happens to use)
Qualified Teacher	Teacher ID (your school may use social security number)

Now your task is to define among which of those entity classes relationships exist and then write some verbs that describe each relationship just as we did in Figure C.2. We've drawn rectangles for each of the four entity classes. Connect the rectangles with dotted lines where relationships exist and write the appropriate verbs to describe the relationships.

Seminar

Seminar Section

Qualified Teacher

Student

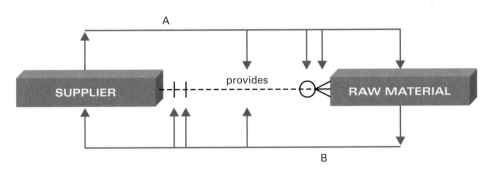

Figure C.3

Reading an Entity-
Relationship (E-R)
Diagram

Once you determine that a relationship does exist, you must then determine the numerical nature of the relationship, what we refer to as "minimum and maximum cardinality." To describe this, you use a | to denote a single relationship, a 0 to denote a zero or optional relationship, and/or a crow's foot (<) to denote a multiple relationship. By way of illustration, let's consider the portion of your E-R diagram in Figure C.3. To help you read the symbols and diagram, we've added blue lines and arrows. Following the line marked A, you would read the E-R diagram as:

"A *Supplier* may not provide any *Raw Material* (denoted with the 0) but may provide more than one *Raw Material* (denoted with the crow's foot)."

So, that part of the E-R diagram states that the logical relationship between *Supplier* and *Raw Material* is that a *Supplier* may provide no *Raw Material* currently in inventory but may provide more than one *Raw Material* currently in inventory. This is exactly what business rule 4 (on page 163) states.

Following the blue line marked B, you would read the E-R diagram as:

"A *Raw Material* must be provided by a *Supplier* and can only be provided by one *Supplier*."

That statement again reinforces business rule 4.

Similarly, you can also develop statements that describe the numerical relationships between *Concrete Type* and *Raw Material* based on that part of the E-R diagram in Figure C.2. Those numerical relationships would be as follows:

- A *Concrete Type* is composed of more than one *Raw Material* and must be composed of at least one *Raw Material*.
- A *Raw Material* can be used to create more than one *Concrete Type* but is not required to be used to create any *Concrete Type*.

Again, these statements reinforce business rules 1 and 2 on page 163.

To properly develop the numerical relationships (cardinality) among entity classes, you must clearly understand the business situation at hand. That's why it's so important to write down all the business rules.

DEFINING THE CARDINALITY AMONG ENTITY CLASSES

As we continue with the design of the relational database at your school, it's time to define the cardinality among the entity classes. If you correctly completed the Team Work project on page 166, the relationships among the entity classes are as follows.

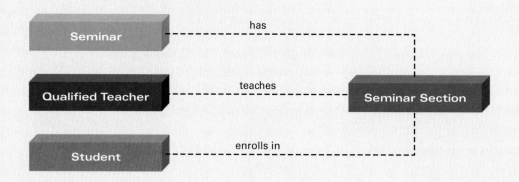

Your task is to create the numerical relationships by adding the symbols of |, O, and crow's foot in the appropriate places. Once you do, complete the table that follows by providing a narrative description of each numerical relationship.

Relationship	Narrative Description
Seminar–Seminar Section	
Seminar Section–Seminar	
Qualified Teacher–Seminar Section	
Seminar Section–Qualified Teacher	
Student–Seminar Section	
Seminar Section–Student	

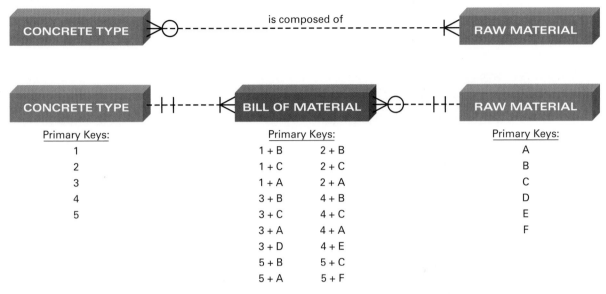

Figure C.4

Creating an Intersection Relation to Remove a Many-to-Many Relationship

After developing the initial E-R diagram, it's time to begin the process of normalization. **Normalization** is a process of assuring that a relational database structure can be implemented as a series of two-dimensional relations (remember: relations are the same as files or tables). The complete normalization process is extensive and quite necessary for developing organizationwide databases. For our purposes, we will focus on the following three rules of normalization:

1. Eliminate repeating groups or many-to-many relationships.
2. Assure that each field in a relation depends only on the primary key for that relation.
3. Remove all derived fields from the relations.

The first rule of normalization states that no repeating groups or many-to-many relationships can exist among the entity classes. You can find these many-to-many relationships by simply looking at your E-R diagram and note any relationships that have a crow's foot on each end. If you look back at Figure C.2 on page 165, you'll see that a crow's foot is on each end of the relationship between *Concrete Type* and *Raw Material*. Let's look at how to eliminate it.

In Figure C.4, we've developed the appropriate relationships between *Concrete Type* and *Raw Material* by removing the many-to-many relationship. Notice that we started with the original portion of the E-R diagram and created a new relation between *Concrete Type* and *Raw Material* called *Bill of Material*, which is an intersection relation. An **intersection relation** (sometimes called a **composite relation**) is a relation you create to eliminate a many-to-many relationship. It's called an intersection relation because it represents an intersection of the primary keys between the first two relations. That is, an intersection relation will have a **composite primary key** that consists of the primary key fields from the two intersecting relations. The primary key fields from the two original relations now become foreign keys in the intersection relation. A **foreign key** is a primary key of one file (relation) that appears in another file (relation). When combined, these two foreign keys make up the composite primary key for the intersection relation.

Figure C.5

The Completed E-R
Diagram for the Supply
Chain Management Side
of Solomon's Database

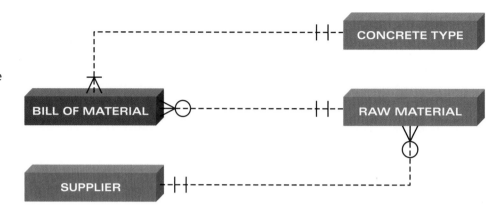

For Solomon's supply chain management portion of its database, the intersection relation *Bill of Material* represents the combination of raw materials that go into each concrete type. Listed on the next page is how you would read the relationships between *Concrete Type* and *Bill of Material* and *Raw Material* and *Bill of Material* (see Figure C.5).

- *Concrete Type–Bill of Material*

  From left to right: A *Concrete Type* can have multiple listings of *Raw Material* in *Bill of Material* and must have a listing of *Raw Material* in *Bill of Material*.

  From right to left: A *Concrete Type* found in *Bill of Material* must be found and can be found only one time in *Concrete Type*.

- *Raw Material–Bill of Material*

  From left to right: A *Raw Material* can be found in many *Bill of Material* listings but may not be found in any *Bill of Material* listing.

  From right to left: A *Raw Material* found in *Bill of Material* must be found and can be found only one time in *Raw Material*.

If you compare the E-R diagram in Figure C.5 to the E-R diagram in Figure C.2, you'll notice that they are very similar. The only difference is that the E-R diagram in Figure C.5 contains an intersection relation to eliminate the many-to-many relationship between *Concrete Type* and *Raw Material*.

And removing many-to-many relationships is the most difficult aspect when designing the appropriate structure of a relational database. If you do find a many-to-many relationship, here are some guidelines for creating an intersection relation:

1. Just as we did in Figure C.4, start by drawing the part of the E-R diagram that contains a many-to-many relationship at the top of a piece of paper.
2. Underneath each relation for which the many-to-many relationship exists, write down some of the primary keys.
3. Create a new E-R diagram (showing no cardinality) with the original two relations on each end and a new one (the intersection relation) in the middle.
4. Underneath the intersection relation, write down some of the composite primary keys (these will be composed of the primary keys from the other two relations).
5. Create a meaningful name (e.g., *Bill of Material*) for the intersection relation.
6. Move the minimum cardinality appearing next to the left relation just to the right of the intersection relation.

CREATING AN INTERSECTION RELATION

Back to work on the project for your school. If you completed the Team Work project on page 168, you are now able to identify a many-to-many relationship between *Student* and *Seminar Section.* That is, a given *Seminar Section* may have many *Students,* and a given *Student* can enroll in many different *Seminar Sections* (two, to be exact). So, that portion of your E-R diagram looks like what follows.

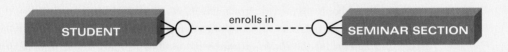

Your task is to eliminate the above many-to-many relationship by creating an intersection relation. As you do, we would encourage you to follow the guidelines given on this page and the previous. What did you name the intersection relation? What does the completed E-R diagram look like?

7. Move the minimum cardinality appearing next to the right relation just to the left of the intersection relation.

8. The maximum cardinality on both sides of the intersection relations will always be "many" (the crow's foot).

9. As a general rule, the new minimum and maximum cardinalities for the two original relations will be one and one.

We would stress again that removing many-to-many relationships is the most difficult aspect when designing the appropriate structure of a relational database.

And the business world is full of many-to-many relationships that must be eliminated before an organization can correctly implement a relational database. Let's talk through another example of a many-to-many relationship to help you better understand how to eliminate them. Consider that Solomon sometimes has to use more than one truck to make a delivery of concrete to a customer. That is, what if—given that a truck can carry at most 8 cubic yards of concrete—Triple A Homes asks for 12 cubic yards of premier marble for a given delivery. In that case, Solomon would have two choices for modeling and storing multiple trucks for the order. First, it could create two separate orders, one for 8 cubic yards of premier marble concrete and the other for 4 cubic yards of premier marble concrete. That option doesn't make business sense—when a customer places an order, then the entire order should be contained in only *one* order, not two.

The second choice—which is the correct one—is to have the ability to specify multiple trucks on a single order. In that case, Solomon would have a many-to-many relationship between *Order* and *Truck.* That is, the revised business rule would be that an *Order* can have multiple *Trucks* assigned to make the delivery and a *Truck* can be assigned to make a delivery on multiple *Orders.*

But it doesn't stop there. Solomon may wish to sometimes send two employees in one truck to deliver one order of concrete. Then, Solomon would need the ability to specify more than one employee per delivery truck.

As you can see, the business world is complex and full of many-to-many relationships. If you can master the art and science of eliminating many-to-many relationships in a database environment, you have created a substantial career opportunity for yourself.

STEP 3: DEFINING INFORMATION (FIELDS) FOR EACH RELATION

Once you've completed steps 1 and 2, you must define the various pieces of information that each relation will contain. Your goal in this step is to make sure that the information in each relation is indeed in the correct relation and that the information cannot be derived from other information—the second and third rules of normalization.

In Figure C.6, we've developed a view of the relational database for Solomon based on the new E-R diagram with the intersection relation. To make sure that each piece of information is in the correct relation, look at each and ask, "Does this piece of information depend only on the primary key for this relation?" If the answer is yes, the information is in the correct relation. If the answer is no, the information is in the wrong relation.

Let's consider the *Raw Material* relation. The primary key is *Raw Material ID,* so each piece of information must depend only on *Raw Material ID.* Does *Raw Material Name* depend on *Raw Material ID?* Yes, because the name of a raw material depends on that particular raw material (as does *QOH* or quantity on hand). Does *Supplier ID* depend only on *Raw Material ID?* Yes, because the particular supplier providing a raw material depends on which raw material you're describing. In fact, *Supplier ID* in the *Raw Material* relation is a foreign key. That is, it is a primary key of one relation (*Supplier*) that appears in another relation (*Raw Material*).

What about *Supplier Name* in the *Raw Material* relation? Does it depend only on *Raw Material ID?* The answer here is no. *Supplier Name* depends only on *Supplier ID.* So, now the question becomes, "In which relation should *Supplier Name* appear?" The answer is in the *Supplier* relation, because *Supplier Name* depends on the primary key (*Supplier ID*) for that relation. Therefore, *Supplier Name* should appear in the *Supplier* relation (as it does) and not in the *Raw Material* relation.

Now, take a look at the intersection relation *Bill of Material.* Notice that it includes the field called *Unit. Unit* is located in this relation because it depends on two things: the concrete type you're describing and the raw material in it. So, *Unit* does depend completely on the composite primary key of *Concrete Type + Raw Material ID* in the *Bill of Material relation.*

If you follow this line of questioning for each relation, you'll find that all other fields are in their correct relations. Now you have to look at each field to see whether you can derive it from other information. If you can, the derived information should not be stored in your database. When we speak of "derived" in this instance, we're referring to information that you can mathematically derive: counts, totals, averages, and the like. Currently, you are storing the raw material total (*Raw Material Total*) in the *Concrete Type* relation. Can you derive that information from other information? The answer is yes—all you have to do is sum the *Units* in the *Bill of Material* relation for a given *Concrete Type.* So, you should not store *Raw Material Total* in your database (anywhere).

CONCRETE TYPE RELATION

Concrete Type	Type Description	Raw Material Total
1	Home foundation and walkways	4.5
2	Commercial foundation and infrastructure	4
3	Premier speckled (with smooth gravel aggregate)	7.5
4	Premier marble (with crushed marble aggregate)	6.5
5	Premier shell (with shell aggregate)	7

RAW MATERIAL RELATION

Raw Material ID	Raw Material Name	QOH	Supplier ID	Supplier Name
A	Water	9999	999	N/A
B	Cement paste	400	412	Wesley Enterprises
C	Sand	1200	499	A&J Brothers
D	Gravel	200	499	A&J Brothers
E	Marble	100	444	Juniper Sand & Gravel
F	Shell	25	444	Juniper Sand & Gravel

SUPPLIER RELATION

Supplier ID	Supplier Name
412	Wesley Enterprises
499	A&J Brothers
444	Juniper Sand & Gravel
999	N/A

BILL OF MATERIAL RELATION

Concrete Type	Raw Material ID	Unit
1	B	1
1	C	2
1	A	1.5
2	B	1
2	C	2
2	A	1
3	B	1
3	C	2
3	A	1.5
3	D	3
4	B	1
4	C	2
4	A	1.5
4	E	2
5	B	1
5	C	2
5	A	1.5
5	F	2.5

Unit belongs in this relation because it depends on a combination of how much of a given raw material *(Raw Material ID)* goes into each type of concrete type *(Concrete Type)*.

Figure C.6

A First Look at the Relations for the Supply Chain Management Side of Solomon's Database

CONCRETE TYPE RELATION

Concrete Type	Type Description
1	Home foundation and walkways
2	Commercial foundation and infrastructure
3	Premier speckled (with smooth gravel aggregate)
4	Premier marble (with crushed marble aggregate)
5	Premier shell (with shell aggregate)

RAW MATERIAL RELATION

Raw Material ID	Raw Material Name	QOH	Supplier ID
A	Water	9999	999
B	Cement paste	400	412
C	Sand	1200	444
D	Gravel	200	444
E	Marble	100	499
F	Shell	25	499

SUPPLIER RELATION

Supplier ID	Supplier Name
412	Wesley Enterprises
499	A&J Brothers
444	Juniper Sand & Gravel
999	N/A

BILL OF MATERIAL RELATION

Concrete Type	Raw Material ID	Unit
1	B	1
1	C	2
1	A	1.5
2	B	1
2	C	2
2	A	1
3	B	1
3	C	2
3	A	1.5
3	D	3
4	B	1
4	C	2
4	A	1.5
4	E	2
5	B	1
5	C	2
5	A	1.5
5	F	2.5

Unit belongs in this relation because it depends on a combination of how much of a given raw material *(Raw Material ID)* goes into each type of concrete type *(Concrete Type).*

Figure C.7

The Correct Structure of the Supply Chain Management Side of Solomon's

Once you've completed step 3, you've completely and correctly defined the structure of your database and identified the information each relation should contain. Figure C.7 shows your database and the information in each relation. Notice that we have removed *Supplier Name* from the *Raw Material* relation and that we have removed *Raw Material Total* from the *Concrete Type* relation.

CREATING THE FINAL STRUCTURE FOR YOUR SCHOOL

Now it's time for you to fly solo and try a task by yourself. If your group successfully completed the Team Work project on page 171, you should have a relational database model with five relations: *Seminar, Seminar Section, Student, Qualified Teacher,* and *Seminar Section Class Roll.* The first four you identified early on. The last one is the result of eliminating the many-to-many relationship between *Seminar Section* and *Student.* We named this intersection relation *Seminar Section Class Roll.* We did so because it represents a list of students enrolling in all of the sections. If you group those students by section, then you get class rolls.

Your task is to complete a table for each relation. We've provided a sample table below. That is, you must first fill in the column headings by identifying what information belongs in each relation. Be sure to follow steps 2 and 3 of normalization. Then, we encourage you to add in some actual data entries.

A word of caution. You could easily identify hundreds of pieces of information that need to be present in this database. For *Qualified Teacher,* for example, you could include birth date, rank, office hours, phone number, e-mail address, office location, employment starting date, and many more. Here, simply identify no more than five key pieces of information for each relation. And, by all means, identify the primary and foreign keys for each relation.

Seminar Relation

STEP 4: USING A DATA DEFINITION LANGUAGE TO CREATE YOUR DATABASE

The final step in developing a relational database is to take the structure you created in steps 1 and 3 and use a data definition language to actually create the relations. Data definition languages are found within a database management system. A **database management system (DBMS)** helps you specify the logical organization for a database and access and use the information within the database. To use a data definition language, you need the data dictionary for your complete database. Recall from Chapter 3 that the **data dictionary** contains the logical structure for the information in a database. Throughout this module and in the first part of Chapter 3, we provided you with the overall structure of Solomon's complete database including the relations of *Order, Truck, Customer, Employee, Concrete Type, Raw Material, Supplier,* and *Bill of Material.*

This is the point at which we'll end this extended learning module. But you shouldn't stop learning. We've written *Extended Learning Module J* to take you through the process of using a data definition language in Access to create the database for Solomon Enterprises. To help you implement this database, we've provided its complete structure and data dictionary on the Web site that supports this text (www.mhhe.com/haag, select "Solomon Enterprises").

Summary: Student Learning Outcomes Revisited

1. **Identify how databases and spreadsheets are both similar and different.** Databases and spreadsheets are similar in that they both store information in two-dimensional files. They are different in one key aspect: physical versus logical. Spreadsheets require that you know the physical location of information, by row number and column character. Databases, on the other hand, require that you know logically what information you want. For example, in a database environment you could easily request total sales for Able Electronics, and you would receive that information. In a spreadsheet, you would have to know the physical location—by row number and column character—of that information.

2. **List and describe the four steps in designing and building a relational database.** The four steps in designing and building a relational database include

   1. Defining entity classes and primary keys
   2. Defining relationships among entity classes
   3. Defining information (fields) for each relation
   4. Using a data definition language to create your database

3. **Define the concepts of entity class, instance, primary key, and foreign key.** An *entity class* is a concept—typically people, places, or things—about which you wish to store information and that you can identify with a unique key (called a primary key). A *primary key* is a field (or group of fields in some cases) that uniquely describes each record. Within the context of database design, we often refer to a record as an instance. An *instance* is an occurrence of an entity class that can be uniquely described. To provide logical relationships among various entity classes, you use *foreign keys*—primary keys of one file (relation) that also appear in another file (relation).

4. **Given a small operating environment, build an entity-relationship (E-R) diagram.** Building an entity-relationship (E-R) diagram starts with knowing and understanding the business rules that govern the situation. These rules will help you identify entity classes, primary keys, and relationships. You then follow the process of · normalization, eliminating many-to-many relationships, assuring that each field is in the correct relation, and removing any derived fields.

5. **List and describe the steps in normalization.** *Normalization* is the process of assuring that a relational database structure can be implemented as a series of two-dimensional tables. The normalization steps include

   1. Eliminate repeating groups or many-to-many relationships
   2. Assure that each field in a relation depends only on the primary key for that relation
   3. Remove all derived fields from the relations

6. **Describe the process of creating an intersection relation to remove a many-to-many relationship.** To create an intersection relation to remove a many-to-many relationship, follow these steps:

   1. Draw the part of the E-R diagram that contains a many-to-many relationship
   2. Create a new E-R diagram with the original two relations on each end and a new one (the intersection relation) in the middle
   3. Create a meaningful name for the intersection relation
   4. Move the minimum cardinality appearing next to the left relation just to the right of the intersection relation
   5. Move the minimum cardinality appearing next to the right relation just to the left of the intersection relation
   6. The maximum cardinality on both sides of the intersection relation will always be "many"
   7. As a general rule, the new minimum and maximum cardinalities for the two original relations will be one and one

Key Terms and Concepts

Composite primary key, 169
Database, 161
Database management system (DBMS), 175
Data dictionary, 175
Entity class, 163
Entity-relationship (E-R) diagram, 164
Foreign key, 169

Instance, 163
Intersection relation (composite relation), 169
Normalization, 169
Primary key, 163
Relational database, 161

Short-Answer Questions

1. How are relational databases and spreadsheets both similar and different?
2. What is a database?
3. What are the four steps in designing and building a relational database?
4. What are some examples of entity classes at your school?
5. What is the role of a primary key?
6. What is an entity-relationship (E-R) diagram?
7. How do business rules help you define minimum and maximum cardinality?
8. What is normalization?
9. What are the three major rules of normalization?
10. What is an intersection relation? Why is it important in designing a relational database?
11. Why must you remove derived information from a database?
12. What is a database management system (DBMS)?

Assignments and Exercises

1. **DEFINING ENTITY CLASSES FOR THE MUSIC INDUSTRY** The music industry tracks and uses all sorts of information related to numerous entity classes. Find a music CD and carefully review the entire contents of the jacket. List as many entity classes as you can find (for just that CD). Now, go to a music store and pick out a CD for a completely different music genre and read its jacket. Did you find any new entity classes? If so, what are they?

2. **DEFINING BUSINESS RULES FOR A VIDEO RENTAL STORE** Think about how your local video rental store works. There are many customers, renting many videos, and many videos sit on the shelves unrented. Customers can rent many videos at one time. And some videos are so popular that the video rental store keeps many copies. Write down all the various business rules that define how a video rental store works with respect to entity classes and their relationships.

3. **CREATING AN E-R DIAGRAM FOR A VIDEO RENTAL STORE** After completing assignment 2 above, draw the initial E-R diagram based on the rules you defined. Don't worry about going through the process of normalization at this point. Simply identify the appropriate relationships among the entity classes and define the minimum and maximum cardinality of each relationship. By the way, how many many-to-many relationships did you define?

4. **ELIMINATING A MANY-TO-MANY RELATIONSHIP** Consider the following situation. At a small auto parts store, customers can buy many parts. And the same part can be bought by many different customers. That's an example of a many-to-many relationship. How would you eliminate it? What would you call the intersection relation? This one is particularly tough: You'll have to actually create two intersection relations to model this correctly.

5. **DEFINING THE CARDINALITY AMONG TWO ENTITY CLASSES** Consider the two entity classes of *Student* and *Advisor* at your school. How would you build an E-R diagram to show the relationship between these two entity classes? What is the minimum and maximum cardinality of the relationship?

CHAPTER FOUR OUTLINE

STUDENT LEARNING OUTCOMES

1. Define decision support system, list its components, and identify the type of applications it's suited to.

2. Define geographic information systems and state how they differ from other decision support tools.

3. Define artificial intelligence and list the different types that are used in business.

4. Define expert systems and describe the types of problems to which they are applicable.

5. Define neural networks, their uses, and a major strength and weakness of these AI systems.

6. Define genetic algorithms and list the concepts on which they are based and the types of problems they solve.

7. Define intelligent agents, list the four types, and identify the types of problems they solve.

CHAPTER FOUR

Decision Support and Artificial Intelligence
Brainpower for Your Business

OPENING CASE STUDY:
A DSS TO KEEP AUTO WORKERS' HEALTH UP AND COSTS DOWN

If you were asked whether General Motors (GM) spends more money on steel or health care, what would your answer be? If you said steel, you'd be wrong. It's actually health care for autoworkers. In 2002, GM spent $4.5 billion and together the Big Three spent $8.4 billion to provide the most comprehensive health coverage in the world, an advantage that U.S. autoworkers have been enjoying for decades. In fact, GM is the largest private buyer of health care in the world with 127 carriers that include HMOs and other insurers, who in turn have major contracts with national hospital and pharmacy chains.

Experts say that part of the reason for the continued migration of auto industry jobs overseas is the comparatively high cost to the auto manufacturing industry of health care for their employees. Auto manufacturers based abroad that compete with U.S. auto manufacturers have the advantage of having their governments help pay the health care tab. GM pays about $1,360 per vehicle for health care and retirees' pensions compared to only $107 per American-built Honda.

While information technology can't reverse the 7 percent annual increase that GM has been experiencing in the cost of health care, it can help slow the escalation. Using decision support systems (DSSs) and data warehouses, managers can sift through cost information, insurance claims, and health care providers. IT can help in all aspects of health care from picking the plans that will be made available to employees to evaluating the health care they receive.

Even for an individual with three or four alternatives, picking a health care plan is daunting. GM, by comparison, has hundreds of vendors with many, many plans each. And GM workers are not a homogeneous group. Their needs vary depending on their age, medical history, and where they live. The GM decision support system estimates costs before they are incurred, and evaluates after the fact how well the money was spent. For example, the DSS compares each patient's diagnosis with the treatment that was prescribed by the doctor. Prescribing an inappropriate drug is surely a sign of poor medical advice, and using an expensive drug when a considerably cheaper generic is available indicates inflated charges. With all this information and the analysis that the OLAP (online analytical processing) system provides, GM can judge which providers are the best.

Combining health care information and worker productivity, GM can correlate absenteeism with specific medical problems. Then, the company can analyze the total cost of health problems and the benefit of health care measures, like "wellness" programs. Furthermore, GM can calculate the return on investment (ROI) of these programs. This is especially important in the auto industry since many employees remain with the company for the duration of their working lives. Identifying what jobs exacerbate or cause specific maladies can help to head off trouble and expense. For example, people with carpel tunnel syndrome shouldn't work at jobs that require repetitive wrist motion for long periods.[1]

Introduction

The objective of decision support systems is to help you analyze information to find business intelligence, which, as you learned in Chapters 2 and 3, is the extraction of the true meaning of information so that you can take creative and powerful steps to ensure a competitive advantage. In the opening case study, you learned how General Motors (GM) uses a decision support system to get the best health care for its auto workers at the best price. GM gathers information and analyzes it to generate business intelligence, and then makes decisions based on this business intelligence.

In this chapter we'll investigate the tools that IT can provide to help you to transform business information into business intelligence and make good decisions. According to *Management Review*, the big winners in tomorrow's business race will be those organizations that are "big of brain and small of mass."[2]

For many years, computers have been crunching numbers faster and more accurately than people can. A computer can unerringly calculate a payroll for 1,000 people in the time it takes a pencil to fall from your desk to the floor. Because of IT, knowledge workers have been freed from much of the drudgery of manually handling day-to-day transactions. And now, IT power is augmenting brainpower and thought processes in ways previously seen only in science fiction. In some cases, IT power is actually *replacing* human brainpower to a limited degree.

Businesses, like individuals, use brainpower to make decisions, some big, some small, some relatively simple, and some very complex. As an effective knowledge worker, you'll have to make decisions on issues such as whether to expand the workforce, extend business hours, use different raw materials, or start a new product line. IT can help you in most, if not all, of these decisions. The extended brainpower that IT offers you as a decision maker comes in the form of decision support systems and artificial intelligence.

Whether to use a decision support system or some form of artificial intelligence depends on the type of decision you have to make and how you plan to go about making it. So let's first look at different types of decisions and the process you go through to make a decision. Then we'll discuss decision support systems and artificial intelligence—IT brainpower (see Figure 4.1). To learn even more about decision support systems and artificial intelligence, visit the Web site that supports this text at www.mhhe.com/haag.

Figure 4.1

The Two Categories of Computer-Aided Decision Support

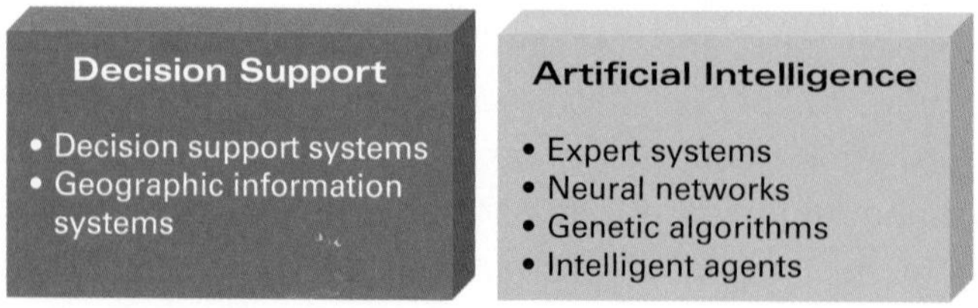

Decision Support

- Decision support systems
- Geographic information systems

Artificial Intelligence

- Expert systems
- Neural networks
- Genetic algorithms
- Intelligent agents

Decisions, Decisions, Decisions

You make many decisions every day from the simplest to the very complex. For example, you may want to make a decision on what mozzarella cheese to buy based on cost. Contrast that decision with the one where you try to decide which job offer to take. Choosing the right job is definitely a more complex decision because it has multiple decision criteria, not all of which are quantifiable. Therefore, it's much more difficult to select the "best" of the alternatives.

Decision making is one of the most significant and important activities in business. Organizations devote vast resources of time and money to the process. In this section, we'll consider the phases of decision making and different decision types to help you better understand how IT can benefit that process.

HOW YOU MAKE A DECISION

In business, decision making has four distinct phases (see Figure 4.2).[3] These four phases are as follows:

1. **Intelligence** (find what to fix): Find or recognize a problem, need, or opportunity (also called the diagnostic phase of decision making). The intelligence phase involves detecting and interpreting signs that indicate a situation which needs your attention. These "signs" come in many forms: consistent customer requests for new-product features, the threat of new competition, declining sales, rising costs, an offer from a company to handle your distribution needs, and so on.

2. **Design** (find fixes): Consider possible ways of solving the problem, filling the need, or taking advantage of the opportunity. In this phase, you develop all the possible solutions you can.

3. **Choice** (pick a fix): Examine and weigh the merits of each solution, estimate the consequences of each, and choose the best one (which may be to do nothing at all). The "best" solution may depend on such factors as cost, ease of implementation, staffing requirements, and timing. This is the prescriptive phase of decision making—it's the stage at which a course of action is prescribed.

4. **Implementation** (apply the fix): Carry out the chosen solution, monitor the results, and make adjustments as necessary. Simply implementing a solution is seldom enough. Your chosen solution will always need fine-tuning, especially for complex problems or changing environments.

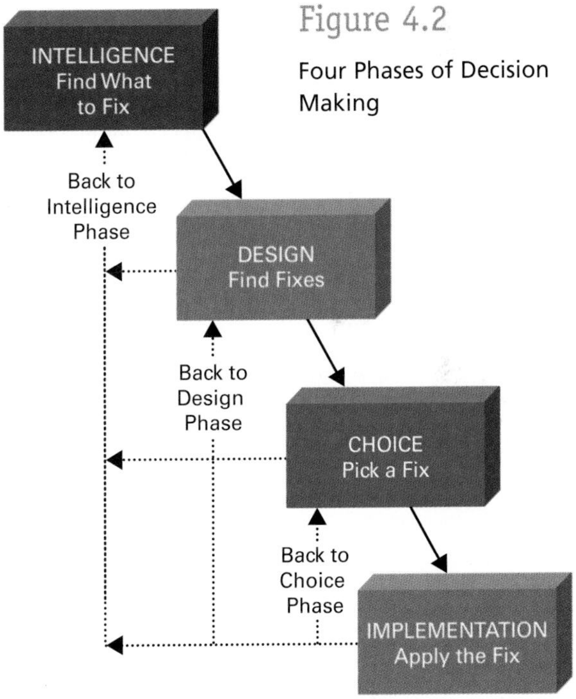

Figure 4.2

Four Phases of Decision Making

INTELLIGENCE
Find What to Fix

Back to Intelligence Phase

DESIGN
Find Fixes

Back to Design Phase

CHOICE
Pick a Fix

Back to Choice Phase

IMPLEMENTATION
Apply the Fix

This four-phase process is not necessarily linear: You'll often find it useful or necessary to cycle back to an earlier phase. When choosing an alternative in the choice phase, for example, you might become aware of another possible solution. Then you would go back to the design phase, include the newly found solution, return to the choice phase, and compare the new solution to the others you generated.

TYPES OF DECISIONS YOU FACE

It's pretty clear that deciding which cheese to buy when you want the cheapest is a decision with a simple comparison that leads to a correct answer. Thus, it is an example of a structured decision, whereas choosing the right job is an example of a decision with nonstructured and structured elements. That is, some parts are quantifiable and some are not.

A ***structured decision*** involves processing a certain kind of information in a specified way so that you will always get the right answer. No "feel" or intuition is necessary. These are the kinds of decisions that you can program—if you use a certain set of inputs and process them in a precise way, you'll arrive at the correct result. Calculating gross pay for hourly workers is an example. You can easily automate these types of structured decisions with IT.

A ***nonstructured decision*** is one for which there may be several "right" answers, and there is no precise way to get a right answer. No rules or criteria exist that guarantee you a good solution. Deciding whether to introduce a new product line, employ a new marketing campaign, or change the corporate image are all examples of decisions with nonstructured elements.

In reality, most decisions fall somewhere between structured and nonstructured. The job choice decision is an example (see Figure 4.3). In choosing the right job, the salary part of the decision is structured, whereas the other criteria involve nonstructured aspects (for example, your perception of which job has the best advancement opportunity). Stock market investment analysis is another example of "somewhere in between" because you can calculate financial ratios and use past performance indicators. However, you still have to consider nonstructured aspects of the companies, such as projected prime interest rate, unemployment rates, and competition.

Another way to view decisions is by the frequency with which the decision has to be made. The decision as to which job to take is the sort of decision you don't make on a regular basis; this is a nonrecurring, or ad hoc, decision. On the other hand, determining pay for hourly employees is a routine decision that businesses face periodically. Therefore, determining gross pay for hourly employees is a recurring decision.

A ***recurring decision*** is one that happens repeatedly, and often periodically, whether weekly, monthly, quarterly, or yearly. You'll usually use the same set of rules each time. When you calculate pay for hourly employees, the calculation is always the same regardless of the employee or time period. A ***nonrecurring,*** or ***ad hoc, decision*** is one that you make infrequently (perhaps only once), and you may even have different criteria for determining the best solution each time. A company merger is an example. These don't happen often, although they are becoming more frequent. And if the managers of a company need to make the merger decision more than once, they will most likely have to evaluate a different set of criteria each time. The criteria depend on the needs of the companies considering the merger, the comparability of their products and services, their debt structure, and so on.

Figure 4.3

Viewing Structured versus Nonstructured Decision Making as a Continuum

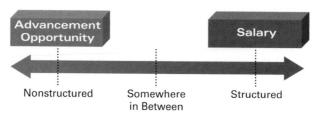

MESSING WITH "GEORGIA HOME BOY"

On a Saturday night in the emergency ward of a large city hospital, two young men brought in an unconscious young woman. Having told the medical staff on duty that the young woman had been "messing with 'Georgia Home Boy,'" they left. The health care workers didn't know what that meant. Was it a fight, had she been assaulted, or was it something else? It turns out that she had taken an illegal drug.

Fortunately for the young woman, this hospital had a DSS that includes a searchable database of more than 4,000 slang street drug terms that allows medical personnel to quickly determine the medical term that corresponds to the street name. The underlying database, which can be accessed using a notebook computer or a hand-held device, has more than 70 slang terms for am-

phetamines and more than 130 common street names for crack cocaine.

In our case of the young woman, the drug was Gamma Hydroxybutyic Acid, or GHB—"Georgia Home Boy"—an illegal drug that gives the user a sense of euphoria and intoxication. When this drug is mixed with alcohol, the result can be respiratory distress and coma. Because their DSS gave them speedy access to the name of the drug, along with its symptoms, likely uses or misuses (for example, use with alcohol), the ER staff could quickly determine the best treatment. With this DSS, the medical staff has a system that can save precious seconds in deciding how best to help patients—seconds that can save lives.[4]

Decision Support Systems

In Chapter 3, you saw how data mining can help you make business decisions by giving you the ability to slice and dice your way through massive amounts of information. Actually, a data warehouse with data mining tools is a form of decision support. The term *decision support system,* used broadly, means any computerized system that helps you make decisions. However, there's also a more restrictive definition. It's rather like the term *medicine.* Medicine can mean the whole health care industry or it can mean cough syrup, depending on the context.

Narrowly defined, a **decision support system (DSS)** is a highly flexible and interactive IT system that is designed to support decision making when the problem is not structured. A DSS is an alliance between you, the decision maker, and specialized support provided by IT (see Figure 4.4). IT brings speed, vast amounts of information, and

What You Bring	Advantages of a DSS	What IT Brings
Experience	Increased productivity	Speed
Intuition	Increased understanding	Information
Judgment	Increased speed	Processing capabilities
Knowledge	Increased flexibility	
	Reduced problem complexity	
	Reduced cost	

Figure 4.4

The Alliance between You and a Decision Support System

sophisticated processing capabilities to help you create information useful in making a decision. You bring know-how in the form of your experience, intuition, judgment, and knowledge of the relevant factors. IT provides great power, but you—as the decision maker—must know what kinds of questions to ask of the information and how to process the information to get those questions answered. In fact, the primary objective of a DSS is to improve your effectiveness as a decision maker by providing you with assistance that will complement your insights. This union of your know-how and IT power helps you generate business intelligence so that you can quickly respond to changes in the marketplace and manage resources in the most effective and efficient ways possible. Following are some examples of the varied applications of DSSs:

- A national insurance company uses a DSS to analyze its risk exposure when insuring drivers with histories of driving under the influence. The DSS revealed that married male homeowners in their forties with one DUI conviction were rarely repeat offenders. By lowering its rates to this group the company increased it market share without increasing its risk exposure.[5]

- Burlington Northern and Santa Fe (BNSF) railroad regularly tests the rails its trains ride on to prevent accidents. Worn out or defective rails result in hundreds of derailments every year, so it's important to address the problem. Using a decision support system to schedule rail testing, BNSF decreased its rail-caused derailments by 33 percent in 2000, while the other three large railroad companies had a 16 percent rise in such accidents.[6]

- Customer relationship management (CRM), as you saw in Chapter 2, is an important part of any successful company's strategy. Decision support is an important part of CRM. On Wall Street, retail brokerage companies analyze customers' behaviors and goals with decision support, which highlights opportunities and alerts brokers to beginning problems.[7]

COMPONENTS OF A DECISION SUPPORT SYSTEM

DSSs vary greatly in application and complexity, but they all share specific features. A typical DSS has three components (see below and Figure 4.5): model management, data management, and user interface management.

Before we look at these three components individually, let's get a quick overview of how they work together. When you begin your analysis, you tell the DSS, using the user interface management component, which model (in the model management component) to use on what information (in the data management component). The model requests the information from the data management component, analyzes that information, and sends the result to the user interface management component, which in turn passes the results back to you (see Figure 4.5). Here's an example of a decision support system at Lands' End clothing business.

- *Model management:* The DSS at Lands' End has to have models to analyze information. The models create new information that decision makers need to plan product lines and inventory levels. For example, Lands' End uses a statistical model called regression analysis to determine trends in customer buying patterns and forecasting models to predict sales levels.

- *Data management:* The DSS's data management component stores Lands' End's customer and product information. In addition to this organizational information, the company also needs external information, such as demographic information and industry and style trend information.

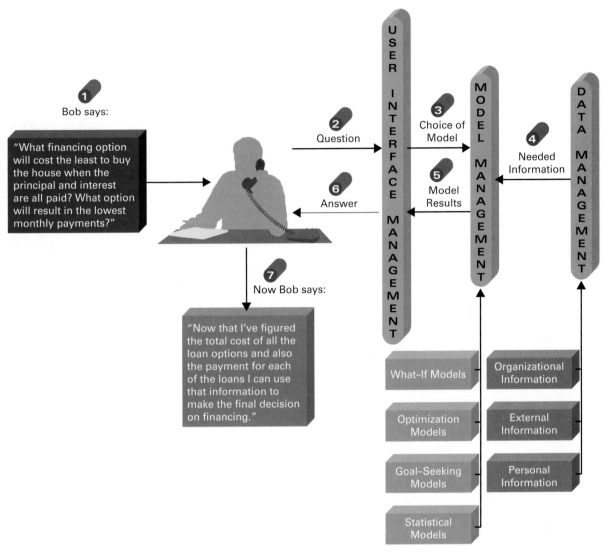

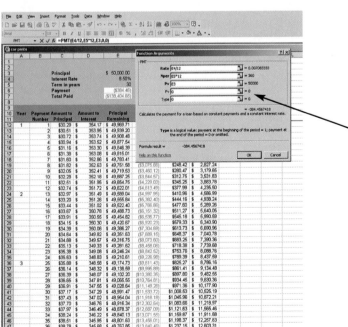

The PMT function calculates the monthly payment on the mortgage. The Rate (interest rate) is usually quoted as an annual rate so you have to divide by 12 to get the monthly rate. Similarly, the NPER (number of periods) is in years so you have to multiply by 12 for monthly payments.

Figure 4.5

Components of a Decision Support System

- *User interface management:* A user interface enables Lands' End decision makers to access information and specify the models they want to use to create the information they need.

Now we'll examine the three DSS components in more general terms.

MODEL MANAGEMENT COMPONENT   The *model management* component consists of both the DSS models and the DSS model management system. A model is a representation of some event, fact, or situation. Businesses use models to represent variables and their relationships. For example, you would use a statistical model called analysis of variance to determine whether newspaper, television, and billboard advertising are equally effective in increasing sales. DSSs help in various decision-making situations by utilizing models that allow you to analyze information in many different ways. The models you use in a DSS depend on the decision you're making and, consequently, the kind of analysis you require. For example, you would use what-if analysis to see what effect the change of one or more variables will have on other variables, or optimization to find the most profitable solution given operating restrictions and limited resources. You can use spreadsheet software such as Excel to create a simple DSS for what-if analysis. Figure 4.5 (on the previous page) has an example of a spreadsheet DSS you might build to compare how much you'd pay for a house at different interest rates and payback periods.

The model management system stores and maintains the DSS's models. Its function of managing models is similar to that of a database management system. The model management component can't select the best model for you to use for a particular problem—that requires your expertise—but it can help you create and manipulate models quickly and easily.

DATA MANAGEMENT COMPONENT   The *data management* component performs the function of storing and maintaining the information that you want your DSS to use. The data management component, therefore, consists of both the DSS information and the DSS database management system. The information you use in your DSS comes from one or more of three sources:

1. *Organizational information:* You may want to use virtually any information available in the organization for your DSS. You can design your DSS to access this information directly from your company's databases and data warehouses.
2. *External information:* Some decisions require input from external sources of information. Various branches of the federal government, Dow Jones, and the Internet, to mention just a few, can provide additional information for use with a DSS.
3. *Personal information:* You can incorporate your own insights and experience—your personal information—into your DSS.

USER INTERFACE MANAGEMENT COMPONENT   The *user interface management* component allows you to communicate with the DSS. It consists of the user interface and the user interface management system. This is the component that allows you to combine your know-how with the storage and processing capabilities of the computer. The user interface is the part of the system you see; through it you enter information, commands, and models. If you have a DSS with a poorly designed user interface—if it's too rigid or too cumbersome to use—you simply won't use it no matter what its capabilities. The best user interface uses your terminology and methods and is flexible, consistent, simple, and adaptable.

PROFITING BY HELPING PRESERVE THE ENVIRONMENT

Kappa Packaging, based in Holland, is a company that turns waste paper into cardboard. The company has 17 paper and board mills across Europe. Each mill has a giant multimillion-pound paper machine that converts pulp into reels of paper for board-making.

When it first goes into this paper machine, the pulp is 99 percent water that is progressively squeezed out by passing the pulp over a series of about 20 mesh screening belts. These belts are varyingly made from stainless steel, polypropylene, and polyethylene and cost over $20,000 each. So you would think that with 17 branches all doing the same job, Kappa would be able to get a good price on volume purchases of the belts. That's what Kappa thought too. The big obstacle was that each plant had its own preferences as to types of belts and suppliers.

Kappa developed a DSS to analyze information on all the combinations of belts used by plants and the suppliers they liked, along with the prices and options available. Each plant was asked to identify which belts it was buying from which suppliers and to specify an acceptable alternative for each belt.

Kappa then fed all this information into its DSS with the intention of reducing the overall number of belt types as much as possible. Thus, Kappa had business intelligence, which it used to negotiate a deal with suppliers to minimize costs by maximizing-volume discounts for the belts. The end result was an annual saving of over $500,000 per year. In terms of the highly competitive commodity cardboard market, this is a huge advantage for Kappa.[8]

Geographic Information Systems

In 1992, Hurricane Andrew attacked the east coast of the United States leaving devastation throughout several states in its wake. One of the places hardest hit was Miami, Florida, where the hurricane came on land smashing businesses and private buildings and causing billions of dollars in damage. Reporters at the *Miami Herald* believed that not all the damage was due to Andrew. They hypothesized that at least some of the harm was a result of shoddy construction of homes built after 1980.

Four months after Hurricane Andrew, the paper ran a series of reports and used geographic information system maps to make its point. A *geographic information system (GIS)* is a decision support system designed specifically to analyze spatial information. Spatial information is any information that can be shown in map form, such as roads, the distribution of the bald eagle population, sewer systems, or the path of a hurricane.

The *Miami Herald* plotted the arrival point of the hurricane where winds were strongest and charted the progress of Andrew inland, where it lost some of its initial punch. Then the reporters plotted the damaged houses with one dot representing 10 homes. These dots were color-coded to show level of damage—blue showed 10 repairable homes and orange dots represented 10 destroyed homes. When the two maps were laid over each other, it was clear that the wind strength did not match up with damage as it should have. That is, the reporters showed that Hurricane Andrew alone was not responsible for all the devastation. The net result was that building codes in Dade County were tightened so that contractors had to use more nails and install stronger windows, doors, and shutters on homes. The *Miami Herald* received the Pulitzer Prize for its investigative work.

Businesses use GIS software too to analyze information, generate business intelligence, and make decisions. GIS is a powerful combination of database and graphics technology. There is virtually no limit to the sort of information you can plot with a GIS,

Figure 4.6

San Diego Shown in
ArcExplorer 2, GIS
Software from ESRI[9]

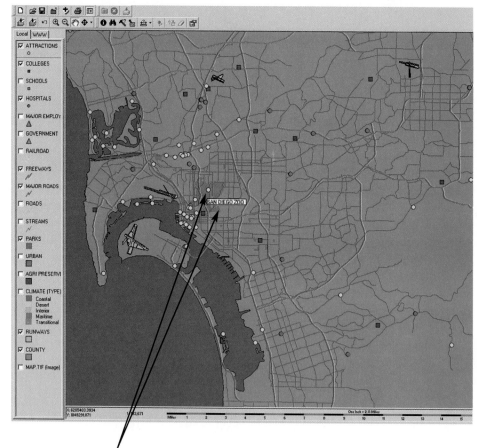

The ArcExplorer software allows you to choose which
features you want to view. The Active Theme, which in this
case is ATTRACTIONS, allows you to see the name of
attraction by placing the cursor on the symbol.

including the placement of roads, rivers, income levels, health conditions, areas of high
or low crime, and so on. Of course, you can do this with paper maps too. The strength
of an electronic GIS is in the ability you get to layer information with a mouse click.

Figure 4.6 is a map of San Diego shown in ESRI's ArcExplorer 2 GIS software. On
the left-hand side you can see the layers (or type of information) that can be shown on
the map. In our figure we have shown the *Attractions, Colleges, Hospitals, Freeways,
Major Roads, Parks,* and *Runways.* Each type of information has its own symbol and is
called a *theme.* When a theme is active, as *Attractions* is in our example, and you move
the cursor over the little yellow circle, you can see the name of the attraction—in our
case, the San Diego Zoo.

This is an example of the feature of GIS software that represents information themat-
ically (i.e., in map or theme form). With themes, you can show the layers in combination
as we did in our example and as the *Miami Herald* reporters did for Hurricane Andrew.
You can represent either statistical information, such as the average salary of homeowners, or point information, such as the location of a bank's customers.

When businesses use GIS software to generate maps showing information of interest
to them, we call it *business geography.* You can find a wealth of information to incorporate into your GIS from various sources. For example, the U.S. Census Bureau has a vast
database of demographic information and the Bureau of Labor Statistics has employ-

ment information. Both of these would be statistical information. In the private sector, many research companies would be happy to sell you consumer habit information.

Studies show that how information is presented significantly impacts the effectiveness and efficiency of the decision-making process.[10] Here are other examples of GISs in use:

- Clean Harbor is the company that hauled away potentially anthrax-tainted debris from the offices of the NCB during the anthrax scare of 2001. Since hazardous waste removal is such a dangerous job, the company had to keep track of the shipment every minute. Clean Harbor used software that incorporated a GIS map and GPS information to monitor the trucks along their journey.[11]

- Branson, Missouri, is a small town in the Ozark Mountains that boasts more than two dozen theaters offering 75 performances per day to the 5 to 7 million visitors the town hosts every year. The town's motto is "the show must go on." But the show can't go on without electricity. The White River Valley Electric Cooperative (WRVEC) that supplies power to the area has a Web-based GIS where employees can access all the information they need, such as the precise location of poles, meters, transformers, capacitors, and underground facilities.[12]

Artificial Intelligence

DSSs and GISs are IT systems that augment business brainpower. IT can further expand business brainpower by means of artificial intelligence—the techniques and software that enable computers to mimic human behavior in various ways. Financial analysts use a variety of artificial intelligence systems to manage assets, invest in the stock market, and perform other financial operations.[13] Hospitals use artificial intelligence in many capacities, from scheduling staff, to assigning beds to patients, to diagnosing and treating illness. Many government agencies use artificial intelligence, including the IRS and the armed forces. Credit card companies use artificial intelligence to detect credit card fraud, and insurance companies use artificial intelligence to spot fraudulent claims.[14] Artificial intelligence lends itself to tasks as diverse as airline ticket pricing, food preparation, oil exploration, and child protection. It is widely used in the insurance, meteorology, engineering, and aerospace industries and by the military. It was artificial intelligence that guided cruise missiles during the Gulf War in 1991.[15]

Artificial intelligence (AI) is the science of making machines imitate human thinking and behavior. For example, an expert system is an artificial intelligence system that makes computers capable of reasoning through a problem to reach a conclusion. We use the process of reasoning to find out, from what we already know, something that we don't know.

Today computers can see, hear, smell, and, important for business, think (in a manner of speaking). Robots are a well-known form of AI. A *robot* is a mechanical device equipped with simulated human senses and the capability of taking action on its own (in contrast to a mechanical device such as an automobile, which requires direction from the driver for its every action). Robots are in use in many industries. For example, Piedmont Hospital's Pharmacy Dosage Dispenser is a robotic prescription-filling system. Using bar code technology, this pharmaceutical robot receives medication orders online, retrieves prepackaged doses of drugs, and sends them to hospital patients.[16] One of the most exciting new areas of research in robotics is the development of microrobots that can be introduced into human veins and arteries to perform surgery.

A recent U.S. Commerce Department survey reported that 70 percent of the top 500 companies use artificial intelligence as part of decision support, and the sale of artificial intelligence software is rapidly approaching the $1 billion mark. The AI systems that businesses use most can be classified into the following major categories:

- *Expert systems,* which reason through problems and offer advice in the form of a conclusion or recommendation.
- *Neural networks,* which can be "trained" to recognize patterns.
- *Genetic algorithms,* which can generate increasingly better solutions to problems by generating many, many solutions, choosing the best ones, and using those to generate even better solutions.
- *Intelligent agents,* which are adaptive systems that work independently, carrying out specific, repetitive, or predictable tasks.

Expert Systems

Suppose you own a real estate business, and you generate more than 40 percent of your revenue from appraising commercial real estate. Consider further that only one person in your firm is capable of performing these appraisals. What if that person were to quit? How do you replace that expertise? How fast can you find someone else? How much business would you lose if it took you a month to find a suitable replacement?

In business, people are valuable because they perform important business tasks. Many of these business tasks require expertise, and people often carry expertise in their heads—and often that's the only place it can be found in the organization. AI can provide you with an expert system that can capture expertise, thus making it available to those who are not experts so that they can use it, either to solve a problem or to learn how to solve a problem.

An **expert system,** also called a **knowledge-based system,** is an artificial intelligence system that applies reasoning capabilities to reach a conclusion. Expert systems are excellent for diagnostic and prescriptive problems. Diagnostic problems are those requiring an answer to the question, "What's wrong?" and correspond to the intelligence phase of decision making. Prescriptive problems are those that require an answer to the question, "What to do?" and correspond to the choice phase of decision making.

An expert system is usually built for a specific application area called a *domain.* You can find expert systems in the following domains:

- *Accounting*—for auditing, tax planning, management consulting, and training.
- *Medicine*—to prescribe antibiotics where many considerations must be taken into account (such as the patient's medical history, the source of the infection, and the price of available drugs).
- *Process control*—to control offset lithographic printing, for example.
- *Human resource management*—to help personnel managers determine whether they are in compliance with an array of federal employment laws.
- *Financial management*—to identify delinquency-prone accounts in the loan departments of banks.
- *Production*—to guide the manufacture of all sorts of products, such as aircraft parts.
- *Forestry management*—to help with harvesting timber on forest lands.

AN EXPERT SYSTEM TO HAUL FREIGHT AROUND NORTH AMERICA

Would you like to be in charge of getting 50,000 shipments of heavy freight on 2,100 trucks to 200 locations across 25 U.S. states and Canada every 12 hours with your boss demanding that you do it as fast and as cheaply as possible? Never mind all the customer requests for service that keep coming in while you're trying to deal with the set you started with. Then there are road conditions and other considerations, for example, ice and snow somewhere causing traffic to be diverted. While you're thinking about your problems and how to solve them, the trucks and drivers are standing idle in the depots waiting for orders on when to move out and where to go.

This is exactly how the dispatchers of Con-Way Central Express's line-haul company operated for years and years. It was a case of working feverishly from clock-in to clock-out. The eight dispatchers were constantly shouting at each other questions like "Have you got anyone in your area who can divert to Indianapolis for two units?" If not, a driver would have to make a trip of 130 miles that wouldn't generate any revenue.

People at Con-Way realized that there must be a better way to go. So they hired YaFeng Du, a former Chinese army rocket scientist and industrial engineer, to develop an expert system to help with their gargantuan task. YaFeng figured it would take six months, but he told his boss a year to give himself some wiggle room. In fact it ended up taking five years and $3 million.

The dispatchers, who were the domain experts, worked hard and long to help YaFeng understand how they did their jobs and what they had learned from years of on-the-job training. The system expanded to thousands of rules that had to be developed and tested. Since it sometimes took more than a month for a problem to surface, such as that on a certain route a driver would be stranded so far from home he was unable to make it home by the end of the shift, the testing process was grueling.

Despite the rocky road to the end product, all agree that it was worth it. Now, instead of frantically trying to make up schedules based only on experience and what seemed right at the time, the expert system provides a routing plan for 95 percent of the shipments in seven minutes. The dispatchers then use their time to look into possible problems and discrepancies at a finer level, like freight size or weight that seems out of line, and they readjust the schedule accordingly. One of the big benefits of the expert system is better customer relationship management. With the automated system, Con-Way can take orders much later than its competition and has improved its on-time delivery rate.

Con-Way has become the perennial earning leader in its niche of less-than-full-truckload, time-and-day-definite freight delivery.[17]

A DSS sometimes incorporates expert systems, but an expert system is fundamentally different from a DSS. To use a DSS, you must have considerable knowledge or expertise about the situation with which you're dealing. As you saw earlier in this chapter, a DSS *assists* you in making decisions. That means that you must know how to reason through the problem. You must know which questions to ask, how to get the answers, and how to proceed to the next step. However, when you use an expert system, the know-how is in the system—you need only provide the expert system with the facts and symptoms of the problem for which you need an answer. The know-how, or expertise, that actually solves the problem came from someone else—an expert in the field. What does it mean to have expertise? When someone has expertise in a given subject, that person not only knows a lot of facts about the topic but also can apply that knowledge to analyze and make judgments about related topics. It's this human expertise that an expert system captures.

Rule	Symptom or Fact	Yes	No	Explanation
1	Is the light green?	Go through the intersection.	Go to Rule 2.	Should be safe if light is green. If not, need more information.
2	Is the light red?	Go to Rule 4.	Go to Rule 3.	Should stop, may not be able to.
3	Is the light likely to change to red before you get through the intersection?	Go to Rule 4.	Go through the intersection.	Will only reach this point if light is yellow, then you'll have two choices.
4	Can you stop before entering the intersection?	Stop.	Go to Rule 5.	Should stop, but there may be a problem if you can't.
5	Is traffic approaching from either side?	Prepare to crash.	Go through the intersection.	Unless the intersection is clear of traffic, you're likely to crash.

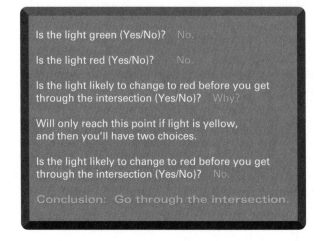

Figure 4.7

Traffic Light Expert System Rules

Let's look at a very simple expert system that would tell a driver what to do when approaching a traffic light. Dealing with traffic lights is an example of the type of problem to which an expert system is well-suited. It is a recurring problem, and to solve it you follow a well-defined set of steps. You've probably gone through the following mental question-and-answer session hundreds of times without even realizing it (see Figure 4.7).

When you approach a green traffic light, you proceed on through. If the light is red, you try to stop. If you're unable to stop, and if traffic is approaching from either side, you'll probably be in trouble. Similarly, if the light is yellow, you may be able to make it through the intersection before the light turns red. If not, you will again be faced with the problem of approaching traffic.

Let's say that you know very little about what to do when you come to a traffic light, but you know that there are experts in the field. You want to capture their expertise in an expert system so that you can refer to it whenever the traffic light situation arises. To gain an understanding of what's involved in the creation and use of an expert system, let's now consider the components of an expert system individually with the traffic light example in mind.

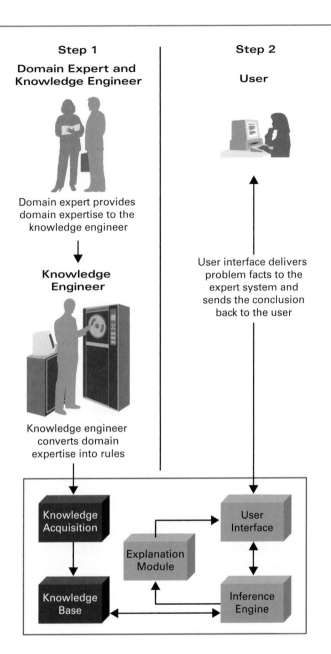

Figure 4.8

Developing and Using an
Expert System

COMPONENTS OF AN EXPERT SYSTEM

An expert system, like any IT system, combines information, people, and IT components.

Information types	People	IT components
Domain expertise	Domain expert	Knowledge acquisition
"Why?" information	Knowledge engineer	Explanation module
Problem facts	Knowledge worker	User interface
		Inference engine
		Knowledge base

These components and their relationships are shown in Figure 4.8.

INFORMATION TYPES   The traffic light *domain expertise* is the core of the expert system, because it's the set of problem-solving steps—the reasoning process that will solve the problem. You'll also want to ask the expert system how it reached its conclusion, or why it asked you a question. The "Why" information included in the expert system allows it to give you the answers. It's information that's provided by the expert—the traffic expert in our example. With the domain expertise and the "Why" information, the expert system is now ready to solve traffic light problems. So now you need to enter the *problem facts,* which are the specifics of your traffic light situation. Problem facts are the symptoms of and assertions about your problem. You'll enter these problem facts as answers to the expert system's questions during your consultation.

PEOPLE   Three separate roles must be filled in the development and use of an expert system. The first role is that of the domain expert, who knows how to solve the problem. The *domain expert* provides the domain expertise in the form of problem-solving strategies. In our traffic light expert system, the domain expert could be an official from the department of motor vehicles. This official, turned domain expert, would also be able to indicate where to gather further domain expertise, and might direct you to the local police station or give you a booklet with the rules of the road. Eventually, the combination of these sources will produce the five steps shown in Figure 4.7.

The domain expert usually works with an IT specialist, a *knowledge engineer,* who formulates the domain expertise into an expert system. In this case, the knowledge engineer might consider it best to represent the five steps in the form of rules, making a *rule-based expert system.* The knowledge engineer will see to it that the rules are in the correct order and that the system works properly.

The knowledge worker or user—that's you—will then apply the expert system to the problem of what to do when approaching a traffic light. When you face the traffic light problem, you would run a *consultation* (see again Figure 4.7) and provide the expert system with the problem facts. You would answer the questions as they appear on the screen, with the expert system applying the appropriate rules and asking you more questions. This process continues until the expert system presents you with a conclusion (telling you what to do) or indicates that it can't reach a conclusion (telling you that it doesn't know what you should do).

IT COMPONENTS   When the knowledge engineer has converted the domain expertise into rules, the *knowledge base* stores the rules of the expert system (see Figure 4.8 on the previous page). All the rules must be in place before a consultation, because the expert system won't be able to offer a conclusion in a situation for which it has no rules. For example, if the traffic light is broken and has been replaced by a four-way stop sign, the expert system, as it stands, would not be able to reach a conclusion. The knowledge engineer could, of course, go back to the domain expert and enter rules about four-way stops. The knowledge engineer uses the *knowledge acquisition* component of the expert system to enter the traffic light rules. The domain expertise for the rules can come from many sources, including human experts, books, organizational databases, data warehouses, internal reports, diagrams, and so on.

The *inference engine* is the part of the expert system that takes your problem facts and searches the knowledge base for rules that fit. This process is called *inferencing.* The inference engine organizes and controls the rules; it "reasons" through your problem to reach a conclusion. It delivers its conclusion or recommendation based on (1) the problem facts of your specific traffic light situation and (2) the rules that came from the domain expert about traffic light procedures in general. The user interface is the part of the expert system that you use to run a consultation. Through the user interface, the ex-

TRAFFIC LIGHTS REVISITED

Create a table similar to Figure 4.7 to extend the traffic light expert system. Include the following situations in the table:

1. There is a wreck in the middle of the intersection.
2. You are turning left at the intersection.
3. You are turning right at the intersection.
4. A pedestrian is crossing in front of you.
5. A dog has wandered into the intersection.
6. A ball belonging to children playing near the intersection has rolled into the street.
7. The car in front of you has stalled.

pert system asks you questions, and you enter problem facts by answering the questions. In the traffic light expert system, you would enter yes or no. These answers are used by the inference engine to solve the problem.

The domain expert supplies the "Why" information, which is entered by the knowledge engineer into the ***explanation module,*** where it is stored. During a consultation, you—as the knowledge worker or user—can ask why a question was posed and how the expert system reached its conclusion. If you're using the expert system as a training tool, then you'll be very interested in how it solved the problem.

In Figure 4.8 you can clearly see the distinction between the development and use of an expert system. The domain expert and the knowledge engineer develop the expert system; then the knowledge worker can apply the expert system to a particular set of circumstances.

WHAT EXPERT SYSTEMS CAN AND CAN'T DO

An expert system uses IT to capture and apply human expertise. For problems with clear rules and procedures, expert systems work very well and can provide your company with great advantages. An expert system can

- Handle massive amounts of information
- Reduce errors
- Aggregate information from various sources
- Improve customer service
- Provide consistency in decision making
- Provide new information
- Decrease personnel time spent on tasks
- Reduce cost

You can run into trouble, however, in building and using an expert system. Difficulties can include the following:

1. Transferring domain expertise to the expert system is sometimes difficult because domain experts cannot always explain how they know what they know. Often experts are not aware of their complete reasoning processes. Experience has given them a feel for the problem, and they just "know."

2. Even if the domain expert can explain the whole reasoning process, automating that process may be impossible. The process may be too complex, requiring an excessive number of rules, or it may be too vague or imprecise. In using an

expert system, keep in mind that it can solve only the problems for which it was designed. It cannot deal with inconsistency or a newly encountered problem situation. An expert system can't learn from previous experience and can't apply previously acquired expertise to new problems the way humans can.

3. An expert system has no common sense or judgment. One of the early expert systems built into an F-16 fighter plane allowed the pilot to retract the landing gear while the plane was still on the ground and to jettison bombs while the plane was flying upside down, both highly dangerous actions.

Neural Networks

Suppose you see a breed of dog you've never encountered before. Would you know it's a dog? For that matter, would you know it's an animal? Probably so. You know, because you've learned by example. You've seen lots of living things, have learned to classify them, and so can recognize a dog when you see one. A neural network simulates this human ability to classify things without taking prescribed steps leading to the solution. A *neural network* (often called an *artificial neural network* or *ANN*) is an artificial intelligence system that is capable of finding and differentiating patterns. Your brain has learned to consider many factors in combination to recognize and differentiate objects. This is also the case with a neural network. A neural network can learn by example and can adapt to new concepts and knowledge. Neural networks are widely used for visual pattern and speech recognition systems. If you've used a PDA that deciphered your handwriting, it was probably a neural network that analyzed the characters you wrote.[18]

Neural networks are useful to a variety of other situations, too. For example, bomb detection systems in U.S. airports use neural networks that sense trace elements in the air that may indicate the presence of explosives. The Chicago Police Department uses neural networks to identify corruption within its ranks.[19] In medicine, neural networks check 50 million electrocardiograms per year, check for drug interactions, and detect anomalies in tissue samples that may signify the onset of cancer and other diseases. Neural networks can detect heart attacks and even differentiate between the subtly different symptoms of heart attacks in men and women.[20,21,22] In business, neural networks are very popular for securities trading, fraud detection, real estate appraisal, evaluating loan applications, and target marketing, to mention a few. Neural networks are even used to control machinery, adjust temperature settings, and identify malfunctioning machinery.

Neural networks are most useful for identification, classification, and prediction when a vast amount of information is available. By examining hundreds, or even thousands of examples, a neural network detects important relationships and patterns in the information. For example, if you provide a neural network with the details of numerous credit card transactions and tell it which ones are fraudulent, eventually it will learn to identify suspicious transaction patterns.

Here are some examples of the uses of neural networks:

- Many banks and financial institutions use neural networks. For example, Citibank uses neural networks to find opportunities in financial markets.[23] By carefully examining historical stock market data with neural network software, Citibank financial managers learn of interesting coincidences or small anomalies (called market inefficiencies). For example, it could be that whenever IBM stock goes up, so does Unisys stock. Or it might be that a U.S. Treasury note is selling for 1 cent less in Japan than it is in the United States. These snippets of information can make a big difference to Citibank's bottom line in a very competitive financial market.

HOW WOULD YOU CLASSIFY PEOPLE?

Some people have suggested that neural networks could be applied to people to indicate how likely they are to develop disease or even become criminals. The idea is to input a child's personal characteristics, demographics, and genealogy into a neural network, and the neural network will classify that youngster as being at risk for a disease or for aberrant behavior.

Choose either susceptibility to disease or to criminal behavior, discuss it with your group, and make the following lists, explaining why you chose each one.

1. What personal characteristics would be useful?
2. What demographic factors would strongly influence a person's future?
3. What, if any, inherited characteristics can predict a child's future?

Would such classification on a large scale be legal? Would it be ethical? Would it be effective? Why? Why not? (to all three questions).

- In Westminster, California, a community of 87,000 people, police use neural network software to fight crime. With crime reports as input, the system detects and maps local crime patterns. Police say that with this system they can better predict crime trends, improve patrol assignments, and develop better crime-prevention programs.[24]

- Fingerhut, the mail order company based in Minnesota, has 6 million people on its customer list. To determine which customers were and were not likely to order from its catalog, Fingerhut recently switched to neural network software. The company finds that the new software is more effective and expects to generate millions of dollars by fine-tuning its mailing lists.[25]

- Fraud detection is one of the areas in which neural networks are used the most. Visa, MasterCard, and many other credit card companies use a neural network to spot peculiarities in individual accounts. MasterCard estimates neural networks save them $50 million annually.[26]

- Many insurance companies (Cigna, AIG, Travelers, Liberty Mutual, Hartford) along with state compensation funds and other carriers use neural network software to identify fraud. The system searches for patterns in billing charges, laboratory tests, and frequency of office visits. A claim for which the diagnosis was a sprained ankle and which included an electrocardiogram would be flagged for the account manager.[27]

- FleetBoston Financial Corporation uses a neural network to watch transactions with customers. The neural network can detect patterns that may indicate a customer's growing dissatisfaction with the company. The neural network looks for signs like a decrease in the number of transactions or in the account balance of one of Fleet's high-value customers.[28]

All of the above situations have pattern recognition in common. They all require identification and/or classification, which may then be used to predict a finding or outcome. Neural networks are often called predictive systems since they can see patterns in huge volumes of information.

INSIDE A NEURAL NETWORK

Neural networks are so called because they attempt to mimic the structure and functioning of the human brain. Conceptually, neural networks consist of three layers of virtual nerve cells, or neurons. There's an input layer and an output layer and between them is a hidden layer, although there may be more than one hidden layer. The input and output layers are connected to the middle layer(s) by connections called weights of various strengths (see Figure 4.9). If you were to train a neural network to recognize a "good" stock portfolio, you would input many, many examples of good and bad portfolios, telling the neural network which was which. As the neural network is learning to differentiate between good and bad, the weights change. The flow of information to the output layer also changes. After you have fed the system enough examples, the weights stabilize, and the neural network then consistently classifies portfolios correctly.

So, you may be asking, how is a neural network different from an expert system, since both can take input and produce an answer as to which group the input belongs? An expert system, as we saw, can also classify; that is, it asks questions and, based on the answers, can diagnose or prescribe. The difference is that an expert system does not adjust by itself and is rigid in its application of the rules. For example, if a credit card fraud detection expert system had a rule that said to flag a purchase over a certain amount on certain types of accounts, the expert system would flag a transaction that was even one penny over. A neural network, on the other hand, would learn the spending behavior of cardholders and would be better able to evaluate whether deviations were large enough to be queried or not. A neural network can even adjust to situations not explicitly used in training. For example, if when the neural network was learning, mortgage rates were between 6 percent and 10 percent, the system could interpolate if the rate were to drop to 5 percent.

Figure 4.9

The Layers of a Neural Network

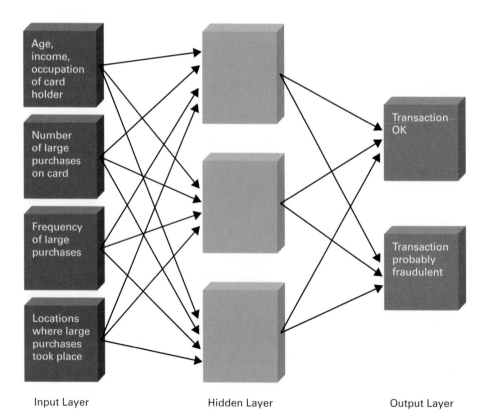

Input Layer   Hidden Layer   Output Layer

Neural networks have many advantages. For example, neural networks can

- Learn and adjust to new circumstances on their own.
- Lend themselves to massive parallel processing.
- Function without complete or well-structured information.
- Cope with huge volumes of information with many dependent variables.
- Analyze nonlinear relationships in information and have been called fancy regression analysis systems.

The biggest problem with neural networks to date has been the fact that the hidden layers are "hidden." That is, you can't see how the neural network is learning and how the neurons are interacting. Newer neural networks no longer hide the middle layers. With these systems you can manually adjust the weights or connections giving you more flexibility and control.

Genetic Algorithms

Have you ever wondered how chefs around the world create recipes for great-tasting foods? For example, how did the Chinese discover that cashew nuts and chicken taste good when combined? How did Mexican chefs arrive at combining tomatoes, onions, cilantro, and other spices to create pica de gallo? All those great recipes came about through *evolutionary processes*. Someone decided to put together a few ingredients and taste the result. Undoubtedly, many of those combinations resulted in unpalatable concoctions that were quickly discarded. Others were tasty enough to warrant further experimentation of combinations.

Today significant research in AI is devoted to creating software capable of following a similar trial-and-error process, leading to the evolution of a good result. Such a software system is called a genetic algorithm. A ***genetic algorithm*** is an artificial intelligence system that mimics the evolutionary, survival-of-the-fittest process to generate increasingly better solutions to a problem. In other words, a genetic algorithm is an optimizing system: It finds the combination of inputs that give the best outputs.

Here's an example. Suppose you were trying to decide what to put into your stock portfolio. You have countless stocks to choose from but a limited amount of money to invest. You might decide that you'd like to start with 20 stocks and you want a portfolio growth rate of 7.5 percent.

Probably you'd start by examining historic information on the stocks. You would take some number of stocks and combine them, 20 at a time, to see what happens with each grouping. If you wanted to choose from a pool of 30 stocks, you would have to examine 30,045,015 different combinations. For a 40-stock pool, the number of combinations rises to 137,846,500,000. It would be an impossibly time-consuming, not to mention numbingly tedious, task to look at this many combinations and evaluate your overall return for each one. However, this is just the sort of repetitive number-crunching task at which computers excel.

So, instead of a pencil, paper, and calculator, you might use a genetic algorithm. You could input the appropriate information on the stocks, including the number of years the company has been in business, the performance of the stock over the last five years, price to earnings ratios, and other information.

You would also have to tell the genetic algorithm your exact "success" criteria. For example, you might use a growth rate in the company over the last year of at least 10 percent, a presence in the marketplace going back at least three years, a connection to the

THE EVOLUTION OF FARMING EQUIPMENT

There is an almost infinite number of combinations possible for features on a car. This is true for many products, as Deere, a company that makes agricultural equipment, knows all too well. Deere's customers demand all sorts of variations in planters. These different combinations of features make creating a good manufacturing schedule by hand all but impossible. Deere found that genetic algorithm software not only makes the task manageable but can compute the best schedule that offers the easiest and fastest way to utilize the production line to optimize production.

The initial stages of the huge project were very expensive, but the software gave the company a way to meet customer demand quickly and to gain competitive advantage. It worked so well for Deere that the company's supplier, Auburn Consolidated Industries, is also using it and Deere is reaping the benefits of improved supply chain management.

As always, technology alone is not the answer. To benefit significantly from technology, the production and business processes have to be efficient and effective.[29,30]

computer industry, and so forth. The genetic algorithm would simply combine and recombine stocks eliminating any combinations that don't fit your criteria and continuing to the next iteration with the acceptable combinations—those that give an aggregate growth rate of at least 7.5 percent while aiming for as high a growth rate as possible.

Genetic algorithms use three concepts of evolution:

1. *Selection*—or survival of the fittest. The key to selection is to give preference to better outcomes.

2. *Crossover*—or combining portions of good outcomes in the hope of creating an even better outcome.

3. *Mutation*—or randomly trying combinations and evaluating the success (or failure) of the outcome.

Genetic algorithms are best suited to decision-making environments in which thousands, or perhaps millions, of solutions are possible. Genetic algorithms can find and evaluate solutions intelligently and can get through many more possibilities more thoroughly and faster than a human can. As you might imagine, businesses face decision-making environments for all sorts of problems like engineering design, computer graphics, strategies for game playing, anything, in fact, that requires optimization techniques. Here are some other examples.

- Genetic algorithms are used by business executives to help them decide which combination of projects a firm should invest in, taking complicated tax considerations into account.[31]

- They're used by investment companies to help in trading choices and decisions.[32]

- In any garment that you buy, the fabric alone accounts for between 35 percent and 40 percent of the selling price. So, when cutting out the fabric to make the garment, it's important that there be as little waste as possible. Genetic algorithms are used to solve this problem of laying out the pieces of the garment and cutting fabric in a way that leaves as little waste as possible.[33]

BE A GENETIC ALGORITHM AND PUT NAILS IN BOXES

This project involves packaging nails so that you make the most profit possible (this is a profit maximizing problem). Say you have five types of nails and can make as many as you need of each. These are 4-inch, 3.5-inch, 3-inch, 2.5-inch, 2-inch, and 1.5-inch nails. The cost of making each type of nail depends on how big a nail it is. Those cost and selling prices are listed in the table below along with the weights. The nails will be sold in boxes of up to 30 nails. There must be no more than 10, but no less than 5, of each of three types of nails in each box. The nails in each box should weigh no more than 20 ounces. You're looking for the combination with the highest profit using a trial-and-error method.

A spreadsheet would be helpful for completing this project. You'll most likely find that you identify some promising paths to follow right away and will concentrate on those to reach the best one.

Nail	Weight	Cost	Selling price
4 inch	1 oz	4 cents	8 cents
3.5 inch	0.85 oz	3.5 cents	6 cents
3 inch	0.7 oz	3 cents	5 cents
2.5 inch	0.5 oz	2.5 cents	4 cents
2 inch	0.25 oz	2 cents	3 cents
1.5 inch	0.1 oz	1.5 cents	2 cents

- US West uses a genetic algorithm to determine the optimal configuration of fiber-optic cable in a network that may include as many as 100,000 connection points. By using selection, crossover, and mutation, the genetic algorithm can generate and evaluate millions of cable configurations and select the one that uses the least amount of cable. At US West, this process used to take an experienced design engineer almost two months. US West's genetic algorithm can solve the problem in two days and saves the company $1 million to $10 million each time it's used.[34]

Genetic algorithms are good for these types of problems because they use selection, crossover, and mutation as methods of exploring countless solutions and the respective worth of each.

You have to tell the genetic algorithm what constitutes a "good" solution. That could be low cost, high return, among other factors, since many potential solutions are useless or absurd. If you created a genetic algorithm to make bread, for example, it might try to boil flour to create moistness. That obviously won't work, so the genetic algorithm would simply throw away that solution and try something else. Other solutions would eventually be good, and some of them would even be wonderful. According to David Goldbert, a genetic algorithm pioneer at the University of Illinois at Urbana–Champaign, evolution is the oldest and most powerful algorithm there is, and "three billion years of evolution can't be wrong!"[35]

Intelligent Agents

Do you have a favorite restaurant? Is there someone there who knows you and remembers that you like Italian dressing, but not croutons, on your salad; and ice cream and a slice of cheddar cheese with your apple pie? Does this person familiar with your tastes put a glass of diet cola on your favorite table when you come in the door? If so, he or she has the qualities that artificial intelligence scientists are working on incorporating into intelligent agents. An ***intelligent agent*** is software that assists you, or acts on your behalf, in performing repetitive computer-related tasks. Future intelligent agents will most likely be autonomous, acting independently, and will learn and adapt to changing circumstances.

You may not realize it, but you're probably already familiar with a primitive type of intelligent agent—the shifty-eyed paper clip that pops up in some versions of Word. For example, if your document looks as if it is going to be a business letter—that is, you type in a date, name, and address—the animated paper clip will offer helpful suggestions on how to proceed.

You can find hundreds of intelligent agents, or bots, for a wide variety of tasks. The BotSpot and SmartBot Web sites at www.botspot.com and www.smartbots.com are good places to look for the different types of agents available.

Essentially there are four types of intelligent agents:

1. Buyer agents or shopping bots
2. User or personal agents
3. Monitoring-and-surveillance agents
4. Data-mining agents

BUYER AGENTS

Buyer agents travel around a network (very likely the Internet) finding information and bringing it back to you. Buyer agents are also called shopping bots. These agents search the Internet for goods and services that you need and bring you back the information.

A ***buyer agent*** or ***shopping bot*** is an intelligent agent on a Web site that helps you, the customer, find products and services you want. Shopping bots work very efficiently for commodity products such as CDs, books, electronic components, and other one-size-fits-all products.

Shopping bots make money by selling advertising space, conducting special promotions in cooperation with merchants, or charging click-through fees, which are payments to the site that provided the link to the merchant site. Some shopping bots give preference to certain sites for a financial consideration. The people who run shopping bot sites have two competing objectives. They want to present as many listings as possible to the consumer in the most useful way, but they also want to make money doing it.

MySimon.com is the most successful shopping bot to date with more than a million visitors a month according to Nielsen/NetRatings. MySimon searches for millions of products on thousands of Web sites.[36]

Government sites have search-and-retrieve agents you can use to get the information you need. FERRET (Federal Electronic Research and Review Extraction Tool) was developed jointly by the Census Bureau and the Bureau of Labor Statistics. With FERRET you can find information on employment, health care, education, race and ethnicity, health insurance, housing, income and poverty, aging, and marriage and family.

You may have encountered a shopping bot without having specifically requested its services. For example, Amazon.com will offer you a list of books that you might like to buy based on what you're buying now and what you have bought in the past. The Amazon site uses an intelligent agent—a shopping bot—to provide this service. As you saw in Chapter 2, Amazon's agent uses collaborative filtering, which consists of matching each customer with a group of users who have similar tastes and presenting choices common in that group.

USER AGENTS

User agents (sometimes called *personal agents*) are intelligent agents that take action on your behalf. In this category belong those intelligent agents that already perform, or will shortly perform, the following tasks:

- Check your e-mail, sort it according to priority (your priority), and alert you when good stuff comes through—like college acceptance letters.
- Play computer games as your opponent or patrol game areas for you.
- Assemble customized news reports for you. There are several versions of these. A CNN Custom News bot will gather news from CNN on the topics you want to read about—and only those topics.
- Find information for you on the subject of your choice.
- Fill out forms on the Web automatically for you. They even store your information for future reference.
- Scan Web pages looking for and highlighting the text that constitutes the "important" part of the information there.
- "Discuss" topics with you from your deepest fears to sports.

One expanding application of intelligent agent technology is in automating business functions. For example, Mission Hockey, a company that manufacturers and distributes in-line and ice hockey skates and other gear, uses software from Sweden called Movex that has a user agent component. Movex will search the Internet or a company intranet or extranet to negotiate and make deals with suppliers and distributors. An *intranet* is an internal organizational Internet that is guarded against outside access by a special security feature called a firewall. An *extranet* is an intranet that is restricted to an organization and certain outsiders, such as customers and suppliers. You can read more on intranets and extranets in Chapter 7. In the Movex case, the intelligent agent is incorporated into an enterprise resource planning system. *Enterprise resource planning (ERP)* is a very important concept in today's business world. The term refers to a method of getting and keeping an overview of every part of the business (a bird's eye view, so to speak), so that production, development, selling, and servicing of goods and services will all be coordinated to contribute to the company's goals and objectives.

In the future, user agents for personal use will be available for both your wired and your wireless computer devices. Sprint has recently announced an e-assistant that will carry out verbal requests.[37] In the future, we'll see personal agents that

- Interact with the personal agents of colleagues to set up a meeting time.
- Incorporate shopping bots that can take your preferences for features on a new car (or anything else) along with a price range and then haggle with car dealers (or their personal agents) to find you the best deal.

GO BARGAIN HUNTING ONLINE

Try out shopping bots for yourself. Choose three items to search for: one music item, one item of clothing, and one household item. Search for them with each of the following sites.

- Bottom Dollar at www.bottomdollar.com
- MySimon at www.mysimon.com
- R U Sure at www.rusure.com
- Yahoo! Shopping at shopping.yahoo.com
- Prescan at www.prescan.com

Answer these questions . . .

- How many hits did you get at each site for each item?
- Are tax, postage, and handling charges included in the quoted price?
- Can you sort in order of price?
- Does the shopping site specialize in a particular kind of item?

MONITORING-AND-SURVEILLANCE AGENTS

Monitoring-and-surveillance agents (also called ***predictive agents***) are intelligent agents that observe and report on equipment. For example, NASA's Jet Propulsion Laboratory has an agent that monitors inventory, planning, and scheduling equipment ordering to keep costs down.[38] Other monitoring agents work on the manufacturing shop floor, finding equipment problems and locating other machinery that will do the same job.

Monitoring-and-surveillance agents are often used to monitor complex computer networks. Allstate Insurance has a network with 2,000 computers. The company uses a network monitoring agent from Computer Associates International called Neugent that watches its huge networks 24 hours a day. Every 5 seconds, the agent measures 1,200 data points and can predict a system crash 45 minutes before it happens. Neugent combines intelligent agent technology with neural network technology to look for patterns of activity or problems. The neural network part can learn what conditions predict a downturn in network efficiency or a slowing in network traffic. Neugent also watches for electronic attacks from hackers, detecting them early so that they can be stopped.

Another type of monitoring-and-surveillance agent that works on computer networks keeps track of the configuration of each computer connected to the network. It tracks and updates the central configuration database when anything on any computer changes, like the number or type of disk drive changes. An important task in managing networks is in prioritizing traffic and shaping bandwidth. That means sending enough network capacity or bandwidth to the most important tasks over those tasks that are of secondary importance. At a university, for example, processing end-of-semester grades might take precedence over net surfing.

Some further types of monitoring-and-surveillance agents include agents that

- Watch your competition and bring back price changes and special offer information.
- Monitor Internet sites, discussion groups, mailing lists, and so on, for stock manipulation, insider training, and rumors that might affect stock prices.
- Monitor sites for updated information on the topic of your choice.

INDUSTRY PERSPECTIVE

INTELLIGENT AGENTS DO BACKGROUND CHECKS

The Army hires a lot of people who will have access to sensitive and potentially lethal information and hardware and who, therefore, need security clearance. This involves a thorough background check for each soldier, a process which, even with all the resources and experience that the investigators have, can take days or even weeks to complete.

In 2002, the Army started to use intelligent agents to automate the data gathering. The intelligent agent searches through electronic records collecting information. It places all this information in an electronic file and then inspects the contents looking for anything that looks suspicious or might be a precursor to later problems. Such warning signs would be arrests, financial problems, or anything else that could indicate personal weakness exploitable by unauthorized interested parties.

The effects of this electronic investigator have been dramatic. The Army Central Clearance Facility in Fort Meade, MD, can now process a background check in 24 hours, has cleared some of its year-long backlog, and can handle almost one-third more checks per year.[39]

- Watch particular products and bring back price or term changes.
- Monitor auction sites for products or prices that you want.

DATA-MINING AGENTS

A *data-mining agent* operates in a data warehouse discovering information. A data warehouse brings together information from lots of different sources. Data mining is the process of looking through the data warehouse to find information that you can use to take action, like ways to increase sales or retain customers who are considering defecting to the competition. Data mining is so called because you have to sift through a lot of information for the gold nuggets that will affect the bottom line. This sort of nugget spotting is similar to what the FBI and CIA do when they bring together little bits of information from diverse sources and use the overall pattern to spot trouble brewing.

As you learned in Chapter 3, database queries answer questions such as, How much did we spend on transportation in March of this year? Multidimensional analysis is the next step in complexity and answers questions such as, How much did we spend on transportation in the Southeast during March of the last five years? Data mining goes deeper and finds answers to questions you may not even have asked such as, What else do young men buy on Friday afternoons when they come in to buy diapers? The answer, culled by data-mining tools, is beer.[40]

One of the most common types of data mining is classification, which finds patterns in information and categorizes items into those classes. You may remember that this is just what neural networks do best. So, not surprisingly, neural networks are part of many data-mining tools. And data-mining agents are another integral part, since data-mining agents search for information in a data warehouse.

A data-mining agent may detect a major shift in a trend or a key indicator. It can also detect the presence of new information and alert you. Volkswagen uses an intelligent agent system that acts as an early-warning system about market conditions. If conditions become such that the assumptions underlying the company's strategy are no longer true, the intelligent agent alerts managers.[41] For example, the intelligent agent might see a problem in some part of the country that is or will shortly cause payments to slow down. Having that information early on lets managers formulate a plan to protect themselves.

Summary: Student Learning Outcomes Revisited

1. **Define decision support system, list its components, and identify the type of applications it's suited to.** A *decision support system (DSS)* is a highly flexible and interactive IT system that is designed to support decision making when the problem is not structured. A DSS has three components: model management, data management, and user interface management. It's primarily an analysis tool to support your decision making, but you make the final decision.

2. **Define geographic information systems and state how they differ from other decision support tools.** A *geographic information system (GIS)* is a decision support system designed specifically to work with spatial information. It's used for the analysis of information in map form. Information is stored in layers which can be overlaid as appropriate. It's the layering and presentation that separates a GIS from other decision support tools.

3. **Define artificial intelligence and list the different types that are used in business.** *Artificial intelligence* is the science of making machines imitate human thinking and behavior. The types used in business include expert systems, neural networks, genetic algorithms, and intelligent agents.

4. **Define expert systems and describe the types of problems to which they are applicable.** An *expert system* (or *knowledge-based system*) is an artificial intelligence system that applies reasoning capabilities to reach a conclusion. A rule-based expert system asks the user questions and, based on the answers, asks other questions until it has enough information to make a decision or a recommendation. Expert systems are good for diagnostic (what's wrong) and prescriptive problems (what to do). For example, you could use an expert system to diagnose illness or to figure out why a machine is malfunctioning. And you could use an expert system to determine what to do about the problem.

5. **Define neural networks, their uses, and a major strength and weakness of these AI systems.** A *neural network* (also called an *artificial neural network* or *ANN*) is an artificial intelligence system that is capable of finding and differentiating patterns. Neural networks are good for finding commonalities in situations that have many variables. The major strength of a neural network is that it can learn and adapt. Its major weakness is that it's not usually clear how the system reached its result and it's hard, therefore, to verify its solutions.

6. **Define genetic algorithms and list the concepts on which they are based and the types of problems they solve.** A *genetic algorithm* is an artificial intelligence system that mimics the evolutionary, survival-of-the-fittest process to generate increasingly better solutions to a problem. Genetic algorithms use the principles of *selection, crossover,* and *mutation* from evolution theory. These systems are best suited to problems where hundreds or thousands of solutions are possible and you need an optimum solution.

7. **Define intelligent agents, list the four types, and identify the types of problems they solve.** An *intelligent agent* is software that assists you, or acts on your behalf, in performing repetitive computer-related tasks. The four types are

   - *Buyer agents* (or *shopping bots*) search the Web for products and services
   - *User agents* (or *personal agents*) take action for you, particularly in repetitive tasks like sorting e-mail
   - *Monitoring-and-surveillance agents* (or *predictive agents*) track conditions, perhaps on a network, and signal changes or troublesome conditions
   - *Data-mining agents* search data warehouses to discover information

CLOSING CASE STUDY ONE

SHUTTLE DEBRIS, TREES, AND SNIPER ATTACKS

What do shuttle debris, trees, and possible locations of sniper attacks have in common? They can all be mapped and managed using a geographic information system (GIS). A GIS, as you learned in this chapter, allows you to see information spatially. Being able to visualize the physical location of objects and their proximity to each other greatly aids the decision-making process. Following are some examples that will give you an idea of how diverse the application of GIS is.

THE ILL-FATED SPACESHIP COLUMBIA

On January 31, 2003, after 16 days of intensive research conducted while orbiting the earth, the seven-member crew of the space shuttle Columbia shut down all experiments, packed up their stuff, and ran tests of the systems they would need to land the next day. On February 1, the shuttle headed for home, but something went terribly wrong and the shuttle exploded over East Texas and arrived on earth in small pieces. To try to figure out what had happened, it was necessary to gather the pieces and try to reconstruct the sequence of events that led to the disaster. So, within hours of the terrible tragedy, while many of us were still too stunned to think, researchers and students at Stephen F. Austin State University in Nacogdoches, Texas, collected their GPS (global positioning system) gear and headed out looking for the debris. The field crews wanted to pinpoint exactly where all the debris fell—they didn't move or even touch anything they found. Within days there were 60 to 70 teams with up to 200 people collecting the information.

The GPS system they used is accurate to 100 feet, but with further processing the accuracy can be increased to within 3 feet. Using ArchInfo from ESRI, they were able to plot all the data points on a digital map that showed topological features, as well as roads and other man-made structures. In all, the volunteers collected 70 megabytes of information that they turned over to the federal agencies that had set up a central command post in Lufkin, Texas.

TREES IN CHATTANOOGA

In Chattanooga, people take the natural beauty and environmental benefits of their trees seriously. The city has created a GIS that maps the location of the 6,000 trees located in and around the business district. Along with this basic information, the GIS also has details on each tree that include its species, tree-pit dimensions, irrigation status, and trunk diameter. This information is very helpful when working out a maintenance plan to keep the trees healthy. For example, the size of a tree determines how many pruning hours it will need. Having an accurate map of where trees are allows the city to plan for future foliage. The city doesn't want to have more than 10 percent of any one species in such a small area since any insect infestation or disease that takes hold on one tree could spread more easily and potentially eliminate the whole tree population.

With the GIS system, which cost about $7,000 in labor to develop, the city can make more accurate estimates of the cost of materials and labor that are necessary to maintain the trees. This keeps the city from wasting resources or getting nasty surprises at the end of the fiscal reporting period.

RICHMOND MAPS BUS STOPS AND TRACKS BUSES

When GRTC Transit, the public transportation agency serving the City of Richmond and Chesterfield County, in Virginia, created a GIS of its bus routes and stops, it was not part of the plan to use it to protect its ridership from snipers. The idea was to improve its planning process designed to serve its rapidly expanding customer base.

GRTC's first step was to map its 2,500 bus stops. The agency wanted to know the details about each one, such as curb length, type and condition of the signs, benches, shelters, ramps, and trashcans at each stop. Within months of collecting this information, GRTC was using the GIS to analyze its bus routes and to consider requests from customers for changes and additions to the routes and also for amenities at the stops. With the ease of viewing lots of information in context that the GIS provides, the agency has implemented many improvements to its service.

In November 2001, the northern and central parts of Virginia were beset by sniper attacks, and no one knew where they were coming from, why they were occurring, or how to stop them. GRTC Transit was able to use its GIS to quickly provide the police with information on bus stops where passengers' lives could have been at risk from sniper attacks because of on/off highway ramps close by.[42,43,44]

Questions

1. You saw examples in this case of a city that used a GIS to keep track of trees and one that mapped its bus stops to better serve its residents. Cities provide many other benefits, for example, firefighting and ambulance services. What sort of city features would a city incorporate into a GIS so that emergency dispatchers could more efficiently send out ambulances and fire trucks?

2. How would NASA use the information that students and other volunteers collected on the widely dispersed bits of the space shuttle Columbia? Why is it so important for NASA and for the Federal Aviation Authority (FAA) to map the location of, collect, and reassemble, as far as possible, this debris?

3. How might a business such as a bank use a GIS to determine where to put a new branch? What sort of information would the bank want to have about the area surrounding the proposed site?

4. Thematic GIS maps show a statistical value for certain locations and link those locations to an underlying geographic feature, such as the distribution of population within a county, or the areas in a nature reserve where birds and animals congregate. A point map shows the location of specific data items, like where your customers live or where fire hydrants are located. For each of the three examples in this case, specify whether each one uses thematic or point maps, or some combination.

CLOSING CASE STUDY TWO

USING NEURAL NETWORKS TO CATEGORIZE PEOPLE

Would your banker give you an A, B, or C? What about your supermarket? You know you're being graded in your classes, but did you know that you're also being graded by businesses?

Special treatment for certain customers is not new. Airline customers who fly first class have always received preferential treatment, even when flights were cancelled or delayed. You won't find them napping on a stone floor with their backpacks as pillows. This makes business sense to the airlines, since these are the customers who are most profitable.

Although companies have always offered preferential treatment to their more profitable customers, the speed and capacity of computers today are making the segmenting of customers possible to a degree unheard of just a few years ago. Part of the reason for this is neural networks. Using neural network software, businesses now have the ability to look for patterns in their customer information and classify customers according to how they affect the company's bottom line and thus to gauge whether it's worth the trouble of making them happy.

BANKS

The First Union Bank uses software that categorizes people into red, green, and yellow classes depending on the customer's history and value to the bank. Customers who are green might get better credit card rates than customers who are red and are judged to add less to the bank's bottom line.

Say you called the bank that issued you your credit card and said that you didn't want to pay the annual fee anymore. The bank could look at your credit card activity and decide whether it's more profitable to the bank to waive your fee rather than risk your not using the credit card anymore.

CREDIT CARD COMPANIES

Visa has saved millions of dollars using neural network software to spot fraud and to determine which of their customers might default or go bankrupt. Neural networks are good at spotting patterns, and if your profile looks like that of people who have defaulted, you'll be tossed into that category.

SUPPLIERS

Neural network classifying software can be applied to finding the best suppliers, too. Weyerhaueser Corporation's door factory executives have software to rank suppliers and distributors based on price, speed of delivery, and innovation. Using this information, Weyerhaueser doubled its sales and increased its return on net assets from 2 percent to 24 percent.

SUPERMARKETS

Catalina Supermarkets keeps track of what customers buy which products, how frequently, and what price they pay. Using neural network software, the supermarket chain can identify high-value customers and work at retaining them with offers of services such as free home delivery.

MOVIES

Even the movie business is getting in on the act. Twentieth Century Fox slices and dices its information in its databases to determine the most popular movies, actors, and plots in certain theaters, cities, and areas of the country. The aim is to show movies in those areas that will add the most to the bottom line. The result may be that people in certain areas will not get the chance to see certain movies.

There was a time when certain neighborhoods or geographic regions were redlined. That meant that banks and other businesses wouldn't deal with anyone who lived there. Some people think that this sort of market segmentation is a new form of redlining. Do you? Following are some questions for you to answer regarding this practice.[45]

Questions

1. A neural network learns to recognize patterns based on past information. Is this fair or reliable when applied to people? How accurate is it for a business to predict the future behavior of customers on the basis of historic information? Don't people change? Have you ever changed your behavior in the course of your life?

2. Customers are not likely ever to see the information that companies are using to pigeonhole them. Even the company executives may not know what criteria the neural network uses. How important are the assumptions underlying the software (i.e., the facts that the neural network is given about customers)? Even the IT specialists who design neural networks can't always vouch for their accuracy or specify exactly how the neural network reaches its conclusions. Is this safe for businesses? What are the possible business consequences of using neural networks without assurances of their reliability?

3. Businesses can use segmenting to suggest products and services to you, or if you request it, prevent your getting junk mail you don't want. Is that good? Would receiving wanted information or avoiding junk mail be worth the price of being categorized?

4. Say you run a business that supplies medical equipment (not prescription drugs)—wheelchairs, hospital beds, heating packs. You're trying to determine which customers you should give preferential treatment to. What assumptions or variables would you use (for example, age, income, and so on) to segment your customer population?

5. Do you think that this segmentation practice is fair? First, consider the business's stockholders, then consider the customers. Does it matter whether it's fair or not? Why or why not? Should there be laws against it, or laws controlling it, or none at all? Explain and justify your answer.

6. Does this differentiating practice make business sense? If you owned stock in a company, how would you feel about this practice? Do you think you should get better treatment if you're a better customer? Do you think people who are not such good customers should get the same deal that you get? Would it make any difference whether the company collected the information and did the neural network analysis itself, or bought the information or the whole package from a third party?

7. Is this practice of classifying the same as "redlining," or is it okay because it looks at behavior to classify people rather than assuming characteristics based on membership in a particular group?

Key Terms and Concepts

Artificial intelligence (AI), 189
Buyer agent (shopping bot), 202
Choice, 181
Crossover, 200
Data management, 186
Data-mining agent, 205
Decision support system (DSS), 183
Design, 181
Domain expert, 194
Domain expertise, 194
Expert system (knowledge-based system), 190
Explanation module, 195
Extranet, 203
Genetic algorithm, 199
Geographic information system (GIS), 187
Implementation, 181
Inference engine, 194
Intelligence, 181
Intelligent agent, 202

Intranet, 203
Knowledge acquisition, 194
Knowledge base, 194
Knowledge engineer, 194
Model management, 186
Monitoring-and-surveillance agent (predictive agent), 204
Mutation, 200
Neural network (artificial neural network, ANN), 196
Nonrecurring (ad hoc) decision, 182
Nonstructured decision, 182
Recurring decision, 182
Robot, 189
Rule-based expert system, 194
Selection, 200
Structured decision, 182
User agent (personal agent), 203
User interface management, 186

Short-Answer Questions

1. What are the four types of decisions discussed in this chapter? Give an example of each.
2. What are the four steps in making a decision?
3. What is a DSS? Describe its components.
4. What is a geographic information system used for?
5. How is information represented in a geographic information system?
6. What is artificial intelligence? Name the artificial intelligence systems used widely in business.

7. What are the components of an expert system?
8. What does the domain expert do?
9. How does a neural network work?
10. What three concepts of evolution are used by the genetic algorithm?
11. What are intelligent agents? What tasks can they perform?
12. What do shopping bots do?
13. What do monitoring-and-surveillance agents do?

Assignments and Exercises

1. **MAKE A GIS** Make a GIS-type map using transparencies. Draw a map of your campus on one plastic transparency sheet. You can use software or felt-tip pens to do the actual drawing of the map. Next, use a second sheet as an overlay and mark on it what classes you have taken in what buildings. Take a third sheet and enter the type of classroom you had the course in (i.e., auditorium, lab, small, medium, large room). Make a fourth layer with special facilities, like a computer lab or a biology lab, and so on. What problems did you encounter while designing your GIS? What other information would you like to see in a real GIS of this type? Would this handmade GIS be helpful for new students? What layers would you keep for general use? What layers would you keep for sentimental value when your college days are over?

2. **CHOOSE A FINANCING OPTION** Using a spreadsheet (like Excel, for example) evaluate your options for a $12,000 car. Compare the payments (use the =pmt function in Excel), the total amount of interest, and the total you'll pay for the car under the following four options:

a. 3 years at 0 percent interest

b. 2 years at 1.99 percent annual percent rate (APR)

c. 4 years at 5 percent APR

d. 6 years at 6 percent APR

What other considerations would you take into account if you were going to buy a new car? Are there considerations other than the interest rate and the other parts that can be calculated? What are they? How is a car different from other purchases, such as CDs or TV sets or computers?

3. **WHICH SOFTWARE WOULD YOU USE?** Which type or types of computer-aided decision support software would you use for each of the situations in the table below? Note why you think each of your choices is appropriate. The decision support alternatives are

- Decision support system
- Geographic information system
- Expert system
- Neural network
- Genetic algorithm
- Intelligent agent

Problem	Type of Decision Support
You and another marketing executive on a different continent want to develop a new pricing structure for products	
You want to predict when customers are about to take their business elsewhere	
You want to fill out a short tax form	
You want to determine the fastest route for package delivery to 23 different addresses in a city	
You want to decide where to spend advertising dollars (TV, radio, newspaper, direct mail, e-mail)	
You want to keep track of competitors' prices for comparable goods and services	

4. **WHAT SHOULD THE MUSIC STORE OWNER DO?** A music store owner wants to have enough of the hottest CDs in stock so that people who come in to buy a particular CD won't be disappointed—and the store won't lose the profit. CDs that are not sold within a certain length of time go onto the sale table where they may have to be sold at cost, if they sell at all.

The owner wants to design a decision support system to predict how many copies she should purchase and what information she will need. List some of the considerations that would go into such a system. Here are a couple to start you off: (1) the population of the target market; (2) sales for particular types of music in similar markets.

Discussion Questions

1. Some experts claim that if a business gets 52 percent of its decisions right, it will be successful. Would using a decision support system guarantee better results? Why or why not? What does the quality of any decision depend on? Do you think it matters what type of decisions are included in this 52 percent? For example, would getting the right type of paper clips be as influential a decision as deciding where to locate the business? Can you think of a situation where the type of paper clip matters a great deal?

2. Consider the topic of data warehouses in Chapter 3. In the future, AI systems will be increasingly applied to data warehouse processing. Which AI systems do you think might be helpful? For which tasks, or situations, might they best be applied? Do you think that AI systems will someday play a greater role in the design of databases and data warehouses? Why or why not?

3. Consider the differences and similarities among the four AI techniques discussed in this chapter. Name some problems that might be amenable to more than one type of AI system. Say you sell baseballs from your Web site. What types of AI systems could you use to generate information that would be useful to you in deciding what direction to take your company in the future? If you were pretty successful at selling baseballs, would you expect to have the amount of information on customers that, say, Wal-Mart has? Why or why not?

4. AI systems are relatively new approaches to solving business problems. What are the difficulties with new IT approaches in general? For each of the systems we discussed, identify some advantages and disadvantages of AI systems over traditional business processes. Say you were selling specialty teas and had both brick and click stores. Would you use the same type of AI systems for each part of your business? In what way would you use them or why would you not? Is there a place for decision support and artificial intelligence techniques in small specialty businesses? In what way would decision support add value? Can you think of how a DSS or an AI system would be value reducing (in terms of Porter's value chain theory)? What do you see as the major differences between running a mammoth concern and a small specialty business?

5. Neural networks recognize and categorize patterns. If someone were to have a neural network that could scan information on all aspects of your life, where would that neural network potentially be able to find information about you? Consider confidential (doctor's office) as well as publicly available (department of motor vehicles) information.

6. What type of AI systems could your school use to help with registration? Intelligent agents find vast amounts of information very quickly. Neural networks can classify patterns instantaneously. What sort of information might your school administration be able to generate using these (or other AI systems) with all of its student information?

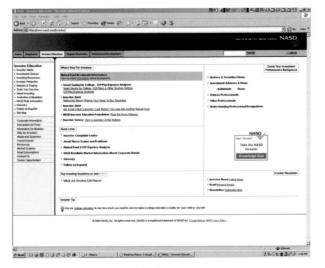

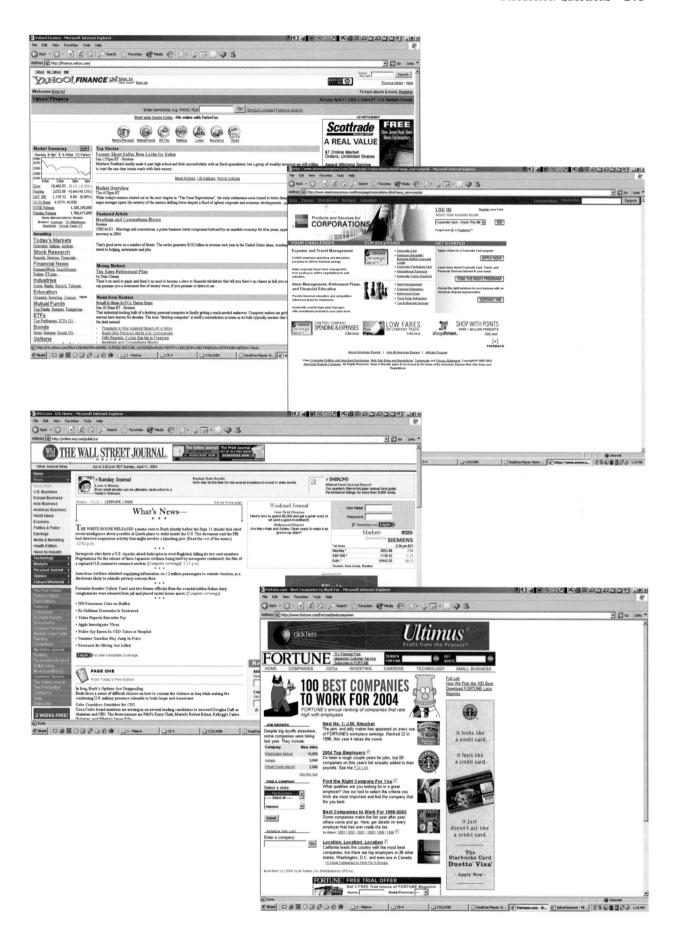

Finding Investment Opportunities on the Internet

When you buy stock in a company, you're betting on the success of that firm. Sometimes that bet is a good one, and sometimes it's not. Finding a company that's a good bet involves lots of research. To further complicate matters, some people prefer investing in large, safe companies, whereas others prefer the higher return of a small, more risky firm. So how do you make sense of all the options? Well, now you have access to financial information that professional investors use to evaluate stocks. The Internet brings together information-hungry investors with companies that have been anxiously looking to reach out to investors online. More than 900 companies now offer investment information on the World Wide Web, and the number is increasing rapidly. Remember, though, you must proceed with caution. Do your best to verify the source of any information.

You'll find many links on the Web site that supports this textbook (www.mhhe.com/haag, and select "Electronic Commerce Projects").

LEARNING ABOUT INVESTING

Investing can be as simple as finding a company that performs well financially and buying some of their stock. Or, if you want to spread your investment over a number of stocks and you don't want to select each stock personally, you can invest in a mutual fund. Of course, there are thousands of mutual funds with all types of investment objectives. So, any way you go you must pick your investment wisely. To help you get up to speed quickly, you'll find many helpful Web sites on the Internet.

For starters, you might explore the National Association of Securities Dealers (NASD) at www.nasdr.com. Check out their Investor Resources with its Education and Tools. You might also want to retrieve more general information from the online versions of traditional print media such as *The Wall Street Journal* or *Money* magazine.

Find three investment reference sites and explore what information is available. Then answer the following questions.

A. Is the site designed for first-time investors or those that are more experienced?

B. Can you search for a specific topic?

C. Are specific stocks or mutual funds reviewed or evaluated?

D. Does the site provide direct links to brokerage or stock quoting sites?

E. Is a forum for submitting questions available? If so, are frequently asked questions (FAQs) posted?

F. Who sponsors the site? Does it seem as if the sponsor is using the site to advertise its own products or services?

G. Can you download reference documents to read later?

RESEARCHING THE COMPANY BEHIND THE STOCK

One excellent way to pick a stock investment is to research the company behind that stock. Focusing on items such as sales revenues and profits to pick a stock is called *fundamental research*. So you might choose to invest in Hughes stock because you've discovered their sales revenues have been climbing steadily for the last three years. Or you might initially consider buying some Disney stock but change your mind when you find that EuroDisney revenues have been below expectations.

Now that you're ready to research a stock investment, connect to four different company sites. You can find your own or go to the Web site that supports this text where you will find a list of many other company sites. As you connect to the four sites, look up each company's financials and answer the questions that follow. You'll probably want to include at least two companies with which you are familiar and two that are new to you. In addition to reviewing company financials, look around each company site and see to what degree the site is investor oriented.

A. Do all the company sites offer financial information?

B. Is the information targeted at investors? How can you tell?

C. Can you download financial information to your computer and use it in a spreadsheet?

D. Can you download the company's annual report? Is it a full-color version?

E. Does the site provide direct links to e-mail addresses for requesting additional information?

F. Do the companies provide comparisons to others in their industry?

G. Does the site provide stock quotes as well as financials?

H. Can you search the site for financial-related information such as press releases?

I. Was there a charge for retrieving the financial information?

RETRIEVING STOCK QUOTES

Once you find the right stock to buy, you'll then be asking yourself, How much will this stock cost me? Stocks and mutual funds are both offered by the share and so you can easily buy as much or as little of the stock or mutual fund as you like. Still, some individual shares are priced in the hundreds or thousands of dollars, and that alone might make the purchase undesirable to you.

In addition to pricing individual shares to assess the affordability of an investment, you'll probably want to see how the price has varied over time. Even though most financial advisors will tell you that historical price variations provide no indication of future performance, most everyone uses price history to get a feel for whether the investment is trading at all-time highs or lows. So finding a chart of a stock price online might be helpful when deciding to make your purchase.

And even after you've made your purchase, you'll probably want to follow how your investment is doing. The thrill of realizing a "paper profit" is enough to keep many investors checking their investments daily. Of course, realizing a "paper loss" can be equally disappointing. And even if daily tracking isn't for you, you'll certainly want to check on your investments regularly, and doing so online can be quick and painless.

Pick three stock quoting services, examine what it takes to retrieve a stock or mutual fund quote, and answer the following questions.

A. Are the quotes provided free of charge or for a fee?

B. Does the site require a ticker symbol (the abbreviation used by experienced investors) or can you type in a company name?

C. Are the quotes in real time or are they delayed (15 to 20 minutes old)?

D. Does the site require registration?

E. Are historical prices available?

F. Are price charts available? Can you customize the chart display?

G. Can you create and save a personal portfolio of stocks?

EXTENDED LEARNING MODULE D

DECISION ANALYSIS WITH SPREADSHEET SOFTWARE

Student Learning Outcomes

1. DEFINE A LIST AND LIST DEFINITION TABLE WITHIN THE CONTEXT OF SPREADSHEET SOFTWARE AND DESCRIBE THE IMPORTANCE OF EACH.

2. COMPARE AND CONTRAST THE AUTOFILTER FUNCTION AND CUSTOM AUTOFILTER FUNCTION IN SPREADSHEET SOFTWARE.

3. DESCRIBE THE PURPOSE OF USING CONDITIONAL FORMATTING.

4. DEFINE A PIVOT TABLE AND DESCRIBE HOW YOU CAN USE IT TO VIEW SUMMARIZED INFORMATION BY DIMENSION.

Introduction

As you just read in Chapter 4, technology can and does play a vitally important role in both supporting decision making and, in some instances, actually making decisions or recommendations. In this module, we'll focus on decision-making support, by exploring many of the advanced and productive features of Microsoft Excel.

Microsoft Excel is spreadsheet software that allows you to work with any kind of information, with each individual piece of information located in a cell. A cell is the intersection of a row and column and is uniquely identified by its column character and row number. In Figure D.1 you can see a simple workbook (the terms *workbook* and *spreadsheet* are used interchangeably). It shows the number of customers by region (North, South, East, and West) and by rent versus own.

There are a total of 487 customers (cell D9), of which 262 own a home (cell B9) and 225 rent (cell C9). Within this workbook, you can easily see some interesting information. For example, there are 148 customers in the East region while only 98 live in the South region. By region and ownership status, 82 own a home in the East region while only 47 rent in the South region.

Of course, now the question becomes, How is that information helpful? Well, it depends on the nature of your decision-making task. If you believe that home owners spend more money than those who rent and want to target advertising to the largest region, the information in Figure D.1 might be helpful. Then again, it might not be. It could very well be that home owners actually spend less than customers who rent. And, perhaps you generate more sales in regions with a lower number of customers.

Let's see how spreadsheet software can help you make better decisions. As we do, we'll introduce you to some spreadsheet features including AutoFilter, conditional formatting, and pivot tables. Our goal here is not to provide in great detail how each of these

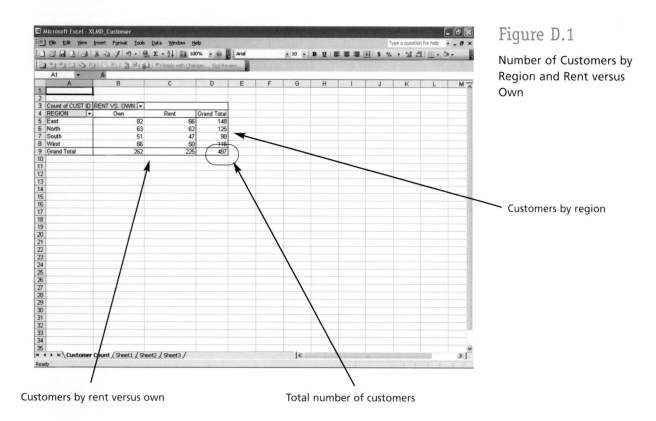

Figure D.1

Number of Customers by Region and Rent versus Own

Customers by region

Customers by rent versus own

Total number of customers

work, but rather what's most important about each one of them in supporting your decision-making tasks. After completing this module, you'll definitely be able to use all features in their basic forms. We recommend that you continue to explore them in detail.

Lists

What we showed in Figure D.1 was a pivot table. A pivot table is a spreadsheet function that summarizes information by category. In our case, it summarized information by region and rent versus own. To create a pivot table (and use many of the other features we'll discuss in this module), you have to first build a list. You should work along with us on this. Connect to the Web site that supports this text (www.mhhe.com/haag and select XLM/D). There, you can download the file called XLMD_Customer.xls.

A **_list_** is a collection of information arranged in columns and rows in which each column displays one particular type of information. In spreadsheet software, a list possesses the following characteristics:

1. Each column has only one type of information.
2. The first row in the list contains the labels or column headings.
3. The list does not contain any blank rows.
4. The list is bordered on all four sides by blank rows and blank columns (it may not have a blank line above it, if it starts in the first row).

Take a look at the workbook in Figure D.2. It contains detailed information about our customers. In fact, we used this very list to generate the pivot table in Figure D.1.

First, notice that each column contains only one type of information: column A contains _CUST ID_, column B contains _REGION_, and so on. Second, notice that the first row (row 1) contains the labels or column headings. Third, if you scroll down completely

Figure D.2

The Complete List of Customers

Labels or column headings

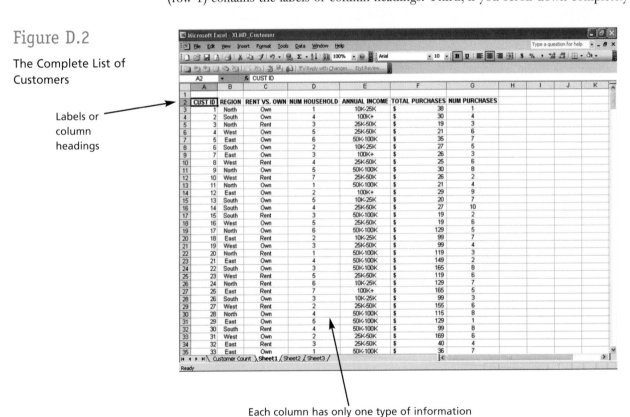

Each column has only one type of information

through the list, you'll notice that there are 487 customers and there are no blank rows. Finally, notice that the list is bordered on all sides (except the top) by blank rows and columns. So, this is a list according to the four characteristics we listed.

We're going to be working extensively with this list throughout this module, so let's take a little time to explore the information in it. The columns of information include

A. *CUST ID*—A unique ID for each customer

B. *REGION*—The region in which the customer lives (North, South, East, or West)

C. *RENT VS. OWN*—Whether the customer rents or owns a home

D. *NUM HOUSEHOLD*—Number of family members in the household

E. *ANNUAL INCOME*—Total combined annual income of all family members

F. *TOTAL PURCHASES*—Dollar total of all purchases made by the customer within the last six months

G. *NUM PURCHASES*—Count of all purchases made by the customer within the last six months

What we listed above is called a **list definition table,** a description of a list by column. List definition tables are important. If you can create one just as we did, then you can create a list in a workbook with the appropriate characteristics. If you can't, then you may not be able to use many of the features we're about to show you.

With the good solid list in place, you're now ready to start exploring many of the decision support features in Excel. Let's assume that you work for our hypothetical retail company and have been asked to perform the following tasks to aid in various decisions:

1. Show all information for only customers who live in the North region.

2. Show all information for only customers who (a) live in the North region, (b) own their homes, and (c) have only one household member.

3. Show all information for customers who have at least 4 household members.

4. Show all information for customers who (a) have spent less than $20 or (b) more than $100.

5. Show all information for all customers highlighting those customers who have spent more than $100.

6. Provide a two-dimensional table that counts the number of customers by the categories of *REGION* and *RENT VS. OWN.*

7. Provide a two-dimensional table that both (a) counts the number of customers and (b) sums the *TOTAL PURCHASES* of customers by the categories of *REGION* and *RENT VS. OWN.*

8. Provide a three-dimensional table that counts the number of customers by the categories of *REGION, RENT VS. OWN,* and *NUM HOUSEHOLD.*

Basic AutoFilter

Working with small lists that can be displayed in their entirety on a screen is seldom a problem. With a small list you can see the entire domain of information without scrolling up or down. But our list is much larger, containing 487 customers. So, you have to scroll through it to see all the information. If you were looking for specific information, such as all the customers in the North region (your first task in the list above), you could sort using the *REGION* column but you still get all the information (not to mention that customers in the North would come after the customers in the East region, alphabetically).

Figure D.3

Using AutoFilter to See Customers in the North Region

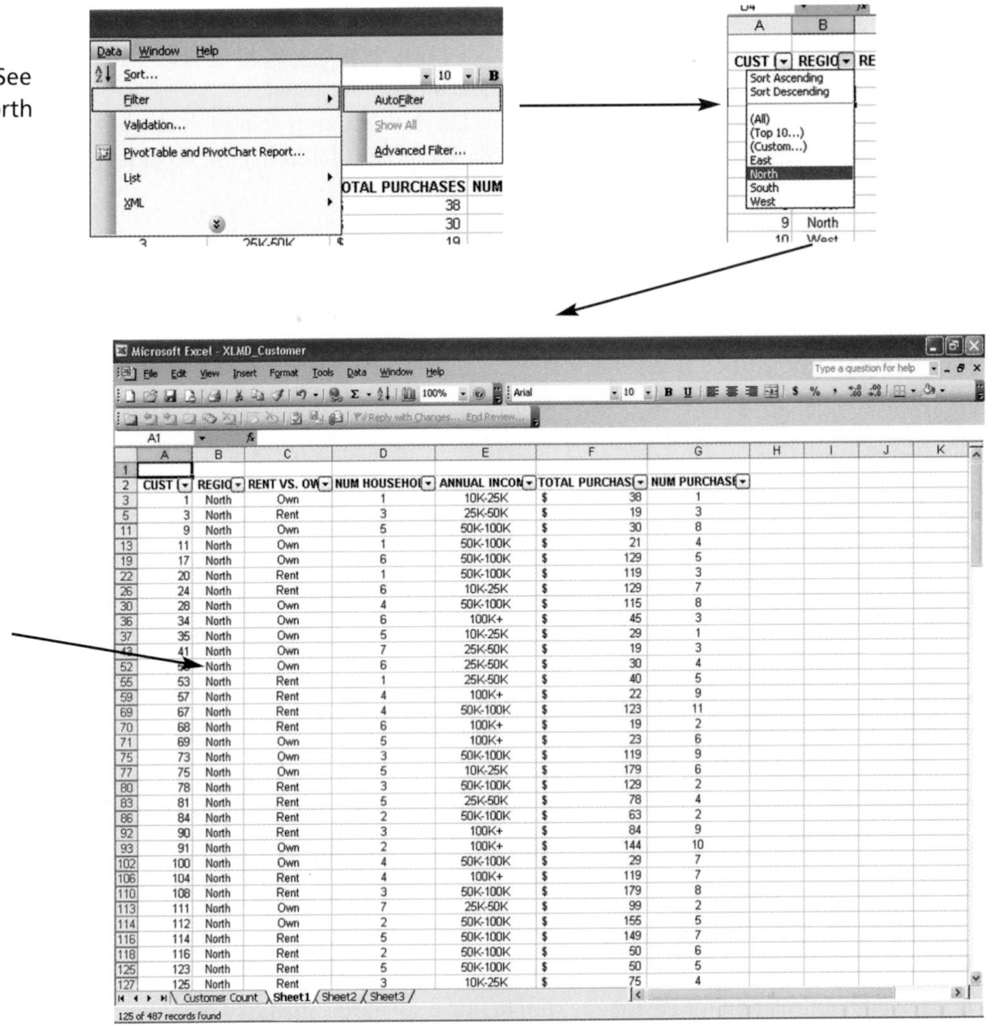

	CUST	REGIO	RENT VS. OW	NUM HOUSEHOL	ANNUAL INCOM	TOTAL PURCHAS		NUM PURCHASE
3	1	North	Own	1	10K-25K	$	38	1
5	3	North	Rent	3	25K-50K	$	19	3
11	9	North	Own	5	50K-100K	$	30	8
13	11	North	Own	1	50K-100K	$	21	4
19	17	North	Own	6	50K-100K	$	129	5
22	20	North	Rent	1	50K-100K	$	119	3
26	24	North	Rent	6	10K-25K	$	129	7
30	28	North	Own	4	50K-100K	$	115	8
36	34	North	Own	6	100K+	$	45	3
37	35	North	Own	5	10K-25K	$	29	1
43	41	North	Own	7	25K-50K	$	19	3
52	[illegible]	North	Own	6	25K-50K	$	30	4
55	53	North	Rent	1	25K-50K	$	40	5
59	57	North	Rent	4	100K+	$	22	9
69	67	North	Rent	4	50K-100K	$	123	11
70	68	North	Rent	6	100K+	$	19	2
71	69	North	Own	5	100K+	$	23	6
75	73	North	Own	3	50K-100K	$	119	9
77	75	North	Own	5	10K-25K	$	179	6
80	78	North	Rent	3	50K-100K	$	129	2
83	81	North	Rent	5	25K-50K	$	78	4
86	84	North	Rent	2	50K-100K	$	63	2
92	90	North	Rent	3	100K+	$	84	9
93	91	North	Own	2	100K+	$	144	10
102	100	North	Own	4	50K-100K	$	29	7
106	104	North	Rent	4	100K+	$	119	7
110	108	North	Rent	3	50K-100K	$	179	8
113	111	North	Own	7	25K-50K	$	99	2
114	112	North	Own	2	50K-100K	$	155	5
116	114	North	Rent	5	50K-100K	$	149	7
118	116	North	Rent	2	50K-100K	$	50	6
125	123	North	Rent	5	50K-100K	$	50	5
127	125	North	Rent	3	10K-25K	$	75	4

Shows only customers in the North *REGION*

To quickly create smaller lists out of a much larger list, you can use the AutoFilter function. The ***AutoFilter function*** filters a list and allows you to hide all the rows in a list except those that match criteria you specify. To filter a list with the AutoFilter function, perform the following steps (see Figure D.3):

1. Click in any cell within the list
2. From the menu bar, click on **Data,** point at **Filter,** and click on **AutoFilter**

Once you complete those two steps, Excel will place list box arrows next to each label or column heading. Now, all you have to do is click on the appropriate list box arrow and select the type of filtering you want. In Figure D.3, you can see that we clicked on the *REGION* list arrow box and chose North. Excel then presented us with a filtered list of only those customers in the North region. Our list is still quite long, but it does show only customers in the North. To turn off the AutoFilter function, from the menu bar, click on **Data,** point at **Filter,** and click on **AutoFilter.**

When using the AutoFilter function, you're not limited to working with just one column. In Figure D.3, we filtered using the *REGION* column. Now, what if you want a filtered list of those customers in the North who own a home and have only one household member (your second task in the list on page 219)? That's easy. Click in the *RENT VS. OWN* list arrow box and choose **Own.** Then, click in the *NUM HOUSEHOLD* list

LISTS, LIST DEFINITION TABLES, AND USING AUTOFILTER

Now it's your turn to practice using the basic AutoFilter function on a list. Go to the Web site that supports this text (www.mhhe.com/haag), select XLM/D, and download the file called XLMD_Customer2.xls. Take a moment and review the information in that workbook.

First, in the table below, create the list definition for it just as we did on page 219.

Now perform the following AutoFilter exercises:

1. Show only those customers in the state of California.

2. Show only those customers whose type of business is nonprofit.

3. Show only those customers in the retail business sector.

4. Show only those customers in Texas whose type of business is government.

5. Show only those customers in the manufacturing business sector.

Column Name	Description

arrow box and choose **1.** That will show you the complete list (4 to be exact) of customers in the North who own a home and have only one household family member (see Figure D.4).

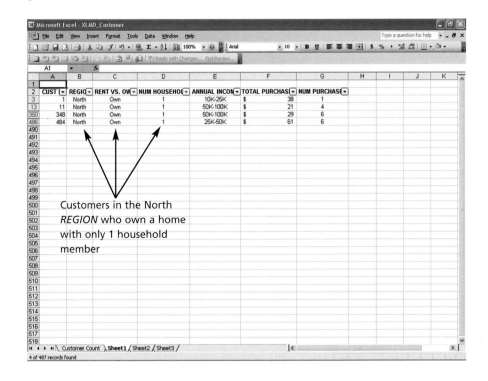

Customers in the North *REGION* who own a home with only 1 household member

Figure D.4

A List Generated with Three Filters

Custom AutoFilter

The basic AutoFilter function allows you to create sublists using exact match criteria: *REGION* must be North, *NUM HOUSEHOLD* must be 1, and so forth. But what if you want to know all those customers who have at least four people in their households (your third task in the list on page 219)? In that case, you can't use the basic AutoFilter function—you need to use the ***Custom AutoFilter function.*** The Custom AutoFilter function allows you to hide all the rows in a list except those that match criteria, besides "is equal to," you specify. Let's see how to use the Custom AutoFilter function.

Figure D.5

Using a Custom
AutoFilter

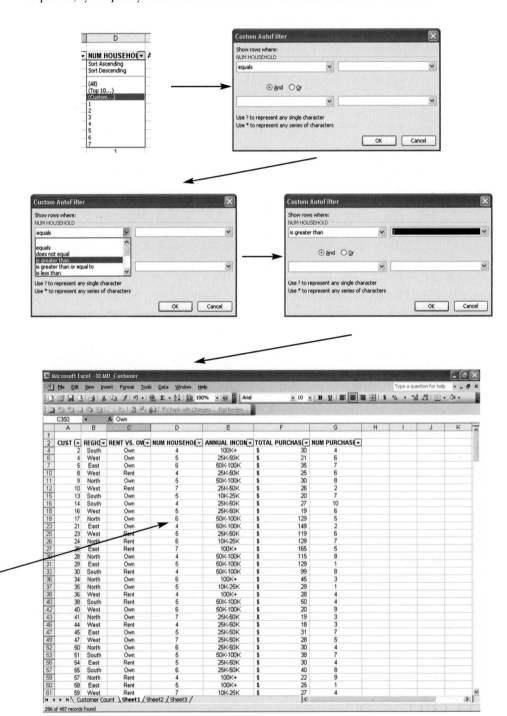

Only customers with
more than four people
in their households

Given that you want to see a list of all customers who have at least four people in their households, perform the following steps:

1. Make sure you can see the entire list with the AutoFilter function turned on
2. Click on the *NUM HOUSEHOLD* list arrow box
3. Select **(Custom . . .)**

What you'll then see is a Custom AutoFilter box (the top right box in Figure D.5). For the top-left entry field, click on its pull-down arrow and select **is greater than.** For the top-right entry box, click on its pull down arrow and select **3** (or type the number **3** directly into the box). Then, all you have to do is click on **OK.** Excel does the rest and shows you the appropriate list of customers with at least four people in their households.

You should notice in Figure D.5 that the Custom AutoFilter box allows you to enter two criteria for creating a filtered list. So, you can easily create a Custom AutoFilter that answers the following question: What customers have spent less than $20 or more than $100 in the past six months (your fourth task in the list on page 219)? In Figure D.6, we've shown you how to do that along with the result.

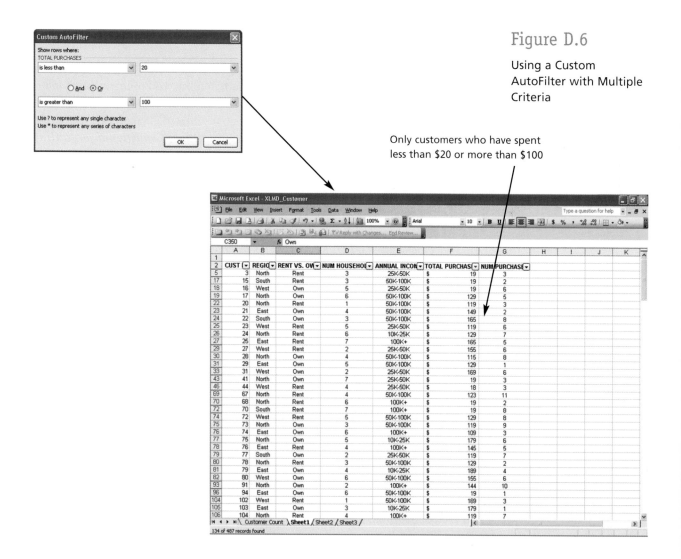

Figure D.6

Using a Custom AutoFilter with Multiple Criteria

Only customers who have spent less than $20 or more than $100

USING CUSTOM AUTOFILTERS

Now it's your turn to practice using the Custom Auto-Filter function on a list. Go to the Web site that supports this text (www.mhhe.com/haag), select XLM/D, and download the file called XLMD_Customer2.xls (the same one you used previously for the On Your Own project). Now perform the following Custom AutoFilter exercises:

1. Show only those customers who have more than 100 employees.

2. Show only those customers who have fewer than 100 employees.

3. Show only those customers who have at least 50 employees but no more than 100 employees.

4. Show only those customers in Tennessee who have fewer than 10 employees.

Conditional Formatting

When you use AutoFilter (either basic or custom), in a way you're highlighting information you want to see by basically hiding the other information you don't. As an alternative, you might want to highlight certain information while still being able to see all the other information. If so, you can use conditional formatting. *Conditional formatting* highlights the information in a cell that meets some criteria you specify.

For example, what if you still wanted to be able to scroll through the entire list of customers but also wanted to have all *TOTAL PURCHASES* greater than $100 highlighted (your fifth task in the list on page 219). This is a simple process in Excel. To do that, perform the following steps (see Figure D.7 on the facing page):

1. Select the entire *TOTAL PURCHASES* column (move the pointer over the F column identifier and click once)

2. From the menu bar, click on **Format** and then click on **Conditional Formatting**

You will then see a Conditional Formatting box as shown in the middle-left of Figure D.7.

Now, click on the pull down arrow for the field second from the left and click on **greater than.** In the field on the right, enter **100.** Finally, you need to select the conditional formatting for the information. To do so, click on the **Format** button. You will then see a Format Cells box. Across the top, you'll see tabs for Font, Border, and Patterns.

In our example, we clicked on the Patterns tab, chose the color red, and clicked on **OK.** Excel returned us to the Conditional Formatting box at which time we clicked on the **OK** button. As you can see in Figure D.8, Excel left the list intact and highlighted all cells in the *TOTAL PURCHASES* column in which the value exceeded $100.

To remove conditional formatting, first highlight the entire column again. Second, from the menu bar, click on **Format** and click on **Conditional Formatting.** Third, click on the **Delete** button in the Conditional Formatting box. Fourth, select **Condition 1** in the Delete Conditional Format box. Finally, click on **OK** in the Delete Conditional Format box, and click on **OK** in the Conditional Format box.

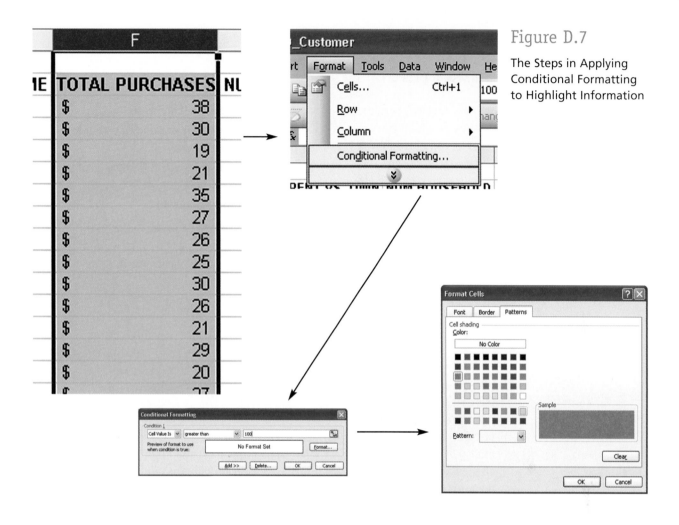

Figure D.7

The Steps in Applying Conditional Formatting to Highlight Information

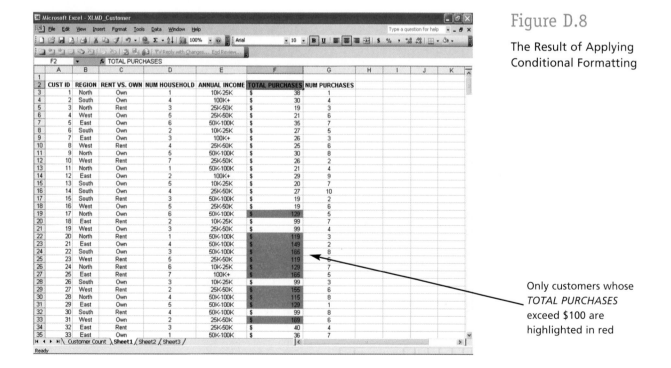

Figure D.8

The Result of Applying Conditional Formatting

Only customers whose *TOTAL PURCHASES* exceed $100 are highlighted in red

TEAM WORK

CONDITIONAL FORMATTING

On the Web site that supports this text (www.mhhe. com/haag and select XLMD), we've provided a workbook titled XLMD_Production.xls. It contains information concerning batches of products produced. Each batch is produced using only one machine by one employee. For each batch, a batch size is provided as well as the number of defective products produced in the batch.

Highlight the following by applying conditional formatting:

1. All batches made by Employee 1111.
2. All batches for which the number of defective products is greater than 10.
3. All batches for which the batch size is greater than 1,000.
4. All batches for Product 10.

Pivot Tables

Now, let's return to our original pivot table in Figure D.1 on page 217. Formally defined, a **pivot table** enables you to group and summarize information. That's just what we did in Figure D.1. We created a two-dimensional pivot table that displayed a count of customers by *REGION* and by *RENT VS. OWN* (your sixth task in the list on page 219). Of all the Excel decision-support features we demonstrate in this module, pivot tables take the most steps to create, but they also tend to yield highly valuable information.

To create a two-dimensional pivot table, first ensure that your list has no conditional formatting and that you do not have the AutoFilter function turned on. To create any two-dimensional pivot table, follow the four steps at the top of the next page (and see Figure D.9).

Figure D.9

The First Steps in Creating a Two-Dimensional Pivot Table

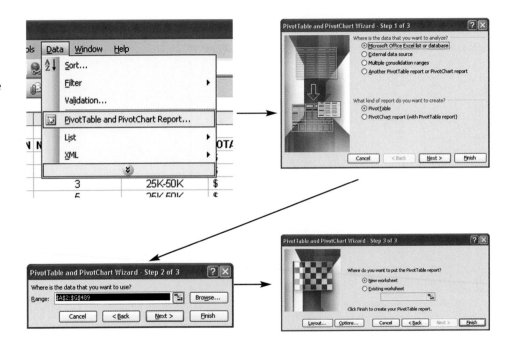

226

1. From the menu bar, click on **Data** and **PivotTable and PivotChart Report**
2. In the Step 1 of 3 box, click on **Next**
3. In the Step 2 of 3 box, click on **Next**
4. In the Step 3 of 3 box, click on **Finish**

What you will then see is the skeletal structure of a pivot table as shown in Figure D.10.

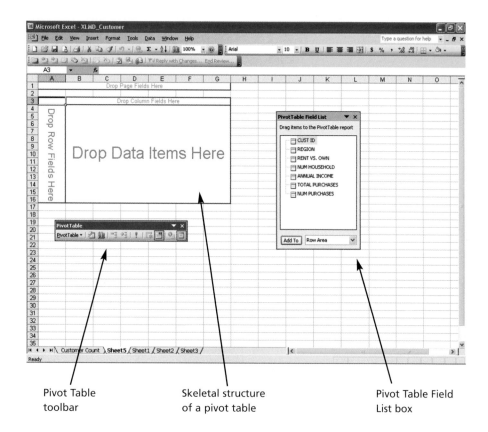

Figure D.10

The Skeletal Structure of a Pivot Table and the Pivot Table Toolbar

Pivot Table toolbar

Skeletal structure of a pivot table

Pivot Table Field List box

BUTTON NAME	PURPOSE
PivotTable	Drop-down that displays shortcut menu of pivot table commands
Format Report	Displays a list of pivot table report styles
Chart Wizard	Creates a chart sheet from a pivot table
MapPoint	Creates map from PivotTable data
Hide Detail	Hides detail lines of a pivot table field
Show Detail	Reveals detail lines of a pivot table field
Refresh Data	Updates a pivot table
Include Hidden Items in Total	Items you have hidden are still counted in the PivotTable totals
Always Display Items	Controls when Excel goes to an external data source to determine a pivot table value
Field Settings	Opens the PivotTable field dialog box containing options you can apply to the selected pivot table field
Hide/Show Field Test	Toggles between hiding and displaying the field list

To provide a brief explanation of what we've done so far, let's examine the three dialog boxes in Figure D.9 on page 226. The first box allows you to choose the location of the information from which you want to build a pivot table. We wanted to use an Excel list so we accepted the default. The first box also gives you the ability to choose between creating a pivot table or a pivot table chart. We wanted a pivot table so we accepted the default.

The second box allows you to choose a range of information from which to build a pivot table. The default is the entire list, which we accepted. Finally, the third box allows you to specify a location for the pivot table. The default is a new worksheet, which we accepted. At some point in time, you should explore the various other options.

What you see in Figure D.10 on page 227 takes some more explaining. In the upper left portion is the skeletal structure of the pivot table. To the right, you can see the Pivot Table Field List box. It includes a list of all the labels or column headings we have in the list.

Near the bottom left, you can see the Pivot Table toolbar. It includes numerous buttons for different functions. The primary one of interest to us now is the **Field Settings** button, the second button from the right in the toolbar. Figure D.10 lists and explains all the buttons in the Pivot Table toolbar.

What you do now is to drag and drop the appropriate labels or columns headings from the Pivot Table Field List box into the appropriate areas of the pivot table itself.

Recall that we are attempting to build a two-dimensional pivot table that looks like the one in Figure D.1 on page 217. So, you know that the row information is by *REGION*. To achieve this, drag the *REGION* label from the Pivot Table Field List box to the pivot table and drop it into the area marked "Drop Row Fields Here" (see Figure D.11). You also know that the column information is by *RENT VS. OWN*. So, drag that label from the Pivot Table Field List box and drop it into the area marked "Drop Column Fields Here."

Figure D.11

Creating a Pivot Table by Dragging and Dropping Information

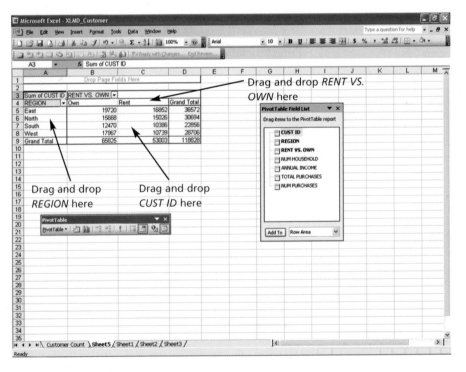

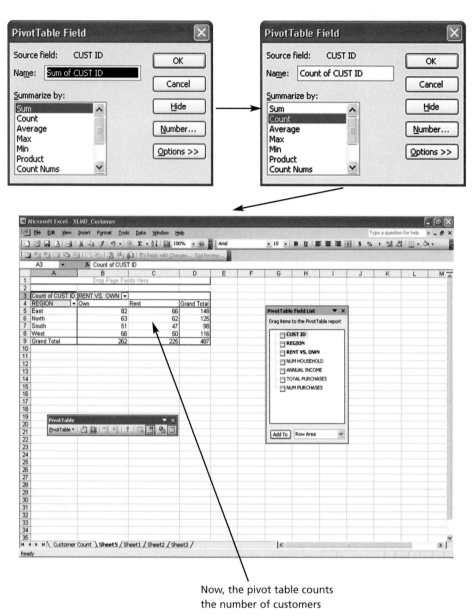

The Pivot Table with the Information You Want

Now, the pivot table counts the number of customers

Finally, you need to place something in the main area of the pivot table that will enable you to count customers by region and rent versus own. The simplest way to achieve this is to drag *CUST ID* from the Pivot Table Field List box and drop it into the area marked "Drop Data Items Here." What you will then have is a pivot table that looks like the screen in Figure D.11, on page 228, which is not at all what we want. Why?

When you drop information into the main area of a pivot table, the default aggregation or summarization is by summation. You don't want to sum customer IDs—that doesn't make any sense. What you want to do is count them. To change this, perform the following steps (see Figure D.12):

1. Click on the **Field Settings** button in the Pivot Table toolbar
2. In the PivotTable Field box, click on **Count** in the **Summarize by** list
3. Click on **OK**

The final screen in Figure D.12 shows the correct information.

CREATING A TWO-DIMENSIONAL PIVOT TABLE

Let's return to our workbook containing production in-formation (XLMD_Production.xls). Using it, create sep-arate pivot tables that show

- The number of different machines used to produce each product

- The number of defective products produced by employee by product

- The total number of products produced by each employee

- The total number of products produced by each employee as well as the total number of defective products produced by each employee

We now have a pivot table that shows a count of customers by *REGION* and *RENT VS. OWN*. But depending on what decision you're trying to make, that may not be enough information. What else might be helpful? Again, depending on the decision, it might be helpful to also know the total of all purchases by *REGION* and *RENT VS. OWN* (your seventh task in the list on page 219). If so, you don't need to create another pivot table. You can simply add the field *TOTAL PURCHASES* to the main area of the pivot table. To do so, drag that label from the Pivot Table Field List box and drop it into the main area of the pivot table. Figure D.13 shows the result.

Figure D.13

An Added Field of Information to a Pivot Table

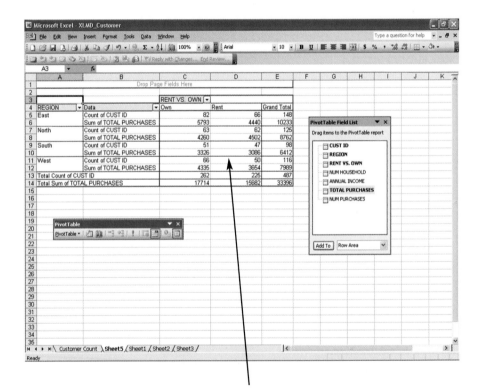

Drag and drop *TOTAL PURCHASES* here to obtain a summary of another dimension of information

Is the information helpful? Again, it depends on the decision you're trying to make. But adding another piece of information to the main area of a pivot table is easy, and it does illustrate the true productivity of spreadsheet software.

Your final task in the list on page 219 is to create a three-dimensional pivot table that counts the number of customers by the categories of *REGION, RENT VS. OWN,* and *NUM HOUSEHOLD.* The result will look similar to the two-dimensional pivot table in Figure D.13 with two exceptions. First, you will not include the sum of *TOTAL PUR-CHASES* in the main area of the pivot table. Second, you will add depth to the pivot table, making it a three-dimensional pivot table. In short, you do this by dragging the *NUM HOUSEHOLD* label from the Pivot Table Field List box to the pivot table and dropping it into the area marked "Drop Page Fields Here."

In Figure D.14, you can see in the upper left screen that we created a two-dimensional pivot table showing a count of customers by *REGION* and *RENT VS. OWN.* This is the same two-dimensional pivot table we created in Figure D.12 on page 229. To add depth to the pivot table, we dragged the *NUM HOUSEHOLD* label from the Pivot Table Field List box to the pivot table and dropped it into the area marked "Drop Page Fields Here." Notice that the new pivot table (the lower right screen in Figure D.14) still looks like a two-dimensional pivot table and provides the same information in the main area of the pivot table. That's because the default display for a three-dimensional pivot table is to show all summarized information for the depth. You can tell this because to the right of *NUM HOUSEHOLD* in cell A1 is the word "All."

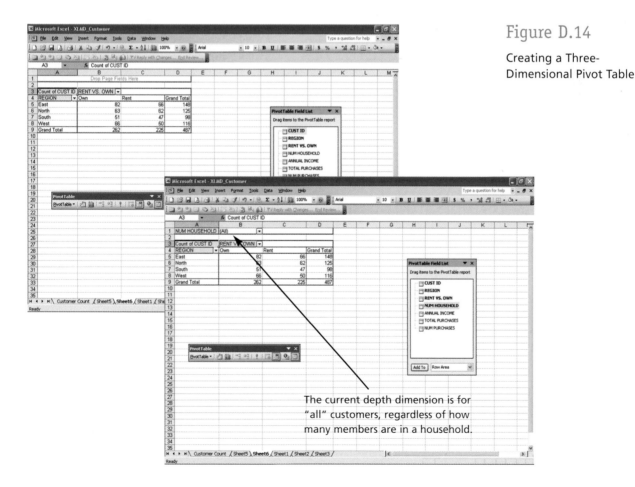

Figure D.14

Creating a Three-Dimensional Pivot Table

The current depth dimension is for "all" customers, regardless of how many members are in a household.

Figure D.15

Viewing Different Depths in a Three-Dimensional Pivot Table

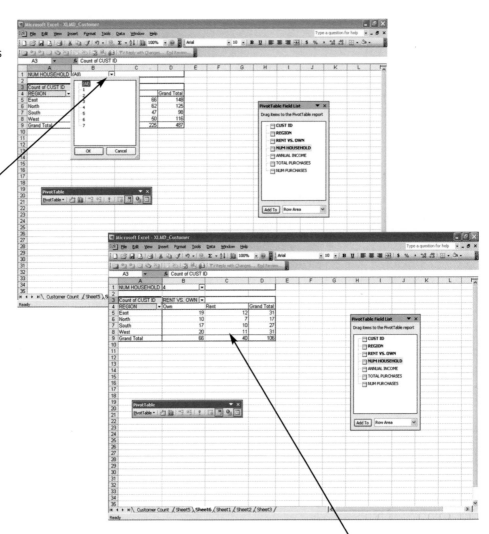

Click on the *NUM HOUSEHOLD* pull-down arrow to see your depth options.

By selecting 4 in the *NUM HOUSEHOLD* depth dimension, you see a summary of customers for only that criteria.

To view the count of your customers according to specific values for *NUM HOUSE-HOLD*, simply click on the list box arrow immediately to the right of the word "All" as we did in the top screen in Figure D.15. You then click on the value you want in *NUM HOUSEHOLD* for displaying the count of customers for that value by *REGION* and *RENT VS. OWN*. We clicked on 4 and then **OK.** The bottom screen in Figure D.15 shows the result. It shows some interesting information that might help you make a decision. For example, in the West region there are 20 customers who own their homes and only 11 who rent their homes. Furthermore, across all regions there are 66 customers who own their homes and only 40 who rent. Again, is this helpful information? That depends on the decision you're trying to make.

The three-dimensional pivot table feature in Excel is a powerful one. If you recall our discussions of data warehouses in Chapter 3, you can actually build a data warehouse with rows, columns, and layers by simply creating a three-dimensional pivot table in Excel. By selecting different values for the page (depth) field, you are actually bringing layers of information to the front.

Back to Decision Support

Let's take a break from the computer for a moment and discuss what we've just demonstrated within the context of decision support. After all, you don't need to learn the various tools of spreadsheet software just because "they are there." You should learn them because they will be beneficial to you.

In general, the spreadsheet features we've just shown you give you the ability to look at vast amounts of information quickly. Indeed, our customer workbook contained information on 487 customers. Can you imagine trying to summarize or aggregate information on 48,700 customers without the use of spreadsheet software? Even creating simple totals and subtotals would be a daunting task.

AUTOFILTER

The AutoFilter function (either basic or custom) helps you quickly create a view of a partial list of information. The basic AutoFilter function creates a partial list based on exact match criteria, while the custom AutoFilter function allows you to specify ranges (e.g., greater than, less than, and so on).

The purpose of the AutoFilter function is really to help you quickly focus on only the information that's important to you by "hiding" the information that isn't. It's rather like having a very good search engine that only gives you a list of useful articles to help you write a term paper.

CONDITIONAL FORMATTING

Conditional formatting maintains the view of the entire list of information but highlights key pieces of information that you may be looking for. This gives you the ability to see the entire list of information but quickly draws your attention to specific information.

PIVOT TABLE

A pivot table (either two- or three-dimensional) helps you quickly aggregate or summarize information by *dimension*. This gives you a nice overview of the information without bogging you down in any of the details.

Further, a pivot table can help you see relationships among the information. If you look back at the pivot table in Figure D.13 on page 230, you can see the relationship between the number of customers and their total purchases within *REGION* and *RENT VS. OWN*. These types of relationships can certainly be insightful.

Can any of these tools or functions make a decision for you? Definitely not. But they can help you make that decision. That's why spreadsheet software is often called *decision support* software.

Summary: Student Learning Outcomes Revisited

1. **Define a list and list definition table within the context of spreadsheet software and describe the importance of each.** A *list* is a collection of information arranged in columns and rows in which each column displays one particular type of information. A *list definition table* is a description of a list by column. Lists are important within the context of spreadsheet software because they enable you to use such spreadsheet features as AutoFilter, conditional formatting, and pivot tables. Creating a list definition table is important because it requires you to adhere to the necessary rules for creating a list.

2. **Compare and contrast the AutoFilter function and Custom AutoFilter function in spreadsheet software.** The *AutoFilter function* filters a list and allows you to hide all the rows in a list except those that match specific criteria you specify. The *Custom AutoFilter function* allows you to hide all the rows in a list except those that

match criteria, besides "is equal to," you specify. So, the basic AutoFilter function makes use of "is equal to" as the criteria, while the Custom AutoFilter function allows you to use other criteria such as greater than, less than, and so on.

3. **Describe the purpose of using conditional formatting.** *Conditional formatting* highlights the information in a cell that meets some criteria you specify. So, conditional formatting allows you to view the entire list while having certain information called to your attention.

4. **Define a pivot table and describe how you can use it to view summarized information by dimension.** A *pivot table* enables you to group and summarize information. When creating a pivot table, you create dimensions of information by specifying how information is to be summarized by dimension. You define the dimensions by dragging and dropping information labels or column headings into the row, column, and page areas of a pivot table.

Key Terms and Concepts

AutoFilter function, 220
Conditional formatting, 224
Custom AutoFilter function, 222

List, 218
List definition table, 219
Pivot table, 226

Assignments and Exercises

1. **WHAT PRODUCTION PROBLEMS DO YOU HAVE?** Throughout this module, you've been practicing some spreadsheet features using XLMD_Production.xls. Its list definition table is as follows:
   A. *BATCH*—A unique number that identifies each batch or group of products produced
   B. *PRODUCT*—A unique number that identifies each product
   C. *MACHINE*—A unique number that identifies each machine on which products are produced
   D. *EMPLOYEE*—A unique number that identifies each employee producing products
   E. *BATCH SIZE*—The number of products produced in a given batch
   F. *NUM DEFECTIVE*—The number of defective products produced in a given batch

   It seems you have some real problems. There are an unacceptable number of defective products being produced. Your task is to use some combination of AutoFilter, conditional formatting, and pivot tables to illustrate where the problems seem to be concentrated, perhaps by product, by employee, by machine, or even by batch size. Based on your analysis, recommend how to correct the problems.

2. **EVALUATING TOTAL PURCHASES AND ANNUAL INCOME** Using XLMD_Customer.xls, create a pivot table that illustrates the relationship between *TOTAL PURCHASES* and *ANNUAL INCOME*. What trends do you see in the information? Suppose your task is to concentrate marketing efforts and resources. On which annual income level would you concentrate? Why? If you were the marketing manager, what additional information would be helpful as you make your decision? Where would you be able to obtain such information?

3. **FINDING OUT INFORMATION ABOUT YOUR EMPLOYEES** Suppose you own a small business and have a workbook with the following list:
   A. *ID*—Unique employee's identification number
   B. *First Name*—Employee's first name
   C. *Last Name*—Employee's last name
   D. *Department*—Employee's department
   E. *Title*—Employee's job title
   F. *Salary*—Employee's annual salary
   G. *Hire Date*—Date employee was hired
   H. *Birth Date*—Employee's birthday
   I. *Gender*—Female (F) or male (M)
   J. *Clearance*—N (none), C (confidential), S (secret), or TS (top secret)
   You can obtain this workbook from the Web site that supports this text (www.mhhe.com/haag and select XLM/D). Its filename is XLMD_Employee.xls. Perform the following tasks:
   a. Create a pivot table that shows average salary by gender within department.
   b. Create a pivot table that shows the number of employees by clearance.
   c. Use conditional formatting to highlight those employees in the Engineering department.
   d. Use conditional formatting to highlight those employees who have no clearance (none).
   e. Use basic AutoFilter to show only those employees who have top secret clearance (TS).
   f. Use Custom AutoFilter to show only those employees who earn more than $50,000.

4. **EXPLORING INFORMATION AT B&B TRAVEL** Benjamin Travis and Brady Austin are co-owners of B&B Travel Consultants, a medium-size business in Seattle with several branch offices. B&B specializes in selling cruise packages. Ben and Brady maintain a workbook that contains the following list for each cruise package sale:
   A. *LOCATION #*—A unique number that identifies which office location recorded the sale
   B. *TRAVEL AGENT #*—A unique number that identifies which travel consultant recorded the sale
   C. *CRUISE LINE*—The name of the cruise line for which the package was sold
   D. *TOTAL PACKAGE PRICE*—The price charged to the customer for the package
   E. *COMMISSION*—The amount of money B&B made from the sale of the package
   Ben and Brady have decided to scale back their operations. So, they're looking to you for help. The workbook name is XLMD_Travel.xls and you can find it on the Web site that supports this text at www.mhhe.com/haag (select XLM/D). Using AutoFilter, conditional formatting, and pivot tables, prepare a short report that answers each of the following questions and illustrates the justification for your answers.
   a. Which, if any, location should be closed?
   b. Which, if any, travel consultants should be downsized?
   c. On which cruise lines should B&B focus its sales efforts?

5. **CREATE A LIST FOR A BOOKSTORE** Suppose that you're the manager for your school's bookstore. Your task is to create a list in a workbook that contains information about the textbooks it sells. In addition to tracking price, first author name, and publisher, identify five other pieces of information for each textbook. For this list, first provide a list definition table. Second, enter some information for 20 textbooks. Third, illustrate the use of the basic AutoFilter function, the Custom AutoFilter function, conditional formatting, and pivot tables. Finally, address how your bookstore might be able to use this information to support its decision-making tasks.

CHAPTER FIVE OUTLINE

STUDENT LEARNING OUTCOMES

1. Define and describe the two major e-commerce business models (Business to Business and Business to Consumer).

2. Summarize Porter's Five Forces Model and how business people can use it to understand the relative attractiveness of an industry.

3. Describe the emerging role of e-marketplaces in B2B e-commerce.

4. Identify the differences and similarities among customers and their perceived value of products and services in the B2B and B2C e-commerce business models.

5. Compare and contrast the development of a marketing mix for customers in the B2B and B2C e-commerce business models.

6. Summarize the various ways of moving money in the world of e-commerce and related issues.

CHAPTER FIVE

Electronic Commerce
Strategies for the New Economy

OPENING CASE STUDY:
IS AMERICA ONLINE (AOL) INCHING
TOWARD BECOMING AN INTERNET
BANK?

In March 2004, America Online (AOL) launched a streamlined new service for online bill payment. No—it doesn't yet provide the capability to pay online bills directly through AOL, but it does seem to be a step by AOL toward making that a reality.

The service—called *AOL Bill Pay*—is free to all AOL members and is provided through an alliance with Yodlee.com, Inc. (www.yodlee.com), a company that provides a variety of online personal financial services. After AOL members sign up for the service, they will receive summaries of their online bills via AOL e-mail messages. The messages will include links directly to the business e-commerce Web sites where members can make their payments.

A nice feature of AOL Bill Pay is that it creates a single portal (the AOL account) with only one user ID and one password. Once inside his or her AOL account, an AOL member does not have to enter a new ID and password at any of the e-commerce Web sites.

AOL members can configure AOL Bill Pay to provide alerts in several different forms: e-mail, instant messaging, or a text-based message to a cell phone. The system can also trigger an alert that is more of a warning message when, for example, an AOL member's bank account balance drops below a certain limit or a credit card transaction exceeds a prespecified amount. It is AOL's hope that its members will see these types of alerts and warnings as value-added services.

AOL Bill Pay connects directly to over 2,500 Web sites that offer bill paying over the Internet. If a certain AOL member makes payments to a Web site not on AOL Bill Pay's list, AOL can easily add the Web site to the list.

Even so, some users may be wary of using such a service. According to Patrick Mahoney, an analyst with The Yankee Group, "Some people may prefer going to individual Web sites instead of having the one password access to everything." But Patrick does think this is a good business model for AOL. He explains, "Although some companies provide this type of service, the market isn't overcrowded and existing offerings haven't been highly publicized. It's not like AOL is coming into a market with a lot of competition."

Just like in the traditional brick-and-mortar business environment, in the world of e-commerce you must constantly strive to stay ahead of the competition. You have to determine innovative ways in which to offer products and services that your customers will perceive add value. You must constantly evaluate industry segments and competitive spaces to determine if there is a lack of competition where you might enter.

In this chapter you'll explore the world of e-commerce, and we'll introduce you to many "special" considerations that you must take into account to be successful. Commerce will always be commerce—the buying and selling of products and services. But the "e" in e-commerce presents new challenges and opportunities.[1]

Introduction

You've probably heard the ancient Chinese curse, "May you live in interesting times." It's a curse because it is often easier to live in times that are not so interesting, when things move along pretty much as expected, as they always have. The past 10 years of the new economy introduced by the World Wide Web have certainly been interesting. There has been an entrepreneurial frenzy unlike anything the world has ever seen. Fortunes have been made and lost. Dot-com millionaires and billionaires were literally created overnight—many became dot-bomb paupers in about the same amount of time.

What fueled this frenzy and is still doing so today? It's electronic commerce enabled by information technology. **Electronic commerce (e-commerce)** is commerce, but it is commerce accelerated and enhanced by IT, in particular the Internet. E-commerce enables customers, consumers, and companies to form powerful new relationships that would not be possible without the enabling technologies. E-commerce breaks down business barriers such as time, geography, language, currency, and culture. In a few short hours, you can set up shop on the Internet and be instantly accessible to millions of consumers worldwide. The Internet facilitates commerce because of its awesome ability to move digital information at low cost.

Is there a catch? The answer is both no and yes. It's "no" because it doesn't take much effort to create your own e-commerce Web site. It's "yes" because you still have to follow sound business fundamentals and principles to be successful. Let's not forget that fundamentally it's still all about commerce, businesses and people buying and selling products and services. It is no "silver bullet," as some entrepreneurs have found out to their chagrin. You must know your competition; you must have insight into your customers' demographics and buying habits; you must offer your products and services at a superior price or at a superior level of service to beat the competition; you must make a profit.

As illustrated in Figure 5.1, there are four main perspectives for e-commerce: Business to Business (B2B), Business to Consumer (B2C), Consumer to Business (C2B), and Consumer to Consumer (C2). We'll focus on B2C and B2B in this chapter as they represent the greatest percentage of revenue dollars in e-commerce. Another emerging and important player is governments—we'll focus on the explosion of e-government in Chapter 9.

To succeed in the e-commerce environment, you must develop a strategic position and execute your business operations well. After introducing you to the basics of the B2B and B2C e-commerce perspectives, we'll cover Porter's Five Forces Model, an

Figure 5.1

Four Perspectives of E-Commerce

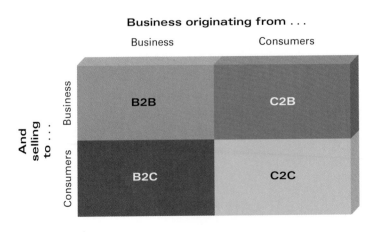

**Top 10 Most Popular Queries
from Google and Yahoo! for 2003[3]**

Rank	Google	Yahoo!
1	Britney Spears	KaZaA
2	Harry Potter	Harry Potter
3	Matrix	American Idol
4	Shakira	Britney Spears
5	David Beckham	50 Cent
6	50 Cent	Eminem
7	Iraq	WWE
8	Lord of the Rings	Paris Hilton
9	Kobe Bryant	NASCAR
10	Tour de France	Christine Aguilera

**E-Mail and Online Advertising
Impressions in 2003[2]**

Q1—136,600,000

Q2—149,800,000

Q3—172,000,000

Q4—203,800,000 (40% increase over Q1)

Average Web Usage (United States) for December 2003[4]

	Home	Work
Number sessions/visits per person	31	63
Number of domains visited per person	55	99
Computer time per person	27:00:53	72:27:48
Duration of a Web page visited	55 seconds	59 seconds

Top Parent Companies for Home Use, December 2003 (United States)[5]

Parent	Number Homes	Time per Session
Microsoft	87,322,000	01:31:43
Time Warner	77,981,000	04:01:58
Yahoo!	75,639,000	01:45:42
Google	41,561,000	00:16:01
eBay	39,424,000	01:21:52
Amazon	27,557,000	00:20:33
U.S. Government	26,172,000	00:16:00
RealNetworks	24,097,000	00:25:43
Terra Lycos	23,364,000	00:08:30
About-Primedia	20,148,000	00:08:59

B2B E-Commerce Statistics[6]

- $823.4 billion in 2002
- $2.4 trillion in 2004 (projected)
- 2,200 B2B Internet-based marketplaces (2001)
- B2B trade accounts for less than 2 percent of all U.S. trade (current)
- Western Europe—B2B purchasing will increase at a compound annual growth rate of 91 percent from 2001 to 2005

**Percentage of Online Purchases
of Music CDs and DVDs[7]**

1997—0.3%

1998—1.1%

1999—2.4%

2000—3.2%

2001—2.9%

2002—3.4%

Figure 5.2

What's Happening in the
World of E-Commerce?

effective tool for determining the relative attractiveness of an industry and developing a strategic position. We'll then cover three important e-commerce critical success factors. There are countless others, but these three in particular will help you execute your business operations well.

E-Commerce Business Models

Of all the variations of e-commerce business models to be found operating in the real world today, Business to Business (B2B) is the most lucrative area. Business to Consumer (B2C) e-commerce, on the other hand, is the most well-known in everyday life.

- ***Business to Business (B2B) e-commerce*** occurs when a business sells products and services to customers who are primarily other businesses.
- ***Business to Consumer (B2C) e-commerce*** occurs when a business sells products and services to customers who are primarily individuals.

So, for example, when Gates Rubber Company sells belts, hoses, and other rubber- and synthetic products to General Motors or any other manufacturer that needs those parts, this is B2B e-commerce. B2C e-commerce, on the other hand, is all about the commerce between a business and an individual end consumer—you, for example, when you buy a music CD from Circuit City online at www.circuitcity.com.

B2B e-commerce is where all the money is right now, accounting for approximately 97 percent of all e-commerce revenues. Business organizations have realized that there are tremendous efficiencies and potential savings from innovations in doing business electronically. Businesses can shorten cycle times and reduce costs in the supply chain. They can more effectively reach a wider audience of potential customers (other businesses, in this case). Via the Web they can reduce traditional barriers such as time, location, language, and currency. But probably you like most people are more familiar with B2C e-commerce. Have you ever bought something on the Internet? B2C e-commerce is typically what you hear about on television or read about in such periodicals as *PC Magazine* and *Wired*.

It's important for you to understand in which environment your organization operates—either in B2B or in B2C (or perhaps a combination of the two), as there are significant differences. Businesses in one area or the other employ different tactics, electronically speaking. For example, as you can see in Figure 5.3, businesses participating in B2B e-commerce are taking advantage of electronic marketplaces, or e-marketplaces. B2B e-marketplaces are virtual marketplaces in which businesses buy and sell products, share information, and perform other important activities. B2B e-marketplaces include many variations such as vertical e-marketplaces, horizontal e-marketplaces, value-added network providers, and many others.

B2B e-marketplaces represent one of the fastest growing trends in the B2B e-commerce model. Businesses are increasingly aware that they must create supply chain management systems, drive out costs, create information partnerships with other businesses, and even collaborate with other businesses on new product and service offerings. B2B e-marketplaces offer tremendous efficiencies to businesses for performing all of these tasks.

Consumers, on the other hand, in the B2C e-commerce business model tend to deal directly with a chosen business on the Internet (see Figure 5.3). That is, consumers usually surf the Web evaluating products and services at numerous separate e-commerce Web sites until they eventually choose one distinct site from which to make a purchase. That is not to say that consumers don't have access to or use e-marketplaces. eBay is a good example of an e-marketplace for consumers, where you can buy and sell just about

GATHERING CONSUMERS AT EPINIONS.COM

Epinions.com (www.epinions.com) "helps people make informed buying decisions." It bills itself as "the Web's premier consumer reviews platform and the most reliable source for valuable consumer insight, unbiased advice, in-depth product evaluations and personalized recommendations." In short, it is a special sort of Business to Consumer (B2C) e-marketplace where consumers gather to read each other's opinions.

Epinions.com actively solicits product reviews from its customer base. It doesn't edit the reviews in any way (unless the comments are slanderous or vulgar). That way, you get unbiased and unedited reviews of products you're considering for purchase. On the basis of those reviews, Epinions.com provides a rating of each product anywhere from one to five stars.

Epinions.com will help you find other consumers with tastes and needs similar to your own. You can learn what they purchased and why. This information can help you decide what to buy because you learn what other people have bought who have needs like yours.

Suppose you have determined a particular product to

buy, and have heard of a Web site that sells it. Epinions.com provides you with comparative shopping information in an easy-to-read table that includes such information as the e-commerce Web site name and a link to it, the address of the e-commerce Web site, the Web site's rating, the product price, tax and shipping, total price, and any other product notes such as "in stock" or "currently on backorder."

After you have made your purchase, Epinions.com encourages you to visit its site again and provide your own product review. That information then becomes additional information the next consumer will use.

Epinions.com, and many other B2C e-marketplaces, represent a growing new trend supporting e-gathering places for consumers on the Web. How do these sites make money? It's simple. If you link to an e-commerce Web site from Epinions.com to make a purchase, that e-commerce Web site gives Epinions.com a commission from the sale. It's an interesting and effective "e-referral" business model.[8]

---

anything you want. As an e-marketplace, eBay brings together many buyers and sellers, offering chat rooms, discussion boards, and a variety of other consumer-centric services. Although eBay is the most well-known of these types of sites, there are other gathering places for individual end consumers such as Epinions.com (www.epinions.com), which you can read about in the accompanying Industry Perspective.

Figure 5.3

Business to Business and Business to Consumer E-Commerce Business Models

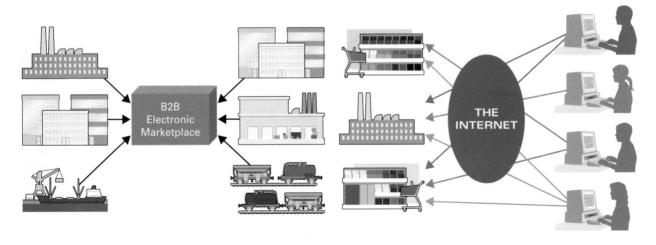

Business to Business E-Commerce Model with an Electronic Marketplace

B2B Electronic Marketplace

Business to Consumer E-Commerce Model

THE INTERNET

The distinction presented in Figure 5.3 is a very important one. If your organization has customers who are primarily other businesses, then you need to find the appropriate e-marketplace or e-marketplaces in which to participate. If your organization has customers who are primarily individual end consumers, then you need to create a marketing mix that will allow as many potential individual consumers as possible to find your organization while they surf and search the Web.

Porter's Five Forces Model: A Framework for Competitive Advantage

To achieve and sustain a competitive advantage in today's information-based and digital business environment, you must take creative steps in the use of information technology. Michael Porter's framework—called the *Five Forces Model*—has long been accepted as a useful tool for business people to use when thinking about business strategy and the impact of IT. Given that the e-commerce environment is so highly competitive, your ability to create and sustain a competitive advantage is essential.

The **Five Forces Model** helps business people understand the relative attractiveness of an industry and includes the following five forces (see Figure 5.4):

1. Buyer power
2. Supplier power
3. Threat of substitute products or services
4. Threat of new entrants
5. Rivalry among existing competitors

You can use Porter's Five Forces Model to decide to (1) enter a particular industry or (2) expand your operations if you are already in it. Most important, the strategies you develop should then be supported by enabling technologies. It doesn't matter if your organization is operating within B2B, B2C or a combination of the two; the Five Forces Model can help.

BUYER POWER

Buyer power in the Five Forces Model is high when buyers have many choices from whom to buy, and low when their choices are few. As a provider of products and services, your organization wishes to reduce buyer power. You create a competitive advantage

Figure 5.4

Michael Porter's Five Forces Model

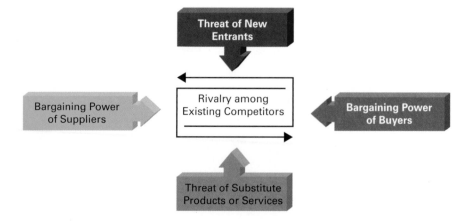

Figure 5.5

Evaluating Buyer and
Supplier Power for Your
Organization

by making it more attractive for customers to buy from you than from your competition. One of the best IT-based examples is the loyalty programs that many organizations offer. *Loyalty programs* reward customers based on the amount of business they do with a particular organization. This depends on keeping track of the activity and accounts of many, perhaps millions of customers, which is not practical—or even feasible—without large-scale IT systems. Loyalty programs use IT to reduce buyer power. They are very common in the travel industry (see the discussion in Chapter 2 on frequent flyer programs). Because of the rewards (e.g., free airline tickets, upgrades, and hotel stays) they receive, travelers are more likely to give most of their business to a single organization.

SUPPLIER POWER

Supplier power in the Five Forces Model is high when buyers have few choices from whom to buy, and low when their choices are many. Supplier power is the converse of buyer power: As a supplier organization in a market, you want buyer power to be low and supplier power to be high. In a typical supply chain, however, as we discussed in Chapters 1 and 2 (see Figure 5.5), your organization will probably be both a supplier (to customer organizations) and a customer (of other supplier organizations).

In the case of being a customer of other supplier organizations, you want to increase your buyer power. You can create a competitive advantage by locating alternative supply sources for your organization. IT-enabled B2B e-marketplaces can help you. B2B e-marketplaces are Internet-based services which bring together many buyers and sellers. We'll talk about implementations of e-marketplaces throughout this chapter.

THREAT OF SUBSTITUTE PRODUCTS OR SERVICES

The *threat of substitute products or services* in the Five Forces Model is high when there are many alternatives to a product or service, and low when there are few alternatives from which to choose. Ideally, your organization would like to be a supplier organization in a market in which there are few substitutes for the products and services you offer. Of course, that's seldom possible in any market today, but you can still create a competitive advantage by increasing *switching costs*. *Switching costs* are costs that make customers reluctant to switch to another product or service supplier. What you need to realize is that a switching cost does not necessarily have to have an actual monetary cost.

As you buy products at Amazon.com over time, for example, Amazon.com develops a unique profile of your shopping and purchasing habits through such techniques as collaborative filtering. When you visit Amazon.com, products are offered to you that have been tailored to your profile. If you choose to do your shopping elsewhere, there is a switching cost because the new site you visit will not have a profile of you nor a record of your past purchases. So, Amazon.com has reduced the threat of substitute products or services, in a market in which there are many substitutes, by tailoring offerings to you, by creating a "cost" to you to switch to another online retailer.

Switching costs can be real monetary costs too. You've probably been introduced to a switching cost when you signed up for the services of a cell phone provider. All the options and plans sound really great. But there is a serious switching cost in that most cell phone providers require you to sign a long-term contract (as long as two years) in order to receive a free phone or unlimited night and weekend calling minutes. These sorts of switching costs, unfortunately, are sometimes hidden in the fine print.

THREAT OF NEW ENTRANTS

The ***threat of new entrants*** in the Five Forces Model is high when it is easy for new competitors to enter a market, and low when there are significant entry barriers to entering a market. An ***entry barrier*** is a product or service feature that customers have come to expect from organizations in a particular industry and that must be offered by an entering organization to compete and survive. Such barriers are erected, overcome, then new ones created again.

For example, if you're thinking of starting a bank, you must nowadays offer your customers an array of IT-enabled services, including ATM use, online bill paying and account monitoring, and the like. These are significant IT-based entry barriers to entering the banking market because you must offer them for free (or for a very small fee). The first bank to offer such services gained a first-mover advantage and established entry barriers, an advantage nullified as other banking competitors developed similar IT-enabling systems and overcame the barriers to entering or expanding in the industry.

RIVALRY AMONG EXISTING COMPETITION

The ***rivalry among existing competitor***s in the Five Forces Model is high when competition is fierce in a market, and low when competition is more complacent. Simply put, competition is more intense in some industries than in others, although the overall trend is toward increased competition in just about every industry.

The retail grocery industry is intensely competitive. While Kroger, Safeway, and Albertson's in the United States compete in many different ways, essentially they try to beat or match the competition on price. For example, most of them have loyalty programs that give shoppers special discounts. Customers get lower prices while the store gathers valuable business intelligence on buying habits to craft pricing and advertising strategies. In the future, you can expect to see grocery stores using wireless technologies to track customer movement throughout the store and match it to products purchased to determine purchasing sequences.

Since margins are quite low in the grocery retail market, grocers build efficiencies into their supply chains, connecting with their suppliers in IT-enabled information partnerships (as we discussed in Chapter 2). Communicating with suppliers over telecommunications networks rather than using paper-based systems makes the procurement process faster, cheaper, and more accurate. That equates to lower prices for customers—and increased rivalry among existing competitors.

CONSIDERING PORTER IN LIGHT OF E-COMMERCE

Porter's Five Forces Model is a valuable tool for considering whether or not to enter any industry, and that holds true in the e-commerce environment as well. However, the "e" in e-commerce implies technology, and technology has even further intensified the competition in almost every industry you care to name.

USING PORTER TO EVALUATE THE MOVIE RENTAL INDUSTRY

One hotly contested and highly competitive industry is the movie rental business. You can rent videos from local video rental stores (usually for a specified number of days), you can order pay-per-view from the comfort of your own home (usually to watch as many times as you want in a given 24-hour period of time), and you can rent videos from the Web at such sites as Netflix (www.netflix.com) and keep the videos as long as you want.

Using Porter's Five Forces Model, evaluate the relative attractiveness of entering the movie rental business. Specifically, answer the following questions and perform the following tasks (and provide the appropriate justification/description for each of your outputs):

1. Is buyer power low or high?
2. Is supplier power low or high?
3. What substitute products and services are perceived as threats?
4. What is the level of threat of new entrants? That is, are the barriers to entry high or low? What are the barriers to entry?
5. What is the level of rivalry among existing competitors? Create a list of the top five competitors in the business.

Finally, what's your overall view of the movie rental business? Is it a good or bad industry to enter? How would you use Porter's Five Forces Model to enter this industry?

Today it will help you be successful in business if you truly understand the impact technology has on the relative attractiveness of an industry. Without referencing a specific industry or industry segment, consider the following statements as they relate to Porter's Five Forces Model.

- Because of technology, buyer power has increased in most industries. It's now far easier for new suppliers to enter a given industry and for all suppliers to reach more potential buyers. That translates into more options for buyers, thus increasing buyer power.

- Because of technology, the entry barriers into many industries have been lessened. Geographic boundaries of markets are a simple yet effective illustration of this. Previously, many markets were difficult—without the aid of technology—to enter because of their geographic location. Technologies such as the Internet have made it easier to enter these markets in distant or inaccessible areas of the country or world.

- The threat of substitute products or services has increased in most industries because of technology. Again, it's easier now because of technology for suppliers to reach more buyers with either directly competing products and services or substitute products and services.

Those statements may not exactly "paint a pretty picture" for the competitive landscape of business today, but they do offer a realistic view of just how competitive business is.

So how can your organization be successful in the business world of e-commerce? We have no magic answer, but we can offer you several guidelines by which your organization should operate, which are the focus of the next several sections in this chapter. As you'll see, each guideline has its own unique set of considerations depending on the focus of your e-business efforts, either as the "B" in Business to Consumer e-commerce or the first "B" in Business to Business e-commerce.

ELIMINATING ENTRY BARRIERS WITH LOCAL NUMBER PORTABILITY

As we discussed in regard to Porter's Five Forces Model and switching costs, cell phone providers want to keep you as a long-term customer. So to receive a free phone or unlimited minutes, you may have to sign a one- or two-year contract. That creates a switching cost for you because, if you change providers before the end of the contract, you have to pay a penalty in terms of real dollars.

But that hasn't been the greatest switching cost working in favor of cell phone providers. Until 2003, if you switched cell phone providers, you couldn't take your number with you. This stopped many customers from switching.

That switching cost went away in late 2003 with the implementation of *Local Number Portability (LNP)* or the ability to "port" your number from one cell phone provider to another.

Within the context of Porter's Five Forces Model, eliminating this switching cost creates a greater threat of substitute products or services. That is, you can now expect to see more new cell phone providers cropping up over the next several years. They will compete on price, quality, and services with the big-name cell phone providers such as AT&T and Verizon because there is no cost to you—in terms of not being able to keep your number—to switch from one provider to another.

When businesses reduce or eliminate switching costs, you—as a consumer—win because you have more options.

Understand Your Business, Products, Services, and Customers

To be successful in any business, you must be able to define exactly the products and services you provide, who your target customers are, and how your customers perceive the use of your products and services within their business activities (for the B2B model) or in their personal lives (for the B2C model). In order to create strategies that will help you gain a competitive advantage you have to clearly articulate the nature of your products and services, customers, and the value that your customers place on your products and services.

For the moment skip over the traditional notions of developing a mission statement and glitzy marketing brochures. Although both of these are essential, first you need to develop an objective, very down-to-earth understanding of what your business does. The reality is you can't be all things to all customers. You must clearly define (1) your target customers and (2) the value of your products and services as perceived by your customers. Let's look at each in turn.

WHO ARE YOUR CUSTOMERS?

Just as in the brick-and-mortar business world, you must focus your efforts on selling to other businesses, individual end consumers, or some combination of the two. If you were like our example earlier in the chapter, Gates Rubber Company, which produces mostly rubber and synthetic products primarily for sale to the automotive industry and other manufacturers that extensively use such items in the manufacture of other products (such as boats and bicycles), you would almost exclusively focus on the B2B e-commerce model, with other businesses as your target customers. If you were to sell résumé and job

Business to Consumer (B2C)	Business to Business (B2B)
• **Convenience**—low-priced but something needed on a frequent basis	• **Maintenance, repair, and operations (MRO) materials**—necessary items that do not relate directly to the company's primary business activities
• **Specialty**—higher-priced, ordered on a less frequent basis, and often requiring customization	• **Direct materials**—materials used in production in a manufacturing company or placed on the shelf for sale in a retail environment
• **Commoditylike**—the same no matter where you buy it	
• **Digital**—the best of all because of low cost of inventory and shipping	

Figure 5.6

B2C and B2B Products and Services

placement services to individuals looking for careers, your customers would be individual end consumers. If you wanted to be like Monster.com (www.monster.com) and provide an electronic marketplace with services catering to both individuals looking for careers and businesses looking for employees, your customer mix would include both end consumers and businesses. In this case, you'd need to carefully consider both groups of customers, their needs, and the value to them of the products and services you sell.

Many businesses in the travel industry, American Express for example, cater to both businesses and end consumers. As an individual consumer, you may work with American Express to plan and pay for a vacation. At the same time, many businesses use the services of American Express to handle all their travel needs.

Whatever the nature of your business, you must know who your customers are. In the world of e-commerce, that means clearly distinguishing between end consumers (B2C) and other businesses (B2B), even if you target both. As you will see throughout this chapter, individual end consumers and other businesses have dramatically different needs. For some different kinds of products and services needed by B2C and B2B, see Figure 5.6, and the discussion that follows.

WHAT IS THE VALUE OF YOUR PRODUCTS AND SERVICES AS PERCEIVED BY YOUR CUSTOMERS?

If a customer orders a product or service from your organization, it is because that customer perceives some value in what you provide—the customer either *wants* or *needs* your product or service. Here, the distinctions between end consumers and businesses as customers become increasingly important and clearly evident, so let's look at each customer group in turn.

B2C: CONVENIENCE VERSUS SPECIALTY   In many respects, you can differentiate between convenience and specialty merchandise (or services) on the basis of price and consumers' frequency of purchase. To end consumers, convenience merchandise is typically lower priced but something they need, usually on a frequent basis. Nonperishable food items such as cereal are a good example. From organizations such as Peapod (www.peapod.com), you can easily order food items and have them delivered to your home within 24 hours of making the order or at predetermined time intervals such as weekly. Consumers might pay more for these low-priced items in order to have them "conveniently."

YOUR PERCEPTION OF PRODUCT AND SERVICE VALUE

Within the Business to Consumer e-commerce model not all consumers are the same. Not only do they have different tastes and needs, but also different perceptions of product and service value. Your task is to evaluate the products and services in the table below according to your own personal preferences and specify (1) your perception of whether each is a convenience or specialty item and (2) whether you require some level of customization for each. Place an X in the appropriate cells for each.

Product/Service	Convenience	Specialty	Customization
Fiction book			
Textbook			
Cell phone			
Internet access			
Job search			
Computer			
Checking account			
Living space (e.g., apartment)			
Music			
Car stereo			
Home stereo			

Specialty merchandise might be such things as home stereo systems, computers, name-brand clothing, furniture, and the like. For consumers, these are higher-priced (than convenience merchandise) items, are typically ordered on a less-frequent basis, and often require some sort of customization or feature specification. For specialty merchandise, consumers will spend more time "shopping around," not only to find the best deal in terms of price but also in terms of customization, warranty, service, and other after-sales features.

B2C: COMMODITYLIKE AND DIGITAL In B2C e-commerce, as a general rule, the best merchandise to sell is either commoditylike, digital, or a combination of the two. This enables you to minimize your internal costs, but requires that you be innovative in how you offer your merchandise and attract consumers to your site.

Commoditylike merchandise, to your customers, is the same regardless of where they purchase it, and it is similar to convenience items in that respect. Books are a good example. No matter where you buy a particular book, it is the same. As a business, you compete in a commoditylike environment on the basis of:

- Price
- Ease and speed of delivery
- Ease of ordering
- Your return policy

Of course, commoditylike business environments are typically easy to enter (i.e., they have low barriers to entry) and thus buyer power is high. Your organization's goals in this type of environment would have to include (1) minimizing price to the end consumer and (2) minimizing your internal costs by creating a tight supply chain management system. You also want to create a "sticky" Web site that not only attracts consumers but also encourages them to return to your site again and again.

Digital merchandise offerings are also important in the B2C e-commerce model. The goal here is to eliminate shipping costs by delivering the digital product over the Internet once a consumer has made a purchase. Music is a good example. Apple's iTunes Web site (www.apple.com/itunes/store/) allows you to select the exact song you want, pay for it, and then download it from the Internet. Apple can offer each song for just 99 cents because it has no physical delivery costs and no physical inventory. As this example illustrates, digital products are also advantageous (to the business and the consumer) because they are customizable. That is, customers don't have to purchase an entire music CD—they can pick only the song or songs they want.

B2C: MASS CUSTOMIZATION   As we've alluded to, end consumers are often interested in customizing their purchases. In the B2C e-commerce model this is the concept of *mass customization*—the ability of an organization to give its customers the opportunity to tailor its product or service to the customer's specifications. Customization can be appropriate and is a key competitive advantage regardless of customer value perception. For example, Dell Computer (www.dell.com) is well regarded in its market for being the best at allowing consumers to customize a computer purchase. Music sites now allow you to pick the songs you want instead of an entire CD. Clothing sites allow you to select from among various styles, colors, and size of clothing to fit your needs.

In a B2C environment, you're potentially dealing with millions of different consumers, each with unique tastes and needs. You must support the concept of mass customization.

B2B: MRO VERSUS DIRECT   *Maintenance, repair, and operations (MRO) materials* (also called *indirect materials*) are materials that are necessary for running a modern corporation, but do not relate to the company's primary business activities. MRO materials include everything from ballpoint pens to three-ring binders, repair parts for equipment, and lubricating oils. Thus, B2B MRO materials are similar to convenience and commoditylike items in the B2C e-commerce model.

In their purchases of these materials, however, business customers (B2B) are very different from end consumers (B2C) in many ways. For example, a business because of its volume of MRO materials purchases can bargain with suppliers for a discount (end consumers in the B2C e-commerce model usually don't have this ability). Many businesses may band together to create even more volume and thus demand an even higher discount from a supplier. This practice is known as *demand aggregation*—the combining of purchase requests from multiple buyers into a single large order, which justifies a discount from the business. If your organization is a supplier of MRO materials in the B2B e-commerce model, you will compete mostly on price (including discounts), delivery, and ease of ordering.

Direct materials are materials that are used in production in a manufacturing company or are placed on the shelf for sale in a retail environment. So, as opposed to MRO materials, direct materials relate to a company's primary business activities. It is critically important that the customer business receives exactly what is needed in terms of quality, quantity, and the timing of delivery of direct materials.

For direct materials acquisition, some businesses participate in a reverse auction (through an electronic marketplace). A *reverse auction* is the process in which a buyer posts its interest in buying a certain quantity of items with notations concerning quality,

BEAUTY AND "VALUE" ARE IN THE EYE OF THE BEHOLDER

Customer "value" is an elusive concept. Sometimes it means low price, other times it means high quality, and yet other times it means convenience.

Consider the joint-venture offering by JCB Co., Japan's largest credit-card issuer, and Fujitsu. The new offering is a cell phone that authenticates the owner of the phone through a fingerprint scanner. As a user of the phone, you can check your JCB account balances and transfer funds. But you don't have to enter a special password or PIN. Instead, you place your finger on the phone's fingerprint scanner and it does the rest.

There is no real competitive advantage to telephone-based banking as most financial institutions already offer that service. The competitive advantage for JCB and Fujitsu (that is, customer value) lies in the phone's ability to recognize who you are without requiring you to provide some sort of validation such as a password or PIN.

What's your perception? As a customer, do you agree—is there value in a phone with a fingerprint scanner?[9]

specification, and delivery timing, and sellers compete for the business by submitting successively lower bids until there is only one seller left. Reverse auctions create tremendous "power" for the buyer because multiple sellers are competing for the same business.

B2B: HORIZONTAL VERSUS VERTICAL   As a supplier to other businesses, you also need to understand whether you are selling in a horizontal or vertical e-marketplace (see Figure 5.7). An *electronic marketplace (e-marketplace)* is an interactive business providing a central market space where multiple buyers and suppliers can engage in e-commerce and/or other e-commerce business activities. E-marketplaces feature a variety of implementations including value-added network providers (which we'll discuss later in the chapter), horizontal e-marketplaces, and vertical e-marketplaces. A ***horizon-***

Figure 5.7

Horizontal and Vertical B2B Electronic Marketplace

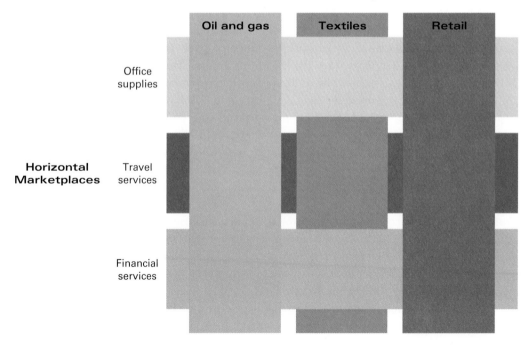

→ WHEN THE INTERNET WORKS AND RETAIL STORES DON'T

As we alluded to in the chapter's introduction, e-commerce brought about an entrepreneurial frenzy like the world has never seen. Venture capitalists poured trillions of dollars into ill-fated, ill-run, and ill-advised e-commerce businesses. Many traditional retail businesses went online in the hope of reaching millions of new customers and making billions of dollars, only later to pull their online shelves because they just couldn't make a profit online.

One company seeming to buck that trend was Gateway, with its famous "cow" boxes. Gateway was successful both in the brick-and-mortar retail world and in the online world. In fact, Gateway is bucking the trend so much that it recently announced it was closing all its retail stores and cutting some 2,500 jobs.

Gateway will focus its marketing and retail efforts more on direct channels, including catalog and online sales. According to Gartner analyst Leslie Fiering, "It's something that a lot of people have been calling for—a total severing of the old business model."

This example is quite interesting. In the short history of e-commerce, very few businesses have opted for a "total severing of the old business model" in favor of operating almost completely online. Most businesses have found it advantageous to operate in both environments, with many deciding just to operate in the brick-and-mortar world. But not Gateway—it's choosing only the virtual world of the Internet.[10]

tal e-marketplace is an electronic marketplace that connects buyers and sellers across many industries, primarily for MRO materials commerce. Again, MRO materials include a broad of range of both products and services including office supplies, travel, shipping, and some financial services. Because horizontal e-marketplaces support MRO materials commerce, much of our previous discussion on B2B e-commerce for MRO materials holds true here.

A *vertical e-marketplace* is an electronic marketplace that connects buyers and sellers in a given industry (e.g., oil and gas, textiles, and retail). Covisint (www.covisint.com) is a good example. Covisint provides a B2B e-marketplace in the automotive industry where buyers and sellers specific to that industry conduct commerce in products and services, share mission-critical information for the development of products and parts, collaborate on new ideas, and deploy infrastructure applications that enable the seamless communication of each other's proprietary IT systems.

To summarize, we would offer you the following for understanding your business, products, services, and customers.

- **Business to Consumer**

    Exhibit greatly varying demographics, lifestyles, wants, and needs

    Distinctions of products and services are by convenience versus specialty

    Works best for commoditylike and digital products and services

    Includes mass customization in some instances

- **Business to Business**

    Distinctions of products and services are by maintenance, repair, and operations (MRO) materials versus direct materials

    Includes demand aggregation and negotiation capabilities on the part of businesses as customers

    Supports e-marketplaces including horizontal e-marketplaces (primarily for MRO materials) and vertical e-marketplaces (specific to a given industry)

Find Customers and Establish Relationships

The most important preselling activity in commerce is finding and reaching your customers and establishing a relationship with them—otherwise you can't make a sale. People generally refer to this as *marketing;* there are added considerations to keep in mind about marketing in e-commerce that can create a competitive advantage for you.

BUSINESS TO CONSUMER

With almost one billion people on the Internet, you'd think it would be easy to find and attract customers to your B2C e-commerce site. But that's not necessarily true because all your competition is trying to do the same thing—drive customers to their Web site and encourage them to make a purchase.

Here, you need to determine your appropriate *marketing mix*—the set of marketing tools that your organization will use to pursue its marketing objectives in reaching and attracting potential customers. In B2C e-commerce, your marketing mix will probably include some or all of the following: registering with search engines, online ads, viral marketing, and affiliate programs.

Many Web surfers use *search engines* to find information and products and services. While some search engines will include your site for free (FreeSearch.com at www. freesearch.com is an example), almost all the popular search engines such as Yahoo! and Google require you to pay a fee. Most of these sites will guarantee that your site appears in the top portion of a search list for an additional fee.

Online ads (often called *banner ads*) are small advertisements that appear on other sites (see Figure 5.8). Variations of online ads include pop-up and pop-under ads. A *pop-up ad* is a small Web page containing an advertisement that appears on your screen outside the current Web site loaded into your browser. A *pop-under ad* is a form of a

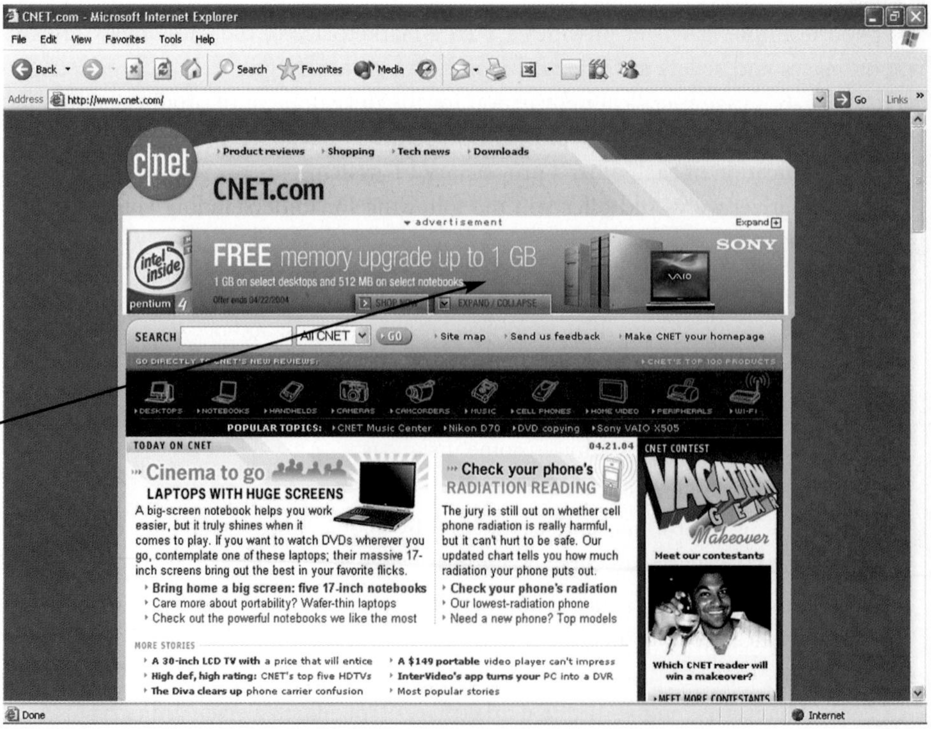

Figure 5.8

An Online Ad at Cnet.com

Banner ad for Sony

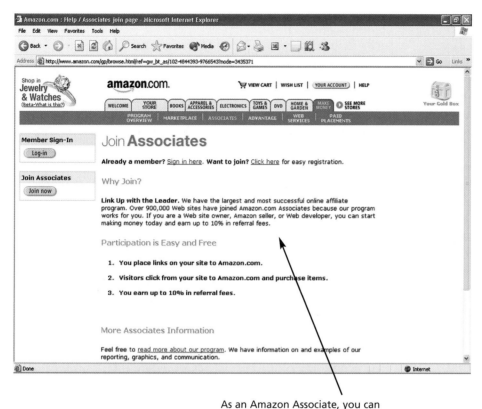

Figure 5.9

Amazon.com's Affiliate
Program Is Called
Associates

As an Amazon Associate, you can
earn up to 10% for referrals.

pop-up ad that you do not see until you close your current browser window. A word of
caution here: Most people don't mind banner ads because they appear as a part of the
site they're visiting. However, most people consider pop-up and pop-under ads to be
very annoying.

Viral marketing encourages users of a product or service supplied by a B2C
e-commerce business to encourage friends to join in as well. Blue Mountain Arts
(www.bluemountain.com) is a good example. When you use Blue Mountain to send an
e-birthday card (or some other type of card), the intended recipient will receive an e-mail
directing him or her to Blue Mountain's site. Once the recipient views the card, Blue
Mountain provides a link so that person can send you a card in return. Of course, Blue
Mountain charges for each card sent, so it makes money both ways.

An *affiliate program* is an arrangement made between two e-commerce sites that directs viewers from one site to the other. Amazon.com is the most well-known creator of
an affiliate program. If you become an Amazon associate, your e-commerce Web site
would direct viewers to Amazon's site for certain purchases. If a sale results, Amazon will
pay you a fee, which is usually a percentage of the sale (see Figure 5.9). Likewise, you
can pay another site to direct traffic to yours, which may be through an online ad. In
some instances, affiliate programs create relationships such that a payment is made for
each click-through. A *click-through* is a count of the number of people who visit one
site, click on an ad, and are taken to the site of the advertiser.

In general, you want your marketing mix to drive as many potential customers as possible to have a look at your B2C e-commerce offerings. From there, however, you need
to focus on your conversion rate. A *conversion rate* is the percentage of potential customers who visit your site who actually buy something. So, while total views or "hits" to
your e-commerce Web site is important, obviously even more so is your conversion rate.

A GLOBAL PARTNERSHIP TO CREATE GLOBAL PARTNERING OPPORTUNITIES

In March 2004, Business Commerce Limited, the Hong Kong subsidiary of Global eXchange Services, and ChinaECNet announced a new business partnership that will establish a B2B electronic marketplace named "e-Hub." E-Hub will connect China-based electronics manufacturers with other China-based manufacturers and international customers and suppliers as well.

ChinaECNet is China's leading digital media and e-commerce network, focused mainly on the electronic manufacturing industry. It represents a joint venture between the China Centre for Industry Information Development, Avnet Inc., and Global Techmart.

Global eXchange Services provides one of the largest B2B e-commerce business networks in the world, supporting over 1 billion transactions annually among over 100,000 trading partners.

E-Hub will provide buyers and sellers with a standards-based transaction environment that will ultimately lead to more efficient and effective sourcing, purchasing, and tracking of inventory. According to Gou Zhongwen, vice-minister of China's Ministry of Infor-

mation Industry, "Strengthening the electronics supply chain and material information management is an important step toward utilizing advanced information technology to reform and improve the manufacturing supply and distribution of electronics enterprises." As Wayne Chao, chairman and CEO of ChinaECNET, further explains, "We anticipate that the e-Hub will be China's premier procurement and logistic data exchange platform to connect Chinese electronics OEMs with other Chinese manufacturers of all sizes, and as importantly, with international customers and suppliers. This will greatly help the Chinese OEM market improve material management efficiency and overcome the challenges caused by the rapid globalization of the Chinese electronics industry."

Sometimes, you build partnerships with other businesses specifically so you can support e-commerce activities among other businesses that also want to build partnerships. In the case of Global eXchange Services and ChinaECNET, their partnership will enable other businesses to create partnerships.[11]

BUSINESS TO BUSINESS

Finding and attracting customers to your B2B e-commerce site is much different. Businesses—customers in the B2B model—don't usually find products and services by surfing the Web or using search engines. Instead, business customers prefer to actively participate in e-marketplaces to find suppliers. Within an e-marketplace, an organization can participate in a reverse auction to find a supplier, as we discussed earlier.

Moreover, an organization can search an e-marketplace for suitable suppliers and then enter into negotiations outside the e-marketplace. This happens for organizations needing to purchase millions of dollars in inventory, parts, or raw materials, and it occurs for organizations wanting to establish a long-term relationship with just one supplier.

Relationships among businesses in B2B are very important. These relationships, characterized by trust and continuity, extend into the IT realm. In the B2B e-commerce business model, you must provide a level of integration of your IT systems with those of your business partners. Once a formal business relationship has been established, the goal is to use IT to streamline the ordering and procurement processes to create tight supply chain management systems and drive out cost, so your IT systems have to work closely together.

DEVELOPING A MARKETING MIX STRATEGY FOR MONSTER.COM

Monster.com (www.monster.com) is a premier service provider in the job placement industry. It exhibits both a B2B e-commerce business model because it provides services for organizations seeking employees and a B2C e-commerce business model because it provides services to individuals hoping to find jobs.

You've been hired by Monster.com to create a marketing mix strategy. Your tasks are many. Complete the table below by filling in the appropriate information. If you feel that it is not in the best interest of Monster.com to advertise in a certain media, leave that part of the table blank.

	B2B	B2C
Television Advertising		
• What type of TV station(s)?		
• What type of shows?		
• What time of day?		
Newspaper Advertising		
• What day of the week?		
• What section of the newspaper?		
Internet Advertising		
• What sites for online ads?		
• What sites for affiliate programs?		
• What types of viral marketing?		
Other Advertising		
• Anything not listed in the above three categories		

To summarize, for marketing, or finding customers and creating relationships with them in e-commerce:

- **Business to Consumer**

    Marketing mix designed to drive potential customers to a Web site

    Includes registering with a search engine, online ads, viral marketing, and affiliate programs

    Focuses on conversion rates as a method of measuring success

- **Business to Business**

    Occurs frequently in an e-marketplace

    Still requires the formal establishment of business relationships that include trust and continuity

    Requires some level of IT system integration between you and your customer

    Includes negotiations for pricing, quality, specifications, and delivery timing

    Doesn't usually include a marketing mix that broadly and generically reaches all businesses that might be potential customers

Move Money Easily and Securely

In the world of e-commerce, you must create IT systems that enable your customers (other businesses or end consumers) to pay electronically, easily, and securely for their purchases. Of course, you can still accept credit cards as the form of payment just like in the brick-and-mortar world, but credit card payments are really an electronic form of payment.

BUSINESS TO CONSUMER PAYMENT SYSTEMS

Your customers in the Business to Consumer e-commerce model will most often pay for products and services using credit cards, smart cards, financial cybermediaries, electronic checks, and Electronic Bill Presentment and Payment (EBPP) (and also smart cards in some instances).

- *Financial cybermediary*—an Internet-based company that makes it easy for one person to pay another person or organization over the Internet. PayPal (www.paypal.com) is the best known example of a financial cybermediary (see Figure 5.10). You create a PayPal account by logging on to the PayPal Web site and providing it with personal, credit card, and banking information. When you want to send money, you go to the PayPal site and enter the amount of money you want to send and provide information for either the person or organization you want to send the money to. You can also accumulate money in your personal PayPal account by accepting money from other people. You can transfer the money to one of your banking accounts, use it for other purposes, send the funds to someone else, or just leave it there for awhile.

- *Electronic check*—a mechanism for sending money from your checking or savings account to another person or organization. There are many implementations of electronic checks, with the most prominent being online banking.

- *Electronic Bill Presentment and Payment (EBPP)*—a system that sends bills (usually to end consumers) over the Internet and provides an easy-to-use mechanism (such as clicking on a button) to pay for them if the amount looks

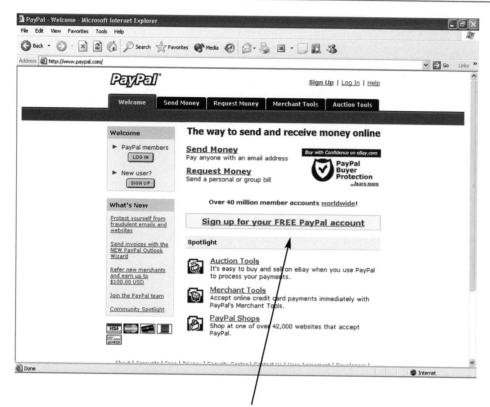

Figure 5.10

PayPal Is the Most Well-Known Financial Cybermediary

Setting up a PayPal account is free.

correct. EBPP systems are available through local banks or online services such as Checkfree (www.checkfree.com) and Quicken (www.quicken.com/banking_and_credit/).

- **Smart card**—plastic card the size of a credit card that contains an embedded chip on which digital information can be stored and updated. The chip, in this case, can contain information about how much money you have. When you swipe your card to pay for a purchase, the swiping device deducts the purchase amount from the amount you have stored on the chip. Some debit cards are implementations of the smart card concept.

The entire payment process encompasses more than accepting a form of payment. It also includes determining the shipping address for your customer. You can create a competitive advantage by having a way of asking each customer only once for his or her delivery information and storing it, thus creating a switching cost because when your customer makes another purchase, you can simply ask him or her to verify the delivery information and not have to provide it all over again. One implementation of this is called a digital wallet. A **digital wallet** is both software and information—the software provides security for the transaction and the information includes payment information (for example, the credit card number and expiration date) and delivery information. Digital wallets can be stored either on the client side or the server side. A *client-side digital wallet* is one that you create and keep on your computer; you can then use it at a variety of e-commerce Web sites. Most browsers such as Internet Explorer and Netscape Communicator support your ability to create this type of digital wallet. A *server-side digital wallet* (sometimes referred to as a *thin wallet*) is one that an organization creates for and about you and maintains on its server. Many credit card issuers use this type of digital wallet to verify your credit card transactions.

SPOOFING EBAY CUSTOMERS TO GET CREDIT CARD INFORMATION

When you register as a user at eBay, you set up a personal account that includes your shipping information and important financial information such as your credit card number. At any time, you can log in with eBay and change your personal and financial information. These are necessary aspects of creating the world's largest online auction e-marketplace.

But there is a drawback. Now thieves are trying to steal your credit card information, not by looking through your trash for a credit card statement or by monitoring your electronic communications but rather by pretending to be eBay.

It's called *spoofing*—the forging of the return address on an e-mail so that the e-mail message appears to come from someone other than the actual sender. The thief will send you an e-mail that looks like one

coming from eBay. The message will instruct you to do something in order to keep your eBay account active, like clicking on a link that will take you to a page so you can update your credit card information.

In reality, you'll be taken to a site that looks very much like eBay but isn't eBay at all. When you type in your credit card information, things will go bad in a big way and in a big hurry. The thief now has your credit card information and can use it online.

Sometimes, thieves simply ask you to enter your eBay user ID and password on a fictitious site. Then, they have that information and can log into your eBay account and take your information that way.

It's up to you to protect your most personal and confidential information.

All of this is significant because your customers in the B2C e-commerce model exhibit some common characteristics when paying for your products and services.

- They tend to make numerous purchases for small amounts.
- They pay for each transaction individually.
- You must validate each transaction.

BUSINESS TO BUSINESS PAYMENT SYSTEMS

Payments for products and services in the Business to Business e-commerce model are usually much different from those in the Business to Consumer e-commerce model. In B2B e-commerce, your customers tend to make very large purchases and will not pay using a credit card or a financial cybermediary such as PayPal. Instead, other businesses will want to pay (1) through financial EDI and (2) often in large, aggregated amounts encompassing many purchases.

ELECTRONIC DATA INTERCHANGE In the B2B model, another business wants to order products and services from your organization via electronic data interchange. *Electronic data interchange (EDI)* is the direct computer-to-computer transfer of transaction information contained in standard business documents, such as invoices and purchase orders, in a standard format. Your organization can implement EDI-facilitated transactions in many ways; one of the more prominent is a B2B e-marketplace that supports EDI through a value-added network. Global eXchange Services (GXS at www.gsx.com) is one such B2B e-marketplace. (We introduced you to GXS in the Global Perspective on page 254.)

GXS, formerly known as General Electric (GE) Information Services, supports one of the largest B2B e-marketplaces in the world with more than 100,000 trading busi-

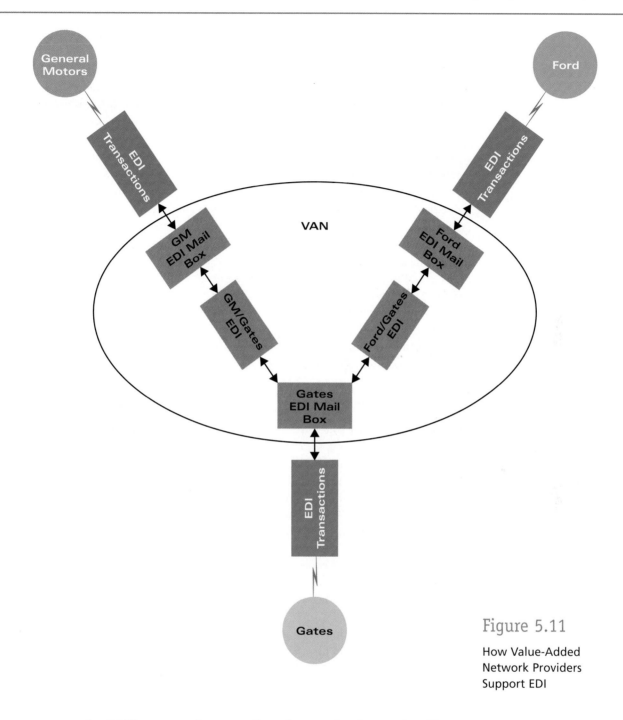

Figure 5.11

How Value-Added
Network Providers
Support EDI

nesses processing 1 billion transactions annually and accounting for over $1 trillion in products and services. GXS focuses on providing value-added network capabilities primarily to supply chain management activities. Figure 5.11 illustrates how General Motors, Ford, and Gates Rubber Company might use GXS's services to support electronic data interchange. In this case, General Motors and Ford would submit orders to Gates through GXS's value-added network (VAN). The VAN supports electronic catalogs (from which orders are placed), EDI-based transactions (the actual orders), security measures such as encryption (which we'll discuss in a moment), and EDI mail boxes (similar to your personal e-mail box). When GM sends an order, for example, to Gates, the order waits in Gates's EDI mail box for processing. Once the order is processed, Gates sends an order confirmation back through the VAN to GM's mail box.

FINANCIAL ELECTRONIC DATA INTERCHANGE   Thereafter, at some predetermined time, Gates would create an invoice totaling many of the orders and purchases from GM. That invoice would be sent through the VAN much like the orders themselves. When the invoice was accepted and approved by GM, GM would make a financial EDI payment to Gates. *Financial EDI (financial electronic data interchange)* is an electronic process used primarily within the Business to Business e-commerce model for the payment of purchases. The actual reconciliation of the funds may occur through a bank or an automated clearing house (ACH) support site such as National Cash Management System (www.ach-eft-ncms.com/index.asp).

As you can see, B2B transactions among businesses are much more involved and complex than B2C transactions between a business and an end consumer such as yourself. Most notably, business to business transactions require a level of system integration between the businesses. Considering our previous example in Figure 5.11, Gates's order fulfillment and processing systems would have to be integrated with similar systems at GM and Ford. That is to say, Gates's order fulfillment and processing systems would have to be able to accept and process EDI-based and standardized electronic order records. GM and Ford would have to have similar systems to create EDI-based and standardized electronic order records. In doing so, costs for order processing among all businesses are minimized as the orders can be handled electronically, without paper and without much human intervention.

SECURITY: THE PERVADING CONCERN

Regardless of whether your customers are other businesses or end consumers, they are all greatly concerned about the security of their transactions. This includes all aspects of electronic information, but focuses mainly on the information associated with payments (e.g., a credit card number) and the payments themselves, that is, the "electronic money." Here, you need to consider such issues as encryption, Secure Sockets Layers, and Secure Electronic Transactions. This is by no means an exhaustive list but rather representative of the broad field of security within electronic commerce.

ENCRYPTION   *Encryption* scrambles the contents of a file so that you can't read it without having the right decryption key. Encryption can be achieved in many ways: by scrambling letters in a known way, replacing letters with other letters or perhaps numbers, and other ways.

Some encryption technologies use multiple keys. In this instance, you would be using *public key encryption (PKE)*—an encryption system that uses two keys: a public key that everyone can have and a private key for only the recipient (see Figure 5.12). When

Figure 5.12

Public Key Encryption
(PKE) System

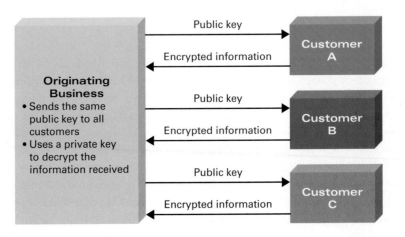

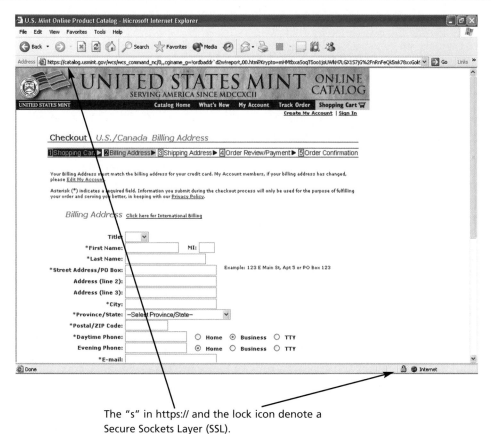

Figure 5.13

Secure Sockets Layer
(SSL) on a Web Site

The "s" in https:// and the lock icon denote a
Secure Sockets Layer (SSL).

implementing security using multiple keys, your organization provides the public key
to all its customers (end consumers and other businesses). The customers use the public key to encrypt their information and send it along the Internet. When it arrives at
its destination, your organization would use the private key to unscramble the encrypted
information.

SECURE SOCKETS LAYERS   A *Secure Sockets Layer (SSL)* (1) creates a secure
and private connection between a Web client computer and a Web server computer,
(2) encrypts the information, and (3) then sends the information over the Internet. SSLs
do provide good security for transferring information and are used widely by B2C
e-commerce Web sites. As an end consumer, you can tell your information is being transferred via SSL if you see either (1) the Web site address starts with https:// (notice the
inclusion of the "s") as opposed to just http:// or (2) the presence of a lock icon in the
bottom portion of your Web browser window (see Figure 5.13).

SECURE ELECTRONIC TRANSACTIONS   A *Secure Electronic Transaction (SET)* is
a transmission security method that ensures transactions are *legitimate* as well as secure.
Much like an SSL, an SET encrypts information before sending it over the Internet. Taking it one step further, an SET enables you, as a merchant, to verify a customer's identity by securely transmitting credit card information to the business that issued the credit
card for verification. SETs are endorsed by major e-commerce players including MasterCard, American Express, Visa, Netscape, and Microsoft.

   To summarize, we would offer the comments on page 263 about moving money easily and securely.

DEFINING YOUR BUSINESS TO CONSUMER E-COMMERCE BUSINESS

It's now time for you to gather everything you've learned in this chapter and use it to create the overall strategy for a B2C e-commerce business. As a group, you are to define a B2C e-commerce business you wish to operate. It can be anything from selling tutoring services to offering music on the Web. First, you need to clearly define your customers according to their demographics and lifestyles. Next, define your products/services according to your customers' perception of their value. Third, define the best marketing mix to reach your customers. Finally, evaluate your new e-commerce business in light of Porter's Five Forces Model. Complete the table below with this information.

Your B2C e-commerce business (provide a one-paragraph description):	_____ _____ _____ _____ _____ _____
Your customers (provide their demographics and lifestyles):	_____ _____ _____ _____
Your customers' perception of value (discussion of convenience versus specialty, commoditylike, digital, and extent of needed customization):	_____ _____ _____ _____ _____
Your marketing mix (where you will advertise, when, etc.):	_____ _____ _____ _____
Porter's Five Forces Model (describe your competitive space according to each of the five forces):	_____ _____ _____ _____ _____

- **Business to Consumer**

  Methods include credit cards, financial cybermediaries, electronic checks, Electronic Bill Presentment and Payment (EBPP), smart cards, and digital wallets.

  Consumers make numerous individual purchases for small amounts that must each be validated.

- **Business to Business**

  The use of electronic data interchange (EDI) facilitates the ordering process.

  Value-added network providers used for EDI and financial EDI.

  Financial EDI used for payment of purchases.

- **Both Business to Consumer and Business to Business**

  Security is an overriding concern.

  Security is provided by the use of encryption, Secure Sockets Layers (SSLs), and Secure Electronic Transactions (SETs).

Summary: Student Learning Outcomes Revisited

1. **Define and describe the two major e-commerce business models (Business to Business and Business to Consumer).** *Business to Business (B2B) e-commerce* occurs when a business sells products and services to customers who are primarily other businesses. B2B e-commerce is all about the commerce interactions among two or more businesses. *Business to Consumer (B2C) e-commerce* occurs when a business sells products and services to customers who are primarily individuals. B2C e-commerce is all about the commerce interactions among a business and an end consumer.

2. **Summarize Porter's Five Forces Model and how business people can use it to understand the relative attractiveness of an industry.** Porter's *Five Forces Model* helps business people understand the relative attractiveness of an industry and includes the following five forces:

   a. *Buyer power*—high when buyers have many choices from whom to buy, and low when their choices are few.

   b. *Supplier power*—high when buyers have few choices from whom to buy, and low when their choices are many.

   c. *Threat of substitute products and services*—high when there are many alternatives to a product or service, and low when there are few alternatives from which to choose.

   d. *Threat of new entrants*—high when it is easy for new competitors to enter a market, and low when there are significant entry barriers to entering a market.

   e. *Rivalry among existing competitors*—high when competition is fierce in a market, and low when competition is more complacent.

3. **Describe the emerging role of e-marketplaces in B2B e-commerce.** An *electronic marketplace (e-marketplace)* is an interactive business providing a central market space where multiple buyers and suppliers can engage in e-commerce and/or other e-commerce business activities, such as sharing mission-critical information for the development of products and parts, collaborating on new ideas, and deploying infrastructure applications. Two variations of B2B e-marketplaces include horizontal and vertical e-marketplaces. A *horizontal e-marketplace* is an electronic marketplace that connects buyers and sellers across many industries, primarily for MRO materials commerce. A *vertical marketplace* is an electronic marketplace that connects buyers and sellers in a given industry (e.g., oil and gas, textiles, and retail).

4. **Identify the differences and similarities among customers and their perceived value of products and services in the B2B and B2C**

e-commerce business models. Customers in the B2C e-commerce business model are end consumers. They (1) exhibit greatly varying demographics, lifestyles, wants, and needs, (2) distinguish products and services by convenience versus specialty, (3) often shop for commoditylike and digital products, and (4) sometimes require a level of *mass customization* to get exactly what they want. Customers in the B2B e-commerce business model are other businesses. They (1) distinguish products and services by *maintenance, repair, and operations (MRO) materials* versus *direct materials*, (2) aggregate demand to create negotiations for volume discounts on large purchases, and (3) most often perform e-commerce activities within an e-marketplace.

5. **Compare and contrast the development of a marketing mix for customers in the B2B and B2C e-commerce business models.** A *marketing mix* is the set of marketing tools that your organization will use to pursue its marketing objectives in reaching and attracting potential customers. In B2B e-commerce, marketing mixes do not usually include broad and generic strategies that reach all potential businesses. Instead, marketing often occurs within the context of an e-marketplace. Once a contact has been made between businesses, the development of the relationship is still formal and often includes negotiations for pricing, quality, specifications, and delivery timing.

   In B2C e-commerce, a marketing mix will include some or all of the following:

   a. Registering your site with a search engine.

   b. *Online ads* (small advertisements that appear on other sites), including *pop-up ads* (small Web pages containing an advertisement that appear on your screen outside the current Web site loaded into your browser) and *pop-under ads* (a form of a pop-up ad that you do not see until you close your current browser session).

   c. *Viral marketing*—encourages users of a product or service supplied by a B2C e-commerce business to encourage friends to join in as well.

   d. *Affiliate program*—arrangement made between two e-commerce sites that directs viewers from one site to the other.

6. **Summarize the various ways of moving money in the world of e-commerce and related issues.** B2C e-commerce payment systems most commonly include credit cards, *financial cybermediaries* (such as PayPal), *electronic checks* (with online banking being an implementation), *Electronic Bill Presentment and Payment (EBPP)*, *smart cards* (credit card with an embedded computer chip on which digital information can be stored and updated), and *digital wallets* (software and instructions for completing a transaction). In the B2B e-commerce business model, financial EDI is the norm. *Financial EDI* is an electronic process used primarily within the Business to Business e-commerce business model for the payment of purchases. Security for the electronic transfer of funds is an overriding concern. Techniques such as *encryption, public key encryption (PKE), Secure Sockets Layers (SSLs),* and *Secure Electronic Transactions (SETs)* all address this issue of security.

CLOSING CASE STUDY ONE

WHEN YOU'RE BIG, YOU CAN BE YOUR OWN B2B E-MARKETPLACE

Business to Business (B2B) e-marketplaces are the growing trend in the B2B e-commerce business model. Businesses from all industries and countries can gather, perform commerce functions, share mission-critical information, and deploy infrastructure applications that allow those organizations to tie their internal systems to each other.

But some companies—the largest ones—don't have to play in the generic B2B e-marketplaces. Instead, they can build their own and literally require that their suppliers participate. Once such company is Volkswagen AG. Its B2B e-marketplace is called VWgroupsupply.com (www.vwgroupsupply.com).

Volkswagen AG offers eight brands of automobiles—Volkswagen (passenger), Volkswagen Commercial Vehicles, Audi, Bentley, Bugatti, Lamborghini, Seat, and Skoda. In 2003, Volkswagen spent almost 60 billion euros, or approximately $77 billion, on components, automotive parts, and MRO materials for its manufacturing operations. When you spend that much money with your suppliers, you can open and run your own B2B e-marketplace.

VWgroupsupply.com handles 90 percent of Volkswagen global purchases. Almost all request for quotes, contract negotiations, catalog updating and buying, purchase-order management, vehicle program management, and payments are handled electronically and online through VWgroupsupply.com.

Gains in efficiency and productivity coupled with material costs reductions have been tremendous. The cost savings alone generated over the last three years were more than 100 million euros, or approximately $127 million.

Volkswagen requires that each of its 5,500 suppliers use VWgroupsupply.com for any interactions. Suppliers place product and pricing catalogs on the system, respond to requests for quotes, and collaborate with Volkswagen engineers on new product designs, all in the safe and secure environment of Volkswagen's proprietary B2B e-marketplace.

By requiring its suppliers to interact with Volkswagen in the e-marketplace, purchasing agents no longer have to spend valuable time searching for information and pricing. Volkswagen has, in essence, created a system that brings the necessary information to the purchasing agents. This new system within VWgroupsupply.com is called iPAD, or Internal Purchasing Agent Desk.

Prior to the implementation of iPAD, purchasing agents entering a purchase order for a vehicle front module had to use numerous separate systems to complete the process. They had to retrieve information from a supplier system and its database, query information in Volkswagen's internal parts information system, obtain information from a request-for-quotes database, enter information into a contract-negotiation transcript system, and interact with several other systems and databases. In all, the purchasing agent had to log into and use seven separate systems. Analysis revealed that Volkswagen purchasing agents were spending 70 percent of their time finding, retrieving, analyzing, validating, and moving information. This

took away valuable time from such tasks as negotiating better prices with suppliers.

Using a form of an integrated collaboration environment, or ICE, which we discussed in Chapter 2, purchasing agents now participate in a simple three-step process. First, iPAD captures and sends a business event to the purchasing agent, such as the need to order vehicle front modules. Second, iPAD attaches to that communication other necessary information such as information about potential suppliers, their costs, and other forms of analysis and descriptive information. Finally, iPAD sends the corresponding business processes and work flows to be completed electronically.

It works much like a digital dashboard, which we also introduced you to in Chapter 2. When purchasing agents log onto the iPAD portal in the morning, they receive a customized Web page with announcements, business alerts, analyses, and digital workflows to be completed. The purchasing agents can set out immediately to complete the tasks for the day, without having to spend 70 percent of their time finding, retrieving, and analyzing information. iPAD even customizes the Web page according to the purchasing agent's native language, something very necessary for a global manufacturer of automobiles with more than 2,000 purchasing agents worldwide.[12]

Questions

1. Volkswagen operates its own proprietary B2B e-marketplace in which its suppliers participate. What are the disadvantages to Volkswagen of not using a generic B2B e-marketplace with even more suppliers? What are the advantages to Volkswagen of developing and using its own proprietary B2B e-marketplace?

2. When Volkswagen needs a new part design, it uses VWsupplygroup.com to get its suppliers involved in the design process early. This creates a tremendous amount of interorganizational collaboration. What are the advantages to the suppliers and to Volkswagen in doing so?

3. How is Volkswagen's VWgroupsupply.com B2B e-marketplace an example of a vertical e-marketplace implementation? How is it an example of a horizontal e-marketplace implementation? Why is it necessary that Volkswagen combine both of these e-marketplaces into one e-marketplace? What would be the drawbacks to creating two different e-marketplaces—one for suppliers of direct materials and one for suppliers of MRO materials?

4. On pages 75–76 in Chapter 2, we alluded to four challenges to successful supply chain management. Pick two of those and discuss how VWgroupsupply.com helps Volkswagen address them. Is there one in the list on pages 75–76 not specifically discussed in this case? If so, which is it? Postulate how Volkswagen has successfully met that challenge as well.

5. To make effective purchasing decisions, Volkswagen's purchasing agents need business intelligence. What kind of business intelligence does iPAD provide to purchasing agents for carrying out their tasks? What additional kinds of business intelligence not discussed in this case could Volkswagen's purchasing agents take advantage of to make more effective decisions?

6. IPAD manages the workflow for purchasing agents. Describe how iPAD manages this process including information provided, steps to be executed, and the presentation of information.

CLOSING CASE STUDY TWO

TOTING THE E-COMMERCE LINE WITH EBAGS

For a true e-commerce success story you don't have to look any further than eBags (www.ebags.com). While many pure-play e-commerce Web sites have fallen by the wayside, eBags is not only surviving, it is thriving. It is the world's leading online provider of bags and accessories for all lifestyles. With 180 brands and over 8,000 products, eBags has sold more than 2.5 million bags since its launch in March 1999. It carries a complete line of premium and popular brands, including Samsonite, JanSport, The North Face, Liz Claiborne, and Adidas. You can buy anything from backpacks and carry-ons to computer cases and handbags at extremely competitive prices from its Web site.

eBags has received several awards for excellence in online retailing, among them:

- Circle of Excellence Platinum Award, Bizrate.com
- Web Site of the Year, *Catalog Age Magazine* (for the second year in a row)
- Email Marketer of the Year, ClickZ.MessageMedia
- Marketer of the Year, Colorado AMA
- Rocky Mountain Portal Award
- Gold Peak Catalog, Colorado AMA
- Entrepreneur of the Year—Rocky Mountain Region, Ernst and Young
- E-Commerce Initiative Award of Merit, Colorado Software and Internet Association
- Best of Show, eTravel World Awards
- 50 Essential Web Sites, *Condé* Naste Traveler

A good part of the reason for eBags's success is its commitment to providing each customer with superior service, 24 hours a day, 365 days a year. eBags provides customers with the ability to contact customer service representatives for personal assistance by telephone or e-mail and also provides convenient, real-time UPS order tracking. According to Jon Nordmark, CEO of eBags.com, "From a customer perspective, we've spent a great deal of time developing pioneering ways to guide our shoppers to the bags and accessories that enhance their lifestyles through function and fashion."

Although you would never know it, this superior customer service is not provided by eBags employees. For the past several years, eBags has outsourced both the handling of phone orders and customer service calls to Finali Corporation (www.finali.com). "The call center is often the only human contact customers have with our brand," says eBags CEO Jon Nordmark. "By maintaining a call center staff that can think on its feet, Finali delivers real value to our customers and a measurable return on our call center investment."

Typically, the conversion rate of inbound customer calls to sales at the call center has been about 25 percent. But during the 2001 holiday season, special training and incentives for Finali call center reps servicing the eBags Web site helped raise that number to 44 percent. In addition, the average size of orders placed through the call center hit $100, topping the average Web order of just over $75. The increased conversion rates and order size meant that for every dollar eBags spent with Finali, Finali generated $3.79 in sales.

eBags' many online services also distinguish it from the rest of the online marketplace. eBags' Laptop Finder searches for compatible laptop cases based on the brand and model number of your computer. And eBags' Airline Approved Carry-On Finder will show you all the carry-on bags that fit in each airline's overhead bins. eBags has also tightly integrated its systems with those of UPS to provide accurate estimated arrival dates and free returns.

eBags announced profits for the first time in December 2001, posting 5.4 percent earnings before interest, taxes, depreciation, and amortization. "Part of that achievement was due to smart outsourcing like the call center," says eBags CFO Eliot Cobb. As of early 2004, eBags had posted seven consecutive profitable quarters.[13]

Questions

1. According to Porter's Five Forces Model how would you characterize the competitive space in which eBags operates according to buyer power, supplier power, threat of substitute products or services, threat of new entrants, and rivalry among existing competitors? You may have to do some research on the Web to determine what other e-commerce Web sites sell similar products. Pick one of Porter's five forces and describe what steps eBags has undertaken to shift that force in a positive way in its direction.
2. In our discussions of customers and their perceptions of value, we noted that customers tend to categorize products and services as either convenience or specialty. How would you characterize what eBags provides—convenience, specialty, or perhaps a combination of the two? Justify your answer.
3. We also noted in this chapter that commoditylike and digital products work extremely well within the B2C e-commerce business model. eBags sells products that are neither. How can it be so successful without selling these types of products?
4. How would you describe the majority of eBags' customers (end consumers)? What sort of demographics would you like to know about eBags' customers if you were an eBags employee?
5. Given that eBags' customers are end consumers, and on the basis of your answer to question 4, what sort of marketing mix would you recommend for eBags? If you specify creating affiliate programs, identify the types of Web sites with which to enter into an affiliate program.
6. What innovative steps could eBags employ to offer mass customization to its customers? Do you think this would have any measurable positive effect on sales? Why or why not?
7. What sort of payment options does eBags accept? You may have to visit its Web site to determine this. Should eBags consider broadening the payment options it accepts? Why or why not?

Key Terms and Concepts

Short-Answer Questions

1. What is electronic commerce? What are the four main perspectives for e-commerce?
2. What is the Five Forces Model? What are the "five forces" of that model?
3. How is a loyalty program an example of reducing buyer power?
4. How can you use a B2B e-marketplace to reduce your dependency on a particular supplier?
5. What are switching costs?
6. What are entry barriers?
7. How do convenience and specialty items differ in the B2C e-commerce business model?
8. Why do commoditylike and digital items sell well in the B2C e-commerce business model?
9. What is mass customization?
10. What are maintenance, repair, and operations (MRO) materials?
11. What is demand aggregation?

12. What are direct materials?
13. How does a reverse auction work?
14. How are vertical and horizontal e-marketplaces different?
15. What is spoofing?
16. What can a marketing mix include for a B2C e-commerce business?
17. How do pop-up and pop-under ads differ?
18. What is a conversion rate?
19. What are the major types of B2C e-commerce payment systems?
20. What is the difference between a client-side digital wallet and a server-side digital wallet?
21. What is financial EDI?
22. How does public key encryption work?
23. How are Secure Sockets Layers (SSLs) and Secure Electronic Transactions (SETs) different? How are they the same?

Assignments and Exercises

1. **PORTER'S FIVE FORCES MODEL AND YOUR SCHOOL** To illustrate the use of Porter's Five Forces Model, let's apply it to your school. Assume that you are a school administrator and want to use Porter's Five Forces Model for evaluating your business program's competitive position in the marketplace. Is buyer power low or high? What are some options other than your school's program that students could choose? Is supplier power low or high? Who are your school's suppliers? Is the threat of substitute products or services low or high? What are possible substitutes to getting an education? Is the threat of new entrants low or high? What entry barriers exist? Is the rivalry among existing competition low or high? Who are your school's competitors?

2. **DEALING WITH THE GREAT DIGITAL DIVIDE** The great digital divide addresses the concerns of many people that the world is becoming one marked by the "have's" and "have not's" with respect to technology—that is, the traditional notion of a "third world" is now also being defined by the extent to which a country has access to and uses technology. Find out what, if anything, the United Nations is doing about this issue and express an opinion on whether or not you believe its efforts will be successful. Determine if there are organizations such as private companies or foundations that have the digital divide high on their agendas. For any such organizations you find, evaluate their efforts and express an opinion as to whether or not

they will be successful. Finally, search for a less developed country that is making significant local efforts to deal with the digital divide. If you can't find one, prepare a list of the countries you reviewed and briefly describe the conditions in one of them with respect to technology.

3. **RESEARCHING A BUSINESS TO BUSINESS E-MARKETPLACE** Biz2Biz (www.biz2biz.com/Marketplace/) is a B2B e-marketplace. Connect to its site and do some looking around. What sort of marketing services does it provide through its Biz2BizCommunication program? What sort of services does it provide for creating and maintaining an electronic catalog? If you owned a business and wanted to join, what process would you have to go through? How much does it cost your organization to join Biz2Biz? What buyer tools does Biz2Biz provide its membership?

4. **DEVELOPING M-COMMERCE SCENARIOS FOR GPS CELL PHONES** Soon, cell phones will be equipped with GPS chips that enable users to be located to within a geographical location about the size of a tennis court. The primary purpose for installing GPS chips in phones is to enable emergency services to locate a cell phone user. For example, if you dial an emergency assistance number (911 in the United States) from your home now, it is possible for a computer system to use your home telephone number to access a database and obtain your address. This could be very useful in situations in which you were unable to give address information to the emergency operator for some reason. The problem with trying to do the same thing with present-day cell phones is that you could be calling from anywhere and that is the problem GPS-enabled cell phones are intended to overcome.

As you might imagine, marketers have been monitoring this development with great interest because GPS-phones will support m-commerce, which we discussed in Chapter 1. When the new cell phones become available, marketers visualize scenarios where they will know who you are (by your telephone number) and where you are (by the GPS chip). One possible way they could use this information, for example, is to give you a call when you are walking past their shop in the mall to let you know of a special sale on items they know you would be interested in buying. Of course, retailers would have to possess IT systems that would permit them to craft such personalized offers, and you would have had to give them permission to call you.

Find out what at least three e-commerce marketers are saying about personalized marketing using GPS-equipped cell phones and prepare an analysis of how the phones will be likely to be used when the technology is widely available.

5. **FINDING THE MOST POPULAR B2C E-COMMERCE SITES** Connect to the Web and do some research to find the most popular B2C e-commerce Web sites in terms of number of hits or views per month. What are the sites? Which of the sites in some way or another supports the concept of an e-marketplace where end consumers can gather?

Discussion Questions

1. In what ways can shopping over the Internet be more convenient for consumers? In what ways can it be less convenient? List at least five products you would have no hesitation buying over the Internet, five products you might want to think about a bit before buying, and five products you would never consider buying over the Internet. Justify your reasons in each case.

2. In your opinion, according to Porter's Five Forces Model, has competition increased or decreased overall as a result of the Internet and e-commerce? Specifically address each of the five forces in Porter's model.

3. Why is the ability to change prices instantaneously considered an advantage for e-commerce Web sites? When might the use of personalized pricing be a disadvantage for an e-commerce Web site?

4. There have been a string of e-commerce Web sites running out of cash, not being able to attract more money from investors, and going out of business as a result. What are some of the main reasons this happened?

5. Under what circumstances would it be appropriate to consider using viral marketing? See if you can think of an organization with

an online presence that could benefit from viral marketing but is not currently using it. It could be your school, for example, or it could be an organization you are involved with. How would you suggest the organization go about using viral marketing in order for it to achieve the desired results? What are some of the other marketing techniques available for an e-commerce Web site to use? Why is it important to consider a mix of techniques rather than just relying on a single one?

6. Describe the services provided by value-added networks that make it easier for companies to exchange EDI transactions with each other. What are the pros and cons of using value-added networks for B2B e-commerce? Why don't more companies use the Internet for EDI since it is much cheaper than using a value-added network? Assume that you work for a telecommunications company that operates a value-added network (AT&T or GXS). What sort of strategies would you encourage your company to explore to deal with the possibility of losing considerable amounts of revenues as your customers leave you in favor of using other Internet-based services?

7. What are the advantages and disadvantages of B2B marketplaces for buyers? For sellers? How could a supplier company play on the relationships that it has with a long-standing customer to avoid getting pulled into a reverse auction in an open B2B marketplace? Why do some observers say that B2B marketplaces can be risky ventures?

8. Throughout this chapter, we've illuminated numerous differences between end consumers and businesses as customers. Review those differences and then write down the three you consider most significant. Discuss those three. For the differences that you did not choose as the three most important, be prepared to justify your decision.

9. In this chapter, we discussed using such technologies as B2B e-marketplaces to create tighter supply chain managements, thereby driving out costs. If you refer back to Chapter 2, you'll recall that another major business initiative is customer relationship management (CRM). How can B2C e-commerce businesses use the Internet to further enhance their CRM initiatives? How can B2B e-commerce businesses use the Internet to further enhance their CRM initiatives? Does it become easier or harder to maintain relationships with customers as businesses move toward more "electronic" commerce? Why?

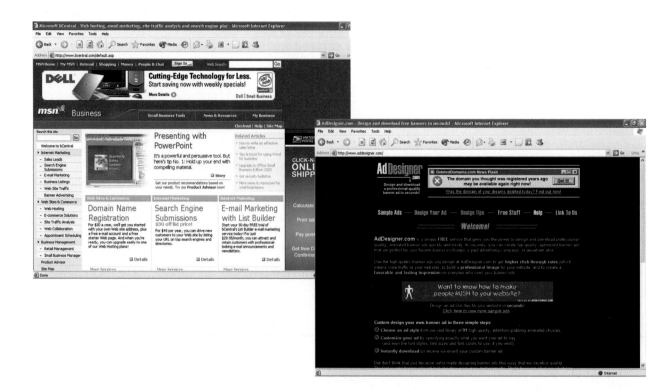

Getting Your Business on the Internet

Let's say you've decided it might be fun (and profitable) to establish a retail-oriented Internet-based business. You can use the one your team created in the Team Work project on page 262 if it's appropriate or you can create a new one. You know that many such e-commerce businesses don't make it, but you'd like to be one that is successful. There are a lot of resources on the Internet that can help you with the tasks of selecting the right business in the first place, getting the site up and running, deciding who should host your site, marketing your site, understanding privacy issues, and obtaining the funds you need to pay your expenses until your business begins to show a profit. On the Web site that supports this text (www.mhhe.com/haag, select "Electronic Commerce Projects"), we've provided direct links to many useful Web sites. These are a great starting point for completing this project. We also encourage you to search the Internet for others.

COMPETITIVE INTELLIGENCE

The first thing you need is an idea for the business. What would you like to sell? A product or a service? Make sure you have expertise, or something special to offer. After you've come up with a candidate, it's time to see how much competition is out there and what they're up to. One of the things many new business owners fail to do is to see how many competitors there are before they launch their business. You may find there are too many and that they would be tough competition for you (review Porter's Five Forces Model). Or, you may find that there are few competitors and the ones who are out there aren't doing a terrific job.

Seek out and look at some of the Web sites of businesses in the competitive space you're thinking of entering. As you do, answer the following questions.

A. How many sites did you find that are offering the same product or service you're planning to offer?

B. How many are in your country and how many are in other countries?

C. Did you come across a site from another country that has a unique approach that you did not see on any of the sites in your own country?

STOREFRONT SOFTWARE

If you decide to sell products, there is software that you can use to make it easy to create a Web site. There are many software products for you to choose from. Some will cost you a lot of money, but others are free. FreeMerchant.com, for example, has a Basic Store for $9.95 per month, a Bronze Package for $24.95 per month, a Silver Package for $49.95 per month, and a Gold Package for $99.95 per month. What you get in each of these packages is listed in detail on the FreeMerchant.com Web site (www.freemerchant.com). Since there are many options to choose from, it would be worth your while to do a little research to see if you can find an article that compares current versions of storefront software. A site like ZDNet.com (www.zdnet.com) would be a good place to start your search. Build up a list of features that you will need for your e-commerce site, and then compare your needs with the features offered by the various software packages. They all sound good when you read about them on the vendors' Web sites so be sure you take a "test drive" of the software before you sign up.

Another possibility would be to sign up for a shopping mall. Find your way to Amazon.com's zShops or Yahoo!Store and see what you think of these alternatives. Finally, you'll need a way for your customers to pay you for what they buy. This involves getting a merchant account which permits you to accept credit cards. Most of the storefront sites will explain how merchant accounts work and will help you get a merchant account (see www. bigstep.com, for example).

    A. What features have you decided your storefront software must provide?

    B. How have you evaluated the pros and cons of using a storefront software package versus the options offered by Amazon.com and Yahoo!?

    C. See if you can track down users of software options you are considering. Send them an e-mail and ask them what they like and dislike. You may be surprised at their answers.

HOSTING SERVICES

You've got some options here. You can decide to acquire the necessary computer and communications hardware and software to manage your own technical infrastructure, or you can let a specialist firm do it for you. Unless you're really into the technical side of things, it's probably better to work with a firm that specializes in it. They are called *Web hosting services* and there are plenty of them around. Cost, reliability, security, and customer service are some of the criteria you might use in selecting a hosting service. If you're planning to have your business located in a country with poor telecommunications services, don't forget that you can choose a hosting service located in a country with a more reliable telecommunications infrastructure, anywhere in the world. Some companies provide directories that make it easy for you to find and compare prices and features of Web hosting companies, sort of like shopping malls for Web hosting services. An example of such a company is FindYourHosting.com (www.findyourhosting.com). Take a look at its site to see some of the options available. As you consider Web hosting services, answer the following questions.

    A. Compare the costs of the various hosting services. Were you able to find one that seems to be within your budget?

    B. How can you evaluate the reliability of the various Web hosting services?

    C. How can you evaluate the quality of a Web hosting company's customer service? What do you have a right to expect in the way of customer service and also security?

MARKETING YOUR SITE

In this chapter, we discussed several options for marketing a Web site: registering with search engines, online ads, viral marketing, and affiliate programs. Deciding on the marketing mix that will be most effective and still permit you to stay within a reasonable budget will be critical to the success of your venture. You may want to consider employing an Internet marketing consultant to help you lay out a marketing plan. One, AdDesigner.com (www.addesigner. com), even offers some free services. Also, you may want to see what marketing services your storefront software or Web hosting service may offer. As you consider how to market your site, answer the following questions.

    A. How have you defined your target market? Who are the people that will be most interested in your product or service?

    B. Which of the available marketing techniques have you selected as being most appropriate to market your site? Why have you selected this particular marketing mix?

    C. What have you decided about using the services of a marketing consultant? How did you justify your decision?

EXTENDED LEARNING MODULE E

NETWORK BASICS

Student Learning Outcomes

1. IDENTIFY AND DESCRIBE THE FOUR BASIC CONCEPTS ON WHICH NETWORKS ARE BUILT.

2. LIST THE COMPONENTS YOU NEED TO SET UP A SMALL PEER-TO-PEER NETWORK AT HOME.

3. COMPARE AND CONTRAST THE VARIOUS INTERNET CONNECTION POSSIBILITIES.

4. DESCRIBE CLIENT/SERVER BUSINESS NETWORKS FROM A BUSINESS AND PHYSICAL POINT OF VIEW.

5. DEFINE LOCAL AREA NETWORKS (LANS), MUNICIPAL AREA NETWORKS (MANS), WIRELESS LOCAL AREA NETWORKS (WLANS), AND WIDE AREA NETWORKS (WANS).

6. COMPARE AND CONTRAST THE TYPES OF COMMUNICATIONS MEDIA.

Taking Advantage of the CD

When you're surfing the Web, accessing software on your school's server, sending e-mail, or letting your roommate use his/her computer to access the files on your computer, your computer is part of a network. A ***computer network*** (which we simply refer to as a network) is two or more computers connected so that they can communicate with each other and share information, software, peripheral devices, and/or processing power. Many networks have dozens, hundreds, or even thousands of computers.

Networks come in all sizes from two computers connected to share a printer, to the Internet, which is the largest network on the planet, joining millions of computers of all kinds all over the world. In between are business networks, which vary in size from a dozen or fewer computers to many thousands.

Some networks are extremely complex with perhaps thousands of computers connected together. These networks require highly skilled professionals to keep them up and running. However, regardless of their size, some basic principles apply to all networks.

1. Each computer on a network must have a network interface (either as an expansion card or integrated into the motherboard or through software for a modem) that provides the entrance or doorway for information traffic to and from other computers.

2. A network usually has at least one connecting device (like a hub or a router) that ties the computers on the network together and acts as a switchboard for passing information.

3. There must be communications media like cables or radio waves connecting network hardware devices. The communications media transport information around the network between computers and the connecting device(s).

4. Each computer must have software that supports the movement of information in and out of it. This could be modem software and/or a network operating system.

We definitely believe that it's worth your time and energy to pop in the CD and read this module. This module is the same as the modules in your text—it includes Team Work and On Your Own projects and great end-of-module Assignments and Exercises. In it, you'll learn many things including

- How to build a peer-to-peer network at home or in your dorm with network cards, cabling and a network connecting device
- Five ways to connect to the Internet
  - Phone line and dial-up modem
  - Phone line and Digital Subscriber Line (DSL) modem
  - Cable TV line and cable modem
  - Satellite dish and satellite modem
  - Wireless access points
- How to add wireless access to a network
- Client/server networks from a business point of view
- Client/server networks from a physical point of view
- What differentiates LANs, MANs, WLANs, and WANs
- The types of telecommunications media that networks use

CHAPTER SIX OUTLINE

STUDENT LEARNING OUTCOMES

1. List the seven steps in the systems development life cycle (SDLC) and associated activities for each step.

2. Describe three keys to success you can use to help ensure a successful systems development effort.

3. Define the three different ways you can staff a systems development project.

4. List the three advantages of selfsourcing.

5. Describe prototyping and profile an example of a prototype.

6. Describe the five advantages of prototyping.

7. Describe the outsourcing process and the current trend toward offshore outsourcing.

CHAPTER SIX

Systems Development
Phases, Tools, and Techniques

OPENING CASE STUDY:
DEVELOPING *ENTER THE MATRIX*

It took four long years of development to build the highly anticipated videogame *Enter the Matrix* based on the movie *The Matrix*. Directors Larry and Andy Wachowski and Shiny Entertainment developed the videogame, which is so realistic that you may begin to believe life on Earth is nothing more than an elaborate facade. The Wachowski brothers wrote an original 244-page script for the game, which includes actual footage shot on location during the filming of the movie. Over 60 developers worked on the system for two years creating the proprietary technology that allows the game to expand beyond the movie. For example, a door that remains unopened on the big screen could be a portal to another level in the game. A few of the amazing new features developed for the game include:

- Motion capture: Every cast member from Keanu Reeves to Jada Pinkett Smith was cyberscanned into a 3-D synthespain. The process took over six months.
- Virtual modeling: The system uses a modeling technique called *alpha-mapping* that allows light to pass through such things as hair and beards and allows virtual skin to stretch in real time, making those deep knee bends and smile lines look real.
- Action: *Enter the Matrix* game characters can make over 3,500 moves, significantly more than the average game character that can perform only around 300 moves.

- Zoom: Wide shots seamlessly fade into close-ups without any loss of clarity, which mimics the Hollywood look and feel. The game automatically knows when to add and subtract details so that, to the player, the adventure always looks the same and runs at a speedy 60 frames per second—more than twice as fast and smooth as movie footage.

Since Atari's *Star Wars* hit arcades 20 years ago, the movie industry has promised multimedia convergence of film and videogames. For the first time the movie industry is living up to its promise with the dual release of *Enter the Matrix* the videogame and *The Matrix Reloaded* the movie on the same day. Jada Pinkett Smith predicts that game acting is going to be one of Hollywood's next big things, noting that husband Will Smith is already investigating a game tie-in for his next movie.

Building new and exciting information systems that have the capacity to change industries, reinvent processes, and reshape organizations is the focus of this chapter. If you are the least bit curious about how to build information systems, then we welcome you to the exciting and challenging world of systems development. This chapter provides a high-level overview of how information systems are developed using the systems development life cycle through either insourcing, selfsourcing, or outsourcing.[1]

Introduction

Have you ever wondered why businesses build information systems or how a business knows when it's time to replace an old information system? Typically, new systems are created because knowledge workers request the systems to help them perform their work. For example, a marketing manager might request a system to produce product information and track customer sales information (CRM activities) or a human resource manager might request a system to track employee vacation and sick days. Almost any position you take in a company today will require you to work with information systems because they are one of the most important parts of any business. In fact, information systems supply the support structure for meeting the company's strategies and goals. This chapter focuses on the many factors that must come together to develop a successful information system.

Insourcing and the Systems Development Life Cycle

The **systems development life cycle (SDLC)** is a structured step-by-step approach for developing information systems. There are literally hundreds of different activities associated with each phase in the SDLC. Typical activities include determining budgets, gathering business requirements, designing models, and writing detailed user documentation. The activities you, as a knowledge worker, perform during each systems development project will vary depending on the type of system you're building and the tools you use to build it. Since we can't possibly cover them all in this brief introduction, we have chosen a few of the more important SDLC activities that you might perform on a systems development project as a knowledge worker. Figure 6.1 displays the seven phases in the SDLC along with the associated activities discussed in this chapter.

Figure 6.1

The Systems Development Life Cycle (SDLC) and Associated Activities

SDLC Phase	Activities
1. Planning	• Define the system to be developed • Set the project scope • Develop the project plan including tasks, resources, and timeframes
2. Analysis	• Gather the business requirements for the system
3. Design	• Design the technical architecture required to support the system • Design system models
4. Development	• Build the technical architecture • Build the database and programs
5. Testing	• Write the test conditions • Perform the testing of the system
6. Implementation	• Write detailed user documentation • Provide training for the system users
7. Maintenance	• Build a help desk to support the system users • Provide an environment to support system changes

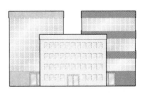

Insourcing	**Selfsourcing**	**Outsourcing**
IT Specialists Within Your Organization	Knowledge Workers	Another Organization

Figure 6.2

Insourcing, Selfsourcing, and Outsourcing

You have three primary choices as to who will build your system (see Figure 6.2). First, you can choose *insourcing,* which involves choosing IT specialists within your organization to develop the system. Second, you can choose *selfsourcing* (also called *knowledge worker development* or *end-user development*), which is the development and support of IT systems by knowledge workers with little or no help from IT specialists. Selfsourcing is becoming quite common in most organizations and is part of the overall concept of knowledge worker development or end-user computing. Third, you can choose *outsourcing,* which is the delegation of specific work to a third party for a specified length of time, at a specified cost, and at a specified level of service.

As we introduce you to the SDLC in this section, we'll focus on how the overall process works, key activities within each phase, roles you may play as a knowledge worker when *insourcing* a project, and opportunities you can capitalize on to ensure that your systems development effort is a success. The remaining sections of this chapter focus on how the SDLC changes when you selfsource and outsource your systems development efforts.

PHASE 1: PLANNING

The *planning phase* of the systems development life cycle involves determining a solid plan for developing your information system. The following are the three primary activities you'll perform during the planning phase:

1. *Define the system to be developed*—You must identify and select the system for development or determine which system is required to support the strategic goals of your organization. A *critical success factor (CSF)* is a factor simply critical to your organization's success. Organizations typically track all the proposed systems and prioritize them based on business impact or critical success factors. This allows the business to strategically decide which systems to build.

2. *Set the project scope*—You must define the project's scope and create a project scope document for your system development effort. The *project scope* clearly defines the high-level system requirements. Scope is often referred to as the 10,000-foot view of the system or the most basic definition of the system. A *project scope document* is a written definition of the project scope and is usually no longer than a paragraph.

3. *Develop the project plan*—You must develop a detailed project plan for your entire systems development effort. The *project plan* defines the *what, when,* and *who* questions of systems development including all activities to be performed, the individuals, or resources, who will perform the activities, and the time required to complete each activity. The project plan is the guiding force behind ensuring the on-time delivery of a complete and successful information system.

ID	Task Name	Duration	Resource Names
1	**Planning**	**3 days**	
2	Set scope	3 days	Scott
3	**Analysis**	**8 days**	
4	Gather Business Requirements	8 days	Anne, Martha
5	**Design**	**3 days**	
6	Model GUI	3 days	David
7	**Development**	**2 days**	
8	Build Database	2 days	Logan
9	**Testing**	**3 days**	
10	Write Test Condition	3 days	Martha
11	**Implementation**	**1 day?**	
12	Install System	1 day?	Leigh
13	**Maintenance**	**6 days**	
14	Setup Help Desk	6 days	Naomi

Figure 6.3

A Sample Project Plan

To learn more about project planning and management, visit the Web site that supports this text at www.mhhe.com/haag.

YOUR ROLE DURING PLANNING   One of the most important activities knowledge workers undertake during the planning phase is defining which systems to develop. We can't stress the importance of this activity enough. Systems development focuses on either solving a problem or taking advantage of an opportunity. Your new system will be successful only if it solves the right problem or takes advantage of the right opportunity.

Developing the project plan is another critical activity in which you'll be directly involved. Figure 6.3 displays a sample project plan. A *project manager* is an individual who is an expert in project planning and management, defines and develops the project plan, and tracks the plan to ensure all key project milestones are completed on time. You must help the project manager define the activities for each phase of the systems development life cycle. The project manager is an expert in project management and you are the expert in the business operations; together the two of you will be able to develop a detailed project plan that meets everyone's needs.

KEY TO SUCCESS—MANAGE YOUR PROJECT PLAN   Continually monitoring and managing your project plan is key to successful systems development. The project plan is the road map you follow during the development of the system. There are many reasons why the project manager must continually review and revise the project plan including employees' vacations and sick leave, adding or removing activities, and changing timeframes. Since the manager must continually update the project plan, it is considered a living document and you can expect it to change almost daily.

Carefully monitoring project milestones is a good way to ensure your project is on the path to success. *Project milestones* represent key dates by which you need a certain group of activities performed. For example, completing the planning phase might be a project milestone. If all your project milestones are completed on time, this is a good indication that your project is on schedule and will be successful. Also, when managing the project plan be sure to watch for scope creep and feature creep. *Scope creep* occurs when the scope of the project increases. *Feature creep* occurs when developers add extra features that were not part of the initial requirements. Closely monitoring scope creep and feature creep will also help ensure your project's success.

PHASE 2: ANALYSIS

Once your organization has decided which systems to develop you can move into the analysis phase. The *analysis phase* of the systems development life cycle involves end

ANALYZING BUSINESS REQUIREMENTS

You have been hired to build an employee tracking system for a new coffee shop. Review the following business requirements and highlight any potential issues.

- All employees must have a unique employee ID.
- The system must track employee hours worked based on employee's last name.
- Employees must be scheduled to work a minimum of 8 hours per day.
- Employee payroll is calculated by multiplying the employee's hours worked by $7.25.

- Managers must be scheduled to work morning shifts.
- Employees cannot be scheduled to work over 8 hours per day.
- Servers cannot be scheduled to work morning, afternoon, or evening shifts.
- The system must allow managers to change and delete employees from the system.

users and IT specialists working together to gather, understand, and document the business requirements for the proposed system. The following is the primary activity you'll perform during the analysis phase:

Gather the business requirements—***Business requirements*** are the detailed set of knowledge worker requests that the system must meet to be successful. A sample business requirement might state, "the CRM system must track all customer sales by product, region, and sales representative." This business requirement states what the system must do from the business perspective.

Gathering business requirements is similar to performing an investigation. You must talk to everyone who has a claim in using the new system to find out what is required. An extremely useful way to gather business requirements is to perform a joint application development session. During a ***joint application development (JAD)*** session knowledge workers and IT specialists meet, sometimes for several days, to define and review the business requirements for the system.

Once you define all the business requirements, you prioritize them in order of business importance and place them in a formal comprehensive document, the ***requirements definition document.*** The knowledge workers receive the requirements definition document for their sign-off. ***Sign-off*** is the knowledge workers' actual signatures indicating they approve all the business requirements. Typically, one of the first major milestones in the project plan is the knowledge workers' sign-off on business requirements.

YOUR ROLE DURING ANALYSIS The most important role you'll play during the analysis phase is performing a detailed review of each business requirement and approving the analysis by signing off on the business requirements. One of the most common reasons why systems development efforts fail is because business requirements are either missing or incorrectly gathered during the analysis phase. For example, assume you're building a student registration system. What would happen if you documented the business requirement as, "System must not allow students to add classes"? This requirement is incorrect and should be stated, "System must allow students to add classes." If you build a student registration system that doesn't allow students to add classes, the system will be a complete failure.

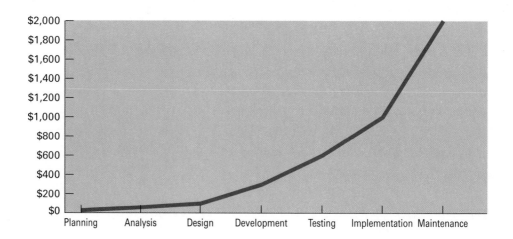

Figure 6.4

The Cost of Finding Errors

The business requirements drive the entire system. If they are not accurate or complete, there is no way the system will be successful. You are the business process expert: That means you know how current processes and current systems work, and you know how things need to change. It's vitally important that you provide this information because the current system model will become the foundation for developing the new system model.

KEY TO SUCCESS—FIND ERRORS EARLY   One of the key things to think about when you are reviewing business requirements is the cost to the company of fixing errors if the business requirements are unclear or inaccurate. An error found during the analysis phase is relatively inexpensive to fix; all you really have to do is change a Word document. An error found during later phases, however, is incredibly expensive to fix because you have to change the actual system. Figure 6.4 displays how the cost to fix an error grows exponentially the later the error is found in the SDLC.

Imagine what will happen if the following business requirement was supposed to have the word "must" instead of "must not": "System must not allow users to change their passwords." Finding this error during analysis is as simple as changing a Word document. But finding this error during a later phase requires the developers to rebuild the system to allow users to change their passwords. For this reason, it is critical that you ensure that every business requirement is accurate and complete.

PHASE 3: DESIGN

The primary goal of the *design phase* of the systems development life cycle is to build a technical blueprint of how the proposed system will work. During the analysis phase, end users and IT specialists work together to develop the business requirements for the proposed system from a logical point of view. That is, during analysis you document business requirements without respect to technology or the technical infrastructure that will support the system. As you move into design, the project team turns its attention to the system from a physical or technical point of view. That is, you take the business requirements generated during the analysis phase and define the supporting technical architecture in the design phase. The following are the primary activities you'll perform during the design phase:

1. *Design the technical architecture*—The ***technical architecture*** defines the hardware, software, and telecommunications equipment required to run the system. Most systems run on a computer network with each employee having a workstation and the application software running on a server. The

telecommunications requirements encompass access to the Internet and the ability for end users to dial-in remotely to the server. You typically explore several different technical architectures before choosing the final technical architecture.

2. *Design the system models*—**Modeling** is the activity of drawing a graphical representation of a design. You model everything you build including screens, reports, software, and databases. There are many different types of modeling activities performed during the design phase including GUI screen design. The *graphical user interface (GUI)* is the interface to an information system. *GUI screen design* is the ability to model the information system screens for an entire system. You must decide many things when modeling a GUI, including the placement of items on the screen and the number of items contained in a drop-down list. You base your decisions on how and where to display menu items on whatever is easiest for the knowledge workers to use. If the menu items are placed incorrectly on the GUI, knowledge workers could waste a significant amount of time just searching the GUI to find the correct item.

YOUR ROLE DURING DESIGN   During design, your role decreases as a business process expert and increases as a quality control analyst. IT specialists perform most of the activities during the design phase, but quality assurance is a key role for you. The IT specialists will develop several alternative technical solutions. It's your job to analyze each and ensure that the recommended solution best meets your business requirements. Design walk-through meetings are a key activity during the design phase. You'll be asked to formally sign off on the detailed design documents indicating that you approve of the proposed technical solution.

KEY TO SUCCESS—DETERMINE FUTURE REQUIREMENTS   You typically explore several different technical architectures before choosing the final technical architecture. The final architecture must meet your needs in terms of time, cost, technical feasibility, and flexibility. One of the most important things to remember during the design phase is that your final architecture must not only meet your current system needs but also meet your future system needs. For example, you want to ensure that your database is large enough to hold the current volume of customers plus all the new customers you expect to gain over the next five years.

PHASE 4: DEVELOPMENT

During the *development phase* of the systems development life cycle, you take all your detailed design documents from the design phase and transform them into an actual system. This phase marks the point at which you go from physical design to physical implementation. The following are the two main activities you'll perform during the development phase:

1. *Build the technical architecture*—For you to build your system, you must first build the platform on which the system is going to operate. In the development phase, you purchase and implement equipment necessary to support the technical architecture you designed during the design phase.

2. *Build the database and programs*—Once the technical architecture is built, you initiate and complete the creating of supporting databases and writing the software required for the system. These tasks are usually undertaken by IT specialists, and it may take months or even years to design and create the databases and write all the software.

CHANGING TECHNOLOGIES

Technology changes at an incredibly fast pace. Here are a few of the new technologies that are already here and changing our world.

- 64-bit chips—Apple's G5 chip and AMD's Athlon's 64-bit processor are giving desktop computers a supercharge with the ability to process as many as 16 billion instructions per second. The 64-bit chip market share in 2003 totaled $260 million, with expectations to increase to $6.6 billion by 2007.

- Voice-Over-Internet Protocol (VOIP)—VOIP technology transmits voice signals over high-bandwidth networks using Internet protocol, the same standard that computers use to exchange data online, offering users less expensive phone calls. The VOIP market share in 2003 totaled $1.2 billion, with expectations to increase to $8.4 billion by 2007.

- Micro hard drives—Micro hard drives have the ability to store gigabyte-level capacity in a tiny casing the size of a matchbook. The micro hard drive market share in 2003 totaled $90 million, with expectations to increase to $1 billion by 2007.[2]

YOUR ROLE DURING DEVELOPMENT   IT specialists complete most of the activities in the development phase. Your role during this phase is to confirm any changes to business requirements and track the progress of tasks on the project plan to ensure timely delivery of the system. Constantly reevaluating the project plan during this phase helps you to determine if you'll be able to meet the final system delivery due date.

You cannot take a passive role during development. For example, you are still responsible for ensuring that the databases contain the information that supports your business requirements. So, you need knowledge of databases and the database design process. If you haven't already, we would encourage you to read *Extended Learning Module C* for additional information on designing and building databases.

KEY TO SUCCESS—TAKE ADVANTAGE OF CHANGING TECHNOLOGIES   Gordon Moore, cofounder of Intel Corporation, observed in 1965 that chip density doubles every 18 months. This observation, known as Moore's law, simply means that memory sizes, processor power, and so forth all follow the same pattern and roughly double in capacity every 18 months. As Moore's law states, technology changes at an incredibly fast pace. It's possible to have to revise your entire project plan in the middle of a project because of a change in technology.

Many of the system examples we discuss in this chapter are small and easy to implement, such as a student registration system we alluded to above. These projects are great for discussion and initial understanding, but they're not indicative of real-world projects. Many real-world projects have hundreds of business requirements, take years to complete, and cost millions of dollars. Technology changes quickly and you must be sure to take advantage of any new technologies that become available during your systems development effort.

PHASE 5: TESTING

The *testing phase* of the systems development life cycle verifies that the system works and meets all the business requirements defined in the analysis phase. Testing is critical. The following are the primary activities you'll perform during the testing phase:

TEAM WORK

WRITING TEST CONDITIONS

Your manager has asked you to test the cut and paste functionality for a word processing application. Write 10 detailed test conditions using the template below. Be sure to think about cutting and pasting such things as different fonts, varying font sizes, bold and italic fonts, graphics, etc. Once you have completed your test conditions, estimate how many test conditions would be required to completely test the cut and paste functionality for Microsoft Word. We have provided a sample for you.

Test Condition Number	Date	Tester Name	Test Condition	Expected Result	Actual Result	Pass/Fail
21	5/27/2004	Hughes	Highlight text	Text highlighted	Text highlighted	Pass

1. *Write the test conditions*—You must have detailed test conditions to perform an exhaustive test. *Test conditions* are the detailed steps the system must perform along with the expected results of each step. The tester will execute each test condition and compare the expected results with the actual results to verify that the system functions correctly. Each time the actual result is different from the expected result, a "bug" is generated, and the system goes back to development for a "bug fix." A typical system development effort has hundreds or thousands of test conditions. You must execute and verify all of these test conditions to ensure the entire system functions correctly.

2. *Perform the testing of the system*—You must perform many different types of tests when you begin testing your new system. A few of the more common tests include:

   - *Unit testing*—tests individual units or pieces of code for a system.
   - *System testing*—verifies that the units or pieces of code written for a system function correctly when integrated into the total system.
   - *Integration testing*—verifies that separate systems can work together.
   - *User acceptance testing (UAT)*—determines if the system satisfies the business requirements and enables knowledge workers to perform their jobs correctly.

YOUR ROLE DURING TESTING IT specialists also perform many of the activities during the testing phase. Your involvement is still critical, as you are the quality assurance expert. You're directly involved with reviewing the test conditions to ensure the IT specialists have tested all the system functionality and that every single test condition has passed.

KEY TO SUCCESS—COMPLETE THE TESTING PHASE   The first thing individuals tend to do when a project falls behind schedule is to start skipping phases in the SDLC, and the most common phase they skip is the testing phase. Failing to test the system can lead to unfound errors, and chances are high that the system will fail. It's critical that you perform all phases in the SDLC during every project. Try not to sacrifice testing time or your system may not work correctly all of the time.

PHASE 6: IMPLEMENTATION

During the ***implementation phase*** of the systems development life cycle you distribute the system to all the knowledge workers and they begin using the system to perform their everyday jobs. The following are the two primary activities you'll perform during the implementation phase:

1. *Write detailed user documentation*—When you install the system, you must also provide the knowledge workers with ***user documentation*** that highlights how to use the system. Knowledge workers find it extremely frustrating to have a new system without documentation.

2. *Provide training for the system users*—You must also provide training for the knowledge workers who are going to use the new system. You can provide several different types of training, and two of the most popular are online training and workshop training. ***Online training*** runs over the Internet or off a CD or DVD. Knowledge workers perform the training at any time, on their own computers, at their own pace. This type of training is convenient for knowledge workers because they can set their own schedule to undergo the training. ***Workshop training*** is held in a classroom environment and is led by an instructor. Workshop training is great for difficult systems for which knowledge workers need one-on-one time with an individual instructor.

YOUR ROLE DURING IMPLEMENTATION   During implementation, you might attend training or help to perform the training. The system may have passed all the tests, but if the knowledge workers don't use the system properly, the system will fail. You must ensure that all the knowledge workers have the required training to use the system correctly.

KEY TO SUCCESS—CHOOSING THE RIGHT IMPLEMENTATION METHOD   You need to choose the right implementation method that best suits your organization, project, and employees to ensure a successful implementation. When you implement the new system, you have four implementation methods you can choose from:

- ***Parallel implementation***—using both the old and new system until you're sure that the new system performs correctly.

- ***Plunge implementation***—discarding the old system completely and immediately using the new system.

- ***Pilot implementation***—having only a small group of people use the new system until you know it works correctly and then adding the remaining people to the system.

- ***Phased implementation***—implementing the new system in phases (e.g., accounts receivables, then accounts payable) until you're sure it works correctly and then implementing the remaining phases of the new system.

MAKING YOUR SOFTWARE WORK

Faulty software installations cost companies billions of dollars. Here are three tips from Mercury Interactive, a testing software company, on how to avoid the common pitfalls of implementation.

1. *Keep it simple*—The trouble with implementing new software is rarely in the software itself. The problems occur when companies purchase software and then attempt to customize it to meet their needs. These unique one-off implementations create complexity and problems. Try to minimize customization of purchased software.

2. *Set clear goals*—You must develop a clear understanding of what the business objectives are for the software, and after implementation ascertain that the software is adding the expected value.

3. *Heed the old adage that less is more*—Historically, IT has the reputation for building bigger, faster, and better software. But organizations should focus on improving the quality of their existing software first to get the biggest bang for their buck.[3]

PHASE 7: MAINTENANCE

Maintaining the system is the final phase of any systems development effort. During the **maintenance phase** of the systems development life cycle, you monitor and support the new system to ensure it continues to meet the business goals. Once a system is in place, it must change as your business changes. Constantly monitoring and supporting the new system involves making minor changes (for example, new reports or information capturing) and reviewing the system to ensure that it continues to move your organization toward its strategic goals. The following are the two primary activities you'll perform during the maintenance phase:

1. *Build a help desk to support the system users*—To create the best support environment, you need to provide a way for knowledge workers to request changes. One of the best ways to support knowledge workers is to create a help desk. A **help desk** is a group of people who respond to knowledge workers' questions. Typically, knowledge workers have a phone number for the help desk they call whenever they have issues or questions about the system. Providing a help desk that answers user questions is a terrific way to provide comprehensive support for knowledge workers using new systems.

2. *Provide an environment to support system changes*—As changes arise in the business environment, you must react to those changes by assessing their impact on the system. It might well be that the system needs to change to meet the ever-changing needs of the business environment. If so, you must modify the system to support the new business environment.

YOUR ROLE DURING MAINTENANCE   During maintenance, your primary role is to be sure that all the knowledge workers have the support they require to use the system. You might be responsible for setting up a help desk or for developing change request forms for your users to fill out if they require a change to the system. Not only do you have to track the change requests but you also must verify that any changes requested for the system are worth performing. Changes cost money, especially once a system has reached the maintenance phase. You must carefully weigh each requested change for merit and monetary worth.

KEY TO SUCCESS—WORKING TOGETHER   It's important to build systems with both the knowledge workers and IT specialists working together because the knowledge workers are the business process experts and quality control analysts, and the IT specialists are highly skilled in designing, implementing, and maintaining the systems. By having knowledge workers and IT specialists combine their unique skills when performing the activities during the SDLC, you'll be sure to build a solid system that supports your organization's strategies and goals.

Selfsourcing and Prototyping

Throughout this text, we have elaborated on the concept of knowledge worker computing—knowledge workers taking an active role in developing and using their own systems to support their efforts in personal and workgroup environments. What we want to look at now is how you, as a knowledge worker, can go about developing your own systems, which we call *selfsourcing*. Recall that ***selfsourcing*** is the development and support of IT systems by knowledge workers with little or no help from IT specialists.

THE SELFSOURCING PROCESS

You can probably create many of the small knowledge worker computing systems in a matter of hours, such as customizing reports, creating macros, and interfacing a letter in a word processing package with a customer database to create individualized mailings. More complicated systems, such as a student registration system or an employee payroll system, require that you follow the formal SDLC process during development.

In Figure 6.5 we've illustrated the selfsourcing process and we've summarized the key tasks within some of the selfsourcing steps. As you can see, the selfsourcing process is similar to the phases in the SDLC. However, you should notice that the selfsourcing process includes *prototyping* (model building, which we'll discuss in detail in the next section). This is key—when you develop a system for yourself, you will most often go through the process of prototyping. As you consider the key tasks in Figure 6.5, we would alert you to several important issues.

Figure 6.5

The Selfsourcing Process and Key Tasks in Selfsourcing

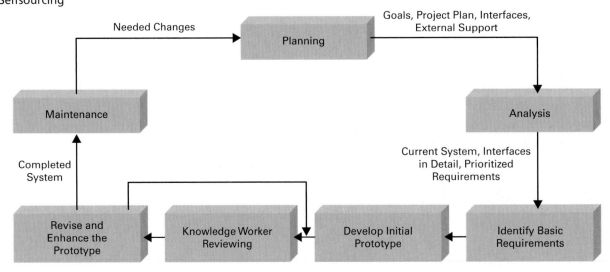

THREE QUESTIONS TO ASK WHEN SELFSOURCING

When developing your own system, ask yourself three questions to be sure you are on the right track. These three questions will help your team's organization and preparation. They also may help higher-level executives who aren't familiar with software development learn a few things about the process.

1. *Who are the intended users of the software?* If your development team doesn't know the answer to this question, go back to the analysis phase and do some more work on business requirements.

2. *What are the functional objectives of the project?* There will be a long list of features, functions, and capabilities that you must prioritize so your team can concentrate on the key ones. If your project manager can't list the top three functions without reference to paper, then he/she isn't in tune with what the project is all about.

3. *Which features should we build first?* Prioritize your development efforts and build the hardest pieces first. This will allow you to determine if you are going to be successful when building the entire system. If you can successfully build the hardest parts, then you should be able to create the remainder of the system.[4]

ALIGNING YOUR SELFSOURCING EFFORTS WITH ORGANIZATIONAL GOALS

When you first begin planning a system you want to develop, you must consider it in light of your organization's goals. If you're considering developing a system for yourself that's counterintuitive to your organization's goals, then you should abandon it immediately. Obviously, you don't want to build a system that reduces sales or decreases the number of customers. You have to consider how you spend your time building systems carefully, since you are busy and your time is extremely valuable. It's important to remember that developing a system through selfsourcing takes time—your time.

So, your first activity should always be to consider what you want to develop in conjunction with what your organization expects you to do.

DETERMINING WHAT EXTERNAL SUPPORT YOU WILL REQUIRE

Some selfsourcing projects may involve support from IT specialists within your organization. Your in-house IT specialists are a valuable resource during the selfsourcing process. Don't forget about them and be sure to include them in the planning phase. The chances of building a successful system increase greatly when you have both knowledge workers and IT specialists working together.

DOCUMENTING THE SYSTEM ONCE COMPLETE

Even if you're developing a system just for yourself, you still need to document how it works. When you get promoted, other people will come in behind you and probably use the system you developed and might even make changes to it. For this reason, you must document how your system works from a technical point of view as well as create an easy-to-read operation manual.

PROVIDING ONGOING SUPPORT

When you develop a system through selfsourcing, you must be prepared to provide your own support and maintenance. Since you are the primary owner and developer of the system, you're solely responsible for ensuring the system continues to function properly and continues to meet all the changing business requirements. You must also be prepared to support other knowledge workers who use your system, as they will be counting on you to help them learn and understand the system you developed. For example, if you develop a customer relationship database using Microsoft Access 2003, you must be prepared to convert it to Microsoft Access 2005 (or whatever the nomanclature happens to be) when it becomes available and your organization adopts it. The systems development process doesn't end with implementation: It continues on a daily basis with support and maintenance.

THE ADVANTAGES OF SELFSOURCING

IMPROVES REQUIREMENTS DETERMINATION   During insourcing, knowledge workers tell IT specialists what they want. In selfsourcing, knowledge workers essentially tell themselves what they want. Potentially, this greatly improves the chances of thoroughly understanding and capturing all the business requirements, and thus the prospect of success for the new system.

INCREASES KNOWLEDGE WORKER PARTICIPATION AND SENSE OF OWNERSHIP   No matter what you do, if you do it yourself, you always take more pride in the result. The same is true when developing an IT system through selfsourcing. If knowledge workers know that they own the system because they developed it and now support it, they are more apt to participate actively in its development and have a greater sense of ownership.

INCREASES SPEED OF SYSTEMS DEVELOPMENT   Many small systems do not lend themselves well to insourcing. These smaller systems may suffer from "analysis paralysis" because they don't require a structured step-by-step approach to their development. In fact, insourcing may be slower than selfsourcing for smaller projects.

POTENTIAL PITFALLS AND RISKS OF SELFSOURCING

INADEQUATE KNOWLEDGE WORKER EXPERTISE LEADS TO INADEQUATELY DEVELOPED SYSTEMS   Many selfsourcing systems are never completed because knowledge workers lack the real expertise with IT tools to develop a complete and fully working system. This might seem like no big deal, since the system couldn't have been that important if the people who needed it never finished developing it. But that's not true. Perhaps it was potentially a good idea. And if knowledge workers choose to try to develop their systems, they must spend time away from their primary duties within the organization. This diverted time may mean lost revenue for the company.

LACK OF ORGANIZATIONAL FOCUS CREATES "PRIVATIZED" IT SYSTEMS   Many selfsourcing projects are done outside the IT systems plan of an organization, meaning there may be many private IT systems that do not interface with other systems and that contain uncontrolled and duplicated information. Such systems serve no meaningful purpose in an organization and can only lead to more problems.

INSUFFICIENT ANALYSIS OF DESIGN ALTERNATIVES LEADS TO SUBPAR IT SYSTEMS   Some knowledge workers jump to immediate conclusions about the hardware and software they should use without carefully analyzing all the possible alternatives. If this happens, knowledge workers may develop systems whose components are inefficient.

LACK OF DOCUMENTATION AND EXTERNAL SUPPORT LEADS TO SHORT-LIVED SYSTEMS   When knowledge workers develop systems, they often forgo documentation of how the system works and fail to realize that they can expect little or no support from IT specialists. All systems—no matter who develops them—must change over time. Knowledge workers must realize that anticipating those changes is their responsibility and making those changes will be easier if they document their system well.

TOSHIBA'S COIN-SIZE HARD DISK PROTOTYPE

Toshiba Corporation plans to begin sample production of a coin-size hard disk that can hold up to 3 GB of data. Currently, the smallest commercial hard disk in mass production have 1-inch platters. Toshiba's new drive contains a disk platter that is 0.85 inches in diameter and the entire drive is about the size of a coin. Toshiba demonstrated a prototype of the drive at the Consumer Electronics Show that took place in Las Vegas in January 2004. The company plans sample pro-duction beginning in the middle of 2004 and commercial production beginning as early as 2005.

According to data from market analysis company Coughlin Associates Inc., the market for 1.8-inch and smaller hard disk will grow exponentially over the next five years. The company estimates shipments of such drives will total 3.3 million drives in 2004 and grow to 23.7 million drives in 2008.[5]

Prototyping

Prototyping is the process of building a model that demonstrates the features of a proposed product, service, or system. A **prototype,** then, is simply a model of a proposed product, service, or system. If you think about it, people prototype all the time. Automobile manufacturers build prototypes of cars to demonstrate safety features, aerodynamics, and comfort. Building contractors construct models of homes and other structures to show layout and fire exits.

In systems development, prototyping can be a valuable tool for you. Prototyping is an iterative process in which you build a model from basic business requirements, have other knowledge workers review the prototype and suggest changes, and further refine and enhance the prototype to include suggestions. Most notably, prototyping is a dynamic process that allows knowledge workers to see, work with, and evaluate a model and suggest changes to that model to increase the likelihood of success of the proposed system.

You can use prototyping to perform a variety of functions in the systems development process:

- *Gathering requirements:* Prototyping is a great requirements gathering tool. You start by simply prototyping the basic system requirements. Then you allow knowledge workers to add more requirements (information and processes) as you revise the prototype.

- *Helping determine requirements:* In many systems development projects, knowledge workers aren't sure what they really want. They simply know that the current system doesn't meet their needs. In this instance, you can use prototyping to help knowledge workers determine their exact requirements.

- *Proving that a system is technically feasible:* Let's face it, there are some things to which you cannot apply technology. And knowing whether you can is often unclear while defining the scope of the proposed system. If you're uncertain about whether something can be done, prototype it first. A prototype you use to prove the technical feasibility of a proposed system is a ***proof-of-concept prototype.***

- *Selling the idea of a proposed system:* Many people resist changes in IT. The current system seems to work fine, and they see no reason to go through the process of developing and learning to use a new system. In this case, you have to convince them that the proposed system will be better than the current one. Because prototyping is relatively fast, you won't have to invest a lot of time to develop a prototype that can convince people of the worth of the proposed system. A prototype you use to convince people of the worth of a proposed system is a ***selling prototype.***

THE PROTOTYPING PROCESS

Prototyping is an excellent tool in systems development. Who uses prototyping and for what purpose determines how the prototyping process occurs. Most often, IT specialists use prototyping in the SDLC to form a technical system blueprint. In selfsourcing, however, you can often continue to refine the prototype until it becomes the final system. The prototyping process for either case is almost the same; only the result differs. Figure 6.6 illustrates the difference between insourcing and selfsourcing prototyping. Regardless of who does the prototyping, the prototyping process involves four steps:

1. *Identify basic requirements:* During the first step, you gather the basic requirements for a proposed system. These basic requirements include input and output information desired and, perhaps, some simple processes. At this point, you're typically unconcerned with editing rules, security issues, or end-of-period processing (for example, producing W-2s for a payroll system at the end of the year).

Figure 6.6

Prototyping Steps for Insourcing and Selfsourcing

INSOURCING PROTOTYPING

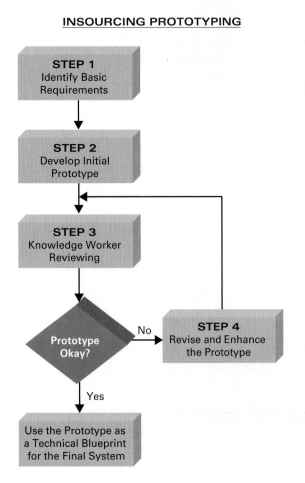

SELFSOURCING PROTOTYPING

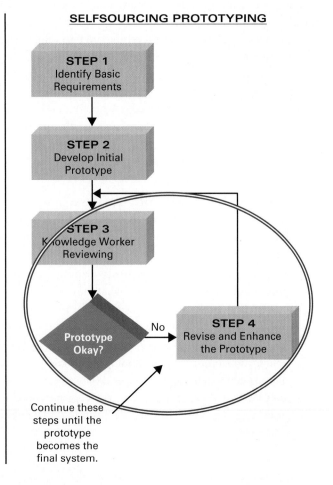

2. *Develop initial prototype:* Having identified the basic requirements, you then set out to develop an initial prototype. Most often, your initial prototype will include only user interfaces, such as data entry screens and reports.

3. *Knowledge worker reviewing:* Step 3 starts the truly iterative process of prototyping. When knowledge workers first initiate this step, they evaluate the prototype and suggest changes or additions. In subsequent returns to step 3 (after step 4), they evaluate new versions of the prototype. It's important to involve as many knowledge workers as possible during this iterative process. This will help resolve any discrepancies in such areas as terminology and operational processes.

4. *Revise and enhance the prototype:* The final sequential step in the prototyping process is to revise and enhance the prototype according to any knowledge worker suggestions. In this step, you make changes to the current prototype and add any new requirements. Next, you return to step 3 and have the knowledge workers review the new prototype; then step 4 again, revision, and so on.

For either insourcing or selfsourcing, you continue the iterative processes of steps 3 and 4 until knowledge workers are happy with the prototype. What happens to the prototype after that, however, differs.

During selfsourcing, you're most likely to use the targeted application software package or application development tool to develop the prototype. This simply means that you can continually refine the prototype until it becomes the final working system. For example, if you choose to develop a simple CRM application using Microsoft Access, you can prototype many of the operational features using Microsoft Access development tools. Because you develop these prototypes using the targeted application development environment, your prototype can eventually become the final system.

That process is not necessarily the same when insourcing. Most often, IT specialists develop prototypes using special prototyping development tools. Many of these tools don't support the creation of a final system—you simply use them to build prototypes. Therefore, the finished prototype becomes a blueprint or technical design for the final system. In the appropriate stages of the SDLC, IT specialists will implement the prototypes in another application development environment better suited to the development of production systems.

THE ADVANTAGES OF PROTOTYPING

ENCOURAGES ACTIVE KNOWLEDGE WORKER PARTICIPATION   First and foremost, prototyping encourages knowledge workers to actively participate in the development process. As opposed to interviewing and reviewing documentation, prototyping allows knowledge workers to see and work with working models of the proposed system.

HELPS RESOLVE DISCREPANCIES AMONG KNOWLEDGE WORKERS   During the prototyping process, many knowledge workers participate in defining the requirements for and reviewing the prototype. The word *many* is key. If several knowledge workers participate in prototyping, you'll find it's much easier to resolve any discrepancies the knowledge workers may encounter.

GIVES KNOWLEDGE WORKERS A FEEL FOR THE FINAL SYSTEM   Prototyping, especially for user interfaces, provides a feel for how the final system will look and work. When knowledge workers understand the look and feel of the final system, they are more apt to see its potential for success.

SSSSSSSSS . . . BUSTED!

Taggertrap, a prototype alarm warning system by Traptec, is activated by the ultrasonic sound of a graffiti artist's spray can. In the past, it has been almost impossible to catch graffiti vandals in the act. Now, thanks to Taggertrap, authorities are instantly alerted to acts of graffiti. The device has wireless sensors that can detect the sound of aerosol sibilance within 200 feet.

Once it has detected the telltale sound, Taggertrap contacts the police via a cell phone and records the vandals with tiny DV cameras. Authorities receive the DV footage immediately via e-mail and dispatch personnel to the area. Early tests in San Diego caught over 20 graffiti vandals red-handed in a single day.[6]

HELPS DETERMINE TECHNICAL FEASIBILITY   Proof-of-concept prototypes are great for determining the technical feasibility of a proposed system.

HELPS SELL THE IDEA OF A PROPOSED SYSTEM   Finally, selling prototypes can help break down resistance barriers. Many people don't want new systems because the old one seems to work just fine, and they're afraid the new system won't meet their expectations and work properly. If you provide them with a working prototype that proves the new system will be successful, they will be more inclined to buy into it.

THE DISADVANTAGES OF PROTOTYPING

LEADS PEOPLE TO BELIEVE THE FINAL SYSTEM WILL FOLLOW SHORTLY
When a prototype is complete, many people believe that the final system will follow shortly. After all, they've seen the system at work in the form of a prototype—how long can it take to bring the system into production? Unfortunately, it may take months or years. You need to be sure that people understand that the prototype is only a model, not the final system missing only a few simple bells and whistles.

GIVES NO INDICATION OF PERFORMANCE UNDER OPERATIONAL CONDITIONS
Prototypes very seldom take all operational conditions into consideration. This problem surfaced for the Department of Motor Vehicles in a state on the East Coast. During prototyping, the system, which handled motor vehicle and driver registration for the entire state, worked fine for 20 workstations at two locations. When the system was finally installed for all locations (which included more than 1,200 workstations), the system spent all its time just managing communications traffic; it had absolutely no time to complete any transactions. This is potentially the most significant drawback to prototyping. You must prototype operational conditions as well as interfaces and processes.

LEADS THE PROJECT TEAM TO FORGO PROPER TESTING AND DOCUMENTATION   You must thoroughly test and document all new systems. Unfortunately, many people believe they can forgo testing and documentation when using prototyping. After all, they've tested the prototype; why not use the prototype as the documentation for the system? Don't make this mistake.

Prototyping is most probably a tool that you will use to develop many knowledge worker information systems. If you stick to the phases of the SLDC, have the correct resources, and learn how to make the most of your prototypes, you will be very successful in your career as a knowledge worker.

Outsourcing

Your final alternative (for *who* will build your system) is to outsource by choosing external employees from another organization, or contractors, to develop a system. However, typically, large systems have both internal and external employees working on the development effort.

DEVELOPING STRATEGIC PARTNERSHIPS

The Outsourcing Research Council recently completed a study indicating that human resources (HR) is a top outsourcing area for many companies. Fifty percent of the companies surveyed said they were already outsourcing some or all of their payroll processing and another 38 percent said they were considering it.

Energizer, the world's largest manufacturer of batteries and flashlights, outsourced its HR operations to ADP, one of the top HR outsourcing companies. Energizer currently has more than 3,500 employees and 2,000 retired employees who all require multiple HR services. ADP provides Energizer with centralized call centers, transaction processing services, and Web-based employee self-service systems. Energizer's Vice President of Human Resources, Peter Conrad, stated, "ADP was clearly the most capable and offered the kind of one-stop shopping our company was looking for." For several of the systems provided by ADP employee usage topped over 80 percent in the first six months the systems were active.[7]

Energizer's choice of using ADP to develop its human resource system is an example of outsourcing. ***Outsourcing*** is the delegation of specific work to a third party for a specified length of time, at a specified cost, and at a specified level of service. IT outsourcing today represents a significant opportunity for your organization to capitalize on the intellectual resources of other organizations by having them take over and perform certain business functions in which they have more expertise than the knowledge workers in your company. IT outsourcing for software development can take one of four forms (see Figure 6.7):

1. Purchasing existing software.
2. Purchasing existing software and paying the publisher to make certain modifications.

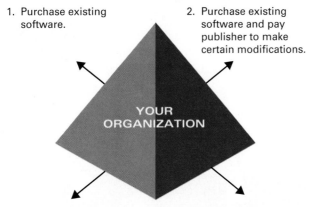

1. Purchase existing software.
2. Purchase existing software and pay publisher to make certain modifications.
4. Outsource the development of an entirely new and unique system for which no software exists.
3. Purchase software and pay publisher for the right to make changes yourself.

YOUR ORGANIZATION

Figure 6.7

Major Forms of Outsourcing Systems Development

3. Purchasing existing software and paying the publisher for the right to make modifications yourself.

4. Outsourcing the development of an entirely new and unique system for which no software exists.

In these instances, we're not talking about personal productivity software you can buy at a local computer store. We're talking about large software packages that may cost millions of dollars. For example, every organization has to track financial information, and there are several different systems they can purchase that help them perform this activity. Have you ever heard of Oracle Financials? This is a great system your organization can buy that tracks all the organizational financial information. Building a financial system would be a waste of time and money since there are several systems already built that probably meet your organizational needs.

THE OUTSOURCING PROCESS

The outsourcing process is both similar to and quite different from the systems development life cycle. It's different in that you turn over much of the design, development, testing, implementation, and maintenance steps to another organization (see Figure 6.8). It's similar in that your organization begins with planning and defining the project scope. It's during one of these phases that your organization may come to understand that it needs a particular system but cannot develop it in-house. If so, that proposed system can be outsourced. Below, we briefly describe the remaining steps of the outsourcing process.

SELECT A TARGET SYSTEM   Once you've identified a potential system to develop by outsourcing, you still have some important questions to answer. For example, will the proposed system manage strategic and sensitive information? If so, you probably wouldn't consider outsourcing it. That is, you don't want another organization seeing and having access to your most vital information. If you're building an order-entry system you might not want people to view your product prices, as they may be a significant part of your strategic advantage.

Figure 6.8

The Outsourcing Process

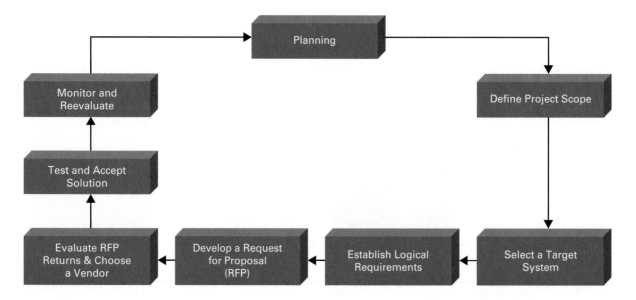

HOW MANY OUTSOURCING COMPANIES ARE THERE?

Assume your company is looking to outsource its payroll activities including calculating the payroll and generating the paychecks each month. Try searching the Internet to find different companies that offer this outsourcing service. Fill in the following table comparing the advantages and disadvantages of the different companies you find. Discuss which one you would choose and why.

Company Name	Advantages	Disadvantages

You should also consider whether the system is small enough to be selfsourced. If so, let knowledge workers within your organization develop the system instead of outsourcing it. On the other hand, if the proposed system is fairly large and supports a routine, nonsensitive business function, then you should target it for outsourcing.

ESTABLISH LOGICAL REQUIREMENTS   Regardless of your choice of insourcing or outsourcing, you must still perform the analysis phase—especially the primary activity of gathering the business requirements for the proposed system. Remember that identification of the business requirements drives the entire system development; if the business requirements are not accurate or complete, there is no way the system will be successful. Regardless of whether you insource or outsource, you must still gather accurate and complete business requirements. If you choose to outsource, part of gathering the business requirements becomes your "request for proposal."

DEVELOP A REQUEST FOR PROPOSAL   Outsourcing involves telling another organization what you want. What you want is essentially the logical requirements for a proposed system, and you convey that information by developing a request for proposal. A *request for proposal (RFP)* is a formal document that describes in detail your logical requirements for a proposed system and invites outsourcing organizations (which we'll refer to as "vendors") to submit bids for its development. An RFP is the most important document in the outsourcing process. For systems of great size, your organization may create an RFP that's hundreds of pages long and requires months of work to complete.

It's vitally important that you take all the time you need to create a complete and thorough RFP. Eventually, your RFP will become the foundation for a legal and binding contract into which your organization and the vendor will enter. At a minimum, your RFP

1. Organizational overview
2. Problem statement
3. Description of current system

   3.1 Underlying business processes
   3.2 Hardware
   3.3 Software (application and system)
   3.4 System processes
   3.5 Information
   3.6 System interfaces

4. Description of proposed system

   4.1 New processes
   4.2 New information

5. Request for new system design

   5.1 Hardware
   5.2 Software
   5.3 Underlying business processes
   5.4 System processes
   5.5 Information
   5.6 System interfaces

6. Request for implementation plan

   6.1 Training
   6.2 Conversion

7. Request for support plan

   7.1 Hardware
   7.2 Software

8. Request for development time frame
9. Request for statement of outsourcing costs
10. How RFP returns will be scored
11. Deadline for RFP returns
12. Primary contact person

Figure 6.9

Outline of a Request for Proposal (RFP)

should contain the elements listed in Figure 6.9. Notice that an RFP includes key information such as an overview of your organization, underlying business processes that the proposed system will support, a request for a development time frame, and a request for a statement of detailed outsourcing costs.

All this information is vitally important to both your organization and the vendors. For your organization, the ability to develop a complete and thorough RFP means that you completely understand what you have and what you want. For the vendors, a complete and thorough RFP makes it easier to propose a system that will meet most, if not all, your needs.

EVALUATE REQUEST FOR PROPOSAL RETURNS AND CHOOSE A VENDOR Your next activity in outsourcing is to evaluate the RFP returns and choose a vendor. You perform this evaluation of the RFP returns according to the scoring method you identified in the RFP. This is not a simple process. No two vendors will ever provide RFP returns in the same format, and the RFP returns you receive are usually longer than the RFP itself.

Once you've thoroughly analyzed the RFP returns, it's time to rank them and determine which vendor to use. Most often, you rank RFP returns according to cost, time, and the scoring mechanism you identified. Again, ranking RFP returns is not simple. Although one vendor may be the cheapest, it may require the longest time to develop the new system. Another vendor may be able to provide a system quickly but without some of the features you have identified as critical.

Once you've chosen the vendor, a lengthy legal process follows. Outsourcing is serious business—and serious business between two organizations almost always requires a lot of negotiating and the use of lawyers. Eventually, your organization has to enter a legal and binding contract that very explicitly states the features of the proposed system, the exact costs, the time frame for development, acceptance criteria, and criteria for breaking the contract for nonperformance or noncompliance.

TEST AND ACCEPT SOLUTION As with all systems, testing and accepting the solution are crucial. Once a vendor installs the new system, it's up to you and your organization to test the entire system before accepting it. You'll need to develop detailed test plans and test conditions that test the entire system. This alone may involve months of running and testing the new system while continuing to operate the old one (the parallel method).

When you "accept" a solution, you're saying that the system performs to your expectations and that the vendor has met its contractual obligations so far. Accepting a solution involves granting your sign-off on the system, which releases the vendor from any further development efforts or modifications to the system. Be careful when you do this because modifications to the system after sign-off can be extremely expensive.

OUTSOURCING HELP DESKS OFFSHORE

There are now two classes of help desk–support customers—high paying and low paying. Today, vendors are tailoring support based on the amount of money customers pay and are transferring the lower-paying customers to offshore support sites. More and more companies, however, are finding that offshore help desks are causing their customers major problems.

Jim Miller, Chief Technology Officer at Creditex Inc., a Wall Street–based credit derivative trading firm, recently requested help with a Microsoft Exchange server that supports users in New York and London. The Microsoft help desk in India answered Jim's call and the technician on the other end of the line merely consulted online Microsoft knowledge-base articles, some-

thing Miller said he could have done himself. The technician told him that the only way to rectify the problem was to rebuild the whole machine and reinstall Exchange, an effort that Miller said would entail ". . . a huge investment in time, the loss of significant data and e-mail down for an extended period of time."

Miller took a pass on the advice and asked the technician to place him back in the call queue, only to end up back in India four times. Finally, Creditex "escalated" its request for help to Microsoft support managers and finally received a call from a knowledgeable technician in Dallas who resolved the problem in 15 minutes.[8]

MONITOR AND REEVALUATE   Just like the systems you develop using the SDLC, systems you obtain through outsourcing need constant monitoring and reevaluation. You must continually evaluate and revise the project plan to ensure the system is going to meet its delivery schedule. In outsourcing, you also have to reassess your working relationship with the vendor. Is the vendor providing maintenance when you need it and according to the contract? Does the system really perform the stated functions? Do month-end and year-end processes work according to your desires? Does the vendor provide acceptable support if something goes wrong? These are all important questions that affect the success of your outsourcing efforts.

The most important questions, though, are, does the system still meet your needs? and how much does it cost to update the system? In many instances, if the system needs updating you must contract with the original vendor. This is potentially one of the greatest drawbacks to outsourcing. When you outsource a system, you create a heavy dependency on a particular vendor to provide updates to the system, and such updates are expensive.

OFFSHORE OUTSOURCING

The recent trend in outsourcing is for organizations to outsource their IT functions offshore. *Offshore outsourcing* is using organizations from other countries to write code and develop systems. Stories about U.S. companies outsourcing work to India have been reported for years; however, it is becoming increasingly apparent that Romania, Bulgaria, Russia, China, Ghana, the Philippines, and dozens of other countries are also clamoring for and getting business from the United States. The value of IT services provided to U.S. businesses from offshore labor will double to $16 billion in 2005 and then almost triple to $46 billion by 2007, according to market research firm IDC.[9]

THE ADVANTAGES AND DISADVANTAGES OF OUTSOURCING

Making the decision to outsource is critical to your organization's success. Throughout this discussion of outsourcing, we've directly or indirectly described many of the advantages and disadvantages of outsourcing. What follows is a summary of the major advantages and disadvantages of outsourcing the systems development process in order to help you make this important decision.

ADVANTAGES   Your organization may benefit from outsourcing because it allows you to

- *Focus on unique core competencies:* By outsourcing systems development efforts that support noncritical business functions, your organization can focus on developing systems that support important, unique core competencies.
- *Exploit the intellect of another organization:* Outsourcing allows your organization to obtain intellectual capital by purchasing it from another organization. Often you won't be able to find individuals with all the expertise required to develop a system. Outsourcing allows you to find those individuals with the expertise you need to get your system developed and implemented.
- *Better predict future costs:* When you outsource a function, whether systems development or some other business function, you know the exact costs.
- *Acquire leading-edge technology:* Outsourcing allows your organization to acquire leading-edge technology without having to acquire technical expertise and the inherent risks of choosing the wrong technology.
- *Reduce costs:* Outsourcing is often seen as a money saver for organizations. Reducing costs is one of the important reasons organizations outsource.
- *Improve performance accountability:* Outsourcing involves delegating work to another organization at a specified level of service. Your organization can use this specified level of service as leverage to guarantee that it gets exactly what it wants from the vendor.

DISADVANTAGES   Your organization may suffer from outsourcing because it

- *Reduces technical know-how for future innovation:* Outsourcing is a way of exploiting the intellect of another organization. It can also mean that your organization will no longer possess that expertise internally. If you outsource because you don't have the necessary technical expertise today, you'll probably have to outsource for the same reason tomorrow.
- *Reduces degree of control:* Outsourcing means giving up control. No matter what you choose to outsource, you are in some way giving up control over that function.
- *Increases vulnerability of your strategic information:* Outsourcing systems development involves telling another organization what information you use and how you use that information. In doing so, you could be giving away strategic information and secrets.
- *Increases dependency on other organizations:* As soon as you start outsourcing, you immediately begin depending on another organization to perform many of your business functions.

A REQUEST FOR PROPOSAL AND THE SYSTEMS DEVELOPMENT LIFE CYCLE

If you review Figure 6.9 closely, you'll notice that an RFP looks very similar to the phases of the SDLC. In the table below, identify which phases of the SDLC correspond to each element of an RFP.

Elements of a Request for Proposal	Phase(s) of the SDLC
1. Organizational overview	
2. Problem statement	
3. Description of current system	
4. Description of proposed system	
5. Request for new system design	
6. Request for implementation plan	
7. Request for support plan	
8. Request for development time frame	
9. Request for statement of outsourcing costs	
10. How RFP returns will be scored	
11. Deadline for RFP returns	
12. Primary contact person	

Summary: Student Learning Outcomes Revisited

1. **List the seven steps in the systems development life cycle (SDLC) and associated activities for each step.** The *systems development life cycle (SDLC)* is a structured step-by-step approach for developing information systems. The seven steps and activities are as follows:

   1. *Planning:* Define system, set project scope, develop project plan.
   2. *Analysis:* Gather business requirements.
   3. *Design:* Design technical architecture, design system models.
   4. *Development:* Build technical architecture, build database and programs.

   5. *Testing:* Write the test conditions, perform testing.
   6. *Implementation:* Perform user training, write user documentation.
   7. *Maintenance:* Provide a help desk, support system changes.

2. **Describe three keys to success you can use to help ensure a successful systems development effort.** This chapter provides you with several keys to success you can use to ensure your systems development efforts are successful. These keys include the following:

   • *Manage your project plan*—Continually monitoring and managing your project plan can ensure your project remains on track and all major project milestones are met.

- *Find errors early*—The sooner you find errors in the systems development life cycle the less costly it is to correct the errors.

- *Determine future requirements*—Establishing requirements for current as well as future needs will help ensure that you do not outgrow your system.

- *Take advantage of changing technology*—Technology changes quickly and you must take advantage of any new technologies to ensure that your project is successful.

- *Complete the testing phase*—It's critical that you perform all phases in the SDLC during every project. Try not to sacrifice testing time or your system may not work correctly all of the time.

- *Choose the right implementation method*—You need to choose the right implementation method that best suits your organization, project, and employees to ensure a successful implementation. Implementation methods include parallel, plunge, pilot, and phased.

- *Work together*—It's important to build systems with both the knowledge workers and IT specialists working together because the knowledge workers are the business process experts and quality control analysts, and the IT specialists are highly skilled in designing, implementing, and maintaining the systems.

3. **Define the three different ways you can staff a systems development project.** Insourcing, selfsourcing, and outsourcing are the three different ways you can staff a system development project. *Insourcing* uses IT specialists within your organization, *selfsourcing* uses knowledge workers, and *outsourcing* uses another organization. It is important to note that most large projects typically use insourcing, selfsourcing, and outsourcing all at the same time.

4. **List the three advantages of selfsourcing.** When you selfsource a project you (1) improve requirements determination, (2) increase knowledge worker participation and sense of ownership, and (3) increase the speed of systems development.

5. **Describe prototyping and profile an example of a prototype.** *Prototyping* is the process of building a model that demonstrates the features of a proposed product, service, or system. A *prototype,* then, is simply a model of a proposed product, service, or system. If you think about it, people prototype all the time. Automobile manufacturers build prototypes of cars to demonstrate safety features, aerodynamics, and comfort. Building contractors construct models of homes and other structures to show layout and fire exits.

6. **Describe the five advantages of prototyping.** First, prototyping encourages active knowledge worker participation. Prototyping encourages knowledge workers to actively participate in the development process. As opposed to interviewing and the reviewing of documentation, prototyping allows knowledge workers to see and work with working models of the proposed system. Second, prototyping helps resolve discrepancies among knowledge workers. During the prototyping process, many knowledge workers participate in defining the requirements for and reviewing the prototype. The word *many* is key. If several knowledge workers participate in prototyping, you'll find it's much easier to resolve any discrepancies the knowledge workers may encounter.

7. **Describe the outsourcing process and the current trend toward offshore outsourcing.** The outsourcing process includes selecting a target system, establishing logical requirements, developing a request for proposal (RFP), evaluating the request for proposal, choosing a vendor, testing and accepting the solution, and monitoring and reevaluating the solution. *Offshore outsourcing* is using organizations from other countries to write code and develop systems. U.S. companies are currently outsourcing IT work to India, Romania, Bulgaria, Russia, China, Ghana, the Philippines, and dozens of other countries.

CLOSING CASE STUDY ONE

THE LUCY PROTOTYPE

Lucy may be only the prototype of a robot baby orang-utan, but someday she will be able to tell us about how the cerebral cortex of the brain works. Steve Grand, Lucy's creator, hopes that she'll be able to help people develop and build new computational architectures inspired by biological systems, as well as applications based on those systems that are more adaptable, intelligent, and robust.

Grand, a recognized authority on artificial life and the founder of Cyberlife Research Ltd., an artificial intelligence research company in Somerset, England, wants to use Lucy to answer the question of how the brain organizes itself into a set of machines that enable it to do all the things that brains do. Lucy is unlike any prototype ever created. Lucy's intelligence is the consequence of the interactions between thousands of simulated neurons. Grand's goal is to develop a machine that can supplement or even supersede the digital computer—a machine that can think and learn.

Grand says the Lucy prototype is developing the ability to learn on her own. She has already learned to point to a banana—any banana: a green banana, a yellow banana, a big banana, a small banana. If you show the Lucy prototype an apple and a banana, she points to the banana. Grand hasn't programmed Lucy to point to bananas; instead, he has given her a model of the bit of cerebral cortex that knows how to do it. Grand states, "It doesn't sound like a huge achievement. Why not just program a computer to recognize yellow? But Lucy solved a whole series of problems by herself like detecting the lines that form the edges of the banana regardless of what position it's in or how far away it is, and she figured out how to point at it."

Thanks to a successful prototype, Grand received a substantial grant from The National Endowment for Science, Technology, and the Arts in London. The grant is allowing Grand to build a new and improved Lucy. Lucy's new body will have a voice, improved eyesight, better hearing, and be able to move arms and legs. Grand hopes Lucy will soon be learning to crawl and ultimately walk. He also hopes she will be able to repeat simple sounds, like toddlers do.

"Lucy won't be very smart, but it won't be far from the truth to say she'll have a mind of her own, albeit a very, very stupid one," Grand says.[10]

Questions

1. The Lucy prototype helped Steve Grand get a grant that is allowing him to develop a more advanced and sophisticated Lucy. Describe how building a prototype helped Steve Grand get a grant to build a new and improved Lucy. What do you think would have happened if Grand hadn't built a prototype? Do you think he still would have received the grant?

2. Research the Web to find this years *Wired* magazine's Vaporware Awards, awarded to the top 10 most eagerly awaited technology products that never made it to consumers. Review the top three products and describe why you believe the products never made it to consumers. What do you think the inventors could have done differently to ensure that the products made it to their customers?

3. Prototyping is an invaluable tool for systems development. Building a prototype allows knowledge workers to see, work with, and evaluate a model and suggest changes to the model. Refer back to the discussion of the cost of fixing errors on page 282 and to Figure 6.4. What do prototyping and Figure 6.4 have in common? How can prototyping help you control your project budget and the cost of fixing errors?

4. Prototyping during the analysis phase can help you gather business requirements. Throughout this chapter we discussed the importance of gathering solid business requirements. How can building a prototype help you gather solid business requirements on an information systems development project?

5. One of the disadvantages of building a prototype is that people will believe that the final system will follow shortly. Why do you think building a prototype will lead people to this inaccurate conclusion? If you were delivering a system prototype, how would you communicate to the system users that the real system would not be ready for another three years?

6. It is important to remember that communication is the primary key to deploying a successful prototype. When Planter's Peanuts first started to market fresh roasted peanuts, the product was a complete failure. Consumers continuously confused the product with coffee and kept taking it home to grind it as they would fresh roasted coffee beans. The words *fresh roasted* are probably what caused the product to fail. If you were in charge of this product, what could you do to change it to help consumers understand the product contained peanuts not coffee beans?

CLOSING CASE STUDY TWO

AL'S BARBEQUE RESTAURANT

Al's Barbeque Restaurant, located in Denver, Colorado, has successfully been in business for over 20 years. Al's specializes in barbeque chicken and beef and includes scrumptious side dishes of potato salad, coleslaw, and baked beans. Customers come from all around for a good old-fashioned barbeque dinner. On a Friday night you can expect the line to be out the door and the wait close to an hour. It is estimated that Al's serves more than 500 barbeque dinners every day.

The restaurant is filled with 20 picnic tables covered in red-and-white cloths. There are a total of 12 wait-staff workers, five of whom have been working at the restaurant since it opened. Al cooks and prepares all of the special barbeque sauce himself along with three other cooks. The restaurant runs today the same as it did 20 years ago. Al can call many of his customers by name. This is definitely part of the charm of the restaurant, but it is also one of the biggest problems with the restaurant. Everything in the restaurant is performed manually from taking orders to ordering inventory.

Al's daughter, Alana, has just graduated from college and has come home to help run the family-owned business. Alana is amazed at how long it takes to perform all of the manual processes required to run the business. Every night she must manually count all of the money in the cash register and compare it to the paper sales tickets that the waitstaff fills out representing the customer orders.

Alana also manually counts the inventory from cans of beans to slices of cheese. Deciding what to order each day is a complete mystery to Alana. Some days the restaurant sells tons of chicken dinners and other days the restaurant sells tons of beef dinners. There doesn't seem to be any pattern to which one is going to sell the best. She continually finds herself ordering too much of one item and not enough of the other. Each week she has to calculate the employee paychecks by reviewing each employee's cardboard handwritten time card. At the end of each month she calculates the sales tax reports. This is an incredibly difficult activity since the reports must match all of the monthly paper tickets, which total close to $45,000.

Alana quickly comes to the conclusion that the restaurant must be automated. Building an information system to support all of these manual processes will not only help the restaurant operate more efficiently but will also give Alana more time to spend talking and dealing with her customers. Alana and Al decide to visit a local restaurant trade show to see what types of information systems are available. The show displays all types of different restaurant systems. One system uses microwave frequencies that allow the waitstaff to carry around a type of PDA that automatically sends orders to a terminal in the kitchen. Some systems can track sales for up to 20 years and generate sales forecasts based on anything from the day of the week to the weather. All of the systems produce daily sales reports and monthly tax reports. This feature alone is a dream come true for Alana as this activity typically takes her from two to three hours a day.

Alana and Al are overwhelmed by the number of restaurant information systems available to purchase. Having no formal training with the SDLC or systems development, they are confused and frustrated with so many choices.

Questions

1. Al is not a believer in technology and he thinks the business works just fine the way it is. How would you convince Al that an information system will help his business become even more successful? How can you explain to Al that using the SDLC will help him successfully implement a new system?

2. Alana realizes that she does not have the expertise required to choose a restaurant information system. Alana decides to ask you for help since you studied this type of information in college. How would you describe to Alana the phases in the SDLC and how she can use them to choose and implement a system?

3. At the beginning of the project you develop a project plan to help guide you through the systems development effort. Alana does not understand the plan or why you continually keep changing it. How can you explain to Alana the benefits of developing a project plan and why it must be continually revised and updated?

4. Al has hired you to help choose and implement the system for the restaurant. From the information you already know about the restaurant, write five of the business requirements. Remember, writing clear and accurate business requirements is critical to the success of the project.

5. Some members of the waitstaff have worked at the restaurant since it began. You're worried that they'll not be receptive to using an automated system. How would you convince the waitstaff that the new system will help them perform their jobs? Why is including them in the requirements gathering activity critical to the systems development effort?

6. Thanks to your help, Al has successfully implemented a new restaurant system. The system is up and running, and Al is extremely pleased with your work. You offer to spend an extra week writing user manuals and system documentation. Al declines your offer as he does not see any benefit in these tools. How would you convince Al that documentation is critical to the continued success of the system?

7. At the restaurant show Al and Alana saw many different restaurant information systems that they could purchase. Research the Web to find two restaurant information systems that might have been at the trade show. Of the systems you found, which one do you think you would choose and why?

Key Terms and Concepts

Analysis phase, 280
Business requirement, 281
Critical success factor (CSF), 279
Design phase, 282
Development phase, 283
Feature creep, 280
Graphical user interface (GUI), 283
GUI screen design, 283
Help desk, 287
Implementation phase, 286
Insourcing, 279
Integration testing, 285
Joint application development (JAD), 281
Maintenance phase, 287
Modeling, 283
Offshore outsourcing, 299
Online training, 286
Outsourcing, 279
Parallel implementation, 286

Phased implementation, 286
Pilot implementation, 286
Planning phase, 279
Plunge implementation, 286
Project manager, 280
Project milestone, 280
Project plan, 279
Project scope, 279
Project scope document, 279
Proof-of-concept prototype, 291
Prototype, 291
Prototyping, 291
Request for proposal (RFP), 297
Requirements definition document, 281
Scope creep, 280
Selfsourcing (knowledge worker development, end-user development), 279
Selling prototype, 292
Sign-off, 281

Short-Answer Questions

1. What is the systems development life cycle (SDLC)?
2. What are the seven steps in the SDLC?
3. What is a critical success factor?
4. What is feature creep?
5. How does a project plan help the project manager do his or her job?
6. In which step in the SDLC do you define business requirements?
7. Why would a company outsource?
8. In which step in the SDLC do you build the technical architecture?
9. How do online training and workshop training differ?
10. Why must you provide sign-off on the business requirements?
11. Will a project be successful if you miss business requirements?
12. What is selfsourcing?
13. Why would you build a prototype?
14. What is a selling prototype?
15. What is an advantage of selfsourcing?
16. What is an advantage of prototyping?

Assignments and Exercises

1. **SDLC AND THE REAL WORLD** Think of the seven steps in the SDLC and try to apply them to one of your daily activities—for example, getting dressed in the morning. First, you plan what you are going to wear. This will vary depending on what you are going to do that day and could include shorts, pants, jeans, and so forth. Second, you analyze what you have in your closet compared to what you plan to wear. Third, you design the outfit. Fourth, you get the clothes out of the closet and assemble them on your bed. Fifth, you test the outfit to ensure it matches. Sixth, you put on the outfit. Seventh, you wear the outfit throughout the day adjusting it as needed.

2. **HOW CREATIVE ARE YOU?** You've been appointed as the manager of the design team for Sneakers-R-Us. Your first activity is to design the GUI for the main system. The only requirements you are given is that the colors must be bold and the following buttons must appear in the screen.
   - Order Inventory
   - Enter Sales
   - Schedule Employees
   - Tax Reports
   - Sales Reports
   - Employee Vacation and Sick Time
   - Administrative Activities

   Create two different potential GUI screen designs for the main system. Provide a brief explanation of the advantages and disadvantages of each design.

3. **REQUEST FOR PROPOSAL** A request for proposal (RFP) is a formal document that describes in detail your logical requirements for a proposed system and invites outsourcing organizations (which we'll refer to as "vendors") to submit bids for its development. Research the Web and find three RFP examples. Please briefly explain in a one-page document what each RFP has in common and how each RFP is different.

4. **UNDERSTANDING INSOURCING** The advantages and disadvantages of selfsourcing and outsourcing are covered throughout this chapter. Compile a list of the different advantages and disadvantages of insourcing compared to selfsourcing and outsourcing.

5. **MANAGING THE PROJECT PLAN** You are in the middle of an interview for your first job. The manager performing the interview asks you to explain why managing a project plan is critical to a project's success. The manager also wants to know what scope creep and feature creep are and how you would manage them during a project. Please write a one-page document stating how you would answer these questions during the interview.

6. **WHY PROTOTYPE?** You are in the middle of the design phase for a new system. Your manager does not understand why it's important to develop a prototype of a proposed system before building the actual system. In a one-page document, explain what potential problems would arise if you didn't develop a prototype and went straight to developing the system.

7. **BUSINESS REQUIREMENTS** Gathering accurate and complete business requirements is critical to the successful development of any system. Review the following requirements and explain any problems they might have.
   - The GUI must be red.
   - There should be three buttons labeled "Start" and "Stop."
   - Buttons 1 through 8 are required for the calculator function.
   - There should be a text field for the user name and a button for the user password.

8. **CONSTRUCTION AND THE SDLC** The systems development life cycle is often compared to the construction industry. Fill in the following chart listing some of the activities performed in building a house and how they relate to the different SDLC steps.

SDLC	Activities for Building a Home
Planning	
Analysis	
Design	
Development	
Testing	
Implementation	
Maintenance	

Discussion Questions

1. Why is it important to develop a logical model of a proposed system before generating a technical architecture? What potential problems would arise if you didn't develop a logical model and went straight to developing the technical design?

2. If you view systems development as a question-and-answer session, another question you could ask is, "Why do organizations develop IT systems?" Consider what you believe to be the five most important reasons organizations develop IT systems. How do these reasons relate to topics in the first five chapters of this book?

3. When deciding how to staff a systems development project, what are some of the primary questions you must be able to answer to determine if you will insource, selfsource, or outsource? What are some of the advantages and disadvantages of each?

4. Your company has just decided to implement a new financial system. Your company's financial needs are almost the same as those of all the other companies in your industry. Would you recommend that your company purchase an existing system or build a custom system? Would you recommend your company insource, selfsource, or outsource the new system?

5. Why do you think system documentation is important? If you had to write system documentation for a word processing application, what would be a few of the main sections? Do you think it would be useful to test the documentation to ensure it's accurate? What do you think happens if you provide system documentation that is inaccurate? What do you think happens if you implement a new system without documentation?

6. What would happen to an organization that refused to follow the systems development life cycle when building systems? If you worked for this organization, what would you do to convince your manager to follow the systems development life cycle?

7. There are seven phases in the systems development life cycle. Which one do you think is the hardest? Which one do you think is the easiest? Which one do you think is the most important? Which one do you think is the least important? If you had to skip one of the phases, which one would it be and why?

8. What would happen to a systems development effort that decided to skip the testing phase? If you were working on this project, what would you do to convince your team members to perform the activities in the testing phase?

9. If you were working on a large systems development effort, and after reviewing the business requirements, you were positive several were missing, would you still sign off on the requirements? If you did, what would happen?

10. You are talking with another student who is complaining about having to learn about the systems development life cycle, because he is not going to work in an IT department. Would you agree with this student? What would you say to him to convince him that learning about the systems development life cycle is important no matter where he works?

11. A company typically has many systems it wants to build, but unfortunately it usually doesn't have the resources to build all the systems. How does a company decide which systems to build?

12. When you start working on a new system, one of your first activities is to define the project scope. Do you think this is an easy activity? Why is the project scope so important? Do you think everyone on the project should know the project's scope? What could happen if people on the project are not familiar with the project scope?

13. People often think that a system is complete once it is implemented. Is this true? What happens after a system is implemented? What can you do to ensure the system continues to meet the knowledge workers' needs?

14. Imagine your friends are about to start their own business and they have asked you for planning and development advice with respect to IT systems. What would you tell them? What if their business idea was completely Internet-based? What if their business idea didn't include using the Internet at all? Would your answers differ? Why or why not?

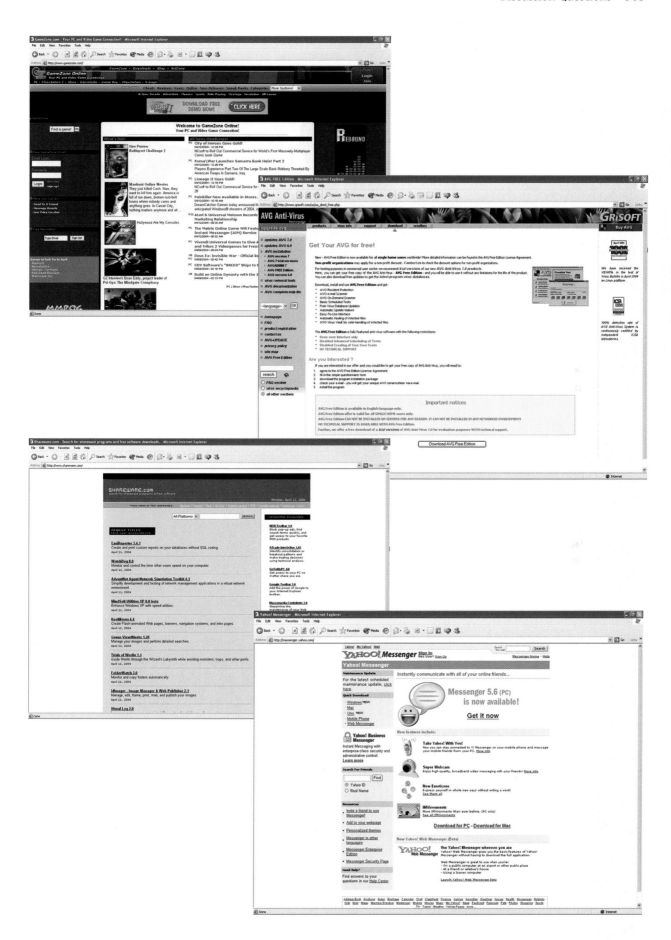

Finding Freeware and Shareware on the Internet

Even upgrading to the latest version of your existing software can make a real dent in your pocketbook. And after installing new software, you may find it simply doesn't meet your needs. That's when you notice that you can't return opened software, you can only exchange it for a new copy. So if it doesn't meet your needs you're out of luck with commercial consumer software.

An alternative to commercial software that you might consider is shareware or freeware. Shareware is sometimes called "try before you buy" software because users are permitted to try the software on their own computer system (generally for a limited time) without any cost or obligation. Then you make a payment if you decide you want to keep using the software beyond the evaluation (trial) period. Freeware is software available at no charge to users for as long as they choose to use the software.

USING YOUR COMPUTER FOR MORE THAN WORK

By far the most popular freeware/shareware applications are games. The quality of these software titles is truly amazing for software that is free to download and begin playing immediately whenever you want. Shareware/freeware games are so numerous on the Internet that you'll often find games grouped by categories. Common categories are action/adventure, board, card, casino, educational, role-playing, simulation, sports, strategy and war, and word games.

Connect to the Internet and several sites that offer freeware and shareware games. Pick at least two games and download them. For each, answer the following questions:

A. Is a description of the game provided?

B. Are system requirements listed?

C. Can you tell if the game is freeware or shareware without downloading it?

D. Are any of the games you selected really commercial software that requires a purchase before you download the game?

E. If the game is shareware, how long are you permitted to use it until registration is required?

F. If the game is shareware, does the game cease to function after the free period is over? How can you tell without waiting that long?

G. How long does it take to download the game? Is it worth it?

PROTECTING YOUR COMPUTER INVESTMENT

Have you ever been frantically typing away, desperately trying to make an assignment deadline, when all of a sudden something goes wrong with your computer? If you're lucky, the problem is something easy to identify, so you correct the problem and go on about your work. At other times the solution eludes you. Most of the time these problems have nice logical explanations such as hardware or software conflicts or failures of some kind. In a few rare instances, the problem may have been caused intentionally by a computer virus, a program that someone develops with malicious intent to harm an IT system.

So how does a computer virus get into your system? Anytime you download software, open a file attachment to an e-mail, or read a file off a diskette from another computer, you stand the chance of contracting a computer virus. And access to the Internet increases your opportunity to download files from many different sources. So on every one of its computers virtually every company installs anti-virus protection software that scans new files for known viruses and purges them from the system. The catch is that traditional anti-virus software can find only viruses that it knows about. As new viruses come along, anti-virus software must be updated. The deviant minds that develop viruses seem to find more and better ways to infiltrate your system every day.

Connect to a site that allows you to download anti-virus software, download the software, and answer the following questions:

A. Is the anti-virus software shareware, freeware, or traditional retail software?

B. What viruses does the software detect?

C. Does the software remove the virus as well as detect it?

D. Are updates for the software available to detect new viruses? How often are they available? At what cost?

E. Does the software detect viruses not yet created? How does it do that?

F. Does the software site offer recommendations to reduce your chance of contracting a virus?

G. Does the site tell you what to do if you have already contracted a virus?

SEARCHING FOR SHAREWARE AND FREEWARE

So maybe the shareware/freeware software concept appeals to you. You'd like to be able to try the software before you buy. If you want software such as screen savers or anti-virus software, you're in luck. But what if you want some shareware to help you compose music or keep track of your soccer team's schedule? Well, then you'll have to go searching for that software. You could use a general-purpose search engine such as Yahoo! and type in shareware and music or soccer. If you do this you will find a few shareware software titles to download. But suppose those few titles don't meet your needs.

Finding shareware/freeware titles can be daunting for two reasons. First, currently there are over 1 million shareware and freeware titles available to you. Unless a search engine is designed specifically for this type of software, you'll probably miss many of these titles using a general-purpose search engine. Second, most shareware/freeware developers don't have their own Web sites. As many don't develop their software as a business, they can't justify the cost of supporting their own Web sites. To address both of these challenges, Web sites have been created that maintain databases of thousands of shareware/freeware software titles. Most also include a search engine to help you navigate through these thousands of titles.

Find a site that maintains a database of freeware and shareware software. As you peruse it, answer the following questions:

A. How does the site group the software?

B. Can you search by operating system or platform?

C. Does the site provide descriptions of the software?

D. Can you search by file size?

E. Are screen captures from the software provided?

F. Are reviews and/or ratings of the software provided?

G. When was the last update for the site?

EXTENDED LEARNING MODULE F

BUILDING A WEB PAGE WITH HTML

Student Learning Outcomes

1. DEFINE AN HTML DOCUMENT AND DESCRIBE ITS RELATIONSHIP TO A WEB SITE.

2. DESCRIBE THE PURPOSE OF TAGS IN HYPERTEXT MARKUP LANGUAGE (HTML).

3. IDENTIFY THE TWO MAJOR SECTIONS IN AN HTML DOCUMENT AND DESCRIBE THE CONTENT WITHIN EACH.

4. DESCRIBE THE USE OF BASIC FORMATTING TAGS AND HEADING TAGS.

5. DESCRIBE HOW TO ADJUST TEXT COLOR AND SIZE WITHIN A WEB SITE.

6. DESCRIBE HOW TO CHANGE THE BACKGROUND OF A WEB SITE.

7. LIST THE THREE TYPES OF LINKS IN A WEB SITE AND DESCRIBE THEIR PURPOSES.

8. DESCRIBE HOW TO INSERT AND MANIPULATE IMAGES IN A WEB SITE.

9. DEMONSTRATE HOW TO INSERT LISTS IN A WEB SITE.

Taking Advantage of the CD

Creating a Web site . . . everyone seems to be doing it. Businesses create Web sites to sell products and services, provide support information, and conduct marketing activities. Individuals build Web sites for a variety of reasons. Some want a family Web site. Some want a Web site for their evening sports leagues. Your instructor has probably built a Web site to support your class. And we've created a Web site to support your use of this text.

Whatever the case, building a basic Web site is actually not that difficult. If you want a Web site that supports product ordering capabilities, then you'll need some specific expertise. But putting up a Web site with just content is simple and easy. In this extended learning module, we'll show you how. You'll find this extended learning module on the CD that accompanies this text. It's just like any other module in this text—it includes Team Work and On Your Own projects and great end-of-module Assignments and Exercises.

Before we begin, let's discuss several important issues. First, be careful what sort of private personal information you include on your Web site. We definitely recommend that you do not include your social security number, your address, or your telephone number. You always need to keep in mind that there are almost 1 billion people on the Internet. Do you really want them to know where you live?

You also need to consider your target audience and their ethics. Having a Web site with profanity and obscene images will offend many people. And, more than likely, your school won't allow you to build a Web site of questionable content. Even more basic than that, you need to consider your target audience and their viewing preferences. For example, if you're building a Web site for school-age children, you'll want to use a lot of bright colors such as red, blue, green, and yellow. If you're targeting college students to advertise concerts and other events, you'll want your Web site to be more edgy and include sharp contrasting colors (including black).

Just remember this: The most elegant solution is almost always the simplest. If you consider eBay, it uses a very simple and elegant presentation of information. The background is basic white. You'll see very little if any flashy movement. You'll hear very little sound. eBay is one of the most visited sites on the Web today. And it's making money with a very simple and elegant Web site.

We definitely believe it's worth your time and energy to pop in the CD and read this module. You'll learn many things including

- How to build and view a Web site on your own computer without connecting to the Web
- How to use a simple text editor to create a Web site
- How to size and position images in your Web site
- How to include e-mail links in your Web site
- How to change the background color or insert a textured background for your Web site
- How to change the color and size of text

If you're interested in learning more about what you can do with a Web site, we recommend that you connect to the Web site that supports this text at www.mhhe.com/haag (and select XLM/F). There, we've included more about building a Web site and useful resources on the Web.

CHAPTER SEVEN OUTLINE

STUDENT LEARNING OUTCOMES

1. Explain the relationship between the organization's roles and goals and its IT infrastructure.

2. Describe the difference between a 2-tier and 3-tier infrastructure.

3. Describe system integration.

4. Describe Web services and Microsoft's .NET.

5. Explain the difference between network area storage (NAS) and storage area networks (SAN).

6. List and describe the seven "-ilities."

CHAPTER SEVEN

IT Infrastructures
Business-Driven Technology

How much time do you spend on the telephone each month? More important, how much is your monthly telephone bill? Do you want to make phone calls to anywhere in the world for free? If so, then all you need to do is make your phone calls over the Internet instead of using a traditional telephone service provider.

Originally, Internet telephony had a reputation of poor call quality, lame user interfaces, and low call-completion rates. With new and improved technology and IT infrastructures, Internet phone now offers similar quality to traditional telephone. Today, many consumers are making phone calls over the Internet by using voice over Internet protocol (VoIP). VoIP transmits over 10 percent of all phone calls and this number is growing exponentially.

If you want to make VoIP phone calls over the Internet, you need to find a vendor that offers VoIP services such as Skype at www.skype.com or Free World Dialup at www.freeworlddialup.com. The way that VoIP works is very similar to e-mail. You simply send your call over the Internet in packets of audio tagged with the same destination. VoIP reassembles the packets once they arrive at their final destination.

There are numerous vendors offering VoIP services. The service works differently depending on the vendor's IT infrastructure. The start-up Skype pairs P2P (point-to-point) technology with your PC's soundcard to create a voice service, which you can use to call other Skype users. Unfortunately, you can talk only to other Skype users. Vonage lets you place calls to any person who has a mobile or landline (regular telephone) number. Vonage sends the call over a cable or DSL connection via a digital-to-analog converter. A few providers even offer an adapter for a traditional handset that plugs right into your broadband modem. Which VoIP vendor would you prefer? All vendors are providing the same VoIP service, but depending on their IT infrastructure the service features vary significantly from vendor to vendor.

You can see then how its IT infrastructure affects a company's product on service offering. Designing and building the correct IT infrastructure is critical to the success of any business. By *IT infrastructure* we mean all the hardware, software, and telecommunications equipment that your organization employs to support its goals, processes, and strategies. As you can see, its IT infrastructure can easily make or break a company, as in the example of the Internet phone providers, the nature of whose service to the customer depends on infrastructure.

At a more basic level, what do you think happens to a company that can't provide its knowledge workers Internet access at all—or the access it does provide is extremely slow? A company must build a solid IT infrastructure that can handle all its current and future technological needs. Its IT infrastructure will play a major role in helping the company achieve success.[1]

Introduction

An *IT infrastructure* is a concept that means different things to different organizations at different times. Organizations today can choose from thousands of components to build their IT infrastructures—from individual software to strategic functions. An ***IT infrastructure*** includes the hardware, software, and telecommunications equipment that, when combined, provide the underlying foundation to support the organization's goals. Figure 7.1 shows a model of how the various components of an IT infrastructure support an organization's goals.

Your organization's goals should drive everything, from how your organization is structured, to how it designs its IT infrastructure. Depending on its goals, your organization may have a flat or hierarchical structure. A flat organizational structure has only a few managerial layers, while a hierarchical organizational structure has many managerial layers. The structure of your organization will, in part, determine the necessary IT infrastructure.

As a knowledge worker, you'll be continually faced with questions regarding how the IT infrastructure can best support your organizational goals. You'll be asked to make decisions regarding which type of IT infrastructure components to purchase, and how to implement them. Of the many technologies available, how will you choose the ones that best meet your organization's needs? As both business and technology continue to change, you'll face such questions again and again.

This chapter discusses a few of the primary IT infrastructure components your organization can use to build a solid foundation that supports everything it does or plans to do. Intranets, Web services, storage area networks (SAN), and application service

Figure 7.1

IT infrastructure Supports Organization Goals

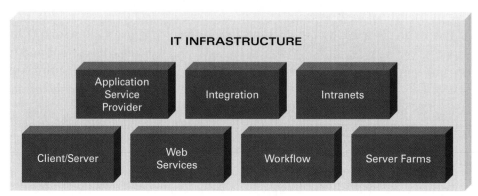

providers (ASP) are just a few of the components we'll discuss in the following pages. After reading this chapter, you'll have enough basic knowledge to understand how each one works.

IT Infrastructure Overview

Organizations spend a great deal of their time determining primary goals, objectives, structures, and strategies. These critical components help them determine how they will operate in the marketplace, what their strategic directions or competitive advantages will be, and how they will achieve unlimited success. A good IT infrastructure will support all of these, supplying all your organization's business and information needs. An IT infrastructure that ignores your organization's business or information needs (reflecting its main goals and strategies) will cause certain failure.

Building a solid IT infrastructure requires you to understand the fundamental IT infrastructure components. The primary components of any IT infrastructure include *client/server networks, the Internet,* and *n-tier infrastructures.*

CLIENT/SERVER NETWORKS

A *client/server network* is a network in which one or more computers are *servers* and provide services to the other computers, called *clients.* The server or servers have hardware, software, and/or information that the client computers can access. Figure 7.2 illustrates a client/server network. You can see that several clients access a single server and a single printer. The server can perform some or almost all of the information processing, which may allow your organization to purchase thin clients. A *thin client* is a workstation with a small amount of processing power and costs less than a full-powered workstation. The new realm of thin clients also includes Web-enabled cell phones, tablet PCs, and PDAs. Purchasing thin clients can save your organization a tremendous

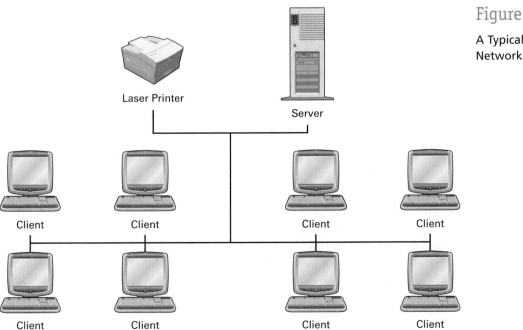

Laser Printer

Server

Client   Client   Client   Client

Client   Client   Client   Client

Figure 7.2

A Typical Client/Server Network

EMPLOYEES' ABUSE OF THE INTERNET

The Internet doesn't always guarantee increased employee productivity. Employee abuse of the Internet can significantly *decrease* productivity. Shawn Vidmar is the IT director of Vidmar Motor Company, a $40 million, 85-employee, automotive dealership in Pueblo, Colorado. Shawn discovered that several employees were spending as many as six hours a day on the Internet playing games, gambling, buying and selling stocks, and sending personal e-mails. Shawn stated, "Employees obviously weren't doing their jobs, and if they're trying to trade online and they're not doing their job, that's a problem. Productivity was being compromised and I was worried about corporate liability. If somebody gets offended by an e-mail, they could go after the company."

Shawn implemented new policies, employee education, and Internet monitoring software to help solve the problem. He decided to install Vericept Corporation's Vericept VIEW, a network abuse management system that tracks and analyzes network traffic. Shawn explained, "Sending out an e-mail from here is like sending it out on Vidmar letterhead. I would hate to lose the business my grandfather started 60 years ago over a bad Internet joke."[2]

---

amount of money when you consider that every single knowledge worker in the company needs a client. A client/server network can also allow your company to save money by purchasing a single printer (or other peripheral device such as a scanner) that serves many individuals. Please review *Extended Learning Module E* for a detailed discussion of the many different types of client/server networks.

THE INTERNET

It's impossible to count the number of ways the Internet makes an organization successful—we discussed many of these in Chapters 2 and 5. Today, in the information age, most employees require an Internet connection to perform their jobs. The Internet allows employees to send e-mail to customers, suppliers, and other employees for a fraction of the cost of a telephone call or surface (snail) mail. Employees also receive the benefit of being able to search through volumes of information from organizations and libraries all over the world in a matter of minutes.

One thing to mention about the Internet is that it's *not* guaranteed to increase employee productivity. Sometimes it can actually decrease employee productivity. The Computer Security Institute/FBI recently reported that 78 percent of companies detected employee abuse of their Internet access privileges. The abuse included playing games, downloading movies, listening to music, gambling, trading stocks, e-mailing jokes, and even distributing critical company information. Employees also abuse the Internet by spending significant time sending personal e-mails to friends and family members. This sounds like a tiny problem, but studies indicate that the amount of time employees spend abusing the Internet directly affects productivity.[3]

One of the decisions you'll make regarding your IT infrastructure is how you're going to design your Internet access. Some companies implement full Internet access to all employees, while other companies provide full Internet access for only certain employees. Deciding which Internet infrastructure to develop will depend on your employee needs and how much control the organization wants to have over how employees use the Internet.

N-TIER INFRASTRUCTURES

Personal computers (PCs) came out of isolation with the emergence of client/server networks. Basic client/server computing is a **2-tier infrastructure** since there are only two tiers—the client and the server. The server primarily supports data storage or access to peripherals such as printers, with limited access to application software. In a 2-tier infrastructure, the majority of the system logic and intelligence (application software) is located on the client PC. This can lead to information sharing issues since the users must maintain the majority of the important corporate information on their PCs. This information, then, may not be accessible to all other employees. These types of networks do, however, have their place in our lives; as you read in *Extended Learning Module E,* you can set up a home network, which is essentially a 2-tier infrastructure.

You can address the problems of information and software sharing by moving to a 3-tier infrastructure, which moves the system logic and intelligence (and much of the information) from the clients to the server. A **3-tier infrastructure** contains clients, application servers, and data servers. The primary differences between a 2-tier and 3-tier infrastructure are (1) the presence of the application servers for maintaining shared application software and (2) the presence of data servers for maintaining shared information.

Client/server networks, the Internet, and n-tier infrastructure considerations are central to any decision you make concerning your organization's IT infrastructure. We'll now spend the rest of this chapter focusing on other elements of IT infrastructures. Figure 7.3 displays these in three general categories:

1. Information views
2. Business logic
3. Data storage and manipulation

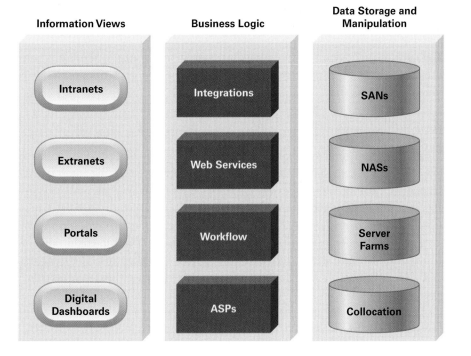

Figure 7.3

IT Infrastructure Components

Information Views

The IT infrastructure components contained in the information views category are responsible for the presentation of information and receiving user events. These components include—but are not limited to—intranets, extranets, portals, and digital dashboards.

INTRANETS AND EXTRANETS

An *intranet* is an internal organizational Internet that is guarded against outside access by a special security feature called a *firewall* (which can be software, hardware, or a combination of the two). The primary characteristic of an intranet is that people outside the organization can't access it. Employees must have a user name and password to logon to a company intranet.

An intranet is an invaluable tool for presenting organizational information as it provides a central location where employees can find information. An intranet can host all kinds of company-related information such as benefits, schedules, strategic directions, and employee directories. At many companies, each department has its own Web page on the company intranet for departmental information sharing. The advantages an intranet gives an organization are tremendous and it should probably be a major component of your IT infrastructure.

An *extranet* is an intranet that is restricted to an organization and certain outsiders, such as customers and suppliers. Many companies are building extranets as they begin to realize the tremendous benefit of offering individuals outside the organization access to intranet-based information and application software such as ordering processing. When looking at the IT systems you're building, be sure to ask yourself, "What value could be added if employees, partners, vendors, and customers could access this system's information and processing capabilities?" If giving partners, vendors, and customers access to system information and processing helps your business, then you need to consider building an extranet. Finding new ways to present organizational information to and enable application software usage by external individuals is another important component of your IT infrastructure. We discussed the important roles of intranets and extranets in Chapter 5.

PORTALS

"Portal" is a very generic term for what is in essence a technology that provides access to information. There are many specific implementations of portals, including enterprise information portals, collaborative-processing enterprise information portals, and decision-processing enterprise information portals.

Enterprise information portals (EIPs) allow knowledge workers to access company information via a Web interface. An EIP is similar to an Internet search engine such as Google, Yahoo!, or Alta Vista, except the only information stored on an EIP is company information. An EIP presents knowledge workers with enterprisewide business information based on a simple search.

The primary difference between intranets and EIPs is that intranets are more of a corporate newsletter or static database of corporate information, while EIPs

- Are dynamic and serve as an electronic workspace for knowledge workers.
- Provide personalized access to key information and applications and real-time notification of important new information via e-mail.
- Can present critical information in the form of graphics and charts that are continuously updated.

There are two primary categories of EIPs—collaborative-processing EIPs and decision-processing EIPs. A ***collaborative-processing enterprise information portal*** presents knowledge workers with access to workgroup information such as e-mails, reports, meeting minutes, and memos. A ***decision-processing enterprise information portal*** presents knowledge workers with corporate information for making key business decisions. EIPs are becoming increasingly popular in the workforce because of the amount of information sharing they provide for knowledge workers.

Both these categories of EIPs support integrated collaboration environments (ICEs), which we discussed in Chapter 2, and provide environments in which virtual teams do their work.

DIGITAL DASHBOARDS

Digital dashboards display key information gathered from several sources on a computer screen in a format tailored to the needs and wants of an individual knowledge worker. Digital dashboards commonly use indicators to help executives quickly identify the status of key information. Key information typically includes such things as critical success factors that you can monitor, measure, and compare. These fall within the realm of business intelligence, which we discussed in Chapters 1, 2, and 3.

Digital dashboards, whether basic or comprehensive, deliver results quickly. As digital dashboards become easier to use, they will enable executives to perform their own analyses of business intelligence without inundating IT people with requests for special analysis, queries, and reports. Digital dashboards help managers view and react to business intelligence as it becomes available, which allows them to make decisions, solve problems, and change strategies quickly. Figure 7.4 displays an example of business intelligence presented in a digital dashboard.

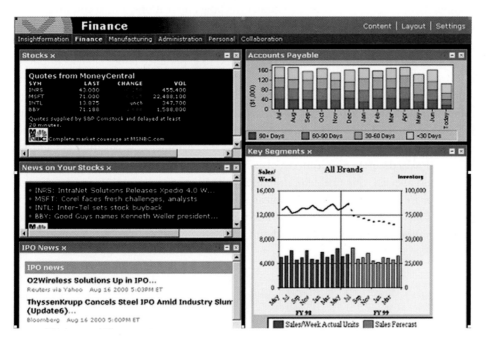

Figure 7.4

Digital Dashboard Example

1,900 GAP STORES COMMUNICATING

The GAP has 1,900 stores around the world, employing more than 13,000 people, which generated $6.2 billion in revenue in 2003. The company's primary goal is to achieve and maintain a 20 percent growth rate each year. To maintain this goal, the Gap needs to keep all employees connected with immediate access to real-time information by sharing information between several different legacy systems and new applications. The Gap chose to implement CORBA middleware to build the integrations between the different systems. CORBA stands for *Common Object Request Broker Architecture* and it allows programs at different locations developed by different vendors to communicate through integrations.

Building an IT infrastructure based on CORBA integrations and the use of the Internet has allowed the Gap to exchange real-time sales, inventory, and shipping information among all its information systems and employees. The new infrastructure also allows the Gap to send information to and from any IT system in the world, which has increased employee and company performance.[4,5]

Business Logic

The IT infrastructure components contained in the business logic category are responsible for maintaining the business rules (e.g., application software) and protecting corporate information from unauthorized direct access by the clients. These components include integrations, Web services, workflow systems, and application service providers (ASPs).

INTEGRATIONS

Many organizations typically maintain separate applications for different departments. For example, marketing might have its own pricing and market-forecasting applications, sales might have its own sales and customer tracking applications, and accounting might have its own financial applications. Some organizations have hundreds of different applications operating across all departments.

Organizations with multiple applications tend to experience issues such as duplicate information and conflicting information. Let's consider a customer address change example to demonstrate the problems that arise from having multiple applications. If a customer moves and sends a change of address form to your company, this information must be entered into every single application that maintains the customer's address. Chances are some of the applications will be missed, and the customer now has different address information in different applications, or conflicting address information.

To help alleviate this problem, organizations build integrations. An ***integration*** allows separate applications to communicate directly with each other by automatically exporting data files from one application and importing them into another. In short, building integrations between applications helps an organization maintain better control of its information.

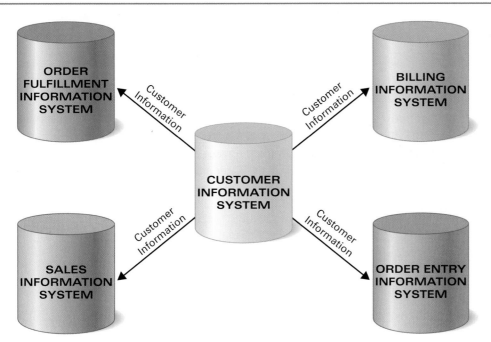

Figure 7.5

Integrating Customer Information

Figure 7.5 illustrates how an organization can integrate customer information. Each time new entries, or changes, occur, the information is integrated, or automatically passed, to all the other applications that maintain customer information, eliminating the problem of having to enter the same customer information into multiple applications, thus reducing conflicting information.

WEB SERVICES

Web services promise to be the next major frontier in computing. Prior to Web services, organizations had trouble with interoperability. *Interoperability* is the concept that different computer systems and applications can talk to each other. For example, if your supply chain management (SCM) system can talk to (share information with) your customer relationship management (CRM) system, then you have interoperability between the two systems. One way organizations achieved interoperability was to build integrations. Now, an organization can use Web services to perform the same task.

Web services encompass all the technologies that are used to transmit and process information on and across a network, most specifically the Internet. You can think of an individual Web service as software that performs a specific task, with that task being made available to any user who needs its service. For example, a *Deposit* Web service for a banking system might allow customers to perform the task of depositing money to their accounts. The *Deposit* Web service could be used by a bank teller when you go inside, by you at an ATM, and/or by you when perform online banking with your Web browser.

The *Deposit* Web service demonstrates one of the great advantages of using the Web service model to develop applications. That is, you don't have to reinvent the wheel every time you need to incorporate a needed functionality. A Web service is really a piece of reusable software code. A software developer can quickly build a new application by using many of these pieces of reusable code. As you learned in the previous chapter on systems development, most of the time spent in the systems development life cycle (SDLC) focuses on writing and testing software. In a Web services environment, because you can reuse existing pieces of software, your organization can greatly reduce the time it takes to write and test software.

THE COMPETITION BETWEEN .NET AND J2EE

When building Web services you need to make a decision between using .NET and Java 2 Enterprise Edition (J2EE). Your decision to select .NET or J2EE will probably hinge on two or three factors including performance, scalability, and expense. *Computerworld* magazine recently held a competition between .NET and J2EE to determine which technology was superior in relation to the above-mentioned factors.

Surprisingly, .NET and J2EE were both declared winners in the software development competition. The competition was held in New Zealand where two pairs of programmers using .NET and J2EE were assigned two projects: (1) to build a course registration application in three hours; (2) to build a system that found errors in Web material in a day. The .NET team produced a working course registration application before the three-hour deadline and won as the preferred infrastructure choice. The J2EE team won as the preferred infrastructure choice for the system that found errors in Web material.[6]

MICROSOFT .NET *.NET* is Microsoft's version of Web services. Microsoft's vision is to make applications available any time, any place, on any device. Microsoft has devoted an enormous amount of resources to .NET. .NET is a pretty big deal when you consider that applications created using the .NET platform are available any time, any place, and on any device. It also means that developers of intranets and extranets can now use Web services to include all kinds of amazing functionalities without having to reinvent the wheel and without needing to know anything about the business or complexity of the Web service they are using. The three primary components of .NET include the .NET platform, .NET framework, and Visual Studio .NET.

- *.NET platform*—Microsoft's entire suite of tools, technologies, and services that support Microsoft's vision of connected applications, which includes Web services. The .NET platform includes the .NET framework.

- *.NET framework*—Microsoft's set of services that are used to support Web services, such as Common Language Runtime (CLR). Web services cannot work without the .NET framework.

- *Visual Studio .NET*—The development tool that is used to create applications for the .NET platform, including Web services.

.NET COMPETITORS When most people hear the term Web services, they typically think of Microsoft's .NET. However, many other companies support Web services. When Web services were first invented, Microsoft, along with a number of other companies, submitted a joint specification document as a standard for passing data over the Internet to the World Wide Web Consortium (known as W3C). The specification for Web services was adopted by the W3C, which makes it an open and publicly available standard. Other companies developing Web services include:

- Sun Microsystems: Sun supports Web services with its *ONE (Open Net Environment)* architecture. *Java 2 Enterprise Edition (J2EE)* is Sun Microsystems' development tool for building Web services applications. The primary difference between .NET and J2EE is that J2EE is Java-centric and has the ability to run on any operating system, while .NET runs on Microsoft operating systems only. You can find more information about Sun Microsystems Web services at www.sun.com/webservices.

- Hewlett Packard (HP): HP supports Web services with its *HP Web Services Platform.* You can find more information about HP's Web services at www.hp.com/go/webservices.
- IBM: IBM supports Web services with its *WebSphere.* You can find more information about IBM's Web services at www3.ibm.com/software/solution/webservices.
- Oracle: Oracle supports Web services with its *Oracle9iAS Web Services Platform.* You can find more information about Oracle's Web services at http://otn.oracle.com/tech/webservices/content.html.

Web services are poised for rapid growth and the Gartner Group estimates a $21 billion market worldwide by 2005 for Web service applications. Currently, the two biggest players in the Web services market are Microsoft's .NET and Sun's J2EE.[7]

WORKFLOW SYSTEMS

We discussed the importance of workflow systems in Chapter 2. As a review, a **workflow** defines all the steps or business rules, from beginning to end, required for a business process. Therefore, **workflow systems** facilitate the automation and management of business processes. When you execute a process, a workflow system dictates the presentation of the information, tracks the information, and maintains the information's status. Let's look at how you could use a workflow system to help you complete a group project. The following are four steps you usually take when completing a group project:

1. Find out what information and deliverables are required for the project and when they are due.
2. Divide the work among the group members.
3. Determine due dates for the different pieces of work.
4. Compile all the work together into a single project.

One of the hardest parts of a team project is presenting information in a unified format and sending it to the various team members. Often one group member can't perform his or her work until another group member has finished, or until work has been uniformly reformatted. Group members waste a lot of time reformatting information and waiting to receive information from other group members. This same situation happens in the "real world." You'll find the actual work is sitting idle waiting for an employee to pick it up to either approve it, continue working on it, or reformat it. Workflow systems help to automate the process of presenting and passing information around the organization.

A workflow system can automatically pass documents around to different team members in the required order. There are two primary types of workflow systems: messaging-based and database-based. *Messaging-based workflow systems* send work assignments through an e-mail system. The workflow system automatically tracks the order for the work to be assigned and, each time a step is completed, the system automatically sends the work to the next individual in line. If you use this type of workflow system to complete your group project, it will automatically distribute the work to each group member via e-mail. For example, each time you completed a piece of the project the system would automatically send the document to the next group member.

Database-based workflow systems store documents in a central location and automatically ask the knowledge workers to access the document when it's their turn to edit the document. If you use this type of workflow system to perform your group project, the project documentation is stored in a central location and you are notified by the system when it is your turn to login and work on your portion of the project.

Either type of workflow system helps to present information in a unified format, improves teamwork by providing automated process support, and allows knowledge workers to communicate and collaborate within a unified environment.

APPLICATION SERVICE PROVIDERS

An *application service provider (ASP)* supplies software applications (and other related services such as maintenance, technical support, and the like) over the Internet that would otherwise reside on its customers' in-house computers. If you employ the services of an ASP, you are outsourcing some of your business logic. Hiring an ASP to manage your organization's software allows you to hand over the operation, maintenance, and upgrade responsibilities for a system to the ASP.

Companies can outsource both application and infrastructure components. Application components include business functions such as payroll, accounting, intranets, and e-mail. Infrastructure components include large systems such as customer relationship management systems, enterprise resource planning systems, and customer service call centers.

Figure 7.6 (on the facing page) represents how your IT infrastructure might support using an ASP. Your company receives access to the application servers through the Internet. The company knowledge workers can login to the applications from their offices, laptops, and sometimes cellular equipment depending on how the software works. The ASP stores, maintains, and upgrades the applications to ensure security and backups.

One of the most important agreements between the customer and the ASP is the service level agreement. *Service level agreements (SLAs)* define the specific responsibilities of the application service provider and set the customer expectations. SLAs include such items as availability, accessibility, performance, maintenance, backup/recovery, upgrades, equipment ownership, software ownership, security, and confidentiality. For example, an SLA might state that the ASP must have the software available and accessible from 7:00 A.M. to 7:00 P.M. Monday through Friday. It might also state that if the system is down for more than 60 minutes, the charge for that day of service will be removed.

Most industry analysts agree that the ASP market is growing rapidly. International Data Corporation estimates the worldwide ASP market will grow from around $693.5

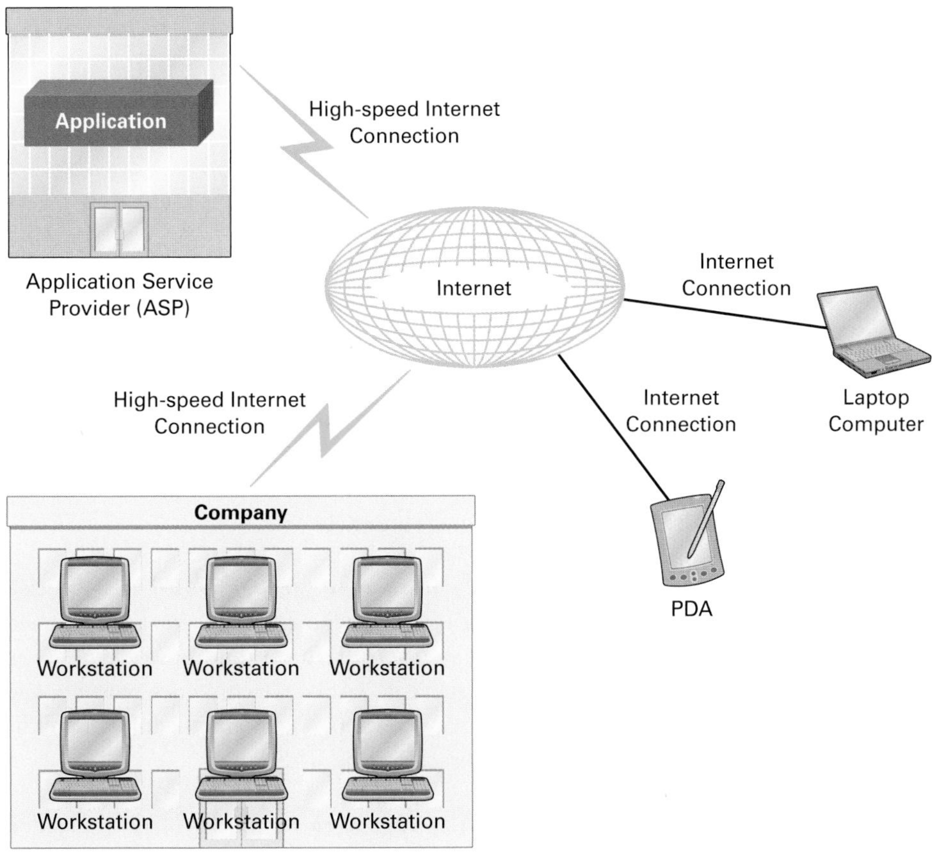

Figure 7.6

A Sample ASP
Infrastructure

million in 2000 to $13 billion by 2005. The Aberdeen group predicts the ASP market will grow to $16.1 billion in 2005. Zona research (now the Sageza group) reported that 63 percent of the companies it surveyed are already using an ASP to access an average of two to six applications. As a knowledge worker, you'll find yourself working with ASPs and outsourced applications. You might even find yourself in the position of having to make the decision to outsource one of your business applications to an ASP.[8]

Data Storage and Manipulation

The IT infrastructure components contained in the data storage and manipulation category are responsible for data storage and manipulation. These components include network area storage, storage area networks, server farms, and collocation.

DATA STORAGE

Making informed decisions sometimes requires reviewing past information as well as current information (both of which can be business intelligence). Viewing historical information, or archived information, allows a company to perform detailed analysis on sales trends, customer trends, product trends, employee trends, and so forth. There is a wealth of business intelligence in historical information.

Therefore, your IT infrastructure must define a storage architecture. A storage architecture takes into account the types and sizes of devices where information is stored. Storage technology continues to improve at a rapid pace, as does the demand for storage

Figure 7.7

Network Area Storage
(NAS)

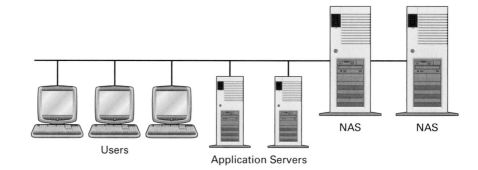

capacity. Organizations are demanding new ways to manage storage at the enterprise level. Once an organization's data requirements pass the million megabyte mark, traditional storage devices simply will not work. Two new storage architectures are dominating the market: network area storage and storage area networks.

NETWORK AREA STORAGE (NAS) *Network area storage (NAS)* is a special-purpose server aimed at providing file storage to users who access the device over a network. A NAS server contains an operating system, disk drives, and power supplies in one integrated package. From a user perspective, a NAS server provides recovery and automated backup software. Figure 7.7 displays a sample NAS architecture where the users and application servers are attached directly to the NAS.

STORAGE AREA NETWORKS (SAN) A *storage area network (SAN)* is an infrastructure for building special, dedicated networks that allow rapid and reliable access to storage devises by multiple servers. Figure 7.8 displays a sample SAN architecture. The system users and application servers attach to a SAN server that distributes the data across several different storage disks.

Both NAS and SAN architectures share several objectives including the ability to provide large amounts of storage capacity, the ability to serve multiple users, and support 24 hours a day, 7 days a week. The two approaches are distinguished primarily by the location of the network that connects these three elements: users and applications, file servers, and a collection of disk drives (see Figures 7.7 and 7.8).

Figure 7.8

Storage Area Network
(SAN)

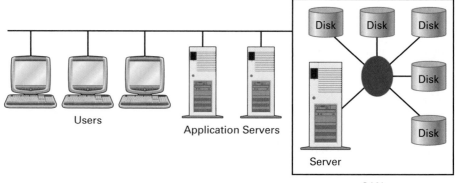

DETERMINING ISSUES IN AN APPLICATION INFRASTRUCTURE

You are a senior manager at Brewers.com, a start-up online coffee supply company. The company is just beginning to develop its IT infrastructure, which must house the primary applications for e-mail, payroll, and Web sites. One of your colleagues has put together the following diagram listing the IT Infrastructure components that are currently available. In a group, assemble the IT infrastructure that will best support your organization.

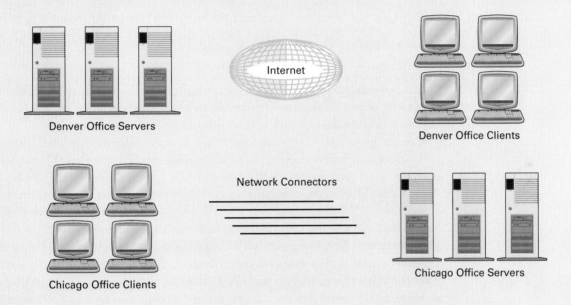

Denver Office Servers

Internet

Denver Office Clients

Network Connectors

Chicago Office Clients

Chicago Office Servers

SERVER FARM

A **server farm** is the name of a location that stores a group of servers in a single place. Server farms are also referred to as *server clusters*. A server farm, or cluster, provides centralized access to and control of files, printers, and backups for each server. The advantage of having a server farm is that if a single server fails there are other servers that can perform the work and the knowledge workers don't experience any downtime because of failed equipment or software. Server farms are often located in collocation facilities (which we'll discuss in a moment).

A **Web farm** is either a Web site that has multiple servers or an ISP that provides Web site outsourcing services using multiple servers. For the most part, you can use a single server to handle user requests for files on a Web site. For large Web sites, you might require multiple servers to handle user requests for files.

COLLOCATION FACILITIES

It's hard to believe but the correct spelling of the word *collocation* is yet to be defined. You could find collocation spelled co-location, colocation, or collocation. Regardless of the way you choose to spell it, the word **collocation** simply means that a company rents space and telecommunications equipment from another company, or a collocation vendor. For example, if a company places a server that contains the company's Web site in a building owned by another company, the company has collocated its server with another company. Collocation facilities are typically large warehouse buildings where hundreds of different companies can store computer hardware and software.

Can you guess why a company would want to use a collocation facility? It saves the company money because buying or renting an office can be expensive. For example, if a company has a central office in Chicago and sales personnel in Chicago, Boston, and Toronto, the IT infrastructure must support all of the employees even if there is not a central office in the town where they work. By placing a server in a collocation facility in Boston and Toronto, the sales personnel in these places could dial in to the server and be connected to the Chicago office's intranet and information systems. This saves the company a great deal of time and energy because the alternative to this configuration would be to have the employees dial a long distance number to the Chicago office or rent an office in each location to maintain the servers. Renting space from a collocation facility is cheap and easy compared to setting up an entire office.

Supporting an IT Infrastructure

Now that you have a fundamental understanding of a few of the important IT infrastructure components, let's turn our attention to how you can support your IT infrastructure, which includes such things as backup/recovery, disaster recovery, and infrastructure *-ilities*.

BACKUP/RECOVERY

How many times have you lost a document on your computer because your computer crashed and you hadn't saved or backed up the document? How many times have you accidentally deleted a file you needed? **Backup** is the process of making a copy of the information stored on a computer. **Recovery** is the process of reinstalling the backup information in the event the information was lost. There are many different media your organization can choose to back up information including tapes, disks, CD-ROMs, SANs, and NASs.

We cannot stress enough the importance of making backups. How many times do you think knowledge workers have lost information because they didn't have a backup? How often do you think knowledge workers should back up their files? The answer to these questions varies depending on your organization's goals. For example, if your organization deals with large volumes of critical information, it might require daily backups. If

BACKUP/RECOVERY OF YOUR COMPUTER

We are sure that most of you would agree that backing up your computer information is critical. However, how many of you are actually making backups of the information stored on your computer? What would happen if your computer crashed right now and you couldn't recover any of the information? How many papers, projects, and course notes would you lose? If you did decide to perform a back up, would you know what information you need to back up and where to find this information on your computer?

There are numerous ways that you can back up the information on your computer including saving your information to disks, CDs, external hard drives, and remote locations such as www.mydocsonline.com. Research the Internet and determine the following:

- What is the best way for you to back up your computer information?
- How frequently do you need to back up your computer information?
- What is the exact location of the information you need to back up?

your organization deals with small amounts of noncritical information, it might require only weekly backups. Deciding how often to back up computer information is a critical decision for any organization.

DISASTER RECOVERY PLAN

Unfortunately, disasters—such as power outages, floods, and even harmful hacking—occur all the time. Therefore, your organization needs to develop a disaster recovery plan. A **disaster recovery plan** is a detailed process for recovering information or an IT system in the event of a catastrophic disaster such as a fire or flood.

A good disaster recovery plan takes into consideration the location of the backup information. Many organizations choose to store backup information in an off-site storage facility, or a place that is separately located from the company and often owned by another company, such as a collocation facility. StorageTek is a company that specializes in providing off-site data storage and disaster recovery solutions.

A good disaster recovery plan also considers the actual facility where knowledge workers will work. A **hot site** is a separate and fully equipped facility where the company can move immediately after the disaster and resume business. A **cold site** is a separate facility that does not have any computer equipment but is a place where the knowledge workers can move after the disaster.

A part of your disaster recovery plan should include a disaster recovery cost curve (see Figure 7.9). A **disaster recovery cost curve** charts (1) the cost to your organization of the unavailability of information and technology and (2) the cost to your organization of recovering from a disaster over time. Where the two intersect is, in fact, the best recovery plan in terms of cost and time. Being able to restore information and IT systems quickly in the event of a disaster is a great way to provide an IT infrastructure that helps to continually increase employee productivity.

Figure 7.9

Deciding How Much to Spend on Disaster Recovery

Abercrombie & Fitch uses the Internet to market its distinctive image of being a fashion trendsetter to one of its largest customer segments, college students. The company designed its Web services infrastructure with the help of IBM, which ensured that www.abercrombie.com paralleled the same sleek but simple design of *A&F Quarterly,* the company's flagship magazine.

Abercrombie & Fitch knew that its Web site had to be accessible, available, reliable, and scalable to meet the demands of its young customers. Young customers tend to be Internet savvy and their purchasing habits vary from shopping for sale items at midnight to knowing exactly what they want immediately. The highly successful Web site gives customers not only an opportunity to shop online, but also a taste of the Abercrombie & Fitch lifestyle through downloadable MP3s, calendars, and desktop accessories.[10]

INFRASTRUCTURE "-ILITIES"

There are a number of factors that you should consider whenever you are developing an IT infrastructure. These factors are commonly referred to as the *-ilities* and include availability, accessibility, reliability, scalability, flexibility, performance, and capacity planning.

AVAILABILITY Many knowledge workers work mainly from 9 A.M. to 5 P.M. It's not uncommon though for a knowledge worker to arrive at work early, or to stay late, or to work on the weekend to meet a deadline. For this reason, it's crucial that the IT infrastructure support knowledge workers' varied schedules.

"Availability" is determining when your IT system will be available for knowledge workers to access. Most companies have IT systems available 24 × 7, or 24 hours a day, 7 days a week. One reason why a company might support 24 × 7 system availability is time zones. Imagine you work for a company based in Denver, Colorado, and the company also has an office in London, England. When the London employees are finishing work, the Colorado employees are just starting work. The same IT systems are worked on by both sets of employees so they must be available around the clock. Supporting global customers mandates that a system be available 24 × 7 in order to support all of the customers in the different time zones.

ACCESSIBILITY "Accessibility" is determining who has the right to access different types of IT systems and information. Imagine what would happen if all employees had access to payroll information or bonus information. Payroll and bonus information is typically confidential, and at some companies you can be fired for having knowledge of or sharing this type of information.

Accessibility means not only who can access the information, but also how they can access or manipulate the information, whether they can create, read, update, and/or delete information, or what is often referred to as *CRUD* in the technology world. It's important that you define how each person can access information.

RELIABILITY "Reliability" ensures your IT systems are functioning correctly and providing accurate information. Inaccurate information exists for many reasons, from the information being entered incorrectly to the information becoming corrupt. Whatever the reason, if employees can't receive reliable information, then they can't perform their jobs.

RANKING THE "-ILITIES"

Understanding and ensuring each of the "-ilities" is critical to any organization's success. In a group, review the list of IT infrastructure -ilities and rank them in order of their impact on an organization's success. Use a rating system of 1 to 7, where 1 indicates the biggest impact and 7 indicates the least impact. Be prepared to justify your rankings.

IT Infrastructure -ilities	Business Impact
Availability	
Accessibility	
Reliability	
Scalability	
Flexibility	
Performance	
Capacity Planning	

Ensuring information is reliable is a critical and difficult task for all organizations. ***Data cleansing*** is the term that describes the process of ensuring that all information is accurate. The more an organization can do to ensure its IT infrastructure promotes reliable information, the more money it will save by catching errors before they occur.

SCALABILITY   Estimating how much growth your organization is expected to experience over the next few years is an almost impossible task. ***Scalability*** refers to how well your system can adapt to increased demands. A number of factors can affect organizational growth including the market, the industry, and the economy. If your organization grows faster than anticipated, you might find your systems experiencing all types of issues including running out of disk space to a slowing in transaction performance speed. To keep employees working and productive, your organization must try to anticipate expected growth and ensure the IT infrastructure supports it.

FLEXIBILITY   A single system can be designed in a number of different ways to perform exactly the same function. When you choose which design you want to implement, you must think about the system's flexibility, or the system's ability to change quickly. Building an inflexible system will cost your company money because it won't be able to handle market, business, or economic changes.

PERFORMANCE   ***Performance*** measures how quickly an IT system performs a certain process. ***Benchmarks*** are baseline values a system seeks to attain. ***Benchmarking*** is a process of continuously measuring system results, comparing those results to optimal system performance (benchmark values), and identifying steps and procedures to improve system performance. Many factors affect the performance of an IT system, ranging from the design of the system to the hardware that supports it, and especially its IT infrastructure.

One of the most common performance problems you'll find occurs because of uncontrolled growth. For example, if business is booming and your company doubles the size of its order entry department, it must ensure the system performs at the same speed with twice as many users. If you had 50 order entry specialists and you now have 100 order entry specialists, your IT systems might not function correctly because of the increased number of users.

CAPACITY PLANNING *Capacity planning* determines the future IT infrastructure requirements for new equipment and additional network capacity. It's cheaper for an organization to implement an IT infrastructure that considers capacity growth at the beginning of a system launch than to try to upgrade equipment and networks after the system has already been implemented. Not having enough capacity leads to performance issues and hinders the ability of knowledge workers to perform their jobs. For example, if you have 100 workers using the Internet to perform their jobs and you purchase modems that are too slow and the network capacity is too small, your workers will spend a great deal of time just waiting to get information from the Internet. Waiting for an Internet site to return information is not the most productive way for knowledge workers to spend their time.

To learn more about capacity planning, visit the Web site that supports this text at www.mhhe.com/haag.

IT Infrastructures and the Real World

Components of a solid IT infrastructure include everything from documentation to business concepts to software and hardware. In this chapter, we've discussed many different IT infrastructure components including client/server networks, ASPs, Web services, and integrations. It may seem that we covered a great deal of material in this chapter, but there are actually thousands of additional components that are important in building a solid IT infrastructure. Deciding which components to implement and how to implement them can be a challenge.

New IT components are released daily, and business needs continually change. An IT infrastructure that meets your organization's needs today may not meet those needs tomorrow. Building an IT infrastructure that is scalable, flexible, available, accessible, and reliable is key to your organization's success.

As a knowledge worker, you'll be responsible for approving the designs for the IT infrastructure for your systems. Remember to ask yourself the following questions before approving the IT infrastructure designs:

- How big is my department going to grow? Will the system be able to handle additional users?

- How are my customers going to grow? How much additional information do I expect to store each year?

- How long will I maintain information in the systems? How much history do I want to keep on each customer?

- When do the people in my department work? What are the hours I need the system to be available?

- How often do I need the information to be backed up?

- What will happen to my system if there is a disaster? What is the disaster recovery plan for my system?

- How easy is it to change the system? How flexible is the system?

Seeing to it that your system designs address each of these questions will put you on the path toward building an IT infrastructure that supports your organization today and will do so tomorrow.

Summary: Student Learning Outcomes Revisited

1. **Explain the relationship between the organization's roles and goals and its IT infrastructure.** An *IT infrastructure* includes the hardware, software, and telecommunications equipment that, when combined, provide the underlying foundation to support the organization's goals. Organizational goals should drive everything about the organization, from how it's structured to how it designs its IT infrastructure. An organization can have many structures including flat or hierarchical. A flat organizational structure has only a couple of managerial layers while a hierarchical organizational structure has many managerial layers. The organization's structure in turn influences IT infrastructure.

2. **Describe the difference between a 2-tier and 3-tier infrastructure.** A *2-tier infrastructure* consists of two layers or tiers—clients and the server. A *3-tier infrastructure* contains clients, application servers, and data servers. The primary differences between a 2-tier infrastructure and a 3-tier infrastructure are (1) the presence of application servers for

maintaining shared application software and (2) the presence of data servers for maintaining shared information.

3. **Describe system integration.** Organizations often have a separate system for each department. Some organizations end up with hundreds of different systems that do not communicate with each other. To alleviate the problem of so many separate systems containing discrete information, organizations build integrations. An *integration* allows separate systems to communicate directly with each other by automatically exporting data files from one system and importing them into another system. Building integrations between systems helps the organization maintain better control of its information and helps it quickly gather information across multiple systems.

4. **Describe Web services and Microsoft's .NET.** *Web services* encompass all the technologies that are used to transmit and process information on and across a network, most specifically the Internet. You can think of an individual Web service as software that performs a specific task and makes that task available along with

335

additional functionality that can be performed with the task. For example, a deposit Web service for a banking system might allow customers to perform the task of depositing money to their accounts. *.NET* is Microsoft's version of Web services and has the vision for making applications available any time, any place, on any device.

5. **Explain the difference between network area storage (NAS) and storage area networks (SAN).** *Network area storage (NAS)* is a special-purpose server aimed at providing file storage to users who access the device over a network. A NAS server contains an operating system, disk drives, and power supplies in one integrated package. A *storage area network (SAN)* is an infrastructure for building special, dedicated networks that allow rapid and reliable access to storage devices by multiple servers. Both NAS and SAN architectures share several objectives including the ability to provide large amounts of storage capacity, the ability to serve multiple users, and support 24 hours a day, 7 days a week. The two approaches are distinguished primarily by the location of the network that connects these three elements: users and applications, file servers, and a collection of disk drives.

6. List and describe the seven "-ilities."

   1. Availability is determining when your IT system will be available for knowledge workers to access.

   2. Accessibility is determining who has the right to access different types of IT systems and information.

   3. Reliability ensures your IT systems are functioning correctly and providing accurate information.

   4. *Scalability* refers to how well your system can adapt to increased demands.

   5. Flexibility ensures the system is designed with the ability to quickly change.

   6. *Performance* measures how quickly an IT system performs a certain process.

   7. *Capacity planning* determines the future IT infrastructure requirements for new equipment and additional network capacity.

CLOSING CASE STUDY ONE

USING LINUX TO SUPPORT YOUR IT INFRASTRUCTURE

Linux has proved itself the most revolutionary software undertaking of the past decade, and estimates predict that Linux spending will reach $280 million by 2006. Linus Torvalds wrote the kernel (the core) of the Linux operating system at age 21. Torvalds posted the operating system on the Internet and invited other programmers to improve his code and users to download his operating system for free. Since then, tens of thousands of people have, making Linux perhaps the single largest collaborative project in the planet's history.

Today, Linux is everywhere. You can find Linux inside a boggling array of computers, machines, and devices. Linux is robust enough to run the world's most powerful supercomputers yet sleek and versatile enough to run inside consumer toys like TiVo, television set-top boxes (e.g., cable TV box), cell phones, and hand-held portable devices. Even more impressive than Linux's in-

creasing prevalence in living rooms and pockets is its growth in the market for corporate computers. According to a recent poll by CIO.com, 39 percent of IT managers agree that Linux will dominate corporate systems by 2007.

Since its introduction in 1991, no other operating system in history has spread as quickly across such a broad range of systems as Linux, and it has finally achieved critical mass. One of the primary reasons for its popularity is its unique open-source format that allows anyone to update, change, and delete its source code. According to studies by market research firm IDC, Linux is currently the fastest-growing server operating system, with shipments expected to grow by over 34 percent per year over the next four years. With its innovative open-source approach, strong security, reliability, and scalability, Linux can help companies achieve the agility they need to respond to changing consumer needs and stay ahead of the game. Gartner Dataquest estimates Linux's server market share will grow seven times faster than Windows.[12]

Questions

1. The Linux operating system is a competitor to Microsoft's operating systems. Research the Internet to find information on the ongoing competition between Linux and Microsoft and discuss the similarities and differences between the two operating systems.

2. An IT infrastructure includes the hardware, software, and telecommunications equipment that, when combined, provide the underlying foundation to support the organization's goals. A good IT infrastructure will support all your organization's business and information needs. An IT infrastructure that ignores your organization's business or information needs will cause certain failure. Describe how you could use the Linux operating system in your IT infrastructure. You may use your school's IT infrastructure as an example.

3. Almost anything you do in an organization is performed in a team. Very few tasks and activities are performed individually in the working world. Improving knowledge workers' ability to collaborate can be a huge benefit for organizations. Linux has a unique open-source format that allows anyone to update, change, and delete its source code. Research the Internet to determine some of the advantages and disadvantages of allowing open-source systems in an organization.

4. What is workflow? What is a workflow system? How can Linux developers use workflow systems to improve communication among developers?

5. Enterprise information portals (EIPs) allow knowledge workers to access company information via a Web interface. How could Linux users benefit from using an EIP?

6. Linux is growing rapidly and chances are high that you will encounter it in your career. You'll find Linux articles and advertisements in all kinds of magazines from *Business Week* to *Fortune*. Research the Internet and find out as much information as you can about Linux. Put together a small PowerPoint presentation describing what Linux is and how corporations today are using it.

CLOSING CASE STUDY TWO

TRANSFORMING THE ENTERTAINMENT INDUSTRY— NETFLIX

The online DVD rental pioneer Netflix is transforming the movie business with its unique business model, streamlined shipping strategy, and unique application infrastructure. Netflix is quickly becoming one of Hollywood's most promising new business partners and is experiencing staggering growth with over 1 million subscribers, which accounts for 3 to 5 percent of all U.S. home video rentals.

Typically, traditional video rental stores focus on major films and ignore older movies and smaller titles with niche audiences. Netflix is turning that idea upside down by offering a serious market for every movie, not just blockbusters. How? Netflix attributes its success to its proprietary software, called the Netflix Recommendation System, which constantly suggests movies you might like, based on how you rate any of the 15,000 titles in the company's catalog. Beyond recommendations, Netflix has figured out how to get DVDs from one subscriber to the next with unbelievable efficiency with its corporate application infrastructure.

Netflix operates by allowing its subscribers to rent unlimited videos for $20 a month, as long as they have no more than three DVDs rented at a time. Currently there are more than 3 million discs in the hands of its customers at any given time, with an average of 300,000 DVDs shipped out of the company's 20 leased distribution centers daily. Netflix's unique application infrastructure allows it to track, monitor, and maintain detailed information on each of its discs, customers, and shippers. At any point in time the company can tell you the exact location of each of its discs, a critical component for Netflix's business model.

To handle the rental logistics for its 5.5 million DVD library the company created several proprietary applications. One of its most successful systems is its Web-based supply chain management system. The system works by having operators scan a bar code on each label for every single disc that arrives in its warehouses. The software then retrieves the name and address of the next person on the wait list for that DVD, prints out a label, and the disc is dropped back into the mail. The custom-built systems have allowed Netflix to slow hiring and reduce labor costs by 15 percent, and the vast majority of its DVDs never touch a warehouse shelf. On any given day, 98 percent of the 15,000 titles in Netflix's inventory are in circulation with its customers.[13]

Questions

1. Netflix makes the majority of its sales over the Internet. Having a great Web site and a solid IT infrastructure is critical to Netflix's business model. Do you think the company uses Web services to build its applications? Briefly describe what Web services are and how Netflix might use them to improve its business.

2. There are two primary types of EIPs: collaborative processing and decision processing. Explain the main difference between the two types. Which type of EIP would you recommend Netflix implement? Why?

3. The -*ilities* are important factors for supporting IT infrastructures. Describe each of the seven -ilities and their importance to Netflix's IT infrastructure.

4. Netflix has hired you as its IT infrastructure expert. Netflix would like you to explain how a solid IT infrastructure can help the company support its primary goals. Netflix also wants you to explain what a 3-tiered infrastructure is and how it can help the organization.

5. Netflix has a massive amount of inventory that it must distribute around the country daily. Explain why a disaster recovery plan is critical to its business operations. Also, explain what might happen to Netflix if it lost all its customer information.

6. Netflix requires several different departments to make its business work. What types of systems do you think Netflix maintains in its different departments? Can you explain why Netflix would want to integrate the system information among its different departments?

Key Terms and Concepts

Short-Answer Questions

1. What is an IT infrastructure?
2. What are the three tiers in a 3-tier infrastructure?
3. What are the primary differences between a 2-tier and 3-tier infrastructure?
4. Why do you need a backup of information?
5. Why would you need to recover information?
6. Name two of the *-ilities.*
7. What are integrations and how are they used to enhance decision making?
8. Why does a business need a disaster recovery plan?
9. What are Web services?
10. Why would an organization use a collocation facility?
11. What is a SAN?
12. What is the difference between J2EE and .NET?
13. How can a digital dashboard help an executive?
14. What is the difference between a server farm and a Web farm?
15. What is the difference between a SAN and a NAS?
16. What are the three components of .NET?
17. What is interoperability?
18. What is the difference between benchmarks and benchmarking?
19. Who is a competitor to .NET?
20. What is the difference between a hot and a cold site?

Assignments and Exercises

1. **AN EIP FOR YOUR COURSE** Enterprise information portals (EIPs) allow knowledge workers to access company information via a Web interface. You have been asked to create an EIP for this course. Answer the following questions in order to determine how the EIP should be developed.
   - What type of information would be contained on the EIP?
   - Who would have access to the EIP?
   - How long would information remain on the EIP?
   - What is the difference between a collaborative processing EIP and a decision processing EIP?
   - Which type of EIP would you implement and why?
2. **SPONSOR OF THE IT INFRASTRUCTURE** To build a solid IT infrastructure you must have executive sponsorship. Your current boss doesn't understand the importance of building a solid IT infrastructure. In fact, your boss doesn't even understand the term IT infrastructure. First, explain to your boss what an IT infrastructure is and why it is critical for any organization. Second, explain three primary components of an IT infrastructure.
3. **IT INFRASTRUCTURE COMPONENTS AND THE REAL WORLD**   Throughout this chapter we discussed several IT infrastructure components including client/server, Web services, integrations, among others. Pick two of the components discussed in this chapter and try to find business examples of how companies are using these components in the real world. We also mentioned that there are thousands of additional components you can use to build an IT infrastructure. Research the Internet to see if you can find two additional IT infrastructure components that were not discussed in this chapter along with business examples of how businesses are using the components in the real world.
4. **CREATING THE IDEAL INFRASTRUCTURE** This chapter focused on many different IT infrastructure components. Choose three of the different components discussed in this chapter and explain how you could use them to improve the IT infrastructure at your school. Be sure to think of current requirements as well as future requirements for the IT infrastructure.

5. **MONITORING THE INTERNET** Providing Internet access to employees is a great way to increase employee productivity. It's also a great way to decrease employee productivity if the employees abuse their Internet privileges. What does it mean to have employees abuse the Internet? What can you do as a manager to prevent your employees from abusing their Internet privileges? What would happen if all of the students in your school spent 10 hours a day surfing the Internet? Use the Internet to find two different types of network monitoring software that you would recommend your school purchase to help deter Internet abuse.

6. **INTEGRATING INFORMATION** Imagine you are working for a large cookie manufacturing company. The company is 75 years old and is just starting to implement technology to help improve operations. Your direct manager has asked you to put together a presentation discussing integrations. In your presentation you must include the definition of integration along with an example of the problems associated with unintegrated systems. You must also explain Web service along with a "real-world" example of how Web services will help your company become more successful.

7. **CREATING A CAMPUS IT INFRASTRUCTURE** You have been assigned the role as student IT infrastructure manager. Your first assignment is to approve the designs for the new on-campus Internet infrastructure. You're having a meeting at 9:00 AM tomorrow morning to review the designs with the student IT employees. To prepare for the meeting, you must understand the student requirements and their current use of the Internet, along with future requirements. The following is a list of questions you must answer before attending the meeting. Please provide your answer to each question.
   - Do you need to have a disaster recovery plan? If so what might it include?
   - Does the system require backup equipment?
   - When will the system need to be available to the students?
   - What types of access levels will the students need?
   - How will you ensure the system is reliable?
   - How will you build scalability into the system?
   - How will you build flexibility into the system?
   - What are the minimum performance requirements for the system?
   - How will the system handle future growth?

Discussion Questions

1. IT infrastructures often mimic organizational hierarchies. Describe two different types of organizational hierarchies and how the IT infrastructure would be built in order to support them.

2. IT infrastructure components can include anything from software to strategic functions. After reading this chapter and learning about a few of the primary IT infrastructure components, explain why a company's IT infrastructure can include so many different components.

3. Organizations tend to spend a great deal of time determining their primary goals, objectives, structures, and strategies. Define your school's goals. Define your school's objectives, structure, and strategies that support these goals. Explain how your school's IT infrastructure supports its goals.

4. The two primary types of data storage infrastructures are storage area networks (SAN) and network area storage (NAS). What is the difference between these two IT infrastructure components? What do these two components have in common? Would a company use both of these components? If it did, why would it want to implement both, and what would be the advantage of having both?

5. Your good friend, Lou Baker, has decided to open his own golf supply company. Lou has come to you for advice on IT infrastructures, especially Web services. Lou has heard of Web services, but he is not sure what they are and how he can use them to help get his business started the right way. Explain Web services to Lou along with an explanation of how Lou can use them to help start his business.

6. A fellow student is trying to write a paper on third-party vendors for IT infrastructure components. Throughout this chapter we have discussed several different third-party vendors including ASPs, collocation facilities, and server farms. Explain each one of these components to your fellow student along with a "real-world" example of each.

7. IT infrastructures should support the creation of flexible and scalable systems that can quickly adapt to support new business requirements. What would be an example of an IT infrastructure that is inflexible and not scalable and a barrier to supporting a changing business? What is an example of an IT infrastructure that is flexible and scalable and supports expanding a business?

8. What is a client/server network? Does your school have a client/server network? How does your school's client/server network increase student productivity? How does your school's client/server network decrease student productivity?

→ Living Life on the Internet

The personal computer is quickly becoming a household necessity as much as a stove or a refrigerator. The primary reason the personal computer has become such an important part of our lives is the Internet. There are literally thousands of ways people use the Internet to perform tasks. Many great Web sites are available, and all of them can help you accomplish things such as finding movie times, cooking a delicious meal, or seeking medical advice.

In this section we'll provide you with a few key Web sites you can use to help you live your life, and you can find many more sites on the Web site that supports this text at www.mhhe.com/haag.

ONLINE MAGAZINES

Each year people spend an incredible amount of money buying magazines. Many of these magazines are received through the mail and are never read. These end up in a giant pile—a giant recycling pile. The following is a list of a few of the many hundreds of magazines available on the Internet:

- *National Geographic*—www.nationalgeographic.com
- *Rolling Stone*—www.rollingstone.com
- *Sports Illustrated*—sportsillustrated.cnn.com
- *Cosmopolitan*—http://magazines.ivillage.com/cosmopolitan
- *Newsweek*—www.newsweek.com
- *PC Magazine*—www.pcmagazine.com
- *TV Guide*—www.tvguide.com
- *Popular Mechanics*—www.popularmechanics.com

Connect to a few of these magazines and try answering the following questions.

A. Does the Web site contain the most recent magazine version?

B. Is it easy to view past issues or search for articles on a particular topic?

C. Can you find three additional magazines you enjoy that are not listed above?

D. Are there any additional features in the online version of the magazine that are not available in the paper version?

E. Do you enjoy reading the magazine online better than reading a paper magazine? Why?

ONLINE MOVIE LISTINGS AND REVIEWS

Your time is incredibly valuable and so is your money. Wasting time and money on a bad movie happens to us all, but there is a way to eliminate this problem, the Internet.

The Internet has a wealth of information regarding movies including theater locations, movie times, and movie ratings and reviews. Spending a few minutes on the Internet researching the movie you want to see or browsing movie lists will save you time and money. You can check out detailed movie reviews at the Movie Review Query Engine Web site, www.mrqe.com. If you want a quick overview of a movie from a wide variety of critics, visit Check The Grid, www.checkthegrid.com. If you are interested in what movies are coming out over the next few month, try the Coming Attractions Web site, corona.bc.ca/films/main.html. You can search for movie times at your local theaters by visiting the Moviefone Web site, www.moviefone.com. Lastly, you must visit the Internet Movie Database, www.imdb.com, for tons of information on any movie ever made.

A. Can you find the movies that are currently playing at a theater near you?

B. Try to research a classic movie such as *Grease* or *Animal House* to find out the movie's rating and the year it was released.

C. Try to locate three new movies that are coming out over the next year.

D. Log in to the Internet Movie Database and search for all the movies made by your favorite actor or actress. Were any movies listed that you have not seen?

E. Log in to the Internet Movie Database and try to research the top 10 movies of all time.

COOKING FROM THE INTERNET

There are hundreds of cooking Web sites that provide recipes, detailed cooking instructions, and nutritional information. The first site you should visit is the Nutrition Analysis Tool (NAT) Web site, www.nat.uiuc.edu. NAT analyzes the foods you eat for various different nutrients and gives you recommendations on the types of food that are missing from your diet. Next, visit www.cooking.com for information on everything from cookbooks and cookware to recipes and cooking tips. For those of you interested in healthy meals try www.cookinglight.com, and those of you interested in gourmet cooking try www.goodcooking.com.

A. Try to find a recipe for barbequed chicken and mashed potatoes on one of the above Web sites.

B. Try logging into the Nutritional Analysis Tool and find out the nutritional value of your last meal.

C. Try to find a Web site that will help you plan a menu for a dinner party of six people.

D. Log in to the gourmet Web site and see how many different recipes you can find for your favorite food.

E. Log in to the cooking light Web site and find a few tips on how you can decrease cholesterol in your diet.

HIGHLY USEFUL MISCELLANEOUS SITES

There are so many helpful Web sites available that it's impossible to share them all with you. We did, however, want to point you in the direction of a few key sites that can help you as you make choices in your everyday life.

- Ever need to find out the exact time? Try the official U.S. time site at www.time.gov.
- If you need to find out the weather forecast quickly try weather.yahoo.com.
- You can also find the full text of more than 16,000 books online for free at digital.library.upenn.edu/books/.
- You can visit an online museum in Paris, France, at www.oir.ucf.edu/wm/.
- If you are sick and wondering if you should visit the doctor, try to seek advice at the world-famous mayo clinic, www.mayoclinic.com.
- A great site that can help you purchase or trade in a car is *Kelley's Blue Book* Web site, www.kbb.com.

A. Log in to the Mayo clinic and research remedies for the common cold.

B. Log in to *Kelley's Blue Book* Web site and determine the current value of your car or a car you would like to purchase.

C. Log in to the online museum in Paris and view the most current art exhibit.

D. We have listed a few helpful Web sites for living your life on the Internet. Try to find three additional Web sites that you and your classmates will find useful.

EXTENDED LEARNING MODULE G

OBJECT-ORIENTED TECHNOLOGIES

Student Learning Outcomes

1. EXPLAIN THE PRIMARY DIFFERENCE BETWEEN THE TRADITIONAL TECHNOLOGY APPROACH AND THE OBJECT-ORIENTED TECHNOLOGY APPROACH.

2. LIST AND DESCRIBE THE FIVE PRIMARY OBJECT-ORIENTED CONCEPTS.

3. EXPLAIN HOW CLASSES AND OBJECTS ARE RELATED.

4. DESCRIBE THE THREE FUNDAMENTAL PRINCIPLES OF OBJECT-ORIENTED TECHNOLOGIES.

5. LIST AND DESCRIBE TWO TYPES OF OBJECT-ORIENTED TECHNOLOGIES.

Taking Advantage of the CD

The explosion of object-oriented technologies is radically changing the way businesses view information and develop information systems. Object-oriented technologies are everywhere in the business world today. It's difficult to find a business or IT department that isn't using object-oriented concepts and technologies. Every single Fortune 500 company is using some type of object-oriented technology. System developers everywhere are quickly learning how to write software in object-oriented programming languages, create databases using object-oriented database management systems, and design new systems using object-oriented analysis and design techniques. The race to learn and understand object-oriented concepts began many years ago and is still going strong.

Extended Learning Module G, found on the CD that accompanies this text, provides an explanation of object-oriented technologies. This module is the same as the modules in your text—it includes Team Work and On Your Own projects and end-of-module Assignments and Exercises. The best part of this module is that it explains object-oriented concepts and terms in an easy and understandable way.

One of the primary goals of this module is to introduce you to the object-oriented approach for developing information systems. By taking a look at the traditional technology approach for developing systems you'll quickly understand the advantages you can gain by using an object-oriented approach. The **object-oriented (OO) approach** combines information and procedures into a single view. This statement probably seems a bit confusing but, after reading this module, it will become crystal clear. Just remember the key to understanding the object-oriented approach is to recognize that combining information and procedures is quite different from the traditional technology approach in which information is separated from procedures. Some of the other important object-oriented concepts you'll be introduced to include:

- The **traditional technology approach,** which has two primary views of any system—information and procedures—and it keeps these two views separate and distinct at all times.
- The five primary concepts of object-oriented technologies including:
  1. Information as key characteristics stored within a system.
  2. A **procedure** that manipulates or changes information.
  3. A **class** that contains information and procedures and acts as a template to create objects (instances of a class).
  4. An **object** which is an instance of a class.
  5. **Messages** that allow objects to communicate with each other.

- The three fundamental principles of object-oriented technologies including inheritance, encapsulation, and polymorphism.
- Several real-world object-oriented examples.
- A detailed business case example, Ice Blue Snowboards, Inc., in which you can apply your object-oriented knowledge.
- Three types of object-oriented technologies including object-oriented programming languages, object-oriented databases, and object-oriented technologies and client/server environments.

Be sure to take advantage of this module on your CD. You'll be taking a giant leap towards understanding object-oriented concepts. You might already be familiar with a few of the key concepts related to object-oriented technologies—information, procedures, classes, objects, or messages. If you're unfamiliar with these concepts there's no need to worry, because you'll gain a solid understanding of each one of these important concepts in this module.

CHAPTER EIGHT OUTLINE

STUDENT LEARNING OUTCOMES

1. Define ethics and describe the two factors that affect how you make a decision concerning an ethical issue.

2. Define and describe intellectual property, copyright, Fair Use Doctrine, and pirated and counterfeit software.

3. Define privacy and describe the ways in which it can be threatened.

4. Describe the two ways that information is valuable to business.

5. Describe the ways in which information on your computer or network is vulnerable.

6. Define risk management and risk assessment and describe the seven security measures that companies can take to protect their information.

WEB SUPPORT

www.mhhe.com/haag

- Air travel
- Rental cars
- Lodging
- One-stop travel sites
- Security
- Privacy

CHAPTER EIGHT

Protecting People and Information
Threats and Safeguards

OPENING CASE STUDY:
THEY KNOW ABOUT 96 PERCENT
OF AMERICAN HOUSEHOLDS

There's a company in Little Rock, Arkansas, called Acxiom, that handles consumer information, mainly for marketing purposes. That is to say that Acxiom stores and analyzes information, both its own and its clients'. Acxiom gets the information it sells from many sources, including the three major credit bureaus (TransUnion, Equifax Inc., and Experian Inc.). Nine of the country's 10 largest credit-card issuers are clients along with many other high profile financial companies in the banking and insurance industries. Forty percent of Acxiom's revenue comes from banking alone.

The company's inventory includes 20 billion records on consumers that include names, addresses, Social Security numbers, and public-record information. In fact, Acxiom has a database with information on about 110 million Americans, or 96 percent of U.S. households. The company categorizes consumers into one of 70 lifestyle clusters that include such groups as "Rolling Stones," "Single City Struggles," and "Timeless Elders." In any given year, about 33 percent of the people in the database move from one cluster to another when they change their lives in some significant way, as when they get married, have children, or retire.

Acxiom was one of the first companies to use grid-based computing ". . . enabling data analysis, modeling and applications at previously unachievable speed—and with a lowered cost," according to Charles Morgan, Chairman and CEO of Acxiom. With so much information belonging to so many clients, it made sense to have a very scalable and flexible system.

To help clients react quickly to changing market conditions, Acxiom offers hundreds of lists. One of these is a daily updated "pre-movers file" which lists people who are about to change residences. Another list is of people who use credit cards, and the list is sorted in order of frequency of use. A further list is sorted according to the square footage of consumers' homes. This type of information helps companies selling goods and services to target their customers and develop solid marketing strategies.

For example, Capital One Financial Corporation, a financial services company based in Virginia, spent $290 million (about 14 percent of its revenue) on marketing for the last quarter of 2003. The company sends out about 1 billion pieces of mail every year that largely consist of advertising intended to entice consumers to sign up for credit cards. Acxiom's information and analysis help Capital One send credit card solicitations only to those who are likely to want another credit card.

Another service that Acxiom provides is the merging of huge databases. The merger of Bank One and J. P. Morgan is a case in point. Both companies had huge, independent databases, and merging such mountains of information is Acxiom's specialty. First the information must be cleaned (called "data hygiene" in the industry), that is, duplicate records must be identified and combined. Acxiom also adds records from its own database to those of its clients, complementing and completing the clients' customer information.

To support these information services, Acxiom has thousands of servers and storage units. Some clients request that their information be kept separate, and so Acxiom supplies a locked room for that purpose. Another client company wants its information stored underground and far away from Acxiom's main site and, again, Acxiom fills the need.[1,2,3,4]

Introduction

As you've already learned, the three components of an IT system are people, information, and information technology. Most of what you've seen in previous chapters has dealt with IT and how it stores and processes information. In this chapter we're going to concentrate on information—its use, ownership, role, and protection. The best environment for handling information is one that has stability without stagnation and change without chaos.

To handle information in a responsible way (see Figure 8.1) you must understand

- The importance of ethics in the ownership and use of information.
- The importance to people of personal privacy and the ways in which it can be compromised.
- The value of information to an organization.
- Threats to information and how to protect against them (security).

The most important part of any IT system consists of the people who use it and are affected by it. How people treat each other has always been important, but in this information-based and digital age, with huge computing power at our fingertips, we can affect more people's lives in more ways than ever before. How we act toward each other, and this includes how we view and handle information, is largely determined by our ethics.

You don't have to look far to see examples of computer use that is questionable from an ethical viewpoint. For example,

- People copy, use, and distribute software they have no right to.
- Employees search organizational databases for information on celebrities and friends.
- Organizations collect, buy, and use information and don't check the validity or accuracy of that information.
- People create and spread viruses that cause trouble for those using and maintaining IT systems.
- Information system developers put systems on the market before they're completely tested. A few years ago, the developers of an incubator thermostat control program didn't test it fully, and two infants died as a result.[5]
- People break into computer systems and steal passwords, information, and proprietary information.
- Employees destroy or steal proprietary schematics, sketches, customer lists, and reports from their employers.
- People snoop on each other and read each other's e-mail and other private documents.

Figure 8.1

Chapter Overview

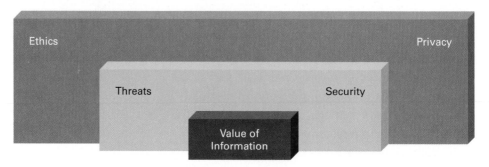

Ethics

Ethical people have integrity. They're people who are just as careful of the rights of others as they are of their own rights. They have a strong sense of what's fair and right and what isn't. But even the most ethical people sometimes face difficult choices.

Ethics are the principles and standards that guide our behavior toward other people. Acting ethically means behaving in a principled fashion and treating other people with respect and dignity. It's simple to say, but not so simple to do since some situations are complex or ambiguous. The important role of ethics in our lives has long been recognized. As far back as 44 B.C., Cicero said that ethics are indispensable to anyone who wants to have a good career. Having said that, Cicero, along with some of the greatest minds over the centuries, struggled with what the rules of ethics should be.

Our ethics are rooted in our history, culture, and religion, and our sense of ethics may shift over time. In this electronic age there's a new dimension in the ethics debate—the amount of personal information that we can collect and store, and the speed with which we can access and process that information.

TWO FACTORS THAT DETERMINE HOW YOU DECIDE ETHICAL ISSUES

How you collect, store, access, and use information depends to a large extent on your sense of ethics—what you perceive as right and wrong. Two factors affect how you make your decision when you're faced with an ethical dilemma. The first is your basic ethical structure, which you developed as you grew up. The second is the set of practical circumstances involved in the decision that you're trying to make, that is, all the shades of gray in what are rarely black or white decisions.

Your ethical structure and the ethical challenges you'll face exist at several levels (see Figure 8.2).[6] At the outside level are things that most people wouldn't consider bad, such as taking a couple of paper clips or sending an occasional personal e-mail on company time. Do these things really matter? At the middle level are more significant ethical challenges. One example might be accessing personnel records for personal reasons.

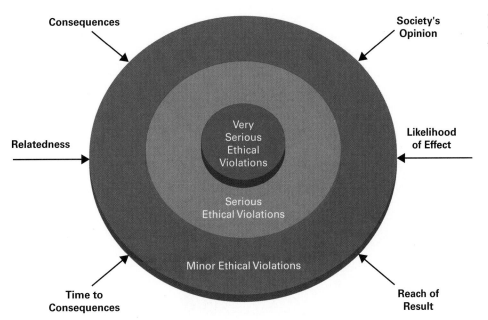

Figure 8.2

Your Ethical Structure

Could there ever be a personal reason so compelling that you would not feel ethical discomfort doing this? Reading someone else's e-mail might be another middle-level example. At the innermost ethical level are ethical violations that you'd surely consider very serious, such as embezzling funds or selling company records to a competitor. And yet, over time, your ethical structure can change so that even such acts as these could seem more or less acceptable. For example, if everyone around you is accessing confidential records for their own purposes, in time you might come to think such an act is no big deal. And this might spell big trouble for you.

It would be nice if every decision were crystal clear, and considerations such as these needn't be taken into account, but ethical decisions are seldom so easy. The practical circumstances surrounding your decisions always influence you in an ethical dilemma.[7]

1. *Consequences.* How much or how little benefit or harm will come from a particular decision?
2. *Society's opinion.* What is your perception of what society really thinks of your intended action?
3. *Likelihood of effect.* What is the probability of the harm or benefit that will occur if you take the action?
4. *Time to consequences.* How long will it take for the benefit or harm to take effect?
5. *Relatedness.* How much do you identify with the person or persons who will receive the benefit or suffer the harm?
6. *Reach of result.* How many people will be affected by your action?

Hopefully, your basic sense of right and wrong will steer you in the right direction. But no matter what your sense of ethics is or how strong it is, practical aspects of the situation may affect you as you make your decision—perhaps unduly, perhaps quite justifiably. Ethical dilemmas usually arise, not out of simple situations, but from a clash between competing goals, responsibilities, and loyalties. Ethical decisions are complex judgments that balance rewards for yourself and others against responsibilities to yourself and others. Inevitably, your decision process is influenced by uncertainty about the magnitude of the outcome, by your estimate of the importance of the situation, sometimes by your perception of conflicting "right reactions," and more than one socially acceptable "correct" decision.

GUIDELINES FOR ETHICAL COMPUTER SYSTEM USE

It's sometimes difficult to decide what to do since there are few hard and fast rules. Knowing the law doesn't always help because what's legal is not always ethical and vice versa. In Figure 8.3 you see the four quadrants of ethical and legal behavior. You're safe if you can manage to stay in quadrant I.

Figure 8.3

Acting Ethically and Acting Legally Are Not Necessarily the Same Thing[8]

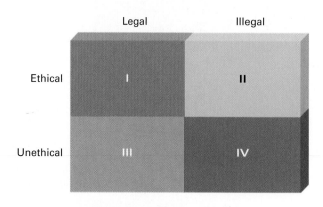

	Legal	Illegal
Ethical	I	II
Unethical	III	IV

So, what do you do then if you're faced with a choice that is not perfectly ethically clear? If you think you are in an ethical quandary, you probably are. If you find you're giving the situation a whole lot of thought, the situation very likely deserves it. You may wish to talk to a friend, a teacher, a supervisor, or a mentor. Know that we're all faced with such dilemmas, they are real, and they do have consequences. And there *is* a line that you shouldn't cross, and most of us know where it is.

Let's look at an example. Say your organization is developing a decision support system (DSS) to help formulate treatments for an infectious disease. Other companies in the industry are working on similar projects. The first system on the market will most likely reap huge profits. You may know that your DSS doesn't yet work properly; it's good, but not yet totally reliable. But you're feeling extreme pressure from your boss to get the system onto the market immediately. You're worried about the harm that might come to a patient because of your DSS; but, on the other hand, it does work well most of the time. You have a family to support and student loans to repay. And you like being employed. Can you hold out and get more information on the system's reliability? What do you do? Where can you get help?

You can certainly ask questions about what you're being asked to do—and you should. Sometimes legitimate actions look unethical, but if you find out more about the situation, you might find that it's perfectly all right. For instance, in the case mentioned, management may be planning to leave out the dubious part of the system or to warn customers of the problem. But you must keep digging until you're very sure and comfortable with what you're being asked to do.

If you really believe that what you're expected to do is wrong, you'll have to say so to your boss and be prepared to quit if you have to. But first, explain what you think is so bad and couch it in terms of the company's future and reputation if at all possible.[9] Be sure to think also of your own future and reputation (many former Enron employees wish they had taken a firmer stand when they had the chance).

Your company may well have an office or person (sometimes called an ombudsman) whose job it is to give advice on work-related ethical dilemmas. Failing that, you could look up your company's code of ethics. If you can't find that or don't think it's taken seriously in your place of work, you can check your profession's ethical code. The ACM (Association for Computing Machinery), for example, has a code of ethics for IT employees. Or you can go to the Computer Ethics Institute Web site for its guidelines ("Ten Commandments") at www.cspr.org/program/ethics.htm.

INTELLECTUAL PROPERTY

An ethical issue you will almost certainly encounter is one related to the use or copying of proprietary software. Software is a type of intellectual property. ***Intellectual property*** is intangible creative work that is embodied in physical form.[10] Music, novels, paintings, and sculptures are all examples of intellectual property. So also are your company's product sketches and schematics and other proprietary documents. These documents along with music, novels, and so on are worth much more than the physical form in which they are delivered. For example, a single U2 song is worth far more than the CD on which it's purchased. The song is also an example of intellectual property that is covered by copyright law.

Copyright law protects the authorship of literary and dramatic works, musical and theatrical compositions, and works of art. ***Copyright*** is the legal protection afforded an expression of an idea, such as a song, video game, and some types of proprietary documents. Having a copyright means that no one can use your song or video game without your permission. As a form of intellectual property, software is usually protected by

WHAT PRICE AN IDEA?

A patent protects a form of intellectual property. A patent applies to the implementation of an idea, such as how to construct an ergonomic mouse. IBM, the computer industry's giant, has for nine years filed more patents with the U.S. Patent and Trademark Office than any other company. In 2001, IBM received 3,454 patents. That's almost 10 new patents *every* day. IBM has always been proud of its patent record, and it certainly gives stockholders and the public in general the impression that the company is working hard and is producing future technology. However, good press is not the only reason IBM files so many patent applications. There are many other reasons—1.5 billion of them, in fact. That's the number of dollars that IBM got from licensing income in 2001 alone, money the company put back into research and development. Since it's very hard to tell which new technology will ultimately be successful, IBM patents everything, and then licenses out those ideas that other companies want to use.

IBM isn't the only technology company to take patents seriously. Also busy in the technology-patent-generating race are Hewlett-Packard, Lucent Technologies, NEC, and Microsoft. Many other industries are realizing great return on the licensing of patents, too. For example,

- Bayer AG, a German drug company, clears profits of 78 percent after expenses on its intellectual property licensing fees.
- Du Pont revenues from intellectual property were $100 million in 1996 and grew to $450 million in 2001.
- Eastman Kodak even created a separate company, Eastman Chemical's Global Technology Ventures (GTV) to extract value from the company's intellectual assets. Since 1999, the company has made 20 deals worth more than $50 million with a further $100 million in net present value of future earnings.[11,12]

copyright law, although sometimes it falls under patent law, which protects an idea, such as the design of a sewing machine or an industrial pump valve.

Copyright law doesn't forbid the use of intellectual property completely. It has some notable exceptions. For example, a TV program could show a video game you created without your permission. This would be an example of the use of copyrighted material for the creation of new material, i.e., the TV program. And that's legal; it falls under the Fair Use Doctrine. The *Fair Use Doctrine* says that you may use copyrighted material in certain situations, for example, in the creation of new work or, within certain limits, for teaching purposes. One of those limits is on the amount of the copyrighted material you may use.

Generally, the determining factor in legal decisions on copyright disputes is whether the copyright holder has been or is likely to be denied income because of the infringement. Courts will consider factors such as how much of the work was used and how, and when and on what basis the decision was made to use it.

Remember that copyright infringement is *illegal*. That means it's against the law, outside of a fair use situation, to simply copy a copyrighted picture, text, or anything else without permission, whether the copyrighted material is on the Internet or not. In particular, it's illegal to copy copyrighted software. But there's one exception to that rule: In the United States, you may always make one copy of copyrighted software to keep for backup purposes. When you buy copyrighted software, what you're paying for is the right to use it—and that's all.

How many more copies you may make depends on the copyright agreement that comes with the software package. Some software companies state emphatically that you may not even put the software on a second computer, even if they're both yours and no one else uses either one. Other companies are less restrictive, and agree to let you put a copy of software on multiple machines—as long as only one person is using that software package at any given time. In this instance, the company considers software to be like a book in that you can have it in different places and you can loan it out, but only one person at a time may use it.

If you copy copyrighted software and give it to another person or persons, you're pirating the software. ***Pirated software*** is the unauthorized use, duplication, distribution, or sale of copyrighted software.[13] Software piracy costs businesses an estimated $12 billion a year in lost revenue. Microsoft gets more than 25,000 reports of software piracy every year, and the company reportedly follows up on all of them. Countries that experience the greatest losses are (in rank order) the United States, Japan, the United Kingdom, Germany, China, France, Canada, Italy, Brazil, and the Netherlands. One in four business applications in the United States is thought to be pirated.[14] In some parts of the world, more than 90 percent of business software is pirated. The Software and Information Industry Association (SIIA) and the Business Software Alliance (BSA) say that pirated software means lost jobs, wages, and tax revenues, and is a potential barrier to success for software start-ups around the globe.

With the crackdown by software manufacturers and the growing awareness of corporations, the amount of illegally copied software is actually declining in businesses. But a new threat is emerging in the form of counterfeit software. ***Counterfeit software*** is software that is manufactured to look like the real thing and sold as such. Counterfeit software is being sold by sophisticated crime organizations, and sometimes the counterfeit is so good that the software even includes a valid certificate of authenticity.[15] The results of counterfeit software are greater than just lost revenue, which in itself is considerable. Many resellers unwittingly buy counterfeit software from distributors and then find that they've sold buggy or infected software to their customers. The legitimate manufacturers have to deal with irate customers who believe that their software and its problems came directly from the software company. It's a public relations nightmare.

You should especially beware when buying software from the Internet. The BSA estimates that there are close to 950,000 Internet sites selling software illegally.[16] If you buy from a shady site, you might never receive your software at all. Or, you might get counterfeit software that has a virus. So, you need to be careful.

Privacy

Privacy is the right to be left alone when you want to be, to have control over your own personal possessions, and not to be observed without your consent. It's the right to be free of unwanted intrusion into your private life. Privacy has several dimensions. Psychologically, it's a need for personal space. All of us, to a greater or lesser extent, need to feel in control of our most personal possessions, and personal information belongs on that list. Legally, privacy is necessary for self-protection.[17] If you put the key to your house in a special hiding place in your yard, you want to keep that information private. This information could be abused and cause you grief. In this section, we'll examine some specific areas of privacy: individuals snooping on each other; employers' collection of information about employees; businesses' collection of information about consumers; government collection of personal information; and the issue of privacy in international trade.

TRACE THE ROUTE OF YOUR JOURNEY TO A WEB SITE

When you send e-mail or visit a Web site, your request for service goes through lots of computers after your own. First, it goes from your computer to the server that's connecting you to the Internet. It may even move between computers within your school or service provider.

The **tracert** function in DOS (which stands for Disk Operating System, the operating system that we used before Windows) allows you to see that journey. To get to DOS, you have to go to the **Command Prompt** option in Windows.

Click on the **Start** button

Click on **All Programs**

Click on **Accessories**

Click on **Command Prompt**

You'll get a DOS screen window and the first thing you'll see is a note about the version of Windows you're using and a declaration of Microsoft's copyright. Next comes the C:\ prompt with the name of the folder you're currently in. It will look something like this (regular text—not the bold):

Microsoft Windows XP [Version 5.1.2600]

<C> Copyright 1985-2001 Microsoft Corp

C:\Documents and Settings\Maeve>**tracert www.pittstate.edu**

DOS is a command-driven user interface—there's no click-and-point capability—so you have to type in commands. At the last greater-than symbol (>) type in the word **tracert** and the address of a Web site (see the boldface in the example above).

You'll get a listing (up to 30 hops) of the computers that your message went through to get to its destination. You'll see the number of the hop (1,2,3, etc.), the time in milliseconds it took to get there, and the address of each computer it encountered on the way along with the computer's IP address (digits grouped in 4 sets consisting of 1 to 3 digits each—example: 192.168.1.50). When you're finished close the window as always or type **exit** at the C:\ prompt.

Try this for your own school and two other Web site addresses. To print out your results, capture the screen with the **Print Screen** key on your keyboard (usually on the top right-hand side), then paste it into Word or Paint, and print from there.

PRIVACY AND OTHER INDIVIDUALS

Other individuals, like family members, associates, fellow employees, and hackers, could be electronically invading your privacy. Their motives might be simple curiosity, an attempt to get your password, or to access something they have no right to. Obviously, there are situations in which you're well within your rights, and would be well advised to see what's going on. Examples may be if you suspect that your child is in electronic contact with someone or something undesirable, or if you think that someone is using your computer without permission. Many Web sites are offering programs, collectively referred to as snoopware, to help people monitor what's happening on a computer.

For general snooping you can get key logger software and install it on the computer you want to monitor. *Key logger,* or *key trapper, software,* is a program that, when installed on a computer, records every keystroke and mouse click. It records all e-mail (whether you're using Eudora or Microsoft Outlook), instant messages, chat room exchanges, Web sites you visit, applications you run, and passwords you type in on that computer.

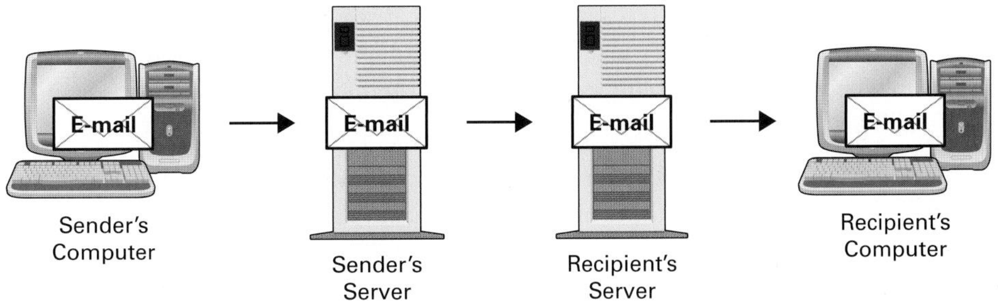

Figure 8.4

The E-Mail You Send Is Stored on Many Computers

Sender's Computer

Sender's Server

Recipient's Server

Recipient's Computer

Also available for monitoring computer use are screen capture programs that periodically record what's on the screen. (They get the information straight from the video card.) These programs don't trap every single screen, just whatever is on the screen when the capturing program activates. But they still give whoever is doing the monitoring a pretty good idea of what the computer user is up to. Other tools for monitoring include packet sniffers (that examine the information passing by) on switches, hubs, or routers (the devices on networks that connect computers to each other), and log analysis tools that keep track of logons, deletions, and so forth.

As you're probably already aware, e-mail is completely insecure. E-mail content might as well be written on a postcard for all the privacy it has. Not only that, but each e-mail you send results in at least three or four copies being stored on different computers (see Figure 8.4). It's stored first in the computer you're using. Second, it's stored by the e-mail server, the computer through which it gets onto the Internet. Third, it's stored on the recipient's computer, and may also be archived on the recipient's e-mail server.

IDENTITY THEFT

In 2001, the Federal Trade Commission (FTC) reported that more than 1 million people had been the victims of identity theft. By 2002, that number had tripled to 3 million, and by 2003, it had ballooned to 10 million. On average, this crime costs victims a total of about $5 billion and businesses about $48 million per year. Here are some examples:

- An 82-year-old woman in Fort Worth, Texas, discovered that her identity had been stolen when the woman using her name was involved in a four-car collision. For 18 months, she kept getting notices of lawsuits and overdue medical bills that were really meant for someone else. It took seven years for her to get her financial good name restored after the identity thief charged over $100,000 on her 12 fraudulently acquired credit cards.

- A 42-year-old retired Army captain in Rocky Hill, Connecticut, found that an identity thief had spent $260,000 buying goods and services that included two trucks, a Harley-Davidson motorcycle, and a time-share vacation home in South Carolina. The victim discovered his problem only when his retirement pay was garnished to pay the outstanding bills.

- In New York, members of a pickpocket ring forged the driver's licenses of their victims within hours of snatching the women's purses. If you steal someone's purse, your haul usually won't be more than $200, probably much less. On the other hand, if you steal the person's identity, you can net on average between $4,000 and $10,000.

- Another crime gang took out $8 million worth of second mortgages on victims' homes. It turned out the source of all the instances of identity theft came from a car dealership.

• The largest identity-theft scam to date in U.S. history was broken up by police in 2002 when they discovered that three men had downloaded credit reports using stolen passwords and sold them to criminals on the street for $60 each. Many millions of dollars were stolen from people in all 50 states.

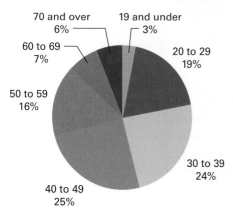

Identity Theft Complaints (by Age) Received by the FTC in 2002

70 and over 6%
19 and under 3%
60 to 69 7%
20 to 29 19%
50 to 59 16%
30 to 39 24%
40 to 49 25%

Figure 8.5

The FTC Had 140,763 Complaints in 2002 and 64 Percent of the Complainants Gave Their Ages

Identity theft is the forging of someone's identity for the purpose of fraud. The fraud is often financial fraud, to apply for and use credit cards in the victim's name or to apply for a loan. But it can also be simply to disguise the thief's own identity, particularly if the thief is hiding from law enforcement or is running some sort of scam. Figure 8.5 shows that about half of all identity theft victims are between the ages of 30 and 50.

A common way to steal identities online is called phishing. *Phishing* (also called *carding* or *brand spoofing*) is a technique to gain personal information for the purpose of identity theft, usually by means of fraudulent e-mail. One way this is done is to send out e-mail messages that look as though they came from legitimate businesses like AOL, MSN, eBay, PayPal, insurance companies, or online retailers like Amazon.com. The messages look genuine with official-looking formats and logos. These e-mails typically ask for verification of important information like passwords and account numbers. The reason given is often that this personal information is needed for accounting or auditing purposes. Since the e-mails look authentic, up to one in five recipients responds with the information, and subsequently becomes a victim of identity theft and other fraud.

Legitimate businesses hardly ever send out such e-mails. If you get such an e-mail, DON'T send any information without checking further. For example, you could call the company and ask about it. Another clue is bad grammar and misspellings. More than one typo in an official communication is a warning sign.

A second kind of phishing is to persuade people in an e-mail to click on a Web site included in the message, and provide personal information there. This is what happened on November 17, 2003, to customers of eBay's auction site. On that day, many eBay customers got notice by e-mail that their accounts had been compromised and they were asked to click on a Web site and reregister by providing their credit card number, ATM number, Social Security number, date of birth, and their mother's maiden name. eBay had not, of course, sent the e-mails.[18]

Usually there's something a bit off about the addresses of these kinds of Web addresses, so look carefully. For example, one from PayPal may arrive as PayPa1 with a "1" (one) instead of the letter "l." The letter "O" and zero can also be interchanged, and the longer the Web site address, the easier it is to fake.[19,20,21]

PRIVACY AND EMPLOYEES

Companies need information about their employees and customers to be effective in the marketplace. But people often object to having so many details about their lives available to others. If you're applying for a job, you'll most likely fill out a job application, but that's not the only information a potential employer can get about you. For a small fee, employers, or anyone else, can find out about your credit standing, your telephone usage, your insurance coverage, and many other interesting things. An employer can also get information on what you said on the Internet from companies who collect and collate chat room exchanges. And an employer can ask a job applicant to take drug and psychological tests, the results of which are the property of the company.

After you're hired, your employer can monitor where you go, what you do, what you say, and what you write in e-mails—at least during working hours. The American Man-

IDENTITY THEFT SHIELDS ILLEGAL ALIEN

Not all identity theft is used solely for financial fraud. An illegal alien assumed one of the many identities stolen in 2001 so that he could elude the Immigration and Naturalization Service and law enforcement. The thief had once been in the United States legally, but was deported in 1996 after being convicted on a charge of possession of marijuana. The identity he stole belonged to a minister who had been killed in the 9/11 disaster.

Sean Booker, 35, worked for Xerox servicing printers at March & McLennan, an insurance company that had its offices on the 93rd floor of the north tower of the World Trade Center. After the twin towers came crashing down, his wife, Sharon, was told that he was missing, presumed dead, but there was no body and no real proof that he was dead.

As if this weren't bad enough, eight months later, several letters arrived from lawyers in North Carolina offering their services to her husband who, they said, had been in a minor traffic accident in that state and had received a traffic ticket for failure to yield.

Sharon was very shocked and wondered if her husband were alive after all. She finally decided to call one of the lawyers to see what she could find out. The lawyer consulted the police, who said that the man to whom they had given a ticket was not the same person whose picture had been posted on the Internet with the other World Trade Center victims. The police in North Carolina followed up by investigating further and eventually found some information about the mystery man's children, which led them to the man's real name.[22]

---

agement Association says that in 2001, 63 percent of companies monitored employee Internet connections including about two-thirds of the 60 billion electronic messages sent by 40 million e-mail users.[23] One reason that companies monitor employees' e-mail is that they can be sued for what their employees send to each other and to people outside the company.

Chevron Corporation and Microsoft settled sexual harassment lawsuits for $2.2 million each because employees sent offensive e-mail to other employees and management didn't intervene. Other companies such as Dow Chemical Company, Xerox, the New York Times Company, and Edward Jones took preemptive action by firing people who sent or stored pornographic or violent e-mail messages.[24]

Another reason employers monitor their workers' use of IT resources is to avoid misuse of resources. Cyberslacking is a form of misuse of organizational resources, and includes visiting pornographic sites and news sites, chatting, gaming, stock trading, auction participation, shopping, checking sports scores, or anything else not related to your job. In May 2000, Victoria's Secret had an online fashion show at three o'clock in the afternoon on a weekday. About 2 million people watched the show, presumably many of them on their companies' computers. One employee watching the fashion show used as much bandwidth as it would take to download the entire *Encyclopedia Britannica*.[25] So, not only were the viewers wasting company time, but they were also slowing down the work of others.

About 70 percent of Web traffic occurs during work hours, and this is reason enough for companies to monitor what, and for how long, employees are surfing the Web. The FBI reports that 78 percent of surveyed companies indicated that employees had abused Internet privileges by downloading pornography, pirating software, or some other activity that wasn't work related. Also, 60 percent of employees said that they visit Web sites or surf for personal use at work. Again, various software packages are available to keep track of people's Web surfing. Some software actually blocks access to certain sites.

WHAT WOULD YOU DO?

Analyze the following situation. You have access to the sales and customer information in a flower shop. You discover that the boyfriend of a woman you know is sending roses to three other women on a regular basis. The woman you know is on the flower list, but she believes that she's the only woman in his romantic life. You really think you should tell the woman. Your dilemma is that you have a professional responsibility to keep the company's information private. However, you also believe that you have a responsibility to the woman. Do you tell her?

Are there factors that would change your decision? Each team member should individually consider the additional information below. Indicate whether any one or more of these factors would change your decision. Then form a consensus with your team.

Additional Facts	Yes	No	Why?
1. The woman is your sister.			
2. The man is your brother.			
3. The woman is about to give the man her life savings as a down payment on a house in the belief that they will soon be married.			
4. The woman is already married.			

Businesses have good reasons for seeking and storing personal information on employees. They

- Want to hire the best people possible and to avoid being sued for failing to adequately investigate the backgrounds of employees.
- Want to ensure that staff members are conducting themselves appropriately and not wasting or misusing company resources. Financial institutions are even required by law to monitor all communications including e-mail and telephone conversations.
- Can be held liable for the actions of employees.

MONITORING TECHNOLOGY Numerous vendors sell software products that scan e-mail, both incoming and outgoing. The software can look for specific words or phrases in the subject lines or in the body of the text. An e-mail-scanning program can sneak into your computer in Trojan-horse software. That is, it can hide in an innocent-looking e-mail or some other file or software.

Some companies use an approach less invasive than actually reading employees' e-mail. Their e-mail inspection programs just check for a certain level of e-mail to and from the same address. This indicates that there may be a problem, and the employee is informed of the situation and asked to remedy it. No intrusive supervisory snooping is necessary.[26]

An employer can track your keyboard and mouse activity with the type of key logger software that you read about in the previous section. An alternative that's sometimes harder to detect is a hardware key logger. A **hardware key logger** is a hardware device that captures keystrokes on their journey from the keyboard to the motherboard. These devices can be in the form of a connector on the system-unit end of the cable between the keyboard and the system unit. There's another type of hardware key logger that you can install into the keyboard. Both have enough memory to store about a year's worth of typing. These devices can't capture anything that's not typed, but they do capture every keystroke, including backspace, delete, insert, and all the others. To defeat them you'd have to copy the password (or whatever you want kept secret) and paste it into its new location. The key logger keeps a record of the keystrokes you use, if any, in your copy-and-paste operation, but not what you copied and pasted.

There is little sympathy in the legal system for the estimated 27 million employees whom the American Management Association says are under surveillance. Employers have the legal right to monitor the use of their resources and that includes the time they're paying you for. In contrast to your home, you have no expectation of privacy when using the company's resources.

The most recent federal bill that addressed electronic monitoring of employees is the Electronic Communications Privacy Act of 1986. Although, in general, it forbids the interception of wired or electronic communications, it has exceptions for both prior consent and business use.

Some state laws have addressed the issue of how far employers can go and what they can do to monitor employees. Connecticut has a law that took effect in 1999 that requires employers in the private sector to notify employees in writing of electronic monitoring. And Pennsylvania, a year earlier, permitted telephone marketers to listen in on calls for quality control purposes as long as at least one of the parties is aware of the action.[27]

PRIVACY AND CONSUMERS

Businesses face a dilemma.

- Customers want businesses to know who they are, but, at the same time, they want them to leave them alone.
- Customers want businesses to provide what they want, but, at the same time, they don't want businesses knowing too much about their habits and preferences.
- Customers want businesses to tell them about products and services they might like to have, but they don't want to be inundated with ads.

Like it or not, massive amounts of personal information are available to businesses from various sources. A relatively large Web site may get about 100 million hits per day, which means that the site gets about 200 bytes of information for each hit. That's about 20 gigabytes of information per day.[28] This level of information load has helped to make electronic customer relationship management (eCRM) systems one of the fastest-growing areas of software development. Part of managing customer relationships is personalization. Web sites that greet you by name and Amazon.com's famous recommendations that "People who bought this product also bought . . . " are examples of personalization, which is made possible by the Web site's knowledge about you.[29]

Apart from being able to collect its own information about you, a company can readily access consumer information elsewhere. Credit card companies sell information, as do the Census Bureau and mailing list companies. Web traffic tracking companies such as DoubleClick follow you (and other surfers) around the Web and then sell the information about where you went and for how long. DoubleClick can collect information about you over time and provide its customers with a highly refined profile on you. DoubleClick is also an intermediary for companies that want to advertise to Web surfers. When hired by a company wanting to sell something, DoubleClick identifies people who might be receptive and sends the ad to them as a banner or pop-up ad. Proponents of this practice claim that it's good for the surfers because they get targeted advertising and less unwanted advertising. You can judge for yourself how true this claim is. DoubleClick, at first, undertook to track consumers without attaching their identity to the information. Then, in 1999, DoubleClick changed its policy and announced that it would attach consumer names to personal information and e-mail addresses. However, in response to negative consumer reaction, DoubleClick withdrew its proposed change. Interestingly, DoubleClick didn't state it would never resume the abandoned policy, but agreed only to wait until standards for such activity are in place.[30]

COOKIES   The basic tool of consumer Web monitoring is the cookie. A *cookie* is a small file that contains information about you and your Web activities, which a Web site you visit places on your computer. A cookie has many uses. For example, it's used to keep ID and password information so that you don't have to go through the whole verification process every time you log onto a Web site. It's also used to store the contents of electronic shopping carts, so that the next time you log on, the Web site will be able to see your wish list (which is stored on your computer in a cookie).

A cookie can also be used to track your Web activity. It can monitor and record what sites you visit, how long you stay there, what Web pages you visited, what site you came from and the next site you went to. This type of cookie is called a *unique cookie*. Some cookies are temporary and some stay on your computer indefinitely.

Third-party or *common cookies* are the ones that have many privacy advocates disturbed. These are different from the unique cookies that a Web site you visit puts onto your hard disk. A common cookie is one that started out as a unique cookie, but the original site sold access to it to a third party, like DoubleClick, that can then change the cookie so that the third party can track the surfer's activity across many sites. The third party collects information about surfers without names or other identifiable personal information. They usually collect an IP address, which they then link to a random identifying ID so that the surfer can be identified at other sites. Surveys have shown that the vast majority of people (91 percent) don't like the idea of unknown companies gathering information about them that they have provided to sites with whom they chose to interact.[31]

You have two options if you want to block cookies. First, you can set your browser to accept or reject all cookies. Or you can get it to warn you when a site wants to put a cookie on your computer. Second, you can get cookie management software with additional options that are not available on your browser. For example, CookieCop 2, from *PC Magazine,* will let you accept or reject cookies on a per-site basis. It also allows you to replace banner ads with the image of your choice and to block ads for sites you find offensive. With this or other cookie-stopper software, you can disable pop-up windows, and stipulate that certain cookies can stay on your hard drive for the duration of one session only.

SPAM   *Spam* is unsolicited e-mail (electronic junk mail) from businesses that advertise goods and services. Often spam mass mailings advertise pornography, get-rich-quick schemes, and miracle cures. If you haven't been inundated with spam, you're either very lucky or you don't use the Internet much. Spam has become a severe irritant to consumers and a costly matter for businesses, who must sort through hundreds of e-mail messages every day deleting spam and hoping that they don't delete e-mail messages that are actually legitimate customer orders.

You can get spam filters to block out spam, but spammers are clever about including nonprinting characters in their subject lines and addresses that fool the filters into letting them pass. For example, say a spammer wanted to send out a message about a new weight loss drug called *Off.* The spammer would alter the spelling of the word or add in-

SPAM BUSTER

Mary Youngblood is a spam buster at Earthlink, a nationwide Internet service provider (ISP). But she might as well be trying to get rid of ghosts since spammers are very elusive phantoms. Earthlink estimates that 40 percent of the e-mail it gets to pass on is spam; other providers, like America Online, estimate that spam is 70 to 80 percent.

One spammer Mary was trying to catch was the Buffalo spammer. The first thing that she noticed was that certain key words kept coming up in get-rich-quick schemes. She found that all these e-mails originated from one e-mail account, and so she shut down that account only to find that the same e-mail was being distributed under another name. Again she shut down the account and again it popped up from somewhere else. During the next year Mary and her team each spent about 10 hours a week trying to track down the originator of the e-mails, and they estimate that the spammer sent about 825 million spam e-mails using 343 stolen identities to sign up for e-mail accounts. He also taunted the investigators on his trail by phone and managed to avoid subpoena servers for three months.

This story highlights the problem of catching spammers. They are hard to find because they spoof every e-mail message, and spam sent from computers located overseas is almost impossible to trace. Software is also available to send spam out in batches small enough that the ISPs don't detect them. Spammers are usually not jailed even when they do get caught even though junk e-mail is illegal in most states.

Joseph Welborn, another spam buster with Earthlink, and also a lawyer, filed suit against multiple "John Doe" spammers and was able to get access to phone and mail drop addresses. This eventually led him to a spammer, whom he hired to distribute spams for a herbal stimulant, agreeing to pay $10 per sale the spam generated. The spammer claimed that he had sent out 10 million e-mails that generated 36 sales. And with that admission, Joseph was able to pursue the spammer under anti-spam statutes.[32]

visible HTML tags so that the subject line would be: O*F*F or O<i></i>F<u></u>F. The HTML tags <i> and <u> would normally italicize and underline text, respectively, and the </i> and </u> would undo the italicizing and bolding, but since there's no text in between the tags do nothing except evade the filter.

Experts estimate that almost two-thirds of e-mail traffic in 2003 was spam, costing organizations worldwide about $20 billion per year.[33] An individual spammer can send out 80 million or so spams per day. AOL and Microsoft say that their servers block a billion spam messages every day.[34] Many states have passed laws to regulate spam and the Federal Government passed an anti-spam law in 2003 called the CAN-Spam Act (see Figure 8.7 on page 367), which was widely criticized by anti-spam activists as legitimizing spam, since it set down rules for spamming rather than banning it altogether.

Most experts doubt that the CAN-Spam Act will hurt the spammers who are the source of most of the spam. They say that it will just cost legitimate businesses time and money since they have to maintain do-not-spam lists and follow the legal guidelines when sending out e-mails to customers. Since the bulk of spam comes from spammers who spoof (disguise) the origin of the e-mail, they can usually operate for a long time in defiance of the law. Irate spam trackers, some of whom have become cyber vigilantes, have gone so far as to "out" spammers and publicize information about them on the Web in an effort to stop them.

One trick that spammers use to collect addresses for spamming is to send out e-mail purporting to add you to a general do-not-spam list if you reply. In fact, what it does is add your e-mail address to the list of "live" ones.

Figure 8.6

Adware in a Free Version of Eudora, an E-Mail Application from Qualcomm

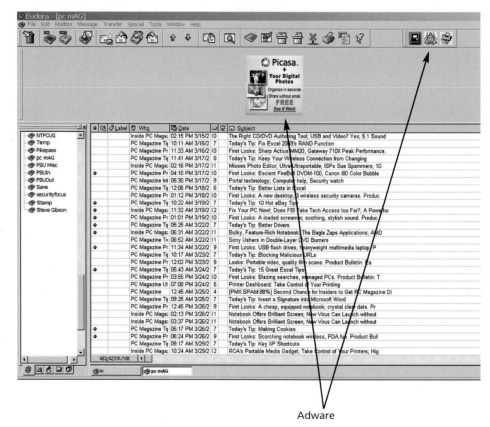

Adware

ADWARE AND SPYWARE   If you've downloaded a game or other software from the Web for free, you may have noticed that it came with banner ads. These ads are collectively known as adware. *Adware* is software to generate ads that installs itself on your computer when you download some other (usually free) program from the Web (see Figure 8.6). Adware is a type of *Trojan horse software,* meaning that it's software you don't want hidden inside software you do want. There's usually a disclaimer, buried somewhere in the multiple "I agree" screens, saying that the software includes this adware. At the bottom of several small-print screens you're asked to agree to the terms. Very few people read the whole agreement, and advertisers count on that. This sort of product is sometimes called *click-wrap* because it's like commercial software that has an agreement that you agree to by breaking the shrink-wrap.

Most people don't get upset about pure adware, since they feel it's worth having to view ads to get software for free. However, there's a more insidious extra that's often bundled with free downloadable software called spyware. *Spyware* (also called *sneakware* or *stealthware*) is software that comes hidden in free downloadable software and tracks your online movements, mines the information stored on your computer, or uses your computer's CPU and storage for some task you know nothing about. The first release of RealNetworks' RealJukebox sent information back to the company about what CDs the people who downloaded the software were playing on that computer. This information collection was going on when the customer wasn't even on the Web.[35]

Spyware is fast becoming the hidden cost of free software. Software such as Kazaa Media Desktop and Audiogalaxy, the successors to Napster for sharing music and other files online, include spyware. If you download free software and it has banner ads, it's quite possible that it has spyware, too. There's usually something in the "I agree" screens telling you about spyware, but it can be hard to find.[36] Spyware can stay on your computer long after you've uninstalled the original software.

You can detect various kinds of Trojan horse software with The Cleaner from www.moosoft.com. Also check out www.wilders.org for Trojan First Aid Kit (TFAK). The best-known spyware detection programs, also called stealthware blockers, are Ad-Aware (free from www.lavasoftUSA.com) and PestPatrol. The software scans your whole computer, identifies spyware programs, and offers to delete them. If you want to check out free software for spyware before you download it, go online to www.spychecker.com, a site that will tell you if particular free software includes adware or spyware.

Even without spyware, a Web site can tell a lot about its Web visitors from its Web log.[37] A **Web log** consists of one line of information for every visitor to a Web site and is usually stored on a Web server. At the very least, a Web log can provide a Web site company with a record of your clickstream.

A *clickstream* records information about you during a Web surfing session such as what Web sites you visited, how long you were there, what ads you looked at, and what you bought. If, as a consumer, you want to protect information about your surfing habits, you can use various software packages to do so. Apart from cookie management software you can avail yourself of *anonymous Web browsing (AWB)* services, which, in effect, hide your identity from the Web sites you visit. An example is Anonymizer at www.anonymizer.com. This site, and others like it, sends your Web browsing through its server and removes all identifying information. Some of the ABW services that are available include disabling pop-up promotions, defeating tracking programs, and erasing browsing history files. If you don't want to go through an outside server, you can download software to do the job. SurfSecret is a shareware antitracking package available from www.surfsecret.com.

As a final note on the subject, remember that even if a company promises, and fully intends, to keep its customer information protected, it may not be possible. When faced with a subpoena, the company will have to relinquish customer records. Furthermore, courts have ruled in bankruptcy cases that customer files are assets that may be sold to pay debts.

PRIVACY AND GOVERNMENT AGENCIES

Government agencies have about 2,000 databases containing personal information on individuals.[38] The various branches of government need information to administer entitlement programs, such as social security, welfare, student loans, law enforcement, and so on.

LAW ENFORCEMENT   You've often heard about someone being apprehended for a grievous crime after a routine traffic stop for something like a broken taillight. The arrest most likely ensued because the arresting officer ran a check on the license plate and driver's license. The officer probably checked the National Crime Information Center (NCIC) database and found the outstanding warrant there. This is how the culprits responsible for the Oklahoma City bombing were caught.

The NCIC database contains information on the criminal records of more than 20 million people. It also stores information on outstanding warrants, missing children, gang members, juvenile delinquents, stolen guns and cars, and so on. The NCIC has links to other government and private databases, and guardians of the law all over the country can access NCIC information. Sometimes they do so in response to something suspicious, and other times it's just routine. For example, Americans returning from outside the country are routinely checked through the NCIC when they come through customs.

Given the wealth of information and accessibility, it's not surprising that NCIC information has been abused. Several police departments have found that a significant number of employees illegally snooped for criminal records on people they knew or wanted to know.

The Federal Bureau of Investigation (FBI) has caused a stir lately because of its electronic surveillance methods. First there was Carnivore (a rather unfortunate name, which has since been changed to DCS-1000, which sounds much more innocuous). DCS-1000 connects hardware to an ISP to trap all e-mail sent to or received by the target of the investigation. It takes a court order to use DCS-1000, and, of course, the target is typically unaware of the surveillance. Intercepting communications is not new: The FBI put the first tap on a phone in 1885, just four years after the invention of the telephone.[39] DCS-1000, with a court order, traps all communications involving the individual named in the court order.

Because it can be hard to identify the data packets of one individual's e-mail amongst all the other Internet traffic, it's entirely possible that other people's e-mail might be scooped up in the net. And this is what happened in March 2000 when FBI agents were legally intercepting messages of a suspect, but someone else was caught in the trap. The information on the innocent party was obtained under the Freedom of Information Act. The FBI said the incident was an honest mistake and a result of miscommunication between it and the ISP.[40] But, this is the sort of mistake that scares people. Most people want law enforcement to be able to watch the bad guys—that's necessary for our collective safety. But the prospect of information being collected on law-abiding citizens who are minding their own business worries a lot of people.

In 2001, the FBI acknowledged an enhancement to DCS-1000 called Magic Lantern, which is key logger software. The FBI installs it by sending the target an innocent-looking Trojan-horse e-mail, which contains the key logger software. The hidden software then sends information back to the FBI periodically.[41]

Another federal agency, the National Security Agency (NSA), uses a system called Echelon that uses a global network of satellites and surveillance stations to trap phone, e-mail, and fax transmissions. The system then screens all this information looking for certain keywords and phrases and analyzes the messages that fit the search criteria.[42]

At the local level, the actions of the Tampa Police Department at the 2001 Super Bowl caused an outcry from privacy advocates. Police, with the agreement of the NFL, focused video cameras on the faces of tens of thousands of spectators as they entered the stadium. The images were sent to computers which, using facial recognition software, compared the images to a database of pictures of suspected criminals and terrorists. The police spokesperson said that the action was legal since it's permissible to take pictures of people in public places. That's true in so far as you have no expectation of privacy in a public place. Indeed surveillance of people has been going on for years without much protest in gambling casinos, Wal-Mart stores, and other businesses in the private sector. But the American Civil Liberties Union (ACLU) protested the surveillance of Super Bowl spectators on the grounds that it was surveillance by a government agency without court-ordered authorization.[43] The fact that the state was involved made it unacceptable to the ACLU.

OTHER FEDERAL AGENCIES   The Internal Revenue Service (IRS) gets income information from taxpayers. But the agency has access to other databases, too. For example, the IRS keeps track of vehicle registration information so that it can check up on people buying expensive cars and boats to make sure they're reporting an income level that corresponds to their purchases. The IRS can go to outside government databases as well. Verizon says that it gets 22,000 requests for phone records from the IRS, FBI, and other government agencies per year. It seldom informs the customer of the request.[44] America Online (AOL) has a special fax number reserved just for subpoenas.

"SHORTY" SHOT, STABBED, AND RAN OVER ME

"It was 'Shorty' that shot, stabbed, and ran over me," the victim told police. That was all he knew, but that was enough for CopLink, software used by the Tucson police to help them solve crimes. Having received this fragment of information at 10:00 A.M., they were able to have a suspect in custody by 5:00 that evening.

Described as a "Google for cops," CopLink, which costs about $60,000, searches through 911 records, arrest records, and police reports for names, license plate numbers, lists of stolen items, fingerprint records, and so on, to find links, suspects, and even leads.

For example, with an approximate height, weight, hair color and an "N" in the a license plate, police can quickly find possible suspects in an arson case. In the past, law enforcement had to search through each database separately and could find links only after many hours of studying all clues from different angles. Just going through paper-based fingerprint records can be a daunting task. Boston, for example, has 350,000 sets of fingerprints on file. It takes a long time to find anything in that many sets of paper records, but it takes only seconds with a computer.

CopLink employs neural network techniques to associate information and find patterns. The program also creates a detailed audit trail. There are two good reasons for having such a capability. First, officers are able to demonstrate the facts that led to the questioning or arrest of a suspect. Second, it allows the law enforcement agency to monitor the system for signs of abuse and to stop it quickly.

CopLink has six components: one to associate relationships, a second to search through all the information, a third to represent its findings graphically, a fourth to manage security, a fifth to allow the use of updated information and to share information with other agencies, and a sixth that allows officers to wirelessly connect to the system when in the field.[45,46]

The Census Bureau collects information on all the U.S. inhabitants it can find every 10 years. All citizens are requested to fill out a census form, and some people get a very long and detailed form requiring them to disclose a lot of personal information. The information that the Census Bureau collects is available to other government agencies and even to commercial enterprises. The bureau doesn't link the information to respondents' names but sells summarized information about geographic regions. Some of these regions are relatively small, however, consisting of fewer than 100 city blocks.

It's fairly safe to assume that anytime you have contact with any branch of government, information about you will be subsequently stored somewhere. For example, if you get a government-backed student loan, you provide personal information such as your name, address, income, parents' income, and so on. Some of the information nuggets attached to the loan would be the school you're attending, the bank dispersing the loan, your repayment schedule, and later, your repayment pattern.

PRIVACY AND INTERNATIONAL TRADE

If a customer in Europe buys books from Amazon.com's U.K. division, you'd probably be surprised to find out that Amazon, U.K., may not transfer the customer's credit card information to Amazon in the United States without being in compliance with "safe-harbor principles." *Safe-harbor principles* are a set of rules to which U.S. businesses that want to trade with the European Union (EU) must adhere. You probably wouldn't think twice about sending customer information, such as a name and address, via e-mail from one part of the company to another. But if you're in a subsidiary in an EU country and the recipient is in the United States you might have a problem.

The EU has very stringent rules about the collection of personal information and in 1998 implemented a Directive on the Protection of Personal Data. This means that the EU set privacy goals and to comply, each member country had to make laws, based on its own culture and customs, to achieve these goals. There are still differences in privacy laws among European countries, but in general, the rights granted to EU citizens include the consumer's right to

- Know the marketer's source of information.
- Check personally identifiable information for accuracy.
- Correct any incorrect information.
- Specify that information can't be transferred to a third party without the consumer's consent.
- Know the purpose for which the information is being collected.

If information can be linked to you—either directly or indirectly—it's personally identifiable information. The list of identifying tags includes names, ID numbers, and unique physical characteristics.[47]

The United States and the European Union began negotiations on the heels of the EU directive to create safe-harbor principles for U.S.-based companies to be able to transfer personal information out of European countries. The safe-harbor rules cover every industry and almost all types of personal information. After extensive negotiations, in June 2000, the United States became the first country outside the EU to be recognized as meeting information privacy requirements of EU states.[48] Without this agreement, disruption of the $350 billion in trade between the United States and Europe would have been a distinct possibility.

So for your company to be able to transfer personal information out of EU countries, you'd have to first register with the U.S. Department of Commerce and agree to adhere to the safe-harbor principles. Although participation is theoretically voluntary, if you transfer personal information without having registered, you're risking punitive action from the U.S. Federal Trade Commission as well as from the European country from which you transferred the information.[49] See Closing Case Study Two for more information on the European Directive on the Protection of Personal Data and the Safe Harbor Agreement.

LAWS ON PRIVACY

The United States doesn't have a comprehensive or consistent set of laws governing the use of information. However, some laws are in place. Recent legislation includes the Health Insurance Portability and Accountability Act (HIPAA) and the Financial Service Modernization Act. HIPAA, enacted in 1996, requires that the health care industry formulate and implement the first regulations to keep patient information confidential. The act seeks to

- Limit the release and use of your health information without your consent.
- Give you the right to access your medical records and find out who else has accessed them.
- Overhaul the circumstances under which researchers and others can review medical records.
- Release health information on a need-to-know basis only.
- Allow the disclosure of protected health information for business reasons as long as the recipient undertakes, in writing, to protect the information.

- **Privacy Act,** 1974, restricts what information the federal government can collect; allows people to access and correct information on themselves; requires procedures to protect the security of personal information; and forbids the disclosure of name-linked information without permission.
- **Family Education Rights and Privacy Act,** 1974, regulates access to personal education records by government agencies and other third parties and ensures the right of students to see their own records.
- **Cable Communications Act,** 1984, requires written or electronic consent from viewers before cable TV providers can release viewing choices or other personally identifiable information.
- **Electronic Communications Privacy Act,** 1986, allows the reading of communications by a firm and says that employees have no right to privacy when using their companies' computers.
- **Computer Fraud and Abuse Act,** 1986, prohibits unauthorized access to computers used for financial institutions, the United States government, or interstate and international trade.
- **Bork Bill** (officially known as the **Video Privacy Protection Act,** 1988) prohibits the use of video rental information on customers for any purpose other than that of making marketing goods and services directly to the customer.
- **Communications Assistance for Law Enforcement Act,** 1994, requires that telecommunications equipment be designed so that authorized government agents are able to intercept all wired and wireless communications being sent or received by any subscriber. The Act also requires that subscriber call-identifying information be transmitted to a government when and if required.
- **Freedom of Information Act,** 1967, 1975, 1994, and 1998, allows any person to examine government records unless it would cause an invasion of privacy. It was amended in 1974 to apply to the FBI, and again in 1994 to allow citizens to monitor government activities and information gathering, and once again in 1998 to access government information on the Internet.
- **Identity Theft and Assumption Deterrence Act,** 1998, strengthened the criminal laws governing identity theft, making it a federal crime to use or transfer identification belonging to another. It also established a central federal service for victims.
- **USA Patriot Act,** 2001 and 2003, allows law enforcement to get access to almost any information, including library records, video rentals, bookstore purchases, and business records when investigating any act of terrorism or hostile intelligence activities. In 2003 Patriot II broadened the original law.
- **Homeland Security Act,** 2002, provided new authority to government agencies to mine data on individuals and groups including e-mails and Web site visits; put limits on the information available under the Freedom of Information Act; and gave new powers to government agencies to declare national heath emergencies.
- **Sarbanes-Oxley Act,** 2002, sought to protect investors by improving the accuracy and reliability of corporate disclosures and requires companies to (1) implement extensive and detailed policies to prevent illegal activity within the company and (2) respond in a timely manner to investigate illegal activity. (You'll find more about the business implications of Sarbanes-Oxley in *Extended Learning Module H: Computer Crime and Forensics.*)
- **Fair and Accurate Credit Transactions Act,** 2003, included provisions for the prevention of identity theft including consumers' right to get a credit report free each year, requiring merchants to leave all but the last five digits of a credit card number off a receipt, and requiring lenders and credit agencies to take action even before a victim knows a crime has occurred when they notice any circumstances that might indicate identity theft.
- **CAN-Spam Act,** 2003, sought to regulate interstate commerce by imposing limitations and penalties on businesses sending unsolicited e-mail to consumers. The law forbids deceptive subject lines, headers, return addresses, etc., as well as harvesting e-mail addresses from Web sites. It requires businesses that send spam to maintain a do-not-spam list and to include a postal mailing address in the message.

Figure 8.7

Information-Related Laws

The Financial Services Modernization Act requires that financial institutions protect personal customer information and that they have customer permission before sharing such information with other businesses. However, the act contains a clause that allows the sharing of information for "legitimate business purposes." See Figure 8.7 for more information-related laws.

Information

In this section we'll consider the dual roles of information in an organization. Nothing else is as universal or as versatile as information. What else can you sell or lease to someone else—and simultaneously retain for yourself? This unique resource called "information" has two functions in an organization: as raw material and as capital (see Figure 8.8).

INFORMATION AS RAW MATERIAL

Raw materials are the components from which a product is made. For example, the raw materials for a chair might be wood, glue, and screws. But almost everything you buy has information as part of the product. If you doubt this, wander through a store and see how many products incorporate absolutely no information. Even bananas have stickers telling you something about them or their distributor. Of course, the amount of information varies. You get a lot more information if you buy a jet airplane than if you buy a cake mix. Sometimes it's the information that makes a product particularly valuable. Take the example of two identical pairs of sports shoes that were originally made by the same company but sold under different logos. It's very likely that the shoes with the more widely known or prestigious logo will sell for a higher price than those with the lesser logo. The more desirable logo doesn't increase the functional value of the shoes. They're the same shoes. But the information (in this case the logo) proclaims something to the world that the wearer wants to be associated with. For that statement, whatever it is, the customer is prepared to pay extra.

The most successful companies place the highest value on information. United Parcel Service (UPS) is an example. The company's IT budget is second only to its expenditures on aircraft. This is because UPS is selling not only a shipping service, but also information. You can connect to the UPS Web site and track your package. As UPS Chief Information Officer (CIO) Frank Ergbrick puts it, "A package without information has no value."[50]

General Motors doesn't just sell vehicles. Many GM cars feature an option called OnStar that combines a global positioning system (GPS), which identifies your position anywhere on earth, with networked sensors, a cell phone, and a link to customer support centers. With the OnStar system you can get directions to any destination and even receive advice on where to dine. OnStar also contributes to your safety. If the car's air bag inflates, the sensor sends a signal to the customer support center, which tries to contact you by phone. If there's no response, the support center uses the GPS component to locate your car, then alerts the emergency service nearest to you. The OnStar system can also help track your car if it's stolen. So a Cadillac is not just a car—it's an IT system on wheels.

INFORMATION AS CAPITAL

Capital is the asset you use to produce a product or service. Buildings, trucks, and machinery are examples of capital. For our chair manufacturer, the capital would be

Figure 8.8

Information as Raw Material and as Capital

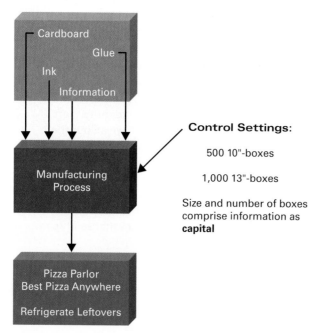

Control Settings:

500 10"-boxes

1,000 13"-boxes

Size and number of boxes comprise information as **capital**

Information as **raw material** becomes part of the product

the factory building, the saw, the glue dispenser, screw drivers, and so on. These items are not part of the chair, but they're necessary to build it. You incur a cost in acquiring capital, and you expect a return on your investment. Additionally, you can sell or lease capital assets.

You can think of information as capital. It's used by companies to provide products and services. Organizations need information to provide what their target market wants. They need information in the form of manufacturing schedules, sales reports, marketing plans, accounting reports, and so on.

Information capital is one of the most important and universal types of capital in an organization. Not every company has a building or a truck, but every single one has information. We cannot state the case too strongly; an organization cannot exist without information any more than you can survive without oxygen.

Security

So, what can put your important information resource in jeopardy? Well, countless things. Hard disks can crash, computer parts can fail, hackers and crackers can gain access and do mischief, thieves engaged in industrial espionage can steal your information, and disgruntled employees or associates can cause damage. The FBI estimates that computer sabotage costs businesses somewhere close to $10 billion every year. Companies are increasing their spending on Internet security software, already having spent more than $4 billion in 2000; this figure is expected to increase substantially in the future.[51]

SECURITY AND EMPLOYEES

Most of the press reports are about outside attacks on computer systems, but actually, companies are in far more danger of losing money from employee misconduct than they are from outsiders. It's a problem that's not restricted to computer misuse. A 300-restaurant chain with 30 employees in each location loses, on average, $218 per employee.

But white-collar crime is where the big bucks are lost (see Figure 8.9). White-collar crime in general, from Fortune 100 firms to video stores to construction companies, accounts for about $400 billion in losses every year—and information technology makes it much easier to accomplish and conceal. ($400 billion is $108 billion more than the whole federal defense budget.) Of all white collar fraud, the biggest losses are those incurred by management misconduct. Manager theft of various kinds is about four times that of other employees. Take embezzlement, for example. The average cost of a non-managerial employee's theft is $60,000, while that for managerial employees is $250,000. The most astonishing aspect of this is that most insider fraud (up to two-thirds) is never reported to the legal authorities, according to the Association of Certified Fraud Examiners (ACFE). A survey by Ernst & Young disclosed that two out of five businesses suffered more than five fraud losses, and fully one-quarter of those resulted in a loss of over $1 million. The reasons most often cited for lack of legal action was fear of damaging the company's reputation or brand name.[52]

- White-collar crime costs an estimated $400 billion per year
- Average nonmanagerial embezzlement is $60,000
- Average managerial embezzlement is $250,000
- Two-thirds of insider fraud is not reported
- Of the known losses, one-quarter cost more than $1 million

Figure 8.9

Statistics on White-Collar Crime

WOULD YOU LIKE YOUR E-MAIL AVAILABLE TO ALL ON THE WEB?

That's exactly what happened not only to Enron employees, who were being investigated by the Federal Energy Regulatory Commission (FERC), but to anyone who sent an e-mail to an Enron e-mail address. So, people who were never accused of wrongdoing and didn't even work at Enron suddenly found their e-mail messages displayed for all the world to see, even if the message was as innocent as a confirmation of a golf date.

FERC gathered a boatload of records, paper and electronic, during its investigation of Enron's alleged energy-market manipulation. In March 2003, FERC posted 1.6 million e-mail messages and other documents on the Web in a searchable database. The e-mails are from the period 2000—2003. So anyone can go to the Web site (www.ferc.gov/industries/electric/indus-act/wem/03-26-03-release.asp) and easily view the e-mails and calendars of 176 current and former Enron employees. The e-mails appear in full—including sender and receiver names.

Among the e-mail messages were lots of personal communications like executives discussing employees and vice versa; romantic messages; discussions of breakups (liaisons and marriages); in-law problems; personal photos, and so on.

FERC said that, since Enron owned the messages, it was incumbent on the company to identify personal communications and request their exclusion.

A couple of days after the e-mail database appeared on the Web, FERC agreed to take off the most sensitive documents, like a document that listed the Social Security number of every employee. In early April, on the order of a U.S. Court of Appeals, the database was shut down for 10 days to allow Enron to examine all the documents and make up a list of documents it wanted removed.

About 100 Enron volunteers spent 350 hours going through hundreds of thousands of e-mails looking for specific terms like "Social Security Number," "credit card number," "kids," and "divorce." FERC removed about 8 percent of the database which amounted to about 141,000 documents.

Think about the Enron e-mail the next time you sit down to write something sensitive in an e-mail message. You just never know where it might end up.[53]

Computer-aided fraud includes the old standby crimes like vendor fraud (sending payment to a nonexistent vendor or payment for goods not delivered), writing payroll checks to fictitious employees, claiming expense reimbursements for costs never incurred, and so on. In addition, there are newer crimes such as stealing security codes, credit card numbers, and proprietary files. Intellectual property is one of the favorite targets of theft by insiders. In fact, the companies that make surveillance software say that employers are buying and installing the software not so much to monitor employees as to track how intellectual property, like product design sketches, schematics, and so on, are moving around the network.[54]

Fraud examiners have a rule of thumb that in any group of employees, about 10 percent are completely honest, 10 percent will steal, and, for the remaining 80 percent, it will depend on circumstances. Most theft is committed by people who are strapped for cash, have access to funds that are poorly protected, and perceive a low risk of getting caught.

SECURITY AND COLLABORATION PARTNERS

Computer security was once considered to be an internal matter. It concerned only the company and those who actually used the computers. If you use collaboration systems, however, many representatives of other companies gain access to your computer systems. It's very important to be sure that the computer system of the company you're giving access to is at least as secure as yours, otherwise you'll create a backdoor into your own system. So now you need to be concerned about your partners', suppliers', and customers' computer security as well as your own.

Goodrich Corporation, an aerospace company that uses collaboration systems, has cut costs dramatically with its file-sharing capabilities allowing suppliers to view design drawings. A large portion of Goodrich's $4 billion in annual sales comes from the Department of Defense, so espionage is a real threat. Before a supplier can be part of the team, Goodrich checks out the newcomer's security measures. The Goodrich people examine firewalls and encryption, and even how physically secure the information on the system is. Then if everything meets its tough standards, the Goodrich team sets up a detailed procedure to be followed in case there's a security breach. The moral of the story is: If you want to do business with Goodrich, or many other companies, you'd better have a secure computer system.[55]

As Groove networks become more popular, the need for better security and trust will increase. Microsoft has invested $51 million in the Groove company and the two have agreed on a strategic alliance to offer peer-to-peer systems to businesses. The basic concept of Groove and other peer-to-peer systems is that computers are connected without a central server. This is the Napster concept, whereby computers are connected to each other as needed, to swap files. However, unlike Napster, participation in Groove networks is by invitation only and is not open to the general public. The Groove groupware tools allow people from different companies—partners, suppliers, distributors, and customers—to work together.[56]

GRID COMPUTING   A new kind of computer infrastructure is beginning to take hold of the business world. Grid computing creates a way to tap remote computing resources. *Grid computing* harnesses far-flung computers together by way of the Internet or a virtual private network to share CPU power, databases, and storage. The government is already engaged in grid computing as evidenced by the National Science Foundation's National Technology Grid and NASA's Information Power Grid. Grid computing software is in development by IBM, Sun Microsystems, and Hewlett-Packard. Grid computing includes peer-to-peer file sharing, but it's much more. The core of grid software is its common interface that allows any computer on the grid to tap into the CPU power or storage of other available computers. Companies as diverse as Pratt & Whitney, Bristol-Myers Squibb, and American Express are using grid computing. Analysts say that grid computing will turn computing power into a utility; the provider will simply send you as much or as little power or storage as you happen to need at that moment.[57]

The issues still to be resolved before grid computing becomes widespread are many and complex, but not least among them is security. Security issues involving computers from multiple locations span cultural and technical issues, ranging from rights of access to data sharing to legal and departmental policies.

SECURITY AND OUTSIDE THREATS

An FBI Computer Security Institute survey found that the computer systems of 85 percent of large companies and governmental agencies were broken into during 2001. Of those, 64 percent said they had suffered financial loss, but only 35 percent wanted to put a figure on the loss. Even so, the total of reported losses came to more than $375 million. "There's no Fortune 500 company that hasn't been hacked, I don't care what they tell you," says one hacker.[58] "Hacking" means unauthorized access to computers and computer information. 3Com gets "thousands of attacks a week. From kids to criminals to foreign governments," says David Starr, senior vice president.[59] Even Microsoft's computers have been hacked.

Figure 8.10

Hacker Types

- White-hat hackers find vulnerabilities in systems and plug the holes. They work at the request of the owners of the computer systems.
- Black-hat hackers break into other people's computer systems and may just look around, or they may steal credit card numbers or destroy information, or otherwise do damage.
- Hacktivists have philosophical and political reasons for breaking into systems. They often deface a Web site as a protest.
- Script kiddies, or script bunnies, find hacking code on the Internet and click-and-point their way into systems, to cause damage or spread viruses.
- Crackers are hackers for hire and are the hackers who engage in corporate espionage.
- Cyberterrorists are those who seek to cause harm to people or to destroy critical systems or information. They try to use the Internet as a weapon of mass destruction.

The threats from outside are many and varied. Competitors could try to get your customer lists or the prototype for your new project. Cyber vandals could be joyriding in cyberspace looking for something interesting to see, steal, or destroy. You could become the victim of a generalized attack from a virus or worm, or could suffer a targeted attack like a denial-of-service attack. If you have something worth stealing or manipulating on your system, there could be people after that, too. For example, the online gambling industry is plagued by attacks where hackers have illicitly gained access to the servers that control the gambling, corrupting games to win millions of dollars. Exploiting well-known system weaknesses accounts for 95 percent of hacker damage, while only 5 percent results from breaking into systems in new ways.[60,61]

The people who break into the computer systems of others are "hackers" (see Figure 8.10). *Hackers* are generally very knowledgeable computer users who use their knowledge to invade other people's computers. They have varying motives. Some just do it for the fun of it. Others (called hacktivists) have a philosophical or political message they want to share, and still others (called crackers) are hired guns who illegally break in, usually to steal information, for a fee. The latter can be a very lucrative undertaking. Some highly skilled crackers charge up to $1 million per job. There are also "good guys," called white-hat hackers, who test the vulnerability of systems so that protective measures may be taken.

TYPES OF CYBER CRIME   Cyber crimes range from electronically breaking and entering to cyberstalking and murder. In October 1999, a 21-year-old woman was shot and killed outside the building where she worked. Her killer had been electronically stalking her for two years. He became obsessed with the young lady and had even posted a Web site dedicated to her on which he announced his intention to kill her. He got her Social Security number online, found out where she worked, tracked her down, and shot her, after which he shot himself.

Most cyber crimes are not as bad as murder, but they can be serious nonetheless. Computer viruses and denial-of-service attacks are the two most common types of cyber crime against which companies need to protect themselves.

A *computer virus* (or simply a *virus*) is software that is written with malicious intent to cause annoyance or damage. A virus can be benign or malicious. The benign ones just display a message on the screen or slow the computer down, but don't do any damage. The malicious kind targets a specific application or set of file types and corrupts or destroys them.

Figure 8.11

The Genealogy of Viruses

- **1980s:** The first viruses in the 1980s were boot-sector viruses that attacked the operating system and spread when people traded floppy disks.
- **1990s:** In the 1990s, macro viruses were all the rage. They spread when people traded disks or e-mail with attachments. The virus was part of the Word or Excel attachment and corrupted either the Word or Excel application respectively.
- **2000s:** Polymorphic worms that change their form and are hard to detect started to appear. Also, viruses such as Klez that spoof the return address make it very difficult to track down the source of the virus.

Today, worms are the most prevalent type of virus (see Figure 8.11 for the genealogy of viruses). Worms are viruses that spread themselves; they don't need your help, just your carelessness.

A *worm* is a type of virus that spreads itself, not just from file to file, but from computer to computer via e-mail and other Internet traffic. It finds your e-mail address book and helps itself to the addresses and sends itself to your contacts, using your e-mail address as the return address. The Love Bug worm was one of the early worms that did a lot of damage and got major press coverage. It's estimated that the Love Bug and its variants affected 300,000 Internet host computers and millions of individual PC users causing file damage, lost time, and high-cost emergency repairs costing about $8.7 billion.[62,63] Ford Motor Company, H. J. Heinz, Merrill Lynch, AT&T, Capitol Hill, and the British Parliament all fell victim to the Love Bug worm. Newer versions of worms include Klez, a very rapidly spreading worm, Nimda, and Sircam.

A *denial-of-service attack (DoS)* floods a Web site with so many requests for service that it slows down or crashes. The objective is to prevent legitimate customers from accessing the target site. E*Trade, Yahoo!, and Amazon.com have all been victims of this type of attack. For more information about viruses and DoSs see *Extended Learning Module H.*

As well as knowing what viruses can do, you need to know what they can't do. Computer viruses can't

- Hurt your hardware, such as your monitor, or processor.
- Hurt any files they weren't designed to attack. A virus designed for Microsoft's Outlook, for example, generally doesn't infect Qualcomm's Eudora, or any other e-mail application.
- Infect files on write-protected disks.

SECURITY PRECAUTIONS

It has been said that while in years past, managers had nightmares about takeover bids, they now have nightmares about teenagers with computers and Internet access. Lloyd's of London says that 70 percent of risk managers see the Internet and e-commerce as the biggest emerging risks in this new century.[64] Worldwide security software revenue is expected to grow from $6.3 billion in 2001 to $11.9 billion by 2004.[65]

The only really safe computer system is one that is never connected to any other computer and is locked away so that almost no one can get to it. In today's business world that's just not practical. Computers are like motor vehicles, they can be used to cause harm both unintentionally and maliciously, and just driving one puts you at risk, especially when you're on the road with other cars. However, we still use motor vehicles, although we build in safety features and take precautions to lessen the risk. So it is with computers. The big difference is that security threats in cyberspace are always changing.

WHY DO HACKERS CREATE MALICIOUS CODE?

The answer to why hackers create malicious code in the form of viruses, worms, and denial-of-service attacks (you'll find these attacks on computers discussed further in *Extended Learning Module H: Computer Crime and Forensics*) is not simple. Some create malware (malicious code that does damage to a computer or a network) because they find a community of hackers where they fit in, because they're bored, because they want revenge, or because they can.

The first example is a sixteen-year-old, who lives in Austria and writes viruses and worms when he's bored. So far, he has written over 150 such mini-programs. He has even tried his hand at code that automatically creates viruses. He says he doesn't create malware that causes damage because he likes to "be friendly."

In Toronto, Canada, lives our second example, who started writing malware when he found himself out of college with no job (despite having sent out 400 résumés), no friends, and not much family. He had an unsuccessful brush with suicide and then he found the hacker community. Here people were interested in him and what he did and he felt as though he had found a home.

He then decided to turn his new hobby against the people who refused to hire him. He admits that this was an act of revenge to show these companies that they should have hired him since he's probably a much better programmer than whomever they hired instead of him. The point he seems to have missed is that there's more to keeping a job than being a good programmer, and many people would say that the prospective employers had been right about him.

The third example is a young man who lives in Detroit and directs his ire toward another group of hackers who, he believes, stole his code. He created malware that he intended them to steal. The code did no damage; it just had pop-up messages insulting the malware thieves.

Many of the more talented malware writers don't circulate their code themselves. Since it's not illegal to write malware—only to circulate it and cause damage—they make it available so that script kiddies (those who cut and paste, then circulate viruses) can access it. This procedure has been compared to drug dealers who use young teenagers to carry the illegal wares so that they are insulated from direct responsibility. However, it doesn't absolve them from culpability.[66]

Given the extraordinary importance of information in an organization, it's imperative that companies make their best efforts to protect that information; that is, they should practice risk management. **Risk management** consists of the identification of risks or threats, the implementation of security measures, and the monitoring of those measures for effectiveness. The first step in the process is establishing the extent of the potential threats and identifying the parts of the system that are vulnerable. That process is called risk assessment. **Risk assessment** is the process of evaluating IT assets, their importance to the organization, and their susceptibility to threats, to measure the risk exposure of these assets. In simple terms, risk assessment asks (1) What can go wrong? (2) How likely is it to go wrong? and (3) What are the possible consequences if it does go wrong?[67]

Implementing the correct amount and type of security is not an easy matter. Too much security can hamper employees' ability to do their jobs, resulting in decreased revenue. Too little security leaves your organization vulnerable. You need security strong enough to protect your IT systems but not so much that authorized people can't access the information they need in a timely fashion. Generally, security consists of a combination of measures such as backup procedures, anti-virus software, firewalls, access authentication, encryption, intrusion-detection software, and system auditing.

BACKUPS   As always, an ounce of prevention is worth a pound of cure. The easiest and most basic way to prevent loss of information is to make backups of all your infor-

HOW PROTECTED ARE COMPUTERS IN YOUR PART OF THE WORLD?

The Firewall Guide Web site at www.firewallguide.com has the following advice on protecting your computer.

- First line of defense—Choose an Internet service provider (ISP), an e-mail service, and/or a Web site hosting service that offers online virus, spam, and content filters.
- Second line of defense—Install a hardware *router* with a built-in firewall between your modem and your computer or network.
- Third line of defense—Use personal firewall, anti-virus, anti-Trojan, anti-spyware, anti-spam, and privacy software on your desktop computer.
- Important tips—After installing any security software, immediately check for updates at the

vendor's Web site. After installing a firewall, use an online testing service to make sure that it is working correctly.

Do a survey to get an idea of how many people you know implement any of the above safeguards. Each person in your group must ask five people (don't ask anyone who is taking this class with you) which of these protective measures they use. For each person, list the software or hardware they use to protect their computers. Some software has multiple uses; for example, anti-virus software might protect against worms and Trojan horse viruses. See if they really know specifically what their protection software protects against.

mation. **Backup** is the process of making a copy of the information stored on a computer. There's no action you can take that's more rudimentary or essential than making copies of important information methodically and regularly (at least once a week). Employee carelessness and ignorance cause about two-thirds of the financial cost of lost or damaged information.[68]

Take the example of one company whose accounting server went down the day that paychecks should have been distributed. The crisis arose during an administration transition. The people who had been temporarily running the system thought that backup occurred automatically. It didn't, so all payroll information was lost. To get the system up and running again, the company had to pay thousands of dollars to consultants to restore the network application, and had to pay four people for 300 hours of overtime to reenter information. In addition, it cost $48,000 for a disk-recovery company to retrieve the information from the damaged disk drive. And all this trouble and expense could have been avoided if backup procedures had been followed.

Make sure you back up *all* information. It's easy to forget about the information that's not stored in the main computer system or network, such as correspondence and customer information kept only by administrative assistants and receptionists, and private information not kept in the main organizational databases or data warehouses. Your backup schedule should include not only your information, but also your software. See Chapter 7 for more on backup and recovery.

ANTI-VIRUS SOFTWARE   Anti-virus software is an absolute must. *Anti-virus software* detects and removes or quarantines computer viruses. New viruses are created every day and each new generation is more deadly (or potentially deadly) than the previous one. When you're looking for virus protection, *PC World* magazine[69] has the following advice. Look for virus protection that finds

- Viruses on removable media like floppies, CDs, and Zip disks, as well as on the hard disk.
- Trojan-horse viruses (viruses hiding inside good software) and backdoor programs (viruses that open a way into the network for future attacks).
- Polymorphic viruses and worms, which are sometimes hard for anti-virus programs to find because they change their form as they propagate.
- Viruses in .zip or compressed files, and even .zip files inside other .zip files.
- Viruses in e-mail attachments.

Two final points: First, your anti-virus software should be able to get rid of the virus without destroying the software or information it came with. Second, you must update your anti-virus software frequently since new viruses come along every day. Some software sites will automatically send updates to your anti-virus software, if you set up the software to accept it.

FIREWALLS   A *firewall* is hardware and/or software that protects a computer or network from intruders. The firewall examines each message as it seeks entrance to the network, like a border guard checking passports. Unless the message has the "right" markings, the firewall blocks the way and prevents it from entering. Any competent network administrator will have at least one firewall on the network to keep out unwelcome guests.

A firewall will also detect your computer communicating with the Internet without your approval, as spyware on your computer may be attempting to do. A very popular software firewall is ZoneAlarm from www.zonealarm.com. ZoneAlarm also offers protection from ads and cookies.

ACCESS AUTHENTICATION   While firewalls keep outsiders out, they don't necessarily keep insiders out. In other words, unauthorized employees may try to access computers or files. One of the ways that companies try to protect computer systems is with authentication systems that check who you are before they let you have access.

There are three basic ways of proving your access rights: (1) what you know, like a password; (2) what you have, like an ATM card; (3) what you look like (more specifically what your fingerprint or some other physical characteristic looks like).

Passwords are very popular and have been used since there were computers. You can password-protect the whole network, a single computer, a folder, or a file. But passwords are not by any means a perfect way to protect a computer system. People forget their passwords, so someone has to get them new passwords or find the old one. Banks spend $15 per call to help customers who forget their passwords. Then if a hacker breaks into the system and steals a password list, everyone has to get a new password. One bank had to change 5,000 passwords in the course of a single month at a cost of $12.50 each.[70]

Which brings us to biometrics, or what you look like. *Biometrics* is the use of physiological characteristics—such as your fingerprint, the blood vessels in the iris of your eye, the sound of your voice, or perhaps even your breath—to provide identification. Roughly a dozen different types of biometric devices are available at the moment, with fingerprint readers being the most popular. About 44 percent of the biometric systems sold are fingerprint systems. It works just like the law enforcement system where your fingerprint is stored in the database, and when you come along, your finger is scanned, and the scan is compared to the entry in the database. If they match, you're in.

In Fresno, California, and elsewhere customers are buying lunch without producing any cash or credit cards. When they order, they press a finger on a fingerprint scanner and are asked what credit card they'd like to use. The McDonald's system then matches the fingerprint to a credit card number.[71]

Another promising type of biometric system is facial recognition. Chicago's O'Hare airport, the busiest in the world, has been using biometrics for years to authenticate employees' identity.[72] Many U.S. airport security officials are proposing biometric systems to check that passengers are who they say they are. Most envision the system as a voluntary recording of passengers' biological characteristics, so that frequent flyers could sign up, have their physical characteristic scanned, then in the future bypass the long manual clearing process. See Chapter 9 for more information on biometrics.

ENCRYPTION   If you want to protect your messages and files and hide them from prying eyes, you can encrypt them. *Encryption* scrambles the contents of a file so that you can't read it without having the right decryption key. There are various ways of encrypting messages. You can switch the order of the characters, replace characters with other characters, or insert or remove characters. All of these methods alter the look of the message, but used alone, each one is fairly simple to figure out. So most encryption methods use a combination.

Companies that get sensitive information from customers, such as credit card numbers, need some way of allowing all their customers to use encryption to send the information. But they don't want everyone to be able to decrypt the message, so they might use public key encryption. *Public key encryption (PKE)* is an encryption system that uses two keys: a public key that everyone can have and a private key for only the recipient. So if you do online banking, the bank will give you the public key to encrypt the information you send them, but only the bank has the key to decrypt your information. It works rather like a wall safe, where anyone can lock it (just shut the door and twirl the knob), but only the person with the right combination can open it again.

INTRUSION-DETECTION AND SECURITY-AUDITING SOFTWARE   Two other types of security software are intrusion-detection and security-auditing software. *Intrusion-detection software* looks for people on the network who shouldn't be there or who are acting suspiciously. For example, someone might be trying lots of passwords trying to gain access. "Honey pots" are a type of intrusion-detection software that creates attractive, but nonexistent, targets for hackers. What actually happens is that hackers' keystrokes are recorded instead.

Security-auditing software checks out your computer or network for potential weaknesses. The idea is to find out where hackers could get in and to plug up the hole. Many third parties, such as accounting firms or computer security companies, also provide this service.

Summary: Student Learning Outcomes Revisited

1. **Define ethics and describe the two factors that affect how you make a decision concerning an ethical issue.** *Ethics* are the principles and standards that guide our behavior toward other people. How you decide ethical issues depends on your basic ethical structure and the practical circumstances surrounding your decision. Your basic ethical structure is your sense of ethics that you acquired growing up. The practical circumstances surrounding your decision include

   - *Consequences.* How much or how little benefit or harm will come from a particular decision?
   - *Society's opinion.* What is your perception of what society really thinks of your intended action?
   - *Likelihood of effect.* What is the probability of the harm or benefit that will occur if you take the action?
   - *Time to consequences.* How long will it take for the benefit or harm to take effect?
   - *Relatedness.* How much do you identify with the person or persons who will receive the benefit or suffer the harm?
   - *Reach of result.* How many people will be affected by your action?

2. **Define and describe intellectual property, copyright, Fair Use Doctrine, and pirated and counterfeit software.** *Intellectual property* is intangible creative work that is embodied in physical form. *Copyright* is the legal protection afforded an expression of an idea, such as a song or a video game and some types of proprietary documents. The *Fair Use Doctrine* says that you may use copyrighted material in certain situations. *Pirated software* is the unauthorized use, duplication, distribution or sale of copyrighted software. *Counterfeit software* is software that is manufactured to look like the real thing and sold as such.

3. **Define privacy and describe ways in which it can be threatened.** *Privacy* is the right to be left alone when you want to be, to have control over your own personal possessions, and not to be observed without your consent. Your privacy can be compromised by other individuals snooping on you; by employers monitoring your actions; by businesses that collect information on your needs, preferences, and surfing practices; and by the various government agencies that collect information on citizens.

4. **Describe the two ways that information is valuable to business.** Information is valuable as raw material, which uses information as part of the product, and as capital, which is something that goes into the production of goods and services, but which is not actually part of the product.

5. **Describe the ways in which information on your computer or network is vulnerable.**

   - Employees can embezzle and perpetrate fraud of other types. Most of the financial losses due to computer fraud that is suffered by companies is caused by employees.
   - You give access to your computer information to collaboration partners who could do damage.
   - Grid computing will mean many computers working together with the potential for information to move between computers when it shouldn't.
   - Hackers and crackers try to break into computers and steal, destroy, or compromise information.
   - Hackers can spread *computer viruses* or launch *denial-of-service attacks (DoS)* that can cost millions in prevention and cleanup.

6. **Define risk management and risk assessment and describe the seven security measures that**

companies can take to protect their information. ***Risk management*** consists of the identification of risks or threats, the implementation of security measures, and the monitoring of those measures for effectiveness. ***Risk assessment*** is the process of evaluating IT assets, their importance to the organization, and their susceptibility to threats, to measure the risk exposure of these assets. The seven security measures are as follows

- ***Backups.*** Make sure there is more than one copy of everything, including files not on the main servers, like correspondence and other information stored on the computers of individual employees.

- ***Anti-virus software*** detects and removes or quarantines computer viruses. You can set your software to perform this task automatically. However, to be effective it must be updated regularly and often. Antivirus software should check *all* files that are introduced to your computer.

- A ***firewall*** is hardware and/or software that protects a computer or network from intruders.

- Access authorization makes sure that those who have access to information have the authorization to do so with password or biometrics. ***Biometrics*** is the use of physiological characteristics—such as your fingerprint, the blood vessels in the iris of your eye, the sound of your voice, or perhaps even your breath—to provide identification.

- ***Encryption*** scrambles the contents of a file so that you can't read it without having the right decryption key.

- ***Intrusion-detection software*** looks for people on the network who shouldn't be there or who are acting suspiciously.

- ***Security-auditing software*** checks out your computer or network for possible weaknesses.

CLOSING CASE STUDY ONE

BIOMETRIC BORDERS

The movie *Minority Report* chronicled a futuristic world where people are uniquely identifiable by their eyes. A scan of each person's eyes gives or denies them access to rooms, computers, and anything else with restrictions. The movie was a bit far-fetched with people running a black market in changing eyeballs to help people hide from the authorities. (Why didn't they just change the database entry instead? That would have been much easier, but a lot less dramatic.) However, the idea of using a biological signature is not at all implausible since biometrics is currently being widely used and is expected to gain wider acceptance in the near future.

In fact, the next time you get a new passport, it may incorporate a chip that has your biometric information encoded on it. The reason is that forging documents has become much easier with the advances in computer graphics programs and color printers. The Office of Special Investigations (OSI) sent out some agents with such fake documents and found that it was relatively easy to enter this country from Canada, Mexico and Jamaica, by land, sea, and air.

The task of policing the borders is daunting in that there are 500 million foreigners who enter the country every year and go through identity checkpoints. More than 13 million permanent-resident and border-crossing cards have been issued by the U.S. government. Adding another complication is the fact that there are 27 countries whose citizens do not need visas to enter this country. They will also be expected to have passports that comply with U.S. specifications so that they will also be readable at the border.

In the post-9/11 atmosphere of tightened security, unrestricted border crossing is simply not acceptable. The Department of Homeland Security (DHS) is charged with securing the nation's borders, and as part of this plan, new entry/exit procedures were put in place at the beginning of 2003. An integrated system, using biometrics, which was given another three years, until the end of 2005, to be fully operational, will be used to identify foreign visitors to the United States and reduce the likelihood of terrorists entering the country.

Early in 2003, after 6 million biometric border-crossing cards had been issued, a pilot test conducted at the Canadian border detected more than 250 imposters. The testing started with two biometric identifiers: photographs for facial recognition and fingerprint scans. As people enter and leave the country, their actual fingerprints and facial features are compared to the data on the biometric chip in the passport.

Part of the awesome challenge facing the DHS is the sheer volume of information that has to be catalogued, stored, and retrieved. Current estimates are that it will take about 5 petabytes (that's 5,000,000,000,000,000 characters) of space to store all that information, and this requirement is likely to expand with time. This information must be available on demand—and quickly. The exit information must be matched against the entry information and then be stored so that it can be retrieved the next time the individual enters the country.

IT specialists are still working on providing an extremely fast database system and a very extensive network to accommodate the mammoth task. Some of the more remote border crossings, for example, on the Mexico/United States border, may need wireless access. Then there are the security considerations. The information must be kept safe from network intruders and other types of misuse.

The first contracts for equipment to implement the new biometric identity verification system included a $3.5 million agreement to buy 1,000 optical-stripe read/write drives with biometric verification systems and a contract for biometric fingerprint scanning technology worth about $27 million.[73,74,75,76]

Questions

1. How do you feel about having your fingerprints, facial features, and perhaps more of your biometric features encoded in documents like your passport? Explain your answer.
2. Would you feel the same way about having biometric information on your driver's license as on your passport? If so, why? And if not, why not?
3. Is it reasonable to have different requirements for visitors from different nations? Explain your answer. What would you recommend as criteria for deciding which countries fall into what categories?
4. If you've ever been out of the United States, you know that there are checkpoints that you go through when returning. These checkpoints vary greatly in the depth of the checks and the time you have to spend. The simplest involves simply walking past the border guards who may or may not ask you your citizenship. The other end of the spectrum requires that you put up with long waits in airports where you have to line up with hundreds of other passengers while each person is questioned and must produce a passport to be scanned. Would you welcome biometric information on passports if it would speed the checkup process and get you through faster, or do you think that the disadvantages of the reduction in privacy outweigh the advantages of better security and faster border processing? Explain your answer.

CLOSING CASE STUDY TWO

IS THE SAFE HARBOR SAFE FOR U.S. BUSINESSES?

European countries and Australia have passed laws protecting the privacy of name-linked consumer information. In Europe this law is the European Union Directive 95/46/EC, which was adopted in 1998, and in Australia it's the Privacy Amendment Act of 2000. The

Australian law says that personal information can be collected only with the consent of the person about whom it's being collected. The law goes further and forbids personal information being transferred to any other country that does not have privacy protection.

The result of this is that U.S. companies with an Australian subsidiary cannot transfer personal information it collected back to the United States since this country has no privacy protection of this type.

In Europe, the 15 countries that belong to the European Union are supposed to have passed laws by now requiring that personal information can only be collected with the express and unambiguous consent of the person to whom the information applies. And this rule applies to invisible information collection such as the information collected in cookies and details on a person's Web surfing activities.

An individual's information can only be collected without consent under the following circumstances:

1. It's necessary to fulfill a contract.
2. It's necessary to save a life, as when a procedure is necessary on an unconscious person.
3. It's necessary for a greater good, such as tax collection.
4. The processing of the information is required by a legal contract.
5. The third party to the information has a lawful right to do so as in an arbitration situation.

Even within these guidelines there is certain "sensitive information" that cannot be requested and cannot be processed without specific consent. This sensitive information includes a person's racial or ethnic origin, political and religious affiliations, trade union membership, and sexual preferences. This exception of sensitive information was deemed necessary in the light of hundreds of years of persecution in Europe of one ethnic or religious group by another.

The EU directive also says that people must be informed when information about them is to be used for direct mailings, and the rules apply anytime the information is being processed within the European Union, even if those who are providing the information are located elsewhere. So why does it matter to U.S. businesses what privacy laws the Europeans choose to have? It matters because it threatens the annual $350 billion in trade between the United States and the European Union, since European countries may refuse to allow the transfer of customer information. So, the U.S. Department of Commerce and the European Commission agreed on voluntary, so-called Safe Harbor provisions, which represented a compromise between the strict consumer privacy requirements of Europe and the more relaxed attitude of American law. At its inception, the Safe Harbor agreement was hailed as a great breakthrough and a guarantee that business would indeed continue to thrive.

However, the Safe Harbor agreement no longer seems to be quite as wonderful as it did at first. There are several reasons for this. First, it's a voluntary program and U.S. companies are slow in signing up. The problem for U.S. companies may be that, by signing up, they open themselves to scrutiny by the Federal Trade Commission (FTC), which is the agency that will investigate complaints. Second, not all European countries have actually passed laws yet to comply with the directive. (An EU directive is simply a statement of intent and each member country must enact its own laws to ensure the outcome of the directive.) France, Ireland and Luxembourg are still working on passing laws. Third, some European countries think that the Safe Harbor agreement is much too weak, and is not in keeping with the intent of the directive. The worry for U.S. companies is that countries like Sweden might refuse to allow information transfer to countries they deem to be deficient. Fourth, the Safe Harbor agreement may not be enforceable by law since the FTC doesn't have the authority to protect European consumers' rights within the United States. And finally, EU authorities have the power to intervene in cases of serious violations and suspend the transfer of information to that country until the matter has been resolved.

Many privacy advocates in the United States hope that companies in this country will be inclined to self-regulate in order to comply with the stricter laws of Europe and Australia. They argue that such compliance would be in the best interests of U.S. companies and would ensure their continued trade and good name. In fact, Microsoft, Intel, Hewlett-Packard, and Procter & Gamble have all promised to provide their customers outside the European Union with privacy protection as strong as the EU demands. This commitment might give these companies a competitive advantage even in the United States as consumers here become more privacy conscious.[77]

Questions

1. Imagine, for a moment, that a federal law, very similar to the EU directive were to take effect in the United States at the beginning of next year. What would the implications be for companies that collect huge amounts of personal information about their customers and clients?
2. Would you like to have stronger privacy laws in this country? If so, what form should they take? If not, do you have any reservations about your personal information being bought and sold like any other commodity? Should there be limits on

who can buy what information and for what purposes? If so, what should they be? If not, provide some examples of the advantages of having all personal information available to anyone with the means to acquire it.

3. Strangely enough, the European Union is considering a law that appears to fly squarely in the face of the philosophy of the privacy directive. The proposal is to give border police access to e-mail and Internet use by citizens. The law would mean that police would be able to access any and all e-mail and Internet usage information from ISPs simply by requesting it. No court order would be needed. There would be no restrictions on the amount or type of information that the police could access on people's personal and business lives. What do you think of this law? What do the privacy directive and the proposed law imply about the European attitude toward access to personal information? Whom do the Europeans see as the abusers of personal information and who are the good guys? Is the attitude the same in the United States? How do the European and American philosophies differ?

4. Do you think that the United States should have stricter border laws? At airports the focus tends to be on luggage. Should there be more emphasis on who is traveling? For instance, should everyone, citizens included, be fingerprinted and checked out before they enter or leave the country? If so, would you be prepared to have a special ID card with your fingerprints or some other biometric feature on it to allow you to pass through the checkpoints at ports of entry faster?

5. Given that bankruptcy courts in the United States have ruled that customer information—even personal information—is an asset for the purposes of paying off debts, many privacy advocates question the safety of personal information even if a company promises privacy and fully intends to keep that promise. What do you think about this ruling? Would your opinion change if you were owed a lot of money by a company that just filed for bankruptcy protection?

Key Terms and Concepts

Adware, 362
Anonymous Web browsing (AWB), 363
Anti-virus software, 375
Backup, 375
Biometrics, 376
Clickstream, 363
Computer virus (virus), 372
Cookie, 360
Copyright, 351
Counterfeit software, 353
Denial-of-service attack (DoS), 373
Encryption, 377
Ethics, 349
Fair Use Doctrine, 352
Firewall, 376
Grid computing, 371
Hacker, 372
Hardware key logger, 358

Identity theft, 356
Intellectual property, 351
Intrusion-detection software, 377
Key logger software (key trapper software), 354
Phishing (carding or brand spoofing), 356
Pirated software, 353
Privacy, 353
Public key encryption (PKE), 377
Risk assessment, 374
Risk management, 374
Safe-harbor principles, 365
Security-auditing software, 377
Spam, 360
Spyware (sneakware or stealthware), 362
Trojan horse software, 362
Web log, 363
Worm, 373

Short-Answer Questions

1. What are ethics, and how do ethics apply to business?
2. What are the two factors that determine how you decide ethical issues?
3. Six practical circumstances affect how you decide ethical issues. What are they?
4. What situation would qualify as an exception to the copyright law?
5. What is privacy?
6. What is pirated software?
7. What is the difference between counterfeit software and pirated software?
8. What does a key logger do?
9. What is spyware?
10. What did the Bork Bill do?
11. What is grid computing?
12. What is a denial-of-service attack?

Assignments and Exercises

1. **HELPING A FRIEND** Suppose you fully intend to spend the evening working on an Excel assignment that's due the next day. Then a friend calls. Your friend is stranded miles from home and desperately needs your help. It will take most of the evening to pick up your friend, bring him home, and return to your studying. Not only that, but you're very tired when you get home and just fall into bed. The next day your friend, who completed his assignment earlier, suggests you just make a copy, put your own name on the cover, and hand it in as your own work. Should you do it? Isn't it only fair that since you helped your friend, the friend should do something about making sure you don't lose points because of your generosity? What if your friend promises not to hand in his or her own work so that you can't be accused of copying? Your friend wrote the assignment and gave it to you, so there's no question of copyright infringement.

2. **FIND OUT WHAT HAPPENED** In December 2001, British Telecom (BT) filed a lawsuit against Prodigy in New York federal court, claiming it owns the hyperlinking process. If BT wins this lawsuit then the company will be able to collect licensing revenue from the 100 billion or so links on the Web. BT has a patent that it says amounts to ownership of the hyperlinking process. Prodigy (and everyone else in the world) stores Web pages with a displayed part, which the browser shows, and a hidden part that the viewer doesn't see, and which contains hidden information including the addresses that are used by the displayed portion. This, BT said, is the essence of its U.S. patent No. 4873662. In reference to this case, answer the following questions:
   A. Has a ruling been handed down on this matter yet? If so, what was the result?
   B. If any kind of hyperlinking is, in fact, the essence of the patent held by BT, what about library card catalogs; are they infringements, too? Why or why not? What else could be?

3. **INVESTIGATE MONITORING SYSTEMS** The text listed several monitoring systems, other systems that defeat them, and an e-mail encryption program. Find two more of the following:
   A. Programs that monitor keyboard activity
   B. Programs that find keyboard monitoring programs
   C. E-mail encryption programs

4. **CHECK OUT THE COMPUTER ETHICS INSTITUTE'S ADVICE** The Computer Ethics Institute's Web site at www.cspr.org/program/ethics.htm offers the "Ten Commandments of Computer Ethics" to guide you in the general direction of ethical computer use. The first two are
   • *Thou shalt not use a computer to harm other people.* This one is the bedrock for all the others.
   • *Thou shalt not interfere with other people's computer work.* This one includes small sins like sending frivolous e-mail, big ones like spreading viruses, and the really big ones like electronic stalking.

   Look up the other eight and give at least two examples of acts that would be in violation of these guidelines.

Discussion Questions

1. When selling antiques, you can usually obtain a higher price for those that have a provenance, which is information detailing the origin and history of the object. For example, property owned by Jacqueline Kennedy Onassis and Princess Diana sold for much more than face value. What kinds of products have value over and above a comparable product because of such information? What kind of information makes products valuable? Consider both tangible (resale value) and intangible value (sentimental appeal).

2. Personal checks that you use to buy merchandise have a standard format. Checks have very few different sizes, and almost no variation in format. Consider what would happen if everyone could create his or her own size, shape, and layout of personal check. What would the costs and benefits be to business and the consumer in terms of buying checks, exchanging them for merchandise, and bank check processing?

3. Consider society as a business that takes steps to protect itself from the harm of illegal acts. Discuss the mechanisms and costs that are involved. Examine ways in which our society would be different if no one ever broke a law. Are there ever benefits to our society when people break the law, for example, when they claim that the law itself is unethical or unjust?

4. Can you access all the IT systems at your college or university? What about payroll or grade information on yourself or others? What kinds of controls has your college or university implemented to prevent the misuse of information?

5. You know that you generally can't use a PC to access the information stored on a Macintosh-formatted disk. What other instances of the lack of difficulty in accessing information have you experienced personally or heard of? For example, have you used different versions of MS PowerPoint or MS Access that won't work on all the PCs that you have access to?

6. Have you, or someone you know, experienced computer problems caused by a virus? What did the virus do? Where do you think you got it? How did you fix the problem? What was the cost to you in time, trouble, and stress?

7. What laws do you think the United States should pass to protect personal information? None? Laws such as the European Union has? Stricter laws than the EU? Why? Should some personal information be more protected than other information? Why or why not?

8. The issue of pirated software is one that the software industry fights on a daily basis. The major centers of software piracy are in places like Russia and China where salaries and disposable income are comparatively low. Given that people in developing and economically depressed countries will fall behind the industrialized world technologically if they can't afford access to new generations of software, is it reasonable to blame someone for using pirated software when it costs two months' salary to buy a legal copy of MS Office? If you answered no, specify at what income level it's okay to make or buy illegal copies of software. What approach could software companies use to combat the problem apart from punitive measures, like pressuring the government to impose sanctions on transgressors?

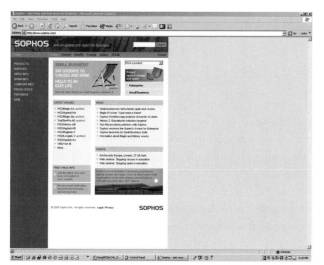

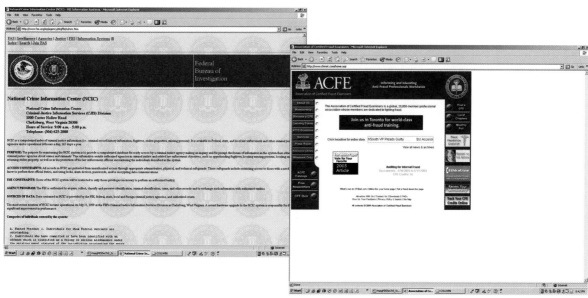

Making Travel Arrangements on the Internet

It's very likely that in the course of business you'll be expected to travel either within the United States or abroad. You can use the Internet to check out all aspects of your journey, from mode of travel to the shopping opportunities that are available. The Internet can also give you pointers and directions about aspects of the trip you might not even have thought about.

In this section, we've included a number of Web sites related to making travel arrangements on the Internet. On the Web site that supports this text (www.mhhe.com/haag, click on "Electronic Commerce Projects"), we've provided direct links to all these Web sites as well as many, many more. This is a great starting point for completing this section. We would also encourage you to search the Internet for other sites.

AIR TRAVEL

Some people are happy to travel with whatever airline provides the flight that fits into their schedule. Others insist on certain airlines, or won't travel on particular airlines. No matter how you feel, the Internet can help you find a flight. On the Internet, you can even get maps of the airports you'll be using. Many airports have sites on the Internet, such as Dallas/Ft. Worth International Airport at www.dfwairport.com. These sites can help you with provisions at the airport for disabled people, among other available services.

The Federal Aviation Authority site (www.faa.com) has a comprehensive list of airlines in this country and all over the world. Find five appropriate Web sites and answer the following questions.

A. Can you make a flight reservation online at this site?

B. If you can book flights, does the site ask you to type in your departure and destination cities, or can you choose from a menu?

C. Again, if you can book flights at this site, on a scale of 1 to 10, rate how difficult it is to get to the flight schedule. That is, how many questions do you have to answer, how many clicks does it take, how much do you have to type in?

D. Is there information on when the lowest fares apply (for example, three-week advance booking, staying over Saturday night, etc.)?

E. Does the site offer to send you information on special deals via e-mail?

F. Does the site offer information on frequent flier mileage? Can you check your frequent flier account online?

G. Does the site offer you a map of the airports you will be using?

RENTAL CARS

When you arrive at your destination, you may need a car. Some sites such as Rental Car Info's site at www.bnm.com have information on multiple companies, and all the large car rental companies have sites on the Internet. Find six Web sites that rent cars and answer the following questions.

A. Can you reserve a car at the Web site?

B. Can you search by city?

C. Is there a cancellation penalty? If so, how much?

D. Can you get a list of car types? Does this company rent sports utility vehicles?

E. Are there special weekend rates?

F. What does the site say about collision insurance purchased from that company in addition to your own insurance?

G. Can you get maps from the site?

H. Are special corporate rates specified on the site?

ONE-STOP TRAVEL SITES

Some travel sites on the Internet allow you to book your entire trip from start to finish, offering a combination of airline, hotel, and other helpful information. Two of the most widely used are Microsoft's Expedia at expedia.msn.com and Preview at www.previewtravel.com. Choose five Web sites and answer the following questions.

A. How many different booking services are offered from this site (airlines, hotels, rental cars, rail travel, etc.)?

B. If the site offers flight booking, how many flight alternatives does it offer? 3? 10? 20? 30? More than 30?

C. Does the site have information on low-cost specials for airlines, hotels, and/or rental cars?

D. Is there a traveler's assistance section?

E. Will the site answer your specific questions?

F. Can you search by destination or company for flights and lodging?

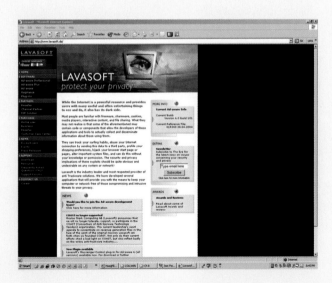

EXTENDED LEARNING MODULE H
COMPUTER CRIME AND FORENSICS

Student Learning Outcomes

1. DEFINE COMPUTER CRIME AND LIST THREE TYPES OF COMPUTER CRIME THAT CAN BE PERPETRATED FROM INSIDE AND THREE FROM OUTSIDE THE ORGANIZATION.

2. IDENTIFY THE SEVEN TYPES OF HACKERS AND EXPLAIN WHAT MOTIVATES EACH GROUP.

3. DEFINE COMPUTER FORENSICS AND DESCRIBE THE TWO PHASES OF A FORENSIC INVESTIGATION.

4. IDENTIFY AND DESCRIBE FOUR PLACES ON A HARD DISK WHERE YOU CAN FIND USEFUL INFORMATION.

5. IDENTIFY AND DESCRIBE SEVEN WAYS OF HIDING INFORMATION.

6. DESCRIBE TWO WAYS IN WHICH CORPORATIONS USE COMPUTER FORENSICS.

Introduction

Computers play a big part in crime: they're used both to commit and to solve crimes. This should be no surprise since they're such a big part of almost every other part of our lives. Computers are involved primarily two ways in the commission of a crime or misdeed: as targets and as weapons or tools. A computer or network is a target when someone wants to bring it down or make it malfunction, as in a denial-of-service attack or a computer virus infection. Crimes that use a computer as a weapon or tool would include acts such as changing computer records to commit embezzlement, breaking into a computer system to damage information, and stealing customer lists. See Figure H.1 for examples of computer-related offenses that use computers as weapons/tools and targets of crime.

Some crimes are clearly what we'd call computer crimes, like Web defacing, denial-of-service attacks, and so on. But, as is the case in so many parts of our modern lives, computers are so integrated into crime that it's sometimes hard to separate them out. Here's an example from the case files of Walt Manning, an expert in computer forensic investigation.

A member of a crime syndicate was sprayed with drive-by gunfire and was severely wounded. Believing that his services were no longer wanted by his crime gang, he switched sides, agreeing to become a witness for the state. The police secured an isolated intensive care unit room for him and guarded it heavily, allowing access only to medical staff and those on a very short list of visitors. Because the man was so badly wounded, there was a distinct danger of infection, and since he was allergic to penicillin, the doctor prescribed a synthetic alternative.

One evening, a nurse wheeling a medicine cart went through the police cordon and into the man's room. He injected the patient with penicillin, and the patient died shortly thereafter. An investigation started immediately and the nurse was potentially in big trouble. He insisted that when he looked at the patient's chart on the computer, there was an order there for penicillin. Subsequent examination of the computer records showed no such order. Eventually, it occurred to someone that perhaps a computer forensics expert should look at the computer angle more closely. Having retrieved the backup tapes (nightly backups are standard operating procedure in most places), the expert found evidence that exonerated the nurse. The patient chart had been changed in the computer to indicate penicillin and later changed back to its original form. Examination further revealed the point and time of access, and indicated that the medical record was changed by someone outside the hospital. A hacker had electronically slipped into the hospital's network unnoticed, made the change, and slipped out again—twice.

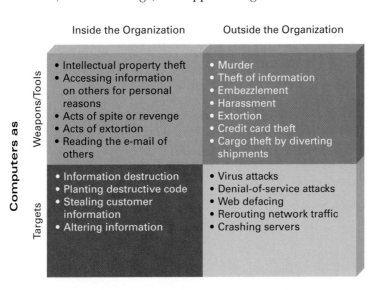

Figure H.1

Examples of Computer Crimes That Organizations Need to Defend Against

389

Most crimes involving a computer are not as lethal as murder, but that doesn't mean they're insignificant. Organizations want to make sure their networks' defenses are strong and can prevent their computers from being used for unlawful or unethical acts. That's why so much time, money, and effort goes into security. We discussed that in Chapter 8.

This module focuses on the sort of threats that computer systems are susceptible to and the examination of electronic evidence. The latter is called computer forensics.

Computer Crime

For our purposes, a ***computer crime*** is a crime in which a computer, or computers, play a significant part. See Figure H.2 for a list of crimes in which computers, although perhaps not essential, usually play a large part.

In this section we'll focus on crime from the organization's viewpoint. First, we'll examine some of the more high-profile types of computer crime committed against organizations that are perpetrated from the outside. Then we'll discuss the varying motivations of people who commit these acts. Lastly, we'll briefly discuss computer crime within the organization.

OUTSIDE THE ORGANIZATION

Businesses are very concerned about the threat of people breaking into their computers and causing damage. The Computer Security Institute conducted a survey in 2003 to determine the extent of the problem. It found that 82 percent of companies had experienced a virus attack during 2002; 80 percent had uncovered insider abuse of Internet access (costing a total of over $11 million for 251 of the companies); and 45 percent had experienced unauthorized access by insiders. The costs are staggering. In 2003 alone, companies reported a total of over $70 million lost in the theft of proprietary information for 251 companies. Denial-of-service attacks for the same group cost over $65 million, and the detection and cleanup of viruses cost over $27 million. The companies further reported that the infection of viruses came, in 86 percent of the cases, from e-mail attachments.[1] To combat these and other attacks, businesses spent about $7.5 billion in 2000 on security software.[2] That market is expected to triple to $21 billion by the end of 2005.

Figure H.2

Crimes in Which Computers Usually Play a Part

- Illegal gambling
- Forgery
- Money laundering
- Child pornography
- Hate message propagation
- Electronic stalking
- Racketeering
- Fencing stolen goods
- Loan sharking
- Drug trafficking
- Union infiltration

VIRUSES

The term *computer virus* is a generic term for lots of different types of destructive software. A **computer virus** (or **virus**) is software that was written with malicious intent to cause annoyance or damage. Two hundred new ones are developed every day.[3] There are two categories of viruses. The first category comprises benign viruses that display a message or slow down the computer but don't destroy any information.

Malignant viruses belong in the second category. These viruses do damage to your computer system. Some will scramble or delete your files. Others will shut your computer down, or make your Word software malfunction, or damage flash memory in your digital camera so that it won't store pictures anymore until you reformat it. Obviously, these are the viruses that cause IT staff (and everyone else) the most headaches.

The macro virus is one very common type of malignant computer virus. **Macro viruses** spread by binding themselves to software such as Word or Excel. When they infect a computer, they make copies of themselves (replicate) and spread from file to file destroying or changing the file in some way.

This type of virus needs human help to move to another computer. If you have a macro virus on your system and you e-mail an infected document as an attachment, the person who gets the e-mail gets the virus as soon as the infected attachment is opened. When you click on the attachment, Word (or the appropriate program) also loads, thereby setting the executable statements in motion.

Worms are the most prevalent type of malignant virus. A **worm** is a computer virus that replicates and spreads itself, not only from file to file, but from computer to computer via e-mail and other Internet traffic. Worms don't need your help to spread. They find your e-mail address book and help themselves to the addresses, sending themselves to your contacts. The first worm to attract the attention of the popular press was the Love Bug worm, and permutations of it are still out there.

THE LOVE BUG WORM

Released on an unsuspecting world in 2000, the Love Bug worm caused the Massachusetts state government to shut down its e-mail, affecting 20,000 workers. It also caused problems on Capitol Hill and shut down e-mail in the British Parliament building. Companies as diverse as Ford Motor Company, H. J. Heinz, Merrill Lynch & Company, and AT&T were infected.[4] All in all, the Love Bug and its variants affected 300,000 Internet host computers and millions of individual PC users causing file damage, lost time, and high-cost emergency repairs totaling about $8.7 billion.[5,6]

A closer look at the Love Bug worm will give you a general idea of what worms do. The Love Bug arrives in your e-mail as an attachment to an e-mail message. The subject of the e-mail is "I LOVE YOU"—a very alluring message to be sure. The text says to open the attached love letter, the name of which is, appropriately, LOVE LETTER. However, what's attached is anything but love. It's a mean piece of software that is set loose in your computer system as soon as you open the attachment.

The Love Bug has three objectives: to spread itself as far and as fast as it can, to destroy your files, and to gather passwords and other information (see Figure H.3 on the next page). First, it spreads itself by mailing itself to everyone in your Outlook address book. (A previous worm of the same type named Melissa sent itself only to the first 50 people listed in Outlook's address book.) And, as if that weren't enough, it also uses your Internet chat software to spread itself to chat rooms.

Second, the Love Bug locates files on your computer that have certain extensions, .MP3 music files, .jpg picture files, .doc Word files, .xls Excel files, .wav sound files, .html browser files, and many others. Having found these files it wipes them out and puts itself in their place, appending .vbs to the end of the filename. For example, if you had a

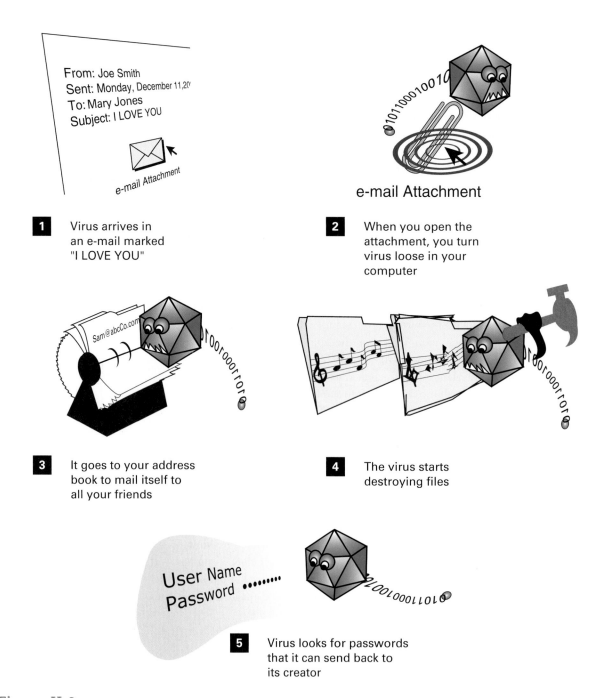

1 Virus arrives in an e-mail marked "I LOVE YOU"

2 When you open the attachment, you turn virus loose in your computer

3 It goes to your address book to mail itself to all your friends

4 The virus starts destroying files

5 Virus looks for passwords that it can send back to its creator

Figure H.3

The Love Bug Worm

file called MySong.wav on your hard disk drive, the Love Bug virus would change the name to MySong.wav.vbs after it had done its dirty work.

Before it's done, the Love Bug worm changes your Internet Explorer start page and downloads a program that looks for passwords and network information, sending this information off by e-mail to the virus originator.[7]

There are at least 29 versions of the Love Bug virus. After people were warned not to open the LOVE LETTER attachment, the originators of the virus changed the name of it to something else. For example, one version is MOTHER'S DAY, and the body of the text says that the receiver has been charged hundreds of dollars for a Mother's Day "diamond special." You have to open the attachment to print the invoice, and then the virus goes into action.

The moral of the story is that you should be very careful about opening an attachment if you're not sure what it is and where it came from. That won't necessarily save you from all virus attacks, but it will certainly help a great deal.

SOBIG, SLAMMER, AND BLASTER

The year 2003 was called the "worst year ever" for viruses and worms. Among the biggest, in terms of cost and name recognition, were the SoBig virus and the Slammer and Blaster worms.

There are several variations of mass-mailer viruses, but the SoBig virus is probably the best known. On Tuesday, August 19, 2003, the SoBig virus began spreading through networks generating e-mail traffic at levels never seen before. It arrived as an attachment in the victim's inbox with varying subject lines like "Your details," "Your application," and "Wicked screensaver." When the recipient opened the attachment, the virus searched through hard drives for e-mail addresses in document files, cached Web pages, and Microsoft Outlook Express databases. Then it sent out huge numbers of useless e-mail messages. At its peak, security experts estimate that 1 out of every 17 e-mail messages carried the SoBig virus, even more than the Love Bug's 1 in 20. It was estimated that SoBig sent out a mass mailing from infected computers—there were about 100,000 of those—at the rate of one every 10 minutes.

Postrini Inc., an e-mail management and screening company, intercepted 1.9 million SoBig e-mails on their way to the company's customers on the first day of the virus's activation. By the next day the volume had increased to 3.5 million.

Whirlpool, a company with $11 billion a year in sales, says that about 95 percent of its sales come through the Internet and that its fast response to protect its 20,000 computers and 800 servers saved the company from suffering much damage. Others weren't so lucky. Experts say that part of the reason that SoBig was so effective was that it incorporated a line in its header that said "X-Scanner: Found to be clean," fooling a popular antivirus application that many Internet service providers use into letting the virus through.

SoBig was preprogrammed to stop replicating itself on September 10, 2003. By that time, it had infected more than 5 million e-mails. About eight times as many private computers were infected as corporate systems, since organizations moved faster to apply the patch that blocked the destruction.

Two of the many worms that hit networks in 2003 were the Slammer worm that hit in January and the Blaster worm that arrived in August. A worm looks for some flaw, or way to enter a computer, in software (often a Microsoft network operating system product) and sneaks in to do damage. Slammer kept flooding the victim server until its buffer memory was full, then it could trick that computer into sending out thousands of new copies to other servers that were vulnerable. Slammer sent out 55 million bursts of information per second onto the Internet and at that rate it took only 10 minutes for the worm to find and invade almost all the vulnerable servers. Microsoft had a patch (a way of plugging the entry point) available on its Web site, but if the network administrators didn't download and apply it, their networks remained vulnerable until they did.

The Blaster worm appeared only 26 days after Microsoft publicized the vulnerability that the worm utilized. Blaster spread like wildfire and among the thousands of companies that were affected were CSX, the third largest railroad company in North America, Amtrak, the commuter train company, and Air Canada. Passengers and freight in all three organizations experienced delays as their network traffic ground to a halt. Commuter trains in Washington, D.C., were delayed for two hours while IT experts worked feverishly to clean out the worm's effects while Air Canada's phone-reservation system and some check-in processes were slowed down.[8,9,10,11]

STAND-ALONE VIRUSES

In any given month, between 200 and 300 viruses are traveling from system to system around the world, seeking a way in to spread mayhem.[12] And they're getting more deadly. Whereas the Love Bug worm was a Visual Basic script virus (i.e., it needed Visual Basic to run), the latest worms can stand alone and run on any computer that can run Win32 programs (Windows 98 or later versions). Examples are SirCam, Nimda, and Klez. Nimda adds JavaScript to every home page on the server it infects, then passes it on to visitors to the site. Viruses of this independent type are very numerous.

The Klez virus is actually a family of worms that introduced a new kind of confusion into the virus business. They spoof e-mail addresses. *Spoofing* is the forging of the return address on an e-mail so that the e-mail message appears to come from someone other than the actual sender. Previous worms went to the recipient from the infected sender's computer and contained the infected person's return e-mail address. The worm found recipient addresses in the infected computer's address book.

Klez goes a step further and uses the address book to randomly find a return address as well as recipient addresses. The result is that people who are not infected with the virus get e-mail from the irate recipients and spend time looking for a virus they may not have. Even worse, some of the virus-laden e-mails look as though they came from a technical support person, leading an unsuspecting victim to open them, believing them to be safe.

TROJAN HORSE VIRUSES

A type of virus that doesn't replicate is a Trojan-horse virus. A *Trojan horse virus* hides inside other software, usually an attachment or download. The principle of any Trojan horse software is that there's software you don't want hidden inside software you do want. For example, Trojan horse software can carry the ping-of-death program that hides in a server until the originators are ready to launch a DoS attack to crash a Web site.

Key-logger software is usually available in Trojan horse form, so that you can hide it in e-mail or other Internet traffic. *Key logger,* or *key trapper, software* is a program that, when installed on a computer, records every keystroke and mouse click. Key logger software is used to snoop on people to find out what they're doing on a particular computer. You can find out more in Chapter 8.

MISLEADING E-MAIL

One type of misleading e-mail is a virus hoax. This is e-mail sent intending to frighten people about a virus threat that is, in fact, bogus. People who get such an alert will usually tell others, who react in the same way. The virus is nonexistent, but the hoax causes people to get scared and lose time and productivity. Within companies the losses can be very severe since computer professionals must spend precious time and effort looking for a nonexistent problem.

Following are some general guidelines for identifying a virus hoax.[13]

- Urges you to forward it to everyone you know, immediately.
- Describes the awful consequences of not acting immediately.
- Quotes a well-known authority in the computer industry.

These are signs that the e-mail is not meant to help but to cause harm. If you get such an e-mail, delete it immediately.

Another type of misleading e-mail is designed to get people to actually take action that results in setting a virus loose or to do something that will disrupt the functioning of their own computers. The first step is usually to make people believe that they have inadvertently e-mailed a virus to others. They get a message (maybe it purports to come from Microsoft) that they have sent out a virus and that they need to run an attached program or delete a file to fix the problem. They then do what the e-mail says believing it to be genuine, and furthermore, they e-mail everyone they sent messages to telling them about the problem. The recipients e-mail the people in their address books and so on. Be advised that Microsoft *never* sends out attachments in any official e-mail in a public mass mailing. It's possible that Microsoft may e-mail you warning you of a problem, but it will only indicate where you can download a file to take care of it. Before you delete a file from your computer, which may be an important system file without which your computer can't function, ask someone who knows or check out the various Web sites that keep up with the latest viruses, like www.symantec.com.

DENIAL-OF-SERVICE ATTACKS

Many organizations have been hit with denial-of-service attacks. *Denial-of-service (DoS) attacks* flood a Web site with so many requests for service that it slows down or crashes. The objective is to prevent legitimate customers from getting into the site to do business. There are several types of DoS attacks. A DoS attack can come from a lone computer that tries continuously to access the target computer, or from many, perhaps even thousands, of computers simultaneously. The latter is called a distributed denial-of-service attack and is considerably more devastating.

DISTRIBUTED DENIAL-OF-SERVICE ATTACKS

Distributed denial-of-service (DDos) attacks are attacks from multiple computers that flood a Web site with so many requests for service that it slows down or crashes. A common type is the Ping of Death, in which thousands of computers try to access a Web site at the same time, overloading it and shutting it down. A ping attack can also bring down the firewall server (the computer that protects the network), giving free access to the intruders. E*Trade, Amazon.com, and Yahoo!, among others, have been victims of this nasty little game. The process is actually very simple (see Figure H.4 on the next page).

The plan starts with the hackers planting a program in network servers that aren't protected well enough. Then, on a signal sent to the servers from the attackers, the program activates and each server "pings" every computer. A ping is a standard operation that networks use to check that all computers are functioning properly. It's a sort of roll call for the network computers. The server asks, "Are you there?" and each computer in turn answers, "Yes, I'm here." But the hacker ping is different in that the return address of the are-you-there? message is not the originating server, but the intended victim's server. So on a signal from the hackers, thousands of computers try to access E*Trade or Amazon.com, to say "Yes, I'm here." The flood of calls overloads the online companies' computers and they can't conduct business.

For many companies, a forced shutdown is embarrassing and costly but for others it's much more than that. For an online stockbroker, for example, denial-of-service attacks can be disastrous. It may make a huge difference whether you buy shares of stock today or tomorrow. And since stockbrokers need a high level of trust from customers to do business, the effect of having been seen to be so vulnerable is very bad for business.

COMBINATION WORM/DOS

Code Red, discovered in 2001, was the first virus that combined a worm and DoS attack. Code Red attacked servers running a specific type of system software. It used e-mail address books to send itself to lots of computers, and it was very efficient, with the ability to infect as many as 500,000 new servers per day. Its first action was to deface the Web site it infected. Then it went about finding other servers to infect. The last part of the plan was for all the infected servers to attack the White House Web site and shut it down. Having been warned of the impending attack, the White House changed the IP

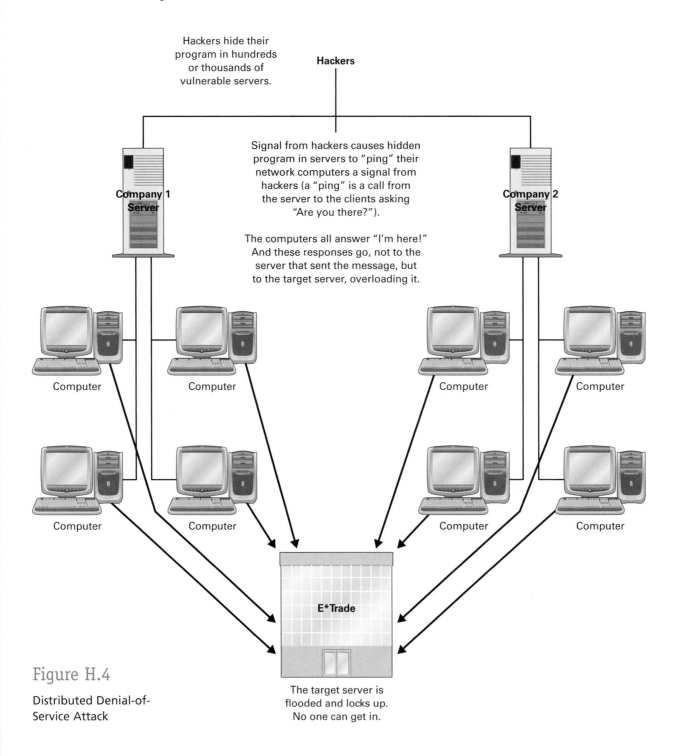

Hackers hide their program in hundreds or thousands of vulnerable servers.

Hackers

Signal from hackers causes hidden program in servers to "ping" their network computers a signal from hackers (a "ping" is a call from the server to the clients asking "Are you there?").

The computers all answer "I'm here!" And these responses go, not to the server that sent the message, but to the target server, overloading it.

Company 1 Server

Company 2 Server

Computer

Computer

Computer

Computer

Computer

Computer

Computer

Computer

E*Trade

The target server is flooded and locks up. No one can get in.

Figure H.4

Distributed Denial-of-Service Attack

address of its Web site. Before it was all over, Code Red cost an estimated $2.4 billion in prevention, detection, and cleanup even though it didn't destroy files or otherwise do much damage. However, this type of attack power is potentially very dangerous.

The Blaster worm in 2003 was also of the combination worm/DoS type. Blaster was programmed to launch a DoS against Microsoft's upgrade page on the Internet on August 16. Microsoft changed the address of its page so that the attempt would fail.

WEB DEFACING

Web defacing is a favorite sport of some of the people who break into computer systems. They replace the site with a substitute that's neither attractive nor complimentary (see Figure H.5). Or perhaps they convert the Web site to a mostly blank screen with an abusive or obscene message, or the message may just read "So-and-so was here." In essence, Web site defacing is electronic graffiti, where a computer keyboard and mouse takes the place of a paint spray can.

In 2000, during a flair-up in tensions between Israel and the Palestinians, Israelis defaced the Web sites of Hezbollah and Hamas. In retaliation, Palestinians brought down Israeli government sites and then turned their attention to Web sites of pro-Israeli groups in the United States.

Web site defacing is becoming increasingly popular, and sites that are accessed by many people worldwide are particular favorites. The USAToday.com Web site was attacked in July 2002, causing the newspaper to shut down the whole site for three hours to fix the problem. The hackers replaced several news stories on the site with bogus stories that were full of spelling errors. One story said that the Pope had called Christianity "a sham." The phony stories were only on the site for 15 minutes before they were spotted and the site was taken offline.[14]

Figure H.5

The Defacing of the Department of Justice's Web Site

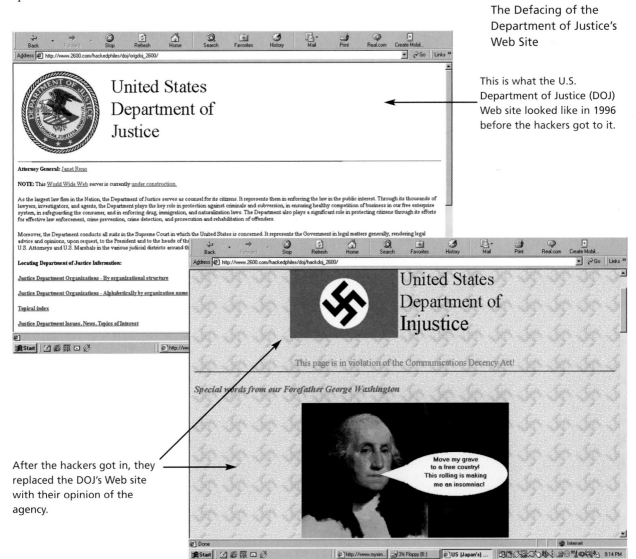

This is what the U.S. Department of Justice (DOJ) Web site looked like in 1996 before the hackers got to it.

After the hackers got in, they replaced the DOJ's Web site with their opinion of the agency.

THE PLAYERS

Who's spreading all this havoc? The answer is hackers. This is the popular name for people who break into computer systems. *Hackers* are knowledgeable computer users who use their knowledge to invade other people's computers. There are several categories of hackers, and their labels change over time. The important thing to note in the following discussion is that the motivation and reasons for hacking are as many and varied as the people who engage in it.

THRILL-SEEKER HACKERS

Thrill-seeker hackers break into computer systems for entertainment. Sometimes, they consider themselves to be the "good guys" since they expose vulnerabilities and some even follow a "hackers' code." Although they break into computers they have no right to access, they may report the security leaks to the victims. Their thrill is in being able to get into someone else's computer. Their reward is usually the admiration of their fellow hackers. There's plenty of information on the Web for those who want to know how to hack into a system—about 2,000 sites offer free hacking tools, according to security experts.

WHITE-HAT HACKERS

The thrill-seeker hackers used to be called white-hat hackers. But lately, the term *white-hat* is being increasingly used to describe the hackers who legitimately, with the knowledge of the owners of the IT system, try to break in to find and fix vulnerable areas of the system. These *white-hat hackers,* or *ethical hackers* are computer security professionals who are hired by a company to break into a computer system. These hackers are also called counter hackers, or penetration testers.

BLACK-HAT HACKERS

Black-hat hackers are cyber vandals. They exploit or destroy the information they find, steal passwords, or otherwise cause harm. They deliberately cause trouble for people just for the fun of it. They create viruses, bring down computer systems, and steal or destroy information.

A 16-year-old black-hat hacker was sentenced to detention for six months after he hacked into military and NASA networks. He caused the systems to shut down for three weeks. He intercepted more than 3,000 e-mails and stole the names and passwords of 19 defense agency employees. He also downloaded temperature and humidity control software worth $1.7 billion that helps control the environment in the international space station's living quarters.[15]

CRACKERS

Crackers are hackers for hire and are the people who engage in electronic corporate espionage. This can be a pretty lucrative undertaking, paying up to $1 million per gig. Typically an espionage job will take about three weeks and may involve unpleasant tasks like dumpster diving to find passwords and other useful information and "social engineering." *Social engineering* is conning your way into acquiring information that you have no right to. Social engineering methods include calling someone in a company and pretending to be a technical support person and getting that person to type in a login and password, sweet talking an employee to get information, and for difficult jobs, perhaps even setting up a fake office and identity. Often when crackers have accumulated about $500 million, they retire to some country that doesn't have an extradition agreement with the country they cracked in.[16]

MAKE UP A GOOD PASSWORD

One way to protect files, folders, entry into stock trading, banking, and other sites is to have a good password. That's the theory anyway. The problem is that most people choose passwords that are easy to remember, and consequently they're easy for others, who perhaps have malevolent intentions, to crack. Others write passwords down, which makes them very accessible to anyone who comes near your desk. Often hackers can get access to a server by way of a legitimate user's ID and password.

Another problem that companies face is that people seem to be unaware of how important it is to keep passwords secret. In a London underground (subway) station, an experiment was conducted in which commuters were offered a cheap pen if they would disclose the password to their company's system. A very large number of people took the deal. Of course, there's no way to know whether they actually gave their real passwords or not, but based on other studies, it's not unlikely that they did.

ZDNet offers some good advice on picking passwords. You should never pick a password that has a word from any dictionary, or one that is a pet's name or a person's. Instead, you should pick a phrase and use the first letter of each word. Then capitalize some letters and substitute punctuations and digits for others.

For example, the saying "just hang loose, just have fun, you only live once" would become JhL?H6+oLo. If you can remember the mnemonic and your substitutions, you'll certainly have a password that will be hard to break.

To find out about breaking passwords, look on the Web for information about "Jack the Ripper," which is a well-known password-cracking problem. Find three more password-cracking programs and note whether they're public domain, freeware, shareware, or whether you have to pay for them. At www.elcomsoft.com you'll find all sorts of password crackers for Microsoft and other popular products. The stated purpose of this site is to help you recover lost corporate files. What other "helpful" products do this and other similar sites have and what do they do?

HACKTIVISTS

Hacktivists are politically motivated hackers who use the Internet to send a political message of some kind. The message can be a call to end world hunger, or it can involve an alteration of a political party's Web site so that it touts another party's candidate. It can be a slogan for a particular cause or some sort of diatribe inserted into a Web site to mock a particular religious or national group.

Hacktivism, in the form of Web defacing, is becoming a common response to disagreements between nations. When the U.S. military plane made an emergency landing in China and a dispute arose about the return of the crew and plane, U.S. hackers started to attack Chinese Web sites, and Chinese hackers returned the favor, targeting government-related sites.

CYBERTERRORISTS

Since September 11, 2001, officials have become increasingly worried about the threat of cyberterrorists. This group of hackers, like the hacktivists, is politically motivated, but its agenda is more sinister. A *cyberterrorist* is one who seeks to cause harm to people or destroy critical systems or information. Possible targets of violent attacks would be air traffic control systems and nuclear power plants, and anything else that could harm the infrastructure of a nation. At a less lethal level, cyberterrorist acts would include shutting down e-mail or even part of the Internet itself, or destroying government records, say on social security benefits or criminals.

However, the FBI and other government agencies are very much aware of the threats they face from computer-based attacks, and have taken steps to protect the infrastructure

DIGITAL SIGNATURES AND CERTIFICATES

Digital signatures are a way of protecting electronic messages, like e-mails, on their journey through cyberspace. They are antitampering devices. The basis of a digital signature is that a set of characters in the message is used in arithmetic operations to generate a unique "key" for that message. When the message arrives, the recipient repeats the operations in the exact order. The result should be the original key. If it's not, then the message has been tampered with.

Digital signatures are often used in conjunction with digital certificates. What are digital certificates? Do some research and write a one-page report on digital certificates and how they're used.

that supports cyberspace. They can enjoy a reasonable expectation of success since a computer system is a lot easier to protect than public structures like buildings and bridges.

SCRIPT KIDDIES

Script kiddies or *script bunnies* are people who would like to be hackers but don't have much technical expertise. They download click-and-point software that automatically does the hacking for them. An example of this was the young man in Holland who found a virus toolkit on the Web and started the Kournikova worm. It was very similar to the Love Bug worm in that it sent itself to all the people in the Outlook address book. Tens of millions of people got the virus after opening the attachment hoping to see a picture of Anna Kournikova.[17]

The concern about script kiddies, according to the experts, apart from the fact that they can unleash viruses and denial-of-service attacks, is that they can be used by more sinister hackers. These people manipulate the script kiddies, egging them on in chat rooms, encouraging and helping them to be more destructive.

INSIDE THE ORGANIZATION

There are plenty of attacks visited on an organization's computer system from outside the organization but insider fraud and embezzlement are where the big bucks are lost. You can find more information on insider crime in Chapter 8.

Along with the traditional crimes of fraud and other types of theft managers sometimes have to deal with harassment of one employee by another. Chevron Corporation and Microsoft settled sexual harassment lawsuits for $2.2 million each because employees sent offensive e-mail to other employees and management didn't intervene. Other companies such as Dow Chemical Company, Xerox, the New York Times Company, and Edward Jones took preemptive action by firing people who sent or stored pornographic or violent e-mail messages.

But companies have learned to be careful when investigating harassment complaints, as the following example from Walt's case file shows. One company had a complaint from a woman who claimed a male colleague was sending her offensive e-mail. The colleague denied it, but when his computer was checked, the pornographic pictures that the woman claimed she had received from him in e-mails, were found. This could have meant his dismissal. But, fortunately for the man, a computer forensics expert was called in. The expert looked beyond the pictures and discovered that the times and dates the e-mails were downloaded and sent corresponded with times the man was out of town.

Later, the woman admitted that she had downloaded the pictures and e-mailed them to herself from the man's computer. If the company hadn't been as thorough in its investigation, it could have escaped a harassment lawsuit only to find itself facing a wrongful termination lawsuit. So what exactly did the computer forensics expert do? We'll discuss that in the next two sections.

Computer Forensics

You may remember some of the following recent news stories:

- Federal Bureau of Prisons intern Chandra Levy had not been seen since April 30, 2001. She had used the Internet when making travel plans to return to California and had e-mailed her parents about her travel plans. The police found partly packed suitcases and her wallet and credit cards in her apartment. She was later found dead.

- A search that ended on March 5, 2002, found 339 discarded bodies on the grounds of Tri-State Funeral home in Walker Country. Ray Brent Marsh was formally charged with multiple counts of abusing a corpse and almost two hundred counts of fraud for allegedly taking money for cremations that were not performed and for giving loved ones fake remains. Photos of the dead bodies arranged in lewd poses appeared on the Internet.

- An engineer left Company A and went to Company B. Company A suspected that he had illegally brought intellectual property in the form of designs to his new employer. On his home computer, investigators found evidence that this was true. The engineer claimed that the clock on his home computer had malfunctioned and that the transfer of the designs occurred during the course of his work for Company A. However, his girlfriend's computer and a letter he wrote about the same time exposed this lie.[18]

- A *USA Today* veteran reporter was discovered to have fabricated many of his stories over the period 1993 to 2003. Furthermore, an examination of his company-owned computer revealed pieces that he had written to mislead investigators. This finding indicated consciousness of guilt.[19]

What all of these news stories have in common is the investigative technique that unearthed information—the process of the finding, examining, and analyzing electronic information saved on computer storage media. This process is called *computer forensics.* Many computer forensic investigations involve intellectual property cases, where a company believes that an employee is secretly copying and perhaps selling proprietary information like schematics, customer lists, financial statements, product designs, or notes on private meetings. Other investigations involve child exploitation domestic disputes, labor relations, and employee misconduct cases. In all such cases, computer forensics is usually the appropriate response strategy.

Computer forensics is the collection, authentication, preservation, and examination of electronic information for presentation in court. Electronic evidence can be found on any type of computer media, such as hard disks, floppy disks, or CDs and also on digital cameras, PDAs, cell phones, and pagers. Computer forensic experts are trained in finding and interpreting electronic evidence to discover or reconstruct computer-related activities.

There are basically two motivations for engaging in computer forensics. The first is to gather and preserve evidence to present in court. The second is to establish what activities have occurred on a computer, often for the purposes of a dispute settlement. You probably know that if you're going to court, you must meet different evidentiary standards for criminal and civil cases. In criminal cases, the standard is "beyond a reasonable doubt." In civil cases, it's the "preponderance of evidence." If you don't have to, and don't want to, involve the legal system, your standard can be lower, perhaps just enough to release someone from employment while reducing the risk of being caught in a wrongful termination lawsuit.

In a well-conducted computer forensics investigation, there are two major phases: (1) collecting, authenticating, and preserving electronic evidence; and (2) analyzing the findings.

THE COLLECTION PHASE

Step one of the collection phase is to get physical access to the computer and related items. Thus, the computer forensic team collects computers, disks, printouts, post-it notes, and so on and take them back to the lab. This process is similar to what police do when investigating crime in the physical world, collecting hair, clothing fibers, blood-stained articles, papers, and anything else that they think might be useful. The crime investigators usually take these potential clue carriers with them and secure them under lock and key, where only authorized personnel may have access, and even they must sign in and out.

Computer forensic experts use the same kind of protocol. To conduct a thorough investigation, they first take digital photos of the surrounding environment and start developing extensive documentation. Then they start collecting anything that might store information. The hard disk is an obvious place to look, but computer forensic investigators also collect any other media where information might be stored (see Figure H.6). If they can't take a clue source with them, they secure it and create an exact copy of the contents of the original media.

As well as electronic media, investigators collect any other potentially helpful items, especially passwords, for use in case any of the files they come across are encrypted or are otherwise difficult to access. Apparently, a favorite hiding place for passwords that people write down (which you should *not* do) is under the keyboard, so that's the first place that investigators look. Then they look in desk drawers and anywhere else that

Figure H.6

Where You Might Find Electronic Evidence

- Floppy disks
- CDs
- DVDs
- Zip disks
- Backup tapes of other media
- USB mass storage devices such as Thumb drives
- Flash memory cards, like an xD-Picture card, CompactFlash card, or similar storage medium for digital cameras and other devices
- Voice mail
- Electronic calendars
- Scanners
- Photocopiers
- Fax machines

passwords might be, perhaps on post-it notes or slips of paper. Other helpful items might be printouts and business cards of associates or contacts of the person being investigated.

Step two of the collection process is to make a forensic image copy of all the information. A *forensic image copy* is an exact copy or snapshot of the contents of an electronic medium. It is sometimes referred to as a bit-stream image copy. To get a forensic image copy, specialized forensic software copies every fragment of information, bit-by-bit, on every storage medium—every hard disk (if there's more than one), every floppy disk, every CD, every Zip disk. That's usually a lot of stuff. Remember that a CD holds about a half a gigabyte of information, and you can build a hard disk array (several hard disks tied together into one unit) that holds a terabyte (one trillion bytes) or more. It can take a long, long time to copy it all. And the investigator must be able to swear in court that he or she supervised the entire copying process, and that no one and nothing interfered with the evidence. This could mean sitting in the lab literally for days just copying files. Also, many experts advise that the investigator make two copies of everything in case there's a problem later with the first copy.

THE AUTHENTICATION AND PRESERVATION PROCESS

To get a forensic image copy of hard disk and other media contents, investigators physically remove the hard disk from the computer. They never turn the suspect computer on, because when the PC is turned on, Windows performs more than 400 changes to files. Access dates change, and so do temporary files, and so on. So, once turned on, the hard drive is no longer exactly the same as it was when it was shut down.[20] Thus, opposing counsel could argue that this is not the same hard disk that the suspect used.

Having removed the hard disk, investigators connect it to a special forensic computer that can read files but can't write or rewrite any medium. (They prefer to remove storage devices, but if that's not possible, they copy the contents in place using cables.) Then they use forensic software like EnCase to extract a forensic image copy of the original medium without changing the files in any way.

How do we know that nothing changed on any disk during the entire investigation, from the time the computer was seized up to the present time? That's the question that opposing counsel will ask the computer forensic expert on the witness stand. So, during the collection phase and later, the analysis phase, the investigators have to make absolutely sure that evidence to be used in a trial could not have been planted, eliminated, contaminated, or altered in any way. This is a basic evidentiary rule for all court proceedings. They have to be able to document a chain of custody and be able to account for the whereabouts and protection of evidence. To help establish a complete chronology of activity, investigators also check the BIOS, which a computer uses to time and date stamp files and actions like deleting, updating, and so on.

In a computer forensic investigation, investigators use an authentication process so that they can show sometime in the future—perhaps even two years later—that nothing changed on the hard drive or other storage medium since seizure. They can do this with an MD5 hash value. An *MD5 hash value* is a mathematically generated string of 32 letters and digits that is unique for an individual storage medium at a specific point in time. The MD5 hash value is based on the contents of that medium. Any change in the content changes the MD5 hash value.

A hash value is a seemingly meaningless set of characters. An example of a hash value would be the sum of the ISBNs and the number of pages in all the books on a bookstore shelf. The result, which would be a mixture of ISBN codes and quantities of pages, would be meaningless for anything except identification. If a book, or even a page, were added to or removed from the shelf, the hash total would change, so the contents of the shelf could be shown not to be the same as they were when the hash value was originally

Figure H.7

MD5 Hash Value

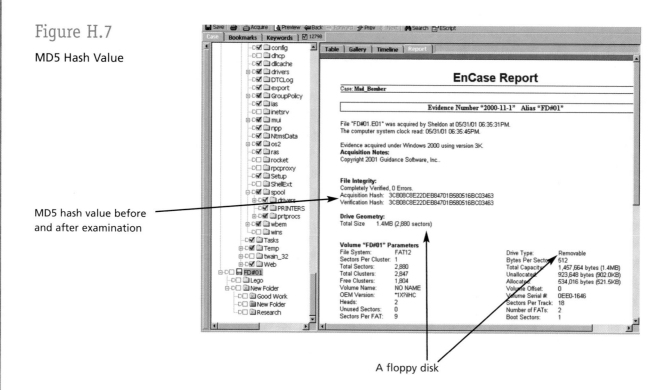

MD5 hash value before and after examination

A floppy disk

computed. Similarly, adding so much as one space in one tiny Word document on a disk will change the MD5 hash value. See Figure H.7 for an example of an MD5 hash value generated by EnCase forensic software.

MD5 hash values are considered very reliable and have become an industry standard accepted by the FBI, the U.S. Marshall Service, and most other law enforcement authorities, as well as private professional firms, as a way of uniquely authenticating a set of contents on a particular storage medium. This confidence in MD5 hash values is based on the fact that the probability of two hard disks with different contents having the same MD5 hash value is 1 in 10 to the 38th power: that's 1 with 38 zeros behind it. This makes the MD5 hash value a sort of DNA or fingerprint for computer media contents. Actually, it's more reliable than those physiological identifiers, since the probability of two sets of hard disk contents resulting in the same MD5 hash value are less than the odds of two individuals' DNA and fingerprints being identical. As an example of this probability, consider that you would have better odds of winning the Powerball lottery 39 times in your lifetime than you would of finding two hard disks with different contents that have matching MD5 hash values.

FORENSIC HARDWARE AND SOFTWARE TOOLS

As we've already mentioned, computer forensic experts use special hardware and software to conduct investigations. Usually the computer system has more power than the standard computer on a desktop and much more RAM, as well as much more hard disk capacity. This is to speed up the copying and analysis process. Computer forensic experts are also very careful not to let static electricity cause any damage or changes to magnetic media (like hard disks, Zips, and floppies). Therefore they use nonconductive mats under all computer parts, and wear wristbands that connect by wire to the ground of an electrical outlet. And just in case they need a tool, such as a screwdriver, they have a special nonmagnetic set of tools nearby, too.

There are many kinds of software in a computer forensics toolkit, in addition to forensic software, that can help in computer forensic investigations. Quick View Plus, used by many forensic experts, is an example. This is software that will load Word, Excel, image, and many other file formats. If it comes across a file with an .xls extension, which is actually an image and not a spreadsheet file, Quick View will show the file as an image regardless of its extension. That saves the investigator having to try it in multiple programs after loading fails in Excel. Conversions Plus is a package that does the same sort of thing. Other helpful software includes Mailbag Assistant, which reads many e-mail formats, and IrfanView, which is an image viewer that will read most picture files.

For investigations that might be headed toward litigation, computer forensic experts often use EnCase, since it's widely accepted as robust and reliable. EnCase has routinely been judged acceptable by the courts in meeting the legal standard for producing reliable evidence.

THE ANALYSIS PHASE

The second phase of the investigation is the analysis phase when the investigator follows the trail of clues and builds the evidence into a crime story. This is the phase that really tests the skill and experience of the investigators. The analysis phase consists of the recovery and interpretation of the information that's been collected and authenticated. If all the necessary files were there in plain sight with names and extensions indicating their contents, life would be much easier for the forensic investigator, but that's seldom the case. Usually, particularly if those being investigated know that they're doing something wrong, the incriminating files will have been deleted or hidden.

Investigators can recover all of a deleted file pretty easily as long as no new information has been written to the space where the file was. But, they can also recover fragments—perhaps rather large fragments—of files in parts of a disk where new files have been written, but have not completely filled the space where the old file was. With the appropriate software they can recover files or fragments of files from virtually any part of any storage medium (see Figure H.8).

E-Mail Files
• E-mail messages • Deleted e-mail messages
Program Files and Data Files
• Word (.doc) and backup (.wbk) files • Excel files • Deleted files of all kinds • Files hidden in image and music files • Encrypted files • Compressed files
Web Activity Files
• Web history • Cache files • Cookies
Network Server Files
• Backup e-mail files • Other backup and archived files • System history files • Web log files

Figure H.8

Some of the Files Recoverable from Storage Media

Figure H.9

History of File Activity

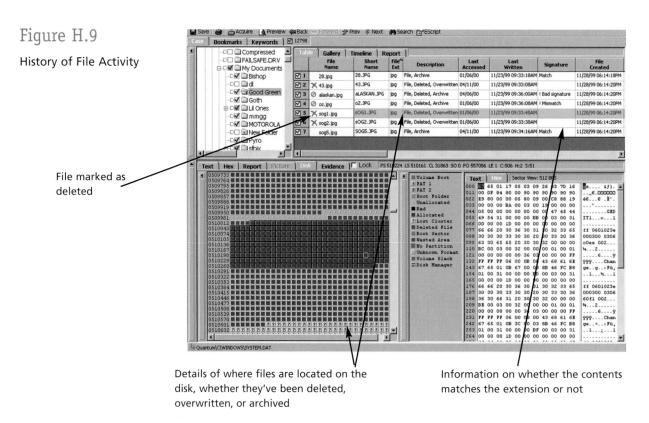

File marked as deleted

Details of where files are located on the disk, whether they've been deleted, overwritten, or archived

Information on whether the contents matches the extension or not

Computer forensic programs can pinpoint a file's location on the disk, its creator, the date it was created, the date of last access, and sometimes the date it was deleted, as well as file formatting, and notes embedded or hidden in a document (see Figure H.9).

Also stored on the hard disk is information about where the computer user went on the Web. For example, every graphic image you view on the Internet is copied to your hard disk, usually without your knowledge. In addition, Web servers have information on which computer connected to the Web and when. The same server can also tell you the sites visited by the user of that computer, the date and time of the visits, and the actions of the user at the site. These attributes are useful if the suspect claims to have reached an inappropriate site by accident, since delving deeper into the site implies a deliberate action. And, of course, if a password was required to reach the material in question, you can rest your case. With all the development in computing and investigative techniques, computer forensics experts need a forum to exchange ideas and information. Professional organizations provide such a forum (see Figure H.10).

Recovery and Interpretation

As with all evidence, the analysis of the electronic clues and the assembling of the pieces into a credible and likely scenario of what happened are very important. Much of the information may come from recovered deleted files, currently unused disk space, and deliberately hidden information or files. Some people's e-mail that was recovered to their extreme embarrassment (or worse) but arguably to society's benefit is shown in Figure H.11.

Following is a discussion, not necessarily exhaustive, of places from which computer forensic experts can recover information.

Professional organizations exist that support computer forensic experts in doing their jobs. The organizations below provide interaction between members who share information, experience, and methods. Such organizations also provide ethical guidelines and certification.

- IACIS (International Association of Computer Investigation Specialists) is open to law enforcement personnel and sets standards and guidelines for computer forensic investigations.
- ACFE (Association of Certified Fraud Examiners) focuses on serving those who investigate fraud. Members include people in law enforcement, auditors, accountants, and computer forensic experts.
- The HTCIA (High Technology Crime Investigation Association) is open to law enforcement and corporate investigators alike and facilitates the sharing of resources among its members.

A group called the Sedona Conference Working Group on Electronic Document Production published *The Sedona Principles: Best Practices, Recommendations & Principles for Addressing Electronic Document Production*. The document, the first draft of which emerged in 2003, is a new set of standards pertaining to properly conducting a computer forensic investigation. These principles were developed by lawyers, consultants, academics, and jurists to address the many issues involved in antitrust suits, intellectual property disputes, and other types of complex litigation.

Figure H.10

Professional Organizations and Standards

"... something could get screwed up enough ... and then you are in a world of hurt ..."

and

"I can only hope the folks ... are listening ..."

Figure H.11

Recovered E-mail Messages (continued on next page)

Excerpts of e-mail traffic that flew back and forth only two days before the February 1, 2003, Columbia shuttle disaster, in which an engineer discussed his misgivings about the possibility of a disaster

One of the "smoking gun" e-mails that helped sink Andersen Consulting and Enron

To:	David B. Duncan
Cc:	Michael C. Odom @ ANDERSEN WO: Richard Corgci @ ANDERSEN WO
BCC:	
Date:	10/16/2001 08:39 PM
From:	Nancy A. Temple
Subject:	Re: Press Release draft
Attachments:	ATT&ICIQ: 3rd qtr press release memo.doc

Dave - Here are a few suggested comments for consideration.

- I recommend deleting reference to consultation with the legal group and deleting my name on the memo. Reference to the legal group consultation arguably is a waiver of attorney-client privileged advice and if my name is mentioned it increases the chances that I might be a witness, which I prefer to avoid.

- I suggested deleting some language that might suggest we have concluded the release is misleading.

- In light of the "non-recurring" characterization, the lack of any suggestion that this characterization is not in accordance with GAAP, and the lack of income statements in accordance with GAAP, I will consult further within the legal group as to whether we should do anything more to protect ourselves from potential Section 10A issues.

Figure H.11

Recovered E-mail
Messages
(continued from previous
page)

From Monica Lewinsky to
Linda Tripp

From:	Lewinsky, Monica, OSD/PA	833-DC-00009446
To:	Tripp, Linda, , OSD/PA	
Subject:	I'm back!	
Date:	Wednesday, February 19, 1997 8:09AM	
Priority:	High	

LRT— Hi, I missed you!!!! I hope you enjoyed your few days of sanity with me gone because I'm back and NOT in good spirits.

1. I have a small present for you. Everything was SOOOOO expensive so I'm sorry it's small.

2. Nice that the Big Creep didn't even try to call me on V-day and he didn't know for sure that I was going back to London.

3. He could have called last night and didn't. He was out of town.

4. Finally, the ????? went away and it was the same night he was gone. ████ me!!!!

HHHEEELLPPP!!!!

Maybe we can have lunch or meet sometime today cuz I want to give you your present.

Bye...msl

From the arresting
officer in the Rodney
King beating

"oops I haven't beaten anyone so bad in a long time...."

From Bill Gates in an
intraoffice e-mail about
a competitor in the
Microsoft antitrust action

" . . . do we have a clear plan on what we want Apple to do to undermine Sun . . . ?"

PLACES TO LOOK FOR USEFUL INFORMATION

Information is written all over a disk, not only when you save a file, but also when you create folders, print documents, repartition the disk, and so on. System and application software alike continually create temporary files resulting in space and file locations being rearranged. Leftover information stays on the disk until another file writes over it, and is often recoverable with forensic software. Next, we'll examine three places where files or file remnants could be: slack space, unallocated disk space, and unused disk space.

DELETED FILES AND SLACK SPACE

It's actually not very easy to get rid of electronically stored information completely. A surprising number of people think that if they delete a file it's gone. It's not—at least not immediately, and perhaps never. When you delete a file, all you're actually doing is marking it as deleted in the disk's directory. The actual file contents are not affected *at all* by a delete action.

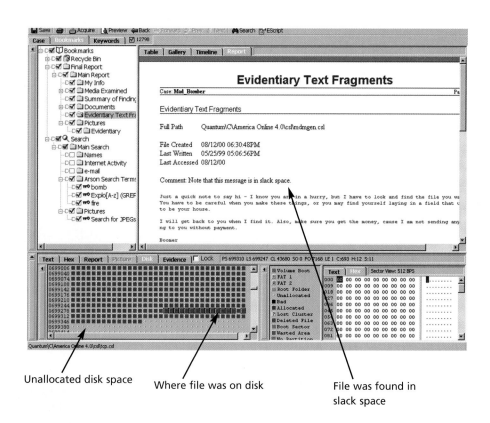

Unallocated disk space

Where file was on disk

File was found in
slack space

If you delete a file from a hard disk you usually get a message asking you if you want it in the *Recycle Bin* and then you can recover it simply by using the *Undelete* option. On a removable medium, like a Zip or floppy disk, it's a little harder, but not much. The message you get asks whether you're sure you want to delete the file because it may not be recoverable. Actually that message should read "not as easily recoverable as files in the recycle bin," since you can get it back with utility programs such as Norton Utilities, and of course, forensic software.

When you mark a file as deleted, the space is freed up for use by some other file. So, another file may shortly be written to that space. However, it's not quite that straightforward. The operating system divides storage space into sectors of bytes or characters. The sectors are grouped into clusters. A file is assigned a whole number of clusters for storage, whether it completely fills the last cluster or not. This storage allocation method usually leaves unused portions of clusters. This is analogous to writing a three and one-half page report. You'd have to use the top half of the fourth page and leave the rest of the page blank. So, the fourth page is allocated to the report but not completely used. If the previously stored file (the deleted one) was bigger and used that last part of the space, then the remnants of the deleted file remain and can be recovered using the appropriate software. The space left over from the end of the file to the end of the cluster is called **slack space,** and information left there from previous files can be recovered by forensic software (see Figure H.12).

SYSTEM AND REGISTRY FILES

Operating system files manage the hardware and software of your computer and let your application software access hardware without having to know how all the various types of hardware function. As one of its many functions, the operating system controls virtual memory. Virtual memory is hard disk space that is used when RAM is full. Details of virtual memory activity are stored in system files. For example, if you have several applications running and you're instant messaging someone, that exchange may be stored on the hard disk without your knowing it simply because there wasn't room for it in RAM.

The Registry is the database that Windows uses to store configuration information. Registry files have information such as preferences for users of the system, settings for the hardware, system software, and installed programs. This information can be very valuable. For example, even if you uninstall a program, remnants of the install process remain in the registry file. Registry files also contain the MAC (Media Access Control) address, which is a special ID for a computer on a network. When this MAC address is contained in a file, as it is in a Word document, it links that document file to its "owner" computer.

UNALLOCATED DISK SPACE

If your hard disk gets a lot of use, it's probable that each sector has had information put into it many times. The operating system is always moving files around, and if you changed a Word file and resaved it, the previous version is marked as deleted and the space becomes unallocated. *Unallocated space* is the set of clusters that has been marked as available to store information, but has not yet received a file, or still contains some or all of a file marked as deleted. Until the new information takes up residence, the old information remains. The bigger the hard disk, the longer it usually takes for old space to be used.

UNUSED DISK SPACE

Unused space results from rearranging disk space. For example, when a hard drive is repartitioned, the new partitioning may not use all the space on the hard disk. So, again, those unused portions are not overwritten. The partition table and other operating system information are stored on their own tracks and are not visible under normal circumstances, but may have once stored a Word document. To be able to see the fragments of files tucked away in these tracks the user needs forensic software.

ERASED INFORMATION

By now you may be asking whether it's possible to completely erase information from a storage medium. It is possible, but you need to know what you're doing. You can get disk-wiping programs that erase information from a disk by writing nonsense information over the previous contents. Utilities like Norton have this feature. However, erasing a disk takes a lot of time. A 10-gigabyte hard disk (not very big) would take several hours to clean. Even then you're not necessarily safe, for three reasons:

- A single overwrite may not erase the information completely. The Department of Justice recommends that government agencies write over old information seven times to be sure it's completely gone.
- Some programs keep track of what was deleted by whom, and that record is viewable if you know where to look.
- Disk-wiping programs vary greatly in which parts of the hard disk they clean. For most of them, you have to change the settings to reach certain parts of the disk. Some claim to go through the wipe process up to 35 times, but that still doesn't erase the areas that the software isn't set to erase. Also keep in mind that if you're trying to erase information because of some illicit activity, traces may still be left of the information you're trying to discard, and unless you are very careful, you'll leave traces of your attempt to wipe the disk. At the very least, you'll most likely leave a record in the Registry that you installed the wiping program.

WAYS OF HIDING INFORMATION

There are many ways of deliberately hiding information (other than deleting the file) and some are easy to defeat and others are not so easy. Following is a sampling of methods that people use to try to hide files.

RENAME THE FILE

The simplest, and most easily detected, way of deliberately hiding a file in Windows is to change the extension of the file. Say you had an Excel file that had calculations you didn't want anyone to know about, you could name the file Space Needle.jpg. Then it would appear in Explorer in the list of files as a .jpeg image file, with the name implying that it's just a vacation photo or something else innocuous.

However, if you try to click on that file, Windows will try to load it with the default .jpg viewer. And, of course, it won't load. What computer forensic experts usually do is load the file into a program that accommodates many file formats. This way, you save a lot of time trying to load the renamed file into lots of different types of software. Even more helpful is a forensic tool like EnCase that actually flags files with extensions that don't match the contents and also show files in their true formats.

MAKE THE INFORMATION INVISIBLE

They always say that the best hiding place is in plain sight. A very simple way to hide information inside a file, say a Word document, is to make the information the same color as the background. This works in Excel and other types of files, too. So if you suspect that something interesting is hidden this way, you could check the size of the file to see if it looks consistent with the contents. Also, software like EnCase is not affected by formatting. So, even white-on-white text will be easily searchable and readable by the forensic investigator.

USE WINDOWS TO HIDE FILES

Windows has a utility to hide files of a specific type. You simply open up that drive or folder, choose *View,* then *Options,* and hide the files by indicating what extensions you want hidden. If you go through this process, you'll probably see that there's a list of hidden files already on your computer. These are files that have to do with the correct functioning of your computer and to list them would just clutter up Windows Explorer and risk their being changed or deleted by accident. Again, forensic software takes special note of hidden files and flags them for further investigation.

PROTECT THE FILE WITH A PASSWORD

Word lets you password protect files so that when someone tries to open the file a pop-up window asks for the password. Unless you know the password, you won't be able to read the file. Forensic software can view the contents of many file types without opening the file, eliminating the effectiveness of many types of password protection.

ENCRYPT THE FILE

Encryption scrambles the contents of a file so that you can't read it without the right decryption key. Often investigators can find the decryption key in a password file or on a bit of paper somewhere around the keyboard. There are also password-cracking programs that will find many passwords very easily (alarmingly easily, in fact). They have dictionaries of words from multiple languages, so whole words from any language are not hard to crack. Some people put a digit or two on the front or back of a word. That doesn't fool password-cracking programs at all.

Sometimes investigators can figure out passwords from knowing something about the person. That's why birthdays, anniversaries, children's or pet's names are not good passwords. Also, since you usually need passwords for lots of reasons and it's hard to remember lots of different random ones, many people use just two or three different passwords. So if investigators find one password, they can try that in multiple places. Also, having one password often offers a clue as to what the other passwords might be. For example, if one password an investigator discovers is a fragment of a nursery rhyme, then the others might be, too.

USE STEGANOGRAPHY

Steganography is the hiding of information inside other information. Paper money is a good example of steganography. If you hold a dollar bill up to the light you'll see a watermark. The watermark image is hidden inside the other markings on the bill, but can be viewed if you know what to do to see it.

You can electronically hide information using this method. For example, if you want to hide a text file inside an image file, you can use a program called Steganos that does the work for you. Steganos takes nonessential parts of the image and replaces them with the hidden file. "Nonessential" means that these are parts of the picture that you can't see anyway, so changing those to the hidden message makes the message invisible (see Figure H.13). Steganography is a process is similar to file compression, where nonessential information is removed to save space, rather than to hide it.

The FBI and other law enforcement agencies believe that worldwide terrorist networks communicate using steganography. They set up a Web site and find pictures in which they can hide messages. When the message is hidden, the innocent-looking picture goes back up on the Web site. Fellow terrorists can download the picture, and open

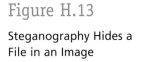

Figure H.13

Steganography Hides a
File in an Image

You can't see the parts of the picture that were changed to encode the hidden
message. You'll only be able to access the hidden file when you put the right
password into a pop-up window.

it with special software. With the correct password, the hidden message appears. Forensic investigators look for clues about steganography by searching for the names of steg programs.

COMPRESS THE FILE

Compressing a file makes it invisible to keyword searches. To find out what's in it you'll have to decompress it with the right software or use a newer version of EnCase that reads compressed files. This decompression software may be on the hard disk or on another disk somewhere around the suspect's desk. That's why investigators take all media for examination.

Who Needs Computer Forensics Investigators?

Computer forensics is widely used wherever and whenever the investigation of electronically stored files is warranted, such as:

- In the military, both as part of national security intelligence gathering and analysis and for internal investigations of military personnel.
- In law enforcement, when the FBI, state investigatory agencies, and local police departments need to gather electronic evidence for criminal investigations.
- Inside corporations or not-for-profit organizations, when conducting internal audits, for example, or investigating internal incidents.
- In consulting firms that specialize in providing computer forensic services to corporations and law enforcement.

Computer forensics experts work both proactively, educating and warning people about possible problems, and reactively, when they're called in to help in response to an incident. The need for such expertise is growing, especially considering that in 1999 it was estimated that 93 percent of all information generated was in digital form.

PROACTIVE COMPUTER FORENSICS EDUCATION FOR PROBLEM PREVENTION

Companies are increasingly providing proactive education for two reasons: first, to educate employees on what to do and not to do with computer resources and why; and second, to teach employees what to do if they suspect wrongdoing, and how not to make things worse by destroying evidence.

People who use computers every day are often not very knowledgeable about what, when, and how information is stored on computers. For example, many corporations have strict policies on how long e-mails will be kept on the system (or in the form of backups). Usually the period of time is about 60 days. You might decide to save your e-mails on your hard disk so that you'll have them indefinitely. This might not be wise since the reason that companies have this policy is that should the company find itself involved in litigation, all electronic information, including e-mail, may be discoverable. That is, the company may have to hand it over to opposing counsel. The more there is, the more it costs to collect, organize, and deliver it.

In Chapter 8 you saw the Industry Perspective box detailing Enron's e-mail situation. Lots of personal information that was not directly related to the legal case became public information and was put on the Internet. See the nearby On Your Own project to see what you know about some basic issues that face employees.

It's been said that what you don't know can't hurt you. That may be true in some circumstances but not in the cyber world. What you don't know about what happens on your computer can cause you all kinds of trouble. Test your knowledge about what goes on inside your computer. If someone asked you to respond as to the wisdom or foolishness of the following statements, what would you say (include explanations of your answers)?

1. My computer at work is safe, secure, and private.

2. When I delete a file from my hard disk, it's removed from the disk.

3. I'll be safe from any investigators as long as I use a disk-wiping program on my hard disk.

4. Computers store files only when you explicitly save them.

5. As long as I don't save the inappropriate images I view on the Web, no one will ever be the wiser.

6. Sending a joke from my work e-mail will be fine as long as I put a smiley face emoticon after it.

7. As long as I don't open e-mail attachments I don't recognize, I can't possibly get a virus.

The second reason for providing some education in computer forensics has to do with conducting internal investigations properly. Say a company wants to file a complaint with law enforcement about the suspected illegal activity of an employee. Before law enforcement can look into the situation, however, it needs to have sufficient cause to do so. It can happen that in collecting relevant information the company inadvertently contaminates or destroys the "crime scene." The result may be that law enforcement can't prosecute after all because of lack of evidence.

REACTIVE COMPUTER FORENSICS FOR INCIDENT RESPONSE

Companies need computer forensics, in a reactive mode, to track what employees have been doing with company resources. You saw in Chapter 8 that employees may be using the Internet to such an extent during working hours that their productivity is affected, and the level of personal traffic on the company network may be such that people who are actually working are slowed down. This is just one example of misuse of the company computer system. The evidence of such misappropriation of computer resources can be found on the system itself—on individual client computers and on the servers.

A second reason for reactive computer forensics is changes in laws and government regulations and new laws passed as a consequence of recent corporate crime and misbehavior, probably the most important being the Sarbanes-Oxley Act of 2002, signed into law by President Bush. Known as "Sarbanes-Oxley," the law requires companies to (1) implement extensive and detailed policies to prevent illegal activity within the company and (2) to respond in a timely manner to investigate illegal activity.

The act expressly states that executives must certify that their financial statements are accurate. They will be held criminally liable for fraudulent reporting, removing the insulation that executives previously had of being able to say that they didn't know about misstatements. Sarbanes-Oxley also specifically requires publicly traded companies to provide anonymous hotlines so that employees and others can report suspicious activity.

The provision that suspicious activity must be investigated in a timely manner in many instances automatically requires computer forensics. In earlier litigation, courts have determined that computer-stored evidence is crucial to the proper investigation of alleged corporate fraud. Add to that the fact that delay in investigating alleged wrongdoing meets with severe penalties and that courts impose severe sanctions on those judged guilty of destroying evidence including electronic information.

A DAY IN THE LIFE OF A COMPUTER FORENSICS EXPERT

You may be considering computer forensics as a profession. If so, you're contemplating a vocation that's very demanding but very rewarding. You have to know a lot about computers, and you have to keep learning to keep up with the fast pace of the computer world. You have to have infinite patience and be very detail-oriented. You also have to be good at explaining to lawyers, juries, and other nonexperts how computers work. You have to be able to remain very cool under pressure and think fast since some of the situations you face will be quite adversarial. Lanny Morrow has these qualities.

Lanny is a computer forensics expert with the Forensic and Dispute Consulting division of BKD, LLP, one of the largest accounting firms in the United States. All sorts of organizations, both for-profit and not-for-profit, and legal firms needing detective work done inside computers hire BKD's computer forensics services called Data Probe.

Lanny's cases are many and varied, making his life very interesting. Some cases take a long time and others are resolved pretty fast like the divorce case where the wife believed that her husband was hiding assets and that the records were on their home computer. No one (wife, lawyers, friends) could find anything incriminating on the hard drive or on any other storage medium. But the wife was adamant that the records were there. Lanny was called in. His first step as always was to open up the computer and have a look inside to see if anything in there looked unusual. And there it was—a second hard drive that wasn't plugged in, and was just sitting inside the system unit. When the husband wanted to do his secret accounting, he just opened up the box and swapped hard disk connections, reversing the process when he was done.

Sometimes Lanny can save a reputation, rather than proving wrongdoing, as in the case of the popular schoolteacher. As a lark, some of the teacher's female students, who were using his computer, decided to search for .jpg image files. They found some pornography and were very upset. They told their parents who immediately contacted a lawyer who in turn contacted the school. The school's information technology staff confirmed that there were many pornographic pictures on the computer. The local media picked up the story and, as outrage spread across the community, the teacher was suspended. The teacher then hired a lawyer who called Lanny in to get the facts.

When Lanny investigated the computer, he found that things weren't quite as they seemed. Having looked at the dates and origins of the images and examined their origins, he found that these images had come as pop-ups in e-mails that the teacher had opened, but had only viewed for seconds. The teacher had not gone searching for this material and had not perused it when it arrived in his e-mail. The reason he even saw the pictures was that, instead of looking at the subject line of the e-mails (which, in many cases, specified the nature of the contents) and then choosing which ones to open, he had simply pushed the *Next* button to view his e-mail messages in order of arrival. The teacher was absolved of any wrongdoing and was subsequently reinstated.

A sales representative who changed jobs and was suspected by his former employer of stealing intellectual property didn't fare so well. The suspicious manager viewed all the videotape footage of the former employee coming in and going out of the building without finding anything suspicious. The other possibility was, of course, that the information had been spirited out electronically.

When he started looking into it, Lanny found a trail of where the former employee had been viewing customer lists, product specifications, and other information that he wouldn't have needed in the normal course of doing his job. Interestingly, these files had been accessed during the lunch hour and had left a trail showing that someone had been burning large numbers of files to a CD. The final confirmation was that when the CD copying box had popped up asking the employee whether he wanted to save his CD project to the hard disk, he inadvertently had answered "Yes" so that all the file names were saved to his hard disk in the *My Documents* folder. Having realized his mistake, the salesman deleted all these file names to the recycle bin where they were easily retrievable. The manager remarked that the employee had left with a dolly-load of information, not in the physical sense, of course, but with a more modern dolly in the form of a CD.

Summary: Student Learning Outcomes Revisited

1. **Define computer crime and list three types of computer crime that can be perpetrated from inside and three from outside the organization.** *Computer crime* is a crime in which a computer, or computers, played a significant part in its commission. Crimes perpetrated outside the organization include

   - *Computer viruses*
   - *Denial-of-service (DoS) attacks*
   - Web defacing
   - *Trojan-horse virus*

   Crimes perpetrated inside the organization include

   - Fraud
   - Embezzlement
   - Harassment

2. **Identify the seven types of hackers and explain what motivates each group.** *Hackers* are knowledgeable computer users who use their knowledge to invade other people's computers. The seven types are

   - *Thrill-seeker hackers,* who are motivated by the entertainment value of breaking into computers
   - *White-hat hackers,* who are hired by a company to find the vulnerabilities in its network
   - *Black-hat hackers,* who are cyber vandals and cause damage for fun
   - *Crackers,* who are hackers for hire and are the people who engage in electronic corporate espionage

   - *Hacktivists,* who are politically motivated hackers who use the Internet to send a political message of some kind
   - *Cyberterrorists,* who seek to cause harm to people or destroy critical systems or information for political reasons
   - *Script kiddies* or *script bunnies,* who would like to be hackers but don't have much technical expertise

3. **Define computer forensics and describe the two phases of a forensic investigation.** *Computer forensics* is the collection, authentication, preservation, and examination of electronic information for presentation in court. Electronic evidence can be found on any type of computer storage medium. A computer forensic investigation has two phases: (1) collecting, authenticating, and preserving electronic evidence; and (2) analyzing the findings. The collection phase consists of

   - Getting physical access to the computer and any other items that might be helpful
   - Creating a *forensic image copy* of all storage media
   - Authenticating the forensic image copy by generating an *MD5 hash value,* that, when recalculated at a later date will be the exact same number, as long as nothing at all on the storage medium has changed in any way
   - Using forensic hardware that can read storage media but cannot write to them
   - Using forensic software that can find deleted, hidden, and otherwise hard-to-access information

The analysis phase consists of

- Finding all the information and figuring out what it means
- Assembling a crime story that fits the information that has been discovered

4. **Identify and describe four places on a hard disk where you can find useful information.** The four places are
   - *Slack space* which is the space left over from the end of the file to the end of the cluster
   - System and registry files that have lots of information about your hardware, software, and files
   - *Unallocated space,* which is the set of clusters that has been marked as available to store information
   - Unused space that results from actions like repartitioning a disk

5. **Identify and describe seven ways of hiding information.** The seven ways of hiding information are
   - Rename the file to make it look like a different type of file
   - Make information invisible by making it the same color as the background
   - Use the Windows operating system's hide utility to hide files
   - Protect the file with a password, so that the person who wants to see the file must provide the password
   - *Encrypt* the file, scrambling the contents of the file so you have to have the key to unscramble and read it
   - Use *steganography* to hide a file inside another file
   - Compress the file so that a keyword search can't find it

6. **Describe two ways in which corporations use computer forensics.** Corporations use computer forensics for proactive education and for reactive incident response. Education serves to explain to employees what they should and should not do with computer resources and also how to conduct an internal computer forensic investigation. Incident response involves uncovering employee wrongdoing and preserving the evidence so that action can be taken.

Key Terms and Concepts

Black-hat hacker, 398
Computer crime, 390
Computer forensics, 401
Computer virus (virus), 391
Cracker, 398
Cyberterrorist, 399
Denial-of-service (Dos) attack, 395
Distributed denial-of-service (DDoS) attack, 395
Encryption, 411
Forensic image copy, 403
Hacker, 398
Hacktivist, 399
Key logger (key trapper) software, 394

Macro virus, 391
MD5 hash value, 403
Script bunny (script kiddie), 400
Slack space, 409
Social engineering, 398
Spoofing, 394
Steganography, 412
Thrill-seeker hacker, 398
Trojan horse virus, 394
Unallocated space, 410
White-hat hacker (ethical hacker), 398
Worm, 391

Short-Answer Questions

1. In what two ways are computers used in the commission of crimes or misdeeds?
2. What constitutes a computer crime?
3. What kind of software is a computer virus?
4. What differentiates a worm from a macro virus?
5. How does a denial of service attack work?
6. What is the effect of a virus hoax?

7. What is the difference between the Klez family of viruses and previous worms?

8. What is a white-hat hacker?

9. What do crackers do?

10. Is there a difference between a cyberterrorist and a hacktivist? If so, what is it?

11. What is computer forensics?

12. What are the two phases of a computer forensic investigation?

Assignments and Exercises

1. **FIND COMPUTER FORENSICS SOFTWARE** On the Web there are many sites that offer computer forensics software. Find five such software packages and for each one answer the following questions:
   - What does the software do? List five features it advertises.
   - Is the software free? If not, how much does it cost?
   - Is there any indication of the software's target market? If so, what market is it (law enforcement, home use, or something else)?

2. **WHAT EXACTLY ARE THE SEDONA PRINCIPLES?** Figure H.10 mentioned the *Sedona Principles.* These 14 principles were developed by lawyers, consultants, academics, and jurists to address the many issues involved in antitrust suits, intellectual property disputes, and other types of complex litigation.

   Write a report on the stipulations of the *Sedona Principles.* Do some research and find out exactly what the *Sedona Principles* suggest. Here's the first one to get you started:

   1. Electronic data and documents are potentially discoverable under Fed.R. Civ. P. 34 or its state law equivalents. Organizations must properly preserve electronic data and documents that can reasonably be anticipated to be relevant to litigation.

   Be sure to explain in your paper any legal terms, such as "discovery," which appears in the first principle, and "spoliation," in the 14th principle.

3. **THE INTERNATIONAL ANTI-CYBERCRIME TREATY** Find out what the provisions of the international anti-cybercrime treaty are and how they will affect the United States. One of the concerns that will have to be addressed is the issue of whether laws of one country should apply to all. For example, if certain sites are illegal in Saudi Arabia, should they be illegal for all surfers? Or if Germany has a law about hate language, should a German or a U.S. citizen be extradited to stand trial for building a neo-Nazi Web site? What do you think?

4. **DOES THE FOURTH AMENDMENT APPLY TO COMPUTER SEARCH AND SEIZURE?** The U.S. Department of Justice's Computer Crime and Intellectual Property Section has an online manual to guide computer forensics experts through the legal requirements of the search and seizure of electronic information. It's available at www.cybercrime.gov/searchmanual.htm and has a section on "Reasonable Expectation of Privacy." There are four subsections: general principles, reasonable expectation of privacy in computers as storage devices, reasonable expectation of privacy and third-party possession, and private searches. Read and summarize these four subsections.

CHAPTER NINE OUTLINE

STUDENT LEARNING OUTCOMES

1. Describe the emerging trends and technologies that will have an impact on the changing Internet.

2. Define the various types of technologies that are emerging as we move toward physiological interaction with technology.

3. Describe technological innovations and trends that will increase portability and mobility.

4. Describe the coming C2C explosion and the broadening of e-government as they relate to the rebirth of e-commerce.

WEB SUPPORT

www.mhhe.com/haag

- MBA programs
- Specialized MBA programs
- Graduate school information and tips
- Tele-education (distance learning)
- Automatic speech recognition

CHAPTER NINE

Emerging Trends and Technologies
Business, People, and Technology Tomorrow

OPENING CASE STUDY:
THE FUTURE: TECHNOLOGY OUT,
PRINGLES IN

You might hold a future technological innovation in your hand right now if you were eating Pringles. It's true. In 2002, i-sec, a security company in England, built a wireless antenna from a Pringles can, attached it to a computer, and then drove around London's financial district. Because of the particular construction of the can (a long tube with aluminum-type material inside), i-sec employees were able to detect and attach to over two-thirds of the wireless networks in that financial district. More alarming, they were then able to break into the networks because there was no security.

In a rich neighborhood in New York, hackers used a Pringles can antenna and drove around the neighborhood during the late night hours trying to detect home wireless networks. When they found one, they stopped and spray-painted a small dot on the curb in front of the house. On a later date, the hackers drove around (in the middle of the day) in a construction van, stopped at every marked house, and attempted to break into the wireless network. If they were successful (and many times they were), they were able to steal bank account numbers, passwords, and other personal and sensitive information.

Technology of the future will take on many forms, with a can of Pringles being an extreme example. Some of the more plausible and helpful coming technological innovations include:

- Digital cash that you can use on the Internet just like folding cash without a credit card or traditional money transfer.
- Renting personal productivity software from an application service provider for only a few pennies while you use your PDA.
- CAVEs that re-create 3-D likenesses of people so you believe they are in the room with you.
- Biometrics that will use your physiological characteristics (such as your iris scan) to determine your identity and perhaps even tell if you have low blood sugar.
- Biochips that will help blind people regain some of their sight.

The list is really endless. In this chapter, we want to introduce you to several such upcoming technological innovations. The primary focus of the chapter isn't just on the technology, however, but on what future technologies will enable you to do. Equally important, we want you to think about the societal ramifications of these technologies. As we've emphasized throughout this book, technology is important but how you choose to use it is far more important.

By the way, some schools now teach hacking with a Pringles can. One such school is Intense School, which provides CEH (Certified Ethical Hacker) Certification courses. There, you can learn the right way to use an empty can of Pringles.[1,2]

Introduction

Technology is changing every day. But even more important than simply staying up with the changes in technology, you need to think about how those changes will affect your life. It's often fun to read and learn about "leading- and bleeding-edge" technologies. It is something that we would encourage you to do. The consequences of those technology changes, however, may have an impact on all our lives more far reaching than you can imagine.

In this final chapter, we will take a look at several leading- and bleeding-edge technologies, including speech recognition, biometrics, implant chips, and digital cash, among others. These new technologies can and will impact your personal and business life. Technology for the sake of technology is never a good thing and can even be counter productive. Using technology appropriately to enhance your personal life and to move your organization toward its strategic initiatives, on the other hand, are always both good things.

This has been both an exciting and a challenging chapter for us to write. The excitement is in the opportunity to talk with you about some emerging technological innovations. The challenge has been not to spotlight the technologies themselves overmuch, but rather to help you focus on how those technologies will affect your life.

So, as you read this chapter, have fun but don't get caught up exclusively in the technology advances themselves that are on the horizon. Instead, try to envision how those new technologies will change the things that you do and the way you do them, both from a personal and organizational perspective. As throughout this book, we remind you always to consider how to make new technology relevant and productive for you.

To introduce you to just a few of the many new technologies on the horizon, we've chosen those that we believe will have the greatest impact. We present those emerging technologies within the context of four important trends (see Figure 9.1).

Figure 9.1

Emerging Trends and Technologies

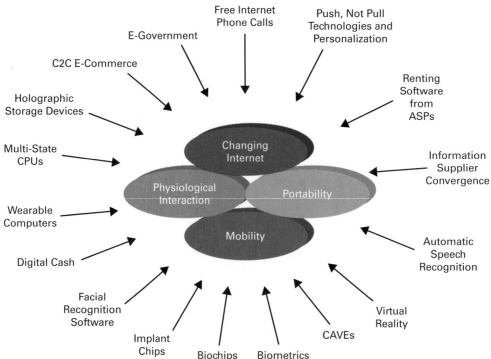

The Changing Internet

Without a doubt, the most explosive and visible aspect of technology is the Internet. Over the next several years, you will witness an unbelievable number of changes with respect to the Internet. You'll see the emergence of many new Internet-based trends and Internet-based technologies. Among those will be free Internet phone calls, push (not pull) technologies and personalization, renting personal productivity software from application service providers, information supplier convergence, and digital cash (which we'll discuss in a later section).

FREE INTERNET PHONE CALLS

Right now, true "free" Internet-based phone calls all over the world are not possible. That will soon come. But you can now use the Internet and your computer to make phone calls, with many of the phone calls you make costing as little as 2.9 cents per minute to many places around the globe.

One such company offering Internet phone calls is Voicenet (www.voicenet.com). To use Voicenet, you connect first to its Web site and download and install some simple software (see Figure 9.2). You also pick a user name and password. You can then use your computer's equipment—microphone and speakers—to make a phone call to anyone, even if they have a cell phone. You can also connect a standard telephone to your computer and use it in conjunction with Voicenet's service.

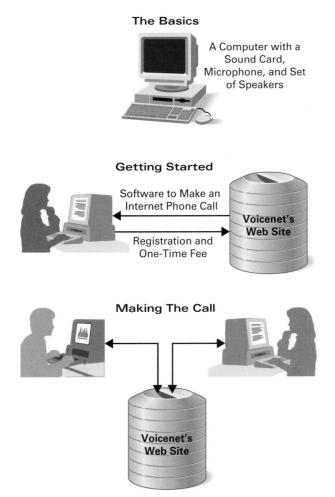

The Basics

A Computer with a Sound Card, Microphone, and Set of Speakers

Getting Started

Software to Make an Internet Phone Call

Registration and One-Time Fee

Voicenet's Web Site

Making The Call

Voicenet's Web Site

Figure 9.2

Making an Internet Phone Call

Internet phone calling will certainly impact every part of your life. You will have greater mobility with your technology and your telephone-calling system. We believe it will eventually greatly reduce your telephone bill. It will increase customer service over the Web, because companies will be able to communicate with you using a "traditional" phone call while you visit their Web sites and consider products and services to purchase.

PUSH, NOT PULL TECHNOLOGIES AND PERSONALIZATION

We live in a *pull* technology environment. That is, you look for, request, and find what you want. On the Internet, for example, you visit a specific site and request information, services, and products. So, you're literally "pulling" what you want. Future emphasis will be on *push* technologies. In a **push technology** environment, businesses and organizations come to you with information, services, and product offerings based on your profile. This isn't spam or mass e-mailings.

For example, in some parts of the country you can subscribe to a cell service that pushes information to you in the form of video rental information. Whenever you pass near a video store, your cell phone (which is GPS-enabled) triggers a computer within the video store that evaluates your rental history to see if any new videos have arrived that you might be interested in viewing. In this case, the system generates a personal data warehouse of rental history—including dimensions for the day of the week, the time of the day, and video categories—concerning you and then evaluates information in the smaller cubes (see Figure 9.3). The evaluation seeks to affirm that (1) you usually rent videos on that particular day, (2) you usually rent videos during that time of that day, and (3) there is a distinct video category from which you rent videos during that time of the day. If so, the system then checks to see if there are any movies in that category that you haven't rented and that it hasn't previously contacted you about.

Figure 9.3

Tracking What You Want and When You Want It with a Data Warehouse

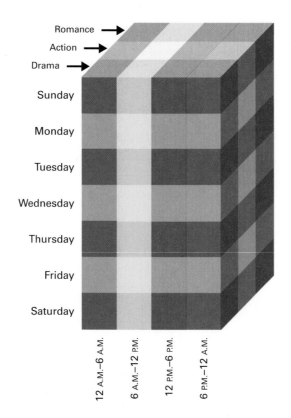

If so, the video store computer will call your cell phone with a message concerning a new release. It will also give you street-by-street directions to the video store and hold the video for you. If the video store doesn't have any new releases that might interest you, you won't receive a phone call.

You might also someday receive a personalized pizza delivery message on your television as you start to watch a ball game. The message might say, "We'll deliver your favorite sausage and mushroom pizza to your doorstep before the game begins. On your remote control, press the ORDER NOW button."

Of course, situations such as these rely on IT's ability to store vast amounts of information about you. Technologies such as databases and data warehouses will definitely play an important role in the development of push technologies that do more than just push spam and mass e-mail. In the instance of the pizza delivery message on your television, a local pizza store would have determined that you like sausage and mushroom pizza and that you order it most often while watching a ball game.

RENTING SOFTWARE FROM APPLICATION SERVICE PROVIDERS

As more technology choices become available to you (smart phones, PDAs, tablet PCs, and the like), you'll probably opt to use many different devices to satisfy your computing needs. As technology becomes increasingly small, you may not have the capacity necessary on every device to store all your software needs. This has given rise to the notion of renting personal productivity software instead of buying it. Many businesses—as you learned in previous chapters—now do rent some software instead of buying it and installing it on every single technology device within the organization. Those businesses are using an application service provider (ASP), or some variation of one.

Let's focus for a moment on your personal use of an ASP (see Figure 9.4). In the future, ASPs will provide personal productivity software for you to use (for a fee, perhaps $.25 per session) and storage so you can store your files on their Web servers as opposed to your personal technologies.

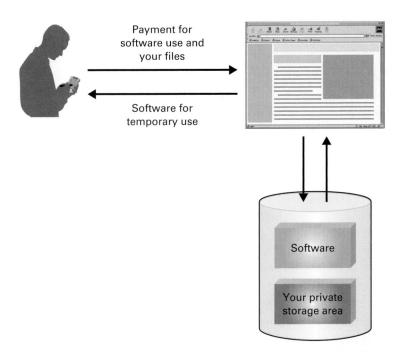

Payment for software use and your files

Software for temporary use

Software

Your private storage area

Figure 9.4

Renting Personal Productivity Software from an Application Service Provider (ASP)

THE FUTURE OF INFORMATION SUPPLIER CONVERGENCE

Information supplier convergence, through the process of mergers and acquisitions (M&A), seems to be an already foregone conclusion in the business world. Cable TV providers are acquiring telephone service providers, and vice versa. Internet conglomerates, such as America Online, are merging with entertainment giants such as Time Warner. Other information conglomerates are composed of TV stations, newspapers, radio stations, and countless other types of information suppliers.

What will be interesting to see is the M&A deals that occur within the next several years. Here are a few possibilities as predicted by Erick Schonfeld and On Malik in a recent issue of *Business 2.0* magazine. Which do you think will become a reality?

- AT&T Wireless and Cingular—creating a company with over 40 million wireless users
- Apple and Roxio—you know Apple; Roxio provides the most popular CD- and DVD-burning software
- Yahoo! and Overture—you know Yahoo!; Overture is one of the largest paid-search providers on the Internet
- Yahoo!, Overture, and Diller's Interactive—see previous bullet; Diller's is the parent company of Citysearch, Expedia, the Home Shopping Network, Hotels.com, Match.com, and Ticketmaster[3]

For example, you may be in an airport and need to build a spreadsheet with your PDA. Your PDA, however, may not have a complete version of Excel. So, you would use your PDA to connect to the Internet and a personal ASP. With your PDA, you would then use the personal ASP's Excel software to create your spreadsheet and save it on the ASP's Web server. When you finally get back to the office, you would use your computer there, connect to the same ASP, and retrieve your spreadsheet and save it on your computer.

There are many issues you'll have to consider when determining whether or not to use a personal ASP, with privacy and reliability definitely being important ones. If all your information is on a Web-based server, it will be easier for someone to gain access to it (for the wrong reasons) than if you stored all your information on your home or office computer. When considering reliability, you need to think about what happens if the personal ASP's Web site goes down. How will you perform your work? In spite of many potential drawbacks, we believe personal ASPs will become a part of your everyday life in the future.

INFORMATION SUPPLIER CONVERGENCE

You'll notice many benefits when we see the convergence of information suppliers. "Information suppliers" provide you with magazines, newspapers, Internet access, telephone service, cable TV, books, business news, and many other types of information. For example, as you read in the opening case study in Chapter 5, America Online is now providing its customers with bill payment information and reminders. Right now, you probably receive information products and services from numerous suppliers. It's difficult therefore for any one of them to help you organize and filter information, because it's coming from so many sources.

You may already be suffering from the information glut of the information age. You may receive hundreds of e-mails, text messages, and phone calls each day. Moreover, when faced with a business problem or opportunity you may have too *much* information, and may suffer from "analysis paralysis," which can occur because you simply have too much information to analyze and you never really get around to actually solving the problem or taking advantage of the opportunity, or at least not as optimally as you might with better focus. Information filtering in the future will be key.

When you start to receive the majority of your information from a single supplier, you'll notice a greater ability to filter the information. For example, if you receive your newspaper from the same organization that provides you Internet access, that organization could determine your preferences and provide you with a personal portal and a customized electronic newspaper tailored to just the topics you want to read about. For example, if the organization operated a worldwide news source it would search the international news and provide you news content appropriate to your interests.

You may already be seeing this convergence happen. Perhaps your cable TV provider is also your telephone service provider. Perhaps you use an information service on the Web that delivers daily articles to you based on your reading preferences. That information service is probably gathering information from numerous other news services, filtering it, and providing only what you want.

Physiological Interaction

Right now, your primary physical interfaces to your computer include a keyboard, mouse, monitor, and printer (basically, your input and output devices). These are physical devices, not physiological. Physiological interfaces capture and utilize your real body characteristics, such as you breath, your voice, your height and weight, and even the iris in your eye. Physiological innovations include automatic speech recognition, virtual reality, cave automatic virtual environments, and biometrics, along with many others.

AUTOMATIC SPEECH RECOGNITION

An *automatic speech recognition (ASR)* system not only captures spoken words but also distinguishes word groupings to form sentences. To perform this, an ASR system follows three steps.

1. *Feature analysis*—The system captures your words as you speak into a microphone, eliminates any background noise, and converts the digital signals of your speech into phonemes (syllables).

GETTING SMALL WITH NANOTECHNOLOGIES

One of the single greatest drawbacks to technological advances is size. The best chip manufacturers can do is to make circuit elements with a width of 130 nanometers. A nanometer is one-hundred-thousandth the width of a human hair. That may seem very, very small, but current manufacturing technologies are beginning to limit the size of computer chips, and thus their speed and capacity.

Nanotechnologies aim to change all that. In nanotechnology, everything is simply atoms. Nanotechnology researchers are attempting to move atoms and encourage them to "self-assemble" into new forms.

Nanotechnology is a bleeding-edge technology worth watching. The changes it will bring about will be unbelievable. Consider these:

Change the molecular structure of the materials used to make computer chips, for instance, and electronics could become as cheap and plentiful as bar codes on packaging. Lightweight vests enmeshed with sensors could measure a person's vital signs. Analysis of a patient's DNA could be done so quickly and precisely that designer drugs would be fabricated on the fly. A computer the size of your library card could store everything you ever saw or read.[4]

2. *Pattern classification*—The system matches your spoken phonemes to a phoneme sequence stored in an acoustic model database. For example, if your phoneme was "dü," the system would match it to the words do and due.

3. *Language processing*—The system attempts to make sense of what you're saying by comparing the word phonemes generated in step 2 with a language model database. For example, if you were asking a question and started with the phoneme "dü," the system would determine that the appropriate word is do and not due.

ASR is certainly now taking its place in computing environments. For example, Microsoft's Office XP and Office 2003 include easy-to-use speech recognition capabilities for both content and commands. The important point is that ASR allows you to speak in a normal voice; thus it supports physiological interaction. Visit the Web site that supports this text (www.mhhe.com/haag) to learn more about ASR systems.

VIRTUAL REALITY

On the horizon (and in some instances here today) is a new technology that will virtually place you in any experience you desire. That new technology is *virtual reality,* a three-dimensional computer simulation in which you actively and physically participate. In a virtual reality system, you make use of special input and output devices that capture your physiological movements and send physiological responses back to you. These devices include a

- *Glove*—An input device that captures and records the shape and movement of your hand and fingers and the strength of your hand and finger movements.
- *Headset (head-mounted display)*—A combined input and output device that (1) captures and records the movement of your head and (2) contains a screen that covers your entire field of vision and displays various views of an environment based on your movements.
- *Walker*—An input device that captures and records the movement of your feet as you walk or turn in different directions.

APPLICATIONS OF VIRTUAL REALITY   Virtual reality applications are popping up everywhere, sometimes in odd places. The most common applications are found in the entertainment industry. There are a number of virtual reality games on the market, including downhill Olympic skiing, race-car driving, golf, air combat, and marksmanship. Other applications include

- Matsushita Electric Works—You design your kitchen in virtual reality and then choose the appliances you want and even request color changes.
- Volvo—For demonstrating the safety features of its cars.
- Airlines—To train pilots how to handle adverse weather conditions.
- Motorola—To train assembly-line workers in the steps of manufacturing a new product.[5]
- Health care—To train doctors how to perform surgery using virtual cadavers.[6]

Let's consider the potential ramifications of virtual reality and how you might someday interact with your computer. New virtual reality systems include aroma-producing devices and devices that secrete fluid through a mouthpiece that you have in your mouth. So, you could virtually experience a Hawaiian luau. The aroma-producing device would generate various smells and the mouthpiece would secrete a fluid that tastes like pineapple or roasted pig. If you were using virtual reality to surf big waves, the mouthpiece would secrete a fluid that tastes like salt water.

Those examples are the "fun" uses of virtual reality. In business, building contractors would use virtual reality to show a new building and the location of fire exits. Managers may be able to experience how a proposed "downsizing" effort would affect productivity. The possibilities are virtually limitless.

CAVE AUTOMATIC VIRTUAL ENVIRONMENTS

A ***CAVE (cave automatic virtual environment)*** is a special 3-D virtual reality room that can display images of other people and objects located in other CAVEs all over the world. CAVEs are ***holographic devices,*** devices that create, capture, and/or display images in true three-dimensional form. If you watch any of the *Star Trek* movies, you'll see an example of a holographic device called the holodeck.

In working form, you would enter a CAVE room. At the same time, someone else would enter another CAVE room in another location (see Figure 9.5). Numerous digital video cameras would capture the likenesses of both participants and re-create and

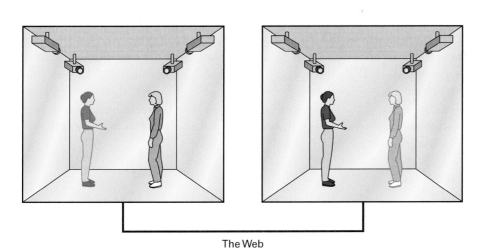

The Web

Figure 9.5

CAVEs (Cave Automatic Virtual Environments)

FINDING APPLICATIONS OF VIRTUAL REALITY

Virtual reality is quickly taking its place in the technology world. In our discussion of it, we listed several well-known applications of virtual reality.

Your task is twofold in this project. First, search the Web for more applications of virtual reality. Find at least three and provide a brief description of each. Only one of these applications can be in the area of entertainment. That is, you cannot use more than one game-oriented application of virtual reality.

Second, identify five potential applications for virtual reality. For each application, describe how virtual reality would be used and why it would be beneficial. Each of these potential applications must relate to the use of virtual reality by an organization. As you describe each of the potential applications, list the type of organization or industry that would use it.

send those images to the other CAVEs. Then, you and the other person could see and carry on a normal conversation with each other, and you would feel as if that other person were in the same room with you.

Current CAVE research is also working on the challenges of having other physical objects in the room. For example, if you sat on a couch in your CAVE, the couch would capture the indentation you made in it and pass it to the couch in the other CAVE. That couch would respond by constricting a mesh of rubber inside it so that your indentation would also appear there. And what about playing catch? Which person would have the virtual ball and which person would have the real ball? The answer is that both would have a virtual ball. When throwing it, the CAVE would capture your arm movement to determine the speed, arc, and direction of the ball. That information would be transmitted to the other CAVE, and it would use that information to make the virtual ball fly through the air accordingly.

Unlike virtual reality, you don't need any special gear in a CAVE. Let your imagination run wild and think about the potential applications of CAVEs. An unhappy customer could call a business to complain. Within seconds, a customer service representative would not answer the phone but rather appear in the room with the unhappy customer. That's an example of great customer service. Your teacher might never attend your class. Instead the teacher would enter a CAVE and have his or her image broadcast into the classroom. You might not really be in class either but rather a holographic likeness of you. Are CAVEs a realistic possibility? The answer is definitely yes. We believe that CAVEs are the successor to virtual reality. So, virtual reality may not be a long-term technological innovation but rather a stepping-stone to the more advanced CAVE. Whatever the case, CAVEs will not only significantly alter how you interact with your computer (can you imagine the thrill of video games in a CAVE?), they will even more significantly alter how you interact with other people. With CAVE technologies, you can visit your friends and relatives on a daily basis no matter where they live. You may even have television shows and movies piped into your home CAVE.

BIOMETRICS

Biometrics is the use of physiological characteristics—such as your fingerprint, the blood vessels in the iris of your eye, the sound of your voice, or perhaps even your breath—to provide identification. That's the strict and narrow definition, but biometrics

Figure 9.6

Custom-Fit Clothes
through Biometrics

is beginning to encompass more than just identification. Consider these real-world applications in place today (see Figure 9.6):

- *Internet-enabled toilets*—These toilets use your physiological output to capture readings (e.g., white-cell count, red-cell count, sodium level, sugar level, the presence of certain types of drugs, etc.) and send that information via the Internet to your doctor's computer. Your doctor's computer can then analyze that information to determine if you're getting sick or perhaps using the wrong type of medication. Of course, you have to plug an Internet-enabled toilet into both an electrical outlet and an Internet connection. Internet-enabled toilets are finding their way into assisted-care living facilities in which older people need 24-hour monitoring of their physiological characteristics.

- *Custom shoes*—Several shoe stores, especially those that offer fine Italian leather shoes, no longer carry any inventory. When you select a shoe style you like, you place your bare feet into a box that scans the shape of your feet. That information is then used to make a custom pair of shoes for you. It works extremely well if your feet are slightly different from each other in size or shape (as is the case with most people).

- *Custom wedding gowns*—Following the custom-fit shoe idea, many bridal boutiques now do the same thing for wedding dresses. Once the bride chooses the style she likes, she steps into a small room that scans her entire body. That information is used to create a wedding dress that fits perfectly.

- *Custom bathrobes*—Some high-end spa resorts now actually have patrons walk through a body-scanning device upon check-in. The scanning device measures the patron's body characteristics and then sends that information to a sewing and fabricating facility that automatically creates a custom-fit bathrobe. Some of these same spa resorts are using the readings from Internet-enabled toilets to design nutritionally optimal meal selections for patrons.

BIOMETRIC SECURITY   The best form of security for personal identification encompasses three aspects:

1. What you know
2. What you have
3. Who you are

The first—*what you know*—is something like a password, something that everyone can create and has. The second—*what you have*—is something like a card such as an ATM card you use at an ATM (in conjunction with your password, what you know). Unfortunately, most personal identification security systems stop there. That is, they do not include *who you are*, which is some form of a biometric.

It's no wonder crimes like identity theft are spiraling out of control. Without much effort, a thief can steal your password (often through social engineering) and steal what you have. For the latter, the thief doesn't actually have to steal your physical card; he or she simply has to copy the information on it. However, stealing a biometric—such as your fingerprint or iris scan—is much more difficult.

Many banks are currently converting ATMs to the use of biometrics, specifically an iris scan, as the third level of personal identification security. When you open an account and request ATM use, the bank will issue you an ATM card (you pick the password). The bank will also scan your iris and create a unique 512-byte representation of the scan. To use an ATM, you must insert your card, type in your password, and allow the machine to scan your iris. The ATM uses all three forms of identification to match you to your account. You can then perform whatever transaction you wish.

Some private schools for young children now require parents and guardians to submit to iris scans. Once the scan is captured and the person is verified as a parent or guardian, the information is entered into a security database. Then, when the parent or guardian comes to the school to pick up a child, his or her iris scan is compared to the one stored in the database. Parents and guardians cannot, under any circumstances, take a child from the school without first going through verification via an iris scan.

INTEGRATING BIOMETRIC PROCESSING AND TRANSACTION PROCESSING
Once society accepts the use of biometrics for security and identification purposes, organizations of all types will be able to add another dimension of business intelligence to their data warehouses—that dimension will capture and record changes in physiological characteristics (see Figure 9.7).

Consider, as a hypothetical example, a woman using an ATM—equipped with iris scanning capabilities—to withdraw cash. Current research suggests that it might be possible to use an iris scan to determine not only that a woman is pregnant but also the sex of the unborn child. (That is a very true statement.) When the woman has her iris

Figure 9.7

Integrating Biometric and Transaction Processing to Create Business Intelligence

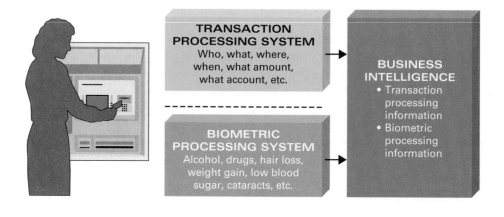

FACIAL RECOGNITION SOFTWARE AT AIRPORTS AROUND THE WORLD

Airport security is now a must. And most airports and airlines are no longer relying on government-issued forms of identification for determining who should and who should not be allowed on a plane. Instead, they're relying on facial recognition software such as FaceIt, a joint-venture product of ARINC and Visionics Corporation. FaceIt creates a digital map of a person's face and compares it to a database that contains the facial images of unwanted fliers and known terrorists.

Facial recognition software plays an important role in the use of biometrics for providing and authenticating identification. FaceIt's ARGUS system can handle an unlimited number of video cameras capturing facial images and comparing them to a database that is also unlimited in size. To learn more about FaceIt, visit ARINC at www.arinc.com and Visionics at www.visionics.com.

Facial recognition software has made great strides over the past couple of years. Consider these facts:

- Tests conducted in 2002 showed a 50 percent reduction in error rates over those conducted in 2000.
- In determining if a person is who he or she claims to be, the best facial recognition systems yield a 90 percent verification rate, with only a 1 percent false-acceptance rate.
- Males are still easier to identify than females.
- Older people are still easier to identify than younger people.[7,8]

---

scanned, the bank might be able to tell that she is pregnant and expecting a boy. When the woman receives her cash and receipt, the receipt would have a coupon printed on the back for 10 percent off any purchase at Babies "Я" Us. Furthermore, the ATM would generate another receipt that says "buy blue."

The key here is for you to consider that transaction processing systems (TPSs) of the future will be integrated with biometric processing systems (BPSs). The TPS will capture and process the "events" of the transaction—when, by whom, where, and so on. The BPS will capture and process the physiological characteristics of the person performing the transaction. Those physiological characteristics may include the presence of alcohol or illegal drugs, hair loss, weight gain, low blood sugar, vitamin deficiencies, cataracts, and yes—even pregnancy.

When businesses start to gather this type of intelligence, you can leave it to your imagination to envision what will happen. For example, because of the noted pregnancy in our previous example of the woman using an ATM, the bank might offer financing for a mini-van, evaluate the size of the family's home and perhaps offer special financing for a second mortgage so another room can be added, or establish a tuition account for the child and place $25 in it. These possibilities will further intensify competition in almost all industries.

OTHER BIOMETRICS AND BIOMETRIC DEVICES   Biometrics is a "hot topic" in research circles right now. Although we haven't the space to discuss them all, you might want to watch for these:

- *Biochip*—a technology chip that can perform a variety of physiological functions when inserted into the human body. Biochips have been proven in some cases to block pain for people who suffer severe spinal injuries, help paralyzed people regain some portion of their motor skills, and help partially blind people see better.

- *Implant chip*—a technology-enabled microchip implanted into the human body that stores important information about you (such as your identification and medical history) and that may be GPS-enabled to offer a method of tracking.
- *Facial recognition software*—software that provides identification by evaluating facial characteristics (see the accompanying Global Perspective on the previous page).

Whatever becomes a reality in the field of biometrics promises to forever change your life and how you interact with technology.

Increasing Portability and Mobility

Portability and mobility go hand-in-hand. *Portability*, in this instance, refers to how easy it is for you to carry around your technology. *Mobility* is much broader and encompasses what you have the ability to do with your technology while carrying it around. For example, PDAs are very portable; they weigh less than a pound and easily fit in your pocket or purse. However, your mobility may be limited with a PDA. That is, while you can manage your schedule, take some notes, and even use e-mail with a PDA, you certainly can't generate spreadsheets with elaborate graphs. You want technology that is no more intrusive than your wallet or purse. Ideally, your watch would really be a powerful computer system with speech and holographic capabilities (it may happen someday). If your watch is a powerful computer system, then it maximizes your mobility.

It goes without saying that to achieve maximum portability and mobility we'll need completely wireless communications. This is a vast and dynamically changing field. We won't delve into it here, but we will need it for portability and mobility. You can learn more about wireless communications in *Extended Learning Module E*.

To further advance the portability and mobility of technology, you can expect to find digital cash, wearable computers, multi-state CPUs, and holographic storage devices in the future.

DIGITAL CASH

When the digital economy arrives, so must digital money. Coins and folding cash have little or no value themselves; they are representations of value. They became the standard on which the economy works because it's much easier to pay for products and services with them than it is to use gold and silver or some other precious metal. *Digital cash* (also called *electronic cash* or *e-cash*) is an electronic representation of cash.

To use digital cash, you must first purchase it from an electronic bank (see Figure 9.8 on the facing page). You can do this by sending real cash in the mail, using a debit or credit card, or actually opening an account with the electronic bank and requesting that an amount of digital cash be deducted from your balance and sent to you. Whatever the case, the electronic bank will electronically send you your digital cash files. For example, you could request $100 in digital cash in $20 increments. What you would end up with is five digital cash files, each representing $20 on your hard disk.

Now all you have to do is find a product or service on the Internet you want to buy. You would send the merchant the appropriate number of digital cash files to equal the purchase amount. The merchant could then use those digital cash files to buy other merchandise or return it to the electronic bank for real money.

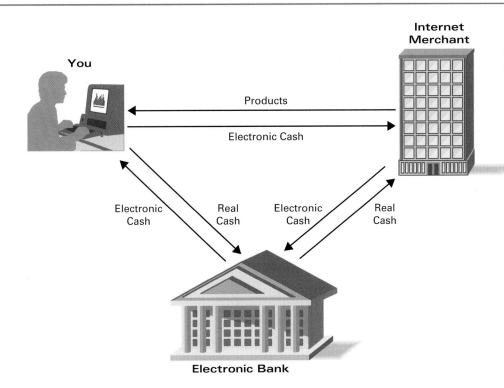

Figure 9.8

How Digital Cash Will Work on the Internet

The concept seems quite simple when you think about it. The implementation, however, has turned out to be extremely difficult for many reasons including the following:

- If your system crashes and your digital cash files are wiped clean, you've lost your money. It's rather like losing your wallet. The electronic bank will not replace the files.

- There is no standard for how digital cash should look. So, a digital cash file from one electronic bank may not look like digital cash from another electronic bank. That makes many merchants very hesitant to accept digital cash.

- Digital cash makes money laundering easy. Because none of your personal information travels with the digital cash when you use it to make a purchase, it's extremely difficult to tell where it came from. So, illegally obtained cash can be easily exchanged for digital cash.

- Digital cash travels across the vast Internet and is susceptible to being stolen. Digital information (which includes digital cash) is easy to steal and hard to trace. This may be the single biggest obstacle to the widespread use of digital cash.

In spite of the above challenges and many others, digital cash is destined to take its place as a standard technology. The real question is how soon.

WEARABLE COMPUTERS

Focusing on portability now, let's turn our attention to wearable computers. A ***wearable computer*** is a fully equipped computer that you wear as a piece of clothing or attached to a piece of clothing similar to the way you would carry your cell phone on your belt.

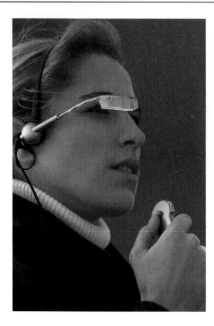

Figure 9.9

Wearable Computers

In reality, wearable computers are not some far-fetched cutting-edge technology that will take years to arrive. Today, Charmed Technologies and Xybernaut® (just to name a few) are already manufacturing and selling wearable computers (see Figure 9.9). The leader in this area is Xybernaut (www.xybernaut.com) with its many lines of wearable computers designed for manufacturing environments, disaster areas, and even children at school.

For schoolchildren, Xybernaut offers XyberKids, a fully functional computer in the form of a pen-based flat-panel display that can be easily held in hand or set on a desk along with a lightweight backpack for carrying the other computer components such as the system unit and hard disk. At the time we wrote this text, Xybernaut's XyberKids computer included a 500MHz processor; 128MB RAM expandable to 256MB; 1GB Compact Flash card; Compact Flash, USB, and Firewire ports; an 800×600 color SVGA flat-panel display with an 8.4-inch viewable screen; and an onscreen keyboard and built-in handwriting recognition. What's really nice is that the technology components in the backpack (i.e., everything but the flat-panel display) weigh less than one pound total.

Again, the focus of wearable computers is portability first and mobility second. Right now, wearable computers are very nonintrusive (portability). But they do have limited processing capabilities, so your mobility is limited. You can certainly expect that to change very soon. As technology increases in capability and decreases in price and size, wearable computers will offer you as much processing capability (mobility) as a standard desktop or notebook computer.

Let your imagination run wild again. Imagine carrying and using your wearable computer as if it were a cell phone. You would have high-speed wireless access to the Internet. You could use one eye to view your headset and work on a spreadsheet application while using your other eye to watch a baseball game. No matter where you were or what you were doing, you could still use your wearable computer to write term papers, send and receive e-mail, buy products on the Internet (m-commerce using micro-payments or digital cash, which we'll discuss in a moment), or just have fun surfing the Web.

Figure 9.10

3-D Crystal-Like Objects in a Holographic Storage Device

MULTI-STATE CPUS AND HOLOGRAPHIC STORAGE DEVICES

To increase portability and mobility, technology will have to become increasingly faster and capable of storing more information in exceedingly smaller spaces. Multi-state CPUs and holographic storage devices are two technological innovations on the horizon that promise to help in those areas.

Right now, CPUs are binary-state, capable of working only with information represented by a 1 or a 0. That greatly slows processing. What we really need to increase speed are CPUs that are multi-state. **Multi-state CPUs** work with information represented in more than just two states, probably 10 states with each state representing a digit between 0 and 9. When multi-state CPUs do become a reality, your computer will no longer have to go through many of the processes associated with translating characters into binary and then reversing the translation process later. This will make them much faster. Of course, the true goal is to create multi-state CPUs that can also handle letters and special characters without converting them to their binary equivalents.

Again, right now, storage devices store information on a two-dimensional surface, but research in the holographic realm will change that, and **holographic storage devices** will store information on a storage medium that is composed of 3-D crystal-like objects with many sides or faces (see Figure 9.10). This is similar in concept to small cards that you may have seen which change the picture or image as you view the cards from different angles.

If and when holographic storage devices do become a reality, you may be able to store an entire set of encyclopedias on a single crystal that may have as many as several hundred faces. Think how small technology will become then.

Rebirth of E-Commerce

In the late twentieth century and into the first years of the new century, e-commerce was highly touted as the next big business frontier. Venture capitalists and individuals alike poured literally trillions of dollars into dot-com businesses. Most of those dot-coms had no idea what they were doing and could very seldom show a clear and reasonable path to profitability (P2P). Of course, the e-commerce balloon popped in the middle of the year 2000 and you know the rest of the story.

But e-commerce as a business principle survived, although the dot-coms that failed to implement it correctly did not and became dot-bombs. Over the next 10 years or so we will see a strong resurgence in the e-commerce area, this time by companies backed by sound business principles and clear paths to profitability. As you witness this, you'll see some interesting trends, including the explosion of Consumer to Consumer (C2C) e-commerce and the broadening of e-government.

BUYING SODA WITH A CELL PHONE

In many countries in Europe, especially in Scandinavian countries, you can't find a slot on a vending machine to insert money to buy a soda. No, it's not because the sodas are free or because there's an extremely high criminal and vandalism rate. But you have to buy the soda with your cell phone.

On the soda machine is a telephone number that you call. When you do, the telephone call automatically triggers the soda machine so you can make a selection. The best part is that the cost of the soda is charged to your cell phone bill. No more trying to find the right change when the "CORRECT CHANGE" message is blinking. No more trying to get the creases out of a dollar bill. You simply charge the cost of the soda to your cell phone. Of course, at the end of every month you still have to pay for it, but it is indeed convenient.

This is an example of how B2C (Business to Consumer) e-commerce is beginning to incorporate non-traditional computing technologies. Within the context of C2C (Consumer to Consumer) e-commerce, this example should help you expand your mind and think of endless wild possibilities for selling products and services to other consumers.

Could you set up some sort of product-selling business that requires consumers to use a cell phone to charge the cost of the product to their cell phone bill? If you answer no, then our next question to you is, Have you actually contacted an ISP and cell phone service provider to determine that you can't do it? How would you answer that question?

C2C e-commerce will require that everyone "think outside the box" or "beyond your ears" as we like to put it. Don't rule out any idea, no matter how strange or far-fetched. Thomas Watson, CEO and Chairman of IBM in 1943, stated, "I think there is a world market for maybe five computers." He was definitely wrong and, to some extent, narrow-minded in his futuristic views. Don't make the same mistake.

EXPLOSION OF C2C E-COMMERCE

Of all the types of private-sector e-commerce activities—B2B, B2C, C2C, C2B, and the government venues—the least amount of revenue dollars right now is in the C2C (Consumer to Consumer) space. But we expect that to change rather dramatically in the next several years. *Consumer to Consumer (C2C) e-commerce* occurs when an individual sells products and services to customers who are primarily other individuals. eBay is a good example. It's really just an e-marketplace in which consumers buy and sell products from and to each other. eBay doesn't guarantee the quality or authenticity of any products or services sold in its auction format. It simply provides a convenient mechanism for allowing consumers to gather and buy and sell products and services.

But consider the impacts of push technologies, m-commerce, digital cash, wearable computers, and even GPS-enabled implant chips. You could drive around your neighborhood in search of garage sales, for example. As you neared one, your GPS-enabled implant chip would trigger someone's personal computer that would call you on your cell phone and notify you what they have for sale and even provide you with driving directions. Once you arrived at the garage sale and found something to buy, you could make a digital cash transfer with your cell phone or PDA.

Far beyond garage sales, someday you may be able to create and store a C2C Web site on a personal digital assistant (PDA). People would access your PDA, view the products you have to sell, and then make digital cash payments. Throughout the day, your PDA would constantly update your inventory records and notify you instantly of any stockouts. At the end of the day, your PDA would show you all the necessary delivery and shipping information.

These are not far-fetched ideas. Right now, we think in terms of setting up e-commerce Web sites and hosting them on Web server computers. That will change someday, and your home computer, wearable computer, or even PDA will become a server computer that hosts your Web site and includes all the necessary e-commerce software. When that happens, expect C2C e-commerce to explode.

BROADENING OF E-GOVERNMENT

In Chapter 5, we briefly alluded to the fact that the major players in e-commerce include businesses (B), consumers (C), and the government (G). Within the electronic government (e-government) arena, there are four primary focuses (see Figure 9.11).

1. *Government to Government (**G2G,** also called **intra-G2G**)*—The electronic commerce activities performed within a single nation's government focusing on vertical integration (local, city, state, and federal) and horizontal integration (within or among the various branches and agencies). If you consider the United States government, a vertical integration example would include the Environmental Protection Agency interacting with local, city, and state government entities for the enforcement and monitoring of environmentally focused legislation and statutes. A horizontal integration example would include the interaction and information transfer between a branch of the military and the Veteran's Administration (VA) when military personnel retire.

2. *Government to Business (G2B)*—The electronic commerce activities performed between a government and its business partners for such purposes as purchasing direct and MRO materials, soliciting bids for work, and accepting bids for work.

3. *Government to Consumer (G2C)*—The electronic commerce activities performed between a government and its citizens or consumers including paying taxes, registering vehicles, and providing information and services.

4. *International Government to Government (inter-G2G)*—The electronic commerce activities performed between two or more governments including providing foreign aid.

There are substantial career opportunities in the e-government arena. Governments of all types desperately need motivated knowledge workers skilled in the creation and execution of all types of e-commerce initiatives. It's a business segment worth looking into.

Figure 9.11

The Primary Focuses of E-Government

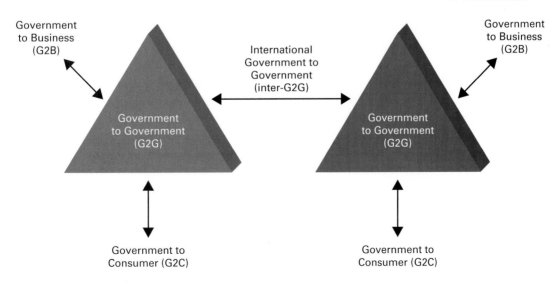

Government to Business (G2B)

International Government to Government (inter-G2G)

Government to Business (G2B)

Government to Government (G2G)

Government to Government (G2G)

Government to Consumer (G2C)

Government to Consumer (G2C)

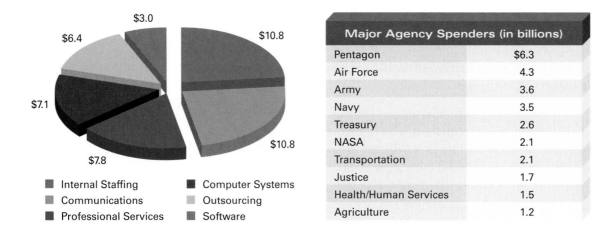

Major Agency Spenders (in billions)	
Pentagon	$6.3
Air Force	4.3
Army	3.6
Navy	3.5
Treasury	2.6
NASA	2.1
Transportation	2.1
Justice	1.7
Health/Human Services	1.5
Agriculture	1.2

Figure 9.12

How the U.S. Federal Government Spends Its IT Dollars ($46 Billion in 2002)[9]

Consider that the U.S. federal government is the single largest acquirer and user of information technology and related services (see Figure 9.12). In 2002, the U.S. federal government spent just over $46 billion on IT and related services. Almost 25 percent of that $46 billion went to internal staffing, which is essentially IT personnel. So, there are substantial career opportunities in e-government. Even if you don't want to work for the federal government but perhaps as an IT consultant to the federal government, notice in Figure 9.12 that over 25 percent of federal government IT dollars went to professional services ($7.8 billion) and outsourcing ($6.4 billion). Current estimates within the U.S. federal government have IT spending increasing at a rate of 10 percent annually for the next several years.

In Figure 9.12 you can also see the allocation of IT dollars across the major spending agencies. Defense and the armed forces are at the top, followed by the Treasury Department (it accepts and distributes all government monies), NASA (heavily involved in research), and then a series of more socially oriented agencies such as Health and Human Services and Agriculture. The table in Figure 9.12, because it includes 2002 data, does not show the positioning of the Homeland Security Department, which has an IT budget of approximately $3 billion.

The goal of the federal government right now is to become a true click-and-mortar enterprise. ***Click-and-mortar*** refers to those organizations that have a presence in the physical world, that is, buildings you can visit and representatives you can talk to, and also a presence in the virtual world of the Internet. That latter presence will be Web sites with which you can interact in order to deal with the federal government at all levels and in all areas.

We offer you this insight into e-government for two good reasons. Many e-government applications will have a direct impact (1) on your personal life and (2) your business life. In the not-too-distant future, the IRS will no longer accept paper-based income tax returns. That is, you'll be using G2C e-commerce to submit your tax forms electronically. Most state governments now allow you to renew your driver's license online and file your state income tax returns online. In addition, many governmental agencies are also using G2B to send out and accept bids for work. Those government agencies simply refuse to work with businesses that cannot perform this electronic commerce activity. If your organization can't, don't rely on getting any government contracts.

BUYING ELECTRONIC SAVINGS BONDS AT TREASURYDIRECT

Savings bonds, specifically Series EE and I, have long been a safe and solid investment. Parents buy them for their children. Many people purchase them as gifts. Workers enroll in payroll-deduction programs with the money going toward the purchase of savings bonds.

That will all remain the same; however, the Treasury Department now wants you to purchase your savings bonds online. Not only that, you will no longer receive the paper bonds in the mail. Instead, you'll have an account in which the bonds reside.

It's called *TreasuryDirect* (www.treasurydirect.gov). When you first visit the site, you create a personal account and provide such information as your checking or savings account number and other personal information. You can then buy savings bonds in any denomination offered. You pay with a credit card. Then, at any point in time, you can visit your account and the system will tell you exactly what your savings bonds are worth should you redeem them on that day. If you choose to do so, you instruct the system into which bank account to transfer the money. Your money will arrive within two working days.

Parents can set up accounts for their children. They can create different accounts for their children such as "College Tuition," "First Car," or "Happy 16th Birthday." Once the accounts are created, anyone can log into the system and buy bonds for the child. So, friends, grandparents, and other relatives can buy bonds for a child and place them in the appropriate account.

When the bonds mature, *TreasuryDirect* will send an e-mail notifying you that the bonds are mature and will accrue no more interest.

Most Important Considerations

Throughout this chapter, we've discussed some key emerging trends and technologies. They certainly are exciting and promise that the future will be different and dynamic, to say the least. We have suggested that you anticipate these changes and how they will affect you personally and in your career.

As we close this chapter (and perhaps your studies in this course), let's take a close look at five key topics. Each is a culmination in some way of the material you've learned in this course. Each is inescapable in that it will happen and you must deal with it. Finally, each is vitally important and reaches far beyond the technologies that either necessitate or support it. For you, these last few pages are a chance to reflect on what you've learned and to place that knowledge within the bigger picture.

THE NECESSITY OF TECHNOLOGY

Like it or not, technology is a necessity today. It's hard to imagine a world without it. Just as we need electricity to function on an everyday basis, we need technology as well.

Of course, that doesn't mean you should adopt technology just for the sake of the technology or because it sounds fun. Rather, you need to carefully evaluate each technology and determine if it will make you more productive, enhance your personal life, enrich your learning, or move your organization in the direction of its strategic goals and initiatives.

Technology is not a panacea. If you throw technology at a business process that doesn't work correctly, the result will be that you'll perform that process incorrectly millions of times faster per second. At the same time, you can ill afford to ignore technology when it really will help you and your organization become more efficient, effective, and innovative.

HOW MANY COMPUTERS DO YOU RELY ON IN A WEEK?

Technology is certainly a necessity in today's society. If computers and computer systems go down, trains stop running, airline flights are delayed, and stoplights may not work. Your everyday life depends on the use of computers. According to one study, the average American relies on approximately 264 computers every day.

You won't have to think long or hard to come up with a list of computers that you depend on in your everyday life—that's your task for this project. Your team is to develop a list of computers that you rely on in a week's time. Did you recently go to the movies? If

so, you relied on the computer that issued your ticket, the cash register computer that totaled your concession bill, and the computer that showed the movie. (No—most movie theaters don't show movies from rolls of film anymore.)

As you create your list, critically evaluate the importance of each computer. Although it might be a nuisance to have the computer go down that's showing you a movie, it's much more critical that other computers in your life be working all the time, without fail.

CLOSING THE GREAT DIGITAL DIVIDE

We must, as a human race, completely eliminate the great digital divide. As we alluded to in Chapter 5, the *great digital divide* addresses the concerns of many people that the world is becoming one marked by the "have's" and "have not's" with respect to technology. That is, the traditional notion of a third world economy is now being defined by the extent to which a country has access to and uses technology.

The power of technology needs to be realized on a worldwide scale. We cannot afford to have any technology-challenged nation or culture (within reason). If you live and work in a technology-rich country, don't keep it to yourself. When possible, take it to other countries by creating international business partnerships and strategic alliances. The world will benefit greatly from your efforts.

TECHNOLOGY FOR THE BETTERMENT OF SOCIETY

Life isn't just about making money. As you approach the development and use of technological innovations (or even standard technologies), think in terms of the betterment of people and society in general. (Making money and helping people often go hand in hand, in fact.)

Medical research is performing marvelous work in the use of technology to treat ailments and cure diseases. But if these efforts are purely profit-driven, we may never wholly realize the fruits of them. For example, therapists are using virtual reality to teach autistic people to cope with increasingly complex situations (see the accompanying Industry Perspective). We know for a fact that this use of technology isn't making anyone a lot of money. But it isn't always about making money. It's about helping people who face daily challenges far greater than ours. You're fortunate to be in an environment of learning. Give back when you have the chance.

EXCHANGING PRIVACY FOR CONVENIENCE

On a personal level, you need to consider how much of your personal privacy you're giving up in exchange for convenience. The extreme example is GPS-enabled implant chips. The convenience is knowing where you are and being able to get directions to

VIRTUAL REALITY SIMPLIFIES PATIENT'S WORLD

Imagine a world in which the color blue feels like sandpaper, the only furniture you can sit on must be green, or the sound of a pin dropping on the floor sounds like the cracking of thunder. Fortunately, most of us can't, but unfortunately, that's the real world for a person with autism. Autism is a disease that interferes with the development of the part of the brain that processes sensory perceptions. So, autistic people may feel sandpaper grinding across their skin when they see a color or they may be unable to correlate objects, such as chairs, bar stools, couches, and love seats (all items on which you can sit).

For autistic people, the world is a mishmash of objects that make no sense to them when they have to deal with them all at once. That makes teaching autistic people very difficult. For example, if you place two differently colored chairs in front of an autistic person and tell him or her that they are both chairs, that person may become confused and disoriented.

A simple world is the best world for individuals suffering from autism. Unfortunately, the real world is not so simple. So Dorothy Strickland and many others are researching ways to use virtual reality to teach people with autism. In a virtual reality simulation, researchers can eliminate all forms of background noise, colors, and objects, except those that they want the autistic person to focus on. As the autistic person becomes comfortable with the virtual reality simulation, new objects or colors can be introduced without the usual adverse effects.

Technology is really great—it can help an organization gain a competitive advantage in the marketplace or help you get a job in the future. But the greatest uses of technology may never make anyone rich; instead those uses will help many mentally and physically challenged individuals cope with daily life.[10,11]

---

your destination. But you're obviously giving up some privacy. Is this okay? Convenience takes on many forms. When you use a discount card at a grocery store to take advantage of sales, that grocery store then tracks your purchasing history in great detail. You can bet that the grocery store will use that information to sell you more tailored products.

It really is a trade-off. In today's technology-based world, you give up privacy when you register for sweepstakes on certain Web sites. You give up privacy just surfing the Web because tracking software monitors your activities. Even when you click on a banner ad, the Web site you go to knows where you came from. Although such trade-offs may seem insignificant, small trade-offs can add up to a big trade-off over time.

Because you are very much a part of this trend, it's often hard to see the big picture and understand that every day you're giving up just a little more privacy in exchange for a little more convenience. Don't ever think that organizations won't use the information they're capturing about you. They're capturing it so they can use it. Of course, much of it will be used to better serve you as a customer, but some of it may not.

ETHICS, ETHICS, ETHICS

As our final note to you, we cannot stress enough again the importance of ethics as they guide your behavior toward other people in your career. We realize that business is business and that businesses need to make money to survive. But the recent scandals involving Enron and others in the corporate world should be a reminder of how important your personal ethical compass is to you. Success shouldn't come to the detriment of other people. It's quite possible to be very ethical and very successful. That's our challenge to you.

NECESSITY, CONVENIENCE, AND PRIVACY

As you consider your own use of technology, it's important that you consider that use within the context of necessity, convenience, and your own privacy. You really have two questions to answer. They are

1. *Necessity*—If you truly need technology to perform a personal task, how much of your personal privacy are you willing to forgo?

2. *Convenience*—If you can use technology to make your life more convenient (but your use of it isn't an absolute necessity), how much of your personal privacy are you willing to forgo?

Regarding question 1, provide your answer on a scale of 1 to 5. A 1 represents the fact that you would relinquish all your privacy to use technology that is a necessity. A 5 represents the fact that you would not relinquish any privacy even if it meant not being able to use a technology that was a necessity.

Regarding question 2, also provide your answer on a scale of 1 to 5. A 1 represents the fact that you would relinquish all your privacy in exchange for using technologies that would make your life more convenient. A 5 represents the fact that you would not relinquish any of your privacy even if it meant not being able to use a technology that made your life more convenient.

Compare your answers with those of several classmates. How do your answers compare to everyone else's?

Summary: Student Learning Outcomes Revisited

1. **Describe the emerging trends and technologies that will have an impact on the changing Internet.** The Internet is the single most visible aspect of technology and is changing every day. In the future, you can expect to see a number of emerging trends and technologies including:

   - Free Internet phone calls—using your computer and Internet connection to make phone calls over the Internet.
   - *Push technology*—when businesses and organizations come to you with information, services, and product offerings based on your profile.
   - Personalization—the tailoring of products and services to your needs.
   - Renting software from ASPs—especially while using portable devices such as PDAs to work with various types of personal productivity software.
   - Information supplier convergence—the mergers and acquisition processes that will combine many information suppliers into one may help you organize and filter information.

2. **Define the various types of technologies that are emerging as we move toward physiological interaction with technology.** Emerging technologies in the area of physiological interaction include

   - *Automatic speech recognition (ASR)*—a system that not only captures spoken words but also distinguishes word groupings to form sentences.
   - *Virtual reality*—a three-dimensional computer simulation in which you actively and physically participate.
   - *Cave automatic virtual environments (CAVEs)*—holographic devices that create, capture, and/or display images in true three-dimensional form.
   - *Biometrics*—the use of physiological characteristics—such as your fingerprint, the blood vessels in the iris of your eye, the sound of your voice, or perhaps even your breath—to provide identification.

3. **Describe technological innovations and trends that will increase portability and mobility.**

Technological innovations that will focus on increasing portability and mobility include:

- *Digital cash*—an electronic representation of cash.
- *Wearable computers*—fully equipped computers that you wear as a piece of clothing or attached to a piece of clothing similar to the way you would carry your cell phone on your belt.
- *Multi-state CPUs*—work with information represented in more than just two states, probably 10 states with each state representing a digit between 0 and 9.
- *Holographic storage devices*—devices that store information on a storage medium that is composed of 3-D crystal-like objects with many sides or faces.

4. **Describe the coming C2C explosion and the broadening of e-government as they relate to the rebirth of e-commerce.** Consumer to Consumer e-commerce currently generates the least revenue in the e-commerce space. However, with the advancement of portable and mobile technologies, you can expect to see a tremendous increase in the activity and revenue of C2C e-commerce. The broadening of e-government will come in four forms:

- *Government to Government*—the electronic commerce activities performed within a single nation's government focusing on vertical integration and horizontal integration.
- *Government to Business*—the electronic commerce activities performed between a government and its business partners for such purposes as purchasing direct and MRO materials, soliciting bids for work, and accepting bids for work.
- *Government to Consumer*—the electronic commerce activities performed between a government and its citizens or consumers including paying taxes, registering vehicles, and providing information and services.
- *International Government to Government*—the electronic commerce activities performed between two or more governments including providing foreign aid.

CLOSING CASE STUDY ONE

WILDSEED—A CELL PHONE FOR EVERY FASHION

U.S. manufacturers of cell phones and providers of cell phone service are heavily targeting one select group of customers—teenagers. In the United States, only about 38 percent of all teenagers have cell phones, compared to over 80 percent in most European countries and some Asian countries. Cell phone providers and manufacturers know that there is plenty of room to grow in the teenage market, not only because 62 percent don't currently have cell phones but also because teenagers are very quick to embrace and use new technologies. Those same companies know that teenagers aren't as frugal with money and tend to spend much more time talking on a cell phone than adults.

Of course, cell phones aren't really new technologies, but what you can do with them is. Motorola, for example, manufactures a cell phone with FM radio capability (XM radio may not be far behind). Samsung and many others offer cell phone service that includes AOL Instant Messenger (with audio and limited video). Most cell phone providers offer cell phones with cameras and multimedia messaging.

One of the leaders in this dynamic and changing industry is Wildseed. It regularly holds cell phone focus groups just for teenagers. Wildseed has determined that teenagers have three cell phone concerns:

1. *Visual appeal*—A cell phone should make a fashion statement. Teenagers also believe that cell phones should be a statement of individuality ("I want a cell phone that doesn't look like anyone else's").
2. *Functionality*—A cell phone should do more than just support phone-calling capabilities.
3. *Price*—Long-term calling plans are not the way to go.

VISUAL APPEAL

Wildseed has tested numerous cell phone designs on teenagers. One cell phone holder was designed to be worn like a garter belt, and it flopped in a big way. According to one young man in the focus group, "Is a guy supposed to wear that?" And a young girl in the focus group commented, "It looks like something for a prostitute." But Wildseed did hit upon a good idea. It now manufactures "smart skins," cell phone covers that have an embedded computer chip. According to what the teenager is wearing, he or she can quickly change the design of the cell phone face plate. While skateboarding one day, for example, a young man could change his cell phone face plate to a splashy rendition of hard colors such as red, yellow, and green. Teenagers can also choose from among music-oriented themes according to their favorite artist.

FUNCTIONALITY

Cell phones are certainly no longer devices just for talking. Most cell phones have e-mail capabilities and support surfing the Web. Those are no longer a competitive advantage for any cell phone manufacturer. Wildseed tried a couple of new ideas on teenage focus groups; the first failed and the second met with great success. The first additional functionality was a cell phone that supported Morse code. No one liked that because no one knew how to send and interpret Morse code. Additionally, teenage girls stated they would have a problem sending Morse code because their long fingernails made it difficult to type. The second function was "airtexting." Using an airtexting-enabled cell phone, you type in a brief message (e.g., "Call me") and then wave your cell phone back and forth in the air. Blinking red lights on the cell phone are synchronized to display the message in the air. That way, someone across the room can receive your message without having to use a cell phone. You may have seen airtexting clocks that have an arm that moves back and forth through the air and seems to suspend the time and day in the air. As one young lady put it, "That's tight."

PRICE

Price is a major drawback for most teenagers, not necessarily the per-minute charge but rather the long-term contract that must be signed. In the United States, as opposed to most other countries, you must typically sign a six-month or one-year contract for cell phone service. That prohibits many teenagers from getting a cell phone because they have to get their parents to co-sign on the contract. Unfortunately, Wildseed is a manufacturer of cell phones and not a cell phone service provider.[12,13]

Questions

1. The role and purpose of cell phones have certainly changed over the past few years. Not too long ago, business professionals were the only ones to use cell phones. Now, over one in three teenagers in the United States have a cell phone and about 99 percent of them don't use them for business. Are cell phones becoming a technology of convenience and not of necessity? If people use them just for the convenience of communicating anywhere at anytime, are they really a necessity? On the other hand, if you use a cell phone as your primary mode of communication, is it no longer just a convenience?

2. Airtexting sounds like a good idea. From across a room, you'll be able to easily send someone a short message without using your minutes or having the other person's cell phone ring. But you are giving up some privacy. If you airtext your message, everyone in the room will be able to see it. Are you willing to give up some amount of privacy to use an airtexting feature? Why or why not? What about while sitting in a classroom? Should you be able to airtext a message in the middle of class? Does your school have a policy requiring you to turn off your cell phone when entering a classroom? If so, should this policy apply to airtexting? Why or why not?

3. Functionality is very important for cell phones. What types of functionality does your cell phone support beyond making and receiving phone calls? If you could design the "perfect" cell phone, what additional functionality would you include?

4. Do you foresee a day when cell phones will be the standard phone and we'll simply do away with land-based phone lines? It's probably going to happen. If cell phones do become the standard, how will you access the Internet from home?

STADIUMS OF THE FUTURE

There are several industries that always seem to be the leaders in using technological innovations. The movie industry, for example, quickly embraced the use of 3-D technologies and animation to create such movie series as *Shrek, Terminator,* and *The Matrix,* all blockbusters in part because of their use of technological innovations. The movie industry is even exploring how to create and use virtual actors and actresses. Real people may no longer be used in movies; instead, likenesses of them will be computer-generated and controlled.

Another related industry always on the forefront of the use of new technologies is professional sports. It may not be an industry that immediately pops into your mind in this regard, but that industry must strive daily to attract and retain large audiences (just check out the salaries many professional athletes make and you'll understand why). The professional sports industry wants your business in one of two ways: either you watch a sporting event on television or you attend a sporting event in person. For the latter, sports franchises are building some unbelievable arenas and stadiums that make use of technological innovations. Consider these technology-based activities for you in the stadium of the future.

ORDER AND PAY FOR FOOD AND BEVERAGES AT YOUR SEAT

In future stadiums, you won't have to catch the attention of a stadium vendor selling popcorn, beverages, and hot dogs. Instead, you'll use a small keypad at your seat to view a menu and order exactly what you want. You'll use the same keypad to pay for your order by swiping your credit card. Your order will be transmitted to a kitchen where it's made and then given to a runner who will deliver it to you.

WATCH REPLAYS ON A PRIVATE SCREEN

Your seat will also have a private screen that folds down and within your arm rest. At any point during the game, you can unfold the screen and view replays. You'll be able to choose from among a variety of camera angles from which to see the replay, and you'll be able to use a zooming function to see the entire field or just a portion of it.

VIEW HOLOGRAPHIC REPLAYS SUSPENDED IN THE AIR

Ideally, you'll be able to watch replays not on a flat two-dimensional screen but rather suspended in the air in front of you as a holographic image. These holographic images will be completely three-dimensional, allowing you to turn them at different angles to view the replay from different perspectives. Many people believe that much of the audience will opt to watch an entire game in this fashion as opposed to through binoculars.

PARTICIPATE IN REAL-TIME INTERVIEWS WITH PLAYERS

Almost all player interviews occur after the game is over and are primarily viewed by people watching a game on television. In a future stadium, you'll be able to request and participate in a real-time interview with a player during the game. For example, after a player makes a great catch in a baseball game to end the inning, you'll be able to interview that player and ask him or her how the catch was made.

VIEW STATISTICS ON ANY PLAYER

You'll also be able to use your screen and keypad to pull up any statistics you might want to view. These could include career statistics for a specific player, season statistics for a specific team, current game statistics for a specific player, and even records within a particular sport. You'll even be able to request that this type of information be presented in graphical form perhaps accompanied by an audio analysis provided by a sports or statistics expert.

VIEW SCORES AND HIGHLIGHTS OF OTHER GAMES

You certainly won't have to wait for a stadium to display scores and highlights of other games on a hanging big-screen monitor. You'll be able to view scores and highlights of other games at the press of a button. You'll even be able to attend one game and watch another completely on your screen.

SEND MESSAGES TO PEOPLE IN THE STADIUM

If you buy tickets the day before a sports event, it's often difficult to get a group of tickets all in the same area. If you can't get tickets all together, then you miss out on some of the fun associated with attending a sports event with friends. That won't be a problem in future stadiums. You'll soon be able to use videoconferencing software to communicate with any other person in the stadium.

Questions

1. Will this type of stadium of the future further widen the "digital divide"? It makes sense that people who don't have enough money to buy personal technologies will also not have enough money to attend sporting events. Will that group of people fall further behind because they can't take advantage of technological innovations in the stadium of the future? Or is this use of technology one of convenience and not of necessity?

2. How do you think players will react to being interviewed during the middle of a game? Can you think of some professional athletes who would not want to do this? Can you think of some professional athletes who would want to do this? Many governing bodies of professional sports such as the NBA and NFL require that athletes be available before and after the game for interviews. Should those same governing bodies require that athletes be available during games for interviews? Why or why not?

3. Do you believe that stadiums of the future will encourage more people to attend sports events? Why or why not? Right now, you can sit at home, watch picture-in-picture to see multiple games, and change channels to see yet other games. And let's not forget that these stadiums of the future will be extremely expensive to build and maintain, so you can expect ticket prices to go up as well.

4. In this chapter, we introduced you to several leading-edge and bleeding-edge technologies. Which of those that we didn't highlight in this case study do you believe could be used to enhance the experience of attending a sporting event? How would you use them? Would the use of those technologies further encourage you to attend a sporting event? Why or why not?

Key Terms and Concepts

Automatic speech recognition (ASR), 427
Biochip, 433
Biometrics, 430
CAVE (cave automatic virtual environment), 429
Click-and-mortar, 440
Consumer to Consumer (C2C) e-commerce, 438
Digital cash (electronic cash, e-cash), 434
Facial recognition software, 434
Feature analysis, 427
Glove, 428
Government to Business (G2B), 439
Government to Consumer (G2C), 439
Government to Government (G2G, intra-G2G), 439

Headset (head-mounted display), 428
Holographic device, 429
Holographic storage device, 437
Implant chip, 434
International Government to Government (inter-G2G), 439
Language processing, 428
Multi-state CPU, 437
Pattern classification, 428
Push technology, 424
Virtual reality, 428
Walker, 428
Wearable computer, 435

Short-Answer Questions

1. How will free Internet phone calls work?
2. What is a push technology environment?
3. How will push technologies support personalization?
4. Why may you someday rent personal productivity software from an ASP?
5. What is the concept of information supplier convergence?
6. What is the role of physiological interfaces?
7. What are the three steps in automatic speech recognition?
8. What is virtual reality?
9. What type of special input and output devices does virtual reality make use of?
10. What are CAVEs?
11. What are some examples of biometric applications?
12. How will biometrics aid in providing security and identification?
13. What is the function of a biochip?
14. What is the role of an implant chip?
15. How will digital cash someday work on the Internet?
16. What is a wearable computer?
17. How do multi-state CPUs differ from today's standard CPUs?
18. Why will holographic storage devices be able to store more information than today's storage devices?
19. Why will we see an explosion of C2C e-commerce?
20. What are the four primary focuses of e-government?
21. What is the great digital divide?

Assignments and Exercises

1. **SELLING THE IDEA OF IMPLANT CHIPS AT YOUR SCHOOL** Let's assume for a moment that your team is in favor of using implant chips that contain vitally important information such as identification and medical information. Your task is to put together a sales presentation to your school that would require all students obtain implant chips. Within your presentation, include the following:
   A. The school-related information that each implant chip would contain
   B. The nonschool-related information that each implant chip would contain
   C. The processes within your school that would use the information on the implant chips
   D. The benefits your school would realize by requiring implant chips
   E. The benefits students would realize by having implant chips
   Your presentation should be no more than five minutes, so it must be a powerful selling presentation.

2. **RESEARCHING WEARABLE COMPUTERS** One of the leading-edge manufacturers of wearable computers is Xybernaut. Connect to its Web site at www.xybernaut.com and research its various lines of wearable computers. What are the names of the lines of Xybernaut's wearable computers? What are their CPU speeds? How much RAM do they include? What functions can you perform with them? What sort of technology devices (e.g., wireless Internet access) can you add to each line? Is there any line advanced enough and cheap enough that you would consider buying one? Why or why not?

3. **FINDING A GOOD AUTOMATIC SPEECH RECOGNITION SYSTEM** Research the Web for automatic speech recognition (ASR) systems. Make a list of the ones you find. What are the prices of each? Are they speaker-independent or speaker-dependent? Do they support continuous speech recognition or discrete speech recognition? What sort of add-on vocabularies can you purchase? How comfortable would you feel speaking the contents of a term paper as opposed to typing it? Would you have to be more or less organized **to use speech recognition as opposed to typing? Why?**

4. **UNDERSTANDING THE RELATIONSHIPS BETWEEN TRENDS AND TECHNOLOGICAL INNOVATIONS** In this chapter, we presented you with numerous key technologies and how they relate to six important trends. (See Figure 9.1 on page 422 for the list of technologies and trends.) For each trend, identify all the technologies presented in this chapter that can have an impact. For each technology that you do identify, provide a short discussion of how it might have an impact.

5. **LEARNING ABOUT E-GOVERNMENT** Visit the Web site for Government Computer News (GCN) at www.gcn.com. GCN is a periodical devoted to the use of technology within various governmental agencies in the United States. Click on some of the "hot topics" listed on the left side of the screen. Pick a couple of articles that detail how a government agency is using some type of technology. Now, prepare a short report for your class on the differences between two groups—governments and for-profit businesses. Your report should show how each uses technology to achieve some type of "competitive advantage."

6. **RESEARCHING INTELLIGENT HOME APPLIANCES** Visit a local appliance store in your area and find three home appliances that contain some sort of intelligence (i.e., an embedded computer chip that takes over some of the functionality and decision making). For each appliance, prepare a short report that includes the following information:
   - A description and price for the intelligent home appliance
   - The "intelligent" features of the appliance
   - How those features make the appliance better than the nonintelligent version

Discussion Questions

1. There is currently much legislation pending right now in many states that would make it illegal for people to use a cell phone while driving a car. The reason is that society has already noticed a significant increase in the number of traffic accidents in which one of the drivers involved in the accident was using a cell phone. Think beyond that for a moment and include wearable computers. As this new technology becomes more widely available, isn't it possible for someone to be driving a car while using a computer? Should the government enact legislation to prevent it? Why or why not?

2. In a push technology environment, businesses and organizations will come to you with information, services, and product offerings based on your profile. How is a push technology environment different from mass mailings and spam? Is it an invasion of your privacy to have organizations calling you on your cell phone every time you come near a store? Why or why not? Should you be able to "opt in" or "opt out" of these offerings? Is this really any different from someone leaving a flyer at your house or on your car while it's parked in a parking lot?

3. There are three steps in automatic speech recognition (ASR): feature analysis, pattern classification, and language processing. Which of those three steps is the most challenging for a computer to perform? Why? Which of those three steps is the least challenging for a computer to perform? Why? If ASR systems are to become automatic speech understanding systems, which step must undergo the greatest improvement in its capabilities? Why?

4. Much debate surrounds the use of biometrics. Many people like it because biometrics can provide identification and increase security. Other people see it as a tremendous invasion of your privacy. Just as you read in this chapter, a bank—by using biometric identification—may be able to tell if a woman is pregnant. So, the greatest challenge to overcome is not technological but rather societal. What do you think needs to happen for society to accept the use of biometrics? How long do you think it will be before society accepts the use of biometrics? In what year do you believe the U.S. federal government will begin requiring a biometric of every newborn child?

5. Digital cash is destined to greatly impact the use of coins and folding cash. What sort of future do you foresee if we do away completely with traditional forms of currency and just use electronic forms? Will this help eliminate the digital divide or will the digital divide provide a barrier to the widespread use of electronic forms of payment? Justify your answer.

6. What are the ethical dilemmas associated with using facial recognition software? Is the use of this type of software really any different from a store asking to see your driver's license when

you use your credit card? Why or why not? Should the government be able to place digital video cameras on every street corner and use facial recognition software to monitor your movements? Why or why not?

7. When (and if) CAVEs become a common reality, you'll be able to visit your family and friends anytime you want no matter where they live. What sort of impact will this have on the travel industry? If you can see your relatives in a CAVE as often as you want, will you be more or less inclined to buy a plane ticket and visit them in person? Why or why not?

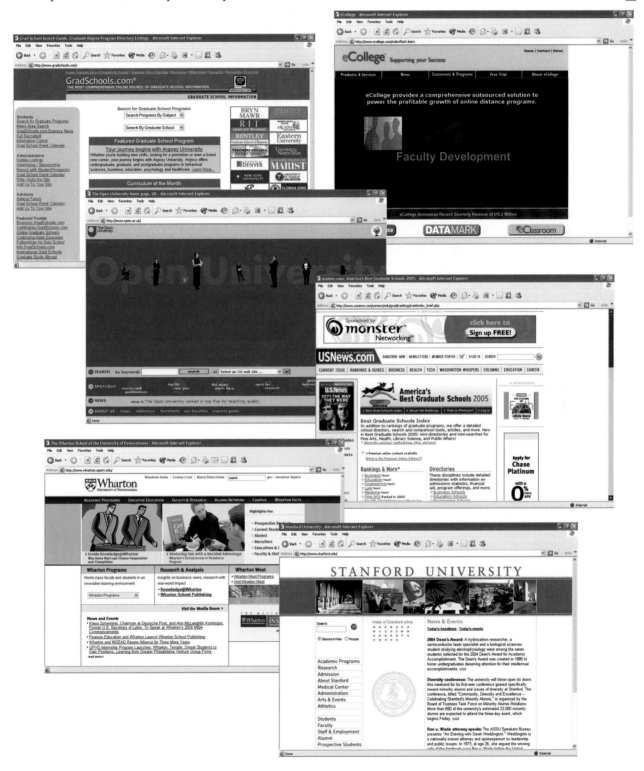

Continuing Your Education Through the Internet

To be perfectly honest, it's a dog-eat-dog world out there. The competitive landscape of business is more intense than it ever has been. And that competitiveness spills into your personal life. Many of you are in school right now to get an education to better compete in the job market. But many knowledge workers are finding out that an undergraduate degree is simply not enough to compete in the business world, and so they wish to acquire more education.

Just like businesses, graduate schools (and all schools in general) are using the Internet as a way to communicate information to you. Many of these schools are even offering you online courses through the Internet to further your education.

MBA PROGRAMS

Many of you will undoubtedly choose to continue your education by obtaining an MBA. And you probably should. The market for the best business positions is extremely competitive, with hiring organizations seeking individuals who can speak more than one language, have job experience, and have extended their educational endeavors beyond just getting an undergraduate degree.

Each year, *U.S. News & World Report* ranks the top business schools in the nation. On the Web site that supports this text, you'll find a list of the Web sites for some of the top 50 business schools in the nation.

Choose a couple of different business schools from the list of 50, visit their Web sites, and answer the following questions for each:

A. What business school did you choose?

B. Does that school offer a graduate program in your area of interest?

C. Can you apply online?

D. Does the site list tuition and fee costs?

E. Does the site contain a list of the graduate courses offered in your area of interest?

SPECIALIZED MBA PROGRAMS

In the previous section, you explored a few of the top 50 business schools in the nation. Those schools were ranked irrespective of any specialization, focusing rather on overall academic reputation. *U.S. News & World Report* also compiles an annual list of the best business schools in 10 specializations: accounting, entrepreneurship, finance, health services administration, management information systems, international business, general business, marketing, nonprofit organizations, and production/operations. If you're interested in a specialized MBA, you should consider viewing schools in these lists.

Choose at least three schools that offer a specialization in your area of interest and visit their Web sites. Based on what you find, rank those three schools according to your first, second, and third choices. What factors did you consider? Was cost an overriding concern? Before you began your analysis, did you already have a preconceived notion of the best school? Did you change your mind once you visited the schools' sites?

GRADUATE SCHOOL INFORMATION AND TIPS

Before you begin your decision-making process concerning which graduate school to attend, you should gather a variety of material. For example, obtaining a directory of universities (both domestic and international) would be helpful. Perhaps even more important, you should ask yourself several questions. Are you ready for graduate school? Why are you considering going to graduate school? How do you determine which school is best for you based on such issues as price, location, and area of specialization?

Many of these questions are very personal to you. For example, we can't help you determine if you're really ready for graduate school or answer why you're considering going to graduate school. But what we can do is point you toward some valuable resources on the Internet to help you answer some of your questions and find a wealth of information relating to universities. On the Web site that supports this text, we've included many links to those types of sites.

At your leisure, we recommend that you connect to several of these sites and see what they have to offer. Some simply provide a list of universities, whereas others may be particularly useful as you make that all-important decision.

TELE-EDUCATION (DISTANCE LEARNING)

Throughout this text, you've explored the concept of 24×7 connectivity through information technology. Using IT (part of which is the Internet), organizations today are sending out telecommuting employees, and medical and health facilities are establishing telemedicine practices.

Tele-education, which goes by a number of names including e-education, distance learning, distributed learning, and online learning, enables you to get an education without "going" to school. Quite literally, you can enroll in a school on the East Coast and live in Denver, enjoying great winter skiing. Using various forms of IT (videoconferencing, e-mail, chat rooms, and the Internet), you can take courses from schools all over the world. Some of those schools even offer complete degree programs via IT.

These schools include graduate programs in business. For example, the Massachusetts Institute of Technology and Duke University have graduate programs that combine traditional classroom instruction courses and computer-delivered courses. In 1997, Ohio University (Athens) introduced MBA without Boundaries, an MBA program that is completely online except for a required six-week orientation session.

Connect to at least five of these sites and explore the possibilities of tele-education. As you do, consider the issues below.

A. Can you just take courses or enroll in a complete degree program?
B. What is the cost of tele-education?
C. What process do you go through to enroll in a tele-education program?
D. How would you feel about staying at home instead of going to class?
E. How do tele-education programs foster interactivity between students and teachers?

EXTENDED LEARNING MODULE I

BUILDING AN E-PORTFOLIO

Student Learning Outcomes

1. DESCRIBE THE TYPES OF ELECTRONIC RÉSUMÉS AND WHEN EACH IS APPROPRIATE.

2. DISCUSS NETWORKING STRATEGIES YOU CAN USE DURING A JOB SEARCH.

3. EXPLAIN HOW SELF-ASSESSMENT IS VALUABLE TO RÉSUMÉ WRITING.

4. USE THE INTERNET TO RESEARCH CAREER OPPORTUNITIES AND POTENTIAL EMPLOYERS.

5. DEVELOP POWERFUL JOB SEARCH E-PORTFOLIO CONTENT.

6. DOCUMENT EFFECTIVE WEB SITE STRUCTURE AND DESIGN COMPONENTS.

7. CREATE A JOB SEARCH E-PORTFOLIO WEB SITE AND PLACE IT ON AN INTERNET SERVER.

Introduction

Welcome to the 21st century—the anytime, anywhere job market. In this information age, Internet technology has undoubtedly had an impact on résumé development, job networking, and their effectiveness in uncovering hidden job opportunities. The Internet provides instant access to job-market intelligence, such as: who is hiring, what skills are in demand, and how much those skills are worth—24 hours a day. For the first time ever, individual job seekers have access to the same information once available only to corporate insiders and recruiters.

Although there are many forms of electronic recruitment, this module will concentrate on electronic documents that you as a potential employee need to have prepared to compete in today's electronic job market. The final product is an electronic portfolio designed to help you successfully promote yourself in the electronic job market.

In this module, we assume that you are familiar with the Internet and research tools and have at least a little knowledge of HTML. For a review of the Internet, see *Extended Learning Module B.* For a review of HTML, refer to *Extended Learning Module F.*

The Electronic Job Market— Extending Your Reach

The online recruiting industry has been developing for several years and is poised for explosive growth. It happens all the time. A new industry forms and simmers for a while, and then someone discovers the last piece of the puzzle, the missing link that explodes the industry out of its infancy, into the limelight, and into the mainstream.

Since the early 1990s the term electronic portfolio (e-portfolio) has been described in a range of ways, with most recognizing the primary role of information and communications technologies in describing the "e." Common to most definitions is an assumed continuity of purpose with paper-based portfolios (or résumés) that have been used as documented evidence of experience and achievement. Formally, an ***electronic portfolio (e-portfolio)*** is a cohesive, powerful, and well-designed collection of electronic documents that demonstrate your skills, education, professional development, and the benefits you offer to a hiring organization.

E-portfolios are much more than innovative résumés or scrapbooks. Neither of those forms can show reflection, evolution of thought, or professional development. In education and training contexts e-portfolios are learner-centered and outcomes-based. They are created when individuals selectively compile evidence of their own electronic activities and output as a means to indicate what they have learned or achieved. In this sense, e-portfolios function as a learning record or transcript. But given their developmental character, e-portfolios function as both an archive and a developmental repository that is used for learning management and self-reflective purposes.

The online recruiting industry, or the ***electronic job market,*** makes use of many Internet technologies to recruit employees. The average cost per hire through online recruiting is $152 compared with $1,383 using traditional methods. Additionally, a much broader worldwide selection of candidates can be screened, significantly increasing the likelihood of finding a good match for the hiring organization. As more and more hiring employers turn to the Internet to recruit employees, it is critical that you learn to capitalize on the technologies that help organizations locate and evaluate potential employees. Although the basic parts of your résumé stay the same and the purpose of your résumé is still to present your skills and qualifications, how you do so must change dramatically in the electronic job market.

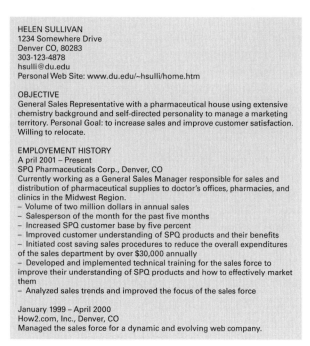

HELEN SULLIVAN
1234 Somewhere Drive
Denver CO, 80283
303-123-4878
hsulli@du.edu
Personal Web Site: www.du.edu/~hsulli/home.htm

OBJECTIVE
General Sales Representative with a pharmaceutical house using extensive chemistry background and self-directed personality to manage a marketing territory. Personal Goal: to increase sales and improve customer satisfaction. Willing to relocate.

EMPLOYEMENT HISTORY
A pril 2001 – Present
SPQ Pharmaceuticals Corp., Denver, CO
Currently working as a General Sales Manager responsible for sales and distribution of pharmaceutical supplies to doctor's offices, pharmacies, and clinics in the Midwest Region.
– Volume of two million dollars in annual sales
– Salesperson of the month for the past five months
– Increased SPQ customer base by five percent
– Improved customer understanding of SPQ products and their benefits
– Initiated cost saving sales procedures to reduce the overall expenditures of the sales department by over $30,000 annually
– Developed and implemented technical training for the sales force to improve their understanding of SPQ products and how to effectively market them
– Analyzed sales trends and improved the focus of the sales force

January 1999 – April 2000
How2.com, Inc., Denver, CO
Managed the sales force for a dynamic and evolving web company.

HELEN SULLIVAN
1234 Somewhere Drive
Denver CO, 80283
Personal Web Site: www.du.edu/~hsulli/home.htm
303-123-4878
hsulli@du.edu

OBJECTIVE
General Sales Representative with a pharmaceutical house using extensive chemistry background and self-directed personality to manage a marketing territory. Personal Goal: to increase sales and improve customer satisfaction. Willing to relocate.

EMPLOYMENT HISTORY
SPQ Pharmaceuticals Corp., Denver, CO — April 2000 – Present

Currently working as a General Sales Manager responsible for sales and distribution of pharmaceutical supplies to doctor's offices, pharmacies, and clinics in the Midwest Region. • Volume of two million dollars in annual sales • Salesperson of the month for the past five months • Increased SPQ customer base by five percent • Improved customer understanding of SPQ products and their benefits	• Initiated cost saving sales procedures to reduce the overall expenditures of the sales department by over $30,000 annually • Developed and implemented technical training for the sales force to improve their understanding of SPQ products and how to effectively market them • Analyzed sales trends and improved the focus of the sales force

How2.com, Inc., Denver, CO — January 1999 – April 2000

Managed the sales force for a dynamic and evolving web company. • Sales force of 8.	• Increased overall sales by 28 percent • Improved sales force morale and productivity using team management

STR Systems, Bloomington, IN — August 1996 – December 1998

Managed the sales force for a dynamic and evolving web company. • Sales force of 8.	• Increased overall sales by 28 percent • Improved sales force morale and productivity using team management

EDUCATION
Indiana University, Bloomington — B.S. in Marketing and Chemistry, 1996

Figure I.1

Sample Electronic Job Search Documents

The Internet provides $24 \times 7 \times 365$ access to information for both the employer and you as a potential employee. During your electronic job search, your effective use of Internet tools is critical to a successful job hunt. Since meeting the needs of employers is the basis for getting hired, your prerésumé tasks must center on gathering information about who is hiring, what skills are in demand, how much those skills are worth, and what you need to do to be considered for the available jobs. With this information in hand, you are prepared to create the electronic documents that will place you in a position to be considered for not just a job, but a career (see Figure I.1).

Résumés are the currency of the recruitment industry. They are the cornerstone of communication between candidates, recruiters, and employers. To put the matter in perspective, ask yourself, "When was the last time you were hired as a professional without submitting a résumé?" If you are like most people, the answer is "never." Technology is automating elements of the recruitment process, but a complete solution requires proper handling of the actual development of all the pieces and parts that comprise not just an e-résumé, but an e-portfolio.

Historically, applicants prospected for jobs by sending out large numbers of unsolicited paper résumés in the hope of uncovering hidden opportunities. Even the best techniques for converting these paper résumés into electronic formats were labor intensive, slow, and prone to inaccuracy.

As all companies large and small expand their operational efficiency with technology, it will be necessary for job seekers to expand their computer competency to online job searching and résumé posting. The Internet also provides job seekers with a way to contact more of the right employers in less time and, therefore, build a larger network of potential job leads.

Convergence of Online Networking and Résumé Development

In the always-available job market created by the Internet, organizations post and remove jobs on a continuous and instantaneous basis. Businesses have many options for where and how to list positions. Most Internet-savvy organizations have recruiting pages on their Web sites. Others use job database Web sites such as www.monster.com that reach a worldwide audience. Some organizations use their intranets to recruit from within.

Even in this all-encompassing electronic job market, some jobs are never posted. Collectively, unposted positions are referred to as the **hidden job market.** It is important to prepare yourself to search for jobs in the traditional (newspaper and magazine), electronic, and hidden job markets to maximize your job opportunities.

Many companies still select candidates to interview by visually reviewing résumés. However, in today's electronic world more and more firms supplement such manual methods with automated résumé tracking systems. Employers use such systems because they drastically reduce the time it takes to manually review, sort, and file large numbers of résumés. Using these systems, employers collect and store text from thousands of résumés in electronic databases. Such databases can then be sorted to find applicant résumés which contain skills, experience or education that match specified job requirements. Selected résumés can then be viewed onscreen, printed in their entirety, or specific information can be extracted from each one.

For job seekers, this new electronic world means that you must have two versions of your résumé: (1) a nicely formatted one for human eyes, which we will refer to as your "visual résumé"; and (2) one designed for computers, which we are calling your "electronic résumé." Later in this module you will learn how to create an electronic résumé by converting your résumé word processing file into "plain text or ASCII format" as well as an HTML format.

To achieve job search success in today's electronic arena, there are two key points to guide you:

1. You want to learn how to create a résumé (which will morph into an e-résumé) that will come to the top when an employer sorts for keywords or areas of experience that he or she needs. You will achieve this by knowing the type of job you want, the skills needed for such a position, and then effectively matching your skills to that position.

2. You want to use Internet job search strategies to find employer Web sites and job postings so that you can apply for them.

START TO NETWORK

If you read the want ads, send out résumés, and wait for employers to discover you, the odds of finding a satisfying job are not very good. According to JobStar (www.jobstar.org), a job board and collection of job search information offered in association with the *Wall Street Journal* (www.CareerJournal.com), "80 percent of all positions are filled without employer advertising. These positions are filled by—or created for—candidates who come to an employer's attention through employee recommendations, referrals from trusted associates, recruiters, or direct contact with the candidate." This means that networking and preparing résumé content targeted to a specific job and industry are critical to your success. Networking involves:

BUILD YOUR 30-SECOND COMMERCIAL

Building a quality 30-second commercial can be tougher than it sounds. The goal is to be able to contact strangers and let them know who you are, what your skills are, and why you are approaching them.

1. Narrow your focus by selecting one job type (a job type can encompass several job titles but the skills are the same) and one industry. Write your job description. For example,

   - Online researcher for a major law firm specializing in corporate contracts and patents.
   - Java and C++ programmer in the Texas oil and gas industry.

2. Start a list of job title synonyms. For example, a Java and C++ programmer could also be called a Web Applet developer or simply a programmer/analyst. This list will help you research and write your résumé.

3. Create a list of words describing your skills and interests. Begin broadly and then narrow your list to skills related to your current job search (see Figure I.2).

4. Put together your script. Include who you are, how you came in contact with this person, your top three skills, and what you would like from this contact. For example,

   > Hello my name is _____. I am working on an Information Technology degree at the University of Denver. You are registered as a mentor in the Career Placement Center and your job title is listed as Java Developer. I am very analytical, have enjoyed all of my programming courses, and am particularly interested in Java programming. Can you give me some advice on how to secure a job?

5. Practice your script before attending face-to-face networking functions. Edit your script as appropriate before using it in electronic communications.

6. Create a list of follow-up questions to use when your contact responds. For example,

   - How did you get your first job in this area?
   - Do you know of any open positions that I should apply for?

- **Creating relationships.** Target people who are in a position to further your career search. Make a list of everyone that you call on the phone, e-mail, electronically chat with, or have even had passing conversations with. This list should be quite long. The goal here is to get a list of potential contacts.

- **Developing a 30-second commercial.** This is a short description of who you are, what job you are looking for, and the skills that make you suited for the job. Having a short script makes it easier to contact people and avoids wasting their time.

- **Employing electronic means.** No matter how you are contacting people, use the technology to further your reach, such as e-mail, and learn how to develop an e-portfolio Web site (which is the basis of this learning module).

- **Avoiding sending bulk e-mails.** The personal touch of sending individual e-mail is more likely to obtain results. Set a goal to contact a specific number of people each week, keep track of whom you have contacted and the responses you have received, and finally make sure you send a follow-up message.

- **Joining mailing lists.** *Mailing lists* are discussion groups organized by area of interest. By subscribing to such a list, you can communicate with members via e-mail. Mailing lists allow you to gain industry information and make contacts that would not otherwise be available. On occasion, job announcements are also circulated through these lists. You can find mailing lists by topic at groups.yahoo.com, www.topica.com, www.tile.net/listserv, and groups.google.com.

PERFORM A SELF-ASSESSMENT

Contrary to popular belief and traditional résumé-writing styles, employers are not really interested in what you have already done; they want to know what you will do for them and to have documented evidence of those skills. To effectively communicate your skills and how they will benefit a potential employer, you must know what those skills are and that means spending some time evaluating yourself. While it is nice to be a "people person," that does not tell an employer that you work well under stress, mediate, negotiate contracts, and follow procedures. Being a "people person" will not get you a job, but detailing your skills in that area may.

Remember that the paper and electronic documents you create are your personal marketing tools. Most people want to jump right in and write a résumé, but you must get employer-focused first. Employers typically process résumés looking for things that exclude candidates by sorting applicants into three groups: Definitely, Maybe, and No. Ideally, you would like to be in the Definitely group, but the Maybe group can result in a position if you have done your homework and documented what you offer an employer.

There are many good tools for self-assessment: personality profiles, checklists (see Figure I.2), strength identification, achievement lists, and any number of writing and projection exercises. You can even ask people what your strengths are. Believe it or not, others are often better at articulating your strengths than you may be. Most colleges and universities have an array of assessment tools available to their students, such as the Myers-Briggs Type Indicator test. There are also many organizations offering testing from the Web. Some are free, for example, www.jobstar.org, and others charge a fee, such as www.careermaze.com. Use the methods that are available and that suit your needs, but do not shortchange this step. Time spent here will pay off when you do begin to write.

The goal of performing a self-assessment exercise is to develop a list of evocative words that you can use to describe your objective and experience in a manner that employers can understand. Typically these words are nouns and adjectives called *skill words* that stress your capabilities, which you should weave into the text of your résumé.

RESEARCH CAREERS, INDUSTRIES, AND COMPANIES

The Web is an incredible resource for researching topics such as résumé writing, career forecasts, job availability, skills required to be hirable, industry trends, and virtual communities. Although there are other approaches, most Web users find that search tools significantly improve the quality of the material located when browsing. We direct you to *Extended Learning Module B* to learn more about how to use electronic search tools.

Many job seekers underestimate the role of research in creating effective documents such as a résumé. A résumé is not simply a history of your education and work, but should be a document targeted to one position and industry.

Research is the key to creating powerful employer-centered résumé content directed to a specific industry. There is so much information available to help you develop powerful résumé content that the task of sifting through it can be overwhelming.

To make the most of the available information, develop a list of search terms based on your goals and then visit job database Web sites, search engines, government sites, and business Web pages. You should be able to find information on planning your career, the education or training needed to be successful, expected earnings by geographic location, the work environment, attire, normal career path, projected number of openings, and current job postings. Additionally you should find specific organizations, contacts, and communities that will help you fine-tune your target.

Figure I.2
Sample Self-Assessment Tool
Transferable Skills

Transferable skills are those that can be applied to any job or work situation. Everyone has them. Each transferable skill has keywords that can be used to describe your strengths. Select each skill below that applies to you and then write how you effectively exhibit that skill.

General Keywords			
___ critical thinking	___ self-discipline	___ general knowledge	___ self-confidence
___ research techniques	___ insight	___ cultural perspective	___ imagination
___ perseverance	___ writing	___ teaching ability	___ leadership

Research Keywords			
___ initiating	___ attaining	___ achieving	___ reviewing
___ updating	___ interpreting	___ analyzing	___ synthesizing
___ communicating	___ planning	___ designing	
___ performing	___ estimating	___ implementing	

Teaching Keywords			
___ organizing	___ assessing	___ public speaking	___ reporting
___ counseling	___ managing	___ coordinating	___ administering
___ motivating	___ problem solving		

Personality Keywords			
___ dynamic	___ sensitive	___ responsible	___ creative
___ imaginative	___ accurate	___ easygoing	___ adept
___ innovative	___ expert	___ successful	___ efficient
___ perceptive	___ astute	___ humanistic	___ honest
___ outstanding	___ calm	___ outgoing	___ self-starting
___ reliable	___ unique	___ experienced	___ talented
___ vigorous	___ versatile	___ diplomatic	

Object Keywords			
___ data	___ systems	___ relations	___ theories
___ recommendations	___ programs	___ events	___ outputs
___ facts	___ conclusions	___ goals	___ surveys
___ procedures	___ methods	___ statistics	___ strategy
___ feelings	___ designs	___ tools	___ journals
___ techniques	___ communications	___ charts	___ presentations
___ reports	___ research projects	___ information	___ human resources

START YOUR RESEARCH

Research is time-consuming and the sheer volume of information available on the Web is daunting. Target your research and stay focused. When you come upon items of interest that will not further your current goal, copy and paste their URLs into an open word processing document and then proceed with the your research.

In a second open word processing document, track career-related data and their sources gathered from your search. Refine your search words as necessary. Remember that you should be gathering as much data as you can about your chosen career, but it may be helpful to search for each type of information separately. For example, salary information may not be available from the sources discussing the projected number of jobs over the next five years or the normal work week in an industry. Use the following list of Web resources as a starting point.

Search Engines

- www.google.com—The largest Web index.
- www.search.com—Search using several search engines at once.
- www.searchengineguide.com—Listing of search engines by topic.
- www.job-search-engine.com—A meta job search engine dedicated to employment.

Media

- www.enews.com—Online magazines on any topic with online forums.
- www.careerpath.com—Online classifieds.
- www.classifieds2000.com—Online classifieds.

Government

- www.bls.gov—Bureau of Labor Statistics. Excellent source for work environment, job forecast, and regional data. Try the kids' pages.

Job Boards

- www.monster.com—Largest job board consistently listed in the top five sites.
- www.hotjobs.com—Job postings by location, industry, or company. International postings and salary wizard.
- www.collegegrad.com—Excellent resource for entry-level job seekers. Offers job search, résumé, and networking strategies.

Other Resources

- www.careers.org—Job search and career resource directory organized by topic and region.

Résumé Building—A Lifelong Process

Electronic résumés, or e-résumés, have moved into the mainstream of today's job market at lightning speed. E-résumés have stepped up the efficiency of job placement to such a point that you could get a call from a recruiter just hours after submitting your e-résumé. With this kind of opportunity, you cannot afford to be left in the dark ages of using only a visual résumé.

A *résumé* is a summary of your qualifications. It is an organized collection of information that will "sell" your skills to an employer. A résumé and accompanying applications correspondence are likely to be the most important documents you will create. They are advertisements that get you noticed in the crowded, competitive job market.

A generation ago it was common to work for a single company throughout your entire career. This type of job security is no longer possible in today's volatile business climate. Most people will end up making at least a half-dozen major job changes in a lifetime of work.

The average employer looks at a résumé less than 34 seconds. In some situations, a computer may actually scan in your résumé looking for specific skill and abilities. Your résumé must then be professionally written, attractive, concise, and demonstrate your skills and value to a potential employer.

CONTENT, CONTENT, CONTENT

Through beginning to network, assessing your skills, and researching, you will gain the knowledge critical for creating targeted résumé content. Use the job titles, skills, and jargon from one industry to describe yourself and your experience. If you are job seeking in multiple industries or in a variety of position titles, you may need to develop a separate résumé for each.

When you begin writing, concentrate on creating solid content that is targeted, is grammatically correct, and convincingly outlines your skills. Since we are concentrating on electronic documents, old rules governing the writing style, length, and content of paper résumés do not apply. For example, creating a résumé that will print on one page (or two at most) is not relevant in this arena.

No one wants to be considered conceited or boastful. When it comes to looking for a job, however, you must emphasize your abilities, focus on your strengths, and create a dynamic first impression. A well-written and neatly organized résumé can do all of that. The topics covered in this section will enable you to analyze the components of a good résumé and to design an effective résumé for yourself.

IMPORTANT CONTACT INFORMATION

You should dedicate the first section of your résumé to your name and how you can be contacted. Although this seems obvious, there are a couple of important contact issues to mention. Contact information must be complete, correct, and permanent. Depending on the policies of the company receiving your résumé, it could remain on file for months or even years. If your résumé is pulled for consideration six months from now, the contact information should still be valid.

Since we are focusing on electronic documents, it is important to note that privacy is a concern. While paper documents are typically routed to a person or department within an organization who has the responsibility of protecting your privacy, electronic documents can be generally distributed with no party directly responsible for privacy. Especially for documents posted to the Internet, it may be preferable to omit your address and phone numbers; instead use an e-mail account devoted to job hunting. If you elect to use an e-mail address, be sure to check your e-mail regularly and then provide the remaining contact information to legitimate organizations who contact you.

KEYWORDS

All résumés stored electronically can be sorted by key skills, experience, or education. Such items are referred to as "keywords." For example, an employer looking for an accountant might enter the following keywords or phrases: Staff Accountant, B.A. Degree in Accounting, Full-Cycle Accounting, Financial Statements and Cost Accounting. A computer query of all résumés in the database could be performed and those that contain all or some of these keywords would be identified. An employer could then read them via the computer screen, print the entire résumés or print abstracted data from some or all of the résumés.

Some automated résumé tracking systems can read and retain an unlimited number of keywords contained in an entire résumé. Other, usually older, systems may only be able to retain 35 to 45 keywords. Either way, you can see why keywords are the "magic door" for generating interviews with employers who use résumé tracking systems. Key-

WRITE YOUR OWN OBJECTIVE STATEMENT

Strong objective statements clearly state the position and industry of interest along with your strongest skills. Do not use "I," "me," or "my." Focus on the benefit to the employer. Here are two examples:

- Pharmaceutical sales representative capitalizing on extensive chemistry background and self-directed personality to manage a marketing territory.
- Researcher in investment and analysis. Interests and skills include securities analysis, financial planning, and portfolio management. Long-range goal: to become a chartered financial analyst. Willing to travel and relocate.

1. Identify the position, industry, skill words, and jargon in the two sample objectives above.

2. Rewrite the following weak objective statement:

   A position in marketing with a progressive firm

3. Create a strong objective statement for your planned career. Start with "I would like a job where I can use my ability to _____ which will result in _____." Rewrite the statement to be employer centered, contain industry jargon, and use skills keywords.

words are, in short, how employers find you in their systems. If you do not supply the right keywords, then your résumé has a limited chance to be found.

Whenever possible, use a minimum of 50 percent of the keywords found in an assortment of ads for the type of position you want. If possible, use all of them as long as you have the skills you are listing. Obviously you never want to lie or exaggerate by adding keywords to describe skills you do not possess. Such an unethical strategy could land you an interview, or a call from an employer, but would backfire when employers see you do not have the skills you have marketed.

Use the following steps to compile keywords and keyword phrases for your e-résumé:

1. Underline all keywords and keyword phrases in each ad.

2. Group keywords and keyword phrases into skill categories.

3. Create skill headings using keywords or keyword phrases for each group of skill categories.

4. Prioritize and number the skill categories.

5. Select the top 35 to 45 keywords to create a keyword section for the top of your e-résumé.

6. Write statements using as many keywords as possible for use in the rest of the e-résumé.

POWERFUL OBJECTIVE STATEMENTS

An objective statement specifies your target market. A well-developed objective statement is a potent tool for getting employers to look more deeply into your potential. Although some résumé styles omit this statement, it can be a critical résumé component when it provides an executive summary of your qualifications. Typical objective statements are short—between one and three sentences—and appear below the contact information.

For first-time job seekers or those changing careers, an objective statement should include a job title, an industry, the top three to five skills that qualify you for the job, and the benefit you will bring to the hiring organization. Using a decisive writing style lets employers know that you understand their business and helps them better determine that your skills can benefit their organization. A well-written, strong objective statement can

Figure I.3

Weak vs. Strong
Objective Statements

Weak Objective Statements	Strong Objective Statements
Management position which will utilize business administration degree and will provide opportunities for rapid advancement.	An entry-level position in software development designing and implementing operating systems.
A position in social services which will allow me to work with people in a helping capacity.	A mid-level public relations position with opportunities to develop and implement programs, organize people and events, and communicate positive ideas and images.
A position in personnel administration with a progressive firm.	Employment counselor/job development position working with disabled clients.
Sales representative with opportunity for advancement.	Entry position in financial analysis with a major financial institution.

provide a focus for organizing your résumé's content. Refer to Figure I.3 for a comparison of weak and strong objective statements.

Experienced job seekers can break this content into two sections: (1) a single-line objective with a job title and (2) industry followed by a summary of qualifications section. The summary of qualifications should highlight your skills and accomplishments that benefited previous employers. We recommend that you present this content in the form of a bulleted list (see Figure I.4).

In addition to basic job skills, it is important to let potential employers know about your cultural, language, and communication talents. While being multilingual may not be a requirement for a position, it is certainly a nice bonus that may get you noticed. Being willing to relocate may allow you to be considered for a wider range of jobs in an organization. Be decisive about what you want to do and showcase your skills whether they have been gained in the classroom, through life experiences, travel, or on the job.

Figure I.4

Objective and Summary
Examples

Entry-level Objective Statement	
Objective	Public accounting auditor position in the Midwest capitalizing on internal and external audit experience gained in a four-month PricewaterhouseCoopers internship. Familiar with payroll, tax, and general ledger processing. Multilingual and willing to travel.
Entry-level Objective Statement with Summary	
Objective Summary	Public accounting auditor position in the Midwest. Accounting coursework and internships • PricewaterhouseCoopers auditor internship with four months of experience in both internal and external general ledger audit techniques • Bookkeeping and coursework experience with payroll, cost, and tax accounting • Spanish fluency gained through extensive travel in Mexico and South America • Willing to travel and relocate

FEEDBACK, FEEDBACK, FEEDBACK!

As you probably learned in your composition courses, it is important to proofread and obtain feedback before submitting written work. This is even more essential for projects as important as your job search e-portfolio. Either formally or informally, create a group of two to three people who will provide constructive feedback throughout the remainder of your e-portfolio development.

1. Begin by each discussing your overall career goals and your work to date on this module.

2. Test your 30-second commercial on the group and solicit feedback.

3. Test your objective on the group and solicit feedback.

4. Discuss the other sections needed for your résumé and how to make your content employer centered.

5. Repeat steps 2 through 4 for the other group members.

Regardless of whether you are writing a stand-alone objective statement, keywords, or a summary of qualifications, write for your audience, or, in other words, write from the hiring organization's perspective. Remember to state what you can do for the organization that hires you using the industry jargon and skill keywords uncovered through networking, self-assessment, and research to describe yourself and what you offer an organization. Do not use words that indicate that you are not competent at a skill, such as entry level or beginner.

Avoid statements that appear self-centered or self-serving. For instance, do not mention money or promotions. Instead state that you are willing to accept increasing levels of responsibility. Money and promotions benefit you, while increasing your responsibility benefits the organization. Do not include statements with "I," "my," or "me," since these personal pronouns focus on you rather than on the organization.

Stay away from canned or hyped phrases normally associated with résumé writing. For example, a "position with a progressive company" and "opportunity for advancement" are commonly seen in résumés but don't communicate anything important about the applicant. Write honestly about your abilities and skills in a way that demonstrates your value to employers.

Most people reviewing résumés visually scan the objectives and summary of qualifications to determine whether or not to review the remaining résumé content. If you do not have enough skills to create competitive objective and summary statements, create a plan to acquire them.

OTHER VALUABLE RÉSUMÉ SECTIONS

Most résumés should include sections outlining your education and work experience. Place the section most important to your marketable skills first. Within each section, organize the information to best present your skills. In general, hiring organizations prefer chronological presentations because they are traditional and easy to follow, but other styles can be effective as long as it does not appear that you are trying to hide or omit anything.

Use the same writing techniques outlined for creating a powerful objective statement to describe and demonstrate your relevant coursework and job skills. It is not enough to list course and job titles. Include descriptions documenting relevant skills and their organizational benefit using jargon relevant to your position and industry. For example, "responsible for coding and testing Visual Basic applications" is an adequate job description for a programmer but "coded Visual Basic applications consisting of thousands of executable lines to solve complex business problems, manage system throughput, and improve end-user satisfaction" demonstrates both the level of skill being offered and how the organization benefited from them.

On most résumés, the last section should present information on references. Commonly this section contains a single statement, "References available upon request." This is common nomenclature to use since references are not needed until you are actually being considered for a position or going through the interview process.

Other sections to consider include Awards, Publications, Personal Information, and anything specific to the particular job being applied for. For example, a "Statement of Belief" could be important when applying for a job with a religious organization but probably should not be included otherwise. Personal information can be troublesome. When applying for a position with a formal organization, too much personal information can make you look informal. However, the same information can make you look like a good fit in a less formal institution. Use your research to determine what to include and omit.

In summary, no résumé is likely to rise to the top of the stack without the following elements:

- **Contact information.** At the very least include your name, phone number, and an e-mail address.
- **Objective.** Describe your purpose for seeking a particular job.
- **Qualifications.** List your abilities and skills that pertain to the job.
- **Education.** Include the name and location of the school(s) you attended, and diploma(s), degree(s), and honors received.
- **Work experience.** Include the name and location of the company, how long you worked there, and your job responsibilities.
- **Activities.** List volunteer activities, organization memberships, and leadership roles.
- **Style.** Use standard fonts, such as 12 point Times, Arial, or Helvetica.
- **Correct spelling and grammar.** Proofread very carefully. Use your word processor's spell-checker, but do not rely on it solely.
- **Clarity.** Use clear, concise, professional language.

SHOW ACTION

Finally, use action verbs to describe your work experiences powerfully. Instead of saying that you "participated in the organization of work teams," say that you "organized work teams." Action verbs should be used abundantly throughout your résumé to promote your talents, skills, and achievements. They help make a strong impression. Action verbs can bring your résumé to life. The intent is to indicate that you are a person of action, a "take charge and get the job done" person. Refer to Figure I.5 for a list of powerful action verbs.

Accelerated	Accomplished	Achieved	Acted
Adapted	Addressed	Administered	Advanced
Advised	Allocated	Analyzed	Appraised
Approved	Arranged	Assembled	Assigned
Assisted	Attained	Audited	Authored
Automated	Balanced	Broadened	Budgeted
Built	Calculated	Catalogued	Chaired
Clarified	Classified	Coached	Collected
Compiled	Completed	Composed	Computed
Conceptualized	Conducted	Consolidated	Contained
Contracted	Contributed	Controlled	Coordinated
Corresponded	Counseled	Created	Critiqued
Cut	Decreased	Delegated	Demonstrated
Designed	Developed	Devised	Diagnosed
Directed	Dispatched	Distinguished	Diversified
Drafted	Earned	Edited	Educated
Enabled	Encouraged	Engineered	Enlisted
Established	Evaluated	Examined	Executed
Expanded	Expedited	Explained	Extracted
Fabricated	Facilitated	Familiarized	Fashioned
Focused	Forecast	Formulated	Founded
Generated	Guided	Headed up	Identified
Illustrated	Implemented	Improved	Increased
Indoctrinated	Influenced	Informed	Initiated
Innovated	Installed	Instituted	Instructed
Integrated	Instigated	Interviewed	Introduced
Invented	Interpreted	Launched	Lectured
Led	Maintained	Managed	Marketed
Mediated	Moderated	Monitored	Motivated
Negotiated	Organized	Originated	Overhauled
Oversaw	Performed	Persuaded	Planned
Prepared	Presented	Prioritized	Processed
Produced	Programmed	Projected	Promoted
Provided	Publicized	Published	Purchased
Pursued	Recommended	Reconciled	Recorded
Recruited	Redesigned	Reduced	Referred
Regulated	Rehabilitated	Remodeled	Represented
Researched	Restored	Restructured	Retrieved
Revitalized	Saved	Scheduled	Schooled
Screened	Serviced	Shaped	Solidified
Solved	Sparked	Specified	Stimulated
Streamlined	Strengthened	Summarized	Supervised
Surveyed	Systemized	Tabulated	Taught
Targeted	Trained	Translated	Trimmed
Upgraded	Validated	Wrote	

Figure I.5

Action Verbs

ELECTRONIC FILE FORMATS

You should prepare your résumés in a variety of electronic file formats. Each format should be incorporated into your e-portfolio. Begin by building an unformatted résumé with solid content and then add formatting to create the other required formats.

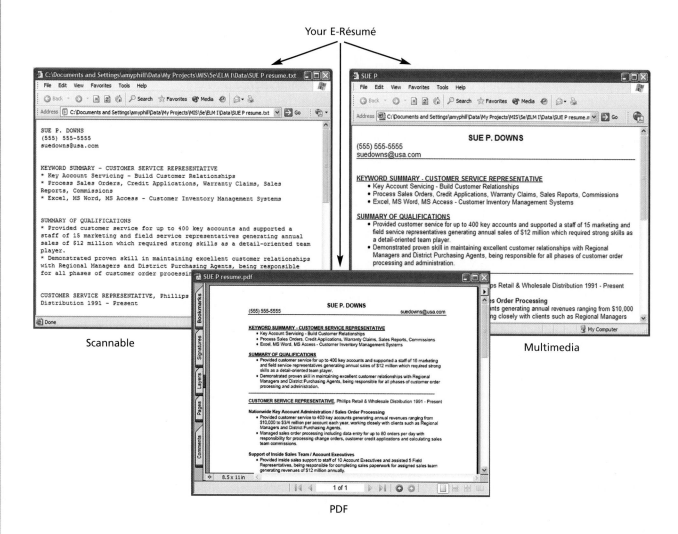

Figure I.6

Electronic File Formats

Just a few years ago, a résumé referred only to a sheet or two of paper that listed your work experience, accomplishments, education and a few other career details. Today, it also means an electronic document that can work for you in cyberspace 24 hours a day. There are three kinds of electronic résumés (these formats are displayed in Figure I.6):

- The *scannable (or ASCII) résumé* is a paper résumé that becomes electronic when it is scanned into a computer.
- The *portable document format résumé (PDF résumé)* is a standard electronic distribution format typically used for e-mailing.
- The *multimedia (or HTML) résumé* uses a multimedia format that exists on the Internet for employers to explore at their convenience.

THE SCANNABLE RÉSUMÉ

Say you create a handsome paper résumé and mail it to a potential employer. Unbeknownst to you, the company has a computerized system for scanning résumés that reach the Human Resources department. Instead of a person reading your application and deciding how to forward or file it, someone will scan it into a computer.

The type is converted into a text file that is stored in an electronic résumé database. The paper version will be filed or discarded. Your résumé may receive the same treatment if you fax it to a potential employer. Instead of printing a hard copy, the employer may store the fax in a computer queue until someone verifies and summarizes its contents in the same computerized database.

A typical Fortune 1000 corporation processes as many as 2,000 electronic résumés a day. Approximately 25 percent come directly through the company's Web site; 25 percent come through major online job banks such as Monster.com; 20 percent arrive via e-mail; and the rest get entered into the company's résumé database through scanning devices.

Medium- and small-sized companies have also become increasingly dependent on the electronic transfer and storage of résumés, as they hook up to online résumé databases or outsource job fulfillment to recruiters who use résumé databases. Even nonprofit organizations receive more résumés through e-mail than ever before.

To design a scannable résumé that improves your hiring prospects, follow these basic guidelines (a demonstration of this format is displayed in Figure I.7):

- Create a text-only file. In Microsoft Word select **File** from the menu, click **Save As,** and then set the Save As Type to Plain Text (*.txt) or use Notepad to create your document.
- Use only Courier or Times New Roman 10 or 12 point font.
- Do not include character formatting such as bold, underline, italics, or text color.
- Do not center or tab-indent text (every line should be left justified).
- Press **Enter** at the end of each line. Line length should be between 65 and 70 characters for optimal skills extraction.

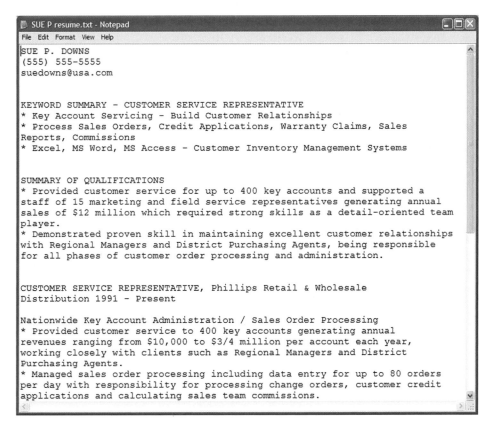

Figure I.7

Scannable Résumé Format

- Do not include tables or graphics.
- Leave two blank lines between sections.
- Capitalize all letters in section headings.
- Use asterisks (*), dashes (—), or another standard keyboard character for bullets (do not use automated bulleted or numbered lists).

THE PDF RÉSUMÉ

When you type words onto a computer screen using word processing software, you are creating a "file" or "document." When you save that file, it includes special formatting codes such as fonts, margins, tab settings, and so on, even if you did not specifically add these codes. Each word processing program (e.g. WordPerfect, Microsoft Word, etc.) automatically saves files in its own native format, making the file readable only to those with the same software or a conversion program. To make sure your document can be read by everyone, ***Portable document format (PDF)*** is the standard electronic distribution file format. The benefit of PDF is that documents created in any application can be shared across platforms and still look exactly as designed. All fonts, indentions, graphics, links, tables, and alignment are retained. This format is widely used to distribute books and forms electronically. For example, most U.S. tax forms are available as PDF downloads from a Web site. You can download Adobe Acrobat Reader from www.adobe.com at no cost to view PDF documents.

Once you convert your presentation résumé to a PFD format, anyone can view and print it exactly as you designed it (as shown in Figure I.8). You can easily distribute your PDF résumé as an e-mail attachment or a Web download. The process of creating a PDF file is simple but requires access to Adobe Acrobat software, which is available in several versions. Currently, a Create Adobe PDF Online link is available from www.adobe.com that will allow you to subscribe and create up to five free PDF files.

Figure I.8

PDF Résumé Format

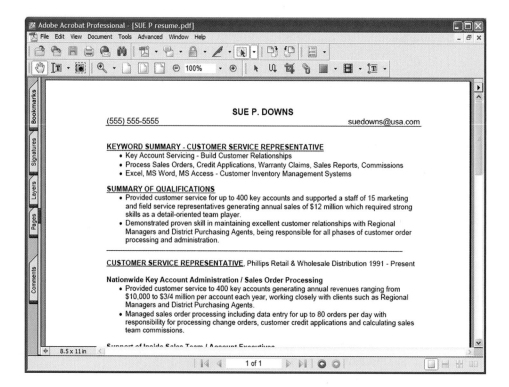

THE MULTIMEDIA (OR HTML) RÉSUMÉ

If you are a computer programmer, Web page developer, graphic designer, artist, sculptor, singer, dancer, actor, model, animator, cartoonist or other professional who would benefit from the photographs, graphics, animation, sound, color and movement possible with a multimedia résumé, then this is the format for you.

As you create and deliver Web content, you create files with either .htm or .html as the file extension. Within these files (called HTML documents), you use hypertext markup language (HTML) tags to provide document formatting instructions to Web browsers such as Microsoft Internet Explorer or Netscape Communicator (see Figure I.9).

A good e-portfolio Web site should include a home page that acts as a site overview and menu, all of your résumé text, and additional supporting materials using HTML tags to format attractive pages. Résumés and supporting content already formatted for other delivery modes (.txt, .pdf, .doc, .ppt, .xls, and so on) for other purposes are usually not converted to HTML. You should refer to *Extended Learning Module F* for using HTML to create a Web site and provide links to downloadable files. In the remainder of this module, we'll specifically address designing and building the pages of your e-portfolio.

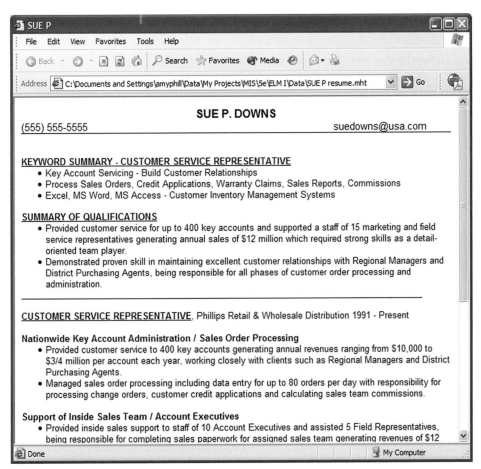

Figure I.9

Multimedia Résumé Format

WHAT IS THE RIGHT RÉSUMÉ STYLE?

Choose a résumé layout that fits your job history and target position (Figure I.10 displays two of these formats).

1. **Chronological.** You easily meet all skill, experience, and education requirements. A chronological résumé arranges work experiences according to time sequence. Generally, your most recent experiences are listed first. Use a chronological résumé:
   - When your work history occupies the same field.
   - When your job history shows real growth or advancement.
   - When your prior job titles and companies are impressive.

2. **Functional.** You are a new graduate, changing fields or industries. A functional résumé focuses on skills, abilities, volunteer experiences, and work experiences. It highlights what you can do. Use a functional résumé:
   - For your first job.
   - When your skills are more impressive than your work history.
   - When you've frequently changed employers or careers.

3. **Curriculum Vitae (or CV).** You are a scientist or educator. A CV is an academic résumé that you use to tell others about your academic qualifications. A CV needs to be as long as it takes to convey the information. For many fourth-year students, the document may be a page or so. For a tenured professor in a medical school, it may cover several hundred pages.

Figure I.10

Chronological and Functional Résumé Layout

Tyler M. Phillips
E-Mail: tmphillips@washington.edu
Web Address: http://www.washington.edu/~tmphillips/

OBJECTIVE	Contribute strong customer-service focus in a creative, exciting marketing-oriented setting.
PROFILE	• Creative marketing problem-solver. • Award-winning customer service provider. • Entrepreneurial self-starter. • Hard-working, dedicated professional.
EDUCATION	Bachelor of Business Administration, University of Washington, Seattle, WA, December 2003 • Major in General Business • Minors in Marketing and Business Law • Grade Point Average: 3.4 • Dean's List • Freshman Honorary Society • Most outstanding academic performance by a junior in the General Business major. • Maintained high G.P.A. while working full-time to finance 100% of tuition.
EXPERIENCE	*Entrepreneur, WIRED ON JAVA!*, Seattle, WA, 1/00 - Present. • Participated on a team of six entrepreneurs through the Quintessential Careers Entrepreneurial Program at Univesity of Washington. • Played instrumental role in creating business idea, formulating a business plan, and operating of business. *Server, OYSTER CREEK INN,* Seattle, WA, 8/99 - Present. • Completed extensive training course that promoted providing excellent service to every guest through both individual and teamwork. • Voted by management as employee of the month for April 2000. *Assistant Manager, ARDOUR & PED,* Seattle, WA, 6/98 - 8/99. • Trained new employees on suggestive selling, creating pleasing displays, computer P.O.S. system, and servicing customers. • Created unique clothing and accessory displays.
COMPUTER SKILLS	Windows, Microsoft Word, Microsoft Excel, PowerPoint, WordPerfect, and HTML programming.
FOREIGN TRAVEL	• Dual citizen of the United Kingdom and U.S. • Extensive European travel.
REFERENCES	Available upon request.

Chronological Résumé Layout

Lory L. Britt
617-555-5555
lbritt@harvard.edu

OBJECTIVE	Highly motivated, intelligent graduate ready to contribute my education and health management skills in a position with a growing and dynamic firm.
EDUCATION	BACHELOR OF SCIENCE Harvard Universit, Cambridge, Massachusetts, May 2003 Major: Health Sciences Minor: Management
RELEVANT COURSES	• Human Anatomy & Physiology I • Human Anatomy & Physiology II • Health Policy • Organizational Analysis and Health Care • Health Care Management • Human Resource Management
Health Management Skills	• Served as Assistant to the Director of the Stacey G. Houndly Breast Cancer Foundation. • Functioned as Public Health Representative for the Cambridge Area Public Health Administration. • Coordinated, Harvard University Public Health Awareness Week, 1996, 1997.
Communications Skills	• Served as a phone-a-thon caller on several occasions, soliciting donations from Harvard alumni and parents for Harvard University. • Volunteered for a political campaign, distributing literature door to door, fielding questions and making phone calls to local constituents.
Management Skills	• Handled all back-office management functions, including employee relations and accounting. • Oversaw client relations, order processing and routine upkeep of the business. • Coordinated efforts between customer needs and group personnel. • Designed all market research analysis and projects for our clients. • Delegated suggestions and duties to other team members. • Presented market research results to client with suggestions of implementation.
Leadership Skills	• Participated in Youth Leadership Boston, a group dedicated to developing leadership skills through diverse programming. • Served as formal/social coordinator for my sorority program council. • Elected Vice President of Risk Management for Panhellenic, a group that oversees and coordinates educational programming for Harvard's Greek system.
Systems Abilities	• Microsoft Office • HTML/Web Publishing • WordPerfect

Functional Résumé Layout

Developing Your E-Portfolio

Your e-portfolio is your living document on the Internet. More than just a homepage, more than just a résumé, the e-portfolio offers you a new, smarter model for self-marketing and networking.

You should design your e-portfolio to provide everything that a prospective employer needs to evaluate your employment potential. That means that it should include several e-résumé formats, permanent contact information, and a gallery designed to demonstrate your skills.

An e-portfolio can be one of the most rewarding marketing tools you will ever use, because it can help you expand your reach in ways never before possible. It shows that you are up-to-date, gives you instant credibility, and expands your market globally and exponentially. But most important of all, your e-portfolio and the World Wide Web makes it possible to have access at anytime to examples of your work. Your prospective employers can get information when they need it without having to wait for you to send it, making it simple for anyone to evaluate you and satisfying the desire for instant gratification that is pervasive in our digital economy.

In this section we will examine several of the techniques you need to use to present yourself successfully, from a marketing point of view, on the Web. Whether you already have a Web site up and running or you are still in the preparation stages, this section will help you make your site one that will achieve your personal marketing goals.

An e-portfolio is one marketing tool that does not live on the back burner. In fact, the opposite is true. Many people have slapped their sites up without much planning, perhaps in preparation for an event or because a client says, "Give me your Web address," or maybe just because everyone else is doing it.

Some people put a site up quickly and then revamp it. In fact, many people who have already created an e-portfolio Web site have transitioned their presentation to a second or third iteration, as they have learned from the comments of visitors and from Web reports what works and what does not.

SELF-PROMOTION

Even if you have no gizmos to sell, the Internet is a powerful tool to get the word out and to increase your visibility. An e-portfolio is not the ultimate marketing tool, but it is an essential one in our digital economy. If you do not have an e-portfolio yet, here are four reasons why you should:

1. *An e-portfolio can give you instant credibility.* Because anyone anywhere can put up a Web site, you must use yours to establish your credibility. A list of projects, examples of your work, and your contact information will show potential employers who you are.

2. *A Web site provides access anytime to you and examples of your work.* Potential employers can go straight to your Web site and get the information they need when they need it.

3. *A Web site shows that you are current and up-to-date.* It is essential that you have either a Web site with your own domain name, or at the very least, an online presence (i.e., Web site) where your e-portfolio is posted.

4. *A Web site expands your exposure and increases your visibility worldwide.* That means your potential reach is wider than it has ever been before because people with whom it was once difficult to communicate are now just a click away.

One of the main principles of self-promotion is this: self-promotion is not just about you; it is also about your prospective employers. Your e-portfolio materials should offer your solutions to their problems, and that applies to your Web site. So instead of focusing all your attention on how to show your work in the best light, ask yourself, "When they visit my site, what do they need to learn more about me and my work, in order to trust that I can do what they need done?"

GIVE THEM WHAT THEY WANT

Some of your future employers are visually oriented, and some are not. Some are Web savvy, and some are not. Some know what they are talking about when they use Internet jargon, and some do not have a clue. And yet, every one of them has an opinion and a perspective that matters. Here is what your future employers are looking for when they visit your Web site (see Figure I.11 for an example):

- *Lots of work.* When your future employers are in their moment of need, they want to see as much work as possible. And they want to see the quality of your work before they decide to invest the time to make contact.
- *Creativity.* Though it is very subjective, employers want creativity from the creative professionals they hire. Anything different or unusual—not boring or "industrial"—will make them stop and take notice.
- *Strategy.* Creativity alone is not enough. Future employers also want to see your marketing savvy. Use your Web site to show how your work will help them build their business.
- *Good architecture.* Future employers do not have time to figure out your Web site, so make it easy to navigate and understand.

Figure I.11

An e-Portfolio Example

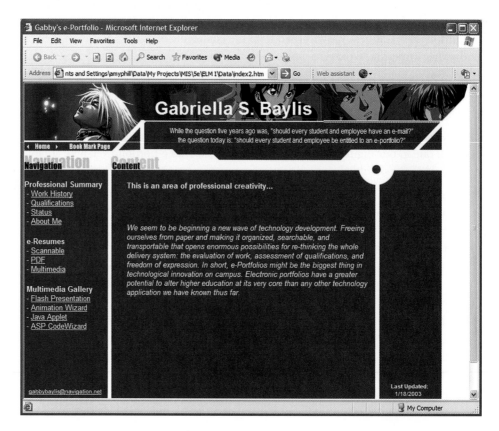

THE SHAPE OF AN E-PORTFOLIO

The e-portfolio has added a new step to the process of hiring online, a step that comes at the very beginning of the getting-to-know-you period and that makes everyone's life—yours and your prospective employer's—easier and more efficient. Your prospective employer can go to your Web site and check you out before making contact, because even a simple online portfolio allows you to convey so much more about yourself and your services than the few examples of your work they would find in a creative directory. The goal of your simple online portfolio, then, is to provide enough of a taste of your work for a prospect to decide whether to take the next step: making contact.

When your online prospective employer arrives at your Web site, the first thing they need to know is how to find the samples of your work. The easier a Web site is to understand and navigate, the longer visitors will stay. And the more they see of your work, the more they will get to know you.

One strategy that helps to orient visitors quickly is to use a metaphorical interface that is familiar and intuitive. With that said, the simplest Web site must have at least:

1. **Biographical information.** Call it what you want—"Profile," "About Me," or "Who I Am"—but provide information about yourself.

2. **Online portfolio.** First and foremost your visitors will be looking for examples of your work and information about your skills and talents. So give them a lot to look at and organize it in a simple way.

3. **Contact information.** Visitors will need to know how to contact you, so make it easy for them. Give them many options—phone, fax, e-mail—and make that information accessible from every page of your site.

E-GALLERY

Besides the ability to deliver your résumé in multiple formats, an e-portfolio provides you with the opportunity to demonstrate your skills through a gallery of works (see Figure I.12). Because the Web allows viewers to click on links to view materials that are of

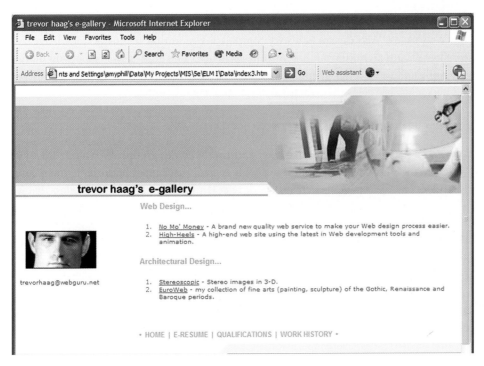

Figure I.12

An e-Gallery Example

interest to them, there is no absolute limit to the number of supporting pages that you can develop.

The simplest way to compose a gallery is to make use of materials that you already have in hand. Remember that the gallery should display your skills, so consider including the following:

- Writing samples
- Spreadsheets or other applications of business tools
- Demonstrations of analytical, planning, or management skills
- Presentations that you have developed

Existing documents may need to be edited to remove confidential materials or to shorten the content. For example, you might include the introduction, problem analysis, and summary sections of a 30-page report since it is unlikely that anyone would read the entire report; they would thereby miss those sections that sufficiently demonstrate your talent. Do not include proprietary employer information or group projects without giving appropriate credit and obtaining permission.

If you do not have existing documents that sufficiently demonstrate your job skills, create them from scratch. This can be time-consuming, but they create a much stronger statement about your talent and dedication than just saying you can do the job. Start small and spend the time to do an excellent job. One of the biggest benefits of a Web-based gallery is that you can add and remove components at any time.

There are no hard-and-fast rules about what to include in your gallery, but remember to keep it focused on your goal of obtaining a job. Label and organize your gallery content so that viewers can click on only what they want to see. For example, provide links from your job and education descriptions to documents demonstrating related skills. Alternatively, a gallery link can lead to a page outlining your skills with links to specific documents.

Web Design Considerations

Web design is the successful blending of text and graphics to create appealing and useable Web pages. Web design is also a complex art requiring technical knowledge, research, skill, and an understanding of your audience. The good news is that you do not have to become a Web designer to have an effective e-portfolio. The sections that follow outline a few basic rules that will help you organize your content.

BASIC WEB DESIGN PRINCIPLES

You need to take advantage of some tried-and-true Web design tips. We will address key Web page design issues and tactics, but with a small disclaimer, because first and foremost, designing Web pages is a creative endeavor. Understand that the parameters that we outline in this module are guidelines. If you search the Web for Web design principles, you will find many lists of suggestions that have only a few elements in common. Every Web design expert has an opinion about what makes a good site and so does everyone browsing the Web. Can they all be right? Probably yes, depending on the context. Here, we will cover effective Web design principles for creating a job search e-portfolio.

The difference between content designed for printed viewing and content designed for electronic viewing on the Web is quite dramatic. You should keep in mind that good print layout does not translate effectively to good Web layout. There are many reasons for this; the primary reasons include:

- Printed pages are designed to be read, while Web pages are designed to be browsed.
- Printed pages are the same size, while Web pages are not. The viewable area of a Web page is also much smaller than a printed page.
- Printed pages stay visually the same, while Web page layout varies depending on the Web browser, screen resolution, operating system, and monitor being used.

Even with the improved resolution of today's monitors, it is more difficult to read from a computer screen than it is from a printed document. Few readers will actually read long passages online; they most often print it or skip it altogether. Consider breaking long text (three or more screens) up so that the user is presented with an overview and can then link to the details. If you need to present long text as a single unit, be sure that it is printer friendly by using the dimensions outlined in Figure I.13.

Web content must be concise, well labeled, and formatted for browsing. Every page needs to contain information about who, what, when, and where, so that a person who just "pops" into that page has a point of reference. The top of each page contains a header that holds the organization's name, logo, and other identifying information. Many sites also include navigational links in the header. The bottom of each page contains a footer outlining the origin (author name or institution), contact point, and the date the page was last updated. Many sites also include navigation in the footer. The middle of each page contains the content, which should be displayed in a manner that helps viewers find topics of interest.

Often the left-hand side of the content zone contains a menu of links. This is particularly important in large sites with long pages. Whether or not you add a menu column to the left of your content, white space to the left and right of your text will make it easier to read. Also, make sure to leave white space between headings and other page elements to avoid a cluttered look.

Safe dimensions for Web page graphics

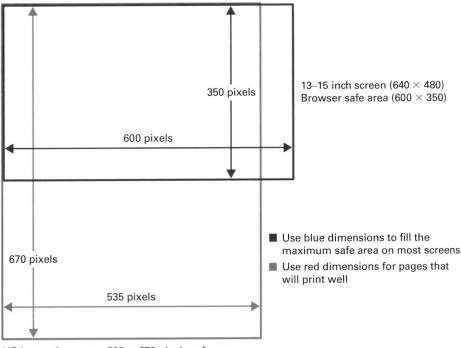

350 pixels

600 pixels

670 pixels

535 pixels

US Letter size page = 535 × 670 pixels safe area

13–15 inch screen (640 × 480)
Browser safe area (600 × 350)

■ Use blue dimensions to fill the maximum safe area on most screens
■ Use red dimensions for pages that will print well

Figure I.13

Printer Friendly Web Page Dimensions

AUDIENCE REIGNS SUPREME

Planning your Web site affects design in a couple of major ways. Specifically, before you design, you should consider your audience and organize your Web page layout and your Web site's structure.

You create and use a job search e-portfolio to market yourself for a job or ranges of related jobs to the hiring organizations of a particular industry. To make this clear, add the industry and job title(s) to your job search e-portfolio. In doing so, you have defined both your audience and your purpose. The key to developing a Web site that will appeal to your audience is to build what they like, not what you like. Again, your research should pay off. Think about the industry and business sites that you visited while researching your chosen career.

Some of the questions you can ask yourself to help gain insight into your target audience are:

- What is the average age of managers (the people who do the hiring)? Employees (the people you would work with)?
- How conservative is this industry?
- Are employees expected to be artistic?
- How will my audience view my page?
- What do the backgrounds, colors, graphics, and navigation of business sites in the industry look like?
- How does this industry promote itself?

There are no absolutes in e-portfolio design. A site that works well for an artist, while beautiful, would probably be inappropriate for an accountant. Remember that this is not a personal site. It should demonstrate your business personality without being too personal.

STORYBOARDING

After you identify your audience but before you start to create your Web pages, you should sketch your Web page's layout as well as any relationships among ancillary pages—this intended visual relationship is called a *storyboard.* In other words, you should illustrate the relationships among your site's pages to ensure that you have created a clear site layout that includes all the related information in an easily accessible format.

You will then need to figure out how best to present yourself electronically. For example, you can organize your site in any number of ways, including the following:

- Alphabetically
- Chronologically
- Graphically
- Hierarchically
- Numerically
- Randomly (not recommended)
- Topically

By far, most sites are organized hierarchically, that is, they present a homepage that contains catchy introductory text and links to the site's main pages.

SITE STRUCTURE

The structure of a Web site is how the various pages of the site are linked together. There are two main schools of thought when it comes to Web page length: scrolling or clicking. Long pages of content require the viewer to scroll to see everything while short pages contain clickable links that provide the full content. Overall, Web users prefer small fast-loading pages that allow them to click directly to the desired content. In other words, most people prefer to click rather than scroll. It is not possible to avoid scrolling altogether, but try not to annoy your users by having them scroll too much.

To create a site of linked pages, you must segment or break your content into usable units. Each segment becomes a separate Web page in your site. Try to think of screens of text rather than pages of text. At 800 × 600 screen resolution, the average Web browser screen displays about one-half page of text when there is nothing else on the screen. The page title, navigation, and footer information can cut that to one-third of a page for text. So, to view one printed page of text, the person reading your e-portfolio would have to scroll down at least two screens. More than three screens of scrolling is beyond the tolerance of the average user unless the text is very interesting or must logically be presented as a unit.

Once you have determined your Web site segments, your next step is to determine how pages will be linked together. The home page is the preferred entry point to your site and should start the navigation. Users should also be able to move from topic to topic in your site without returning to the homepage. Web sites can contain sequence, hierarchical, grid, and Web navigation. Linear sites are the simplest to build and navigate but are appropriate only for sequential information such as a book. Grid structures are appropriate for sites with multiple topics or entry points (see Figure I.14).

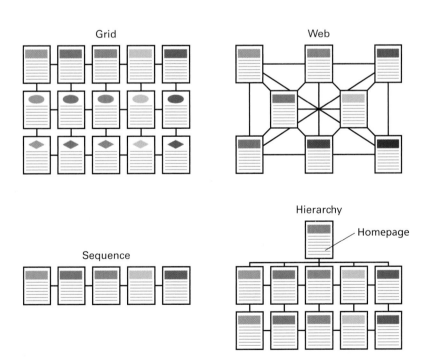

Grid

Web

Sequence

Hierarchy

Homepage

Figure I.14

Documenting Web Site Structure

BUILD YOUR RÉSUMÉS AND VISIT E-PORTFOLIO SITES

Although documents created in Microsoft Windows have filenames that are not case sensitive and handle spaces well (My Résumé.doc), more than likely your e-portfolio will be posted on a UNIX server. UNIX is the most common operating system for Web servers. Make your files UNIX friendly by using consistent capitalization and no spaces in the filenames (MyRésumé.doc). Open a Notepad or Microsoft Word document to create an ASCII résumé. Enter all of your résumé content without any formatting. Be sure to follow the guidelines outlined in the module text. If you use Microsoft Word, be sure to change the **Save As Type** to Plain Text (*.txt).

To create a presentation résumé, open your ASCII résumé in Microsoft Word and save it with a **Save As Type** of Word document (*.doc). Remove all of the extra hard returns (where you pressed Enter) in the document and then select **Theme** from the Format menu. Click the Style Gallery button and select one of the résumé templates. Update the text and formatting to create a résumé that can be printed in one or two pages.

Visit www.adobe.com and register to create free PDF files. Use this service to create a PDF version of your presentation résumé. Create a folder for your Web site development and place copies of all of your résumés there.

To enhance your understanding of job search e-portfolio content, segmenting, navigation, layout, and design, visit www.mhhe.com/haag and select the XLM/I link. Look through the available portfolios paying attention to the content, use of color, fonts, navigation, page layout, and graphics.

1. How important was color in your initial assessment of a site?
2. What attributes made it easy to move through a site?
3. What was your favorite site? Why? Evaluate the way that site content was segmented. Sketch out the navigation structure of this site.
4. What was your least favorite site? Why?

Because an e-portfolio has a structured entry point (the homepage), we recommend using some combination of the hierarchical and Web structures. Simple sites can use a basic hierarchy with just two levels. The homepage would comprise the first level and all second-level HTML pages would be linked back to the homepage. More complex sites will need three hierarchical levels with the level under the homepage representing site topics. At least some of the third-level pages should link back to both the second and third levels, creating a Web hierarchy navigational structure. We do not recommend that your e-portfolio include more than three levels.

Regardless of how you structure your site, it is important for the navigation to be well marked and intuitive. Make sure to label your links descriptively and to group content together that logically belongs together. With few exceptions, each HTML page of a site should contain links to the homepage and other site topics. Non-HTML pages such as Word or Excel documents do not usually contain links. It is important to create a Web site navigation chart to have a checklist of pages and links to build and test.

DESIGN YOUR HOMEPAGE

When designing a group of Web pages that are structured to work together, such as an e-portfolio site, it is critical that each page contain common color, font, navigation, and layout design elements. It should be obvious to a user who has clicked on a link to another Web page that he or she is still in your e-portfolio site. Similarly, someone who has clicked from another Web site into a subpage of your site should be able to easily navigate to content matching their interests. Design your opening or homepage and then apply those navigation, layout, font, and color elements throughout the remaining site pages.

COLOR

You need to pay considerable attention to your Web page's color scheme. A color scheme refers to your site's interface elements, such as title graphics, buttons, background, and text. Ideally, you should limit the number of colors used in you Web page's interface to three or four colors. The key is to use contrasting colors, especially if you are using a colored background.

Color impacts the look and feel of your site. We speak of colors as being warm, cool, muted, light, dark, and garish. Decide what type of color description is appropriate for your audience and then select colors within that description. For example, mocha is a warm color while cyan is a cool color.

In Web page design, browser-safe colors are important since there are 216 different colors that can be displayed by a both a PC and MacIntosh computer. When a Web browser encounters a color that it cannot interpret, it substitutes a color that it knows, resulting in unpredictable Web page displays. For that reason, we recommend that you use *browser-safe colors* that can be displayed by all monitors and Web browsers. You can easily find a chart of browser-safe colors at http://www.lynda.com/hexv.html. Test your color selections on as many systems as possible.

Overall, you should use your color scheme to create balance and unity through your site, but you should also use colors to draw attention to specific areas of your Web page.

FONTS AND FORMATTING

You have the power to control your text's size, color, formatting, and style. Almost universally, Web designers recommend that you use the default size for the main content. This allows viewers to choose the font size via their browser's default settings.

Even though thousands of font styles exist, all font styles can be categorized as either *serif* or *sans serif*. Serif fonts, such as Times, use "hooks" or short lines, on the ends of letters, whereas san serif fonts, like Arial, use plain-edged letters. We generally prefer to use sans serif fonts when creating Web pages because they are easier to read online and tend to be more visually appealing.

Regardless of your preference, you should stick with cross-platform fonts to ensure that users see your text similar to how you designed your page. Cross-platform fonts include the following:

- Arial
- Arial Narrow
- Comic Sans
- Courier New
- Georgia
- Times New Roman (or Times)
- Trebuchet
- Verdana

Titling Images

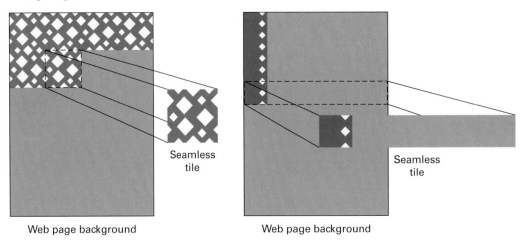

Titles for Web Pages

Initial Caps Cause Pointless Bumps

Start cap with bold omits pointless bumps

Figure I.15

Backgrounds and Titles

As we have already mentioned, reading is more difficult on a computer monitor than on paper. To simplify reading, headings should be easily identified and use sentence case, not title case as they would in a written document. Title case causes unnecessary bumps in a line of text as we show in Figure I.15.

Use tables, bulleted lists, and   (the HTML equivalent to a space) to control the layout of your pages. Tables can provide white space, make columns, and control the placement of graphic elements. For both print and screen reading, three-inch lines of text provide the best readability, so columns are an effective design tool. Bulleted lists make items under a heading easy to identify. The   instruction adds a space to your page and is the most effective way to indent a first line of text. Use the <BLOCK-QUOTE> tag to indent the left (and on some browsers the right) margin of a block of text. Make sure that all the design elements you select work well to create the desired visual impact.

GRAPHICS

Web graphics look fairly similar to print graphics, but some Web-specific factors are relevant when you are creating and using graphics on the Web. Specifically, online graphics require you to consider color limitations, file formats, and files sizes as well as possible transparency, downloading, and animation issues.

You should adhere to the following four practices when using graphical elements on the Web:

1. Avoid large graphics that seem to take days to download on a modem. You might try using *thumbnails* where appropriate. A thumbnail is a small picture that links to a larger image. This gives viewers the choice of viewing the small image or clicking on the thumbnail to view the larger image.

2. Do not use meaningless graphics. Make sure you use graphics that contribute to the user's experience.

3. Ensure that every graphical link has a text link equivalent.

4. Create either GIF (Graphics Interchange Format) or JPEG (Joint Photographic Expert Group) images. These are standard formats used pervasively on the Web.

TEXTUAL ELEMENTS OF YOUR HOMEPAGE

The content for your Web site needs to be segmented into logical units that will become the pages of your Web site. The opening or homepage is the entrance to your Web site and deserves special attention. If at all possible, this page should all be displayed on one screen at 800×600 screen resolution. The goal is to load fast and provide the viewer with enough information to assess the site and navigate to pages of interest. Remember that each Web page should include who, what, when, and where.

Recall that each page of your site should contain the same footer. This is the easiest content to develop. At a minimum, your footer should include your name, e-mail address, and the last time the page was updated. It is often a good idea to include links to the other pages of your site above this information.

Each page of your site should also contain a header or title bar. The header needs to include your name and contact information. If you have a business logo or graphic relevant to your job search, you can incorporate it in your header.

Although it is uncommon to include a photograph in a printed résumé, many people include a high-quality business attire photo in their e-portfolio Web site. However, there is no need to include your photo in the header that will appear on every page of the site, since that would appear egotistical.

Page content is displayed between the header and footer, often with a menu bar down the left-hand side. Since you are developing an e-portfolio site, your objective statement, a description of your ultimate job, or a summary of skills can be effective homepage content. Avoid uninformative text such as "Welcome to my e-Portfolio." Overall, your homepage should be both inviting and informative (refer back to Figure I.11).

DOCUMENT THE SITE DESIGN

After designing your homepage, you should have a good idea of how to segment and link (organize) your remaining e-portfolio content. Ideally, you should create logical groupings of content so that you have no more than eight links on your homepage. For example, you could create a résumé page that, in turn, links to your "30-second commercial" presentation, PDF, and scannable résumés. Similarly, you might provide a gallery page with links to your work.

Be sure that your Web site segments account for all of your gallery content and all résumé file formats before developing a navigational or hierarchy chart. The navigational chart will document the content of each page and how it is linked to the other pages of the site. You will use it to determine the content and links to place on each page during development and then to test each link once you build the site.

The various résumé formats (ASCII, PDF, and HTML) that you have already developed should be placed on the Web site as is, so that potential employers have access to all formats. The navigation chart makes this distinction by including the file extension (.txt, .pdf, .html, and so on) that identifies the file format. You can also place much of the content of your gallery in their native formats since your goal is to demonstrate your skills.

Figure I.16

Sample e-Portfolio
Navigation Chart

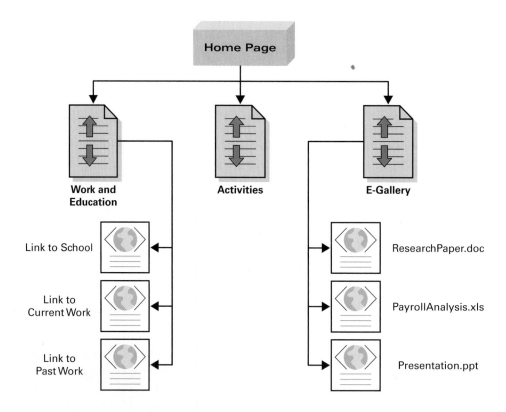

Links using the anchor <A HREF="filename"> tag can link to all of these file formats. We do not recommend that you provide links from these documents back to your e-portfolio site since your site viewers will most likely save them. The navigation chart shows a link to these non-HTML files, but provides no return link (see Figure I.16).

Preparing Web Content

Use the navigation chart (shown in Figure I.16) first to develop and link each page of your site. Begin by placing your existing résumé and gallery files in a site folder and then create an abbreviated HTML document for each HTML Web site page in the same folder. Each abbreviated HTML page should contain a word or two that describes what the page will hold once you fully develop it. You will use these "dummy" pages to test your links on each page as you finish developing them.

One of the trickiest parts of developing a Web site is writing the text and choosing the photos and graphics. This material—the site content—needs to be succinct, informative, and well presented; otherwise you risk being seen as an amateur.

Here are some tips for preparing your Web content:

- Gather all the material you have been preparing through this module, such as your objective statement, résumé formats, and e-gallery examples. It is very helpful to have a printed copy of all these materials.

- Write one key sentence of no more than 30 words describing the essence of your e-portfolio. This could be used to describe who your are when your site is listed in a search directory or even as an introduction element on your homepage.

- Write down at least 10 single keywords and 10 key phrases of two to three words that could be used to reference the site and attract people entering those keywords or phrases into a search engine.

- If you have a special logo, or professional photograph, find the cleanest and largest possible version of it for scanning. You want a physical image that is focused and has an excellent definition of color. Create a digital image of your logo or photograph making sure that you use the highest resolution possible for high definition. You will be able to resize this according to Web standards later.

- Look at other e-portfolios on the Web. Go to a good search engine, such as www.google.com, and enter into the search field the words you would expect someone to use if they were trying to find someone with your skills, talents, and interests. Look at some of the sites that this search produces, and see how they are designed and the words they use. Some will be great, some awful—examine the good ones for ideas.

HTML VERSUS GENERATED CODE

Overwhelmingly, when you are creating your Web pages, you will be spending the greatest amount of time interacting with a text editor or an HTML editor. You can use editors to create HTML files that contain display tags for Web browsers which hold the content of your Web page. When you use an editor, you have the option of working with HTML code manually or using a more advanced what-you-see-is-what-you-get (WYSIWYG) editor which will autogenerate your HTML code while you type, insert images, and drag elements around in a Web page layout view.

When you use a basic text editor, you type in all the HTML commands into a blank document. The most basic of the text editors is Notepad that comes with the Microsoft Windows operating system. Hand-coding Web pages is still considered a feasible option for the following reasons:

- Control
- Quick fixes
- Clean code
- Fine tuning

In general, we believe it is a good idea to get comfortable with some basic HTML before using an HTML editor so that you are familiar enough with the code to read it and apply simple changes manually. Refer to *Extended Learning Module* F for an introduction to building a Web page with HTML.

WEB DESIGN TOOLS

HTML editors enable you to create and edit Web pages by using a graphical interface that will also allow you to view and edit your HTML source code. Although Web authoring software can simplify many tasks, there may be a learning curve to become efficient in their use. Additionally, Web authoring software can generate unnecessary code, making it more difficult for you to make manual modifications and slowing page load time. Sometimes the Web site management portion of this software can introduce errors in Web page links through the default settings and assumptions. A list of the more popular HTML editors are:

- Dreamweaver (www.macromedia.com)
- Microsoft Frontpage (www.microsoft.com/frontpage)
- NewObjects Fusion (www.netobjects.com)
- Adobe GoLive (www.adobe.com)
- HotMetal Pro (www.hotmetalpro.com)

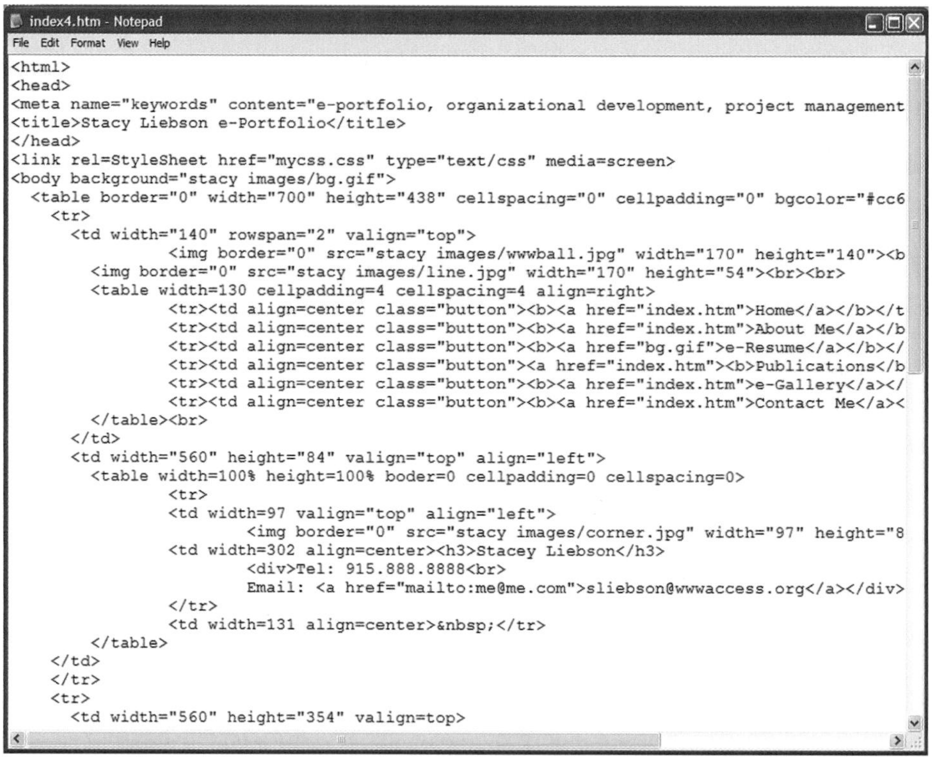

Figure I.17

Sample HTML Code in
Notepad

```
index4.htm - Notepad
File  Edit  Format  View  Help
<html>
<head>
<meta name="keywords" content="e-portfolio, organizational development, project management
<title>Stacy Liebson e-Portfolio</title>
</head>
<link rel=StyleSheet href="mycss.css" type="text/css" media=screen>
<body background="stacy images/bg.gif">
  <table border="0" width="700" height="438" cellspacing="0" cellpadding="0" bgcolor="#cc6
    <tr>
      <td width="140" rowspan="2" valign="top">
              <img border="0" src="stacy images/wwwball.jpg" width="170" height="140"><b
        <img border="0" src="stacy images/line.jpg" width="170" height="54"><br><br>
        <table width=130 cellpadding=4 cellspacing=4 align=right>
              <tr><td align=center class="button"><b><a href="index.htm">Home</a></b></t
              <tr><td align=center class="button"><b><a href="index.htm">About Me</a></b
              <tr><td align=center class="button"><b><a href="bg.gif">e-Resume</a></b></
              <tr><td align=center class="button"><b><a href="index.htm"><b>Publications</b
              <tr><td align=center class="button"><b><a href="index.htm">e-Gallery</a></
              <tr><td align=center class="button"><b><a href="index.htm">Contact Me</a><
        </table><br>
      </td>
      <td width="560" height="84" valign="top" align="left">
        <table width=100% height=100% boder=0 cellpadding=0 cellspacing=0>
              <tr>
              <td width=97 valign="top" align="left">
                      <img border="0" src="stacy images/corner.jpg" width="97" height="8
              <td width=302 align=center><h3>Stacey Liebson</h3>
                      <div>Tel: 915.888.8888<br>
                      Email: <a href="mailto:me@me.com">sliebson@wwwaccess.org</a></div>
              </tr>
              <td width=131 align=center> </tr>
        </table>
      </td>
    </tr>
    <tr>
      <td width="560" height="354" valign=top>
```

You can create or generate HTML code to build Web pages in many ways. In the short history of the Web, the tool that has gained the greatest universal acceptance is Notepad, the simple text editor that comes with the Windows operating system. On the Macintosh, the equivalent tool is called Teach Text or Simple Text. These simple text editing tools are easy to use and are still relied upon by HTML authors as displayed in Figure I.17.

Many of the latest office applications now convert documents to HTML. For example, you can create your résumé in Microsoft Word and export it to create your e-résumé, an HTML page. You can even create a slideshow for an e-gallery in Microsoft Power-Point and export that to HTML.

The learning curve for using an HTML editing program such as Microsoft FrontPage is rather low. The Web page creation capabilities of Microsoft FrontPage are designed for both experienced and beginning Web site developers with a simple yet powerful tool for designing and building great looking, easy-to-navigate Web pages. Microsoft FrontPage is a full-featured HTML editor that uses a number of Web page elements including:

- Button rollover effects
- Image maps
- Marquee text
- Thumbnails
- Counter

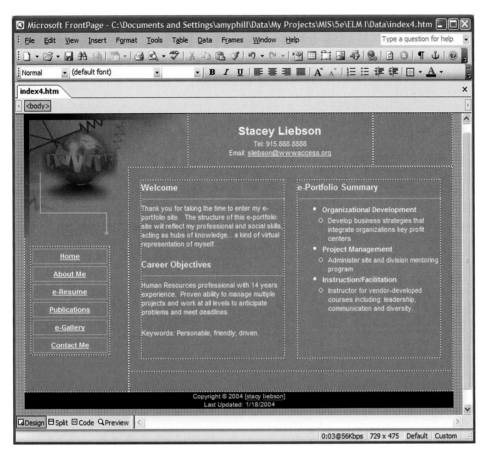

Figure I.18

Sample of FrontPage Interface

With Microsoft FrontPage, you will create Web pages almost as if you were creating them in a word processing environment, with no programming knowledge required (see Figure I.18). For example, formatting attributes such as fonts, borders, and bulleted lists look very close to the way they display in your browser, and many features and options are available using familiar elements such as toolbars, dialog boxes, and templates. Microsoft FrontPage offers two key types of functionality, including:

- *Web page creation.* Microsoft FrontPage allows you to create and edit Web pages without needing to know HTML or other programming languages. FrontPage includes many features that make Web page creation easy, such as templates, graphics, and more.
- *Web site management.* Microsoft FrontPage allows you to view Web pages, publish them to the World Wide Web, and manage existing Web sites. Using FrontPage, you can test and repair hyperlinks on a Web page, view all of the files and folders on a site, and import image files, to name just a few features.

Figure I.19

Sample of Web Page
Created in FrontPage
Imported in Word

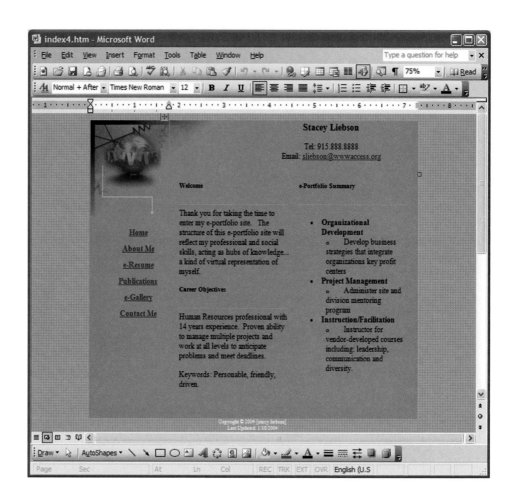

Microsoft Office Web components are not a new technology. Microsoft introduced them in Office 2000. The latest release 2003, however, brings great improvements in the areas of usability, ease of development, and more formatting and functionality. Figure I.19 shows an example of the Web page built in FrontPage that has been imported into Microsoft Word. Because we used Cascading Stylesheets, the formatting is not imported into Word. However, had we used Microsoft Word from the beginning, the formatting would be exactly the same as we intended.

TEST, TEST, TEST

A word of caution: It is critical that you test your Web site many times and from multiple platforms and devices. Statistics gathered in July 2003 indicate that 94 percent of people browsing the Web use Microsoft Internet Explorer (www.w3schools.com). That being the case, 6 percent of your audience is using another Web browser. In addition, about 5 percent of Internet users have a Macintosh. At a minimum, view your site in multiple versions of Internet Explorer and Netscape Communicator to get a feel for how most people will see it.

It is also best to develop your site in its own folder to make it easier to move from your PC as a development platform to an online Web server. The folder should contain all gallery files, HTML pages, and graphics from your site.

Move your site (all files, pages, and graphics) to another computer and test it again. Often links that work on your development computer may not work when pages are moved. These are called broken links and you should definitely repair them before plac-

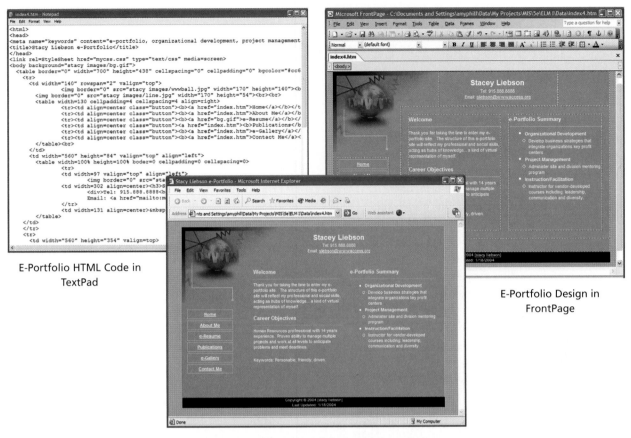

E-Portfolio HTML Code in TextPad

Completed E-Portfolio in Browser

E-Portfolio Design in FrontPage

Figure I.20

View of HTML, FrontPage, and Browser of e-Portfolio Site

ing your site on a Web server. Testing on multiple computers will also let you see color and resolution variances that your viewers will experience.

Finally, when you place your site on a Web server, test it again. Most Web servers use the UNIX operating system. UNIX is case sensitive and prefers filenames without spaces or special characters (!@#$%^&*,. and so on). Microsoft Windows is not case sensitive and accepts filenames with spaces. This is an important difference because Web sites that work on your local computer running a version of Windows may not work when placed in a UNIX environment, mainly due to filename discrepancies. For example, in Windows a link to Page2.htm will work when the file is actually named page2.htm; in UNIX it will not (case sensitivity being the issue).

That ends our module on how to build a job search e-portfolio. If you have been working through the projects in this module and you complete the assignments and exercises to follow, you will be well on your way to developing an effective e-portfolio (see Figure I.20).

As a final note, we highly recommend that you have several people—including classmates, your instructor, and people from your school's career placement center—view your Web site before you send it to the Web for everyone else to see. An effectively designed and well-worded e-portfolio can indeed help you find a really great job. On the other hand, an ineffectively designed and poorly worded e-portfolio can be disastrous. Take some extra time to have other people review your e-portfolio before placing it on the Web for potentially millions of people to see and scrutinize. And by all means—test, test, test.

Summary: Student Learning Outcomes Revisited

1. **Describe the types of electronic résumés and when each is appropriate.** The three types of electronic résumés presented are *scannable* (also called ASCII), *portable document format (PDF),* and *multimedia (HTML).* A scannable résumé can be submitted in print or electronically to organizations using skills extraction software. A PDF résumé is a version of your presentation résumé that can be delivered electronically (via e-mail or a Web page link) without impacting your formatting. A job search e-portfolio contains a multimedia (HTML) résumé, content, and a gallery supporting your skills designed for Web delivery.

2. **Discuss networking strategies you can use during a job search.** Because up to 80 percent of jobs are in the *hidden job market,* networking is critical to a successful job search. Networking involves contacting people and asking them to help you to uncover hidden jobs. Both electronic and face-to-face contacts are necessary to optimize your job opportunities. Strategies involve creating a contact list, developing a 30-second commercial, setting a weekly contact goal, joining *mailing lists,* tracking responses, and following up.

3. **Explain how self-assessment is valuable to résumé writing.** Employers want to hire employees who are focused. Employees want a job that not only produces an income but is satisfying. A good self-assessment will clarify the skills you have to offer an employer, the work environment that best suits you, and employment qualities that lead to your satisfaction.

4. **Use the Internet to research career opportunities and potential employers.** The World Wide Web offers a wide array of tools that can help you research your chosen career. Effective career research should make use of area-specific search engines, job boards, newsgroups, media sites, government statistics, and employer sites. By combining the information provided by these resources, you should be able to get a complete picture of the employment market you

wish to enter and the *skill words* that should be included in your résumé.

5. **Develop powerful job search e-portfolio content.** Powerful job search e-portfolio content is employer-centered and documents the skills that will make you an attractive employee. Quality research and self-assessment are critical to developing content centered on the skills employers want and the benefits these skills provide in an easy-to-use Web site. All traditional résumé content should be developed with these requirements in mind in a manner that does not appear self-centered. Additional e-portfolio content to demonstrate your skills is included as a gallery for potential employees to peruse.

6. **Document effective Web site structure and design components.** Documenting effective Web site structure involves segmenting Web site content and outlining what will be presented on each site page. A navigation chart is developed showing how the various pages of the site will be linked together. Each page of the site should use the same design components outlining the who, what, when, and where of the site. Select a *browser-safe color* scheme for effective viewing by the widest possible audience and use standard content in the header and footer of each page to create a site identity.

7. **Create a job search e-portfolio Web site and place it on an Internet server.** A job search e-portfolio consists of anything that will help a potential employer evaluate your worth as an employee. Use the site navigation chart to develop HTML pages displaying traditional résumé content and linking to your ASCII résumé, PDF résumé, and a gallery of works that demonstrate your skills to allow the evaluator to see how effective you could be in their organization. Once all of your content (HTML pages, supporting documents, résumés, and graphics) has been stored in a folder and tested locally, it can be moved to a Web server using FTP client software. The site should be tested again from the Web.

Key Terms and Concepts

Browser-safe colors, 481
Electronic job market, 455
Electronic portfolio (e-portfolio), 455
Hidden job market, 457
Mailing list, 458
Multimedia (HTML) résumé, 468

Portable document format (PDF), 470
Portable document format résumé (PDF résumé), 468
Résumé, 461
Scannable résumé (ASCII résumé), 468
Skill words, 459
Storyboard, 478

Short-Answer Questions

1. What is the main purpose of a scannable résumé?
2. How is designing a Web page different from designing a print document?
3. Why should multiple résumé formats be included in a job search e-portfolio?
4. What elements of a Web site homepage should be carried throughout the rest of the site pages? Why?
5. Why is the gallery of a job search e-portfolio as important as a well-written and researched résumé?
6. What factors do you believe contribute to 80 percent of available jobs never being publicized?
7. Why is it important to include job and industry-specific skill words in the content of your résumé?
8. What important audience preferences should you consider when designing a job search e-portfolio?
9. Why should a Web site that works on your computer be retested after it is placed on a Web server?
10. How do you know what skill words to include in your résumé? Where do you put these skill words?
11. How do you determine how much content to put on a single Web page?
12. Why is it important to view a newly developed Web site on multiple computers using a variety of browsers?
13. Why should you consider using browser-safe colors on your e-portfolio site?
14. How does the hidden job market complicate the job search?
15. Visit the job board www.monster.com and review the site content. Is this a site that you would recommend for first-time job hunters? Why or why not?

Assignments and Exercises

1. **DESCRIBE YOUR CAREER** Using the research methods we have outlined in the module, locate information about your career. Document your findings in a paper, being sure to include job title synonyms, educational standards, work environment, job forecast statistics, normal work week, and any other pertinent information. Cite your sources.
2. **DEVELOPING JOB CONTACTS** Begin to build a list of job contacts. Consider it a running list. Create a list of your friends; your business associates; teachers; adults in your immediate and extended family; acquaintances; and people who are in the field that interests you.
3. **OCCUPATIONAL OUTLOOK** One important resource you can find online is the *Occupational Outlook Handbook*. Go to the *Occupational Outlook Handbook* Web site www.bls.gov/oco/ and look through the index to get an idea of the many jobs that people actually do. Select three to five jobs from the index that interest you. Write a brief description of each, including as much information as you can find on what kind

of work the job involves; working conditions; qualities and skills you need to get the job; job outlook; earnings; related occupations, including advanced positions; and sources you can contact for more information.

4. **VISIT INDUSTRY WEB SITES** Using the research methods we have outlined in the module, locate and visit at least three business Web sites in the industry you've selected. For each site document the page layout, the colors, and the formality of the site. Did you find press and news releases? If so, what did they tell you about the company? Did you find recruitment pages? If so, what types of positions are available? What skill words did you find on these sites that should be included in your résumé?

5. **ENTRY-LEVEL JOB POSTINGS** Visit www.collegegrad.com and search for entry-level job postings in your area of interest. How many postings did you find? Are you qualified, or will you be qualified for the available positions when you complete your current educational goals? Are the listings for a geographic location that you would consider? What skill words should you include in your résumé to be considered for these positions?

6. **FINALIZE YOUR RÉSUMÉS** If you compiled your résumés as you completed the module, review them for presentation effectiveness and content. If you did not build your résumés as you went through the module, do so now. Start by building all of the content in an unformatted document and then create scannable, PDF, and HTML versions. Unless you have sufficient business experience to use a Summary of Qualifications section, use an objective statement that includes the job title, industry, your best skill words, and the benefit you could provide to the hiring organization. In addition to the objective statement, include Work, Education, and References sections. Other sections can be included to suit your background and career. Solicit feedback from at least one classmate.

7. **SELECT CONTENT FOR YOUR E-PORTFOLIO GALLERY** Look through the files on your computer for work that represents your current skills and could be of interest to a potential employer. Create a list of at least three files that would be appropriate for a job search e-portfolio along with a short description of the skills the files exhibit. What other skills should you develop documents to demonstrate? What types of documents would best showcase these skills?

8. **SEARCH THE WORLD WIDE WEB** Use search tools to locate e-portfolios that have already been posted on the Web. How many e-portfolios did you locate? How many of these e-portfolios were designed for a job search? Pick the best e-portfolio you located and critique its content and design.

9. **BUILD YOUR E-PORTFOLIO SITE** Use either a text editor or Web authoring software to build the HTML pages of your job search e-portfolio Web site. Do not use office productivity software such as a word processor. Include a minimum of three HTML pages, your ASCII résumé, your PDF résumé, and three gallery pages using another document format such as Word or PowerPoint.

EXTENDED LEARNING MODULE J

IMPLEMENTING A DATABASE WITH MICROSOFT ACCESS

Student Learning Outcomes

1. IDENTIFY THE STEPS NECESSARY TO IMPLEMENT THE STRUCTURE OF A RELATIONAL DATABASE USING THE DATA DEFINITION LANGUAGE PROVIDED BY MICROSOFT ACCESS.

2. DEMONSTRATE HOW TO USE THE DATA MANIPULATION SUBSYSTEM IN ACCESS TO ENTER AND CHANGE INFORMATION IN A DATABASE AND HOW TO QUERY THAT INFORMATION.

3. EXPLAIN THE USE OF THE APPLICATION GENERATION SUBSYSTEM IN ACCESS TO CREATE REPORTS AND DATA ENTRY SCREENS.

Taking Advantage of the CD

In Chapter 3 we discussed the important role that databases play in an organization. We followed that with *Extended Learning Module C*, in which you learned how to design the correct structure of a relational database. That module includes four primary steps. They are:

1. Defining entity classes and primary keys.
2. Defining relationships among entity classes.
3. Defining information (fields) for each relation (the term relation is often used to refer to a file while designing a database).
4. Using a data definition language to create your database.

In *Extended Learning Module C*, you followed the process through the first three steps above. In this module, we'll take you through the fourth step—using a data definition language to create your database—by exploring the use of Microsoft Access, today's most popular personal database management system package (it comes as a standard part of Microsoft Office Professional suite).

You'll find this extended learning module on the CD that accompanies this text. In this module, we've included coverage of

- Creating a simple query using one relation
- Creating an advanced query using more than one relation
- Generating a simple report
- Generating a report with grouping, sorting, and totals
- Creating a data input form

We believe this material is vitally important. As the business world increasingly moves toward empowering employees with technology tools, you'll be better prepared for the job market if you know how to design, implement, and access a database. Module C covered how to design a database, and this module covers how to implement and access a database using Microsoft Access.

If you need proof of the growing importance of databases, just connect to any job database Web site and enter "Microsoft Access" as a search term. We did that at Monster.com (www.monster.com) and found over 550 job listings requiring expertise in Microsoft Access. Some of the job titles included

- Financial Analysis Manager
- Education Administrator
- Logistics Engineer
- Military Intelligence
- Corporate Trust Administrator
- Market Research Analyst
- Medical Finance Coordinator
- Guest Satisfaction Agent
- Training Coordinator
- Data Consumption Analyst
- Project Manager
- Retail Support Analyst
- Quality Engineer
- Reinsurance Accountant

If you look carefully at the above list, you'll see that not a single job title is IT-specific. Rather, they represent job openings in such areas as finance, hospitality, logistics, retail sales, medicine, and insurance.

We applaud you for popping in the CD and reading this module.

EXTENDED LEARNING MODULE K

CAREERS IN BUSINESS

Student Learning Outcomes

1. IDENTIFY THE CAREER FIELD AND BUSINESS SPECIALIZATION IN WHICH YOU ARE INTERESTED.

2. PROVIDE TYPICAL JOB TITLES AND DESCRIPTIONS FOR YOUR CAREER FIELD.

3. LIST AND DESCRIBE THE IT SKILLS YOU NEED TO GAIN WHILE IN SCHOOL.

Taking Advantage of the CD

In the business world, you need to be "a jack of all trades and a master of one." That means that you need to excel in a particular business functional area (or specialization), such as finance, accounting, marketing, or any of the other many business specializations. It also means that, while your expertise lies within one functional area, you need to be competent in all the other functional areas.

Think about majoring in marketing, for example. You need expertise in consumer behavior, marketing strategies, branding techniques, and many other marketing-oriented concepts. But as a marketing analyst, you need other skills to be successful. You need knowledge of accounting and finance so you can put together a budget and monitor expenses. You need team and employee management skills so you can work effectively in a group and manage other people. You need knowledge of production and operations management so you can understand works-in-progress information and transportation optimization algorithms.

No matter what your career choice, you need knowledge of information technology tools that will allow you to perform your tasks more efficiently and effectively. This textbook isn't about trying to get you to major in information technology or choose MIS as a career. It's about informing you of the role of information technology and MIS in an organization and enabling you to select and use the right IT tools to carry out your tasks.

In this module, we want to explore with you many of the career specializations in business, including:

- Accounting
- Finance
- Hospitality and tourism management
- Information technology
- Management
- Marketing
- Production and operations management
- Real estate and construction management

At your school, there are probably departments devoted to providing degrees in these specializations. While titles and nomenclatures may differ (e.g., production and operations management is often called management science, operations research, statistics and operations technology, or some other variation), those specializations represent the major functional areas in a typical business.

After providing you with a brief introduction to each specialization, we include the following information:

- List of typical job titles and their descriptions
- IT tools you should focus on learning while in school
- Statistics concerning the job market

It is our hope that, after reading this module, you will come to understand that IT and MIS are important no matter what your career choice. You may be taking this class because it's a required part of the business curriculum. It's required because, no matter what career you choose, you need knowledge of IT and MIS. It's similar to taking a human resource management class. While you may not be majoring in human resource management, you will at some time in your career have to manage people. Knowing how to manage them effectively is a career opportunity for you.

Take the time to pop in the CD that accompanies this textbook and read about careers in business.

CASE 1:
ASSESSING THE VALUE OF INFORMATION

TREVOR TOY AUTO MECHANICS

Trevor Toy Auto Mechanics is an automobile repair shop in Phoenix, Arizona. Over the past few years, Trevor, the owner, has seen his business grow from a two-bay car repair shop with only one other employee to a 15-bay car repair shop with 21 employees.

Up to now, Trevor has always advertised that he will perform any work on any vehicle. But that's becoming problematic as cars are becoming increasingly more complex. Trevor has decided he wants to create a more focused repair shop, and is asking for your help. He has provided you with a spreadsheet file that contains a list of all the repairs his shop has completed over the past year. The spreadsheet file contains the fields provided in the table below.

Column	Name	Description
A	MECHANIC #	A unique number assigned to the mechanic who completed the work
B	CAR TYPE	The type of car on which the work was completed
C	WORK COMPLETED	The type of repair that was performed on the car
D	NUM HOURS	The number of hours it took to complete the work
E	COST OF PARTS	The cost of the parts associated with completing the repair
F	TOTAL CHARGE	The amount charged to the customer for the repair

Trevor is open to any suggestions you might have. So, your analysis could include any combination of (1) keeping only certain mechanics; (2) repairing only certain types of cars; and/or (3) performing only certain types of repairs.

It is your responsibility to analyze the list and make a recommendation to Trevor concerning how he should focus his business.

SOME PARTICULARS YOU SHOULD KNOW

1. As you consider the information provided to you, think in terms of what information is important. You might need to use the existing information to create new information.

2. All mechanics are paid the same hourly wage.

3. Disregard any considerations associated with downsizing such as overhead; simply focus on the information provided to you.

4. Disregard any considerations for potential competition located near Trevor.

5. Upon completing your analysis, please provide concise yet detailed and thorough documentation (in narrative, numeric, and graphic forms) that justifies your recommendations.

6. File: TREVOR.xls (Excel file).

CASE 2:
ASSESSING THE VALUE OF INFORMATION

AFFORDABLE HOMES REAL ESTATE

In late 1995, a national study announced that Eau Claire, Wisconsin, was the safest place to live. Since then, housing development projects have been springing up all around Eau Claire. Six housing development projects are currently dominating the Eau Claire market: Woodland Hills, Granite Mound, Creek Side Huntington, East River Community, Forest Green, and Eau Claire South. These six projects each started with 100 homes, have sold all of them, and are currently developing phase 2.

As one of the three partners and real estate agents of Affordable Homes Real Estate, it is your responsibility to analyze the information concerning the past 600 home sales and choose which development project to focus on for selling homes in phase 2. Because your real estate firm is so small, you and your partners have decided that the firm should focus on selling homes in only one of the development projects.

From the Wisconsin Real Estate Association you have obtained a spreadsheet file that contains information concerning each of the sales for the first 600 homes. It contains the following fields:

Column	Name	Description
A	LOT #	The number assigned to a specific home within each project
B	PROJECT #	A unique number assigned to each of the six housing development projects (see table to follow)
C	ASK PRICE	The initial posted asking price for the home
D	SELL PRICE	The actual price for which the home was sold
E	LIST DATE	The date the home was listed for sale
F	SALE DATE	The date on which the final contract closed and the home was sold
G	SQ. FT.	The total square footage for the home
H	# BATH.	The number of bathrooms in the home
I	# BDRMS	The number of bedrooms in the home

The following numbers have been assigned to each of the housing development projects:

Project Number	Project Name
23	Woodland Hills
47	Granite Mound
61	Creek Side Huntington
78	East River Community
92	Forest Green
97	Eau Claire South

It is your responsibility to analyze the sales list and prepare a report that details which housing development project your real estate firm should focus on. Your analysis should cover as many angles as possible.

SOME PARTICULARS YOU SHOULD KNOW

1. You don't know how many other real estate firms will also be competing for sales in each of the housing development projects.

2. Phase 2 for each housing development project will develop homes similar in style, price, and square footage to their respective first phases.

3. As you consider the information provided to you, think in terms of what information is important and what information is not important. Be prepared to justify how you approach your analysis.

4. Upon completing your analysis, please provide concise, yet detailed and thorough, documentation (in narrative, numeric, and graphic forms) that justifies your decision.

5. File: REALEST.xls (Excel file).

CASE 3:
EXECUTIVE INFORMATION SYSTEM REPORTING

POLITICAL CAMPAIGN FINANCE CONSULTANTS

When it comes to campaign finance, Americans want a system that minimizes the influence of "fat cats" and organized money, which keeps campaign spending at sensible levels, that fosters healthy electoral competition, that doesn't take advantage of wealthy candidates, and that doesn't require candidates to spend all of their waking hours raising money.

Indeed, the much maligned congressional campaign finance system we have now is itself a product of well-intended reform efforts, passed by Congress in 1974 to achieve these ideals. Moreover, dozens of new reform plans have emerged during the 1990s that also reach for these goals. Yet, no reform scheme, however well intended, is likely to produce a perfect congressional campaign finance system.

The city of Highlands Ranch, Colorado, wishes to organize its campaign contributions records in a more linear format. The city council is considering various executive information system packages that can show them overall views of the contribution information as well as give them the ability to access more detailed information. You have been hired to make recommendations about what reports should be available through the soon-to-be-purchased executive information system.

The table below is a list of the information that will be the foundation for the reports in the proposed executive information system. To help you develop realistic reports, the city has provided you with a spreadsheet file that contains specific contributions over the last six months.

Column	Name	Description
A	DATE	The actual date that the contribution was made
B	CONTRIBUTOR	The name of the person or organization that made the contribution
C	DISTRICT	The district number that the councilperson belongs to
D	AMOUNT	The amount of the contribution
E	TYPE	The description type of where the contribution amount was given
F	COUNCILPERSON	The councilperson's name
G	PARTY	The councilperson's political party

What the city council is most interested in is viewing several overall reports and then being able to request more detailed reports. So, as a consultant, your goal is to develop different sets of reports that illustrate the concept of drilling down through information. For example, you should develop a report that shows overall campaign contributions by district (each of the eight different districts) and then also develop more detailed reports that show contribution by political party and contribution by type.

SOME PARTICULARS YOU SHOULD KNOW

1. The council would much rather see information graphically than numerically. So, as you develop your reports, do so in terms of graphs that illustrate the desired relationships.

2. As you consider the information provided to you, think in terms of overall views first and then detailed views second. This will help you develop a logical series of reports.

3. If you wish, you can explore a variety of software tools to help you create the reports. Then prepare your presentation using a presentation graphics package that lets you create a really great presentation of your recommendations.

4. Again, your goal is not to create reports that point toward a particular problem or opportunity. Rather, you are to design sets of logical series of reports that illustrate the concept of drilling down.

5. File: CONTRIBUTE.xls (Excel file).

CASE 4:
BUILDING VALUE CHAINS

STARLIGHT'S CUSTOMERS DEFINE VALUE

StarLight is a Denver-based retailer of high-quality apparel, shoes, and accessories. In 1915, with money earned in the Colorado gold mines, Anne Logan invested in a small downtown Denver shoe store. A few years later, Anne expanded her business by adding fine apparel. Today, StarLight has 97 retail stores and discount outlets throughout the United States. Since the beginning, StarLight's business philosophy has reflected its founder's beliefs in exceptional service, value, selection, and quality. To maintain the level of service StarLight's customers have come to expect, the company empowers its employees to meet any customer demand, no matter how unreasonable it may seem. With so many stores, it's difficult for Cody Sherrod, StarLight's Vice President for Business Information and Planning, to know the level of service customers receive, what customers value, and what they don't. These are important questions for a retailer striving to provide the finest customer experience and products while keeping costs to a minimum.

Cody decided a value chain analysis would be helpful in answering these questions. So, customer surveys were designed, distributed, completed, collected, and compiled into a database. Customers were asked to value their experience with various processes in the StarLight value chain. Specifically, for each value chain process, customers were asked whether this area added value to their experience or reduced the value of their experience. Customers were asked to quantify how much each process added or reduced the value of the services they received. Using a total of 100 points for the value chain, each customer distributed those points among StarLight's processes. The survey results in the database consist of the fields shown in the accompanying table.

Field Name	Description
Survey ID	An ID number uniquely identifying the survey
VA/VR	A field that identifies whether the current row of information reflects a value-added response or a value-reducing response
Date	Survey response date
Mgmt/Acctg/Finance/Legal	Customer value experience, if any, with management, accounting, finance, and the legal departments
HR Mgmt	Customer value of the attitude and general personnel environment
R&D/Tech Dev	Customer perceived value of the quality of research and technology support
Purchasing	Customer value placed on the quality and range of product selection
Receive and Greet Customers	Customer value placed on initial contact with employees
Provide Direction/Advice/Info	Customer value placed on initial information provided by employees
Store Location/Channel Availability & Convenience	Customer value placed on location, availability, and convenience
Product Display/Site or Catalog Layout	Customer value placed on aesthetic appeal of merchandise display and layout
Sales Service	Customer value placed on quality of service provided by sales associates
Marketing	Customer value placed on the effectiveness of marketing material
Customer Follow-up	Customer value placed on postsales service and follow-up

Cody has asked you to gather the raw survey material into two value chains, the value-added chain and the value-reducing chain. You'll create chains that summarize the survey information and size the process areas proportionately as described in Chapter 2. Specifically, your job is to perform the following:

1. Create queries or reports in the provided database to summarize the value-added amounts and the value-reducing amounts for each process.

2. Draw two value chains using that summary information to size the depicted area for each process. Use the value chains in Chapter 2 as reference.

3. Compare the value-added and value-reducing process percentages. Do they correlate in any way? If so, why do you think that is? If not, why not?

4. In the table description provided, a dashed line is drawn between the "purchasing" process and the "receive and greet customers" process. Processes above the line are considered support processes, while processes below are considered primary processes. Create a database query to compare how customers value the total of support processes versus primary processes. Do this for both value-added and value-reducing processes. Do the results make sense or are they surprising? Explain your answer.

SOME PARTICULARS YOU SHOULD KNOW

1. Remember that the total value-added/value-reducing amount for each process must equal 100 percent.
2. The survey values in the database are not percentages although the sum of all responses for a given survey equals 100.
3. File: STARLIGHT.mdb (Access file).

CASE 5:
USING RELATIONAL TECHNOLOGY TO TRACK PROJECTS

PHILLIPS CONSTRUCTION

Phillips Construction Company is a Denver-based construction company that specializes in sub-contracting the development of single family homes. In business since 1993, Phillips Construction Company has maintained a talented pool of certified staff and independent consultants allowing the flexibility and combined experience required to meet the needs of its nearly 300 completed projects in the Denver metropolitan area. The field of operation methods that Phillips Construction is responsible for as it relates to building include structural development, heating and cooling, plumbing, and electricity.

The company charges its clients by billing the hours spent on each contract. The hourly billing rate is dependent on the employee's position according to the field of operations (as noted below).

Figure GP.1 shows a basic report that Phillips Construction managers would like to see every week concerning what projects are being assigned. Phillips Construction organizes its internal

Figure GP.1

Phillips Construction Project Detail

PHILLIPS CONSTRUCTION PROJECT DETAIL

PROJECT NAME	ASSIGN DATE	EMP LAST NAME	EMP FIRST NAME	JOB DESCRIPTION	ASSIGN HOUR	CHARGE/HOUR
Chatfield						
	Tuesday, February 10, 2004	Jones	Anne	Heating and Ventilation	3.4	$84.50
	Tuesday, February 10, 2004	Sullivan	David	Electrical	1.8	$105.00
	Wednesday, February 11, 2004	Frommer	Matt	Plumbing	4.1	$96.75
	Thursday, February 12, 2004	Newman	John	Electrical	1.7	$105.00
	Thursday, February 12, 2004	Bawangi	Terry	Plumbing	4.1	$96.75
Summary of Assignment Hours and Charges					15.10	$1,448.15
Evergreen						
	Tuesday, February 10, 2004	Smithfield	William	Structure	3.0	$35.75
	Tuesday, February 10, 2004	Newman	John	Electrical	2.3	$105.00
	Tuesday, February 10, 2004	Nenior	David	Plumbing	3.3	$96.75
	Wednesday, February 11, 2004	Marbough	Mike	Heating and Ventilation	2.6	$84.50
	Thursday, February 12, 2004	Johnson	Peter	Electrical	2.0	$105.00
	Thursday, February 12, 2004	Newman	John	Electrical	3.6	$105.00
	Thursday, February 12, 2004	Olenkoski	Glenn	Structure	1.9	$35.75
Summary of Assignment Hours and Charges					18.70	$1,543.65
Roxborough						
	Tuesday, February 10, 2004	Washberg	Jeff	Plumbing	3.9	$96.75
	Tuesday, February 10, 2004	Ramora	Anne	Plumbing	2.6	$96.75

Sunday, February 15, 2004

Page 1 of 2

structure in four different operations: Structure (500), Plumbing (501), Electrical (502), and Heating and Ventilation (503). Each of these operational departments can and should have many subcontractors who specialize in that area.

Because of the boom in home sales over the last several years, Phillips Construction has decided to implement a relational database model to track project details according to project name, hours assigned, and charges per hour for each job description. Originally, Phillips Construction decided to let one of its employees handle the construction of the database. However, that employee has not had the time to completely implement the project. Phillips Construction has asked you to take over and complete the development of the database.

The entity classes and primary keys for the database have been identified as the following:

Entity	Primary Key
Project	Project Number
Employee	Employee Number
Job	Job Number
Assign	Assign Number

The following business rules have also been identified:

1. A job can have many employees assigned but must have at least one.
2. An employee must be assigned to one and only one job number.
3. An employee can be assigned to work on one or more projects.
4. A project can be assigned to only one employee but need not be assigned to any employee.

Your job is to be completed in the following phases:

1. Develop and describe the entity-relationship diagram.
2. Use normalization to assure the correctness of the tables (relations).
3. Create the database using a personal DBMS package (preferably Microsoft Access).
4. Use the DBMS package to create the basic report in Figure GP.1.

SOME PARTICULARS YOU SHOULD KNOW

1. You may not be able to develop a report that looks exactly like the one in Figure GP.1. However, your report should include the same information.
2. Complete personnel information is tracked by another database. For this application, include only the minimum employee number, last name, and first name.
3. Information concerning all projects, employees, and jobs is not readily available. You should, however, create information for several fictitious systems to include in your database.
4. File: Not applicable.

CASE 6:
BUILDING A DECISION SUPPORT SYSTEM

CREATING AN INVESTMENT PORTFOLIO

Most experts recommend that if you're devising a long-term investment strategy you should make the stock market part of your plan. You can use a DSS to help you decide what stocks to put into your portfolio. You can use a spreadsheet to do the job. The information you need on 10 stocks is contained in a Word file called STOCKS.doc. This information consists of

1. Two years of weekly price data on 10 different stocks.
2. Stock market indices from
   - The Dow Jones Industrial Average
   - NASDAQ Composite
3. Dividends and cash flow per share over the last 10 years (Source: Yahoo Finance).

Using this information, build a DSS to perform stock analysis consisting of the following tasks:

1. Examine Diversification Benefits
   A. Calculate the average return and standard deviation(s) of each of the 10 stocks.
   B. Form six different portfolios: two with two stocks each; two with three stocks each; two with five stocks each.

   Answer the following questions using your DSS:

   - How does the standard deviation of each portfolio compare to the (average) standard deviation of each stock in the portfolio?
   - How does the average return of the portfolio compare to the average return of each stock in the portfolio?
   - Do the benefits of diversification seem to increase or diminish as the number of stocks in the portfolio gets larger?
   - In the two-stock and five-stock portfolios what happens if you group your stocks toward similar industries?

2. Value Each of the Stocks

   A. Estimate the dividend growth rate based on past dividends.
   B. Estimate next year's dividend using this year's dividend and the estimated growth rate.
   C. Generate two graphs, one for past dividends and one for estimated dividends for the next five years.

SOME PARTICULARS YOU SHOULD KNOW

1. When performing your calculations, use the weekly returns. That is, use the change in the price each week rather than the prices themselves. This gives you a better basis for calculation because the prices themselves don't usually change very much.
2. File: STOCKS.doc (Word file).

CASE 7:
ADVERTISING WITH BANNER ADS

HIGHWAYSANDBYWAYS.COM

Business is booming at HighwaysAndByways, a dot-com firm focusing on selling accessories for car enthusiasts (e.g., floor mats, grill guards, air fresheners, stereos, and so on). Throughout the past year, HighwaysAndByways has had Web site management software tracking what customers buy, the Web sites from which customers came, and the Web sites customers went to after visiting HighwaysAndByways. That information is stored in a spreadsheet file and contains the fields in the accompanying table. Each record in the spreadsheet file represents an individual visit by a customer that resulted in a purchase.

Column	Name	Description
A	CUSTOMER ID	A unique identifier for a customer who made a purchase
B	TOTAL PURCHASE	The total amount of a purchase
C	PREVIOUS WEB SITE	The Web site from which the customer came to visit HighwaysAndByways
D	NEXT WEB SITE	The Web site the customer went to after making a purchase at HighwaysAndByways
E	TIME SPENT	The amount of time that the customer spent at the site

HighwaysAndByways is interested in determining three items and has employed you as a consultant to help. First, HighwaysAndByways wants to know on which Web sites it should purchase banner ad space. Second, HighwaysAndByways wants to know which Web sites it should contact to determine if those Web sites would like to purchase banner ad space on the HighwaysAndByways Web site. Finally, HighwaysAndByways would like to know which Web sites it should develop reciprocal banner ad relationships with; that is, HighwaysAndByways would like a list of Web sites on which it would obtain banner ad space while providing banner ad space on its Web site for those Web sites.

SOME PARTICULARS YOU SHOULD KNOW

1. As you consider the information provided to you, think about the levels of information literacy. In other words, don't jump to conclusions before carefully evaluating the provided information.
2. You don't know if your customers made purchases at the Web site they visited upon leaving HighwaysAndByways.
3. Upon completing your analysis, please provide concise yet detailed and thorough documentation (in narrative, numeric, and graphic forms) that justifies your recommendations.
4. File: CLICKSTREAMS.xls (Excel file).

CASE 8:
OUTSOURCING INFORMATION TECHNOLOGY

A&A SOFTWARE: CREATING FORECASTS

Founded in 1992, A&A Software provides innovative search software, Web site accessibility testing/repair software, and usability testing/repair software. All serve as part of its desktop and enterprise content management solutions for government, corporate, educational, and consumer markets. The company's solutions are used by Web site publishers, digital media publishers, content managers, document managers, business users, consumers, software companies, and consulting services companies. A&A Software solutions help organizations develop long-term strategies to achieve Web content accessibility, enhance usability, and comply with U.S. and international accessibility and search standards.

A&A Software has a 10-year history of approximately 1 percent in turnover a year and its focus has always been on customer service. With the informal motto of "Grow big, but stay small," it takes pride in 100 percent callbacks in customer care, knowing that its personal service has been one thing that makes it outstanding.

A&A Software has experienced rapid growth to six times its original customer-base size and is forced to deal with difficult questions for the first time, such as, "How do we serve this many customers? How do we keep our SOUL—that part of us that honestly cares very much about our customers? How will we know that someone else will care as much and do as good a job as we have done?" In addition, you have just received an e-mail from the company CIO, Sue Downs that the number of phone calls from customers having problems with one of your newer applications is on the increase.

As customer service manager for A&A Software, your overriding goal is to maintain the company's reputation for excellent customer service, and outsourcing may offer an efficient means of keeping up with expanding call volume. A&A Software is reviewing a similar scenario of a major e-BANK company that outsourced its customer service in order to handle a large projected number of customers through several customer interaction channels. Although e-BANK had excellent people, it felt that its competencies were primarily in finance, rather than in customer service and that it needed to have the expertise that a customer-service-focused company could offer. e-BANK also discovered that it was cost effective to outsource its customer service center.

Additionally, the outsourcing approach was relatively hassle-free, since e-BANK did not have to set up its own CIC (customer interaction center/call center).

SOME PARTICULARS YOU SHOULD KNOW

1. Create a weekly analysis from the data provided in FORECAST.xls.
2. The price of the products, the actual product type, and any warranty information is irrelevant.
3. Develop a growth, trend, and forecast analysis. You should use a three-day moving average: a shorter moving average might not display the trend well and a much longer moving average would shorten the trend too much.
4. Upon completing your analysis, please provide concise yet detailed and thorough documentation (in narrative, numeric, and graphic forms) that justifies your recommendations.
5. File: FORECAST.xls (Excel file)

CASE 9:
DEMONSTRATING HOW TO BUILD WEB SITES

WITH HTML

Building a good Web site is simple in some respects and difficult in others. It's relatively easy to learn to write HTML code. Building an effective and eye-catching Web site is a horse of a different color. That is to say, there is a stretch between just using the technology and using the technology to your best advantage.

Your task in this project is to build a presentation (using presentation graphics software such as Microsoft PowerPoint) that achieves two goals. First, your presentation should show your audience how to write simple HTML code to create a Web site. Your presentation should include the HTML code for

- Text formatting (bold, italic, and the like)
- Font families and sizing
- Font colors
- Background colors and images
- Links
- Images
- Numbered and bulleted lists

Next, your presentation should provide the audience with a list of guidelines for creating an *effective* Web site. For this, you should definitely embed links into your presentation that go to Web sites that illustrate good Web site design, displaying examples of both effective and ineffective designs.

SOME PARTICULARS YOU SHOULD KNOW

1. In a file called HTML.doc, we've provided many links to Web sites that teach you how to write HTML code.
2. In a file called DESIGN.doc, we've provided many links to Web sites that teach you how to design Web sites effectively.
3. Files: HTML.doc and DESIGN.doc (Word files).

CASE 10:
MAKING THE CASE WITH PRESENTATION SOFTWARE

INFORMATION TECHNOLOGY ETHICS

Management at your company is concerned about the high cost of computer crime, from lawsuits over e-mail received to denial-of-service attacks and crackers breaking into the corporate network to steal information. You've been asked to make a presentation to inform your colleagues. Develop a presentation using a presentation package such as Microsoft's PowerPoint.

You can choose your presentation's emphasis from the following topics:

- Ethics as it relates to IT systems
- Types of crime aimed at IT systems (such as viruses)
- Types of crime that uses IT systems as weapons (such as electronic theft of funds from one account to another)
- Security measures, how good they are, what they cost, how expensive they are to implement
- Electronic monitoring of employees (from employer and employee standpoints)
- Collection and use of personal information on consumers

SOURCES OF INFORMATION

- In the file ETHICS.doc, you'll find sources for the topics listed above.
- The Web is a great place to find lots of information.
- Most business publications, such as *Business Week, InformationWeek, Fortune,* and *The Wall Street Journal,* frequently have good articles on ethics, cybercrime, and security. You can get some of these articles on the Web.
- General news publications such as *Newsweek* and *USA Today* print articles on these topics.

Your task is to weave the information you find into a coherent presentation using graphs and art where appropriate.

SOME PARTICULARS YOU SHOULD KNOW

1. Content Principles
   - Each slide should have a headline
   - Each slide should express one idea
   - Ideas should follow logically

2. Design Principles
   - Follow the "Rule of 7," which is no more than 7 lines per slide and 7 words per line
   - Keep it simple
   - Keep it organized
   - Create a path for the eye
   - Divide space in an interesting way
   - Use at least 30-point type
   - Use color and graphics carefully, consistently, and for a specific purpose
   - Use high-contrast colors (black/white, deep blue/white, etc.)
3. File: ETHICS.doc (Word file)

CASE 11:
A WEB-BASED CLASSIFIED SYSTEM

E-CLASSIFIED@GABBYGAZETTEER.COM

With the emergence of the Internet as a worldwide standard for communicating information, *Gabby's Gazetteer,* a medium-size community newspaper in central Colorado, is looking to enter the electronic commerce market.

In the listing of classified ads, advertisers place a small ad that lists items they wish to sell and provide a means (e.g., telephone number) by which prospective buyers can contact them.

The nature of a sale via a newspaper classified system goes as follows:

- During the course of the sale, the information flows in different directions at different stages.
- First, there is a downstream flow of information (from seller to buyer)—the listing in print on the newspaper. (Thus, the classified ad listing is just a way of bringing a buyer and seller together.)
- When a potential purchaser's interest has been raised, then that interest must be relayed upstream, usually by telephone or in person.
- Finally, a meeting should result that uses face-to-face negotiation to finalize the sale—if the sale can be agreed upon.

By placing the entire system on the Internet, the upstream and downstream communications are accomplished using a Web browser. The sale becomes more of an auction, because many potential buyers, all with equal status, can bid for the same item. So it's fairer for all purchasers and gets a better deal for the seller.

Any user who is trying to buy an item can

- View items for sale
- Bid on an item they wish to purchase

Any user who is trying to sell an item can

- Place a new item for sale
- Browse a list of the items that he or she is trying to sell, and examine the bids that have been made on each of those items
- Accept a bid on an item that he or she is selling

This system should also allow users to do some very basic administrative tasks, such as

- Browse the listings to see what is for sale
- Register with the system (users can browse without registering; but they must register if they want to sell an item or bid for an item)

Figure GP.2

Gabby's Gazetteer Classified Registration System

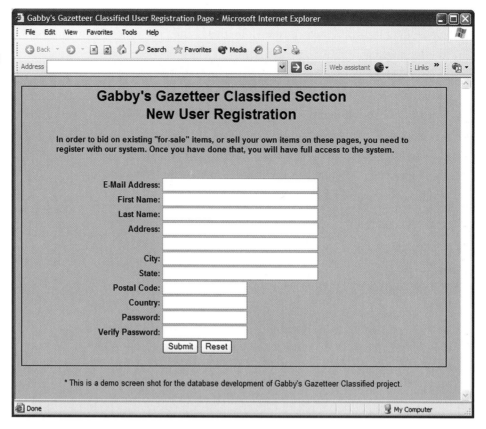

- Log on to the system
- Change their registration details

Your job will be to complete the following:

1. Develop and describe the entity-relationship diagram for the database that will support the above activities.
2. Use normalization to ensure the correctness of the tables.
3. Create the database using a personal DBMS package.

SOME PARTICULARS YOU SHOULD KNOW

1. Use Figure GP.2 as a baseline for your database design.
2. File: Not applicable.

CASE 12:
SHOULD I BUY OR SHOULD I LEASE?

DECISION SUPPORT SYSTEMS

A leading supplier of grapes to the wine-producing industry in California, On the Vine Grapes, wants to expand its delivery services and expand its reach to market by increasing its current fleet of delivery trucks. Some of the older vehicles were acquired through closed-end leases with required down payments, mileage restrictions, and hefty early termination penalties. Other vehicles were purchased using traditional purchase-to-own loans, which often resulted in high depreciation costs and large maintenance fees. All vehicles were acquired one at a time through local dealers.

On the Vine Grapes has asked you to assist in developing a lease/buy cost analysis work sheet in order to make the most cost-effective decision. Currently the director of operations, Bill Smith, has identified a 2004 Ford F-550 4x2 SD Super Cab 161.8 in. WB DRW HD XLT as the truck of choice for the business. This vehicle has a retail price of $34,997.00 or a lease price of $600/month through Ford Motor Credit Company.

Here are some basic fees and costs that you need to factor in:

1. Lease Costs

Refundable security deposit	$500
First month's payment at inception	$500
Other initial costs	$125
Monthly lease payment for remaining term	$600
Last month payment in advance	No
Allowable annual mileage	15,000
Estimated annual miles to be driven	20,000
Per mile charge for excess miles	0.10

2. Purchase Costs

Retail price including sales taxes, title	$34,997
Down payment	$4,000
Loan interest rate	8.75%
Will interest be deductible business or home equity interest?	Yes
Is the gross loaded weight of the vehicle over 6,000 lbs?	Yes

3. Common Costs and Assumptions

Total lease/loan term	36
Discount percent	8.75
Tax bracket—combined federal and state	33%
Business use percentage	100%

SOME PARTICULARS YOU SHOULD KNOW

1. In the file BUYORLEASE.xls is a template you can use to enter the information above. There is also a sheet that has been developed to assist you with the annual depreciation for an automobile.
2. Create a detailed summary sheet of the lease/buy option for On the Vine Grapes.
3. File: BUYORLEASE.xls (Excel file).

CASE 13:
HIGHER EDUCATION PLANNING AND DATA PROCESSING

ERP FOR HIGHER EDUCATION

The State Annual Report on Enterprise Resource Planning and Management was developed to provide a comprehensive view of the management and use of technology by the Higher Educational System of Colorado. This report shows the statewide issues surrounding information technology, priorities for the ensuing two years, initiatives and projects, performance management, and the information technology resources utilized to support the business processes of Higher Education during fiscal year 2002–2003. A comparison report is also generated to produce a percentage change in funds from fiscal year 2001–2002 and fiscal year 2002–2003.

Chief information officer (CIO) for the Department of Higher Education, David Paul, was required to report the estimated expenditures for technology across five appropriation categories: Employee Salaries/Benefits, Other Personal Services (OPS—noncareer service employees with no permanent status), Expenses (all hardware purchases under $1,000, travel, training, and general office expenses), Operating Capital Outlay (OCO), and Data Processing Services. Most of these performance management initiatives have been measured using manual processes. Several reporting units documented the need for automated measurement tools in the future to take advantage of the full opportunities for improvement. David Paul has asked you to assist him in organizing this information and calculating some of the requirements established by the State Board of Education. Along with the appropriation categories mentioned above, each institution is categorized according to status (2 Year, 4 Year Public, or 4 Year Private). This will aid in the overall analysis for current and future resource planning.

SOME PARTICULARS YOU SHOULD KNOW

1. You need to create a detailed report for:
   a. Summary of overall change from 2001–2002 fiscal year (FY) and 2002–2003 FY
   b. Percentage of budget allocated to data processing services
   c. Percentage of 2 year, 4 year public, and 4 year private institutions allocating resources to data processing services
2. Develop a graphical representation of the percentage of 2 year, 4 year public, and 4 year private institutions allocating resources to data processing services
3. File: COLORADOHIGHERED.xls (Excel file)

CASE 14:
ASSESSING A WIRELESS FUTURE

EMERGING TRENDS AND TECHNOLOGY

"Intelligent wireless hand-held devices are going to explode, absolutely explode over the next several years."—Steve Ballmer, CEO, Microsoft.

Wireless, mobility, small form factor, pervasive computing, the anytime network—whatever name you choose—it's here. The price of easy-to-handle devices which provide access to a variety of applications and information is rapidly falling while the efficiencies of such devices are increasing. More and more, the business user is looking to use mobile devices to perform tasks that previously could be handled only by the desktop PC. End user adoption is skyrocketing. The next 18 months will demonstrate a true growing period for mobile computing as the world changes to one characterized by the mobile user.

As this market sector grows, software and information companies are beginning to evolve their products and services. Wireless mobility and associated functionality provide new market opportunities for both established companies and new entrants to increase efficiency and take advantage of new revenue possibilities. The services to Internet-enabled mobile devices create a vast array of new business opportunities for companies as they develop products and services that utilize location, time, and immediate access to information in new and innovative ways.

Some of the lower profile topics that are currently being developed at this time include:

- Hard drives for wireless devices
- Global-roaming movement
- Mobile power supplies that run on next-generation fuel cells.

All three could bring about significant changes in the wireless space.

You have been asked to prepare a presentation using a presentation package such as Microsoft's PowerPoint. Using the list of wireless solution providers and manufacturers provided in WIRELESS.htm, select at least two developers and create a presentation that will emphasize the following topics:

1. What are the current products or services under development?
2. What is the target market for that product or service?
3. What are the key features that product or service will bring to the wireless industry?
4. Which provider/manufacturer/developer seems to be the first to market with their product?
5. How is the wireless product or service content being delivered?
6. Are the products or services able to deploy interactive multimedia applications to any digital wireless device, on any carrier, or across any type of network?
7. Are there any new privacy concerns that are being discussed in relation to the new products or services? (These can include concerns from being able to track users' preferences, purchasing history or browsing preferences, or the capability to track a user's physical location while using a wireless device.)
8. How does this product or solution affect the global marketplace?
9. What is the current retail price for the wireless products or solutions?
10. Is current bandwidth available to the wireless industry a concern?

Your task is to weave the information you find into a coherent presentation using graphs and art where appropriate.

SOME PARTICULARS YOU SHOULD KNOW

1. Content Principles
   - Each slide should have a headline
   - Each slide should express one idea
   - Ideas should follow logically
2. Design Principles
   - Follow the "Rule of 7"—no more than 7 lines per slide and 7 words per line
   - Keep it simple
   - Keep it organized
   - Create a path for the eye
   - Divide space in an interesting way
   - Use at least 30-point type
   - Use color and graphics carefully, consistently, and for a specific purpose
   - Use high-contrast colors (black/white, deep blue/white, etc.)
3. File: WIRELESS.htm (html file)

CASE 15:
E-COMMERCE: THE NEXT GENERATION

DOT-COM ASPS

E-commerce is creating a new set of challenges for dot-com start-ups to well-established brick-and-mortar companies. Driven by the need to capture increasing shares of business online, IT managers take the first step by deciding on a commerce application. Then they face the most important decision: whether to assign implementation, deployment, and application hosting to internal IT resources or to contract for these services with an ASP.

Roughly 24 months ago, no one had even heard the term *application service provider (ASP)*. Now the ASP market is a certified phenomenon. In the short space of two years, the concept of leasing applications to businesses has grown to an interesting but unproven proposition in an ever-expanding industry.

You have been hired by Front Range Car Rental, a major car rental company in Colorado, to research ways to use technology to leverage more business. The company needs a Web Service written which transacts reservations on its back-end mainframe system. This Web Service will need to be made available to airline partners to integrate the travel booking process. When consumers book a flight, they are also given the option to reserve a car from the airline site. The rental details will need to be captured and transported to the car rental company's Web Service, which processes the reservation. This new capability will help the car rental company to drive more bookings and achieve a competitive advantage in a highly commoditized market.

The major task that Front Range Car Rental needs you to research is what the cost benefits would be for in-house implementation and an ASP deployment. You have been given an analysis spreadsheet, DOTCOMASP.xls, with all the detailed information; however, you will need to use the Internet in order to find current price information. Another file, DOTCOMASP_SEARCH.htm, has been developed for you with a list of search engines that will provide you with a focal point for your research.

SOME PARTICULARS YOU SHOULD KNOW

1. All ASPs are not created equal. Here are some questions to help you identify their strengths, weaknesses, capabilities and core competencies.
   - Does the ASP offer full life-cycle services, including proof-of-concept, installation, operations, training, support, and proactive evolution services?
   - What is the ASP's depth and breadth of technical expertise? What are the company's specialties?
   - Where and how did key technical staff obtain their expertise?
   - Does the ASP have actual customers online and if so, what results have they achieved?
   - Does the ASP offer service-level agreements and what are the penalties for SLA violations?
   - Specifically, how does the ASP's infrastructure deliver:
     High availability (uptime)?
     Assured data integrity?
     Scalability?
     Reliability?
     High performance?
     Security and access control?
   - Does the ASP offer 24 × 7 technical support to end users? Escalation procedures? High-priority problem resolution? Dedicated account managers?
   - Can the ASP provide development expertise to customize the applications?
   - How does the ASP handle updates? Adding product modules?
   - Is the ASP capable of assisting with add-on projects such as bringing a new factory online or adding a new supplier?
   - Can the ASP provide a comprehensive suite of integrated applications (versus a single application)?

2. File: DOTCOMASP.xls (Excel File) and DOTCOMASP_SEARCH.htm (html file)

CASE 16:
STRATEGIC AND COMPETITIVE ADVANTAGE: ANALYZING OPERATING LEVERAGE

PONY ESPRESSO

Pony Espresso is a small business that sells specialty coffee drinks at office buildings. Each morning and afternoon, trucks arrive at offices' front entrances, and the office employees purchase various beverages with names such as Java du Jour and Café de Colombia. The business is profitable. But Pony Espresso offices are located to the north of town, where lease rates are less expensive, and the principal sales area is south of town. This means that the trucks must drive cross-town four times each day.

The cost of transportation to and from the sales area, plus the power demands of the trucks' coffee brewing equipment, is a significant portion of the variable costs. Pony Espresso could reduce the amount of driving—and, therefore, the variable costs—if it moves the offices much closer to the sales area.

Pony Espresso presently has fixed costs of $10,000 per month. The lease of a new office, closer to the sales area, would cost an additional $2,200 per month. This would increase the fixed costs to $12,200 per month.

Although the lease of new offices would increase the fixed costs, a careful estimate of the potential savings in gasoline and vehicle maintenance indicates that Pony Espresso could reduce the variable costs from $0.60 per unit to $0.35 per unit. Total sales are unlikely to increase as a result of the move, but the savings in variable costs should increase the annual profit.

You have been hired by Pony Espresso to assist in the cost analysis and new lease options to determine a growth in profit margin. You will also need to calculate a degree of operating leverage to better understand the company's profitability. Degree of operating leverage (DOL) will give the CEO of Pony Espresso, Darian Presley, a great deal of information for setting operating targets and planning profitability.

SOME PARTICULARS YOU SHOULD KNOW

1. Consider the information provided—especially look at the change in the variability of the profit from month to month. From November through January, when it is much more difficult to lure office workers out into the cold to purchase coffee, Pony Espresso barely breaks even. In fact, in December of 2003, the business lost money.

2. First, develop the cost analysis on the existing lease information using the monthly sales figures provided to you in the file PONYESPRESSO.xls. Second, develop the cost analysis from the new lease information provided above.

3. You need to calculate the variability that is reflected in the month-to-month standard deviation of earnings for the current cost structure and the projected cost structure.

4. Do not consider any association with downsizing such as overhead; simply focus on the information provided to you.

5. You will need to calculate the EBIT—earnings before interest and taxes.

6. Would the DOL and business risk increase or decrease if Pony Espresso moved its office? *Note:* Variability in profit levels, whether measured as EBIT, operating income, or net income, does not necessarily increase the level of business risk as the DOL increases.

7. File: PONYESPRESSO.xls (Excel file).

CASE 17:
DECISION SUPPORT SYSTEM

BREAK-EVEN ANALYSIS

Ski-YA! is a Colorado-based company that sells high-performance ski equipment. When it comes to the serious business of sliding downhill, the Ski-YA! dudes of Colorado don't trouble themselves with petty categories; to them, all alpine snow equipment is summed up in one word, AWESOME!

This season's offerings at Ski-YA! are no exception. Skis continue to grow wider for better flotation beyond the groomers, and the sidecuts, the stick's hourglass shape designed to help you turn, now reflect the needs of terrain skiers. Even bindings have been rejiggered: forget the drill and screwdriver; the latest fittings snap or slide into place, extending ski life and improving energy transfer.

The Ski-YA! company wants to begin selling a new pair of skis, labeled the Downhill Demons, in the upcoming ski season. It wants to know how many skis it will have to sell in order to break even on its investment in materials and equipment. The chief financial officer has provided the following information:

Fixed Costs

Metal molding machine:	$200,000
Milling machine:	$150,000
Sander and grinder:	$10,000
Presses:	$25,000
Silkscreen machine:	$50,000

Variable Costs (per Unit)

Packaging material	$5.00
Raw material	$100.00
Shipping	$20.00

The marketing department estimates that it can sell the new skis for $400.00 per unit. Further projections estimate that an average of 200 units will be sold per month. The goal is that the skis will break even and start to earn a profit within the first year. Ski-YA!'s target-profit level for the end of the first fiscal year is $100,000.

SOME PARTICULARS YOU SHOULD KNOW

1. First, create a break-even analysis where your goal is to determine how many units you must sell to recover all of your fixed costs.

2. Then create a target-profit analysis where your goal is to determine how many units you must sell to reach a predefined profit level. The difference between the two is that at breakeven your target-profit is zero, whereas when you specify a target-profit that is greater than zero, you are setting your goal above the break-even point.

3. You will want to create a table sheet that contains the data used to generate the break-even/target-profit chart. This includes 10 data points on either side of the break-even/target-profit point.

4. Finally create a chart where you can visually measure your break-even or target-profit level along with total fixed and variable costs. If you choose to calculate the number of months before you reach a break-even or target-profit, those numbers will be reported here.

5. File: SkiYA.xls (Excel file).

CASE 18:
FINANCING

CREATING A CONVENTIONAL MORTGAGE WORKSHEET

The Foothills Savings Bank (FSB) is a federally insured stock savings bank which was organized in 1982 as a privately insured savings and loan association in Denver, Colorado. It received federal insurance in 1985 and a federal savings bank charter in 1986. FSB is a member of the Federal Home Loan Bank (FHLB) system and its deposits are insured by the Federal Deposit Insurance Corporation (FDIC) to the maximum amount provided by law.

The Foothills Savings Bank offers loans for owner-occupied properties, second homes, and investment homes. FSB offers first trust residential conventional fixed rate and ARM (adjustable rate mortgage) loans. Conventional financing is any mortgage that is not insured or guaranteed by federal, state, or local governments. FSB is now offering an online prequalification worksheet for its customers or prospective customers to use. FSB requires a minimum of 10 percent down, which is generally required for conventional financing.

It is your responsibility to complete a mortgage qualification worksheet and then create a mortgage amortization analysis worksheet from the data in the mortgage qualification worksheet.

SOME PARTICULARS YOU SHOULD KNOW

1. A template for the mortgage qualification worksheet has been created; however, you need to complete the formulas.

2. The Qualifying Section:
   - The first qualifying number needs to calculate the maximum monthly payment, assuming there are no long-term debts. It is computed by multiplying the total income by the housing cost ratio and dividing the result by 12.
   - The second qualifying number takes into account the monthly debt payments, applying the total debt service ratio. It is calculated by multiplying the total debt by the debt service ratio and dividing the result by 12.
   - Mortgage companies usually qualify people for monthly payments that are no higher than the lesser of the two results.
   - By default, your worksheet should assume a housing cost ratio of 0.28 and a total debt service ratio of 0.36, which are standards often used for conventional mortgages.

3. The Loan Amount Section:

   The table created below the qualifying section calculates the amount of a loan you might qualify for with the monthly payment. Depending on the circumstances, some or all of the following will be true:
   - In all cases, the monthly payment will include principal and interest payments.
   - In most cases, it will include a monthly escrow deposit to cover taxes and mortgage insurance, if any. In some cases, homeowner's insurance is also included in this calculation. Use your best guess estimates for these figures.
   - If the customer is buying a condominium or co-op unit, the monthly payment figure may also include the homeowner's dues and/or maintenance fees. You will need to estimate these monthly costs and type them into the appropriate cells.

4. Creating an amortization analysis worksheet:
   - Use the data from the mortgage qualification worksheet to create an amortization table. You will need to calculate beginning balance, principal paid, interest paid, total principal, total interest, and ending balance per payment period for the life of the loan.

5. File: Mortgage.xls (Excel file).

CASE 19:
SCHEDULING

AIRLINE CREW SCHEDULING

Rockies Airline is a new airline company that maintains a schedule of two daily flights between Salt Lake City, Denver, and Chicago. Rockies Airline took to the air on February 11, 2004, with the inauguration of service between Denver International Airport and Salt Lake City. Every Rockies Airline aircraft is outfitted with roomy all-leather seats, each equipped with 24 channels of DIRECTV programming.

Rockies Airline must strategically position itself as a low-cost provider in a very volatile industry. Therefore, it must work toward finding a minimum cost assignment of flight crews to a given flight schedule while satisfying restrictions dictated by the Federal Aviation Administration. Rockies Airline needs to solve the crew scheduling problem that is an involved and time-consuming process.

To begin, you will want to figure out all the possible crew rotations. You will want to find an approximate expected cost of each combination and then solve the traditional crew scheduling problem by using these costs. Second, you will want to calculate the crew constraints in order to determine the decision variables, constraints, and objectives.

You have been given Rockies Airline flight schedule as follows:

From	To	Departure	Arrival	Departure	Arrival
Salt Lake City	Denver	9:00 AM	12:00 PM	2:00 PM	5:00 PM
Salt Lake City	Chicago	10:00 AM	2:00 PM	3:00 PM	7:00 PM
Denver	Salt Lake City	8:00 AM	11:00 PM	2:00 PM	5:00 PM
Denver	Chicago	9:00 AM	11:00 PM	3:00 PM	5:00 PM
Chicago	Salt Lake City	8:00 AM	12:00 PM	2:00 PM	6:00 PM
Chicago	Denver	10:00 AM	12:00 PM	4:00 PM	6:00 PM

SOME PARTICULARS YOU SHOULD KNOW

1. A crew that leaves a city in the morning has to return there at night.
2. The crew can be brought back on another airline. This would always be on an 8 PM flight. There are 6 airplanes in use.
3. When a crew is flying, the cost is $200 per hour.
4. When a crew is waiting or being flown back, the cost is $75 per hour.
5. How should the company schedule its crews to minimize cost?
6. *Hint:* You will want to install the Solver Add-in to assist with this.
7. File: CREWSCHEDULING.xls (Excel file).

CASE 20:
DATABASE MANAGEMENT SYSTEM

MOUNTAIN BIKE RENTALS

Vail Resort in Vail, Colorado, is internationally known as one of the best places in North America for mountain biking. Since 1973, Slopeside Bike Rentals has been a tradition in the area. At Slopeside Bike Rentals you will find the largest selection of bikes, parts, accessories, books, maps, clothing, shocks, helmets, eyewear, shoes, car racks, and touring gear in the area with everything you need for on and off the road. Its state-of-the-art demo and rental program has everything from premium dual suspension to kids' bikes and trailers.

You have been employed for the past three summers by Slopeside Bike Rentals. Recently, there has been a surge in business and the owners need a more accurate way to manage the rental business. You have decided to create a database to help the owners keep track of the bike rentals, who the customers are, amount paid, and any damage to the bikes when they are rented. Currently Slopeside Bike Rentals owns 13 mountain bikes in its fleet of rentals. The bikes vary in type, size, and parts. When customers rent bikes, they are required to leave their driver's license number and to give you a home address, phone number, and credit card number.

You have designed the entity classes and primary keys for the database as the following:

Entity	Primary Key
Bike	Bike_ID
Customer	Customer_ID
Rental	Rental_ID

You have also identified the following business rules:

1. Rentals can have many customers assigned but must have at least one.
2. A bike must be assigned to one and only one rental type.
3. A customer can rent one or more bikes at one time.
4. A bike can be assigned to only one customer but need not be assigned to any customer.

Your job is to be completed in the following phases:

1. Develop and describe the entity-relationship diagram.
2. Use normalization to assure the correctness of the tables (relations).
3. Create the database using a personal DBMS package (preferably Microsoft Access).
4. Slopeside Bike Rentals has the following fee structures for its 13 bike rentals:

Description	Cost Per Hour
Specialized Rockhopper	$12.00
Specialized Rockhopper	$12.00
Trek Fuel 70	$12.00
Trek Fuel 80	$15.00
Trek Fuel 80	$15.00
Trek Fuel 90	$16.00
Marin Downhill FRS	$16.00
Marin Downhill FRS	$16.00
Marin Downhill FRS	$16.00
Specialized Stumpjumper FSR	$18.00
Specialized Stumpjumper FSR	$18.00
Specialized Stumpjumper FSR	$18.00
Specialized Stumpjumper Hardtail	$20.00

Figure GP.3

Slopeside Bike
Rental Report

Slopeside Bike Rental Report

Description	Date	Last Name	First Name	Amount Paid
Specialized Rockhopper				
	5/30/2004	Smith	Sue	$24.00
	6/2/2004	Smith	Sue	$42.00
	7/5/2004	Dunn	David	$72.00
Summary for Specialized Rockhopper (3 detail records)				**$138.00**
Trek Fuel 70				
	6/29/2004	Myers	Mike	$24.00
	6/30/2004	Myers	Mike	$24.00
Summary for Trek Fuel 70 (2 detail records)				**$48.00**
Trek Fuel 80				
	7/5/2004	Elliott	Raymond	$30.00
	7/7/2004	Elliott	Raymond	$15.00
	7/11/2004	Lapierre	Lynne	$225.00
	7/12/2004	Lapierre	Lynne	$37.50
Summary for Trek Fuel 80 (4 detail records)				**$307.50**
Trek Fuel 90				
	7/1/2004	Smith	Sue	$48.00
	7/11/2004	Dunn	David	$32.00
Summary for Trek Fuel 80 (2 detail records)				**$80.00**
Grand Total				**$573.50**

5. Use the DBMS package to create the basic report in Figure GP.3.

SOME PARTICULARS YOU SHOULD KNOW

1. You may not be able to develop a report that looks exactly like the one in Figure GP.3. However, your report should include the same information.
2. One of your tables will need a composite primary key.

2-tier infrastructure a basic client/server computing infrastructure with two tiers—the client and the server.

3-tier infrastructure contains clients, application servers, and data servers.

A

Ad hoc nonrecurring decision decision you make infrequently (perhaps only once) and for which you may even have different criteria for determining the best solution for each time.

Adware software to generate ads that installs itself on your computer when you download some other (usually free) program from the Web.

Affiliate program an arrangement made between two e-commerce sites that directs viewers from one site to the other.

Alliance partner a company your company does business with on a regular basis in a collaborative fashion, usually facilitated by IT systems.

Analysis phase of the systems development life cycle involves end users and IT specialists working together to gather, understand, and document the business requirements for the proposed system.

Anonymous Web browsing (AWB) service hides your identity from the Web sites you visit.

Anti-virus software detects and removes or quarantines computer viruses.

Application generation subsystem of a DBMS contains facilities to help you develop transaction-intensive applications.

Application service provider (ASP) supplies software applications (and often related services such as maintenance, technical support, and the like) over the Internet that would otherwise reside on its customers' in-house computers.

Application software the software that enables you to solve specific problems or perform specific tasks.

Arithmetic logic unit (ALU) a component of the CPU that performs arithmetic, as well as comparison and logic operations.

Artificial intelligence (AI) the science of making machines imitate human thinking and behavior.

Artificial neural network (ANN) (also called a **neural network**) an artificial intelligence system that is capable of finding and differentiating patterns.

ASCII (American Standard Code for Information Interchange) the coding system that most personal computers use to represent, process, and store information.

AutoFilter function filters a list and allows you to hide all the rows in a list except those that match criteria you specify.

Automatic speech recognition (ASR) a system that not only captures spoken words but also distinguishes word groupings to form sentences.

B

Back office system used to fulfill and support customer orders.

Backup the process of making a copy of the information stored on a computer.

Bandwidth capacity of the communications medium, refers to the amount of information that a communications medium can transfer in a given amount of time.

Bar code scanner reads information that is in the form of vertical bars, where their width and spacing represent digits (often used in point-of-sale [POS] systems in retail environments).

Basic formatting tag HTML tag that allows you to specify formatting for text.

Benchmarking a process of continuously measuring system results, comparing those results to optimal system performance (benchmark values), and identifying steps and procedures to improve system performance.

Benchmarks baseline values a system seeks to attain.

Binary digit (bit) the smallest unit of information that your computer can process.

Biochip a technology chip that can perform a variety of physiological functions when inserted into the human body.

Biometric scanner scans some human physical attribute, like your fingerprint or iris, for security purposes.

Biometrics the use of physiological characteristics—such as your fingerprint, the blood vessels in the iris of your eye, the sound of your voice, or perhaps even your breath—to provide identification.

Black-hat hacker a cyber vandal.

Bluetooth a standard for transmitting information in the form of short-range radio waves over distances of up to 30 feet, used for purposes such as wirelessly connecting a cell phone or a PDA to a computer.

Broadband high-capacity telecommunications pipeline capable of providing high-speed Internet service.

Browser-safe colors 215 colors that can be viewed by all browsers and computers.

Business intelligence (BI) knowledge—knowledge about your customers, your competitors, your business partners, your competitive environment, and your own internal operations—that gives you the ability to make effective, important, and often strategic business decisions.

Business intelligence (BI) system the IT applications and tools that support the business intelligence function within an organization.

Business requirement a detailed set of knowledge worker requests that the system must meet to be successful.

Business to Business (B2B) e-commerce when a business sells products and services to customers who are primarily other businesses.

Business to Consumer (B2C) e-commerce   when a business sells products and services to customers who are primarily individuals.

Buyer agent or **shopping bot**   an intelligent agent on a Web site that helps you, the customer, find the products and services you want.

Buyer power   in the Five Forces Model it is high when buyers have many choices from whom to buy, and low when their choices are few.

Byte   a group of eight bits that represents one natural language character.

C

Cable modem   a device that uses your TV cable to deliver an Internet connection.

Capacity planning   determines the future IT infrastructure requirements for new equipment and additional network capacity.

Cat 5 (Category 5) cable   a better-constructed version of the phone twisted-pair cable.

CAVE (cave automatic virtual environment)   a special 3-D virtual reality room that can display images of other people and objects located in other CAVEs all over the world.

CD-R (compact disc-recordable)   an optical or laser disc that you can write to one time only.

CD-ROM (compact disc-read-only memory)   an optical or laser disc whose information cannot be changed. A CD stores up to 800 Meg of information.

CD-RW (compact disc-rewritable)   an optical or laser disc on which you can save, change, and delete files as often as you like.

Central processing unit (CPU)   the hardware that interprets and executes the system and application software instructions and coordinates the operation of all other hardware.

Chief information officer (CIO)   responsible for overseeing an organization's information resource.

Choice   the third step in the decision-making process where you decide on a plan to address the problem or opportunity.

Chronological résumé   arranges work experiences according to time sequence.

Class   contains information and procedures and acts as a template to create objects.

Click-and-mortar   refers to those organizations that have a presence in the physical world such as a building you can visit and a presence in the virtual world of the Internet.

Clickstream   a stored record about your Web surfing session, such as what Web sites you visited, how long you were there, what ads you looked at, and what you bought.

Click-through   a count of the number of people who visit one site, click on an ad, and are taken to the site of the advertiser.

Client/server network   a network in which one or more computers are servers and provide services to the other computers, called *clients*.

Coaxial cable (coax)   one central wire surrounded by insulation, a metallic shield, and a final case of insulating material.

Cold site   a separate facility that does not have any computer equipment but is a place where the knowledge workers can move after the disaster.

Collaboration system   a system that is designed specifically to improve the performance of teams by supporting the sharing and flow of information.

Collaborative planning, forecasting, and replenishment (CPFR)   a concept that encourages and facilitates collaborative processes between supply chain partners.

Collaborative-processing enterprise information portal   presents knowledge workers with access to workgroup information such as e-mails, reports, meeting minutes, and memos.

Collocation   a company rents space and telecommunications equipment from another company, or a collocation vendor.

Communications medium   the path, or physical channel, in a network over which information travels.

Communications protocol (protocol)   a set of rules that every computer follows to transfer information.

Communications satellite   microwave repeater in space.

Communications service provider   third party who furnishes the conduit for information.

Communications software   helps you communicate with other people.

CompactFlash (CF) card   a flash memory card that is slightly larger than a half-dollar, with a capacity of up to 6 gigabytes.

Competitive advantage   providing a product or service in a way that customers value more than what the competition is able to do.

Competitive intelligence (CI)   business intelligence focused on the external competitive environment.

Composite primary key   consists of the primary key fields from the two intersecting relations.

Computer crime   a crime in which a computer, or computers, played a significant part.

Computer forensics   the gathering, authentication, examination, and analysis of electronic information stored on any type of computer media, such as hard drives, floppy disks, or CDs.

Computer network (network)   two or more computers connected so that they can communicate with each other and share information, software, peripheral devices, and/or processing power.

Computer virus (virus)   software that is written with malicious intent to cause annoyance or damage.

Conditional formatting   highlights information in a cell that meets some criteria you specify.

Connectivity software   enables you to use your computer to dial up or connect to another computer.

Consumer to Consumer (C2C) e-commerce   when an individual sells products and services to customers who are primarily other individuals.

Control unit   the component of the CPU that directs what happens in your computer, sends to RAM for instructions and the information it needs.

Conversion rate the percentage of potential customers who visit your site who actually buy something.

Cookie a small record deposited on your hard disk by a Web site containing information about you.

Copyright the legal protection afforded an expression of an idea, such as a song, video game, and some types of proprietary documents.

Counterfeit software software that is manufactured to look like the real thing and sold as such.

CPU cache a type of memory on the CPU where instructions called up by the CPU wait until the CPU is ready to use them.

CPU clock a sliver of quartz that beats at regular intervals in response to an electrical charge.

CPU (machine) cycle consists of retrieving, decoding, and executing the instruction, then returning the result to RAM, if necessary.

Cracker a hacker for hire; a person who engages in electronic corporate espionage.

Crash-proof software utility software that helps you save information if your system crashes and you're forced to turn it off and then back on again.

Critical success factor (CSF) a factor simply critical to your organization's success.

Crossover the process within a genetic algorithm where portions of good outcomes are combined in the hope of creating an even better outcome.

CRT a monitor that looks like a traditional television set.

CRUD (Create, Read, Update, Delete) the four procedures, or ways, a system can manipulate information.

Curriculum Vitae (or CV) an academic résumé that you use to tell others about your academic qualifications. It is used if you are a scientist or educator.

Custom AutoFilter function allows you to hide all the rows in a list except those that match criteria, besides "is equal to," that you specify.

Customer relationship management (CRM) system uses information about customers to gain insights into their needs, wants, and behaviors in order to serve them better.

Customer self-service system an extension of a TPS that places technology in the hands of an organization's customers and allows them to process their own transactions.

Cyberterrorist one who seeks to cause harm to people or destroy critical systems or information.

D

Data raw facts that describe a particular phenomenon.

Data administration the function in an organization that plans for, oversees the development of, and monitors the information resource.

Data administration subsystem of a DBMS helps you manage the overall database environment by providing facilities for backup and recovery, security management, query optimization, concurrency control, and change management.

Data cleansing describes the process of ensuring that all information is accurate.

Data definition subsystem of a DBMS helps you create and maintain the data dictionary and define the structure of the files in a database.

Data dictionary contains the logical structure for the information in a database.

Data management component of a DSS that performs the function of storing and maintaining the information that you want your DSS to use.

Data manipulation subsystem of a DBMS helps you add, change, and delete information in a database and query it for valuable information.

Data mart a subset of a data warehouse in which only a focused portion of the data warehouse information is kept.

Data-mining agent an intelligent agent that operates in a data warehouse discovering information.

Data-mining tool a software tool you use to query information in a data warehouse.

Data warehouse a logical collection of information—gathered from many different operational databases—used to create business intelligence that supports business analysis activities and decision-making tasks.

Database a collection of information that you organize and access according to the logical structure of that information.

Database administration the function in an organization that is responsible for the more technical and operational aspects of managing the information contained in organizational information repositories (databases, data warehouses, and data marts).

Database-based workflow system stores documents in a central location and automatically asks the knowledge workers to access the document when it's their turn to edit the document.

Database management system (DBMS) helps you specify the logical organization for a database and access and use the information within a database.

DBMS engine accepts logical requests from the various other DBMS subsystems, converts them into their physical equivalent, and actually accesses the database and data dictionary as they exist on a storage device.

Decentralized computing an environment in which an organization distributes computing power and locates it in functional business areas as well as on the desktops of knowledge workers.

Decision-processing enterprise information portal presents knowledge workers with corporate information for making key business decisions.

Decision support system (DSS) a highly flexible and interactive IT system that is designed to support decision making when the problem is not structured.

Demand aggregation the combining of purchase requests from multiple buyers into a single larger order, which justifies a discount from the business.

Denial-of-service (DoS) attack floods a Web site with so many requests for service that it slows down or crashes.

Design   where you consider possible ways of solving the problem, filling the need, or taking advantage of the opportunity.

Design phase   of the systems development life cycle builds a technical blueprint of how the proposed system will work.

Desktop computer   the type of computer that is the most popular choice for personal computing needs.

Desktop publishing software   extends word processing software by including design and formatting techniques to enhance the layout and appearance of a document.

Development phase   of the systems development life cycle takes all your detailed design documents from the design phase and transforms them into an actual system.

Digital camera   captures still images or video as a series of 1s and 0s.

Digital cash (electronic cash, e-cash)   an electronic representation of cash.

Digital dashboard   displays key information gathered from several sources on a computer screen in a format tailored to the needs and wants of an individual knowledge worker.

Digital still camera   digitally captures still images in varying resolutions.

Digital Subscriber Line (DSL)   a high speed Internet connection using phone lines, which allows you to use your phone for voice communications at the same time.

Digital video camera   captures video digitally.

Digital wallet   both software and information—the software provides security for the transaction and the information includes payment information (for example, the credit card number and expiration date) and delivery information.

Direct materials   materials that are used in production in a manufacturing company or are placed on the shelf for sale in a retail environment.

Directory search engine   organizes listings of Web sites into hierarchical lists.

Disaster recovery cost curve   charts (1) the cost to your organization of the unavailability of information and technology and (2) the cost to your organization of recovering from a disaster over time.

Disaster recovery plan   a detailed process for recovering information or an IT system in the event of a catastrophic disaster such as a fire or flood.

Disk optimization software   utility software that organizes your information on your hard disk in the most efficient way.

Distributed denial-of-service (DDoS) attack   attack from multiple computers that floods a Web site with so many requests for service that it slows down or crashes.

Distribution chain   the path followed from the originator of a product or service to the end consumer.

Document management system   manages a document through all the stages of its processing.

Domain expert   the person who provides the domain expertise in the form of problem-solving strategies.

Domain expertise   the set of problem-solving steps; it's the reasoning process that will solve the problem.

Domain name   (technical name for a Web site address) identifies a specific computer on the Web and the main page of the entire site.

Dot pitch   the distance between the centers of a pair of like-colored pixels.

DVD-R or DVD+R (DVD – recordable)   a high-capacity optical or laser disc to which you can write one time only.

DVD-ROM   a high-capacity optical or laser disc whose information cannot be changed.

DVD-RW or DVD+RW   (depending on the manufacturer) a high-capacity optical or laser disc on which you can save, change, and delete files.

E

Electronic Bill Presentment and Payment (EBPP)   a system that sends bills (usually to end consumers) over the Internet and provides an easy-to-use mechanism (such as clicking on a button) to pay them if the amount looks correct.

Electronic check   a mechanism for sending money from your checking or savings account to another person or organization.

Electronic commerce (e-commerce)   commerce, but it is commerce accelerated and enhanced by IT, in particular the Internet.

Electronic data interchange (EDI)   the direct computer-to-computer transfer of transaction information contained in standard business documents, such as invoices and purchase orders, in a standard format.

Electronic job market   consists of employers using Internet technologies to advertise and screen potential employees.

Electronic marketplace (e-marketplace)   an interactive business providing a central space where multiple buyers and sellers can engage in e-commerce and/or other e-commerce business activities.

Electronic portfolio (e-portfolio)   collection of Web documents used to support a stated purpose such as demonstrating writing, photography, or job skills.

E-mail (electronic mail) software   enables you to electronically communicate with other people by sending and receiving e-mail.

Encapsulation   information hiding.

Encryption   scrambles the contents of a file so that you can't read it without having the right decryption key.

Enterprise information portal (EIP)   allows knowledge workers to access company information via a Web interface.

Entity class   a concept—typically people, places, or things—about which you wish to store information and that you can identify with a unique key (called a primary key).

Entity-relationship (E-R) diagram   a graphic method of representing entity classes and their relationships.

Entry barrier   a product or service feature that customers have come to expect from organizations in a particular industry and that must be offered by an entering organization to compete and survive.

Ethernet card   the most common type of network interface card.

Ethical (white-hat) hacker a computer security professional who is hired by a company to break into its computer system.

Ethics the principles and standards that guide our behavior toward other people.

Executive information system (EIS) highly interactive IT system that allows you to first view highly summarized information and then choose how you would like to see greater detail, which may alert you to potential problems or opportunities.

Expandability refers to how easy it is to add features and functions to a system.

Expansion bus the set of pathways along which information moves between devices outside the motherboard and the CPU.

Expansion card (board) a circuit board that you insert into the expansion slot on the motherboard and to which you connect a peripheral device.

Expansion slot a long skinny socket on the motherboard into which you insert an expansion card.

Expert system (knowledge-based system) an artificial intelligence system that applies reasoning capabilities to reach a conclusion.

Explanation module the part of an expert system where the "why" information, supplied by the domain expert, is stored to be accessed by knowledge workers who want to know why the expert system asked a question or reached a conclusion.

External information describes the environment surrounding the organization.

Extranet an intranet that is restricted to an organization and certain outsiders, such as customers and suppliers.

F

Facial recognition software software that provides identification by evaluating facial characteristics.

Fair Use Doctrine allows you to use copyrighted material in certain situations.

Feature analysis captures your words as you speak into a microphone, eliminates any background noise, and converts the digital signals of your speech into phonemes (syllables).

Feature creep occurs when developers add extra features that were not part of the initial requirements.

File transfer protocol (ftp) communications protocol that allows you to transfer files of information from one computer to another.

Financial cybermediary an Internet-based company that makes it easy for one person to pay another person or organization over the Internet.

Financial EDI (financial electronic data interchange) an electronic process used primarily within the Business to Business e-commerce model for the payment of purchases.

Firewall software and/or hardware that protects a computer or network from intruders.

Firewire (IEEE 1394 or I-Link) port fits hot-swap, plug-and-play Firewire connectors and you can connect up to 63 Firewire devices to a single Firewire port by daisy-chaining the devices together.

Five Forces Model helps business people understand the relative attractiveness of an industry.

Flash memory card has high-capacity storage laminated inside a small piece of plastic.

Flash memory device a flash memory storage device that is small enough to fit on a key ring and plugs directly into the USB port on your computer.

Flat-panel display thin, lightweight monitor that takes up much less space than a CRT.

Floppy disk a removable magnetic storage medium that holds 1.44 Meg of information.

Foreign key a primary key of one file (relation) that appears in another file (relation).

Forensic image copy an exact copy or snapshot of the contents of an electronic medium.

Front office system the primary interface to customers and sales channels.

Ftp (file transfer protocol) server maintains a collection of files that you can download.

Functional résumé focuses on skills, abilities, volunteer experiences, and work experiences.

G

Game controller used for gaming to better control screen action.

Gamepad a multifunctional input device with programmable buttons, thumb sticks, and a directional pad.

Gaming wheel a steering wheel and foot pedals for virtual driving.

Gas plasma display sends electricity through gas trapped between two layers of glass or plastic to create an image.

Genetic algorithm an artificial intelligence system that mimics the evolutionary, survival-of-the-fittest process to generate increasingly better solutions to a problem.

Geographic information system (GIS) a decision support system designed specifically to work with spatial information.

Gigabyte (GB or Gig) roughly 1 billion bytes.

Gigahertz (GHz) the number of billions of CPU cycles per second that the CPU can handle.

Glove an input device that captures and records the shape and movement of your hand and fingers and the strength of your hand and finger movements.

Government to Business (G2B) the electronic commerce activities performed between a government and its business partners for such purposes as purchasing direct and MRO materials, soliciting bids for work, and accepting bids for work.

Government to Consumer (G2C) the electronic commerce activities performed between a government and its citizens or consumers including paying taxes, registering vehicles, and providing information and services.

Government to Government (G2G, intra-G2G)   the electronic commerce activities performed within a single nation's government focusing on vertical integration (local, city, state, and federal) and horizontal integration (within or among the various branches and agencies).

Graphical user interface (GUI)   the interface to an information system.

Graphics software   helps you create and edit photos and art.

Grid computing   harnesses far-flung computers together by way of the Internet or a virtual private network to share CPU power, databases, and database storage.

GUI screen design   the ability to model the information system screens for an entire system.

H

Hacker   a very knowledgeable person who uses his or her knowledge to invade other people's computers.

Hacktivist   a politically motivated hacker who uses the Internet to send a political message of some kind.

Handspring   a type of PDA that runs on the Palm Operating System (Palm OS).

Hard disk   magnetic storage device with one or more thin metal platters or disks that store information sealed inside the disk drive.

Hardware   the physical devices that make up a computer (often referred to as a computer system).

Hardware key logger   a hardware device that captures keystrokes on their journey from the keyboard to the motherboard.

Heading tag   HTML tag that makes certain information, such as titles, stand out on your Web site.

Headset (head-mounted display)   a combined input and output device that (1) captures and records the movement of your head, and (2) contains a screen that covers your entire field of vision.

Help desk   a group of people who respond to knowledge workers' requests.

Hidden job market   the collective term used to describe jobs that are not advertised.

Holographic device   a device that creates, captures, and/or displays images in true three-dimensional form.

Holographic storage device   stores information on a storage medium that is composed of 3-D crystal-like objects with many sides or faces.

Horizontal e-marketplace   an electronic marketplace that connects buyers and sellers across many industries, primarily for MRO materials commerce.

Horizontal market software   application software that is general enough to be suitable for use in a variety of industries.

Hot site   a separate and fully equipped facility where the company can move immediately after the disaster and resume business.

Hot swap   an operating system feature that allows you—while your computer is running—to unplug a device and plug in a new one without first shutting down your computer.

HTML document   a file that contains your Web site content and HTML formatting instructions.

HTML tag   specifies the formatting and presentation of information on a Web site.

Hypertext markup language (HTML)   the language you use to create a Web site.

Hypertext transfer protocol (http)   the communications protocol that supports the movement of information over the Web.

I

Identity theft   the forging of someone's identity for the purpose of fraud.

Image scanner   captures images, photos, text, and artwork that already exist on paper.

Implant chip   a technology-enabled microchip implanted into the human body that stores important information about you (such as your identification and medical history) and that may be GPS-enabled to offer a method of tracking.

Implementation   the final step in the decision-making process where you put your plan into action.

Implementation phase   of the systems development life cycle distributes the system to all the knowledge workers and they begin using the system to perform their everyday jobs.

Inference engine   the processing component of the expert system. It takes your problem facts and searches the knowledge base for rules that fit your problem facts.

Information   data that have a particular meaning within a specific context.

Information age   a time when knowledge is power.

Information decomposition   breaking down the information and procedures for ease of use and understandability.

Information granularity   the extent of detail within the information.

Information-literate knowledge workers   can define what information they need, know how and where to obtain that information, understand the information once they receive it, and can act appropriately based on the information to help the organization achieve the greatest advantage.

Information technology (IT)   any computer-based tool that people use to work with information and support the information and information-processing needs of an organization.

Information view   includes all of the information stored within a system.

Infrared, IR, or IrDA (infrared data association)   uses red light to send and receive information.

Inheritance   the ability to define superclass and subclass relationships among classes.

Inkjet printer   makes images by forcing ink droplets through nozzles.

Input device   tool you use to enter information and commands.

Insourcing   choosing IT specialists within your organization to develop the system.

Instance   an occurrence of an entity class that can be uniquely described with a primary key.

Integrated collaboration environment (ICE)   the environment in which virtual teams do their work.

Integration   allows separate applications to communicate directly with each other by automatically exporting data files from one application and importing them into another.

Integration testing   verifies that separate systems can work together.

Integrity constraint   rule that helps ensure the quality of the information.

Intellectual property   intangible creative work that is embodied in physical form.

Intelligence   the first step in the decision-making process where you find or recognize a problem, need, or opportunity (also called the diagnostic phase of decision-making).

Intelligent agent   software that assists you, or acts on your behalf, in performing repetitive computer-related tasks.

Interface   any device that calls procedures and can include such things as a keyboard, mouse, and touch screen.

Internal information   describes specific operational aspects of an organization.

International Government to Government (inter-G2G)   the electronic commerce activities performed between two or more governments including providing foreign aid.

International virtual private network (International VPN)   virtual private network that depends on services offered by phone companies of various nationalities.

Internet   a vast network of computers that connects millions of people all over the world.

Internet backbone   the major set of connections for computers on the Internet.

Internet server computer   computer that provides information and services on the Internet.

Internet service provider (ISP)   a company that provides individuals, organizations, and businesses access to the Internet.

Interoperability   the concept that different computer systems and applications can talk to each other.

Intersection relation (composite relation)   a relation you create to eliminate a many-to-many relationship.

Intranet   an internal organizational Internet that is guarded against outside access by a special security feature called a *firewall* (which can be software, hardware, or a combination of the two).

Intrusion-detection software   looks for people on the network who shouldn't be there or who are acting suspiciously.

IRC (Internet Relay Chat) server   supports your use of discussion groups and chat rooms.

IT infrastructure   includes the hardware, software, and telecommunications equipment that, when combined, provide the underlying foundation to support the organization's goals.

J

Java 2 Enterprise Edition (J2EE)   Sun Microsystems' development tool for building Web services applications.

Joint application development (JAD)   occurs when knowledge workers and IT specialists meet, sometimes for several days, to define or review the business requirements for the system.

Joystick   allows you to control action of a game with a vertical handle and programmable buttons.

Just-in-time (JIT)   an approach that produces or delivers a product or service just at the time the customer wants it.

K

Key logger (key trapper) software   software that, when installed on a computer, records every keystroke and mouse click.

Keyboard   the most often used input device for desktop and notebook computers.

Knowledge acquisition   the component of the expert system that the knowledge engineer uses to enter the rules.

Knowledge base   stores the rules of the expert system.

Knowledge-based system (expert system)   an artificial intelligence system that applies reasoning capabilities to reach a conclusion.

Knowledge engineer   the person who formulates the domain expertise into an expert system.

Knowledge management (KM) system   an IT system that supports the capturing, organization, and dissemination of knowledge (i.e., know-how) throughout an organization.

Knowledge worker   a person who works with and produces information as a product.

L

Language processing   attempts to make sense of what you're saying by comparing the word phonemes generated in step 2 with a language model database.

Laser printer   forms images using the same sort of electrostatic process that photocopiers use.

Link (hyperlink)   clickable text or an image that takes you to another site or page on the Web.

Linux   an open-source operating system that provides a rich operating environment for high-end workstations and network servers.

Liquid crystal display (LCD)   makes an image by sending electricity through crystallized liquid trapped between two layers of glass or plastic.

List   a collection of information arranged in columns and rows in which each column displays one particular type of information.

List definition table   a description of a list by column.

Local area network (LAN)   a network that covers a limited geographic distance, such as an office, building, or a group of buildings, in close proximity to each other.

Logical view   focuses on how you as a knowledge worker need to arrange and access information to meet your particular business needs.

Logistics   the set of processes that plans for and controls the efficient and effective transportation and storage of supplies from suppliers to customers.

Loyalty program   rewards customers based on the amount of business they do with a particular organization.

M

Mac OS   the operating system for today's Apple computers.

Macro virus   spreads by binding itself to software such as Word or Excel.

Mail server   provides e-mail services and accounts.

Mainframe computer (mainframe)   a computer designed to meet the computing needs of hundreds of people in a large business environment.

Maintenance phase   of the systems development life cycle monitors and supports the new system to ensure it continues to meet the business requirements.

Maintenance, repair, and operations (MRO) materials (indirect materials)   materials that are necessary for running a modern corporation, but do not relate to the company's primary business activities.

Management information systems (MIS)   deals with the planning for, development, management, and use of information technology tools to help people perform all tasks related to information processing and management.

Marketing mix   the set of marketing tools that your organization will use to pursue its marketing objectives in reaching and attracting potential customers.

Mass customization   the ability of an organization to give its customers the opportunity to tailor its product or service to the customer's specifications.

M-commerce   the term used to describe electronic commerce conducted over a wireless device such as a cell phone, PDA, or notebook.

MD5 hash value   a mathematically generated string of 32 letters and digits that is unique for an individual storage medium at a specific point in time.

Megabyte (MB or **M** or **Meg)**   roughly 1 million bytes.

Memory Stick Media card   elongated flash memory card about the width of a penny developed by Sony with capacities up to 512 megabytes.

Message   how objects communicate with each other.

Messaging-based workflow system   sends work assignments through an e-mail system.

Microphone   captures audio for conversion into electronic form.

Microsoft Windows XP Home   Microsoft's latest upgrade to Windows 2000 ME, with enhanced features for allowing multiple people to use the same computer.

Microsoft Windows XP Professional (Windows XP Pro)   Microsoft's latest upgrade to Windows 2000 Pro.

Microwave   a type of radio transmission used to transmit information.

Minicomputer (mid-range computer)   a computer designed to meet the computing needs of several people simultaneously in a small to medium-size business environment.

Mobile computing   broad general term describing your ability to use technology to wirelessly connect to and use centrally located information and/or application software.

Mobile CPU   a special type of CPU for a notebook computer that changes speed, and therefore power consumption, in response to fluctuation in use.

Model management   component of a DSS that consists of both the DSS models and the DSS model management system.

Modeling   the activity of drawing a graphical representation of a design.

Monitoring-and-surveillance agent (predictive agent)   an intelligent agent that observes and reports on equipment.

Mouse   a pointing device that you use to click on icons or buttons.

Multidimensional analysis (MDA) tool   slice-and-dice technique that allows you to view multidimensional information from different perspectives.

Multifunction printer   a printer that can scan, copy, and fax, as well as print.

Multimedia (HTML) résumé   a multimedia format that exists on the Internet for employers to explore at their convenience.

MultiMediaCard (MMC)   flash memory card that looks identical to an SD card (but SD cards have copy protection built-in), is a little larger than a quarter, and is slightly thicker than a credit card.

Multi-state CPU   works with information represented in more than just two states, probably 10 states with each state representing a digit between 0 and 9.

Multitasking   allows you to work with more than one piece of software at a time.

Municipal (metropolitan) area network (MAN)   covers a metropolitan area.

Mutation   the process within a genetic algorithm of randomly trying combinations and evaluating the success (or failure) of the outcomes.

N

.NET   Microsoft's version of Web services.

.NET framework   Microsoft's set of services that are used to support Web services, such as Common Language Runtime (CLR).

.NET platform   Microsoft's entire suite of tools, technologies, and services that support Microsoft's vision of connected applications, which includes Web services.

Network access point (NAP)   a point on the Internet where several connections converge.

Network area storage (NAS)   a special-purpose server aimed at providing file storage to users who access the device over a network.

Network hub   a device that connects multiple computers into a network.

Network interface card (NIC)   an expansion card or a PC Card (for a notebook computer) that connects your computer to a network and provides the doorway for information to flow in and out.

Network service provider (NSP)   such as MCI or AT&T, owns and maintains routing computers at NAPs and even the lines that connect the NAPs to each other.

Neural network (artificial neural network or ANN)   an artificial intelligence system that is capable of finding and differentiating patterns.

Nonrecurring (ad hoc) decision   one that you make infrequently (perhaps only once) and you may even have different criteria for determining the best solution each time.

Nonstructured decision   a decision for which there may be several "right" answers and there is no precise way to get a right answer.

Normalization   process of assuring that a relational database structure can be implemented as a series of two-dimensional tables.

Notebook computer   a small, portable, fully functional, battery-operated computer.

O

Object   an instance of a class.

Objective information   quantifiably describes something that is known.

Object-oriented approach   combines information and procedures into a single view.

Object-oriented database   works with traditional database information and also complex data types such as diagrams, schematic drawings, video, and sound and text documents.

Object-oriented programming language   a programming language used to develop object-oriented systems.

Offshore outsourcing   using organizations from developing countries to write code and develop systems.

Online ad (banner ad)   small advertisement that appears on other sites.

Online analytical processing (OLAP)   the manipulation of information to support decision making.

Online training   runs over the Internet or off a CD or DVD.

Online transaction processing (OLTP)   the gathering of input information, processing that information, and updating existing information to reflect the gathered and processed information.

Operating system software   system software that controls your application software and manages how your hardware devices work together.

Operational database   a database that supports OLTP.

Operational management   manages and directs the day-to-day operations and implementations of the goals and strategies.

Optical character reader   reads characters that appear on a page or sales tag (often used in point-of-sale [POS] systems in retail environments).

Optical fiber   a telecommunications medium that uses a very thin glass or plastic fiber through which pulses of light travel.

Optical mark reader   detects the presence or absence of a mark in a predetermined spot on the page (often used for true/false and multiple choice exams answers).

Optical storage media   plastic discs on which information is stored, deleted, and/or changed using laser light.

Output device   a tool you use to see, hear, or otherwise recognize the results of your information-processing requests.

Outsourcing   the delegation of specific work to a third party for a specified length of time, at a specified cost, and at a specified level of service.

P

Palm   a type of PDA that runs on the Palm Operating System (Palm OS).

Palm Operating System (Palm OS)   the operating system for Palm and Handspring PDAs.

Parallel implementation   using both the old and new system until you're sure that the new system performs correctly.

Parallel port   fits parallel connectors, which are large flat connectors found almost exclusively on printer cables.

Pattern classification   matches your spoken phonemes to a phoneme sequence stored in an acoustic model database.

PC Card   the expansion card you use to add devices to your notebook computer.

PC Card slot   the opening on the side or front of a notebook, where you connect an external device with a PC Card.

Peer-to-peer collaboration software   permits users to communicate in real time and share files without going through a central server.

Peer-to-peer network   a network in which a small number of computers share hardware (such as a printer), software and/or information.

Performance   measures how quickly an IT system performs a certain process.

Personal agent (user agent)   an intelligent agent that takes action on your behalf.

Personal digital assistant (PDA)   a small hand-held computer that helps you surf the Web and perform simple tasks such as note taking, calendaring, appointment scheduling, and maintaining an address book.

Personal finance software   helps you maintain your checkbook, prepare a budget, track investments, monitor your credit card balances, and pay bills electronically.

Personal information management software (PIM)   helps you create and maintain (1) to-do lists, (2) appointments and calendars, and (3) points of contact.

Personal productivity software   helps you perform personal tasks—such as writing a memo, creating a graph, and creating a slide presentation—that you can usually do even if you don't own a computer.

Phased implementation   implementing the new system in phases (e.g., accounts receivables, then accounts payable) until you're sure it works correctly and then implementing the remaining phases of the new system.

Phishing (carding or brand spoofing)   technique to gain personal information for the purpose of identity theft, usually by means of fraudulent e-mail.

Physical view   deals with how information is physically arranged, stored, and accessed on some type of storage device such as a hard disk.

Pilot implementation   having only a small group of people use the new system until you know it works correctly and then adding the remaining people to the system.

Pirated software   the unauthorized use, duplication, distribution or sale of copyrighted software

Pivot table   enables you to group and summarize information.

Pixels (picture elements)   the dots that make up the image on your screen.

Planning phase   of the systems development life cycle involves determining a solid plan for developing your information system.

Plug and play   an operating feature that finds and installs the device driver for a device that you plug into your computer.

Plunge implementation   discarding the old system completely and immediately using the new system.

Pocket PC   a type of PDA that runs on Pocket PC OS that used to be called Windows CE.

Pocket PC OS (Windows CE)   the operating system for the PocketPC PDA.

Pointing device   a device that is used to input commands into a computer.

Pointing stick   a little rod (like a pencil-top eraser) used almost exclusively on notebook computers.

Polymorphism   to have many forms.

Pop-under ad   a form of a pop-up ad that you do not see until you close your current browser window.

Pop-up ad   small Web page containing an advertisement that appears on your screen outside the current Web site loaded into your browser.

Port   a place on your system unit, monitor, or keyboard through which information and instructions flow to and from your computer system.

Portable document format (PDF) résumé   a standard electronic distribution format typically used for e-mailing.

Presence awareness   a software function which determines whether a user is immediately reachable or is in a less-available status.

Presentation software   helps you create and edit information that will appear in electronic slides.

Primary key   a field (or group of fields in some cases) that uniquely describes each record.

Privacy   the right to be left alone when you want to be, to have control over your own personal possessions, and not to be observed without your consent.

Private network   the communications media that your organization owns or exclusively leases to connect networks or network components.

Procedure   manipulates or changes information.

Procedure view   contains all of the procedures within a system.

Program   a set of instructions that, when executed, cause a computer to behave in a specific manner.

Programming language   the tool developers use to write a program.

Project manager   an individual who is an expert in project planning and management, defines and develops the project plan, and tracks the plan to ensure all key project milestones are completed on time.

Project milestone   represents a key date by which you need a certain group of activities performed.

Project plan   defines the *what, when,* and *who* questions of systems development including all activities to be performed, the individuals, or resources, who will perform the activities, and the time required to complete each activity.

Project scope   clearly defines the high-level system requirements.

Project scope document   a written definition of the project scope and is usually no longer than a paragraph.

Proof-of-concept prototype   a prototype you use to prove the technical feasibility of a proposed system.

Prototype   a model of a proposed product, service, or system.

Prototyping   the process of building a model that demonstrates the features of a proposed product, service, or system.

PS/2 port   fits PS/2 connectors, which you often find on keyboards and mice.

Public key encryption (PKE)   an encryption system that uses two keys: a public key that everyone can have and a private key for only the recipient.

Public network   a network on which your organization competes for time with others.

Push technology   an environment in which businesses and organizations come to you with information, services, and product offerings based on your profile.

Q

Query-and-reporting tool   similar to a QBE tool, SQL, and a report generator in the typical database environment.

Query-by-example (QBE) tool   helps you graphically design the answer to a question.

R

Random access memory (RAM)   a temporary holding area for the information you're working with as well the system and application software instructions that the CPU currently needs.

Recovery   the process of reinstalling the backup information in the event the information was lost.

Recurring decision   a decision that you have to make repeatedly and often periodically, whether weekly, monthly, quarterly, or yearly.

Relation   describes each two-dimensional table or file in the relational model (hence its name *relational* database model).

Relational database   uses a series of logically related two-dimensional tables or files to store information in the form of a database.

Repeater   a device that receives a radio signal, strengthens it, and sends it on.

Report generator   helps you quickly define formats of reports and what information you want to see in a report.

Request for proposal (RFP)   a formal document that describes in detail your logical requirements for a proposed system and invites outsourcing organizations (which we refer to as "vendors") to submit bids for its development.

Requirements definition document   defines all the business requirements and prioritizes them in order of business importance.

Resolution of a printer   the number of dots per inch (dpi) it produces.

Resolution of a screen   the number of pixels it has.

Reverse auction   the process in which a buyer posts its interest in buying a certain quantity of items with notations concerning quality, specification, and delivery timing, and sellers compete for the business by submitting successively lower bids until there is only one seller left.

Risk assessment   the process of evaluating IT assets, their importance to the organization, and their susceptibility to threats to measure the risk exposure of these assets.

Risk management   identification of risks or threats, the implementation of security measures, and the monitoring of those measures for effectiveness.

Rivalry among existing competitors   in the Five Forces Model is high when competition is fierce in a market, and low when competition is more complacent.

Robot   a mechanical device equipped with simulated human senses and the capability of taking action on its own.

Router   device that connects computers into a network using multiple communications links and separating your network from any other network it's connected to.

Rule-based expert system   the type of expert system that expresses the problem-solving process as rules.

S

Safe-harbor principles   the set of rules to which U.S. businesses that want to trade with the European Union (EU) must adhere.

Sales force automation (SFA) system   automatically tracks all of the steps in the sales process.

Satellite modem   modem that allows you to get Internet access from your satellite dish.

Scalability   refers to how well your system can adapt to increased demands.

Scannable (or ASCII) résumé   a paper résumé without any formatting that becomes electronic when it is scanned into a computer.

Scanner   used to convert information that exists in visible form into electronic form.

Scope creep   occurs when the scope of the project increases.

Script bunny (script kiddie)   someone who would like to be a hacker but doesn't have much technical expertise.

Search engine   a facility on the Web that helps you find sites with the information and/or services you want.

Secure Digital (SD) card   flash memory card that looks identical to an MMC card (but SD cards have copy protection built-in), is a little larger than a quarter, and is slightly thicker than a credit card.

Secure Electronic Transaction (SET)   a transmission security method that ensures transactions are legitimate as well as secure.

Secure Sockets Layer (SSL)   creates a secure and private connection between a Web client computer and a Web server computer, encrypts the information, and then sends the information over the Internet.

Security auditing software   checks out your computer or network for potential weaknesses.

Selection   the process within a genetic algorithm that gives preference to better outcomes.

Selfsourcing (knowledge worker development or end-user development)   the development and support of IT systems by knowledge workers with little or no help from IT specialists.

Selling prototype   a prototype you use to convince people of the worth of a proposed system.

Server farm   the name of a location that stores a group of servers in a single place.

Service level agreements (SLAs)   define the specific responsibilities of the application service provider and set the customer expectations.

Shared information   an environment in which an organization's information is organized in one or more central locations, allowing anyone to access and use it as he or she needs to.

Sign-off   the knowledge workers' actual signatures indicating they approve all the business requirements.

Skill words   nouns and adjectives used by organizations to describe jobs skills which should be woven into the text of an applicant's résumé.

Slack space   the space left over from the end of the file to the end of the cluster.

Smart card   a plastic card the size of a credit card that contains an embedded chip on which digital information can be stored and updated.

SmartMedia (SM) card   flash memory card that's a little longer than a CF card and about as thick as a credit card with capacities of up to 512 megabytes.

Social engineering   conning your way into acquiring information that you have no right to.

Social network system   an IT system that links you to people you know and, from there, to people your contacts know.

Software   the set of instructions that your hardware executes to carry out a specific task for you.

Software suite (suite)   bundled software that comes from the same publisher and costs less than buying all the software pieces individually.

Spam   unsolicited e-mail (electronic junk mail) from businesses that advertises goods and services.

Spoofing　the forging of the return address on an e-mail so that the e-mail message appears to come from someone other than the actual sender.

Spreadsheet software　helps you work primarily with numbers, including performing calculations and creating graphs.

Spyware (sneakware, stealthware)　software that comes hidden in free downloadable software and tracks your online movements, mines the information stored on your computer, or uses your computer's CPU and storage for some tasks you know nothing about.

Steganography　the hiding of information inside other information.

Storage area network (SAN)　an infrastructure for building special, dedicated networks that allow rapid and reliable access to storage devises by multiple servers.

Storage device　a tool you use to store information for use at a later time.

Storyboard　a visual representation illustrating relationships of objects on a Web page.

Strategic management　provides an organization with overall direction and guidance.

Structure tag　HTML tag that sets up the necessary sections and specifies that the document is indeed an HTML document.

Structured decision　a decision where processing a certain kind of information in a specified way so that you will always get the right answer.

Structured query language (SQL)　a standardized fourth-generation query language found in most DBMSs.

Stylus　the most frequently used input device for PDAs and tablet PCs.

Subjective information　attempts to describe something that is unknown.

Supercomputer　the fastest, most powerful, and most expensive type of computer.

Supplier power　in the Five Forces Model is high when buyers have few choices from whom to buy, and low when their choices are many.

Supply chain management (SCM)　tracks inventory and information among business processes and across companies.

Supply chain management (SCM) system　an IT system that supports supply chain management activities by automating the tracking of inventory and information among business processes and across companies.

Switch　a device that connects multiple computers into a network in which multiple communications links can be in operation simultaneously.

Switching cost　a cost that makes customers reluctant to switch to another product or service supplier.

System bus　electrical pathways that move information between basic components of the motherboard, including between RAM and the CPU.

System software　handles tasks specific to technology management and coordinates the interaction of all technology devices.

System testing　verifies that the units or pieces of code written for a system function correctly when integrated into the total system.

Systems development life cycle (SDLC)　a structured step-by-step approach for developing information systems.

T

Tablet PC　a pen-based computer that provides the screen capabilities of a PDA with the functional capabilities of a notebook or desktop computer.

Tactical management　develops the goals and strategies outlined by strategic management.

TCP/IP (Transport control protocol/Internet protocol)　the primary protocol for transmitting information over the Internet.

Technical architecture　defines the hardware, software, and telecommunications equipment required to run the system.

Technology-literate knowledge worker　person who knows how and when to apply technology.

Telecommunications device　tool you use to send information to and receive it from another person or computer in a network.

Telecommuting　the use of communications technology (such as the Internet) to work in a place other than a central location.

Telephone modem (modem)　a device that connects your computer to your phone line so that you can access another computer or network.

Terabyte (TB)　roughly 1 trillion bytes.

Test conditions　the detailed steps the system must perform along with the expected results of each step.

Testing phase　of the systems development life cycle verifies that the system works and meets all the business requirements defined in the analysis phase.

Thin client　a workstation with a small amount of processing power and costs less than a full-powered workstation.

Threat of new entrants　in the Five Forces Model is high when it is easy for new competitors to enter a market, and low when there are significant entry barriers to entering a market.

Threat of substitute products or services　in the Five Forces Model is high when there are many alternatives to a product or service, and low when there are few alternatives from which to choose.

Thrill-seeker hacker　a hacker who breaks into computer systems for entertainment.

Top-level domain　three-letter extension of a Web site address that identifies its type.

Touchpad　the little dark rectangle that you use to move the cursor with your finger, often found on notebook computers.

Trackball　similar to a mechanical mouse, but it has the ball on the top.

Traditional technology approach has two primary views of any system—information and procedures—and it keeps these two views separate and distinct at all times.

Transaction processing system (TPS) a system that processes transactions within an organization.

Trojan horse software software you don't want hidden inside software you do want.

Trojan horse virus hides inside other software, usually an attachment or download.

True search engine uses software agent technologies to search the Internet for key words and then places them into indexes.

U

Unallocated space the set of clusters that have been set aside to store information, but have not yet received a file, or still contain some or all of a file marked as deleted.

Uniform resource locator (URL) an address for a specific Web page or document within a Web site.

Uninstaller software utility software that you can use to remove software from your hard disk that you no longer want.

Unit testing tests individual units or pieces of code for a system.

USB (universal serial bus) port fits small flat plug-and-play, hot-swap USB connectors, and, using USB hubs, you can connect up to 127 devices to a single USB port on your computer.

User acceptance testing (UAT) determines if the system satisfies the business requirements and enables knowledge workers to perform their jobs correctly.

User agent (personal agent) an intelligent agent that takes action on your behalf.

User documentation highlights how to use the system.

User interface management component of a DSS that allows you to communicate with the DSS.

User interface of an expert system the component of the expert system that you use to run a consultation.

Utility software software that provides additional functionality to your operating system software.

V

Vertical e-marketplace an electronic marketplace that connects buyers and sellers in a given industry (e.g., oil and gas, textiles, and retail).

Vertical market software application software that is unique to a particular industry.

View allows you to see the contents of a database file, make whatever changes you want, perform simple sorting, and query to find the location of specific information.

Viewable image size (VIS) the size of the image on a monitor.

Viral marketing encourages users of a product or service supplied by a B2C e-commerce business to encourage friends to join in as well.

Virtual private network (VPN) uses software to establish a secure channel on the Internet for transmitting data.

Virtual reality a three-dimensional computer simulation in which you actively and physically participate.

Virtual team a team whose members are located in varied geographic locations and whose work is supported by specialized ICE software or by more basic collaboration systems.

Virus (computer virus) software that is written with malicious intent to cause annoyance or damage.

Visual Studio .NET the development tool that is used to create applications for the .NET platform, including Web services.

W

Walker an input device that captures and records the movement of your feet as you walk or turn in different directions.

Wearable computer a fully equipped computer that you wear as a piece of clothing or attached to a piece of clothing similar to the way you would carry your cell phone on your belt.

Web authoring software helps you design and develop Web sites and pages that you publish on the Web.

Web browser software enables you to surf the Web.

Web farm either a Web site that has multiple servers or an ISP that provides Web site outsourcing services using multiple servers.

Web log consists of one line of information for every visitor to a Web site and is usually stored on a Web server.

Web page a specific portion of a Web site that deals with a certain topic.

Web portal a site that provides a wide range of services, including search engines, free e-mail, chat rooms, discussion boards, and links to hundreds of different sites.

Web server provides information and services to Web surfers.

Web services encompass all the technologies that are used to transmit and process information on and across a network, most specifically the Internet.

Web site a specific location on the Web where you visit, gather information, and perhaps even order products.

Web site address a unique name that identifies a specific site on the Web.

Web space storage area where you keep your Web site.

Webcam captures digital video to upload to the Web.

White-hat (ethical) hacker a computer security professional who is hired by a company to break into its computer system.

Wide area network (WAN) a network that covers large geographic distances, such as a state, a country, or even the entire world.

WiFi (wireless fidelity or IEEE 802.11a, b, or g) a standard for transmitting information in the form of radio waves over distances up to about 300 feet.

Wired communications media transmit information over a closed, connected path.

Wireless communications media transmit information through the air.

Wireless Internet service provider (wireless ISP)   a company that provides the same service as a standard Internet service provider except that the user doesn't need a wired connection for access.

Wireless local area network (WLAN or **LAWN)**   a local area network that uses radio waves rather than wires to transmit information.

Wireless network access point (wireless access point)   a device that allows computers to access a wired network using radio waves.

Word processing software   helps you create papers, letters, memos, and other basic documents.

Workflow   defines all of the steps or business rules, from beginning to end, required for a business process.

Workflow system   facilitates the automation and management of business processes.

Workshop training   held in a classroom environment and is led by an instructor.

World Wide Web (Web)   a multimedia-based collection of information, services, and Web sites supported by the Internet.

Worm   a type of virus that spreads itself, not just from file to file, but from computer to computer via e-mail and other Internet traffic.

X

xD-Picture (xD) card   flash memory card that looks like a rectangular piece of plastic smaller than a penny and about as thick, with one edge slightly curved.

Y

Yield management system   a specialized kind of decision support system designed to maximize the amount of revenue an airline generates on each flight.

Z

Zip disk   a high capacity (100 Meg, 250 Meg, and 750 Meg) removable storage medium.

CHAPTER 1

1. Baca, Ricardo, "Ailing Industry Hears Swan Song of CDs," *Denver Post,* December 18, 2003, from www.denverpost.com/cda/article/print/0,1674,36%7E23827%7E18377 63,00.html, accessed December 26, 2003.

2. Gunderson, Edna, "Downloading Squeezed the Art Out of the Album," *USA Today,* December 5–7, 2003, pp. 1A–2A.

3. Zuckerman, Mortimer, "America's Silent Revolution," *U.S. News & World Report,* July 18, 1994, p. 90.

4. Greenspan, Robyn, "E-Banking, Online Bill Paying Growth Ahead," from http://cyberatlas.internet.com/markets/finance/article/0,,5961_3112511,00.html, accessed December 23, 2003.

5. "Home-Based Telework by U.S. Employees Grows by 40% Since 2001," from www.telecommute.org/news/pr090403.htm, accessed December 23, 2003.

6. Charles Schwab at www.schwab.com, accessed January 23, 2004.

7. Cuneo, Eileen, "Uptick in Care," *InformationWeek,* November 3, 2003, at www.informationweek.com/healthcare/showArticle.jhtml?articleID=15600635, accessed January 23, 2004.

8. "Dr Pepper/Seven Up, Inc.," a company success story provided by Cognos Inc. at www.cognos.com/company/success/index.html, accessed December 20, 2003.

9. Kontzer, Tony, "Brink's Gets Smarter about Learning," *InformationWeek,* December 15, 2003, from www.informationweek.com/story/showArticle.jhtml?articleID=16700281, accessed December 20, 2003.

10. Kallman, Ernest; and John Grillo, *Ethical Decision Making and Information Technology* (San Francisco: McGraw-Hill, 1993).

11. Peyser, Marc; and Steve Rhodes, "When E-Mail Is Ooooops Mail," *Newsweek,* October 16, 1995, p. 82.

12. Global Online Populations, Internet.com, at http://cyberatlas.internet.com/big_picture/geographics/article/0,1323,5911_151151,00.html, accessed January 23, 2004.

13. Bergstein, Brian, "Technology to Take Swipe Out of Credit Cards," *Denver Post,* December 14, 2003, p. 7A.

14. "A Live Link to a Dynamic Brand," a company success story provided by Open Text Corp. at www.opentext.com/customers/success-stories.html, accessed December 26, 2003.

15. "Losses from Identity Theft to Total $221 Billion Worldwide," *CIO Magazine,* May 23, 2003, at www2.cio.com/metrics/2003/metric551.html, accessed April 16, 2004.

16. "Accenture: Customer Satisfaction Driving Egovernment," from www.nua.com/surveys/index.cgi?f=VS&art_id=905358759&rel=true, accessed December 2, 2003.

17. "Traffic Patterns of 2003," from http://cyberatlas.internet.com/big_picture/traffic_patterns/print/0,,5931_3114931,00.html, accessed December 24, 2003.

18. "Benchmarking E-Government: A Global Perspective," United Nations Division for Public Economics and Public Administration, released May 2002, available at www.unpan.org.

CHAPTER 2

1. "Covisint Membership," from www.covisint.com/about/members/, accessed June 10, 2004.

2. Koudal, Peter, et al. "General Motors: Building a Digital Loyalty Network Though Demand and Supply Chain Integration," Stanford Graduate School of Business, Case GS–29, March 17, 2003.

3. "POLK ANNOUNCES AUTOMOTIVE LOYALTY AWARD WINNERS *NUMEROUS NEW WINNERS EMERGE ACROSS SEGMENT-LEVEL CATEGORIES FOR MODEL YEAR 2003,*" Polk Automotive Intelligence, January 4, 2004, at www.polk.com/news/releases/2004_0105.asp, accessed June 10, 2004.

4. Beth, Scott, et al, "Supply Chain Challenges: Building Relationships." *Harvard Business Review,* July 2003, pp. 65–73.

5. "Configuring a 500 Percent ROI for Dell," i2 White Paper, at www.i2.com/customers/hightech_consumer.cfm, accessed May 5, 2004.

6. Luttrel, Sharron Kahn, "Talking Turkey with Perdue's CIO—Supply Chain Management," *CIO Magazine,* November 1, 2003, at www.cio.com/archive/110103/tl_scm.html, accessed June 10, 2004.

7. "CPFR Introduction," CPFR Collaborative Forecasting, Planning and Replenishment, from www.cpfr.org/Intro.html, accessed May 5, 2004.

8. "Gaining Recognition for World Class Supply Chain Management," September 1, 2003, EDB Singapore, from www.sedb.com/edbcorp/sg/en_uk/index/in_the_news/publications/singapore_investment17/singapore_investment2/gaining_recognition.html, accessed May 5, 2004.

9. D'Avanzo, Robert, "The Reward of Supply Chain Excellence," *Orbitzmag.com,* December 2003, p. 76.

10. Beth, Scott, et al, "Supply Chain Challenges: Building Relationships," *Harvard Business Review,* July 2003, pp. 65–73.

11. Navas, Deb, "Supply Chain Software Stands Tough," *Supply Chain Systems Magazine,* December 2003, at www.scsmag.com/reader/2003/2003_12/software1203/index.htm, accessed June 10, 2004.

12. "Websmart 50," *Business Week,* November 24, 2003, p. 96.

13. *"Partnering in the Fight Against Cancer,"* Siebel-American Cancer Society—Case Study, at www.siebel.com/common/includes/case_study.shtm?pdfUrl=/downloads/common/case_studies/Non-Profit/pdf/American_Cancer_Society.pdf&coName=American%20Cancer%20Society, accessed June 10, 2004.

14. Koudal, Peter, et al., "General Motors."

15. Bethune, Gordon, "How to Create Fanatically Loyal Customers," *Business 2.0*, December 2003, p. 86.

16. Schuster, Roy, "Nine Steps to Make the CRM Case," CRMIQ 2004, at www.crmiq.com/resources/tips/148-CRMIQ_shortcuts.html, accessed May 5, 2004.

17. Songini, Marc L. "Companies Skeptical of CRM Success, Wary of Project Rollouts," *Computerworld*, March 4, 2003, at www.computerworld.com/softwaretopics/crm/story/0,10801,79009,00.html, accessed June 10, 2004.

18. Selland, Chris, "Are Companies Responsible for CRM Failures?" *Network World*, July 14, 2003.

19. Dragoon, Alice, "Business Intelligence Gets Smart(er)," *CIO Magazine*, September 15, 2003, at www.cio.com/archive/091503/smart.html, accessed June 10, 2004.

20. Gray, Paul, "Business Intelligence: A New Name or the Future of DSS?" in Bui, T., Sroka, H., Stanek, S., and Goluchowski, J., (eds.) *DSS in the Uncertainty of the Internet Age*, Katowice, Poland, University of Economics in Katowice: 2003.

21. "IBM and Factiva Join Forces to Transform Global Content Business," Press Release, Factiva Press Releases, September 18, 2003, at www.factiva.com/investigative/releases/09182003_ibm.asp?node=menuElem1176, accessed May 5, 2004.

22. Langseth, J., Vivatrat, N. "Why Proactive Business Intelligence Is a Hallmark of the Real-Time Enterprise: Outward Bound," *Intelligent Enterprise*, 5 (18), 2003.

23. Willen, Claudia, "Airborne Opportunities," *Intelligent Enterprise*, 5 (2), January 14, 2002.

24. Gray, "Business Intelligence."

25. Koudal, Peter, et al., "General Motors."

26. Morris, H., "The 5 Principles of High-Impact Analytics," *DM Review*, 13 (4), 2003.

27. Soejarto, Alex, "Tough Times Call for Business Intelligence Services," from VARBusiness, March 20, 2003, at www.varbusiness.com/sections/strategy/strategy.asp?ArticleID=40682, accessed May 5, 2003.

28. Rudin, K., and Cressy, D., "Will the Real Analytics Application Please Stand Up?" *DM Review* 13 (3), 2003.

29. Stodder, D., "Enabling the Intelligent Enterprise: The 2003 Editors' Choice Awards," *Intelligent Enterprise*, 6 (2), 2003.

30. "From Germany to America: SiteScape Connects Siemens AG, a Fortune Global 50 Organization," from SiteScape Testimonial, at www.sitescape.com/next/test_siemens.html, 2004, accessed June 10, 2004.

31. "LinkedIn in Three Steps," at www.linkedin.com/static;jsessionid=CAC221A555830B49D0DF40BA2AE133C5.app01?key=guest_tour, accessed June 10, 2004.

32. Surmacz, Jon, "Collaborate and Save: Collaboration Technology Can Save Big Money for the Oil and Gas Industry," *CIO Magazine*, November 5, 2003, at www2.cio.com/metrics/2003/metric625.html, accessed June 10, 2004.

33. Davenport, Thomas H., and Prusak, Laurence, "What's the Big Idea?: Creating and Capitalizing on the Best Management Thinking," Boston. Harvard Business School Press: 2003.

34. Malhotra, Y., and Galletta, D., "Role of Commitment and Motivation in Knowledge Management Implementation: Theory, Conceptualization and Measurement of Antecedents of Success," *Proceedings of the 36th Hawaii International Conference on System Sciences*, 2003.

35. "The new geography of the IT industry," Economist.com, July 17th, 2003, at www.economist.com/displaystory.cfm?story_id=1925828, accessed June 10, 2004.

36. "The Role of Technology in Knowledge Management," *Internet Strategist*, 1 (2), October 22, 2002, at www.intranetstrategist.com/xq/asp/sid.0/articleid.CD89216B-8E50-4AB1-9E73-77DFB0DB1D1E/qx/display.htm, accessed June 10, 2004.

37. "Social Networks," *New York Times Magazine*, December 14, 2003, page 92.

38. "Big Blue's Big Bet: Less Tech, More Touch," *The New York Times*, January 25, 2004, sec. 3, p. 1.

39. Salesforce.com, Product Features, at www.salesforce.com/us/products/feature.jsp, accessed June 10, 2004.

40. "CRM—Customer Relationship Management," at www.siebel.com, accessed June 10, 2004.

41. Davenport, Thomas H., and Glaser, John, "Just-in-Time Delivery Comes to Knowledge Management," *Harvard Business Review*, July 2002, pp. 107–111.

42. "Health: Best Hospitals Honor Roll 2003," USNews.com, at www.usnews.com/usnews/nycu/health/hosptl/honorroll.htm, accessed June 10, 2004.

CHAPTER 3

1. "Chrysler Manages a Nationwide Supply Chain of Vendors," from IBM at www-1.ibm.com/industries/automotive/doc/content/casestudy/283426108.html, accessed January 19, 2004.

2. Watterson, Karen, "A Data Miner's Tools," *BYTE*, October 1995, pp. 170–72.

3. Cash, James, "Gaining Customer Loyalty," *InformationWeek*, April 10, 1995, p. 88.

4. Dunn, Darrell, "Fancy Footwork Moves Inventory," *InformationWeek*, www.informationweek.com/story/showArticle.jhtml?articleID=1670,0271, December 15, 2003, accessed January, 12, 2004.

5. "Lufthansa Boosts Customer Quality with Its COSMIC," from Oracle at http://oracle.com/customers/profiles/PROFILE9407.HTML, accessed January 20, 2004.

6. Anthes, Gary, "Car Dealer Takes the Personal Out of PCs," *Computerworld,* August 14, 1995, p. 48.

7. Nevins, Scott, "Database Security Breaches on the Rise," *Computerworld,* www.computerworld.com/printthis/2003/0,4814,79883,00.html, March 31, 2003, accessed January 27, 2004.

8. "Israel's Largest Bank Strengthens Customer Relationships with Cognos BI," from Cognos at www.cognos.com/news/release/2003/0115.html, accessed February 2, 2004.

9. Maselli, Jennifer, "Insurers Looks to CRM for Profits," *InformationWeek,* www.informationweek.com/story/IWK20022050250007, May 6, 2002.

10. Kling, Julia, "OLAP Gains Fans among Data-Hungry Firms," *Computerworld,* January 8, 1996, pp. 43, 48.

11. Hutheesing, Nikhil, "Surfing with Sega," *Forbes,* November 4, 1996, pp. 350–51.

12. LaPlante, Alice, "Big Things Come in Smaller Packages," *Computerworld,* June 24, 1996, pp. DW/6–7.

13. "Customer Success: Land O'Lakes," from Informatica at www.informatica.com/Customers/Customer+Success/landolakes.htm, accessed January 2, 2004.

14. Worthen, Ben, "What To Do When Uncle Sam Wants Your Data," *CIO,* www.cio.com/archive/041503/data.html, April 15, 2003, accessed January 10, 2004.

15. Schlosser, Julie, "Tech@Work," *Fortune,* www.fortune.com/fortune/subs/print/0,15935,427294,00.html?cookie=1|1073974157, March 3, 2003, accessed January 10, 2004.

16. Whiting, Rick, "Analysis Gap," *Informationweek,* www.informationweek.com/story/IWK20020418S0007, April 22, 2002, accessed April 24, 2004.

17. "Red Robin International," company success story from Cognos at www.cognos.com/company/success/ss_entertainment.html, accessed January 13, 2004.

18. "Mining the Data of Dining," *Nation's Restaurant News,* May 22, 2000, pp. S22–S24.

19. Brown, Erika, "Analyze This," *Forbes,* April 1, 2002, pp. 96–98.

CHAPTER 4

1. Piszczalski, Martin, "IT & Skyrocketing Health Care Costs," *Automotive Design & Production,* May 2003, pp. 14–15.

2. Gambon, Jill, "A Database that 'Ads' Up," *InformationWeek,* August 7, 1995, pp. 68–69.

3. Simon, Herbert, *The New Science of Management Decisions,* rev. ed. (Englewood Cliffs, NJ: Prentice Hall, 1977).

4. Amsden, David, "Push Technology in the Pharmacy," *Health Management Technology,* January 2003, pp. 28–31.

5. Kauderer, Steven; and Amy Kuehl, "Adding Value with Technology," *Best's Review,* October 2001, p. 130.

6. "M/W Planning: It's All in the Data," *Railway Age,* January 2001, pp. 60–61.

7. Marlin, Steven; Cristina McEachern; and Anthony O'Donnell, "Cross Selling Starts with CRM System," *Wall Street & Technology,* December 2001, pp. A8–A10.

8. Wheatly, Malcolm, "Turning Data into Decisions, *Supply Management,* May 22, 2003, p. 22.

9. Davis, David, *GIS for Everyone,* 3rd ed. (Redlands, CA: ESRI Press, 2003).

10. Smelcer, J. B.; and E. Carmel, "The Effectiveness of Difference Representations for Managerial Problem Solving: Comparing Tables and Maps," *Decision Sciences,* 1997, pp. 391–420.

11. Brewin, Bob, "IT Helps Waste Hauler Handle Anthrax Safely," *Computerworld,* November 12, 2001, p.8.

12. Johnson, Robert, "AM/FM/GIS Moves to the Web," *Transmission & Distribution World,* October 2001, pp. 52–57.

13. Dunkin, Amy, "The Quants May Have Your Numbers," *Business Week,* September 25, 1995, pp. 146–47.

14. Port, Otis, "Computers That Think Are Almost Here," *Business Week,* July 17, 1995, pp. 68–71.

15. Williams, Fred, "Artificial Intelligence Has Small but Loyal Following," *Pensions & Investments,* May 14, 2001, pp. 4, 124.

16. Stuart, Ann, "A Dose of Accuracy," *CIO,* May 15, 1996, pp. 22–24.

17. Pastore, Richard, "Cruise Control; This Freight Delivery Company's Leaders Took Four Years to Get a New Expert System Right; Now They're Watching as the Benefits Roll In," *CIO Magazine,* February 1, 2003, pp. 60–66.

18. Kay, Alexx, "Artificial Neural Networks," *Computerworld,* February 12, 2001, p. 60.

19. Ibid.

20. Perry, William, "What Is Neural Network Software?" *Journal of Systems Management,* September 1994, pp. 12–15.

21. Port, Otis, "Diagnoses That Cast a Wider Net," *Business Week,* May 22, 1995, p. 130.

22. Baxt, William G., and Joyce Skora, "Prospective Validation of Artificial Neural Network Trained to Identify Acute Myocardial Infarction," *The Lancet,* January 6, 1997, pp. 12–15.

23. McCartney, Laton, "Technology for a Better Bottom Line," *InformationWeek,* February 26, 1996, p. 40.

24. Whiting, Rick, "Companies Boost Sales Efforts With Predictive Analysis," *InformationWeek,* February 25, 2002.

25. Ibid.

26. Punch, Linda, "Battling Credit Card Fraud," *Bank Management,* March 1993, pp. 18–22.

27. "Cigna, IBM Tech Tool Targets Health Care Fraud," *National Underwriter Property & Casualty-Risk & Benefits,* October 1994, p. 5.

28. Anthes, Gary H., "Picking Winners and Losers," *Computerworld,* February 18, 2002, p. 34.

29. Moody, Patricia E., "What's Next after Lean Manufacturing?" *Sloan Management Review,* Winter 2001, pp. 12–13.

30. "John Deere Credit Helps Retailers and Farmers Get with the Programs," *Agri Marketing,* October 2003, p. 28.

31. Johnson, Colin, "Breeding Programs," *Financial Management,* February 2001, pp. 18–20.

32. Ruggiero, Murray, "Enhancing Trading with Technology," *Futures,* June 2000, pp. 56–59.

33. Patrick, C. L. Hui; S. F. Ng Frency; and C. C. Chan Keith, "A Study of the Roll Planning of Fabric Spreading Using Genetic Algorithms," *International Journal of Clothing Science & Technology,* 2000, pp. 50–62.

34. Begley, S., "Software au Naturel," *Newsweek,* May 8, 1995, pp. 70–71.

35. Goldbert, David E., "Genetic and Evolutionary Algorithms Come of Age," *Communications of the ACM,* March 1994, pp. 113–19.

36. Baumohl, Bernard, "Can You Really Trust Those Bots?" *Time,* December 11, 2000, p. 80.

37. O'Brien, Mike, "Virtually Helpful," *Telephony,* February 11, 2002, p. 56.

38. Dobbs, Sarah Boehle Kevin; Donna Goldwasser; Gordon Jack; and David Stamps, "The Return of Artificial Intelligence," *Training,* November 2000, p. 26.

39. Overby, Stephanie, "The New, New Intelligence; A Year Ago, the Army Began Using Intelligent Software Agents instead of People to Route the Background Files of Soldiers Who Required Security Clearance to the Proper Authorities for Review," *CIO Magazine,* January 1, 2003, pp. 82–84.

40. Totty, Patrick, "Pinpoint Members with New Data-Mining Tools," *Credit Union Magazine,* April 2002, pp. 32–34.

41. Wolinsky, Howard, "Advisa Helps Companies Get More from Their Data: Helps Managers to Understand Market," *Chicago Sun-Times,* December 20, 2000, p. 81.

42. Brewin, Bob, "IT Goes on a Mission: GPS/GIS Effort Help Pinpoint Shuttle Debris," *Computerworld,* February 10, 2003, pp. 1, 6.

43. Ursery, Stephen, "Chattanooga, Tenn., Builds Tree Inventory," *American City & County,* July 2003, p. 18.

44. "Transit Agency Builds GIS to Plan Bus Routes," *American City & County,* April 2003, pp. 14–16.

45. "Weblining," *Business Week Online,* April 3, 2000, issue at www.BusinessWeek.com.

CHAPTER 5

1. Perez, Juan Carlos, "Update: AOL Launches New Bill-Paying Tool," *TheStandard,* http://www.thestandard.com/article.php?story=20040316172813723, March 16, 2004, accessed April 7, 2004.

2. Greenspan, Robyn, "Online Ads, E-marketing on Upswing," ClickZ Network, Jupiter Media Corporation, www.clickz.com/stats/markets/advetising/article.php/3320671, accessed March 6, 2004.

3. "Top Searches of 2003," ClickZ Network, Jupiter Media Corporation, www.clickz.com/stats/big_picture/traffic_patterns/print.php/3293581, accessed March 10, 2004.

4. "U.S. Web Usage and Traffic," ClickZ Network, Jupiter Media Corporation, www.clickz.com/stats/big_picture/traffic_patterns/print.php/5931_3301321, December 2003, accessed March 2, 2004.

5. Ibid.

6. "B2B E-Commerce Headed for Trillions," ClickZ Network, Jupiter Media Corporation, www.clickz.com/stats/markets/b2b/print.php/986661, accessed March 11, 2004.

7. "2002 Consumer Profile," The Recording Industry Association of America, from www.riaa.com, accessed February 29, 2004.

8. www.epinions.com/about/, accessed April 5, 2004.

9. Rosen, Cheryl, "Passwords Are So Passe," *Optimize,* December 2003, p. 21.

10. Regan, Keith, "Gateway Shuts All Stores, Cuts 2,500 Jobs," *E-Commerce Times,* www.ecommercetimes.com/perl/story/33302.html, April 2, 2004, accessed April 3, 2004.

11. "Global eXchange Services and ChinaECNet Establish B2B Exchange for China's $80 Billion Electronics Industry," Global eXchange Services, Inc., http://www.gxs.com/gxs/press/release/press20040318, accessed April 4, 2004.

12. Hofmann, Martin, "VW Revs Its B2B Engine," *Optimize,* March 2004, pp. 22–30.

13. "eBags.com Celebrates Five Years of Helping Consumers Find the Perfect Bag Online," eBags.com, http://www.ebags.com/info/aboutebags/index.cfm?Fuseaction=pressitem&release_ID=102, accessed April 6, 2004.

EXTENDED LEARNING MODULE E

1. Levy, Steven; and Brad Stone, "The WiFi Wave," *Newsweek,* June 10, 2002, pp. 50–53.

2. "How to Revitalize Host Systems for Client/Server Computing Today and Tomorrow," *Datamation,* April 1, 1995, pp. S1–S24.

3. Schalon, Lisa, "Sales Automation Systems Increase Sales, Productivity," *Best's Review-Life-Health Insurance Edition,* January 1996, pp. 100–2.

CHAPTER 6

1. Guadiosi, John, "Hacking The Matrix," *Wired,* www.wired.com, August 2003, accessed June 10, 2004.

2. "10 Technologies to Watch in 2004," *Business 2.0,* November 2003, www.business2.com, accessed June 10, 2004.

3. "Business Technology Optimization," www.mercuryinteractive.com, accessed June 11, 2004.

4. Boutin, Paul, "Clearing Up The Confusion," *Wired Magazine,* October 2003, www.wired.com, accessed June 10, 2004.

5. Brown, Kenn, "Six Technologies That Will Change the World," *Business 2.0,* August 2003, www.business2.com, accessed June 10, 2004.

6. Davis, Joshua, "ssss busted," *Wired,* October 2003, www.wired.com, accessed June 10, 2004.

7. Panettieri, Joseph, "Lucrative Liaisons," *Wired,* December 2003, www.wired.com, accessed June 10, 2004.

8. Fox, Justin, "Hang-ups in India," *Fortune,* December 22, 2003, www.fortune.com, accessed June 10, 2004.

9. Fisher, Anne, "If All the Jobs Are Going to India, Should I Move to Bangalore?" *Fortune,* January 12, 2004, www.fortune.com, accessed June 10, 2004.

10. Rosencrance, Linda, "AI Loves Lucy," *Computerworld Magazine,* November 10, 2003, www.computerworld.com, accessed June 10, 2004.

CHAPTER 7

1. Jardin, Xeni, "Why Your Next Phone Call May Be Online," *Wired,* January 2004, www.wired.com, accessed June 10, 2004.

2. Gaudin, Sharon, "Employees' Abuse of Internet Rampant," *Internetnews.com,* April 2003, www.internetnews.com, accessed June 10, 2004.

3. Ibid.

4. "The Gap Inc.," www.corba.org/industries/retail.gap.html, September 2003, accessed June 10, 2004.

5. "The Company," www.gapinc.com/about/ataglance/company.htm, accessed June 10, 2004.

6. "The Battle Between .NET and J2EE," *Computerworld,* September 2003, www.computerworld.com, accessed June 10, 2004.

7. Ibid.

8. Surmacz, Jon, "Alive and Kicking," *CIO Magazine,* July 2003, www2.cio.com, accessed June 10, 2004.

9. McDonald, Duff, "A Website as Big (and Cheap) as the Great Outdoors," *Business 2.0,* October 2003, www.business2.com, accessed 10, 2004.

10. "Abercrombie & Fitch Ace the Basics of Selling Lifestyle Online," IBM Corp., www-3.ibm.com, accessed June 10, 2004.

11. Hof, Robert D., "Your Undivided Attention Please," *Business 2.0,* September 2003, www.business2.com, accessed June 10, 2004.

12. Wildstrom, Stephen, "Linux for the Desktop: It's a Contender," *BusinessWeek,* February 2004, www.businessweek.com, accessed June 10, 2004.

13. Null, Christopher, "How Netflix Is Fixing Hollywood," *Business 2.0,* July 2003, www.business2.com, accessed June 10, 2004.

CHAPTER 8

1. Behar, Richard, "Never Heard of Acxiom? Chances Are It's Heard of You," *Fortune,* February 23, 2004, pp. 140–48.

2. Herman, Josh, "Albany, NY, Reflects True Test Market," *Marketing News,* February 1, 2004, p. 34.

3. "American Banker: TransUnion Teams with Acxiom on Anti-Fraud Tool," *American Banker,* February 23, 2004, from www.acxiom.com, accessed June 24, 2004.

4. Bleed, Jake, "Acxiom Thrives on Sorting Bank Megamergers," *Arkansas Democrat-Gazette,* February 8, 2004, from www.acxiom.com, accessed June 24, 2004.

5. Pliagas, Linda, "Learning IT Right from Wrong," *InfoWorld Publications,* October 2, 2000, pp. 39–40.

6. Fogliasso, Christine; and Donald Baack, "The Personal Impact of Ethical Decisions: A Social Penetration Theory Model," *Second*

Annual Conference on Business Ethics Sponsored by the Vincentian Universities in the United States, New York, 1995.

7. Jones, T. M., "Ethical Decision-Making by Individuals in Organizations: An Issue-Contingent Model," *Academy of Management Review,* 1991, pp. 366–95.

8. Kallman, Ernest; and John Grillo, *Ethical Decision-Making and Information Technology* (San Francisco: McGraw-Hill, 1993).

9. Zhivago, Kristin, "Et Tu Enron?" *AdWeek Magazines' Technology Marketing,* April 2002, p. 33.

10. Baase, Sara, *The Gift of Fire: Social, Legal and Ethical Issues in Computing* (Upper Saddle River, NJ: Prentice Hall, 1997).

11. Jonietz, Erika, "Economic Bust Patent Boom," *Technology Review,* May 2002, pp. 71–72.

12. Stevens, Tim, "Cashing In on Knowledge," *Industry Week,* May 2002, pp. 39–43.

13. Moores, Trevor, "Software Piracy: A View from Hong Kong," *Communications of the ACM,* December 2000, pp. 88–93.

14. "New Study Reveals Significant Decline in World Software Piracy Since 1994," June 3, 2003, at www.bsa.org, accessed June 24, 2004.

15. James, Geoffrey, "Organized Crime and the Software Biz," *MC Technology Marketing Intelligence,* January 2000, pp. 40–44.

16. Ibid.

17. Rittenhouse, David, "Privacy and Security on Your PC," *ExtremeTech,* www.extremetech.com, May 28, 2002, accessed June 24, 2004.

18. Russell, Kay, "Phishing," *Computerworld,* January 19, 2004, p. 44.

19. DeBaise, Colleen; and Jochi Dreazen, "Ring of Identity Thieves Is Broken," *The Wall Street Journal,* November 26, 2002, p. A3.

20. Scalet, Sarah, "5 Ways to Fight ID Theft," *CSO,* March 2004, pp. 46–52.

21. Fleck, Carole, "Stealing Your Life," *AARP Bulletin,* February 2004, pp. 3–5.

22. Jones, Charisse, "His Life Was Stolen, Then His Name," *USA Today,* November 15, 2002, p. 3A.

23. Adams, Hall III, "E-Mail Monitoring in the Workplace: The Good, the Bad and the Ugly," *Defense Counsel Journal,* January 2000, pp. 32–46.

24. Corbin, Dana, "Keeping a Virtual Eye on Employees," *Occupational Health & Safety,* November 2000, pp. 24–28.

25. Ibid.

26. Pliagas, "Learning IT Right from Wrong."

27. Vaught, Bobby; Raymond Taylor; and Vaught Steven, "The Attitudes of Managers Regarding the Electronic Monitoring of Employee Behavior: Procedural and Ethical Considerations," *American Business Review,* January 2000, pp. 107–14.

28. Parker, Laura, "Medical-Privacy Law Creates Wide Confusion," *USA Today,* October 17–19, 2003, pp. 1A, 2A.

29. Medford, Cassimir, "Know Who I Am," *PC Magazine,* February 7, 2000, pp. 58–64.

30. Charters, Darren, "Electronic Monitoring and Privacy Issues in Business-Marketing: The Ethics of the DoubleClick Experience," *Journal of Business Ethics,* February 2002, pp. 243–54.

31. Naples, Mark, "Privacy and Cookies," *Target Marketing,* April 2002, pp. 28–30.

32. Blackman, Andrew, "Spam's Easy Target," *The Wall Street Journal,* August 19, 2003, pp. B1, B4.

33. Stone, Brad, "Soaking in Spam," *Newsweek,* November 24, 2003, pp. 66–69.

34. Angwin, Julia, "Elusive Spammer Sends Web Service on a Long Chase," *The Wall Street Journal,* May 7, 2003, pp. A1, A10.

35. Graven, Matthew P., "Leave Me Alone," *PC Magazine,* January 16, 2001, pp. 151–52.

36. Konrad, Racheal; and John Vorland, "Guess What's in Your Hard Drive?" *ZDNet News,* at zdnet.com.com/2100-1104-885792.html, April 18, 2002, accessed April 11, 2004.

37. Mirsky, Dara, "Tap Your Web Site's Log Files to Improve CRM," *Customer Inter@action Solutions,* May 2001, pp. 42–43.

38. Baase, *The Gift of Fire.*

39. Rittenhouse, "Privacy and Security on Your PC."

40. Soat, John, "IT Confidential," *InformationWeek,* June 3, 2002, p. 98.

41. Salkever, Alex, "A Dark Side to the FBI's Magic Lantern," *BusinessWeek Online,* at www.businessweek.com, November 27, 2001, accessed March 14, 2004.

42. Rittenhouse, "Privacy and Security on Your PC."

43. Carey, Jack, "ACLU Decries Super Bowl Surveillance," *USA Today,* February 2, 2001, p. 1C.

44. CopLink at www.coplink,net.

45. Leonard, Bill, "Crime-Data Software for Police May Benefit Employers," *HR Magazine,* January 2003, p. 27.

46. Baase, *The Gift of Fire.*

47. Han, Peter; and Angus Maclaurin, "Do Consumers Really Care about Online Privacy?" *Marketing Management,* January/February 2002, pp. 35–38.

48. De Bony, Elizabeth, "EU Overwhelmingly Approves U.S. Data-Privacy Regulations," *Computerworld,* June 5, 2000, p. 28.

49. Banham, Russ, "Share Data at Your Own Risk," *World Trade,* November 2000, pp. 60–63.

50. Caldwell, Bruce, "We Are the Business," *InformationWeek,* October 28, 1996, pp. 36–50.

51. Mogelefsky, Don, "Security Turns Inward," *Incentive,* May 2000, p. 16.

52. Conley, John, "Knocking the Starch Out of White Collar Crime," *Risk Management,* November 2000, pp. 14–22.

53. Bannen, Karen, "Watching You, Watching Me," *PC Magazine,* July 2002, pp. 100–4.

54. Berman, Dennis, "Online Laundry: Government Posts Enron's E-Mail," *The Wall Street Journal,* October 6, 2003, pp. A1, A12.

55. Hulme, George, "In Lockstep on Security," *InformationWeek,* March 18, 2002, pp. 38–52.

56. Chudnow, Christine, "Grid Computing," *Computer Technology Review,* April 2002, pp. 35–36.

57. Neel, Dan, "Plug-and-Pay Computing," *InfoWorld,* April 15, 2002, pp. 1, 38.

58. Radcliff, Deborah, "Hackers, Terrorists, and Spies," *Software Magazine,* October 1997, pp. 36–47.

59. Hulme, George V.; and Bob Wallace, "Beware Cyberattacks," *InformationWeek,* November 13, 2000, pp. 22–24.

60. "Europe Plans to Jail Hackers," zdnet.com.com/2100-11105-889332.html, April 23, 2002, accessed December 12, 2003.

61. Meyer, Lisa, "Security You Can Live With," *Fortune,* Winter 2002, pp. 94–99.

62. "Fast Times," *Fortune,* Summer 2000, pp. 35–36.

63. Zemke, Ron, "Tech-Savvy and People-Stupid," *Training,* July 2000, pp. 16–18.

64. Thompson, Clive, "The Enemy Within," *The Observer: Review Section,* February 22, 2004, pp. 1–2.

65. Spencer, Vikki, "Risk Management: Danger of the Cyber Deep," *Canadian Underwriter,* September 2000, pp. 10–14.

66. Meyer, "Security You Can Live With."

67. Paul, Brooke, "How Much Risk Is Too Much?" *InformationWeek,* November 6, 2000, pp. 116–24.

68. Eastwood, Alison, "End-Users: The Enemy Within?" *Computing Canada,* January 4, 1996, p. 41.

69. Radcliff, Deborah, "Beyond Passwords," *Computerworld,* January 21, 2002, pp. 52–53.

70. Wagley, John, "Tech Detectives," *Institutional Investor,* August 2001, pp. 18–20.

71. Clark, Ken, "Pointing to the Future," *Chain Store Age,* May 2002, p. 170.

72. "Turn Time into Money in the Blink of an Eye," *InformationWeek,* March 4, 2002, p. 53.

73. Verton, Dan, "IT Systems at U.S. Borders Found Lacking," *Computerworld,* March 17, 2003, pp. 1, 16.

74. Verton, Dan, "DHS Broadens Biometrics Use for Border Control," *Computerworld,* October 13, 2003, p. 22.

75. Gips, Michael, "Home on the Page: www.securitymanagement.com," *Security Management,* May 2003, pp. 24–25.

76. Betts, Mitch, "5 Petabytes of Biometric Data," *Computerworld,* November 17, 2003, p. 52.

77. Fjetland, Michael, "Global Commerce and the Privacy Clash," *Information Management Journal,* January–February 2002, pp. 54–58.

EXTENDED LEARNING MODULE H

1. Richmond, Riva, "How to Find Your Weak Spots," *The Wall Street Journal,* September 29, 2003, p. R3.

2. Savage, Marcia, "The White Hats: Security Consultants," *Computer Reseller News,* November 13, 2000, pp. 137–38.

3. Pack, Thomas, "Virus Protection," *Link-Up,* January/February 2002, p. 25.

4. Meserve, Jason, "People around the World Bitten by 'Love Bug,'" *Network World,* May 8, 2000, pp. 14, 28.

5. Zemke, Ron, "Tech-Savvy and People-Stupid," *Training,* July 2000, pp. 16–18.

6. York, Thomas, "Invasion of Privacy? E-Mail Monitoring Is on the Rise," *InformationWeek,* February 21, 2000, pp. 142–46.

7. Meserve, "People around the World Bitten by 'Love Bug.'"

8. Harris, Shane, "SoBig: A Look Back," *Government Executive,* November 2003, p. 72.

9. Babcock, Charles, "Fast-Moving Virus Slams E-Mail Systems," *InformationWeek,* August 2003, p. 22.

10. Roberts, Paul, "The Year Ahead in Security," *InfoWorld,* January 2004, p. 17.

11. Kirkpatrick, David, "Taking Back the Net," *Fortune,* September 29, 2003, pp. 117–22.

12. Luhn, Robert, "Eliminate Viruses," *PC World,* July 2002, p. 94.

13. Landolt, Sara Cox, "Why the Sky Isn't Falling," *Credit Union Management,* October 2000, pp. 52–54.

14. "Hackers Attack *USA Today* Web Site," *Morning Sun,* July 13, 2002, p. 6.

15. Hulme, George, "Vulnerabilities Beckon Some with a License to Hack," *InformationWeek,* October 23, 2000, pp. 186–92.

16. Bischoff, Glenn, "Fear of a Black Hat," *Telephony,* September 3, 2001, pp. 24–29.

17. Kornblum, Janet, "Kournikova Virus Maker: No Harm Meant," *USA Today,* February 14, 2001, p. 3D.

18. "Firms Increasingly Call on Cyberforensics Teams," cnn.com, January 16, 2002, accessed March 18, 2004.

19. "*USA Today* Says Writer Made Up Part of Stories," *Dallas Morning News,* March 20, 2004, p. 11A.

20. Kruse, Warren G.; and Jay G. Heiser, *Computer Forensics: Incident Response Essentials* (New York: Addison-Wesley, 2002).

CHAPTER 9

1. Ward, Mark, "Hacking with a Pringles Tube," *BBC News,* http://news.bbc.co.uk/1/hi/sci/tech/1860241.stm, March 8, 2002, accessed April 15, 2004.

2. www.intenseschool.com/bootcamps/security/hacking/default.asp?mc=ggass_hacking&GTSE=goog&GTKW=hacking, accessed April 15, 2004.

3. Schonfeld, Erick; and Om Malik, "GULP!" *Business 2.0,* August 2003, pp. 88–95.

4. Corcoran, Elizabeth, "The Next Small Thing," *Forbes,* July 23, 2001, pp. 96–106.

5. Adams, Nina, "Lessons from the Virtual World," *Training,* June 1995, pp. 45–47.

6. Flynn, Laurie, "VR and Virtual Spaces Find a Niche in Real Medicine," *New York Times,* June 5, 1995, p. C3.

7. Chabrow, Eric, "Facial-Recognition Software Gives a Better Picture," *InformationWeek,* www.informationweek.com/story/showArticle.jhtml?articleID=8700238, March 13, 2003, accessed April 13, 2004.

8. www.businesswire.com/webbox/bw.050201/211220321.htm, accessed May 2, 2002.

9. Thomas, Owen, "How to Sell Tech to the Feds," *Business 2.0,* March 2003, pp. 111–112.

10. Weikle, Bobbie, "Riding the Perfect Wave: Putting Virtual Reality to Work with Disabilities," from www.pappanikou.uconn.edu/weikle.html, accessed April 14, 2004.

11. McConnaughey, Janet, "Virtual Reality Used to Treat Autism," *Denver Post,* October 20, 1996, p. 39A.

12. www.nytimes.com/2002/05/30/technology/circuits/30TEEN.html, accessed June 7, 2002.

13. Ouchi, Monica Soto, "Wildseed: A Start-up on the Cusp of Success with Teens," *Seattle Times,* seattletimes.nwsource.com/html/businesstechnology/2001834588_ces12.html, January 12, 2004, accessed April 15, 2004.

PHOTO CREDITS

MODULE A

PA.1a, page 39, PRNewsFoto / Panasonic / AP / Wide World Photos

PA.1b, page 39, Kensington Technology Group

PA.1c, page 39, Photo courtesy of Sanyo Fisher

PA.1d, page 39, Photo courtesy of FOSSIL

PA.1e, page 39, Image Courtesy © Eastman Kodak Company. KODAK is a trademark.

PA.1f, page 39, PRNewsFoto / Gateway Inc/ AP / Wide World Photos

PA.1g, page 39, © 2004, Courtesy of Linksys

PA.1h, page 39, Photo courtesy of www.pocketec.net

PA.2a, page 40, Photo courtesy of Logitech

PA.2b, page 40, © Precise Biometrics

PA.2c, page 40, © Nance S. Trueworthy

PA.2d, page 40, Photo courtesy of Intel Corporation

PA.2e, page 40, Image courtesy of KDS USA

PA.2f, page 40, Image courtesy of ATI Technologies

PA.2g, page 40, © 2004, Courtesy of Linksys

PA.4a, page 43, Courtesy of HP

PA.4b, page 43, PRNewsFoto / Mindjet LLC / AP / Wide World Photos

PA.4c, page 43, Photo courtesy of iBUYPOWER Computer

PA.4d, page 43, Courtesy of Dell Inc.

PA.5a, page 44, Courtesy of HP

PA.5b, page 44, Courtesy of International Business Machines Corporation. Unauthorized use not permitted.

PA.5c, page 44, Photo Courtesy of Cray Inc

PA.9a, page 52, Courtesy of Epson America

PA.9b, page 52, Photo courtesy of Microsoft® Corp

PA.9c, page 52, © Plantronics, Inc.

PA.9d, page 52, PRNewsFoto / Logitech / AP / Wide World Photos

PA.9e, page 52, Photo courtesy of Logitech

PA.9f, page 52, Photo courtesy of Microsoft® Corp

PA.12a, page 54, Photo provided by Samsung Electronics America, Inc.

PA.12b, page 54, Photo provided by Samsung Electronics America, Inc

PA.12c, page 54, Courtesy of HP

PA.13a, page 55, Photo courtesy of GCC Printers

PA.13b, page 55, Courtesy of HP

PA.13c, page 55, Courtesy of Sony Electronics Inc

PA.15a, page 57, Courtesy of International Business Machines Corporation. Unauthorized use not permitted.

PA.15b, page 57, Photo Courtesy of Iomega Corporation

PA.15c, page 57, © RF/ Corbis

PA.16a, page 58, © Nance S. Trueworthy

PA.16b, page 58, © Spencer Grant / PhotoEdit

PA.17a, page 59, SanDisk Corporation

PA.17b, page 59, SanDisk Corporation

PA.17c, page 59, SanDisk Corporation

PA.17d, page 59, SanDisk Corporation

PA.17e, page 59, Trekstor USA

PA.17f, page 59, Photo courtesy of PQI Corporation www.pqi1st.com

PA.18a, page 59, Photo courtesy of Intel Corporation

PA.18b, page 59, Photo courtesy of Kingston Technology Company, Inc.

PA.21a, page 63, Photo by R.D. Cummings, Pittsburg State University

PA.21b, page 63, Photo by R.D. Cummings, Pittsburg State University

PA.21c, page 63, Photo by R.D. Cummings, Pittsburg State University

PA.21d, page 63, Photo by R.D. Cummings, Pittsburg State University

PA.21e, page 63, Photo by R.D. Cummings, Pittsburg State University

PA.21f, page 63, Photo by R.D. Cummings, Pittsburg State University

PA.21g, page 63, Courtesy of Belkin Corporation

PA.21h, page 63, Courtesy of Belkin Corporation

PA.23, page 64, © Francis Dean / The Image Works

CHAPTER 9

Fig. 9.6a, page 431, Euan Myles/Getty Images

Fig. 9.6b, page 431, Andersen Ross/Getty Images

Fig. 9.6c, page 431, © Stockbyte

Fig. 9.9a, page 436, © Forestier Yves/Corbis Sygma

Fig. 9.9b, page 436, Courtesy of Alex Lightman, Charmed Technology

Fig. 9.9c, page 436, Courtesy Xybernaut Corporation